The Directory of
BRITISH TRAMWAYS

As part of our ongoing market research, we are always pleased to receive comments about our books, suggestions for new titles, or requests for catalogues. Please write to: The Editorial Director, Patrick Stephens Limited, Sparkford, Nr Yeovil, Somerset, BA22 7JJ.

The Directory of
BRITISH
TRAMWAYS

Every passenger-carrying tramway, past and present

Keith Turner

Patrick Stephens Limited

Dedication

For Margaret, without whose help, encouragement and forbearance this book
would never have been completed

First published in 1996

British Library Cataloguing-in-Publication Data:
A catalogue record for this book
is available from the British Library

ISBN 1 85260 549 9

Library of Congress catalog card No. 96-075175

Patrick Stephens Limited is an imprint of
Haynes Publishing, Sparkford,
Nr Yeovil, Somerset, BA22 7JJ

Typeset by J. H. Haynes & Co. Ltd

Printed in Great Britain by J. H. Haynes & Co. Ltd

Contents

Preface

As a writer and transport historian I have felt for many years the need for a comprehensive one-volume reference work on the tramways of the British Isles. Not since 1962 in fact, when the fourth edition of Bett & Gillham's *Great British Tramway Networks* appeared, has the tramway enthusiast had easy access to a single, up-to-date basic 'where, what and when' of these lines. So, as much for my own reference purposes as for any other reason, I decided to compile such a work and now that it has been completed I hope it will prove of use to anyone else with an interest in this important aspect of our islands' transport history. Wherever possible I have endeavoured to check and double-check all listed facts and, if any errors have crept in, the responsibility for them is mine alone. As regards the illustrations, these have been chosen to portray as many aspects of tramway history as possible, not just the tramcars themselves, with many being taken from postcards – whose heyday coincided neatly with that of the tramway to reflect the integral part played by trams in the popular life of the period.

K. Turner
Kidderminster, 1996

Acknowledgements

I should like to thank all those archivists, librarians and their staff thoughout the British Isles who have provided valued assistance over the years in helping to compile this directory. Thanks must also go to those organisations and individuals, especially John Hawkins and Andy Maxam, who have kindly supplied material to help illustrate it. Special thanks too to Jan and Lil for coming to the rescue in times of crisis. Finally, and most importantly, grateful acknowledgement must be paid to all those writers, recorders and historians who have gone before; without their dedicated efforts my task would have been an impossible one.

Introduction

This directory is intended to cover all the tramways which have operated within the British Isles: that is Great Britain, Ireland and all the off-shore islands including the Isle of Man and the Channel Islands. It should be pointed out here, at the very beginning, that adjectives of locality are used in their geographical, not political or national sense, so that 'British' hereafter refers to the whole of the British Isles, 'Irish' to the whole of Ireland and 'Welsh' to the Principality of Wales plus Monmouthshire. (Since virtually all British tramways were opened, operated and closed before the 1974 local government reorganisation in Great Britain, the names of the old counties have been used throughout – indeed, at the time of writing it appears highly likely that several, if not most, of them will return shortly.)

The immediate problem facing a compiler of a directory of tramways is one of definition: what exactly is a tramway? In many cases, nomenclature is not a reliable guide – a tramway might well have been titled officially a 'light railway' (eg the Kinver Light Railway) while, conversely, a 'tramway' (eg the Rye & Camber Tramway) might actually have been a railway.

This confusion over identification arises from a number of historical causes. During the early years of the 19th century the terms 'tramway' and 'tramroad' were interchangeable, both denoting a horse-worked railed way (usually for mineral or other goods traffic only, situated in a rural area and feeding a canal, river or port) crossing or occupying public highways without restriction or much inconvenience to other road users, few as they were. As the use of steam traction spread however, so locomotive-worked lines became separated physically from the roadways for safety reasons, thus becoming in the process railways (though the older lines often retained their original names of tramway or tramroad); when

tramroad); when tramways proper arrived on the scene in the latter half of the 19th century they could not command exclusive rights to the term. The confusion was further complicated by the fact that tramways in Britain were built under several different authorizing mechanisms, one of which was the 1896 Light Railways Act.

How then have tramways been defined for the purposes of inclusion here? Three criteria have been employed for main entries. First, any line included must, at some time at least, have operated a regular public passenger service. Secondly, any such tramway must have had a significant part of its route along or beside a public highway without being fenced-off from other traffic and consequently was subject to certain operating restrictions when using mechanical or electric traction in recognition of this fact. Finally, such tramways should be, or have been, discrete entities and worked as such with their own stock despite any physical connections with other systems or even – in some cases – the national railway network.

Obviously, the 'typical' British tramway which could be found in many towns and cities between, say, 1890 and 1940 meets the above criteria without difficulty: a self-contained system operating a passengers-only service through the streets. Add an overhead electric power supply and the stock image of the British tramway is complete. There were however a great many lines which did not conform to this picture – and yet still meet the same criteria. 'Public highway', for example, might in a wider context include both open common and seaside pier decking whilst for some tramways goods traffic was just as, if not more important than passengers. Nor should it be assumed that being a tramway meant catering for the general public at large: some needed a prior qualification on the part of the passengers, such as their having paid the price of admission to a pier. Two criteria

price of admission to a pier. Two criteria which purposefully have not been used are those of gauge and motive power; these are discussed more fully below.

Regardless of its official title (or indeed popular name), a line or system according to the above definition of a tramway has been given a main entry whilst any line or system that meets only the last two criteria (ie was a goods-only tramway) has been given a minor entry. Any other line or system officially entitled Tramway but which was in practice a railway, light railway or tramroad has been given a minor entry if it operated a passenger service and omitted entirely if it did not.

Cross-references to main or minor entries have been made from place name elements other than the first in a tramway's title (eg UPWELL see WISBECH & UPWELL) and to major places served where this might not be evident from the title (eg GREAT ORME TRAMWAY see LLANDUDNO: GREAT ORME TRAMWAY). Cross-references in capital letters refer to entries in the same Section and those in lower case to other Sections.

The arrangement used for setting out main entries is as follows:

AUTHORITY

The legal authority for the construction and operation of the tramway. On a general level, promoting a tramway was very much like promoting a railway: unless the line was to be built on land wholly owned by an individual or company, then some form of national or local governmental permission had to be obtained for its construction. The exact form of this authority varied according to what legislative framework was in existence at the time; to a lesser extent it also varied according to where in the British Isles the line was to be built. For this reason further details of the different authorities are given in the introduction to each Section.

GAUGE

For tramways laid with railway-type rails (ie chaired bullhead or spiked flat-bottomed on sleepers) the gauge given is the distance between the inner edges of the rails as if it were a railway. For tramways laid with tramway-type rails (ie grooved rails set flush with the road surface) the gauge given is the distance between the outer edges of the two grooves (ie between the inner edges of the running surfaces).

The range of gauges used by British tramways is a large one, as the breakdown below shows:

1 1/4 in to 15in – used for miniature tramways.
1ft 8in to 2ft 6in – generally regarded as the lower limit for narrow gauge horse and steam tramways.
2ft 9in – the lower limit for narrow gauge electric tramways.
2ft 11 1/2 in – a gauge which enabled 3ft gauge railway vehicles to run on their (deeper) flanges in the grooves of tramway rails to enable through working to take place.
3ft – Isle of Man 'standard gauge' and the most common gauge for steam-worked light railways and tramways in Ireland.
3ft 6in – the most common narrow gauge for electric working in Great Britain.
4ft – a common horse tramway gauge, less common for electric lines.
4ft 7 3/4 in – a gauge which enabled standard gauge railway vehicles to run in the grooves of tramway rails. Widespread in the Scottish systems along side the River Clyde.
4ft 8 1/2 in – standard railway gauge in Great Britain, though if used with grooved rails through working of railway vehicles could not take place (see above).
5ft 3in – standard railway gauge in Ireland (and subject to the same restriction as above).

Other gauges have been employed, usually as one-off examples, in line with this pattern of usage.

TRACTION

The type(s) of tractive power used on a regular basis to work the system. On British tramways the following were used (ignoring unsuccessful experiments with other movers):

Manual – hand-propelled stock, common on pier tramways.
Horse – narrower gauge lines tended to use a single horse pulling a single-deck car; wider gauge lines did likewise, even for double-deckers on level routes. Where steep gradients and/or heavy double-deck vehicles were involved, two horses were normally used with a third, trace horse being attached at the foot of stiff climbs.
Cable – cars attached permanently to a cable in funicular railway fashion or cars which could engage/disengage a continuously moving cable.
Steam – either trailers hauled by special tramway locomotives or passenger vehicles fitted with steam power units.
Internal combustion – as above but with diesel, petrol or similar fuel engines.
Battery electric – as above but with electric motors powered by accumulators.
Gas – passenger stock fitted with gas-fuelled power units.
Petrol-electric – passenger stock fitted with a petrol engine driving a dynamo to power an electric motor.
Overhead electric – passenger stock fitted with electric motors supplied with current from an overhead wire.
Stud electric – as above but with current from roadway studs.
Conduit electric – as above but with current from a roadway conduit.

Where different methods of traction were in use at the same time they are listed in the main entry thus (for example): Horse, steam. Where one method of traction superseded another with no overlapping period of use, they are listed thus (for example): Horse/steam.

Details of other methods of traction used rarely, briefly or experimentally – including sails and clockwork! – are given in the entries themselves.

A Dick, Kerr trade advertisement showing clearly the difference between railway and grooved tramway rails.

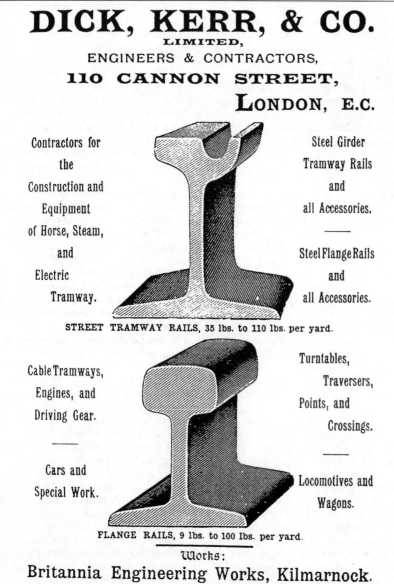

DICK, KERR, & CO.
LIMITED,
ENGINEERS & CONTRACTORS,
110 CANNON STREET,
LONDON, E.C.

Contractors for the Construction and Equipment of Horse, Steam, and Electric Tramway.

Steel Girder Tramway Rails and all Accessories.

Steel Flange Rails and all Accessories.

STREET TRAMWAY RAILS, 35 lbs. to 110 lbs. per yard.

Cable Tramways, Engines, and Driving Gear.

Cars and Special Work.

Turntables, Traversers, Points, and Crossings.

Locomotives and Wagons.

FLANGE RAILS, 9 lbs. to 100 lbs. per yard.

Works:
Britannia Engineering Works, Kilmarnock.

OPENED/TOOK OVER

The date given is that of the first public service. This was often, but not always, the same as that of the official opening ceremony (which occasionally preceded or followed it). Also, especially in the case of larger systems, only part of the tramway might have been opened at this time. In the case of lines taken over from another operator, the date is when services commenced under the new owner-ship, the actual transfer normally being timed from the midnight of the last day of the old ownership.

CLOSED/TAKEN OVER

In the case of a closure, the date of the tramway's last public service over the last section of the line to remain open under that operator (though stock movements often took place after the date of closure). In the case of large systems, usually only a fraction of the whole remained in use by this time. (It should be borne in mind that last journeys were often run late at night, finishing in the early hours of the day following that given.)

In the case of a takeover, the date given is the day the new operator began working the system.

SYSTEM

The physical layout of the tramway system's route(s), codified in a roughly-ascending order of complexity thus (ignoring short spurs to depots, one-way loops in town centres and the like)

Single line – one route from A to B, usually town centre to an outlying district and/or railway station; occasionally from one town to another (an 'interurban').
Split single line – two routes from A to B.
Circle – a single line starting and finishing at the same point.
Branching – a single main line with one or more other lines branching from it.
Cross – two single lines crossing but worked as separate routes.
Radial – a number of routes radiating from a central point (usually a natural focus such as a market square, town hall or railway station).
Radial network – a radial system with one or more linking lines between routes.
Network – a network of crossing and branch-ing routes with no single focus, as found in many large towns and cities.

Combinations of the above are also used, eg branching circle. All systems should be taken to be predominantly urban in nature (though often travelling beyond the original built-up area to serve isolated villages or districts) unless they are described in the notes as rural or interurban.

LENGTH

As far as it can be ascertained, the route mileage of the tramway at its greatest extent is given, correct to the nearest one-hundredth of a mile, based on official returns made by the operators. This may not be the total route mileage worked as, occasionally, a new line might be opened after an earlier section had been abandoned.

STOCK

The total number of vehicles employed by the tramway during its lifetime for passenger services (though not all might have been in use concurrently). Where applicable, the number of locomotives is given first, then the number of single-deck vehicles (sd), then the number of double-deckers (dd). Cars are counted in their original state (eg before conversion from single to double-deck form).

LIVERY

Almost without exception tramcars were painted in what would now be termed a 'two-tone' livery, usually a darker colour such as green, red or blue and a lighter colour such as cream or yellow. There were several aesthetic reasons for this scheme, tried and tested over the years not only on tramcars but on horse buses, railway carriages and even stage-coaches: a dark colour low down gave the vehicle a visual sense of reassuring stability whilst a lighter colour around the windows and higher emphasized the visibility afforded its passengers and the lightness of the car – hence its swiftness – and spaciousness. An added bonus of having dark lower panels was that they did not draw attention to the splash-ings and muddyings they inevitably suffered. Running gear would normally be red oxide or black for the same reasons whilst the roofs would continue the lightening effect by being a very pale neutral colour such as off-white or grey. Steam tramway locomotives tended to be painted with a single dark shade to give an impression of stolid dependability.

The two-tone livery also made the cars highly visible to potential passengers, as did the use of (usually) gold or cream for their ornate lining, numbers and name of the opera-tor.

The difficulty in describing long-vanished liveries is that official records have often not survived, forcing the historian to rely on (sometimes conflicting) eye-witness memories. The problem is compounded by the fact that a colour applied new quickly weath-ered and, if judged unsuitable, was often replaced by a darker shade when the vehicle was repainted. For example, white was frequently used on new horse cars but quickly replaced by off-white (ivory) in the light of experience. Similarly, pale cream was normally darkened into primrose (or even yellow). For this reason the descriptions given

are sometimes a compromise eg red-brown or cream/yellow. The descriptions themselves are of the general livery used during a specific period, ignoring minor variations; in the case of a change from one general scheme to another, this might well have taken months if not years to complete depending on the number of cars involved.

Second-hand vehicles often ran for a while in their old liveries until a new paint job could be arranged whilst during World War I, for reasons of wartime economy, cars would be painted uniformly grey and often remained that way for several years after the war.

LAST CAR

The closure of a tramway was often a very emotional occasion with the last public journey marked by speeches, wreaths and crowds trying to board the 'Last Car'. On many such occasions the identity of this tram was recorded for posterity; on others the line closed without fuss or ceremony and which vehicle made the final trip is not generally known today although the information might well be residing in private films or papers just waiting to be discovered. Sometimes an 'official' Last Car carrying local dignitaries was run behind the last service vehicle, or even on a later date.

BIBLIOGRAPHY

Wherever possible at least one comprehensive history of the tramway which has appeared in book form is cited – for minor lines this might well be part of a wider account – though their accuracy is not guaranteed. Citations are given in the order *Title* (Series and number) Author (Publisher, edition if not the first, date of publication) ISBN.

ABBREVIATIONS

In order to save space and avoid tiresome repetitions, several frequently-occurring names have been given in an abbreviated form (eg companies and other organisations). Company titles are given in concise form, eg '& Co. Ltd' for 'and Company Limited'. Other abbreviations used, if not standard forms or given in full earlier in the same entry, are:

Ashbury – Ashbury Railway Carriage & Iron Co. Ltd, Manchester (later Metropolitan)
Bagnall – W.G. Bagnall Ltd
BB – Balfour, Beatty & Co. Ltd*
BEC – British Electric Car Co. Ltd, Trafford Park
BET – British Electric Traction Co. Ltd*
BH – Black, Hawthorn & Co. Ltd
Birmingham – Birmingham Railway Carriage & Wagon Co. Ltd, Smethwick
BM – Brown Marshalls & Co. Ltd, Birmingham (later Metropolitan)
BNCR – Belfast & Northern Counties Railway

BoT – Board of Trade
BP – Beyer, Peacock & Co. Ltd, Manchester (locomotive builder)
BP – Bruce Peebles & Co. Ltd, Edinburgh (contractor)
BR – British Railways
Brill – J.G. Brill Co., Philadelphia
BTH – British Thomson-Houston Co. Ltd, Rugby*
Brush – Brush Electrical Engineering Co. Ltd, Loughborough
Burrell – Charles Burrell & Sons Ltd, Thetford
CIE – Coras Iompair Eireann
CLC – Cheshire Lines Committee
Cravens – Cravens Railway Carriage & Wagon Co. Ltd, Sheffield
DK – Dick, Kerr & Co. Ltd, Preston
EE – English Electric Co. Ltd, Preston (formerly UEC)
ERTCW – Electric Railway & Tramway Carriage Works Ltd, Preston (a DK subsidiary)
Falcon – Falcon Engine & Car Works, Loughborough (a Brush subsidiary)
Fowler – John Fowler & Co. Ltd
GCR – Great Central Railway
GER – Great Eastern Railway
Gloucester – Gloucester Railway Carriage & Wagon Co. Ltd
GNR – Great Northern Railway
GNR(I) – Great Northern Railway (Ireland)
GNSR – Great North of Scotland Railway
Green – Thomas Green & Sons Ltd, Leeds
GSR – Great Southern Railways
GSWR – Glasgow & South Western Railway
GWR – Great Western Railway
Hardy – Hardy Rail Motors Ltd
Hawthorn – Robert W. Hawthorn & Co. Ltd, Gateshead
Hibberd – F. C. Hibberd & Co. Ltd, London
HN – Hurst, Nelson & Co. Ltd, Motherwell
Hughes – Henry Hughes & Co. Ltd, Loughborough (later Falcon)
Kitson – Kitson & Co. Ltd, Leeds
Krauss – Locomotivfabrik Krauss & Cie, Munich
Lancaster – Lancaster Railway Carriage & Wagon Co. Ltd (later Metropolitan)
LBSCR – London, Brighton & South Coast Railway
LCDR – London, Chatham & Dover Railway
LMS – London, Midland & Scottish Railway
LNER – London & North Eastern Railway
LNWR – London & North Western Railway
LSWR – London & South Western Railway
LYR – Lancashire & Yorkshire Railway
Matthews – James Matthew, Bristol
Merryweather – Merryweather & Sons, London

Metro-Cammell – Metropolitan-Cammell Carriage & Wagon Co. Ltd, Birmingham
Metropolitan – Metropolitan Railway Carriage & Wagon Co. Ltd, Birmingham (later Metro-Cammell)
MGWR – Midland Great Western Railway
Midland – Midland Railway Carriage & Wagon Co. Ltd, Shrewsbury
Milnes – Geo F. Milnes & Co. Ltd, Birkenhead
MR – Midland Railway
MV – G.C. Milnes, Voss & Co. Ltd, Birkenhead
MW – Manning, Wardle & Co. Ltd, Leeds
NBR – North British Railway
NEC – National Electric Construction Co. Ltd*
NER – North Eastern Railway
Oldbury – Oldbury Railway Carriage & Wagon Co. Ltd (later Metropolitan)
Peckham – Peckham Truck & Engineering Co. Ltd

Pickerings – R.Y. Pickering & Co. Ltd, Wishaw
Roberts – Charles Roberts & Co. Ltd, Wakefield
SECR – South Eastern & Chatham Railway
SER – South Eastern Railway
Starbuck – Starbuck Car & Wagon Co. Ltd, Birkenhead
Stephensons – John Stephenson Co., New York
UEC – United Electric Car Co. Ltd, Preston (formerly ERTCW)
Wickham – D. Wickham & Co. Ltd, Ware
Wilkinson – Wilkinson & Co. Ltd, Wigan

* see main entry in Section 1

Other symbols used are:

[ ] – unofficial short title
? – this information is uncertain or lacking
– – not applicable
c – about
* – see text/footnote

Trade advertisement of the 1890s for Bell Punch, one of the major manufacturers of ticket equipment, with a list of systems supplied.

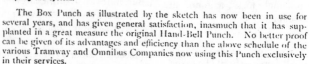

Section 1

Tramways of England

Ignoring anachronistic passenger-carrying tramroads, the history of the tramway in the British Isles is very much the history of the tramway in England. Certainly it was here that the first street tramway was laid (BIRKENHEAD) and here that the first regular use of steam (WANTAGE), cable (LONDON) and safe electric traction (BLACKPOOL) was made.

English tramway history is, in turn, a condensed parallel version of the development and growth of Britain's railways. The urban tramway arrived from the USA (where it was aptly known as a 'street railway') in the early 1860s and, just a quarter of a century later, had employed the same four main motive power systems as had been used on railways over a period four times as long: horse, steam, cable and electricity. Of these four, the first held sway during the 1860s and 1870s. It was familiar and acceptable to the travelling public and the tramcar's journey smoother than that of a horse bus. It was however not very much quicker, hence the introduction (permitted by the 1879 Act for the Use of Mechanical Power on Tramways) of steam traction using specially designed tank locomotives with side skirts to enclose the motion, end fittings to prevent anyone being run over, and a driving cab at each end to allow the driver a clear view of the road ahead. In addition, the BoT required them to burn coke to reduce pollution and to be equipped with condensing apparatus for the waste steam. Because of their power advantage over horses, these steam locomotives could pull much larger trailers (sometimes in multiple) up steeper gradients which meant that many existing horse systems were converted – notably in the major industrial towns and regions – and new, hilly routes opened. Self-contained cars fitted with seats and a steam engine were also experimented with, generally unsuccessfully.

The adoption of steam traction gave birth to the fixed tram stop for their greater momentum meant that, unlike horse cars, steam trams could not stop for prospective passengers wherever hailed in the street – a legacy later passed on to electric tramway and motor bus operators. Steam trams were not however very popular with the general public, being regarded as dirty and noisy, and when reliable electric traction was developed in the 1880s, the use of steam was quickly abandoned with virtually all lines employing it being converted by the early years of the 20th century. (See Appendix 6 for those special cases which used no other form of traction.)

During the steam tram era cable traction was also employed (though on far fewer lines) to cope with gradients that locomotives could not manage. Its use met with mixed fortunes: those climbs which could be tackled by electric trams were soon converted to enable routes to become part of an integrated system (as in BIRMINGHAM and LONDON) whilst those which remained too steep (in England, only MATLOCK) kept faithful to it until closure. (See Appendix 7 for a list of all British cable tramways.)

Undoubtedly, the most successful of the traction systems was electricity. First used on any scale in the British Isles in 1883 on Volk's Electric Railway in Brighton and the Giant's Causeway Tramway in Ireland (see Section 4), it was adopted two years later at BLACKPOOL and from then on almost all new tramways employed it and existing ones which did not were either almost all closed or converted by the outbreak of World War I. (See Appendix 5 for a list of those horse lines never converted.)

Before 1870 tramway construction was normally authorized either by local authority permission or by private Act of Parliament. The former applied when the streets involved were under local authority control and the latter when compulsory purchase of land was required. In return for this power, an Act laid down certain conditions on the company to be formed to build and operate the tramway, notably the amount of capital which could be raised, the time limit for construction to start and finish, the gauge and type of traction to be used and so on. Obtaining an Act of Parliament was an expensive business – and never guaranteed to succeed in the face of opposition from powerful landowners, railway companies and the like – and in 1870 the Tramways Act was passed to make life easier for would-be promoters. Under its provisions an application could be made to the BoT for a Provisional Order which, if sanctioned after a local inquiry, was then confirmed (along with any others outstanding) in a Tramways Confirmation Act.

One important provision of the Act was to have profound consequences, affecting virtually all those lines built under such Orders: after 21 years (and at regular intervals thereafter) from the confirmation of an Order, any local authority with a tramway within its boundaries could purchase the whole undertaking at cost. (Where a tramway crossed municpal boundaries two or more authorities could act jointly in the matter.) This many authorities chose to do, especially as the 21-year period coincided with the possibility of introducing electric traction, often to the intense annoyance of the operating companies, resulting in legal squabbling and the arbitration of the price to be paid. (Originally local authorities were not allowed to operate tramways – though they could build and lease them to private companies – though this prohibition was later dropped.)

Another option was made available from 1896 onwards with the passing of the Light Railways Act in that year. Although intended to facilitate the construction of light railways – often as adjuncts of the national network – in much the same way as the Tramways Act had done for tramways, several private and municipal tramway promoters used its provisions, obtaining Light Railway Orders to authorize their undertakings. (One advantage of doing so for private companies was that no later municipal buy-out was threatened.)

The first great wave of tramway closures came in the 1920s and 1930s when many tracks and vehicles reached the end of their useful life (a situation often hastened by lack of proper maintenance during World War I) at a time when motor buses were claiming a rapidly-increasing share of the public transport market. The situation was not helped by the fact that often the bus operators, private and municipal, were the tramway operators themselves. Some respite was afforded by the demands of World War II but after that the closures came thick and fast with SHEFFIELD, in 1960, the last to go – the last that is except Blackpool which, until 1970 when the SEATON line opened, was England's sole tramway operator. The Seaton Tramway was a special case however and it was not until the opening of the MANCHESTER METROLINK 22 years later, that the resurgence of the tramway in the streets of England began. The South Yorkshire Supertram in Sheffield followed in 1994 and more are planned. Although these are unlikely to be running before the end of this century, the next will almost certainly see the tramways' continuing fight-back with hi-tech light rail systems designed and installed to free our city centre streets from the slow and dirty motor cars which threaten to choke them to death in exactly the same way as horse-drawn traffic did more than a century and a quarter ago.

ACCRINGTON CORPORATION STEAM TRAMWAYS

Authority: Accrington Corporation
  Tramways Act 1882
Gauge: 4ft
Traction: Steam
Opened: 5 April 1886
Taken Over: 20 September 1907
System: Radial
Length: 9.45 miles
Stock: 23 locos, 2 sd? 17+ dd
Livery: ?

The first tramway in the Lancashire town of Accrington was operated by the Accrington Corporation Steam Tramways Co. which leased the track for 21 years from the date of opening from Accrington Corporation. Work began in 1884 with three, mainly single-track, routes being laid from the Market Place. The shortest ran due west along the Blackburn Road past the Town Hall and then the depot in Ellison Street for 1 mile and terminated at the Commercial Hotel, Church, where a connection was later

made with the BLACKBURN CORPORATION TRAM-WAYS (though through running never took place).

The second route ran northwest up Whalley Road for 1¾ miles to The Load of Mischief in the village of Clayton-le-Moors whilst the third ran southeast for 2¼ miles down Abbey Street and the Manchester Road to terminate near the railway station in Baxenden.

Public services began over the Church–Market Place–Clayton portion of the system immediately after the BoT inspection on 5 April 1886 (with an official opening three days later). The Baxenden route followed on 12 June that year and was extended twice in 1887, firstly to the Commercial Hotel, Haslingden on 27 August and on to Lockgate (the Haslingden/Rawtenstall boundary) in November, the track of the extension (2.9 miles) being owned by Haslingden Corporation and leased to the Company. Two years later a connection was made here with the ROSSENDALE STEAM TRAMWAYS line, but again through running did not result.

The initial rolling stock fleet comprised Green tram locomotives Nos 1-9 of 1885 and Nos 10-14 of 1886 hauling roofed bogie double-deck trailers 1-10 from Falcon. These were joined by similar Ashbury cars 11-14 in 1887 and Lancaster ones 15-17 in 1891, while the locomotive stud was increased by Green engines 15 and 16 in 1890, 17 in 1894 and 18 and 6 in 1898 – this last one replacing an older loco. Finally, in

1901 four more Green engines (Nos 19-22) were bought from Blackburn, which system was then being electrified, plus an unknown number of trailers from there and BURNLEY.

In 1905 the Corporation obtained authority to take over and electrify the tramways on expiry of the lease and preparatory work for the conversion began; the purchase price of £2,227 for eleven locos and eleven cars was paid on 20 September 1907, the Corporation thus becoming the system's operator (see below.) Eight locos and seven cars were bought by HASLINGDEN CORPORATION in order to work that authority's portion of the Lockgate route.

Bibliography: *The Tramways of Accrington 1886-1932* Robert W. Rush (The Light Railway Transport League, 1961)

ACCRINGTON CORPORATION TRAMWAYS

Authority: Accrington Corporation Act 1905
Gauge: 4ft
Traction: Overhead electric, steam
Opened: 2 August 1907
Closed: 6 January 1932
System: Radial
Length: 7.02 miles
Stock: 13 sd, 25 dd electric; 11 locos, 11 dd steam
Livery: Bright red & cream
Last Car: No 6

Commemorative postcard of Accrington Corporation's new electric service with car No 11 of 1907, staff and dignitaries. (Lens of Sutton)

Even before it had finalized its takeover of the town's steam tramways (see above), Accrington Corporation had opened its first, double-tracked electric route along the former steam line from the Town Hall to Church where it turned south as a single track down Union Road for another 1¼ miles to Oswaldtwistle. That same month through running between Accrington and BLACK-BURN began. On 20 September the reconstructed Clayton route opened, the mainly single-track line now extended 200yd to the canal bridge there; this was followed on 26 October by a single-track northeastern branch off Whalley Road just north of the Market Place along the Burnley Road to the Cemetery at Huncoat with the line to Baxenden station (a mixture of double and single tracks) opening on 1 January next. It is not known when the last steam tram ran.

The first electric cars were single-deckers 1-4 and top-covered double-deckers 5-18, followed in 1908 by two more single-deckers, Nos 5 and 6 (double-deckers 5 and 6 being renumbered 19 and 20). All were from Brush – as indeed were all subsequent purchases – and housed in the rebuilt steam depot.

Through running to the Commercial Hotel, HASLINGDEN (which Corporation had taken over its portion of the former steam route from 1 January 1908) began on 28 September 1908 and on to Lockgate on 20 October to complete the system. On 1 April 1910 through running began via RAWTENSTALL to Bacup. (Haslingden Corporation retained ownership of its portion of track throughout the tramway's life though it never operated electric services of its own.)

In 1909 top-covered cars 21 and 22 and single-decker 23 were added to the fleet, followed in 1910 by top-covered 24 and 25, in 1912 by top-covered 26 and single-decker 27 and in 1915 by single-deckers 28-30 and enclosed double-deckers 38 and 39, these last five cars being bogie vehicles. Six cars were bought after World War I: bogie single-deckers 31 and 32 and enclosed bogie double-deckers 40 and 41 in 1920 and enclosed lowbridge double-deckers 42 and 43 six years later. By the late 1920s though the future of the tramway was looking bleak, for in 1928 the Corporation began bus operations and on 30 April 1930 the route to Rawtenstall was jointly closed, followed on 26 August that year by the Clayton and Oswaldtwistle routes. This left just the Burnley Road line to survive into the next year.

Several of the cars were disposed of to other systems before and after the closure. Nos 42 and 43 were sold in 1931 to SUNDERLAND, Nos 28-32 in 1932 to the Llandudno & Colwyn Bay Electric Railway (see Section 2), No 39 in 1933 to LYTHAM-ST-ANNES and Nos 38, 40 and 41 in 1934 to SOUTHEND.

Bibliography: as above

ALDERSHOT & FARNBOROUGH TRAMWAYS

Authority: Aldershot and Farnborough
  Tramways Order 1878
Gauge: 4ft 8½in
Traction: Horse
Opened: *
Closed: 1906
System: Single line
Length: 2.69 miles
Stock: 4 sd?
Livery: *
Last Car: ?

The first tramway proposal for Aldershot was made by George Francis Train of BIRKEN-HEAD and LONDON fame whose Aldershot Street Rail Co. Ltd (incorporated 4 December 1861) proposed a line linking that town with Farnborough, though nothing ever came of the scheme. Other proposals followed to provide such a link, the successful one being an 1878 promotion for a single-track line south through the town from close to Farnborough's LSWR station, then along Farnborough Road to the Queens Hotel where it turned east along Lynchford Road past the military establishment known as North Camp (a few miles north of Aldershot itself) to a terminus by the SER's North Camp station.

Extensive extensions to this system were proposed (with subsequent Orders being obtained) but never constructed; the one line opened at an unknown date sometime between its BoT inspection on 15 August 1881 and 30 June 1883 when passenger receipts for the previous twelve months were recorded. The tramway was owned by the Aldershot & Farnborough Tramways Co. (itself owned by the Aldershot & Farnborough Tramways Co. Ltd) and worked with a pair of two-horse single-deckers, complete with 1st and 3rd class compartments, shedded at the Farnborough terminus.

It appears that the line closed just a year or two after it opened, only to re-open again soon after with two open toastracks painted white and two single-deck saloons painted red and white. (These were possibly all new cars as one report says that the original pair were sold to local gypsies following the early closure.)

The tramway was finally abandoned in 1906, by which time only one trip a day was being run (and only as far as the Fir Tree Hotel short of North Camp station). This was not quite the end of the story though for an 1897 company, Power & Traction Ltd, obtained the Aldershot and Farnborough Light Railways Order of 1902 to build a 3ft 6in gauge electric system to serve the area but, although some 300yd of track was laid in Farnborough Road near the station, the scheme never came to fruition (like virtually all the P&T's many tramway and light railway promotions).

ALEXANDRA PARK ELECTRIC RAILWAY see LONDON: ALEXANDRA PARK

ALFORD & SUTTON TRAMWAY

Authority: Alford and Sutton Tramways
  Act 1880
Gauge: 2ft 6in
Traction: Steam
Opened: 2 April 1884
Closed: December 1889
System: Single line
Length: 7.06 miles
Stock: 3 locos, 5 sd?
Livery: Red & Yellow?
Last Car: ?

One of England's most short-lived and poorly-documented tramways connected the Lincolnshire town of Alford to the seaside resort of Sutton-on-Sea some 7 miles away, running as a single track laid with grooved rails from the GNR's station at Alford along the public highway (now the A111) through the villages of Bilsby, Markby and Hannah to the High Street in Sutton. The main depot was at the Alford terminus but a smaller one at Sutton housed at least one locomotive and probably a carriage as well. The line's three locos were typical street tramway engines, No 1 being a Wilkinson's patent engine by BH of 1883, No 2 a Merryweather engine of 1884 and No 3 a DK product bought the following year. Passenger stock consisted of (probably) one bogie and four four-wheeled saloon cars, all single-deck and possibly also by DK. There were also a number of open goods wagons – and possibly vans for the livestock the Alford & Sutton Tramway Co. intended to carry.

Unfortunately for the Company, in 1886 the Willoughby & Sutton Railway opened, linking the resort to the GNR line south of Alford (and worked by the latter company prior to its outright purchase in 1902). It proved too much for the tramway as holiday-makers could now travel to Sutton by rail without recourse to it and closure came in the first week of December 1889 after less than six years' service; for the last two of these it had been operated by the grandly-titled Great Northern, Lincoln & East Coast Railway Ltd (incorporated 5 May 1888), which company changed its name on 31 January 1889 to the Great Northern Tramways Co. Ltd.

DICK, KERR & CO.,
101, LEADENHALL STREET, LONDON, E.C.

Works:—BRITANNIA ENGINEERING WORKS, KILMARNOCK, N.B.

SOLE MAKERS OF MORRISON & KERR'S PATENT TRAMWAY ENGINES
AS SUPPLIED TO THE ALFORD AND SUTTON AND NORTH LONDON STEAM TRAMWAYS.
PRICES AND FULL PARTICULARS ON APPLICATION.
MAKERS OF ALL CLASSES OF CARS & ROLLING STOCK
FOR STREET TRAMWAYS & NARROW GAUGE RAILWAYS.

Above: Alford & Sutton loco No 3 and stock as depicted in a Dick, Kerr trade advertisement.

Right: Before the passing of the 1870 Tramways Act the usual procedure for promoters was to obtain an authorizing Act of Parliament; after 1870 this course of action became less common, though was followed in the case of the Alford & Sutton Tramway.

[43 & 44 VICT.]   *Alford and Sutton Tramways*   [Ch. clxviii.]
Act, 1880.

CHAPTER clxviii.

An Act for incorporating the Alford and Sutton Tramways A.D. 1880
Company and authorising them to construct Tramways
from Alford to Sutton-le-Marsh in the parts of Lindsey in
the county of Lincoln ; and for other purposes.
[12th August 1880.]

WHEREAS the construction of tramways from Alford to Sutton-
le-Marsh in the parts of Lindsey in the county of Lincoln
would be of public and local advantage :

And whereas the persons in that behalf in this Act named, with
others, are willing at their own expense to construct such tramways
on being incorporated into a company with adequate powers for
the purpose, and it is expedient that they be incorporated and
empowered accordingly :

And whereas plans and sections showing the situation, lines, and
levels of the tramways authorised by this Act, and the lands to be
taken for the purposes thereof, with a book of reference to the plans
containing the names of the owners and lessees, or reputed owners
and lessees, and of the occupiers of the lands, were duly deposited
with the clerk of the peace for the parts of Lindsey in the county
of Lincoln, and are herein-after referred to as the deposited plans,
sections, and books of reference :

And whereas the objects of this Act cannot be effected without
the authority of Parliament :

May it therefore please Your Majesty that it may be enacted ;
and be it enacted by the Queen's most Excellent Majesty, by and
with the advice and consent of the Lords Spiritual and Temporal,
and Commons, in this present Parliament assembled, and by the
authority of the same, as follows :

1. This Act may be cited as the Alford and Sutton Tramways Short title.
Act, 1880.

[*Local.–168.*]   A   1

Although short-lived, one feature associated with the tramway lasted until 1970 when the Sutton branch closed: the officially-named Tramway Crossing signal box outside Sutton where the two lines crossed on the level.
Bibliography: *Alford & Sutton Tramway* George Dow (Author, 1984)

APPLEDORE *see* BIDEFORD, WESTWARD HO! & APPLEDORE

ASHBY-DE-LA-ZOUCH *see* BURTON & ASHBY

ASHTON-UNDER-LYNE CORPORATION TRAMWAYS

Authority: Ashton-under-Lyne Corporation Tramways Order 1900; Hurst Urban District Council Tramway Order 1900
Gauge: 4ft 8½in
Traction: Overhead electric
Opened: 16 August 1902
Closed: 1 March 1938
System: Radial network
Length: 6.92 miles
Stock: 14 sd, 25 dd
Livery: Dark blue & cream (plus maroon pre-1905)
Last Car: No 32 *

Prior to the opening of the Corporation's own system, trams had been operating in Ashton since 1881 (MANCHESTER TRAMWAYS horse) and 1899 (OLDHAM, ASHTON & HYDE electric). Then, in 1900, the adjoining local authorities of Ashton and Hurst obtained Orders authorizing their own lines with construction beginning the following year.

The first lines opened formed a circular, single-track route northeast from the Market Place (where there was a connection with the OAH's track) to Hurst Cross, out via Union Road and King Street and back via either Whitacre Road or – further to the south – Queen Street and Mossley Road past the depot. Services began with two open-top double-deckers from ERTCW (probably Nos 1 and 2) followed a week later by another pair (probably 3 and 4); these were joined over the next nine months by open-toppers 11 and 12 and single-deck combination cars 5-10, all from ERTCW again. Route length was 3½ miles of which Hurst UDC owned 1.35 miles.

The Manchester Carriage & Tramways Co's last horse tram to Ashton and on to Stalybridge ran on 31 March 1903 when the lease expired on the line but services recommenced on 23 April and lasted until 14

October, a through electric service commencing the next day from the Audenshaw boundary east along the horse tramway route via the Manchester Road and Stamford Street (across the OAH line) through Ashton and on to Stalybridge Town Hall over STALYBRIDGE, HYDE, MOSSLEY & DUKINFIELD metals. On 22 February 1904 MANCHESTER CORPORATION electric cars began through running beyond The Snipe at the Audenshaw boundary into Ashton to replace the Corporation's cars on this section whilst in March that year a short branch (less than ½ mile) was opened south from Stamford Street down Cavendish Street to the Dukinfield boundary at Alma Bridge, followed by a second, to the east, down Scotland Street twelve months later to meet the SHMD tracks. (In April 1906 the SHMD took over the service in Scotland Street to the centre of Ashton.)

In 1905 ERTCW supplied single-deckers 13-18 and in 1908 UEC supplied top-covered cars 20-22, followed by similar vehicles 23 and 24 in 1912 and 25 and 26 two years later. The final purchases were made in 1921 when top-covered cars 27-38 were bought from EE and 24 OAH vehicles acquired with the Corporation's purchase of part of that system. Only two single-deck combination cars from this batch (Nos 39 and 40) were ever put into service though, such was their generally abysmal condition.

Following the OAH purchase, the track layout in the town centre was rationalized slightly to enable that system's two routes to be integrated into the Corporation's network and the Stamford Road part of the southern section doubled. In March 1923 the Corporation began motor bus services and two years later introduced trolleybuses under the Ashton-under-Lyne Corporation Act 1924; on 26 August 1926 these took over the former OAH northern route to Hathershaw. Also in 1926 Hurst was absorbed by Ashton and with it its nominally separate tramways; the following year the first car scrappings took place.

On 10 January 1928 the southern section from Denton to Hyde was closed, after which the remaining services were cut back gradually. The Hurst lines closed in June 1932 and the Ashton-Denton route in October 1936, leaving just the original horse tramway east-west route through the town to survive another two years. The last Corporation car in service was No 32 on the afternoon of 1 March 1938 though more passengers were carried over its tracks by a Manchester car which left the town later that day.

Bibliography: *A History of Public Transport in Ashton-under-Lyne* W.G.S. Hyde (Manchester Transport Museum Society, 1980)

ASTON *see* BIRMINGHAM & ASTON

BALFOUR, BEATTY & CO. LTD

This firm was established in 1909 by A.H. Balfour of the tramway contractors J.G. White & Co. Ltd and George Balfour, a director of several tramway companies. It eventually owned, operated, or had a substantial interest in, a number of tramway and/or electricity supply companies including the systems of CHELTENHAM, DARTFORD, LEAMINGTON & WARWICK, LUTON, MANSFIELD and NOTTINGHAMSHIRE & DERBYSHIRE in England, Llandudno & Colwyn Bay and Llanelly in Wales and Dunfermline, Falkirk and Wemyss in Scotland.

BARKING TOWN COUNCIL LIGHT RAILWAYS

Authority: Barking and Beckton Light
    Railways Order 1899
Gauge: 4ft 8½in
Traction: Overhead electric
Opened: 1 December 1903
Closed: 16 February 1929*
System: Branching
Length: 1.6 miles
Stock: 10 dd
Livery: Crimson lake & cream to 1906,
    brown & cream to 1907 then green &
    cream
Last Car: ?

The first part of this tiny, municipal single-track tramway on the eastern edge of Greater London in Essex ran from Beckton Gasworks (and the depot) close to the River Thames northwards beside Jenkins Lane across the marshes and over Barking Creek into the town centre via Gascoigne Street to terminate at the corner of Axe Street (1¼ miles). Delays in completing the bascule bridge over the creek meant that the line was worked in two halves for a few days. The initial car fleet was made up of Brush open-toppers Nos 1-7 of which Nos 1-3 and 7 were immediately fitted with top covers.

On 6 June 1905 Barking Council opened an isolated ¼-mile section of single track from the boundary with Ilford at Loxford Bridge (where it connected with ILFORD UDC TRAMWAYS) southeast along Fanshaw Road to Longbridge Road near Barking railway station; this was worked by Ilford cars. A similar arrangement was made with EAST HAM CORPORATION TRAMWAYS to the west when, on 17 November 1905, a double-track line was opened eastwards from that system's terminus in London Road south down the Broadway then northeast (as a single track) along East Street to the railway station. In this case the line was worked by East Ham and WEST HAM cars. The three lines were not connected until early 1907 when a double-track link was laid from Axe Street into the Broadway to meet the line from East Ham and a double-tracked road bridge opened at the station (to replace a level crossing) to enable a link to be made with the Ilford line in Longbridge Road (the working of which was taken over by Barking from 1 October 1907).

Two top-covered Brush cars (Nos 8 and 9) were bought in 1911 and a year later (along with Nos 1-3 and 7) fitted with conduit ploughs in anticipation of through working over LONDON COUNTY COUNCIL lines; at the same time car No 10, similar to Nos 8 and 9, was bought already so equipped. Through running via Ilford to Aldgate in London began on 20 December 1912 but lasted only until 31 May 1914, it proving a loss-maker for the Council. No 10 was then sold to Ilford as was No 8 in 1915 while No 9 went to East Ham. In 1926 Nos 4 and 5 were withdrawn as worn-out and three years later, on 16 February 1929, the Beckton-Broadway section was abandoned in favour of buses and the last cars scrapped. In 1931 track renewals meant that the two leased sections of line (totally 1.23 miles) became separated with the removal of the Broadway/East Street junction and two years later both became part of LONDON TRANSPORT routes.

Bibliography: *The Tramways of East London* 'Rodinglea' (The Tramway & Light Railway Society/The Light Railway Transport League, 1967)

BARNSLEY & DISTRICT ELECTRIC TRAMWAY

Authority: Barnsley and District Light
    Railway Order 1900
Gauge: 4ft 8½in
Traction: Overhead electric
Opened: 31 October 1902
Closed: 3 September 1930
System: Branching
Length: 3.06 miles
Stock: 1 sd, 13 dd
Livery: BET green & white
Last Car: ?

Although of the same gauge as and, at one point only a matter of yards from a possible connection with, this south Yorkshire system always remained physically isolated from the neighbouring SHEFFIELD–ROTHER-HAM–MEXBOROUGH & SWINTON–DEARNE DISTRICT network.

At the close of the 1890s two rival proposals were made for an electric tramway in the town, from Barnsley Corporation and the BET, and it was the latter's scheme that won the day. The line was owned and operated by a BET subsidiary, the Barnsley & District Electric Traction Co. (registered 3 February 1902) and consisted of a mainly single-track main line running south from the Smithies terminus in Monk Bretton just over the borough boundary, along Mill Lane and up Eldon Street to the MR and GCR/LYR stations. (This 1 mile was always worked by a shuttle service.) From here it continued on south through the town centre and out along the Sheffield Road and past the depot to a terminus in Park Road, Worsborough Bridge. The system's one branch was a ½-mile line at the southern end running southeast along Worsborough Dale High Street, making the whole track plan look like an inverted Y.

The first year's services were worked by Brush open-toppers 1-10, joined in 1903 by two more (Nos 11 and 12); all were later fitted with top covers. In 1905 BEC demi-car 59 was loaned by YORKSHIRE (WOOLLEN DISTRICT) for trials and purchased that same year (and renumbered 13); the passenger car fleet was completed in 1912 when No 14, a Brush top-covered car, was bought.

The little system settled down to an uneventful life though in 1919 a pointer to the future came when the Company, by now running motor buses, dropped the word Electric from its name. In 1924 the Dearne District finally reached Barnsley but the Company refused to allow a physical connection to be made and through running to take place in order to protect its bus services which, six years later, killed off its own tramway.

BARROW-IN-FURNESS TRAMWAYS

Authority: Barrow-in-Furness Corporation Act 1881
Gauge: 4ft
Traction: Steam/overhead electric
Opened: 11 July 1885
Closed: 5 April 1932
System: Radial
Length: 6.39 miles
Stock: 10 locos, 10 dd steam; 33 sd, 15 dd electric
Livery: Maroon & white steam?, maroon & cream BET, olive green & cream Corporation
Last Car: No 45

In 1881 Barrow-in-Furness Corporation secured an Act to authorize the construction of tramways which it then leased to a private concern, the Barrow-in-Furness Tramways Co. Ltd. The system comprised three lines radiating from Ramsden Square to the steelworks (northwest), past the Furness Railway's Central station to Abbey (northeast) and to Roose by the FR station there (east) plus a fourth route which branched off the last line by the Town Hall and ran south through Tea House to the FR station at Ramsden Dock (this last opening on 28 July 1886). Total route length was 5½ miles and the system single-track.

Eight Kitson tram locomotives (Nos 1-8) were supplied during 1888-92 and a similar number of Falcon top-covered double-deck bogie trailers (Nos 1-8) were bought in 1885, all based on a depot in Salthouse Road on the Roose route.

In 1898 the BFT Co. went into liquidation and was taken over on 23 December the following year by the BET, the Corporation having declined to purchase the concern. The BET's intention was to electrify the system in accordance with its usual policy but whilst awaiting the appropriate authorization improved the service somewhat by the addition in 1900 of two Wilkinson locos and two more trailers from the NORTH STAFFORDSHIRE TRAMWAYS in the POTTERIES. The next notable event occurred on the night of 27 June 1902 when a fire at the depot destroyed several locos and trailers; these were never replaced and by the time of the system's closure on 13 July 1903 the surviving stock was in very poor shape.

The electrified system – authorized by the Barrow-in-Furness Tramways Order 1903 – opened to the public on 6 February 1904 with the Roose and Abbey routes in service; the Ramsden Dock line followed in June. (The short line to the steelworks was lifted in 1903 having been abandoned early in the steam days).

In October 1904 a new route opened: a short branch midway off the Ramsden Dock line to Walney Ferry. The intention was to extend this line over a new bascule bridge to Walney Island and on to Biggar Bank on its west coast and on 4 August 1911 the whole route was in operation. (The line across the island was actually built by the Corporation.)

All routes were mainly single-track and a new depot was built on the site of the old one. Services were worked initially by a fleet of seven Brush open-top cars (Nos 1-7) and five Brush bogie single-deckers (Nos 8-12); these were joined in 1905 by two more Brush open-toppers (Nos 15 and 16) and two BEC demi-cars (Nos 13 and 14). Later additions to the fleet were four large Brush bogie open-toppers in 1911 (Nos 17-20), four Brush bogie single-deckers in 1913-14 (Nos 21-24), and two Midland bogie single-deckers (Nos 25 and 26) bought c1915 from the Potteries system.

After suffering the customary neglect during World War I the tramway was purchased on 1 January 1920 for the sum of £96,250 by the Corporation who added a further 22 single deck cars over the next two years, numbering them 1-4 (ex-SOUTHPORT), 29-34 (ex-SHEFFIELD) and 35-46 (new from Brush). Several of the life-expired BET cars were scrapped and by 1931 a total of 31 were left in stock. A year later the system closed, replaced by bus services in the face of the cost of modernization.

Bibliography: *Seventy-Five Years on Wheels: The History of Public Transport in Barrow-in-Furness 1885-1960* Ian L. Cormack (The Scottish Tramway Museum Society, 1960)
Barrow-in-Furness Transport – a Century on Wheels Ian L. Cormack (Author, Glasgow, 1977)

BATH TRAMWAYS

Authority: Bath Tramways Order 1880
Gauge: 4ft
Traction: Horse
Opened: 24 December 1880
Closed: 25 July 1902
System: Single line
Length: 1.71 miles
Stock: 14 sd
Livery: Blue & yellow?
Last Car: ?

This short line from the GWR station to Grosvenor College on the London Road was operated in later years by the Bath Road Car & Tramway Co. Ltd, operators of several horse bus routes in the city. (It is thought only the northern half of the line opened in 1880 with the extension to the station following later.) It was originally owned by the Bath Tramways Co. Ltd (incorporated July 1880) who ran it with six (later seven) Starbuck cars before selling out in 1884 to the Patent Cable Tramways Corporation who – despite its name – continued with horse traction (and seven new single-deckers). This concern too experienced financial difficulties

Barrow-in-Furness single-decker No 22 of 1913 photographed during World War I (note the conductress). The job of the boy was to jump off and change the points as needed. (Lens of Sutton)

and four years later sold out to DK who, in turn, sold the line in 1889 to the BRCT Co. who ran it successfully until 1902 when it was purchased by the Corporation for the arbitrated price of £5,210 to make way for electrification. (See below).

Bibliography: *Bath Tramways* (Locomotion Papers No 52) C. Maggs (The Oakwood Press, 2nd rev ed 1992) 0 85361 392 3

BATH ELECTRIC TRAMWAYS
Authority: Bath and District Light Railways Order 1901
Gauge: 4ft 8½in
Traction: Overhead electric
Opened: 2 January 1904
Closed: 6 May 1939
System: Radial
Length: 14.78 miles
Stock: 6 sd, 34 dd
Livery: Bright blue & primrose
Last Car: No 22

Work began on building Bath's new tramway system in November 1902 with routes from the city centre northeast to Bathford, south to Combe Down, southwest to Oldfield Park, west to Twerton and Newton St Loe and northwest to Weston being opened between 2 January 1904 and 5 August of the following year. The operator was the Bath Electric Tramways Ltd (registered 9 July 1902) on whose behalf the Corporation had purchased the old horse line (see above).

No further lines or extensions were constructed although the idea of linking with BRISTOL's network was mooted regularly, the two systems being only half a dozen miles apart at their closest points but very much reflecting the differences between the two cities: that of Bath being smaller, more compact and forced to cope with narrow streets, sharp corners and steep gradients. The latter were particularly in evidence on the Combe Down line (much used by day-trippers) which climbed to over 500ft above sea level. The two systems did achieve one link though in December 1936 when the Bath company was taken over, or rather swallowed, by the Bristol Tramways & Carriage Co. By this date the writing was on the wall: both companies were already operating motor buses and on 3 November 1938 the Newton St Loe route closed. The Twerton line went on 22 April 1939 and the remainder of the system on 6 May of the same year.

After the closure the rolling stock (Milnes open-top cars Nos 1-26 of 1903 and 27-34 of 1904 and single-deck combination cars 50-53 of 1903 and 54 and 55 of 1904) was scrapped without any being bought by other systems. All in all it was an almost indecently swift end to the city's tramways.

Bibliography: as above

BATLEY CORPORATION TRAMWAYS
Authority: Batley Corporation Tramways Order 1900
Gauge: 4ft 8½in
Traction: Overhead electric
Opened: 26 October 1903
Closed: 4 March 1934
System: Radial
Length: 6.65 miles
Stock: 8 dd
Livery: Green & cream to World War I, then maroon & primrose
Last Car: ?

Although a tramway (and tramcar) owner, Batley Corporation was never a tramway operator in its own right. Although it obtained the necessary authorization to construct tramways in 1900, a dispute with the BET over using part of the former DEWSBURY, BATLEY & BIRSTAL line prevented the immediate implementation of its plans to the full. Construction however went ahead and eight cars ordered from BEC.

The dispute with the BET was settled eventually: under the provisions of the BET-promoted Dewsbury Batley and Birstal Tramways Act of 1903 the Corporation was to reconstruct and electrify the relevant portion of the old DBB, then lease the whole system to the BET for 28 years. Trials and inspection were carried out in the summer of 1903 using cars on loan from the BET's YORKSHIRE (WOOLLEN DISTRICT) system (of which the Batley lines were to become a part); the Corporation-owned cars did not arrive until October, delaying the opening.

As built, the system was roughly in the shape of a capital H with the two sides linked to the Bradford Road (in the north) and Halifax Road (in the south) routes of the YWD. A stub branch from one of the upper arms led to the Market Place; all lines were single-track with passing places and short double-track sections. From the opening the system was worked as an integral part of the YWD and the eight Corporation cars absorbed into the larger fleet as Nos 49-56 (whilst retaining their own livery) until the closure.

Bibliography: *The Tramways of Dewsbury and Wakefield* W. Pickles (The Light Rail Transit Association, 1980) 0 900433 73 6

BEXLEY URBAN DISTRICT COUNCIL TRAMWAYS
Authority: Bexley Tramways Act 1901
Gauge: 4ft 8½in
Traction: Overhead electric
Opened: 3 October 1903
Closed: 23 November 1935
System: Branching
Length: 5.1 miles
Stock: 39 dd
Livery: Maroon & cream to World War I, then chocolate & cream
Last Car: ?

In spite of its name this system never actually served the Kent town of old Bexley but rather the district to the north. It was promoted by Bexley UDC and ran from a terminus by the end of the WOOLWICH & SOUTH EAST LONDON (see LONDON) horse line in Plumstead in a general south-easterly direction out across the county

Bexley UDC No 8 of 1903 off the rails at the Welling terminus. Such events were frequently recorded by local photographers for a quick postcard sale. (Courtesy Andrew Maxam)

boundary to Welling and thence to the Market Place in Bexleyheath, beyond which was sited the depot just before the actual terminus at Gravel Hill. A second route northwards from the Market Place through Crayford and along the Erith Road to Northumberland Heath provided (from 1905) a connection with the ERITH system. Both routes were single tracks.

Twelve open-top ERTCW cars were bought to work the system, followed in 1904 by four more (Nos 13-16) to cope with the heavier than expected traffic.

In 1906 DARTFORD's new tramway opened to Gravel Hill and from 27 August that system's cars ran through the few hundred yards to the Market Place. The next connection came in 1908 when LONDON COUNTY COUNCIL, having regauged and electrified the Woolwich horse line, connected with the Bexley line at Plumstead. A deal was then made whereby in return for handing over the 8.69 chains of track actually in London, Bexley UDC were given the right to run cars through to Woolwich.

As at Erith and Dartford, World War I brought increased traffic to the line in the shape of munition workers and in 1915 the UDC hired 17 ERTCW enclosed double-deckers from the LCC, purchasing them outright between 1918 and 1920 when they were numbered 17-33; during that period another six similar cars were hired but never bought. (These were theoretically 34-39 in the fleet list but it is not known how many, if any, were actually renumbered.)

Following the disasterous Dartford fire of 1917, both systems were run as one with Bexley supplying the cars; from 1 April 1921 after BB's lease of the Dartford system expired, both were formally run by a Joint Committee of the two local authorities until 1 July 1933 when both were taken over by the new LONDON TRANSPORT. Thereafter some cars of the old fleet were withdrawn and ex-LCC cars brought in during the short period before the whole Woolwich-Bexleyheath-Dartford route closed two years later, replaced by trolley-buses, two weeks after Erith had suffered a similar fate.

Bibliography: *The Tramways of Woolwich and South East London* 'Southeastern' (The Light Railway Transport League, 1963)

BIDEFORD, WESTWARD HO! & APPLEDORE RAILWAY

Although a light railway, the first 1/4 mile of this 5 1/2-mile standard gauge line ran through the streets of the Devon town of Bideford which necessitated the railway's three Hunslet tank engines being fitted with side skirts (and later cowcatchers). Another

tramway connection was provided by the fact that following the line's authorization in 1896 the Company was acquired by the BET before the first section opened on 24 April 1901; when completed in 1908 it ran westwards from Bideford Quay on the River Torridge to the north Devon coast some 2 miles away, then turned northeast to reach the other two places of its title.

Presumably the BET had second thoughts about its purchase for the line, unlike most of the group's other acquisitions, was never electrified and even if the locomotives had not been requisitioned by the Government in 1917 for war service in France it is doubtful that the railway could have lasted much longer in the face of growing bus competition. The last train ran on 28 March of that year.

Bibliography: *Bideford, Westward Ho! and Appledore Railway* (Oakwood Library of Railway History No 89) Stanley C. Jenkins (The Oakwood Press, 1993) 0 85361 452 0

BIRKDALE & SOUTHPORT TRAMWAYS *see* SOUTHPORT TRAMWAYS

BIRKENHEAD TRAMWAYS

Authority: Local authority permission
Gauge: 5ft 2in/4ft 8½in*
Traction: Horse
Opened: 30 August 1860
Closed: 24 January 1901?
System: Network
Length: 10.64 miles
Stock: 6 sd, 31 dd
Livery: Mahogany, red & cream? (Street Railway light green & cream?)
Last Car: ?

Although rural roadside tramways had been known in Britain for many years (see the Oystermouth Tramroad in Section 3 and STRATFORD & MORETON), Birkenhead's first street tramway was of great historic importance, being the first of its kind in the whole of the British Isles. It was the brainchild of George Francis Train, an American entrepreneur of great drive and enthusiasm who, in 1860, convinced the Birkenhead dock and local authorities that a new-fangled American-style street railway would be just the thing for their town.

Despite considerable opposition from certain interests (notably horse bus operators) the scheme went ahead with a 1½-mile line from Woodside Ferry approach, up Shore Road, Argyle Street and Conway Street to terminate at the entrance to Birkenhead Park. The operator was the Birkenhead Street Railway Co. Ltd (registered 7 May 1860). Two open-top double-

deck cars (Nos 1 and 2) and two closed single-deck saloon cars (Nos 3 and 4) were supplied by an American builder, shipped over in pieces and assembled by Robert Main, a local coachbuilder.

Some confusion exists as to the original gauge of the street railway (for so it was called, in American fashion). Train laid the single-track line using step rails, 6in-wide flat wrought iron rails with a ¾in lip or flange along the outer edge (as opposed to a traditional British plateway where the flanges were usually on the inner edges). It would appear that as the gauge used on the American lines on which Train modelled his was commonly given as 5ft 2in or 5ft 2½in, Train specified the same dimension. Unfortunately, the American measurement was taken between the outsides of the flanges and was actually railway standard gauge if measured between the insides (ie normal British practice) so when the rails were laid they were wider apart than intended. The track was laid by the kerbside (both kerbs in the case of Conway Street) and soon gave rise to complaints from other road users on account of its profile; the line was popular with its passengers though and in late August 1861 a 1-mile extension round Birkenhead Park along Park Road East and Park Road South, then down Palm Grove to Oxton (and the depot) was opened. That year the stretch in Shore Road was abandoned, replaced by a new line in Chester Street and Bridge Street.

The horse bus opposition reached its peak in 1862 when Thomas Evans, a local operator and dignitary of some importance, began running what were in effect private tramcars along the tracks. The problem for Train was that when seeking permission to lay his tramway, he had attempted to mollify any opposition by promising to allow other road users to run vehicles on the rails. Beaten, in early 1862 he leased the line to Evans, only to see it closed down that August – only to re-open that same month newly-leased to Charles Castle of Liverpool.

Improvements came in the summer and autumn of 1864 when the Conway Street line was singled and another line laid in Price Street and Hamilton Street to provide a one-way loop, plus a short extension to the new ferry terminal at Woodside. At the same time the entire line, now just under 2½ miles of mainly single track, was relaid to 4ft 8½in gauge with grooved rails (thought to have been the invention of a Laird's shipyard engineer). Thereafter the line was alternately leased out and operated by the Company until 1876 when it was put up for sale. A new concern, the Birkenhead Tramways Co. was then formed to buy it and in 1877, empowered by the Birkenhead Tramways Act of that year, did so (the BSR

Co. being dissolved at the same time). On 1 August 1878 a 1½-mile route south from Argyle Street along Brough Road past Clifton Park and Higher Tranmere to North Road, Prenton, was opened.

In 1879 the Company purchased its close neighbour, the HOYLAKE & BIRKEN-HEAD TRAMWAY (see below), thus beginning the long process of unifying all the town's tramways. On 1 June 1881 a ½-mile extension from North Road south to Prenton Lane was opened (double tracks like the rest of the Prenton route) and at the end of that year the relatively new Price Street line was closed with cars in both directions then using Conway Street again (doubled again since October 1878).

The Street Railway's original four cars were followed by four American single-deckers (Nos 5-8) in 1861 of which at least two were named, in American fashion, *Young England* and *Young America*. It is thought that most, if not all of the eight were converted to 4ft 8½in gauge in 1864 and withdrawn over a number of years, in effect being replaced by eight Starbuck cars of 1876 (all open-top double-deckers) bought by the BT Co. and numbered 1-8 also. These were followed two years later by eight more slightly smaller Starbuck cars (probably Nos 9-15) and in 1879 by eight H&B double-deckers which took the numbers 17-24 and ran until 1887 when they were withdrawn about the same time as the 1876 Starbuck cars. (No 7 was sold to BIRKDALE & SOUTHPORT but managed to survive until the present day and is now undergoing restoration.) Finally, in 1887-8 five small Milnes double-deckers were bought to replace some of the ex-H&B cars and took their numbers.

By the end of the 1880s the Company was in financial trouble – mainly because of the spread of railways in the area – and in September 1888 it went into liquidation. On 8 August 1889 the Birkenhead United Tramway, Omnibus & Carriage Co. Ltd was formed to buy it (and also the Birkenhead & District Omnibus & Carriage Co. Ltd), the takeover being completed on 15 August 1890 with the purchase price of £37,500 buying amongst other things 27 cars (of which only 17 were serviceable). The track was bought by Birkenhead Corporation for £5,000 (to lease back to the United Company until 31 December 1900) which soon found itself spending large sums on repairing or relaying it and by the late 1890s it had decided to purchase and electrify all the town's horse lines, including the WIRRAL TRAMWAY. The only new cars purchased during this period were two small Milnes double-deckers (which appear to have again taken vacated earlier numbers). All surviving cars were sold by auction after

A car on G. F. Train's historic Birkenhead line, as depicted in the Illustrated London News *of 15 September 1860.*

the system's closure which occurred quietly in early 1901 when the last services, based on the New Ferry Depot, were terminated.

Bibliography: *The Tramways of Birkenhead and Wallasey* T.B. Maund & Martin Jenkins (The Light Rail Transit Association, 1987) 0 948106 03 4

BIRKENHEAD: HOYLAKE & BIRKENHEAD TRAMWAY

Authority: Hoylake and Birkenhead Railway and Tramways Act 1872
Gauge: 4ft 8½in
Traction: Horse
Opened: 6 September 1873
Taken Over: 12 October 1879
System: Single line
Length: 2.29 miles
Stock: 8 dd
Livery: Maroon & cream?

This short line was promoted in 1872 by the Hoylake & Birkenhead Rail & Tramway Co. in order to link Woodside Ferry in Birkenhead with the Dock station of the financially-troubled Hoylake Railway to the northwest. (The HBRT Co. took over the railway company at the same time.) Opened

the following year, it ran from the ferry approach along Canning Street, Bridge Street, Cleveland Street and Beaufort Road to the station where a covered interchange was provided – something rarely found on British tramways and which probably originally housed the tramway's fleet of eight open-top Starbuck cars carrying the legend 'THE HOYLAKE RAILWAY'.

From 2 May 1876 the line was worked by W. W. Townson, a local vet, and it is thought that purpose-built stables and depot by the Docks station were rented by him from the Company; this arrangement ended three years later when, on 12 October 1879, the BIRKENHEAD TRAMWAYS Co. (see above) purchased the line for £27,000 (including the cars but not the depot buildings which the railway company leased to the BT Co).

Bibliography: as above

BIRKENHEAD: WIRRAL TRAMWAY (1)

Authority: Wirral Tramways Order 1874
Gauge: 4ft 8½in
Traction: Horse
Opened: 23 July 1877?

Closed: 22 January 1901
System: Single line
Length: 2.99 miles
Stock: 16 sd, 4 dd
Livery: ?
Last Car: ?

Birkenhead's third independent horse system was owned by the Wirral Tramway Co. Ltd who operated a single-track line south from Woodside Ferry along Chester Street and New Chester Road as far as the depot in New Ferry by New Ferry Road, running close to the Mersey shore and the Tranmere and Rock ferries.

The line was inspected by the BoT on 23 July 1877 but not passed for traffic; nevertheless public services were commenced straightaway and ran for some days before the BoT put a stop to them. It was not until after another inspection on 1 November 1877 that the line was passed fit to open; a short extension (built and owned by the Birkenhead Commissioners but rented to the Company) opened 19 January of the following year and took the tramway onto the Woodside Ferry approach.

The line was an obvious success, for heavier rails were substituted for the originals in 1879 whilst at the same time the original seven small Starbuck single-deckers were replaced by seven longer cars. (A low railway bridge over Chester Street by Tranmere Pool precluded the use of double-deckers.) The 1877 cars are thought to have been sold to the WALLASEY TRAMWAYS and their numbers 1-7 allocated to the new cars. Two more (Nos 8 and 9) were bought in 1880, followed by open-top double-deckers Nos 10 and 11 (1894), 12 (1895) and 13 (1896), all

probably from Milnes. It is presumed the double-deckers worked on the long stretch of the line from NewFerry to the Mersey Railway's Green Lane station just south of the low bridge (and close to the Tranmere Ferry pier and Laird's shipyard).

By now Birkenhead Corporation was planning to purchase and electrify the three horse systems in the town; in 1900 a figure of £22,666 was arbitrated for the price and on 8 May 1900 the last WT trams ran to make way for reconstruction work and eight days later the stock was auctioned off. This was not quite the end of the story though for some of the single-deck cars (including Nos 4, 8 and 9) were purchased by Birkenhead United Tramways (see BIRKENHEAD TRAMWAYS earlier) and put back into makeshift service around the affected track sections until 22 January 1901, after which they were auctioned once again!

Bibliography: as above

BIRKENHEAD CORPORATION TRAMWAYS

Authority: Birkenhead Corporation Act 1897
Gauge: 4ft 8½in
Traction: Overhead electric
Opened: 4 February 1901
Closed: 17 July 1937
System: Network
Length: 79.08 miles
Stock: 13 sd, 52 dd
Livery: Maroon & cream
Last Cars: Nos 31 (service) and 22 (official)

The Corporation's 1897 Act gave it the power to work tramways and the Birkenhead

Corporation Act of 1899 authorized its purchase of the town's existing horse tramways. Reconstruction work took place during 1900-01 and the first route re-opened was the old WIRRAL TRAMWAY's New Ferry line (see above), followed slowly by the bulk of the old horse system plus new routes to Claughton Village in the west and Tranmere to the south, the whole network being mainly double-track. The principal depot (opened 28 July 1903) was at Laird Street on the Claughton Village route whilst a second at New Ferry served the south-eastern side of the system.

The initial car fleet was made up of thirteen single-deckers (Nos 1-13) and 31 open-top double-deckers (Nos 14-44), all from Milnes; during 1908-10 the single-deckers were rebuilt as top-covered double-deckers low enough to pass under the Chester Street railway bridge. In 1902 Milnes supplied a further 15 open-top cars (Nos 45-59), this time bogie vehicles. (Except for No 46, all the double-deckers were later fitted with a variety of top covers.) The last cars bought were Nos 63-68, six HN low top-covered cars of 1913 for the New Ferry route. (Nos 60-62 were works cars.)

In 1919 the Corporation began running motor buses, at first as tramway feeders but later, from 30 August 1925 when they took over from the trams on the Claughton Road route to Claughton, as their replacements. By 1931 the buses were operating a route network in their own right and from 28 December that year they took over from the New Ferry trams. The Tranmere line closed 29 September 1934 and the Prenton route the very next day whilst the Dock route (the old HOYLAKE & BIRKENHEAD line) closed on 1 April 1935, leaving only the long, circular route out through Claughton Village round Oxton and back. The last public service tram to run was No 31, followed by No 22 (converted to an illuminated car for King George VI's Coronation) carrying the official party.

Bibliography: as above

BIRKENHEAD: WIRRAL TRAMWAY (2)

Authority: Wirral Tramway Light Railway Order 1994
Gauge: 4ft 8½in
Traction: Overhead electric
Opened: 14 April 1995
System: Single line
Length: 0.23 miles
Stock: 2 dd
Livery: Maroon

Britain's most recent tramway at the time of writing adds yet another chapter to

Three of Birkenhead Corporation's cars awaiting passengers at the Woodside Ferry terminal. (Lens of Sutton)

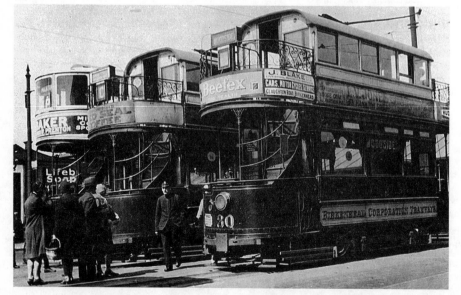

One of the two Hong Kong-built cars on Britain's newest tramway, the Wirral Tramway at Birkenhead.
(Courtesy Wirral Leisure Services & Tourism Department)

Birkenhead's long history of such lines with its opening nearly 60 years after the last trams ran in the town. Again starting from Woodside Ferry terminal (and bus station), it runs northwest as a single track on a roadside reservation for some 400yd along the ferry approach and Shore Road past the depot to a terminus by the corner of Pacific Road; it is intended to extend the line during 1995 another ¼ mile to Egerton Dock (and even further in the future) as part of the docklands redevelopment project. The rail used is from reclaimed Liverpool tramway track. Whilst only a pleasure line at present, it has been included here rather than in Section 7 as it is hoped that it will, when extended, meet a real transport need in serving the variety of different-use sites planned for the area.

The tramway's two enclosed double-deck cars were constructed by Hong Kong Tramways Ltd in 1992 specifically for the line and are numbered 69 and 70 to continue the BIRKENHEAD CORPORA-TION number series (see above) and are painted a similar dark red shade. Both cars ran in BLACKPOOL from mid-1993 until the opening of the line which is operated by Blackpool Transport Services on behalf of the owners, Wirral Metropolitan Borough Council.

BIRMINGHAM & DISTRICT TRAMWAYS

Authority: Birmingham and Staffordshire
 Tramways Act 1870
Gauge: 4ft 8½in
Traction: Horse
Opened: 20 May 1872

Taken Over: 8 December 1885
System: Branching
Length: 6.69 miles
Stock: 8 sd?, 23 dd?
Livery: Crimson & cream

The growth of Birmingham's large tramway system was complicated by the fact that when the first tramways appeared on the scene the city was far smaller in size than it later became and consequently many of the early lines crossed local authority boundaries in order to serve adjoining residential and industrial areas. Lines within the city boundary were always owned by the Corporation and, at first, leased to their operators whilst those outside were owned either by the lessee companies or the local authorities concerned. (Although Birmingham did not become a city until 1889 for the sake of simplicity it is hereafter always referred to as one.)

The first tramway in the region was built and operated by the Birmingham & District Tramways Co. Ltd (registered 29 July 1871) who, in 1872, opened a line from the Birmingham boundary at Hockley Brook running northwest up the Turnpike Road through Handsworth to West Bromwich in Staffordshire. At Carter's Green (the site of the main depot) on the far side of West Bromwich the line forked with the right-hand route going to Hill Top just south of Wednesbury and the left-hand line swinging west through Great Bridge to Dudley Port. Open-top double-deck cars 1-12 were bought from Metropolitan to work the mainly single-track lines. The Company also operated feeder bus services.

On 11 September 1873 Birmingham Corporation, under the Birmingham (Corporation) Tramways Order of 1872, opened a line from Monmouth Street (now Colmore Row) in the city centre via Great Hampton Street and Hockley Hill to meet the B&D line at Hockley Brook; this was leased to the Company and to help work which another (probably) ten double-deckers were bought from Metropolitan and Starbuck.

The line was not a financial success and at the end of 1873 the Dudley Port branch was closed as an economy measure; on 23 November 1874 however a new, shorter branch was opened north of Hockley east along Villa Road to Villa Cross but the following September the Hill Top route was cut back to Carter's Green. Matters did not improve though and on 24 May 1876 a new concern, the Birmingham Tramways & Omnibus Co. Ltd, was formed to buy the line. On 17 June a southern extension (again owned by the Corporation and leased to the Company) was opened along Colmore Road, Anne Street, Paradise Street, Suffolk Street and the Bristol Road for some 2½ miles to the boundary (with a short extension beyond to the Malt Shovel in Bournbrook) to serve the residential south side of the city.

After the Company's leases expired in 1885 on the two-thirds of the system owned by the Corporation the line was taken over by Birmingham Central Tramways (see CITY OF BIRMINGHAM TRAMWAYS later).

Bibliography: *Black Country Tramways Vol 1: 1872-1912* J.S. Webb (Author, Bloxwich, 1974)
Birmingham Transport Vol 1 Alec G. Jenson (The Birmingham Transport Historical Group, 1978) 0 905103 00 9

BIRMINGHAM & ASTON TRAMWAYS

Authority: Birmingham and Aston Tramways Order 1880
Gauge: 3ft 6in
Traction: Steam
Opened: 26 December 1882
Taken Over: 1 January 1904
System: Branching split line
Length: 4.85 miles
Stock: 27 locos, 26 dd
Livery: Locos crimson, cars cream

The next company on the scene in Birmingham, the Birmingham & Aston Tramways Co. Ltd, opened the first narrow gauge line in the city, thereby setting the standard for all subsequent tramways. Its line ran from Aston Street (later Old Square) in the city centre northwards to Aston Cross where two routes to Witton in Aston Manor diverged, one going via Park Road and Witton Lane and the other via Lichfield Road and Church Lane.

Services began with six Kitson tram locomotives (built 1882-83) and ten Starbuck open-top double-deck trailers of the same date. Later in 1883 two Wilkinson locos (Nos 7 and 8) were added and 19 more Kitsons (Nos 9-27) over the next three years. The passenger car stock was similarly increased by a succession of roofed bogie vehicles: Nos 11-18 in 1885 from Midland, Nos 19-22 in 1886 from Metropolitan and Nos 23-26 from Starbuck later that same year. In 1885 a branch was opened continuing up the Lichfield Road to Salford Bridge at the foot of Gravelly Hill from where the Company ran a horse bus service up to Erdington.

On 30 June 1902 Aston Manor UDC purchased its portion of the line, electrified it and leased it to the CITY OF BIRMINGHAM TRAMWAYS (see below) whilst at the beginning of 1904 the lease of the Birmingham portion expired and the Corporation took that section over in order to electrify it.

Bibliography: *A Short Review of Birmingham Corporation Tramways* P.L Hardy & P. Jaques (HJ Publications, Reading, 1971)

CITY OF BIRMINGHAM TRAMWAYS

Authority: Birmingham and Suburban Tramways Order 1882
Gauge: 3ft 6in, 4ft 8½in
Traction: Horse, steam, cable, battery electric, overhead electric
Opened: 11 November 1884
Taken Over: 1 January 1912
System: Radial network
Length: 36.65 miles
Stock: 10 dd horse; 102 locos, 76 dd steam; 10 sd, 38 dd cable; 1 loco?, 12 dd battery electric; 106 dd electric?
Livery: Sage & dark green pre-1896, then various

This system, the last to operate in Birmingham before the Corporation began running its own trams, began with the Birmingham Central Tramway Co. Ltd's horse line to Nechells Park Road from Old Square via Great Lister Street which was followed by a succession of steam-worked routes, the

City of Birmingham Tramways steam loco No 87 and trailer on 31 December 1906, the last day of service to Saltley. (Author's Collection)

principal ones being to Perry Barr, Saltley Road and Lozells in the north and Sparkbrook, Moseley Road and Small Heath in the south. The routes serving the northern half of the city ran from Old Square and those to the south from Station Street by the LNWR's New Street station (to where the Smithfield terminus had been relocated in June 1885). One horse line was also worked: from Albert Street to Nechells Park Road via Curzon Street and Holborn Hill (opened 6 June 1887).

The early steam services were provided by tram locos Nos 1-26, 35 and 36 (Kitson 1884-85), 27-34 and 37-57 (Falcon 1885-86), 58-70 (BP 1886) and 71 (Burrell 1886) hauling roofed double-deck bogie trailers 11-74 supplied by Falcon over the same period. The numbers 1-10 were presumably taken by the Company's ten open-top double-deck horse cars.

In January 1886 the Company bought those portions of the Birmingham Tramways & Omnibus Co.'s system outside Birmingham (see BIRMINGHAM & DISTRICT TRAMWAYS) whilst the Corporation leased it, those lines inside the city, including the Colmore Row–Hockley Brook route which, because of the climb up Hockley Hill, was converted to cable traction (and the 3ft 6in gauge) by the Patent Cable Tramway Co. As rebuilt, this ran from the Grand Hotel in Colmore Row to Hockley Brook from 24 March 1888 until extended on 20 April of the following year to a new, further terminus at the New Inns, Handsworth using open-top bogie cars 75-100 and 113-124, plus ten roofed bogie toastracks Nos 141-150, shedded at Hockley Depot.

The only portion of the system to use the 4ft 8½in gauge was the Bristol Road route to Bournbrook taken over in 1886; this was closed in October 1889 for it to be reconstructed. When it re-opened on 24 July 1890 it was worked by battery electric cars (open-top bogie double-deckers Nos 101-112) which lasted until 14 May 1901 when electric cars using an overhead supply were introduced; there was also at least one short-lived battery loco.

On 29 September 1896 the Company was taken over by a new concern, the City of Birmingham Tramways Co. Ltd; further locos and cars were added in the 1890s (partly as replacements for withdrawn stock), these being new Kitson locos 57, 60-62 and 71-90 together with Nos 91 and 92 (ex-BIRMINGHAM & ASTON) and Nos 93-97 (ex-BIRMINGHAM & MIDLAND) plus roofed double-deck bogie trailers Nos 125-130 from Midland (1899), later joined by Nos 131-136 (the Company's own of 1900).

In June 1902 the BET bought a controlling interest in the Company as part of its grand BLACK COUNTRY design and the next additions to the system came in 1904 when the Company took over the B&A line (worked electrically to Salford Bridge from 14 November and extended to Erdington on 22 April 1907); this was followed by further conversions and new routes (often worked jointly with the Corporation) but, on 31 December 1906, most of its leases expired (this being the last day of steam traction within the city), followed on 30 June 1911 by the last three remaining ones: electric to Cotteridge via the Pershore Road, and Selly Oak via the Bristol Road, and cable to Handsworth (where electric working began the next day). The Company's surviving operating rights passed to the Corporation on 30 December that year, leaving the way clear for it to provide a unified and expanding electric service. (See below.)

Unfortunately complete details of the electric stock (all thought to have been open-top double-deckers) do not seem to have survived. On the basis of the known numbers of the 60 cars taken over the Corporation, and assuming that the whole passenger car fleet was numbered consecutively, it would seem probable that the electric car numbers began in 1901 with Nos 151 to at least 170 (ERTCW) while 178-188 are known to have been 1903 Company-built bogie cars; Nos 193-238 were Brush cars of 1904 and Nos 239 to at least 242 Company-built with the Brush sequence beginning again in 1905 with No 246 (or before) to at least No 251, making a grand total which accords neatly with the 1905 official returns of 106.

Bibliography: as above

BIRMINGHAM CORPORATION TRAMWAYS

Authority: Birmingham Corporation Act 1903
Gauge: 3ft 6in
Traction: Overhead electric
Opened: 4 January 1904
Closed: 4 July 1953
System: Network
Length: 80.42 miles
Stock: 843 dd
Livery: Royal blue & cream
Last Car: No 66

Although Birmingham Corporation always owned the tracks within the city, it did not operate its own trams until 1904 when it re-opened the Steelhouse Lane (end of Colmore Row) to Aston Brook Street (the then boundary) section of the former BIRMINGHAM & ASTON line (see earlier). From then on the network grew slowly as the CITY OF BIRMINGHAM's leases expired (see above) and as the city's boundaries were expanded to swallow up a number of small neighbouring UDCs during the first decade of operations.

The system continued to grow after World War I to become a comprehensive network of long routes extending, from a number of central termini, in all directions to the city boundary with several loops and links between them. Connections to the BLACK COUNTRY network were made northeast of the city at Ladywood (BIRMINGHAM &

Birmingham Corporation No 146 of 1906 in the Stratford Road on the city centre–Sparkhill service. (Author's Collection)

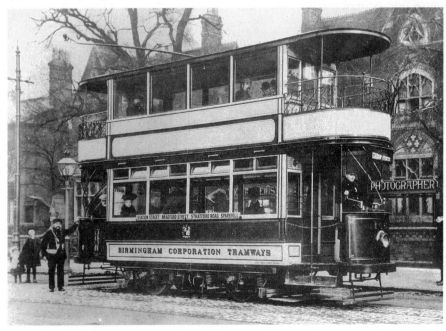

Many tramways illuminated cars for special celebrations. This Birmingham Corporation double-decker was so treated to mark the 1909 visit to the city of King Edward VII to open the new University of Birmingham. (Author's Collection)

MIDLAND) and Handsworth (SOUTH STAFFORDSHIRE). When the latter company's lease of West Bromwich Corporation's lines ran out in 1924, Birmingham took over the working and its trams ran right across the network to Dudley in the west. The last major route to open was east to Stetchford on 26 August 1928 whilst from 1 April that year the Corporation had taken over the former B&M lines.

Although the first route to close (to Nechells) had gone on 26 November 1922, replaced by trolleybuses (the first such substitution in Britain), it was the 1930s which saw serious damage done with the abandonment of the Bolton Road (4 May 1930), Hagley Road (10 August), Lozells via Hampstead Road (7 August 1933), Yardley via Coventry Road (6 January 1934), Stratford Road to Stoney Lane, Hall Green and Acocks Green (5 January 1937), Oxhill Road and West Bromwich (1 April 1939) and the Dudley Road (30 September 1939) routes. Replacement services were provided by motor and trolleybuses.

Although a lot of physical damage was done to the system during the World War II years it kept going (unlike in neighbouring COVENTRY) and the bulk of it remained in use in 1945; after that however the route closures came thick and fast: Lodge Road on 29 March 1947 and Ladywood on 30 August 1947 being the first two to go. By July 1953 only three routes to the northeast were left: up the Lichfield Road to Short Heath, Pype Hayes and Erdington, which all closed on the same day.

As the system expanded, so the car fleet grew in proportion; details of the trams (all double-deckers) were as follows:

Nos 1-20: UEC bogie open-toppers of 1904
Nos 21-70: UEC open-toppers of 1905-06
Nos 71-220: UEC top-covered of 1906-07
Nos 221-300: UEC open-toppers of 1907-08
Nos 301-450: UEC top-covered of 1911-13
Nos 451-511: ex-CB 178, 179, 193-208, 239-242, 181-188, 212-214, 220-227, 229, 231, 233, 234, 236, 246, 247, 249, 251, 152, 154, 156, 158, 160, 162, 164, 168 and 170
Nos 512-586: UEC bogie top-covered of 1913-14
Nos 587-636: Brush bogie top-covered of 1920-21
Nos 637-731: Midland bogie enclosed of 1923
Nos 732-811: Brush bogie enclosed of 1926-28
Nos 812-841: Short Bros bogie enclosed of 1928
No 842: Short Bros bogie lightweight enclosed of 1929
No 843: Brush experimental bogie lightweight enclosed of 1930

Many of the open-top cars were later fitted with top covers and/or rebuilt; of the whole fleet only one (No 395) has been preserved and is now on show in the city's Museum of Science & Industry. Several reminders of the tramways can still be seen in Birmingham today however, most notably the wide central reservations on some routes which carried reserved sleepered tracks – and which might yet carry them again if the Midland Metro proposals come to fruition.

Bibliography: as above

BIRMINGHAM & MIDLAND TRAMWAYS

Authority: Birmingham and Western Districts Tramways Order 1881
Gauge: 3ft 6in
Traction: Steam, horse, overhead electric
Opened: 6 July 1885
Taken Over: 1 July 1904
System: Branching
Length: 12.87 miles*
Stock: 4 sd horse*; 39 locos, 30 dd steam; 8 sd, 50 dd electric*
Livery: Dark green & cream, then BET Munich lake (+ cream for cars)

Promoted by local businessmen to link Birmingham with Dudley in the Black Country to the northwest via Smethwick and Oldbury, this tramway was constructed by the Birmingham & Western Districts Tramways Co. Ltd (incorporated 21 December 1882) but operated by the Birmingham & Midland Tramways Ltd (incorporated 22 November 1883). The plan was for some 35 miles of routes but in the event only a quarter of this was built.

The first section opened, using Kitson tramway locomotives 1-12 and Oldbury roofed bogie trailers 1-16, ran from Summer Row (Lionel Street) on the west side of the centre of Birmingham out along the Dudley Road to the boundary at Cape Hill (which section had been constructed by Birmingham Corporation). The remainder of the system opened in late August 1885 as a continuation of the main line from Cape Hill on through Smethwick, Oldbury and Tividale to Dudley station (8 miles) with two branches to West Bromwich (2½ miles in total). These ran north from Smethwick up Spon Lane and from Oldbury up Bromford Lane with a short link between the two termini along Paradise Street (though it is thought this was never used for passenger services). All lines were single-track with the exception of some stretches at the Birmingham end.

The other locos bought for the tramway were Nos 13 (1885) and 20-24 (1886) from Greens and Nos 14-19 (1886), 13, 22, 24-28 (1896-99), 29-34 (1899) and 1 and 10 (1900) from Kitsons, these last eight being bought from the DUDLEY, STOURBRIDGE & DISTRICT ELECTRIC TRAMWAYS. Trailers added were Nos 17-22 of 1886 (Starbuck), 25-27 of 1897-1900 (Company-built) and 28-32, ex-DSDET bought in 1900; all were roofed bogie vehicles again. The depot was on the main

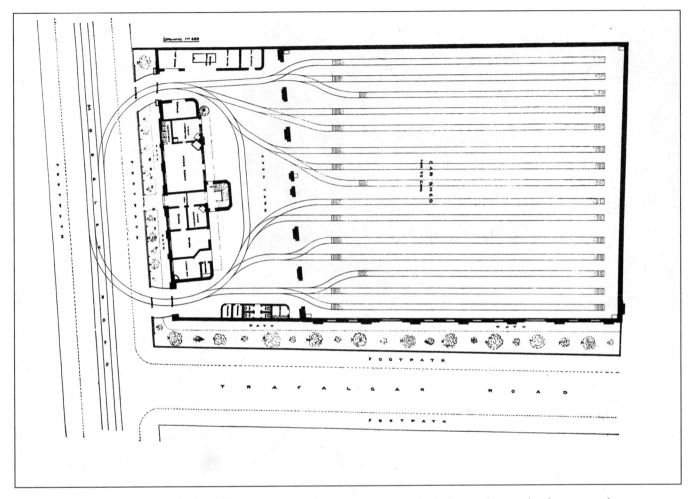

Track plan of Birmingham Corporation's Moseley Road Depot, published in a 1908 commemorative book. Note the unusual oval entrance track.

line in West Smethwick just beyond the Spon Lane junction.

The tramway was not a financial success and by the end of 1892 services over the West Bromwich branches had ceased, though reinstated in late May 1893 using horse trams operated on lease by a Mr B. Crowther of West Bromwich who provided two single-deckers of his own to supplement two Metropolitan single-deckers (Nos 23 and 24) supplied by the Company.

On 29 November 1899 the Company agreed to sell its shares to the BET who wished to electrify the line as part of its grand Black Country scheme and who, by early 1900, had gained control of both the Company and the BWDT Co. Ltd. Agreements were reached with the relevant local authorities (usually of a purchase and lease-back arrangement) and reconstruction began in the summer of 1903; the first portions to re-open, in early November, were the Spon Lane line from Dartmouth Square to the Cape Hotel and the Bromford Lane line from St Michael Street to the canal bridge. These were worked temporarily by

SOUTH STAFFORDSHIRE cars (the systems connected in West Bromwich), no Company cars having yet been ordered. The main Birmingham-Dudley line was re-opened on 24 November 1904, together with a new 1¼-mile double-track branch south from Cape Hill along Bearwood Road to the district of that name, terminating at its junction with the Hagley Road into Birmingham. (The rest of the system was still principally single-track.)

The first electric cars, of 1904, were open-toppers 1-12 (soon top-covered), followed by similar cars 13-18 and open-toppers 19-50 of a different design, all from Brush. Nos 53-60, also of 1904, were single-deckers built by the CITY OF BIRMINGHAM TRAMWAYS Co. On the last day of 1904 a last branch, off the Dudley Road in Birmingham northwest along Heath Street, was opened as far as the city boundary and extended on 24 May 1905 to Soho station in Smethwick (1¼ miles). This was a mixture of single and double tracks and, like the car details, has been included here for the sake of completeness for, from 1 July 1904, the tramway had been

controlled by the BIRMINGHAM & DISTRICT TRAMWAYS JOINT COMMITTEE (see below).

Bibliography: *Black Country Tramways Vol 1: 1872-1912* J.S. Webb (Author, Bloxwich, 1974)

BIRMINGHAM & MIDLAND TRAMWAYS JOINT COMMITTEE

The BMTJC was formed on 4 December 1903 by the BET and its subsidiaries in the Black Country. (This imprecisely-defined area, named after the pall of smoke which once shrouded its mines and metal working industries, is generally accepted to be the roughly square-shaped region of the Midlands bounded by, but not including, Stourbridge to the southwest, Birmingham to the southeast, Wolverhampton to the northwest and Walsall to the northeast. Each of the towns and villages packed cheek-by-jowl within it was noted for its own particular manufacturing industry eg glass around Stourbridge, locks in Willenhall, chains in Dudley and so on.) As from

Black Country car body, latterly used as a chapel, now preserved at the Blists Hill Open Air Museum, Ironbridge. (M. Donnison)

1 July 1904 the CITY OF BIRMINGHAM, BIRMINGHAM & MIDLAND, WOLVERHAMPTON DISTRICT, SOUTH STAFFORDSHIRE and the DUDLEY, STOURBRIDGE & DISTRICT tramways (including the KINVER LIGHT RAILWAY) were all controlled by the new Birmingham-based body with the B&M having bought the BET interests in the four other concerns. The Committee established a common fare structure, a parcels service, through timetabling and running and, in 1907, set up its own car production works at Tividale in the centre of the network just east of Dudley.

Details of cars bought by the companies within the BMTJC have been given in the relevant entries; details of those built by the Committee are given here as its policy was to construct vehicles in batches and allocate

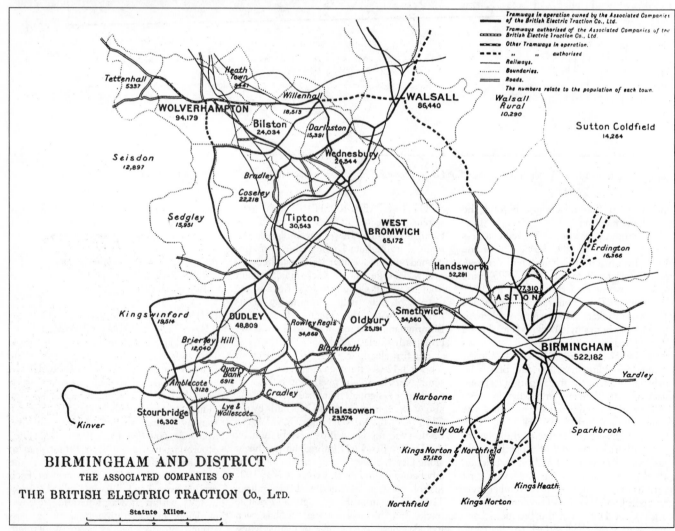

The Black Country tramway network as mapped in the 1903 Manual of Electrical Undertakings.

them as needed to the various nominally-independent systems (numbered in their series). Many were however transferred later between systems, only changing their numbers if confusion would otherwise have resulted.

The original livery was BET orange-yellow and pale cream with many cars being repainted in the 1900s in the BET's new Munich lake and cream; at the end of the decade a green and cream scheme was introduced to replace this. Between 1913 and 1916 the Committee built twelve top-covered double-deckers and between 1917 and 1920 32 single-deckers, this last batch being augmented by ten similar Brush cars (one of which went to the KIDDERMINSTER & STOURPORT line). One of the single-deckers, DSD No 5, is preserved and operational at the Black Country Museum, Dudley. Cars were also contructed for other BET tramways.

The problem facing the Committee was that of holding the whole structure together given the multitude of agreements made with a host of local authorities, three of which (BIRMINGHAM, WALSALL and WOLVERHAMPTON) ran their own systems which they wished to expand. The first cracks appeared in 1924 when West Bromwich Corporation decided not to renew its lease with the SS after 31 March, preferring Birmingham to work its nearly 7 miles of lines. With control of the heart of the network gone, the extremities were now vulnerable to bus (and trolleybus) competition and service cut-backs and abandonments soon followed. On 1 April 1928 the main line to Dudley of the Birmingham District Power & Traction Co. Ltd (the name of the B&MT Co. since 13 August 1912) was taken over by Birmingham Corporation and later that year Wolverhampton purchased the WD in order to substitute a trolleybus service. The DS system finally closed on 1 March 1930 leaving just part of the SS system to operate in the Wednesbury–Darlaston–Walsall area, partly as a joint operation with Walsall Corporation who took over the Walsall lines totally as from 1 October that year, and the Wednesbury area lines on 17 December.

All remaining cars were scrapped after the closure (and many of the bodies sold for garden sheds and the like, hence the survival and rescue of DSD No 5) except for seven double-deckers sold to DOVER CORPORATION and nine to Merthyr Tydfil.

Bibliography: as above, and *Vol 2* (1976)

BIRSTALL *see* DEWSBURY, BATLEY & BIRSTAL

BISLEY COMMON TRAMWAY *see* WIMBLEDON COMMON TRAMWAY

BLACK COUNTRY TRAMWAYS *see* BIRMINGHAM & MIDLAND TRAMWAYS JOINT COMMITTEE

BLACKBURN & OVER DARWEN TRAMWAYS

Authority: Blackburn and Over Darwen
    Tramways Act 1879
Gauge: 4ft
Traction: Steam
Opened: 16 April 1881
Closed: 16 October 1900
System: Single line
Length: 4.93 miles
Stock: 17 locos, 23 dd?
Livery: Red & cream
Last Car: ?

Blackburn's first tramway was a single-track steam line owned and operated by the Blackburn & Over Darwen Tramways Co. which ran south from the centre of Blackburn, south along Darwen Street (with a second terminal spur off this in St Peter Street) and the Bolton Road through Ewood, Earcroft, Hawkshaw (past the depot in Lorne Street) and Darwen to terminate at Whitehall. It was the first British tramway authorized to use steam traction only and had its official opening two days before public services began.

The first stock consisted of Kitson tram locomotives Nos 1-7 of 1881-82 hauling Ashbury open-top double-deck trailers Nos 1-8 of the same period, which were mounted on Eades patent reversible

trucks. These were joined in 1884 by bogie closed double-deckers 9-12, also from Ashbury. During the years 1885-96 another seven locos were bought (Nos 8-14), this time from Greens, plus bogie closed double-deck trailers 13-19 from Lancaster. In 1897-98 three further Kitsons were added (Nos 15, 1 and 2) to complete the locomotive stud. No other cars were bought, though it is thought that four open-top workmen's cars were used in 1883 for a short while.

As from the first day of 1899 the line was purchased jointly by the corporations of Blackburn (see below) and DARWEN for £22,337 and £26,400 respectively as a prelude to electrification – closure taking place the following year – and of the thirteen engines and thirteen cars taken over, Blackburn acquired ten of each and Darwen the remainder.

Bibliography: *The First in the Kingdom: a history of buses and trams in Blackburn and Darwen* R.P. Ferguson, G. Holden & C. Reilly ((Darwen Transport Group, 1981)

BLACKBURN CORPORATION TRAMWAYS

Authority: Blackburn Improvement Act
    1882
Gauge: 4ft 8½in
Traction: Steam, horse, overhead electric
Opened: 28 May 1887
Closed: 3 September 1949
System: Network
Length: 14.73 miles
Stock: 22 locos, 19 dd steam; 8 dd horse;
    13 sd, 48 dd electric
Livery: Holly green & cream
Last Car: No 74

The interior of Blackburn Corporation tramway depot with a range of double-deckers on show. (Lens of Sutton)

Postcard of Blackpool Corporation toastrack 74 of 1912 on a circular sight-seeing tour through the town, once a feature of several seaside resorts. (Author's Collection)

Blackburn's second tramway was an 8¾-mile horse and steam radial system promoted by the Corporation and operated by the Blackburn Corporation Tramways Co. Ltd. Focussed on the Church Street/Railway Street junction in the town centre, two horse routes ran west along Whalley Banks Street to Witton Stocks and along the Preston New Road past the horse tram depot in Simmons Street to Billinge End, while two steam routes ran east along Accrington Road past the steam depot at Intack and the Blackburn Road to Church and northeast up Whalley New Road to the Cemetery. All four routes were single-track and totalled 8.76 miles.

The original steam rolling stock comprised Green tram locomotives Nos 1-15 of 1887-88 and closed Ashbury bogie double-deckers 1-12 of 1887. These were joined in 1888 by similar trailers 13-15 from Falcon and (probably) in 1889 by Nos 16-19 from Milnes. The eight open-top horse cars (Nos 20-27) were also from Milnes. The only addition made to the fleet was the purchase in 1899 of seven Beyer Peacock locos (Nos 16-22) from the NORTH STAFFORD-SHIRE TRAMWAYS in the POTTERIES; these were bought by Blackburn Corporation who, on 24 August 1898, had taken over the system in order to electrify it (for a price of £87,000 agreed the previous year).

The first line to be converted was the 1½-mile Billinge End route which (mainly double-tracked) opened on 20 March 1899, eight Milnes open-top bogie double-deckers (Nos 28-35) having been bought for the purpose and housed in the rebuilt steam depot. This was followed by the electrification of the other horse and steam routes (including an extension of the Witton Stocks line on 31 March 1899 along the Preston Old Road to Witton, extended in 1903 to the Cherry Tree) and the conversion of the the 2½ miles of the BLACKBURN & OVER DARWEN line in Blackburn (see above) which re-opened on 1 December 1900. The Cemetery route re-opened on 1901 (extended to Wilpshire in 1902), the Church route re-opened in 1902 and a new 1½-mile southeast route to Audley was opened in 1903 to complete the mainly double-track system focussed on a long one-way system in the town centre.

To help work the growing electric tramway 40 Milnes bogie open-toppers (Nos 36-75) were added in 1901 (many of which were later top-covered), followed by UEC bogie single-deckers Nos 82-87 in 1907 for the Audley route and a single-deck bogie cross-bench car (No 88) a year later, built by the Corporation.

In August 1907 through running to ACCRINGTON via Church began. Thereafter little changed for more than 20 years, apart from the car rebuilding programme, until the 1930s when many of the tramway's neighbours began to close. It was not long before similar economic and political pressures produced the first Blackburn abandonments: on 13 February 1935 the Audley route went and on 31 March 1939 that to the Cherry Tree, replaced by bus services.

The tramway survived World War II without further cuts but on 5 January 1946 the Preston New Road line closed, followed on 21 December 1947 by the Wilpshire route. On 16 January 1949 the Church route was cut back to the depot and on 2 July 1949 the line to the Darwen boundary was closed, leaving just the Blackburn-Intack depot section to last until the autumn.

Bibliography: as above

BLACKPOOL CORPORATION TRAMWAYS

Authority: Blackpool Corporation
    Tramways Order 1884
Gauge: 4ft 8½in
Traction: Horse, conduit, overhead electric

Blackpool 'Balloon' No 701 of 1934 at Starr Gate, the present southern terminus of the line. Note the station-style nameboard. (Author)

Opened: 12 September 1885
System: Network
Length: 20.97 miles
Stock: 4 sd, 14 dd horse*; 91 sd, 222 dd electric
Livery: Green & teak to 1892, then dark green to c1905, then red, white & teak to 1933, then green & cream

The Blackpool Tramway will always have its place in history – and in the heart of tramway lovers. Not only was it the first electric tramway in England, it somehow managed to survive whilst all its counterparts were abandoned. The purpose of its construction was to assist the growth and development of the town as the premier seaside resort of the region and, in its first form, was a single line conduit tramway running from Cocker Street on the north side of Talbot Square (by the North Pier and close to Blackpool North station) along the Promenade to Dean Street by the South Pier, a distance of some 1¾ miles.

Services actually began with Starbuck open-top double-deck electric cars Nos 1 and 2, similar Lancaster cars 3-6 plus open toastracks Nos 7 and 8 (Starbuck) and 9 and 10 (Lancaster), all horse-drawn without their motors (and the latter pair used as trailers) until 29 September 1885 when electric working began. Nos 9 and 10 were replaced in 1891 by new cars 9 and 10, two Milnes open-toppers. In the following year, on 10 September 1892, the Blackpool Electric Tramway Co.'s lease expired and the owners, Blackpool Corporation, took over the working of the line. In 1895 the first branch was opened, from midway along the Promenade up Lytham Road to meet the LYTHAM ST ANNES line, for which large Lancaster bogie open-toppers 11-14 were bought. In 1897 a link between the two Blackpool routes was laid down Station Road (near Blackpool South station) and the following year, two large Midland bogie open-toppers numbered 15 and 16 and nicknamed 'Dreadnoughts' were purchased.

Although of historic significance in showing that electric street tramways could be operated safely, the Blackpool Conduit Tramway (as it was known) was not a success as regards its method of current supply. The system was prone to all sorts of disruptions caused by sand or water getting into the conduit – a seaside promenade line being just about the worst place possible for such a line – and temporary horse haulage often had to be resorted to. So, in the summer and autumn of 1899 the three lines and the 16 cars were converted to overhead working, and in 1900 linked to the recently-opened BLACKPOOL & FLEETWOOD line at Gynn Square.

After this the system grew steadily, both in terms of routes and stock. By 1 January 1920, when the Corporation took over the B&F line, it operated some 12 miles along the seafront and through the town's streets (mainly as loop lines). Meanwhile, the fleet was built up as follows, with many of the trams constructed by the Corporation under a car-building programme which has continued to this day, based on its main depot and workshops in Blundell Street off the Lytham Road route (although other builders' products are still bought). This is the only non-seafront portion of the system left in Blackpool for ten years after the last extension opened along the South Promenade to Clifton Drive (Starr Gate) in 1926, the cutbacks began of the non-seafront lines.

Nos 17-26: Midland bogie open-toppers of 1900 ('Dreadnoughts')
Nos 27-41: Midland open-toppers of 1901
Nos 42-53: HN bogie open-toppers of 1902
Nos 54-61: Midland Dreadnoughts of 1902
Nos 62-68: UEC bogie balcony cars of 1911-12
Nos 69-92: UEC bogie toastracks of 1911-14
Nos 93-98: Milnes bogie open-toppers bought 1919 ex-LONDON UNITED TRAMWAYS
Nos 28, 33-42, 45, 47-51, 53, 99, 100, 142-145, 153-160: Corporation bogie balcony cars of 1923-29 ('Standards')
Nos 146-152: HN bogie balcony cars of 1924-25
Nos 161-166: Corporation bogie toastracks of 1927
Nos 167-176: EE bogie single-deckers of 1928
Nos 200-224: EE bogie streamlined single-deckers of 1933-34 ('Railcoaches')
Nos 225-236: EE bogie open single-deckers of 1934-35 ('Boats')
Nos 237-249: EE bogie open-toppers of 1934
Nos 250-263: EE bogie enclosed double-deckers of 1934-35 ('Balloons')
Nos 264-283: EE Railcoaches of 1935
Nos 284-303: Brush Railcoaches of 1937
Nos 10-21: EE semi-open Railcoaches of 1939 ('Sun Saloons')
Nos 304-328: Roberts bogie streamlined single-deckers of 1952-53 ('Coronations')
Nos T1-T10: MCW bogie single-deck Railcoach trailers of 1960-61
Nos 761-762 Corporation bogie enclosed double-deckers of 1979 and 1982 respectively
No 641: East Lancashire Coachbuilders bogie single-decker of 1984 ('Centenary Car')
Nos 642-648: ditto of 1986-87

Many of the above vehicles have been, or were, extensively modified over the years, including the fitting of top covers and conversion to one-man operation. In addition, in 1968 the surviving cars were renumbered in a new series so that the 'Boats' became Nos 600-607, the single-unit Railcoaches 610-638, the last Coronation 660, the two-car unit Railcoaches 671-680, their trailers 681-690 and the EE double-deckers 700-726 (all now totally enclosed).

One other feature of the car fleet must be mentioned. Whilst many British tramways have run illuminated cars, usually on special occasions such as coronations, Blackpool has, since 1912, made a grand show of doing so, converting passenger cars into semi-permanent replicas of railway trains, space rockets, hovercraft and the like to complement the town's famous illuminations. Because of the sheer number of cars built for the tramway, and the fact that many of them have been withdrawn only comparatively recently, many survive as preserved vehicles on museum lines up and down the country (see Section 7) and even abroad; in return Blackpool plays host to operational preserved cars from elsewhere, affording visitors the unique sight of vintage tramcars working in their natural urban setting once again.

Bibliography: *Blackpool by Tram* G.S. Palmer & B.R. Turner (The Transport Publishing Co. rev ed 1981) 0 903839 55 5

BLACKPOOL NORTH PIER TRAMWAY
Authority: –
Gauge: 3ft
Traction: Diesel hydraulic
Opened: 2 September 1991
System: Single line
Length: 0.15 miles
Stock: 3 sd
Livery: Burgundy & cream

Blackpool's newest tramway was constructed as part of a £6m refurbishment of the North Pier by its owners, the First Leisure Corporation. The ½-mile long pier first opened in 1863, since when it has been added to and damaged by ships, fire and storms – the last such incident occurring in the winter of 1990-91 when the fishermen's jetty at the pier head and the sun lounge were badly damaged by gales.

The single-track line (with no passing loops or sidings) is laid with flat-bottomed rails laid flush with the decking on the northern side of the mid-section of the pier, partially roped and railed-off from the rest of the promenade area.

The tramway is worked by three similar, enclosed single-deck bogie cars coupled as a train, custom-built by Harry Steer Engineering of Breaston, Derbyshire. The centre car houses a Perkins diesel engine which, via a hydraulic pump, drives wheel

The three-car train on Blackpool's latest tramway, the 1991 North Pier line. (Author)

motors in the cars. (The centre car has four of its eight wheels powered and the driving trailers two each of theirs.) Another unconventional feature of the trams is that they have doors on their north sides only.

Although short in length (just 270yd) the tramway is not simply a pleasure line but serves a useful purpose in ferrying passengers between the landward and seaward structures on the pier in inclement weather – which the cars have been specially built to withstand, there being no shed facilities for them.

Bibliography: *Blackpool North Pier Tramway* Alison Orchard (Lancastrian Transport Publications, Blackpool, 1992) 0 950940 56 9

BLACKPOOL & FLEETWOOD TRAMROAD

Authority: Blackpool and Fleetwood Tramroad Act 1896
Gauge: 4ft 8½in
Traction: Overhead electric
Opened: 14 July 1898
Taken Over: 1 January 1920
System: Single line
Length: 8.21 miles
Stock: 41 sd
Livery: Nut-brown & cream

Following the pioneering success of the BLACKPOOL electric line, a continuation northwards along the Lancashire coast to the fishing port of Fleetwood on the Wyre estuary was promoted by the Blackpool & Fleetwood Tramroad Syndicate (later Company). Construction began from the Fleetwood end in July 1897 and within four

months the line had reached Uncle Tom's Cabin on the northern edge of Blackpool as a mainly reserved sleepered single track (hence the Tramroad rather than Tramway title). The desired route into Blackpool from Gynn Square just south of this point was opposed by Blackpool Corporation so the tramway had to forsake the shoreline and traverse the back streets to the joint Furness Railway and LNWR Talbot Road station (later Blackpool North) though this last mile of the line did not open until 29 September 1898 because of the road-widening works necessitated here. Within Blackpool itself the tramway was constructed by the Corporation and leased to the Company for 21 years.

Initial services were worked by ten cross-bench cars (Nos 1-10) and three cross-bench trailers (Nos 11-13) which were lengthened and motorized c1905, joined in the autumn of 1898 by six saloons (Nos 14-19). In 1899 the fleet was further enlarged by the purchase of five more saloons (Nos 20-24), three cross-bench cars (Nos 25-27) and seven composite cars (Nos 28-34). All were bogie single-deck vehicles and all from Milnes with the exception of the last seven which were from ERTCW. The fleet remained this size until 1910 when three more bogie toastracks were bought, this time from UEC (Nos 35-37), followed four years later by Nos 38-41, four UEC bogie saloons.

The first depots were in Copse Road, Fleetwood and at Bispham near Blackpool; these were joined by a small depot built in 1899 over the terminal road across Bold Street in Fleetwood to house the first and last trams of the day.

The tramway was popular, profitable and undoubtedly led to the growth and development of Fleetwood (and all points south) but as the Company's lease of the Blackpool section expired at the end of 1919 its long-term future looked uncertain. In the event the Company sold the whole line to the Corporation that year for £284,000 (having first failed to interest the LYR in its purchase), it subsequently becoming the major surviving portion of the Blackpool system.

Bibliography: *Blackpool to Fleetwood* Brian Turner (The Light Railway Transport League, 1977) 0 900433 67 1
Blackpool & Fleetwood by Tram Steve Palmer (Platform 5 Publishing, 1988) 0 906579 83 X

BOLTON CORPORATION TRAMWAYS

Authority: Bolton and Suburban Tramways Order 1878
Gauge: 4ft 8½in
Traction: Horse, overhead electric
Opened: 1 September 1880
Closed: 29 March 1947
System: Radial
Length: 32.36 miles
Stock: 48 sd & dd horse?; 3 sd, 162 dd electric
Livery: Maroon & cream
Last Cars: Nos 406 (service) and 440 (official)

Bolton's horse tramways were promoted by Bolton Corporation and the Astley Bridge, Farnworth and Kearsley Local Boards and, when constructed, were leased to Edmund Holden & Co, a local horse bus operator. The first three routes ran from the centre of the town southeast along the Manchester Road to Moses Gate on the boundary with Farnworth, north up the Blackburn Road to Dunscar and northwest along Halliwell Road to the district of that name. By 1882 two further routes had been opened: southwest along Derby Street and Ens Road to Daubhill station and west along Chorley New Road to Lostock Junction Lane, a total of just over 14½ track miles. The depot was in Shiffnall Street off Bradshaw Gate on the east side of the town centre.

By 1899 another 16½ miles of track had been laid on new routes and extensions and that year the Company offered to sell the concern to Bolton Corporation, receiving in June £58,000 for the business and 48 cars, some of which were fitted with reversible bodies. The Corporation was already contemplating electrifying the system (it had opened its own generating station in 1894) and on 9 December 1899 began electric tram services over three new routes: south from the centre for a mile down Fletcher Street,

Grecian Street and Rishton Lane to Lever Edge Lane, Great Lever; east for 1½ miles along the Bury Road as far as Toothill Bridge and northeast up Folds Road and Tonge Moor Road to the district of that name, terminating at Turton Road (2 miles).

The last horse trams ran on 2 January 1900 on the old system, that same day seeing the opening of seven new or converted radial routes to help form the basis of a system which, by 1924 when the last extension opened (as 3 miles of single track along the Wigan Road to Westhoughton on 19 December), comprised thirteen lines focussed on a complex one-way arrangement in the town centre. Originally, the lines were mainly single-track and, where possibly, utilized the old horse tramway rails though these had to be replaced in the 1900s (when a road-widening programme enabled many sections to be double-tracked). The former horse tramway route from Moses Gate to the Black Horse, Farnworth, was electrified by Bolton Corporation and worked by it from 13 April 1900, with an extension opening about January 1902 to Kearsley; from 1 June 1902 however it was worked by FARNWORTH CORPORATION as an independent system.

The first electric cars were ERTCW open-toppers 1-40 which were followed by similar cars 41-49 in 1900 (the last being a bogie vehicle). In 1901 came Brush bogie open-toppers 50-59, followed during 1901-02 by Nos 60-81, similar cars from ERTCW and, in 1903, by top-covered cars 82-86, again from ERTCW. (The open-toppers were later top-covered.) In 1906 ten more of the same (Nos 87-96) were added, this time from Brush. The pre-World War I purchases were completed by Nos 97-103 (top-covered bogie cars), Nos 104-106 (bogie single-deck combination cars) and Nos 107-112 (top-covered bogie cars), all bought 1910-12 from UEC. A depot was built on the site of the former horse stables with a second added in 1909 in Bridgeman Street as the car fleet grew, with three smaller depots added near the Horwich terminus, on the St Helens Road and at Tonge Moor.

In 1921 EE supplied top-covered cars 113-120, followed by ten more, Nos 121-130, in 1923. That year also saw the Corporation commence serious motor bus operations (having experimented with them before the war) and over the next quarter of a century the fleet grew steadily to eventually displace the trams. That was far in the future though and in 1924 eight Brush top-covered cars (Nos 131-138) were bought from SUNDERLAND and in 1927 enclosed cars 139-150 were bought new from EE, followed by similar cars 104-106 a year later which took the running numbers of

Postcard of Oxford Street, Bolton, with Corporation No 32 of 1899 approaching. (Lens of Sutton)

the tramway's only single-deckers.

No further new cars were purchased though twelve more second-hand cars were bought. The first eight, top-covered cars Nos 33-40, were bought in 1933 from the SOUTH LANCASHIRE TRAMWAYS (where they had been numbered 44, 45, 47, 48, 50, 54, 55 and 58) whilst the last four were enclosed cars 331 and 451-453 bought from BURY (Bury 21, 55, 56 and 58) ten years later. (The high numbers resulted from the addition in 1940 of 300 to the existing car numbers.)

On 29 December 1923 the Corporation began a bus service over the route of the short branch to Darcy Lever southeast of the town centre and five years later the trams were withdrawn; further closures followed during the 1930s until World War II offered a brief respite. In 1945 only four routes remained – northeast to Tonge Moor, southwest to Westhoughton, northwest to Horwich and north to Halliwell – of which the Halliwell route went on 5 August that year, the Horwich route on 6 October 1946, the last portion of the Westhoughton route on 8 December 1946 and the Tonge Moor line the following March.

One car from the fleet has been rescued and restored: this is No 66 which is in regular public service at BLACKPOOL.

BOURNEMOUTH CORPORATION TRAMWAYS

Authority: Bournemouth Corporation
   Tramways Act 1901
Gauge: 3ft 6in
Traction: Overhead, conduit electric
Opened: 23 July 1902
Closed: 8 April 1936
System: Radial network
Length: 16.11 miles
Stock: 1 sd, 131 dd
Livery: Chocolate & cream
Last Car: No 115

Although the idea of tramways in the town was originally opposed by Bournemouth Corporation (which resulted in the POOLE & DISTRICT line from the west terminating at the common boundary), it relented at the beginning of the 20th century and sought powers to construct its own system – and take over the Poole line.

The first route opened ran from the Landsdowne in the town centre eastwards along Christchurch Road to Warwick Road, Pokesdown, and by 17 October 1905 when this line was extended via Seabourne Road, Belle Vue Road and over the boundary on Stour Road into Christchurch, the system within the town was complete. Mainly single-track, it stretched as far east as Christchurch, north up Wimbourne Road to Moordown and west to Poole. Between the Christchurch and Moordown routes lay a series of interlinking lines and, by dint of careful planning, it managed to serve (from east to west) the railway stations of Christchurch, Pokesdown, Boscombe, Bournemouth Central, Bournemouth West, Branksome and Poole. As at certain other more genteel seaside resorts, the Corporation wished to avoid the presence of overhead wires on at least part of the system and the central portion of the network from the Landsdowne westwards along Old Christchurch Road, through the Square and on to St Michael's Church, Poole Hill, was laid with a conduit supply which lasted until 1911, an overhead being used here from 13 May onwards.

The only other line added was a Lower Parkstone route in Poole, opened on 3 August 1906 along Castle Hill and Bournemouth

Road, which left and rejoined the Upper Parkstone line.

Services began with bogie cars Nos 2-20 and four-wheelers Nos 21-48 from Milnes, like all Bournemouth's double-deckers open-toppers. These were joined in 1904 by similar bogie cars 49-54 and a year later by former Poole cars 1-17 which were renumbered 55-70 and 82 respectively. To house all these vehicles the Poole depot on Ashley Road was joined by depots at Moordown, Pokesdown and Southcot Road in the town centre, this latest being the Corporation power station as well as the main tramway depot and works.

In 1907 eleven Brush bogie cars were bought (Nos 71-81), the last Bournemouth cars to be equipped for dual current collection. UEC bogie cars 83-92 arrived seven years later and in 1921 and 1926 similar type cars 93-112 and 113-132 were purchased, this time from Brush again, to complete the fleet.

The tramway's only single-decker was No 1, a luxurious Milnes bogie saloon of 1902 which was reserved originally for official inspections, wedding parties and the like. Nicknamed the 'Picnic Car' on account of its wicker armchairs, these were replaced in 1920 when it was put into normal passenger service during peak periods.

In the years immediately after World War I much of the system was double-tracked but by the late 1920s the end was in sight. The first abandonment came on 5 January 1929 when the Lower Parkstone route was closed, replaced by Hants & Dorset Motor Services buses. In 1933 the Corporation began trolleybus operations and two years later the Hants & Dorset purchased the remaining Poole route for £75,000 in order to close it which, on 7 June 1935, it proceeded to do. The trams in Bournemouth lasted less than

another year, to be replaced by Corporation trolleybuses. After the closure Nos 85, 95, 103, 108, 112, 114-116, 121 and 128 were sold to the Llandudno & Colwyn Bay Electric Railway in Wales, together with No 55 which had been converted in 1921 to a rail-grinder. Car 85 is now preserved in Bournemouth, back in its home town again.

Bibliography: *The Tramways of Bournemouth and Poole* R.C. Anderson (The Light Railway Transport League, 1964)

BRADFORD CITY TRAMWAYS
Authority: Bradford Corporation Tramways Order 1880
Gauge: 4ft
Traction: Horse, steam, overhead electric
Opened: 1 February 1882
Closed: 6 May 1950
System: Radial network
Length: 64.54 miles
Stock: 6 sd, 10 dd horse; 44 locos, 39 dd steam*; 2 sd, 410 dd electric
Livery: Locos maroon, horse and steam cars nut-brown & cream; Prussian blue & white to 1937, ultramarine & white to 1942 then light blue & primrose electric
Last Car: No 104

In classic fashion Bradford's tramways progressed through the horse, steam and electric traction phases, beginning with a single horse-operated route running north-west from Rawson Square in the city centre along North Parade, Manningham Lane, Oak Lane, St Mary's Road and North Park Road to Lister Park Gates worked by six Ashbury open-top double-deckers (Nos 1-6). Although built and owned by Bradford Corporation, the line was leased to the

Bradford Tramways Co. (later the Bradford Tramways & Omnibus Co.) for operating purposes.

In 1890 two single-deck cars (Nos 36 and 37) were built locally for the line and two more (Nos 39 and 40) added in 1892, possibly second-hand vehicles from SHIPLEY TRAMWAYS; in 1894 the Company constructed two roofed toastracks (Nos 16 and 17); these could not have been very popular in this part of the country and that year four more Ashbury open-toppers, Nos 16-19, were bought (the toastracks being renumbered 46 and 47). All the horse cars were apparently mounted on Eades reversible trucks.

The horse line closed on 31 January 1902 in order to become part of the Corporation's electric system but by then other routes had been opened – again worked by the BT Co. and bringing the route mileage to 17 – but this time with steam locomotives on account of the steep hills surrounding the city centre. The first, opened 8 August 1882, ran east along the Leeds Road to Stanningley and was followed by other radial lines to Tong Cemetery (southeast), Allerton via Four Lane Ends (west) and from Manningham to Undercliffe as an extension of the horse line. One further steam line, southwest to Odsal and Shelf, was worked by the BRADFORD & SHELF TRAMWAYS Co. (see below).

The first steam locomotives were Nos 1-6 from Kitsons (1882), No 7 from Wilkinsons (1883) and No 8 from Kitsons (1884); a replacement No 7 was bought in 1885 along with Nos 9-11, all from Greens. Green locos 12 (1887), 13-22 (1888) and 23-36 (1896) followed, with second-hand engines 37-40 being bought from the NORTH STAFFORDSHIRE TRAMWAYS in the POTTERIES c1896 and 41-43 from the Bradford & Shelf line in 1887 (B&S Nos 1, 2 and 4, No 3 being broken up for spares).

The passenger fleet was made up of the former double-deck horse cars used as trailers, top-covered and numbered 7-16, joined by Milnes double-deckers 18 and 19 in 1885 with the same firm supplying Nos 20-35 over the next four years. In 1892 the Company rebuilt horse cars 16 and 17 as steam trailer 38 and Nos 18 and 19 as No 41; the last purchases were Nos 21, 49 and 50 from the North Staffs in 1899 and No 51 and 52 bought new in 1901, again all Milnes cars.

By the last years of the 19th century the Corporation had decided to construct and operate an electric tramway system itself and in 1898 opened lines to Bolton Junction (30 July) and Great Horton (27 August). Further new routes and extensions were opened and on 1 February 1902 the Company services were terminated to make way for the electric cars. In 1904 the MID-YORKSHIRE TRAMWAY in SHIPLEY was bought and

General route map of Bradford's tramways, from the 1909 Manual of Electrical Undertakings.

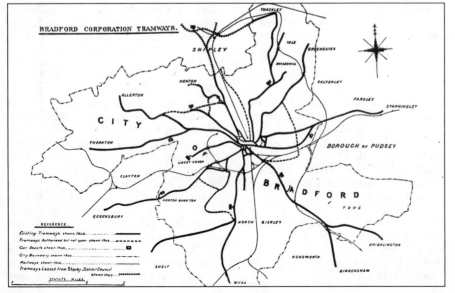

incorporated into the northern part of the system. Ten years later, on 13 October 1914, the last extension (from Bingley to Crossflats) was opened northwest of the city to complete the system. The short distance from here to KEIGHLEY was never bridged (despite pressure from that Corporation) and the only through running agreement made with a neighbouring tramway – from 1907 to 1918 – was with LEEDS via Stanningley using ten cars fitted with sliding axles to negotiate the change of gauge involved.

The first route to close was the section between Undercliffe and Greengates on 11 November 1928, replaced by a motor bus service. A year later, on 29 November 1929, the Allerton trams went, replaced this time by trolleybuses (which the Corporation had been operating since 1911). After that, the remaining routes were closed one by one throughout the 1930s and 1940s, the last to go being the former B&S line from the centre to Odsal and Horsfall Playing Fields.

The system's first electric tramcars were open-top double-deck motor cars 1-24 and similar configuration trailers 25-28, all 1898-99 vehicles from Brush. The trailers were motorized c1900, between when and 1902 the same firm supplied Nos 29-128, a hundred more open-toppers. (Unless otherwise stated, all Bradford's electric cars were double-deckers.) These were joined in 1902-03 by a hundred similar cars (Nos 129-228) from Milnes, all these early cars being later top-covered, rebuilt and/or renumbered. Car No 229 was a short-lived 1903 bogie single-decker constructed from two ex-B&S steam trailers whilst Nos 230-239 were HN open-toppers absorbed into the fleet after the Mid-Yorks takeover.

From 1912 onwards the Corporation began its own car construction programme and between then and 1931 built a total of 140 top-covered cars, the only ones purchased from outside manufacturers being UEC Nos 247-258 of 1920 and 213-232 of 1921, again all top-covered vehicles. (Bradford's cars were numbered and later renumbered in an erratic manner up to No 258 with numbers of withdrawn vehicles being allocated to new cars as and when they became vacant.) The Corporation built one other single-decker at its main Thornbury Works: No 1 of 1926 which was an experimental bogie car with coupled wheels. Put into service in 1927, it proved too long (at nearly 40ft) and too fast for the tracks and in 1930 it was sold to become a holiday home at Filey.

Apart from the Mid-Yorks vehicles, no second-hand cars were bought – presumably because of the Corporation's own construction policy – and only ten were ever disposed of to another operator. Significantly, these were not Bradford-built vehicles, being UEC Nos 237, 242, 243, 251 and 257 of 1920 and

214-217 and 219 of 1921, all sold in 1942 to SHEFFIELD. Later converted to works car 330 there, No 251 is preserved at the National Tramway Museum, Crich, whilst Last Car No 104 of 1925 vintage, which until 1953 served as a scoreboard at Odsal Stadium, is now on show fully restored in the Bradford Industrial Museum.

One other aspect of the Bradford system deserves mention. From 1916 until the end of World War I a specially-laid tramway (comparable to the Mousehold Light Railway in NORWICH) was in operation linking Thornbury Works (turned over to munitions production), the nearby Phoenix Works where aircraft parts were made and the railway exchange sidings in Laisterdyke goods yard. In all, just over a mile of 4ft gauge track was put down with materials and products being moved around the Phoenix Tramway (as it was known) using a combination of goods wagons, Corporation-built electric locos (on tramcar trucks) and cut-down passenger cars.

Bibliography: *Bradford City Tramways 1882-1950* D.M. Coates (Wyvern Publications, Skipton, 1984)
0 907941 12 5

BRADFORD & SHELF TRAMWAY

Authority: Bradford Corporation Tramways Order 1880
Gauge: 4ft
Traction: Steam
Opened: 5 September 1884
Taken Over: 2 September 1903
System: Branching
Length: 7.54 miles
Stock: 21 locos, 7 sd, 12 dd
Livery: Prussian blue & cream to 1892, then chocolate & cream

Although the rest of the Bradford system was operated originally by the Bradford Tramways Co. (see above), one line was not, being operated instead by the Bradford & Shelf Tramway Co. on behalf of the Corporation. The first portion opened ran south from the Town Hall down Manchester Road to Bankfoot where the depot was situated in Rathwell Road.

On 11 June 1886 this single-track line was extended south, under the Bradford and Shelf Tramways Order 1885, through Odsal to Wyke with a branch southwest from Odsal to Shelf via the Halifax Road to complete the tramway. Steam traction was employed from the outset, beginning with Green locomotives 1-5 hauling similarly-numbered Starbuck bogie double-deck trailers. In 1885 loco No 5 met with an accident and was replaced by another No 5, a second-hand purchase ex-NORTH STAFFORDSHIRE TRAMWAYS in the POTTERIES. This was joined that

same year by No 6, a Burrell loco, and between then and 1887 by Nos 7-9, three more from Greens following which Nos 1-4 were sold to the Bradford Tramways Co. Between 1887 and 1894 Greens supplied another eleven locos numbered 10-14 and 1-6, the latter batch replacing withdrawn engines.

In 1885-6 the car fleet grew with the addition of Starbuck bogie double-decker No 6, locally-built single-deck trailers 7-11, Ashbury bogie double-decker 12 and single-deckers 13 and 14 (again constructed locally). Evidently the single-deck cars were not satisfactory for in 1887 six of them were converted into three bogie double-deckers numbered 8, 9 and 13 (renumbered 10 in 1891) whilst another bogie double-decker, No 7, was bought from Ashbury. The last additions to the fleet were Nos 7, 11, 13 and 14 from Milnes in 1893-194, all bogie double-deck vehicles again.

The first cutback to the line came in 1902 when, on 31 January, steam services ceased between the Town Hall and Bankfoot, replaced the next day by the Corporation's new electric trams (the Corporation having paid £12,000 that same day to buy out the Company's lease). On 29 May 1903 the electric cars began running through to Buttershaw on Halifax Road and on 1 September that year the rump steam service stopped altogether, replaced the following day by electric workings.

Bibliography: as above

BRIGHTON CORPORATION TRAMWAYS

Authority: Brighton Corporation Act 1900
Gauge: 3ft 6in
Traction: Overhead electric
Opened: 25 November 1901
Closed: 31 August 1939
System: Network
Length: 9.48 miles
Stock: 165 dd
Livery: Maroon & cream, chocolate & cream 1920s, then plum & cream
Last Car: No 41

This compact system began operations with 25 open-top Milnes double-deckers (Nos 1-25, quickly joined by Nos 26-30) running from Victoria Gardens inland up the Lewes Road, past the depot at the junction with Bear Road, and on to Preston Barracks. Other routes (a mixture of double and single tracks) were soon added during the first half of the decade going west to the LBSCR station via North Road and Queens Road, northwest via New England Road and Dyke Road to Tivoli Gardens, north up Beaconsfield Road and back via Preston Drive and Ditchling Road. Then east along

Two of Brighton Corporation's fleet of double-deckers at the Central station terminus. (Lens of Sutton)

Elm Grove to the racecourse and back from there down Queen's Park Road to the Rock Gardens, and south to Old Steine Gardens near the seafront Aquarium which became the starting point for all routes. (The Corporation refused to allow a route along the seafront itself for fear of spoiling its appearance.)

In 1903 ten more Milnes cars were bought (Nos 31-40), followed over the next two years by another ten open-toppers (Nos 41-50), this time from UEC. Thereafter the Corporation built new and replacement cars in batches at the Lewes Road works, having gained the necessary experience by completely rebuilding the original cars from 1908 onwards. In 1914 open-toppers 51-53 were produced, followed by a rebuilt No 10, which had been damaged in an accident, three years later. (During World War I some, if not all, of the UEC cars had their motors removed temporarily and were used as trailers on services to the town munition works.) Immediately after the war (1919) replacement cars 1, 7, 17 and 26 and new cars 54 and 55 were put into service. Cars built thereafter were 9, 11, 14, 56 (1920); 15, 20, 23, 24, 27, 30, 41, 42, 57, 58 (1921); 46, 49, 50, 59-63 (1922); 2, 36, 43, 44, 47, 48 (1923); 4, 8, 16, 18, 19, 21, 25, 28 (1924); 3, 5, 6, 12, 29, 33, 38, 39 (1925); 31, 32, 34, 35, 37, 40 (1926); 13, 22, 45 (1927); 10, 64-67 (1928); 68-70 (1929); 71-75 (1930); 76-80 (1931); 1, 7, 17, 26 (1932); 9, 11, 41, 55, 57, 58 (1933), 14, 15, 20, 42, 50, 54, 56, 59, 60, 63 (1934); 2, 24, 27, 30, 46, 48 (1935); 21, 23, 25, 43, 49, 74 (1936) and 51-53 (1937).

The system closed just before World War

Map of tramways actual and proposed in the Brighton area, from the 1904 Manual of Electrical Undertakings.

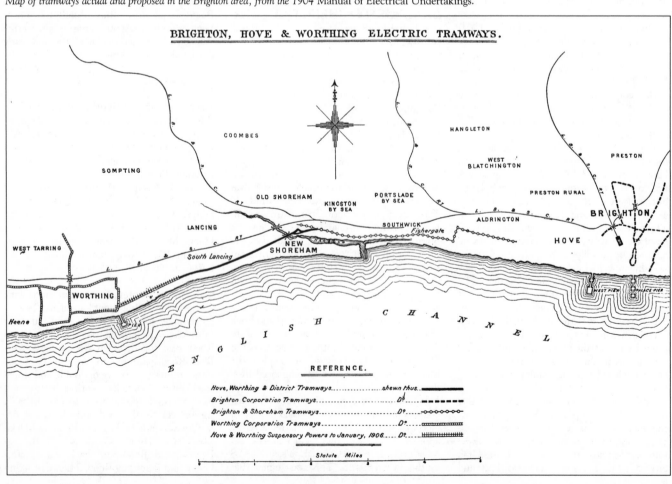

II, the trams replaced by buses and trolley-buses from 26 April 1939 onwards when the Dyke Road line was abandoned, the last service being along Lewes Road to the depot.

BRIGHTON & ROTTINGDEAN SEASHORE ELECTRIC TRAMROAD

Authority: Brighton and Rottingdean
Seashore Electric Tramroad Act 1893
Gauge: 2ft 8½in & 18ft*
Traction: Overhead electric
Opened: 30 November 1896
Closed: January 1901
System: Single line
Length: 2.93 miles
Stock: 1 dd
Livery: Varnished wood & white

Without doubt this line was the most weird and wonderful tramway in the British Isles – if not the whole world. It was the glorious brainchild of Magnus Volk who wished to extend his pioneering electric railway (opened 1883) along the seafront at Brighton to the village of Rottingdean without recourse to an expensive viaduct along the intervening cliff face. His solution was to lay a double line of flat-bottom rails on concrete blocks along the shore (between the high and low water marks) from the Banjo Groyne in Brighton (the then terminus of the Volk's Electric Railway) to a 300ft pier built at Rottingdean. A midway loading stage was provided at Ovingdean Gap.

The track gauge was 2ft 8½in, the same as the VER, with the lines laid 18ft apart as measured between the two outermost rails, this distance being the true 'gauge' of the line as the tramway's one car ran on both tracks in the manner of some dockside cranes. Aptly named *Pioneer*, though popularly known as 'Daddy Longlegs', the car was built by Gloucester and looked like nothing so much as a pier head crossed with a ferry. It weighed 50 tons fully laden, carried 150 passengers and was furnished with a promenade deck surrounding a central saloon some 46ft by 22ft. It stood on four steel legs 24ft high, each of which culmi-nated in an encased four-wheeled bogie. Current from an overhead wire fed two 25hp deck-mounted motors powering the bogies via shafting in two of the hollow legs. (The other two carried the brake rodding). The car was required by the BoT to carry lifebelts and a lifeboat – surely the only tramcar ever to do so!

The line got off to a poor start for in the first week of December 1896, severe storms caused a great deal of damage, capsizing the car, and the tramway did not re-open until 20 July of the following year. The car though proved slow and underpowered (running through 15ft of water at high tide reduced it to a crawl) and the track was given to silting over and by 1900 only short out-and-back novelty trips were being run from the Brighton end of the line. Even these were stopped the following year by Brighton Corporation's removal of part of the track to make way for new sea defences. The rest of the line (and *Pioneer*) were not scrapped until 1910 whilst some of the concrete sleeper blocks remain in situ to be seen today.

Bibliography: *Volk's Railways Brighton: an illustrated history* Alan A. Jackson (Plateway Press, 1993) 1 971980 18 6

BRIGHTON & SHOREHAM TRAMWAYS

Authority: Brighton District Tramways Act 1882
Gauge: 3ft 6in
Traction: Steam, horse
Opened: 3 July 1884
Closed: 6 June 1913
System: Single line
Length: 4.53 miles
Stock: 3 locos, 2 dd steam; 3 sd, 10 dd horse
Livery: Brown & cream
Last Car: No 10

Opened by the Brighton District Tramways Co., this seaside line was unusual in that it began with steam traction but ended up using horses. Despite its title, it had no metals in Brighton at all, running as it did westwards as a single track from Westbourne Gardens, Aldrington, on the boundary with Hove just west of Brighton, along New Church Road through Aldrington to Portslade where it turned south on Station Road before continuing west along Wellington Road, Fishergate Terrace and Albion Street to Southwick, then along Lower Brighton Road and Ham Road through Kingston-by-Sea to Shoreham-by-Sea where it terminated by the LBSCR's station. The depot was in Albion Street between the tramway and Southwick station.

The tramway's first items of rolling stock were Wilkinson tram locomotives Nos 1 and 2 hauling Falcon bogie double-deck trailers Nos 1 and 2 fitted with roof canopies; these were joined in 1885 by three single-deck horse trams which entered service on 23 May. It seems that shortly after this seven double-deck horse cars were acquired and in 1886 locomotive No 3 arrived: this was an Aveling & Porter 0-4-0 geared locomotive (the firm's first) designed for street tramway use but it proved unsuccessful in trials and was returned to the manufacturers. The following year the Company went into receivership – one of its problems was that it closely paralled the LBSCR's railway line – but continued to operate the tramway. (At the same time the Electric Traction Syndicate leased one of the horse cars and converted it to battery power for several months of trials.)

In November 1889 the line was purchased by a new company, the Brighton & Shoreham Tramways Co. who, four years later, sold the steam locos and trailers to WIGAN DISTRICT TRAMWAYS, thereafter using just the horse cars. In 1896 the Company was in turn bought by the BET who wished to electrify the line (and extend it westwards to Worthing) but although the necessary Act of Parliament was obtained (in 1903) and a company registered for the purpose (1904), nothing came of the proposal. In 1900 three open-top double-deckers were bought but before the end of the decade motor bus competition had reduced the tramway to a one-car service using No 10 (one of the 1900 cars), now cut down to single-deck form. In 1912 the eastern third of the line from Hove to Portslade was abandoned with the remainder following a year later.

BRILL TRAMWAY

Never a tramway, this line began life as a private light railway built by the local landowner, the Duke of Buckingham, to link the Buckinghamshire village of Brill with Quainton Road station on the Aylesbury & Buckingham Railway (opened 1868) some 6 miles away. Originally known as the Wootton Tramway, the railway opened in stages during 1871-2 with horse haulage for both passengers and goods until January 1872 when the first of two Aveling & Porter steam engines was purchased (later to be joined by a Bagnall tank).

On 1 April 1894 the line was taken over by the Oxford & Aylesbury Tramroad Co., rebuilt to a heavier standard and more powerful locomotives introduced. From 1 December 1899 it was worked by the Metropolitan Railway as its Brill branch and slowly modernized. It closed on 1 December 1935, by which time the MR had become part of the London Passenger Transport Board.

Bibliography: *The Brill Tramway* Bill Simpson (Oxford Publishing Co., 1985) 0 86093 218 4

BRISTOL TRAMWAYS

Authority: Bristol Corporation Tramways Order 1872
Gauge: 4ft 8½in
Traction: Horse, steam, overhead electric
Opened: 9 August 1875
Closed: 11 April 1941

The Tramways Centre, Bristol, showing much activity – a popular postcard view during the tramway's life. (Lens of Sutton)

System: Radial network
Length: 31.1 miles
Stock: 8 locos, 103 dd steam & horse; 238 dd electric*
Livery: Dark blue & cream
Last Car: ?

The Bristol tramway network grew out of a single horse route on the northern side of the city, running for a little over 1½ miles from the King David Inn in Perry Road out along Queens Road and Whiteladies Road to the district of Redland, where it terminated at the bottom of Blackboy Hill by St John's Church. Owned by Bristol Corporation, the tramway was worked on a lease by the Bristol Tramways Co. Ltd. On 4 December 1874 the line was extended right into the city centre via Colston Street with a new terminus in St Augustine's Parade (to become known later, as the system grew, as the Tramways Centre). Initial services were

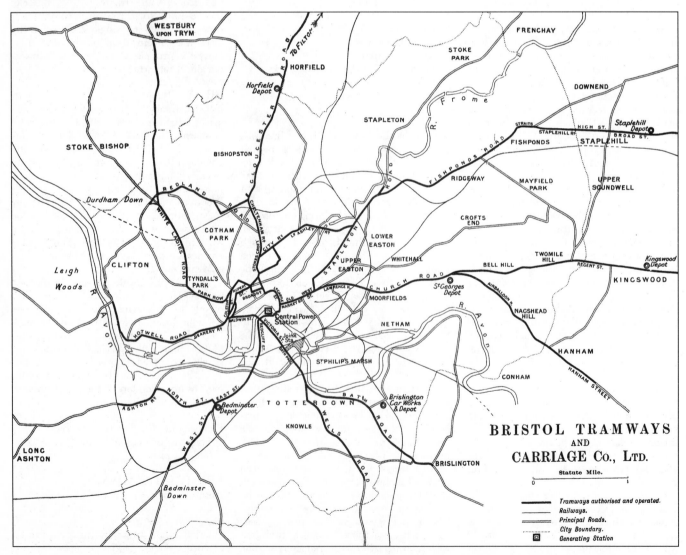

Map of the Bristol tramways system from the 1920-21 Manual of Electrical Undertakings.

worked by six Starbuck open-top double deckers.

Over the ensuing quarter of a century a succession of routes were opened to create a radial network of 9.31 miles of lines stretching out to Eastville and St George (1876) and Kingswood (1892) in the east, Totterdown (1879) and Bedminster (1880) in the south, Hotwells (1880) to the west and Horfield to the north. This last route was worked originally by seven Hughes steam tram locomotives (Nos 1-7) pulling adapted horse cars with primitive roofs, on account of its steep gradients and was opened on 18 November 1880. Apparently the locomotives were not a success and were returned to the manufacturers at the end of their twelve-month contract. An eighth loco, built by Fox, Walker & Co. of Bristol and used on the Redland–Eastville route, fared no better. (All these routes were owned by the Company, as was the original Redland route from 1882 onwards when it was purchased for £8,000 from the Corporation.)

On 1 October 1887 the Company amalgamated with the Bristol Carriage Co. (a local cab and other vehicles for hire firm) to form the Bristol Tramways & Carriage Co. Ltd (soon to become part of the IMPERIAL group) and, by 1898 when the last links and extensions to the system opened, its car fleet had risen to 103 in total, all thought to have been open-top double-deckers numbered 1-85 and 98-115 and housed in a number of depots sited around the system.

By the 1890s the Company was wanting to electrify its lines and on 14 October 1895 the first converted route, from Old Market to Kingswood, opened. The second, from Old Market to Eastville followed on 1 February 1897 (extended later that year to Fishponds, then Staple Hill) and by 2 December 1900 all the former lines had been converted (and in some cases extended). A new, 1½-mile route to the village of Hanham running southeast off the Kingswood route at St George was constructed under a 1898 LRO and known officially as the St George & Hanham Light Railway. Thereafter the only major alterations made to the (nearly all double-track) system were the 1907 extension from Horfield Barracks northwards to Filton and a 1908 extension of the Durdham Downs (Redland) route to Westbury-upon-Trym.

All the electric passenger cars were open-top double-deckers (believed to be the largest such fleet in the British Isles), and numbered in sequence with the horse car fleet. In chronological order of construction they were as follows:

Nos 86-97: Milnes of 1895
Nos 116-118: Milnes of 1895-96

TRAMWAY SERVICES IN THE CITY OF BRISTOL								
Services marked (*) will be replaced by buses during September, 1938								
	Weekdays.		Sundays.			Weekdays.		Sundays.
	First dep. a.m.	Last dep. p.m.	First dep. p.m.	Last dep. p.m.		First dep. a.m.	Last dep. p.m.	First dep. p.m.	Last dep. p.m.
Tramways C. & Durdham D. (via Zet'd Rd)								
From Tramways Centre to Durdham Down	6 30	1115	2 20	1015	***Bristol Bridge and Bedminster Down**			
" Durdham Down to Tramways Centre	7 0	1115	2 30	10 5	From Bedminster Down	5 10	1115	2 15	1020
" Durdham Down to Zetland Road	7 0	1140	2 30	1040	" Bristol Bridge	5 30	1130	2 10	1035
Tramways Centre, Horfield and Filton								
From Ashley Down Rd. to Tramways Centre	4 50	1115	2 0	1020	**Tramways Centre and Kingswood**			
" Tramways Centre to Filton	5 20	1115	2 20	1010	From Kingswood to Old Market	5 15	1035	1 55	10 0
" Filton to Tramways Centre	4 40	11 5	2 10	1010	" Kingswood to Tramways Centre	5 25	1035	1 55	9 50
" Filton to Ashley Down Road	4 40	1140	2 10	1040	" Tramways Centre to Kingswood	6 5	1115	2 35	1025
" Tramways Centre to Horfield Barracks	5 20	1120	2 20	1025	" St. George to Kingswood	5 55	1140	2 0	1050
					" Old Market to Kingswood	5 45	1125	2 25	1035
*Tramways Centre, Eastville & Fishponds								
From Fishponds to Tramways Centre	4 50	1050	2 0	9 55	***Zetland Road and Staple Hill**			
" Warwick Road to Tramways Centre	5 0	11 0	2 0	10 5	From Staple Hill to Old Market	5 0	11 0	1 55	10 5
" Tramways Centre to Fishponds	5 20	1120	2 30	1025	" Fishponds to Old Market	5 5	11 5	2 5	1015
					" Staple Hill to Zetland Road	5 10	1030	2 0	9 30
Tramways Centre and Brislington					" Old Market to Staple Hill	5 35	1130	2 25	1035
From Brislington to Tramways Centre	5 25	1130	2 10	1025	" Warwick Road to Staple Hill	5 40	1140	2 0	1045
" Tramways Centre to Brislington	5 25	1130	2 15	1030	" Zetland Road to Staple Hill	5 55	11 0	2 40	1015
" Tramways Cen. to Temple Meads Stn.	5 25	1140	2 15	1045					
" Temple Meads Stn. to Tramways Cen.	5 10	1130	2 10	1040	**Hanham, Old Market and Knowle**			
					From St. George Depot to Old Market	5 0	1115	2 0	1020
Bristol Bridge and Knowle					" Hanham to Knowle	5 40	1040	2 15	9 40
From Knowle	5 25	1130	2 20	1030	" Old Market to St. George	5 30	1145	2 15	1045
" Bristol Bridge ....(Bath St.)	5 45	1140	2 15	1020	" Old Market to Hanham	5 30	1120	2 15	1030
					" Old Market to Knowle	5 45	11 5	2 15	10 5
*Bristol Bridge and Ashton Road					" Old Market to Nags Head Hill	5 30	1125	2 15	1030
From Ashton Road	5 25	1115	2 10	1030	" Knowle to Old Market	5 25	1125	2 35	1025
" Bristol Bridge	5 30	1130	2 15	1035	" Knowle to Hanham	6 20	11 0	2 35	10 9
					" Knowle to Nags Head Hill	6 20	11 5	2 35	10 0
					" Knowle to St. George	6 20	1125	2 35	1025

The Bristol Tramways & Carriage Co. Ltd bus timetable summer 1938 included just one page for the dwindling tramway service.

Nos 125-140: Milnes of 1897
Nos 141-161: American Car Co. of 1897-98 (No 141 ran as a Manager's car until 1908)
Nos 162-172: Milnes of 1900
Nos 173-202: Midland of 1900-01
Nos 203-232: Bristol of 1900-01

After the withdrawal of the horse cars, the gaps in the sequence were then filled as follows:

Nos 1-85: Milnes of 1900-01
Nos 98-115: Milnes of 1901

The only other passenger cars to be added to the fleet (Bristol prided itself on keeping its aging cars in excellent condition) were six constructed by the Company in 1920 and numbered 233-237 and 86 (this last car replacing the earlier one of that number). In addition, several of the horse cars were used as trailers during the first ten years of electric working. Many of the routes had their own depots with the main one and works being at Bridlington.

The system remained virtually unchanged until the 1930s when the Corporation decided to exercise its option to buy the tramways and did so at a cost of £1,125,000 as from 1 October 1937; the intention was to replace the trams with buses (of which the Company had a large fleet) and, on 8 May 1938, the Hotwells and Westbury routes closed, followed on 3 September by the Staple Hill, Bridlington and Knowle lines.

Further closures followed until by April 1941 only the Kingswood and Hanham routes remained, only to be abandoned ignominiously when a German bomb cut the main power supply, after which all the surviving cars were scrapped.

The Bristol company was one of only two British tramway operators to own a cliff railway (the other being TORQUAY). This was the Clifton Rocks Railway in the Avon Gorge, opened in 1893 and consisting of four tracks running in a tunnel throughout, to lift passengers from the riverside (and the tramway's Hotwells line) up to Sion Hill. The Company purchased the railway in 1912 and closed it in 1934 when it had become no longer profitable.

Bibliography: *Tramways of the West of England* P.W. Gentry (The Light Railway Transport League, 2nd ed 1960)

Edwardian trade advertisement for the British Thomson-Houston Co. Ltd.

BRITISH ELECTRIC TRACTION CO. LTD

The BET was by far and away the biggest of the private owners of tramways in the British Isles. It was formed in 1895 by Emile Garcke and set about, at that timely juncture in tramway history, buying up existing horse and steam lines with a view to extending and electrifying them (usually successfully), creating a number of linked networks in the process (notably in LONDON and the BLACK COUNTRY). The Company also had extensive business interests other than tramways, notably electricity supply and, later, bus operation. In the tramway field it controlled, at one time or another, the METROPOLITAN ELECTRIC and SOUTH METROPOLITAN systems in the London area as well as the BARNSLEY, BARROW-IN-FURNESS, BIRMINGHAM, BIRMINGHAM & MIDLAND, DEVON-PORT, DUDLEY & STOURBRIDGE, GATESHEAD, GRAVESEND, HARTLE-POOLS, JARROW, KIDDERMINSTER & STOURPORT, LEAMINGTON & WARWICK, MIDDLETON, OLDHAM, ASHTON & HYDE, PETERBOROUGH, POOLE, POTTERIES, SHEERNESS, SOUTH STAFFORDSHIRE, SOUTH-PORT, TAUNTON, TYNEMOUTH, WESTON-SUPER-MARE, WOLVER-HAMPTON DISTRICT, WORCESTER and YORKSHIRE (WOOLLEN DISTRICT), electric tramways elsewhere in England plus those of Merthyr Tydfil, Swansea, Swansea & Mumbles and Wrexham in Wales, Airdrie, Greenock & Port Glasgow and Rothesay in Scotland and Cavehill & Whitewell in Ireland. Lines at one time controlled but never electrified by

the Company were those of BRIGHTON & SHOREHAM, CAMBRIDGE, ROSSENDALE VALLEY, SOUTH SHIELDS and YARMOUTH.

BRITISH THOMSON-HOUSTON CO. LTD

The BTH, as well as being a major supplier of tramway equipment and the parent company of the British Tramways & General Construction Co. Ltd, owned or controlled the electric tramway systems at CHATHAM and the ISLE OF THANET in England, Paisley and Lanarkshire in Scotland and Cork in Ireland.

BROADSTAIRS see ISLE OF THANET

BURNLEY & DISTRICT TRAMWAYS

Authority: Burnley and District Tramways Order 1879
Gauge: 4ft 8½in
Traction: Steam/horse/steam
Opened: 17 September 1881
Closed: 17 November 1901
System: Single line
Length: 7.15 miles
Stock: 17 locos, 18 dd steam & horse
Livery: ?
Last Car: ?

Owned and operated by the Burnley & District Tramways Co. Ltd, this otherwise unremarkable steam tramway was taken over (on 1 March 1900) by no less than five local authorities – surely some sort of record. It was built to link Burnley with the tramway systems to the west and north and

ran from Padiham 3 miles west of Burnley along the Padiham Road to the town centre where it swung north past the depot and out along the Colne Road and Manchester Road through Reedley and Brierfield to Nelson where it terminated at Nelson Centre.

Services began with Kitson tram locomotives Nos 1-5 and Starbuck top-covered trailers 1-7; these were joined in 1883 by Falcon locos 6-9, the first in a series of replacements for the Kitsons which had been withdrawn as from 1 March 1882 as unsatisfactory (with horses being used instead until March of the following year when the new engines arrived). More Falcons came later: No 10 in 1884, Nos 11-13 in 1885, No 14 in 1889, No 15 in 1896 and Nos 16 and 17 a year later. Further trailers were also added (all open-top bogie double-deckers): Starbuck cars Nos 8-10 in 1884 and 3, 6, 11 and 12 in 1885, Falcon No 13 in 1888 and 14 and 15 in 1897 and, finally, Metropolitan No 16 in 1900 ex-ST HELENS.

On 1 March 1900 the line was purchased jointly by Burnley and Nelson Corporations, Padiham and Brierfield UDCs and Reedley Hallows Parish Council (which, with just 0.4 miles of track, was the only tramway-owning parish council in Great Britain). The purchase was the prelude to electrification and extension with the BURNLEY CORPORATION system opening just a month after the tramway's final closure (see below).

Bibliography: *Trams in the North West* Peter Hesketh (Ian Allan, 1995) 0 7110 2349 2

BURNLEY CORPORATION TRAMWAYS

Authority: Burnley Corporation Tramways (Etc.) Act 1898
Gauge: 4ft
Traction: Overhead electric
Opened: 16 December 1901
Closed: 7 May 1935
System: Radial
Length: 13.05 miles
Stock: 19 sd, 53 dd
Livery: Chocolate & primrose
Last Car: ?

Burnley's municipal tramway system eventually comprised four principal routes running north, south, east and west from the town centre (Burnley Centre) with all but the southern route having branches off them. Following the 1900 joint purchase of the BURNLEY & DISTRICT TRAMWAYS (see above) the line from Padiham east to Burnley then north to Nelson Centre was re-opened for electric working four weeks later, the track either side of the town in Padiham, Reddley Hallows, Brierfield and Nelson being leased by Burnley Corporation (it having paid £53,000 for its own portion of the B&D).

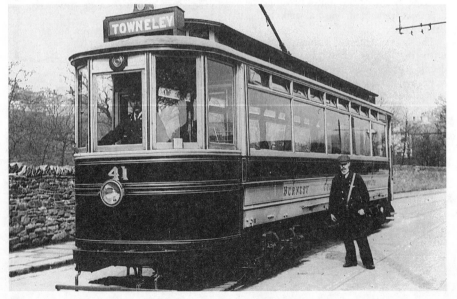

Burnley Corporation No 41 of 1903, one of the single-deckers used on the Towneley service. (Lens of Sutton)

The first services were worked by Milnes open-toppers 1-24, built 1901-02 and based on the reconstructed B&D depot in Queen's Gate. These were joined in 1903 by similar cars 25-38 and ERTCW bogie single-deckers 39-46 bought to work the three new routes opened that year: southwest to Rose Grove via the Accrington Road leaving the Padiham line in Westgate, south down the Manchester Road to Summit and east along Brunshaw Road then south down Todmorden Road to Towneley.

In 1910 another branch was opened, northeast off the Colne Road, up Briercliffe Road to Burnley Lane Head (extended two years later to Harle Syke). By then the car fleet had grown with the addition of UEC single-decker 47 (of 1907), HN bogie balcony cars 48-52 (1909) and UEC bogie single-deckers 53 and 54 (1910), followed by similar cars 55-57 in 1911 and UEC bogie balcony cars 58-67 two years later. The last purchases were Nos 68-72, EE single-deckers of 1921 (by which time all the open cars had been top-covered). The system was completed in 1927 by the construction of a short branch east off the Towneley line, continuing along the Brunshaw Road past the Turf Moor football ground to Brunshaw (and worked, like the Summit and Towneley routes, by single-deck cars). The previous year, car 68 was renumbered 73 with the rebuilding of No 10 and its renumbering as 68 following a crash at Lane Head. (The same car had been involved in an identical accident in 1925!) Another victim was car No 9 which crashed in 1933 and had to be withdrawn.

The first abandonment came in 1932 when the Rose Grove–Harle Syke service was replaced by buses, thus closing two of the branches. On 1 April 1933, following the setting-up of the Burnley, Colne & Nelson Joint Transport Committee Burnley cars began working right through Nelson to Higherford (their numbers suffixed with a B). Remaining routes closed in 1934 (except the original Padiham–Nelson line which lasted another year) after which the surviving cars (all double-deckers) were scrapped.

Bibliography: as above

BURTON-UPON-TRENT CORPORATION TRAMWAYS

Authority: Burton-upon-Trent Corporation Act 1901
Gauge: 3ft 6in
Traction: Overhead electric
Opened: 3 August 1903
Closed: 31 December 1929
System: Radial
Length: 6.66 miles
Stock: 24 dd
Livery: Crimson lake & cream
Last Car: ?

The east Staffordshire town of Burton-upon-Trent was once a transport enthusiast's delight. Not only was it on the MR's Birmingham–Derby main line, it boasted an extensive steam-worked brewery railway network as well as two separate tramway systems. One, the BURTON & ASHBY LIGHT RAILWAY, is dealt with below whilst the other was always Corporation-owned.

Although horse lines were considered as early as 1879, it was not until private proposals were made for electric tramways in the growing town that Burton Corporation decided to build its own. After construction in 1902-03, services were worked by ERTCW open-toppers 1-20 (of which Nos 7-11 and 17 were soon top-covered) from a short terminal spur by the Post Office in Wellington Street. The first route of three ran north through a workers' residential district along Waterloo Street, Victoria Crescent and the Horninglow Road to St John's Church whilst the second went east on Borough Road past the railway station, then along the length of Station Street to the High Street which it joined to run north to Bridge Street before swinging east again to cross the River Trent on the town's sole road bridge, and then up Bearwood Hill Road and Church Hill Street to St Mark's Church, Winshill. The third route ran south from the Winshill side of the Trent Bridge along the edge of the high ground overlooking the river's wide flood plain on Stapenhill Road and Main Street to Ferry Street, Stapenhill. With the exception of Station Street the system was virtually all double-track with the depot in Horninglow Street being reached via a loop line north off Station Street up Guild Street then east along Horninglow Street to the High Street/Bridge Street junction.

As with almost everything else in Burton the tramway was closely linked to the brewing industry. A feature of the latter was its annual outings and in 1909 when 9,000 employees and their families went to Great Yarmouth for the day, the tramway began running at 3am to get them to the station (where the excursion specials departed every ten minutes for a solid three hours). On a less amicable note, the tramway crossed the MR's sidings and the brewery lines a total of eight times and this was blamed for the frequent breaking of the tramcars' axles.

In 1906 the system was linked to the BALR at Winshill and after that led a generally quiet life (apart from the odd accident) with no major changes until August 1918 when eight cars were hired from YARMOUTH, only to be returned the March following and four top-covered cars (Nos 21-24) were bought from EE as replacement vehicles. These were the last additions to the fleet before the tramway closed at the very end of the 1920s to make way for the Corporation's own buses, after which the EE cars were sold to YORK.

Bibliography: *Trams and Buses in Burton 1903-1985* David Stanier, Keith West & Linda Stanier (Carlton Publishing, Derby, 1991) 0 951756 90 7

BURTON & ASHBY LIGHT RAILWAYS

Authority: Burton and Ashby Light Railway Order 1903
Gauge: 3ft 6in
Traction: Overhead electric
Opened: 13 June 1906
Closed: 19 February 1927
System: Branching

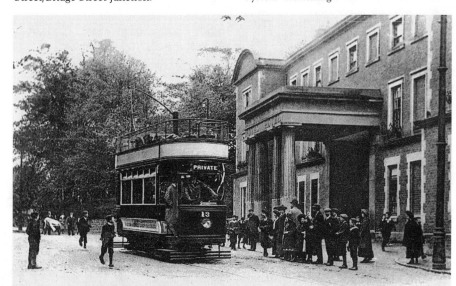

Postcard of Burton & Ashby Light Railways No 13 of 1905 on a private working outside the Royal Hotel, immediately before the Ashby terminus. (Lens of Sutton)

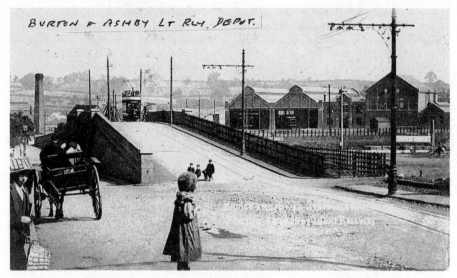

An early postcard view of the newly-built Burton & Ashby depot and power station. The ability to cope with occasional gradients as steep as those on this bridge was just one reason for the supremacy of the electric tram over its rivals. (Lens of Sutton)

Length: 10.12 miles
Stock: 20 dd
Livery: MR crimson lake & white (later
   cream)
Last Car: ?

Built under light railway legislation, the BALR was the MR's only tramway. (Although officially of plural title, the line was normally referred to in the singular.) A large triangular layout centred on Swadlincote in the extreme south of Derbyshire fed three branches to the MR's stations at Gresley (southwest), Ashby-de-la-Zouch in Leicestershire (southeast) and Burton-upon-Trent in Staffordshire (northwest); the final part of the last route was made possible by running powers over BURTON CORPORATION metals from Winshill to the Wellington Street terminus (see above). The system, worked as a Burton–Ashby main line with a branch to Gresley, was mainly single-track but despite this was equipped with parallel overhead wires throughout, one for running in each direction to avoid the need for points in the overhead at the many passing loops.

For most of its route this essentially rural tramway occupied the public highway – hills, bridges and all. Its undulating nature was even more pronounced on the reserved open-field section known as the 'Switchback' between Winshill and Swadlincote where the drivers let the cars go, the resulting swaying and pitching of the short-wheelbase Brush open-toppers (Nos 1-13 of 1905 and 14-20 of 1906) often producing feelings of seasickness in the passengers!

At the 1923 Grouping the line passed with

the MR into the hands of the LMS who, in the face of growing bus competition, closed the system down entirely just four years later with ten of the cars being sold to TYNEMOUTH & DISTRICT. One of the bodies to survive locally, that of No 14, was rescued in the 1970s and restored for use on a heritage line in Detroit.

Bibliography: *Sixpenny Switchback* P.M.
   White & J.W. Storer (J.M. Pearson &
   Son, Burton-on-Trent, 1983)
   0 907864 08 2

BURY CORPORATION TRAMWAYS

Authority: Bury Corporation Act 1899

Gauge: 4ft 8½in
Traction: Overhead electric
Opened: 3 June 1903
Closed: 13 February 1949
System: Radial network
Length: 13.67 miles
Stock: 60 dd electric
Livery: Red & cream
Last Car: No 13

By the 1890s Bury Corporation was eager to take over the lines of the steam-worked MANCHESTER, BURY, ROCHDALE & OLDHAM TRAMWAY within its boundaries and use them as the basis of an electric system. In 1899 it obtained Parliamentary authority to construct its own tramways and in March 1903 work started on converting the MBRO lines with the first route (to Farfield) opening three months later, followed on 19 April 1904 by the line to Heap Bridge and on 20 May by the Walmersley Road line. (Steam services continued to be operated by the steam company on behalf of the Corporation until the changeover.)

The first electric cars, Nos 1-14, were Milnes open-top bogie double-deckers (enclosed 1925-26) shedded in a new depot on Rochdale Road. These were joined in 1903 by Milnes open-toppers 15-28, in 1904 by balcony cars 29-34 from BEC and the following year by a similar vehicle from the local firm of Wilson & Stockall. In 1906 Brush supplied balcony cars 36-41 and between 1907 and 1913 UEC supplied similar cars 42-54; these were joined in 1925 by Nos 55-60, EE fully-enclosed vehicles.

Other, new routes followed. On 20 May 1907 through services began to BOLTON over a southwestern route via Breightmet,

Bury Corporation No 20 of 1902, shortly before receiving a top cover, having its trollypole reversed at the Radcliffe terminus. (Lens of Sutton)

this being part of the western portion of Bury's system operated on behalf of Radcliffe UDC. Through running arrangements were also made with ROCHDALE to the east, SALFORD and MANCHESTER (4 January 1926) to the south and, on 19 May 1928, south to MIDDLETON via HEYWOOD.

The system's decline began in the early 1930s when, on 3 July 1932, the through service to Rochdale ceased; on 18 February 1933 the service to Middleton was likewise abandoned, on 1 May to Rochdale, on 15 October to Salford and Manchester and on 22 January 1934 to Bolton. By the outbreak of World War II only the northern lines to Tottington and Walmersley – both former steam routes – were left, though in 1939 a wartime service down the Manchester Road to Gigg Lane (another former steam route) was re-introduced. This lasted until 6 July 1946, the Tottington service going on 15 February 1948 and the Walmersley one a year later, after which all surviving cars were scrapped. Nos 21, 55, 56 and 58 had however escaped that fate by being sold to Bolton in 1943 and No 30 to SUNDERLAND four years later.

CAMBER *see* RYE & CAMBER

CAMBERWELL *see* LONDON, CAMBERWELL & DULWICH

CAMBORNE & REDRUTH
Authority: Camborne and Redruth
   Tramway Order 1900
Gauge: 3ft 6in
Traction: Overhead electric
Opened: 7 November 1902
Closed: 29 September 1927
System: Single line
Length: 3.45 miles
Stock: 2 sd, 6 dd
Livery: Dark green & cream; later dark
   green
Last Cars: Nos 3 and 4

Cornwall's only tramway, this linked the two towns of its title with nearly 3½ miles of single track down the main road through tin-mining country along the spine of the county. A further ¾ mile of track was laid as spurs to tin mines and smelting works for the line was unusual amongst English street tramways in that it carried freight on a regular, sizeable basis (and unique in that it was mineral traffic). For these workings the owners, the Urban Electric Supply Co. Ltd (owners of the GLOSSOP tramway), employed two small electric locomotives (Nos 1 and 2) and 14 ore wagons. The goods service began in 1903 and actually lasted beyond the closure of the rest of the tramway brought about by the appearance in 1926 of

Postcard of Camborne & Redruth No 2 of 1902 in Roskear, near Camborne. This was Cornwall's only tramway. (Lens of Sutton)

bus competition. The goods trains, which ran over the central mile or so only of the tramway, lasted until 1934 when they were replaced by an aerial ropeway.

The tramway's first six passengers cars were built in 1902 and comprised open-top double-deckers Nos 1-4 and single-deck combination cars Nos 5 and 6; these were joined in 1903 by Nos 7 and 8, two more open-toppers. All the cars (and the two locomotives) were by Milnes and the depot was at Carn Brea, roughly two-thirds of the way along the line from Redruth's West End terminus. The Camborne terminus at the eastern end of the line was in Trelowarren Street.

Bibliography: *Cornwall's Electric Tramcars*
   L. Fisher Barham (Glasney Press, Penryn, 1972)

Like other commercial concerns of the period, tramway companies issued decorative share certificates to investors, this example being one from the Cambridge Street Tramways Co.

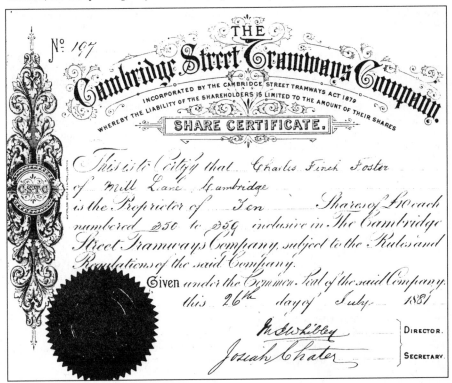

Cartoon postcard marking the end of the horse tramway in Cambridge which lasted until 1914, never to be electrified.

CAMBRIDGE STREET TRAMWAYS

Authority: Cambridge Street Tramways Act
   1879
Gauge: 4ft
Traction: Horse
Opened: 28 October 1880
Closed: 18 February 1914
System: Cross
Length: 2.69 miles
Stock: 4 sd, 4 dd
Livery: Red & cream
Last Car: ?

Apart from the exceptional length of its main platform, the principal claim to fame of Cambridge's railway station is that it was built more than a mile from the city centre, at the insistence of the University authorities. Consequently, with the development of horse tramways it was inevitable that sooner rather than later a proposal would be made to lay one to bridge that gap. In fact, two separate proposals were made with that of the Cambridge Street Tramways Co. succeeding.

The first section of the line opened was from the station down Station Road, Hills Road and Regent Street to terminate outside the Post Office opposite Christ's College. In November 1880 a branch from the Hills Road–Regent Street junction (Hyde Park Corner) opened to Market Hill via Lensfield Road and Trumpington Street, shortly followed by a branch from Hyde Park Corner in the opposite direction along Gonville Place to East Road (and the depot), thus forming a simple + pattern

of lines which thereafter were worked as two separate routes. Both lines were single-track except for a short stretch in Hills Road.

Proposed extensions to outlying parts of the city came to nothing, as did those for other routes through the city centre which were opposed on account of the narrowness of the streets; equally fruitless was the BET-backed proposals to electrify the system before it became an early casualty of motor bus competition. (In this and in many other respects it bore a striking similarity to the OXFORD system.)

Full details of the car fleet are not known but it appears that the tramway operated a total of eight cars during its life, commencing services with double-deckers Nos 1 and 4 and single-deckers 2 and 3 (both later converted to double-deckers). Prior to 1892 another two single-deckers were purchased and numbered 5 and 6; these were followed in 1894 by a Starbuck double-decker (No 7) and in 1909 by another (No 8). All eight were sold by auction following the tramway's closure.

Bibliography: *Cambridge Street Tramways* (Locomotion Papers No 61) S.L. Swingle (The Oakwood Press, 1972)

CANVEY ISLAND TRAMWAY

Authority: –
Gauge: Monorail
Traction: Horse
Opened: 1901?
Closed: 1904?
System: Single line
Length: 3.03 miles
Stock: 1 sd?
Livery: ?
Last Car: ?

A superficial reading of the facts would suggest that the Canvey Island tramway was a typical example of its kind: a horse line is laid to serve a seaside property development – business grows and the line is electrified – financial pressures force its eventual closure. Closer inspection however soon reveals that at no time in its life could this line be considered even faintly typical. The tramway was promoted as a private venture by Frederick Hester who, at the end of the 19th century, was developing Canvey Island on the Essex bank of the Thames estuary as a seaside holiday resort and retirement area. About 1901 a horse monorail was laid from the north side of the island (where it connected with the ferry to Benfleet), past the proposed site of the Winter Gardens in the centre of the island and on to the beach at Leigh Beck on the southern coast. The monorail was of the Caillet type whereby only one rail was used – making it a true monorail – which was laid on the ground and on which the small open car(s) balanced on small, centrally-mounted wheels. A rigid frame on one side of the car held a horse which half-pulled, half-pushed the vehicle along whilst at the same time keeping it upright.

The tramway – the only monorail tramway in the British Isles – was only intended as a stop-gap measure until a 'proper' 3ft 6in gauge electric line could be laid on the same route as demand for Hester's building plots rose. In February 1904 Bruce Peebles were contracted to build such a line, four single-deck cars were ordered from Brush and at least one, carrying the legend 'CANVEY ISLAND ELECTRIC TRAMWAYS', reached the island for trials on the short length of track and overhead actually installed. Severe flooding in 1904 dampened would-be investors' ardour more than somewhat though and the whole scheme collapsed. The electric car(s) went back to Loughborough and, despite being offered elsewhere, apparently the only service any of them ever saw was when two were used to test another BP contract, the Llandudno & Colwyn Bay Electric Railway in Wales, before its 1907 opening.

CITY OF CARLISLE ELECTRIC TRAMWAYS

Authority: Carlisle Tramways Order 1898
Gauge: 3ft 6in
Traction: Overhead electric
Opened: 30 June 1900
Closed: 21 November 1931
System: Radial
Length: 5.73 miles
Stock: 7 sd, 23 dd

Livery: Chocolate & cream to 1912, then
dark green & cream
Last Car: No 8

Although a low-mileage system, the Carlisle
tramways somehow managed to cover the
city more than adequately with no less than
six lines radiating out from the LNWR's
Citadel station. Despite this extensive cover-
age – or perhaps because of it as most of the
branches were well under a mile in length –
the tramway was not a financial success and
in 1910 the owners, the City of Carlisle
Electric Tramways Co. Ltd, agreed to sell out
to Balfour, Beatty. The new owners took
control in November 1911 and promptly set
about renewing the already failing track and
overhead and, in the following year, replaced
the entire fleet of 15 ERTCW cars (single-
deckers Nos 1-3 and open-top double-
deckers Nos 4-15) with twelve new UEC
vehicles (double-deck 1-8 and single-deck 9-
12), later adding three more open-toppers
(Nos 13-15) obtained second-hand from
ILKESTON, another BB operation.
The rebuilt system was inaugurated on
9 December 1912, over £18,000 having been
spent on the improvements.

   After World War I the refusal of the
Company to extend the old routes – or to lay
new ones – meant that as the city expanded,
so motorbus services from the suburbs effectively stole the tramway's trade, a theft the
Company seemingly tolerated as owner of a
bus company in its own right (Percival's
Motor Bus Service). In fact, in 1926 the
Company changed its name to the Carlisle &
District Transport Co. Ltd to reflect its wider
interests.

   Also taking an interest in the existing
public transport situation was the City
Council who, in 1931, purchased the
Company's tram and bus undertakings plus a
number of other bus companies in order to
provide a modern, unified service for the city
and surrounding districts. The trams did not
figure in the Council's grand scheme of
things and, in November of that same year,
they made their last journeys.

Bibliography: *Tramways of the City of
   Carlisle* George S. Hearse (Author,
   Corbridge, 1962)

CASTLEFORD *see* YORKSHIRE (WEST RIDING) ELECTRIC TRAMWAYS

CHATHAM & DISTRICT LIGHT RAILWAYS

Authority: Chatham and District Light
   Railways Order 1899
Gauge: 3ft 6in
Traction: Overhead electric
Opened: 17 June 1902

Postcard of Carlisle Market Place with passengers boarding car No 8 of 1900 bound for Newtown. (Lens of Sutton)

Closed: 30 September 1930
System: Network
Length: 14.98 miles
Stock: 52 dd
Livery: Light green & ivory
Last Car: ?

Promoted by the Rochester, Chatham,
Gillingham & District Electric Railways Co.
Ltd (registered 20 October 1897) to serve
the Medway towns of its title, this system
was authorized originally in a cut-down form
on 17 August 1899 – the day the promoters
cut down their name to the more manage-
able Chatham & District Light Railways Co.
(a subsidiary of BTH who acted as contractors for the project).
   The original intention of linking the

several towns and villages which make up
this important port and dockyard conurbation both sides of the River Medway was
achieved only in stages, the first part to be
opened being centred on Chatham and
Gillingham. This was a kite-shaped circuit
running from Chatham Town Hall on the
western corner northwards along Dock Road
to Brompton, then southeast to Gillingham
High Street, south to Jezreels Corner on
what is now Watling Street where it doubled
back northeastwards down the steep
Chatham Hill to the Town Hall where a
branch ran south along Railway Street and
Maidstone Road to the Cemetery (with a
spur to serve the LCDR station). A second
branch continued up Dock Road in
Brompton to serve the dockyard whilst a

*Souvenir postcard issued to mark the last day of services on the Chatham & District Light Railways. Such
sights were all too common during the 1930s. (Lens of Sutton)*

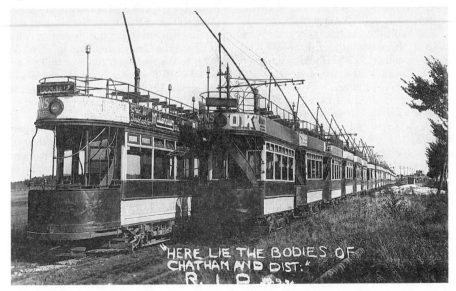

"HERE LIE THE BODIES OF
CHATHAM AND DIST."
R.I.P.

third ran along Gillingham High Street to Gillingham Green. A final branch doubled back southeastwards from the bottom of Chatham Hill to Luton and the depot. Tracks were mainly double and the first cars were 25 Milnes open-top double-deckers.

An agreement was quickly reached between the Company and Rochester City Council whereby the latter would build its own lines and lease them to the former. On 22 December 1904 a branch off Railway Street westwards along New Road into Rochester as far as the foot of Star Hill was opened (with through cars running from Gillingham Green); to cope with the expected extra traffic ten Brush open-toppers (Nos 26-35) had been added to the fleet two years previously. In 1905 five more were bought (Nos 37-41) and on 13 May 1906 this line was extended southwards to Delce. (No 36 was a Milnes car bought in 1903 to replace No 19, damaged in a runaway accident in Old Brompton on 30 October 1902 but later rebuilt as a works car.)

The next addition to the system came on 25 August 1906 when a 3-mile, mainly reserved single-track extension was opened eastwards from Jezreels Corner alongside the main road to Rainham Mark and Rainham; the following year another five Brush open-toppers (Nos 42-46) were purchased.

On 16 April 1908 the Rochester end of the line was extended as a double track along the High Street and across the Medway bridge to a terminus some 200yd beyond the Coach & Horses on the London Road in Strood Hill, whilst on 17 August a single-track extension of the Delce line to the village of Borstal was opened to complete the system. Four more open-top Brush cars (Nos 47-48) were added in 1912 and in 1914 three similar UEC cars (Nos 49-51). Only one other car – No 52 – was added. This was ex-MAIDSTONE No 14, a small UEC 1907 open-top car purchased in 1928 when that system began trolleybus operations.

Inevitably, bus competition after World War I threatened the existence of the tramway and in 1927 BTH sold its interest in the Company to the Maidstone & District Motor Services Ltd and two years later the Company obtained the necessary authorization to close the tramway and run its own buses, which it did from 1 October 1930 onwards.

Bibliography: *The Tramways of Kent Vol 1: West Kent* 'INVICTA' (The Light Railway Transport League, 1971) 1 900433 38 8

CHELTENHAM & DISTRICT LIGHT RAILWAY
Authority: Cheltenham and District Light Railway Order 1900

Gauge: 3ft 6in
Traction: Overhead electric
Opened: 22 August 1901
Closed: 31 December 1930
System: Radial
Length: 10.44 miles
Stock: 2 sd, 23 dd
Livery: Dark red to 1904, then medium lake & cream
Last Car: ?

The Cheltenham tramway system was promoted by an American entrepreneur, Thomas Nevins, who formed the Cheltenham & District Light Railway Co. in 1898 and obtained an initial LRO two years later. The first (and longest) route opened ran for nearly 6 miles in a northeasterly direction from the district of Lansdown along the Gloucester Road past the LMS's Lansdown station and the adjacent LMS&GWR Joint Malvern Road station, through the town centre by way of St George's Road and St George's Place, past the Joint St James station (where a one-way loop was soon put in around Ambrose Street, Lower High Street and Clarence Street) and out along Winchester Street and Prestbury Road on sleepered roadside track to the top of Cleeve Hill.

Services began with eight open-top double-deckers (Nos 1-8) built by Stephensons but the opening was overshadowed by the two deaths which resulted on 29 July when one of the cars ran away down the 1 in 9 Cleeve Hill whilst on trials and overturned. Thereafter, passengers were not permitted to ride on the upper decks of cars on the hill and in 1902 a pair of single-deckers (Nos 9 and 10) were bought from Gloucester to help out.

The system's other two routes from the town centre were opened on 28 March 1905 and ran via Bath Road and Leckhampton Road past the GWR's Leckhampton station to the village of that name in the south and via the High Street, London Road, Copt Elm Road and the Cirencester Road to Charlton Kings to the southeast, terminating by that village's GWR station. Virtually the whole system was single-track with the depot (St Mark's) situated off the Gloucester Road by Lansdown station.

Two further Gloucester cars, open-toppers Nos 11 and 12, were added to the fleet in 1902 and two years later were joined by eight BEC open-toppers (Nos 13-20) bought to work the new routes. No more vehicles were added until 1921 when three EE open-toppers (Nos 21-23) were bought, followed in 1928 by Nos 24 and 25, ex-WORCESTER open-toppers 17 and 16 which took over the Leckhampton route services.

Sometime in the early 1920s No 9 was converted into an open-top double-decker using the appropriate fittings from No 12, which became a single-decker as did No 3 when No 10 was scrapped about this time (and its number taken by No 14 in 1927 when that car was rebuilt). No 19 was similar renumbered 1 the following year.

The Company – which had been taken over in 1914 by BB – decided at the end of the 1920s to replace the trams with trolley-buses but local authority opposition to this idea resulted in the substitution of motor-buses. Services ended quietly with the Cleeve Hill and Leckhampton routes closing in March 1930 and the Lansdown–Charlton Kings route following in the morning of the last day of the year.

Bibliography: *Tramways of the West of England* P.W. Gentry (The Light Railway Transport League, 2nd ed 1960)
Cheltenham's Trams and Buses Remembered J.B. Appleby & F. Lloyd (The Transport Publishing Co., 2nd ed 1973) 0 903839 00 8

CHESTER TRAMWAYS
Authority: Chester Tramways Act 1878
Gauge: 4ft 8½in
Traction: Horse, compressed air
Opened: 10 June 1879
Closed: 27 December 1902
System: Single line
Length: 2.38 miles
Stock: 19 dd?
Livery: Crimson lake & cream
Last Car: ?

The purpose of this single-track line was firstly to link Chester General station (used by the GWR and the LNWR) with the city centre about ½ mile away via City Road and Foregate Street and, secondly, to traverse the centre via Eastgate Street and Grosvenor Street and cross the River Dee on Grosvenor Bridge to serve the district of Saltney by way of Hough Green and Chester Street, terminating close to the Welsh border. The operator was the Chester Tramways Co. and the first Manager T. Lloyd, Manager of the LIVERPOOL horse tramways and whose brainchild the Chester line was. The depot and stables were by the station.

The tramway's original car fleet was made up of eight Eades patent reversible double-deckers, presumably numbered 1-8 and possibly built by Milnes; after that however the rolling stock history becomes somewhat unclear. It seems that these cars did not prove satisfactory (possibly they were too heavy even for two horses) and were soon replaced by eight conventional one-horse double-deckers (also Nos 1-8?) constructed by a local coachbuilder. Two Starbuck cars were bought 1885-86 – again open-top double-deckers – followed by one built by the Company.

In 1886 car No 9 (one of the Starbuck cars?) was made the subject of a curious experiment conducted by the local engineering firm of Hughes & Lancaster. It was fitted with a four-cylinder compressed air engine fed by underfloor wrought iron cyclinders. Proudly emblazoned 'Hughes & Lancaster's Patent Low Pressure Compressed Air Tramcar', it was found to suffer from severe leakage problems, to overcome which an ingenious system was devised. At certain places along the route the driver operated an automatic coupling device to engage an air feed mechanism from a cast iron supply pipe laid beside the track. When the car was restarted the coupling disengaged and the feed closed off. It is not certain whether the whole of the line was so equipped, or merely the Saltney–Grosvenor Bridge section. Certainly by early 1890 the car had been cut down to a single-decker and it actually survived in this state until 1961 having spent most of its life as a cricket pavilion near Wrexham.

By the end of the century Chester Corporation was ready to purchase the line, extend and electrify it and, in 1901, obtained the appropriate Act of Parliament in order to do so (see below). On 1 January 1902 the line came under Corporation control having been bought for £19,866; on 10 November 1902 reconstruction work began at the station end, on 27 December the remaining services ceased and on New Year's Day 1903 what was left was sold.

Bibliography: *Trams and Buses of the City of Chester* W.D. Clark & H.G. Dibdin (Manchester Transport Museum Society, 1979) 0 900857 16 1

CHESTER CORPORATION TRAMWAYS

Authority: Chester Corporation Act 1901
Gauge: 3ft 6in
Traction: Overhead electric
Opened: 6 April 1903
Closed: 15 February 1930
System: Branching
Length: 3.58 miles
Stock: 1 sd, 17 dd
Livery: Apple green & ivory
Last Car: No 10

Following the closure of the Chester horse line (see above) the rebuilding work went speedily ahead and by the end of March 1903 twelve Milnes open-top double-deckers (Nós 1-12) had arrived in the rebuilt horse tram depot. The old northeast–southwest route was faithfully adhered to with the addition of a 77-yard extension at Saltney which brought the line to an abrupt halt in front of a low railway bridge which effectively blocked any hopes of running double-deckers

Chester Corporation No 2 of 1903 at Saltney terminus, close to the Welsh border. (Lens of Sutton)

into Wales. The new line was double-tracked throughout (except for a short stretch in Eastgate), this being made possible by the narrower gauge used.

In 1906 work began on an extension on the other side of the city to serve the district of Boughton. Branching off the existing line at the bottom of City Road (where a full double-track triangular junction was laid), a double-track line ran eastwards along Boughton Road for just over ½ mile to the Fountain Inn; here it divided into two single-track routes to the city boundary along Tarvin Road and Chrisleton Road respectively, each again roughly ½ mile in length. (An authorized line to link the two termini was never built.) Both routes were opened on 22 November 1906 with normal workings

being by cars from St Werburgh Street in the city centre only.

To help cope with the extra traffic generated by the new routes, a one-man operated demi-car (No 13) was bought from Brush in 1906 and five open-top double-deckers (Nos 14-18) from UEC the following year. No 13 was not an operational success – it needed a two-man crew to run to time – and was relegated to odds and ends duties such as helping out when the Chester Races were on and being used as a snow plough when necessary.

No further extensions to the system or additions to the car fleet were made thereafter and the tramway settled down to a quiet life; during the 1920s the system was allowed to gradually wear itself out as it appeared

Electric car No 7 of 1904 appears in this photographic postcard of Chesterfield High Street – see accompanying cartoon card. (Lens of Sutton)

Comic postcard of the Chesterfield electric trams, unusual in that it depicts a recognizable location (see accompanying photograph)

increasingly likely that the future belonged to the motor bus. In 1929 the Chester Corporation Act empowered the city to run its own buses – and abandon the tramways, which it did the following year.

Bibliography: as above

CHESTERFIELD & DISTRICT TRAMWAYS
Authority: Chesterfield Brampton and
   Whittington Tramways Order 1879
Gauge: 4ft 8½in
Traction: Horse
Opened: 8 November 1882
Taken Over: 22 November 1897
System: Single line
Length: 1.25 miles
Stock: 3 sd, 2 dd
Livery: Blue/blue-green & white

Although the 1879 authority was for two tramways (totalling 4½ miles) in the north Derbyshire town of Chesterfield, only a shortened version of one was constructed. This ran from the district of Brampton northeastwards along Old Road and Chatsworth Road (past the depot) into the town centre to terminate in Low Pavement by the Market Place. (The intention had been to continue the line across the centre to the MR station where it would join up with the second route coming in from Whittington Moor to the north.)

Construction of the line (by Joseph Speight of St Helens) was slow and it was not until 1881 that the short line was opened by the impressively-titled Chesterfield & District Tramways Co. with just one single-deck (No 3) and two double-deck cars (Nos

1 and 2), all from Ashburys. The last two of these were fitted with Eades reversible bodies and possibly No 3 was also so equipped.

In February 1885 the Company went into voluntary liquidation and was later acquired by the Chesterfield Tramways Co. (registered 6 December 1886). By 1891 the car fleet had been increased with Nos 4 and 5, probably Milnes single-deckers bought the previous year.

By the late 1890s Chesterfield Corporation was keen to play a part in the tramway scene and on 22 November 1897, in response to the Company's invitation to purchase the under-

taking, did so for the sum of £2,050 (including the Company's winding-up costs).

Bibliography: *Tramtracks and Trolleybooms:
   Chesterfield Trams and Trolleybuses Part 2*
   Barry M. Marsden (Headstock
   Publications, Barnsley, 1988)
   0 951279 33 5

CHESTERFIELD CORPORATION TRAMWAYS
Authority: Chesterfield Brampton and
   Whittington Tramways Order 1879
Gauge: 4ft 8½in
Traction: Horse/overhead electric
Took Over: 22 November 1897
Closed: 23 May 1927
System: Single line
Length: 3.6 miles
Stock: 6 sd, 4 dd horse; 19 dd electric
Livery: Chocolate & yellow/white
Last Car: No 14

Under the Corporation's ownership the Chesterfield horse car fleet was increased again, this time in 1898 by the purchase of No 6, another Milnes single-decker and in 1899 by Nos 7 and 8, a similar pair. In January 1903 two second-hand double-deckers were purchased from SHEFFIELD (and probably not renumbered).

It seems that the line flourished financially under Corporation control and, inevitably, electrification and extension was soon considered, proposed and authorized by the 1904 Chesterfield Corporation Tramways and Improvements Act. Work began on relaying the line in August 1904 and services were temporarily suspended until this was

Chesterfield horse car No 8 of 1899, preserved at the National Tramway Museum, Crich. (M. Donnison)

completed, then the horse cars resumed their trade from Low Pavement as far as Walton Lane, ½ mile short of the Brampton terminus, until the end of the year. The rebuilt line was double the length of the old, the new section running northwards from the former Market Place terminus to Whittington Moor (again mainly as a single track). Rolling stock was twelve Brush open-toppers to begin with, joined in 1907 by another two (Nos 13 and 14).

There is some doubt as to when the new line opened to the public. It was passed by the BoT on 19 December 1904 and different sources give the 20th, 21st and 23rd of that month as the starting date for the electric cars (as the local paper gives the last date, this is probably the most likely) and then only over the horse tramway route. Services as far as Stonegravels on the borough boundary halfway up the Whittington Moor route began on 24 December and throughout from 31 January of the following year.

Although the tramway, like its predecessor, was not a great financial success, in 1914 three Brush balcony cars (Nos 16-18) were bought (No 15 was a 1909 water car) but just two years later, in the early hours of 20 October 1916, a fire in the depot damaged many of the cars, No 8 and one of the 1914 cars having to be scrapped. It seems that two replacement vehicles were acquired in 1920 but details of these are unfortunately sketchy; at the same time seven of the open-toppers were fitted with top covers.

As on many other systems, World War I saw a cut in staff numbers and a serious deterioration in the track as a result of inadequate maintenance and during the 1920s it was decided to replace the trams with trolley-buses. The necessary conversion work commenced in February 1927 and the Brampton route closed on the 28th of that month (replaced by a temporary petrol bus service) with the other half of the system going the same way three months later. The body of No 7, rescued after nearly half a century in a field, is currently undergoing restoration at the National Tramway Museum, Crich, where restored horse car No 8 can also be seen.

Bibliography: as above

CLEETHORPES CORPORATION TRAMWAYS

Authority: Cleethorpes Urban District
    Council Act 1928
Gauge: 4ft 8½in
Traction: Overhead electric
Took Over: 15 July 1936
Closed: 17 July 1937
System: Single line
Length: 1.91 miles
Stock: 1 sd, 24 dd
Livery: Dark blue & primrose*
Last Car: No 38

For just over a year Cleethorpes Corporation operated that portion of the former GRIMSBY system that lay within its boundaries. (Borough status was conferred on 23 September 1936.) With its purchase of the 25 cars which survived from the old Company, the decision was made to adopt a new dark blue and primrose livery and the ex-OLDHAM car, No 38, was so painted although it is not certain how many – if any – of the others were likewise treated. (In the beginning at least paper labels on the cars carried the tramway's new title.)

The intention of the UDC had been to purchase the tramway (powers to work which had been obtained in 1928) in order to abandon it in favour of trolleybuses and the new vehicles entered service the day after the tramway closed.

Bibliography: *The Tramways of Grimsby, Immingham & Cleethorpes* J. H. Price (The Light Rail Transit Association, no date) 0 948106 10 7

COLCHESTER CORPORATION TRAMWAYS

Authority: Colchester Corporation
    Tramways Order 1901
Gauge: 3ft 6in
Traction: Overhead electric
Opened: 28 July 1904
Closed: 8 December 1929
System: Radial
Length: 5.74 miles
Stock: 18 dd
Livery: Maroon/dark brown & cream
Last Car: ?

The Colchester system was an unremarkable example of a corporation-owned tramway which, when major track and rolling stock renewals were needed, was abandoned in favour of motor buses. The only real features of interest were that it was promoted slightly later than was usually the case (after the private construction of a steam tramway had been abandoned in 1883 with ½ mile of track laid) and was closed rather earlier than in many other towns.

The original 16 cars were open-top ERTCW vehicles and were followed in 1906 by a similar pair (Nos 17 & 18) from UEC. The first portion of the system opened consisted of a main, double-track axis a mile long running due south from the GER's North station down North Station Road (where the aborted steam tramway had been laid) and across the River Colne, then up North Hill past the High Street and into Head Street. Here it turned due west to run as a single-track line down Lexden Road and Lexden Street to the suburb of that name. From the main axis a short, double-track section ran due east down the High Street then continued as a single track down East Hill to terminate in East Street just over the river. At the junction of High Street and East Hill another short stretch of double tracks ran due south down Queen Street to St Botolphs station, then eastwards as a single track out to Hythe, terminating on the city side of the river. A final, single-track branch (the building of which was the reason for the purchase of the line's last two cars) opened 28 January 1906 and ran southeastwards for ¾ mile from St Botolphs station to the Recreation Ground.

Bibliograph: *The Tramways of East Anglia* R. C. Anderson (The Light Railway Transport League, 1969) 0 900433 00 0

COLNE & TRAWDEN LIGHT RAILWAYS

Authority: Colne and Trawden Light
    Railways Order 1901
Gauge: 4ft
Traction: Overhead electric
Opened: 28 November 1903
Closed: 6 January 1934
System: Branching
Length: 5.23 miles
Stock: 18 dd
Livery: Light green & cream pre-WWI,
    royal blue & white to 1923, then maroon
    & cream
Last Car: ?

Following the successful promotion of electric tramway services in neighbouring NELSON and BURNLEY, moves to do likewise in the northeast Lancashire town of Colne resulted in the granting of a LRO in 1901 for a line linking the town with Nelson to the southwest and the borough of Trawden to the southeast. The gauge chosen was 4ft, in keeping with the lines of Nelson, Burnley, BLACKBURN and ACCRINGTON close by. The operator was the Colne & Trawden Light Railway Co.

The first section opened ran southwest-wards from Heifer Lane Depot down Keighley Road and Market Street through the centre of Colne and out along Albert Road as far as the junction with Queen Street (about 1¼ miles); the section from here along Burnley Road to the Nelson boundary opened two days later, effectively doubling the length of the mainly single-track line. The 1½ miles of single-track route from the depot down Skipton Road to the Park Hotel in Trawden opened on 22 January 1904 and included a reserved section to bypass a steeper stretch of the roadway. Initial services were worked by cars 1-6, small Milnes open-top double-deckers running from end to end of the tramway.

On an unknown date in December 1904 a 1¼-mile branch from Heifer Lane northeastwards along Keighley Road to the village of Laneshaw Bridge was opened (again single-track) and in April 1905 three small Brush open-toppers (Nos 7-9) were introduced to the growing system. The last length of line opened, in December 1905, was an extension of the Trawden route further on through the village to Lane House Lane. Just over 3 furlongs in length, this was also single-track with another reserved section to avoid a steep hill.

With the system now complete, three further Milnes open-toppers (Nos 10-12) were bought in 1906 and five years later through running to Nelson commenced (though special excursions had been run from Burnley since 1904 using single-deck cars on account of the low MR bridge over the line in Colne and Nos 1-6 fitted with low 'turtle-back' top covers). By now though the Company was looking to sell the tramway and, after first approaching Nelson Corporation, sold it to Colne Corporation for £92,830 as from 25 March 1914. The new owner promptly bought a UEC balcony car (No 13) and set about rebuilding some of the older cars in an attempt to smarten-up the run-down fleet (aided by a new livery). The purchase of further new cars was delayed by the onset of World War I (though three of the other open-toppers were fitted with top covers in 1915) but in 1921 two EE balcony cars were purchased and numbered 2 and 3, those original cars being withdrawn. From 1919 a new, larger depot in Standroyd Road (across the Trawden route from the Heifer Lane depot) was in use, the old one becoming the home of the Corporation's growing bus fleet.

In 1924-25 cars 6 and 11 (and possibly a third) were converted to one-man single-deck vehicles as an economy measure, though three new enclosed double-deckers (Nos 14-16) were bought from Brush in 1926; by now though the growing bus competition and the declining state of the track were irresistible forces and on 19 October 1926 the Laneshaw Bridge branch closed, followed on 3 June 1928 by the Colne–Trawden section of the main line. From 1 April 1933 the tramway was controlled by the Burnley, Colne & Nelson Joint Transport Committee (see BURNLEY) and the car numbers given the suffix C, only to be closed with the Nelson line less than a year later.

Bibliography: *Trams in the North West* Peter Hesketh (Ian Allan, 1995) 0 7110 2349 2

COVENTRY & DISTRICT TRAMWAYS

Authority: Coventry and District Tramways Act 1880

Gauge: 3ft 6in
Traction: Steam
Opened: 1884
Closed: 1893
System: Single line
Length: 5.5 miles
Stock: 7 locos, 6 dd
Livery: ?
Last Car: ?

Operated and owned by the Coventry & District Tramways Co., this single-track steam line ran from Coventry's LNWR station north through the centre of the city via Hertford Street, Broadgate and Bishop Street then out along the Foleshill Road, Longford Road, Bedworth Road and Coventry Road to the village of Bedworth. Services began with tram locomotives Nos 1 and 2 from BP and 3 and 4 from Greens, joined in 1885 by 5 and 6 from Falcon, hauling six Falcon open-top double-deck bogie cars (Nos 1-6). In 1887 loco No 7 was purchased, an 1885 Falcon ex-SOUTH STAFFORDSHIRE.

The tramway was not a success – the steep incline in Bishop Street did not help – and in 1893 services were suspended, never to restart.

Bibliography: *Coventry Transport 1884-1940* A. S. Denton & F. P. Groves (Birmingham Transport Historical Group, 1985) 0 905103 05 X

COVENTRY CORPORATION TRAMWAYS

Authority: Coventry and District Tramways Act 1880
Gauge: 3ft 6in
Traction: Overhead electric

Opened: 5 December 1895
Closed: 24 December 1940*
System: Radial network
Length: 13.33 miles
Stock: 80 dd
Livery: Chocolate & cream to 1933, maroon & cream to 1935, then maroon
Last Car: ?

The former COVENTRY & DISTRICT steam line (see above) was taken over in 1895 by Coventry Electric Tramways Co. Ltd and electrified as a double-track line, the first portion opened being from the station to the depot on Foleshill Road. The northern half of the route on to Bedworth opened exactly a week later. Services began with four Brush open-top double-deckers (Nos 1-4) and these were joined in 1895-96 by Nos 5-8, four converted steam trailers mounted on new trucks. The other two trailers were renumbered 9 and 10 and used as electric trailers until 1898-99 when they too were electrified.

Further routes were authorized under the Coventry Electric Tramways Act of 1897 (and the Coventry Electric Tramways Co., a New General Traction Co. subsidiary, incorporated to buy the CET Co. Ltd) and on 22 July 1899 an easterly route to Stoke from the city centre via Priestley's Bridge, Ford Street and Gosford Green was opened, followed on 27 July by a second route to Gosford Green via Victoria Street. On 18 January 1900 a 2½-mile northeastern extension from Ford Street up Stoney Stanton Road to Bell Green was inaugurated whilst at the same time a new depot was opened at Priestley's Bridge.

During 1898-99 15 more Brush cars were added to the fleet: five were unnumbered trailers and ten (Nos 11-20) were powered cars; all were open-top vehicles again. Two

Coventry Corporation No 34 of 1907 on an early Foleshill working. (Lens of Sutton)

short western extensions (to Earlsdon and Allesley Road) from Broadgate via Smithford Street and Spon Street were opened in March 1905 and to work these twelve ex-WIGAN ERTCW open-toppers (Nos 19-30) were bought in 1904 and the existing Nos 19 and 20 sold to NORWICH (another NGT Co. subsidiary). At the same time the five un-numbered trailers were electrified as Nos 6-10 using the trucks from those aging cars. Six more open-top cars (Nos 31-36) were bought in 1907 from MV; these were followed in 1910 by Nos 37-41, five Brush open-toppers from Norwich.

Shortly after this (from 1 January 1912) Coventry Corporation purchased the tramways for £220,638 and, twelve months later, out-shopped car No 42, another open-topper. After this the new cars added were Brush 43-63 of 1913-25, EE 64-68 of 1928 and Brush 69-73 of 1931, all top-covered vehicles.

The mixed single and double-track system was completed in May 1926 when a short single-track link between the station and Earlsdon routes was opened along Queens Road. By the 1930s though the Corporation, who had been operating bus services since 1914, was preparing to abandon the trams and, on 5 March 1932, closed the Allesley Road route. On 8 March 1936 the Ford Street–Gosford Green link closed, followed on 11 April 1937 by the Earlsdon branch and, three months later, by the Broadgate–station route. The Stoke route service was suspended for twelve months from August 1939 but scarcely had it recommenced than the Corporation, on 24 December 1940, decided to suspend all services for the duration of the war. The city was hit badly at this time by German bombing raids and the decision was an eminently sensible one; in the event though services were never reinstated, it being decided on 25 February 1941 to close the tramways officially and replace them with bus services. All surviving cars were then sold for scrap.

Bibliography: as above

CROYDON TRAMWAYS

Authority: Croydon Tramways Act 1878
Gauge: 4ft 8½in
Traction: Horse
Opened: 9 October 1879
Taken Over: 22 January 1900
System: Network
Length: 6.79 miles
Stock: 7 sd? 24 dd?
Livery: Route colour

Formed by a group of local businessmen, the Croydon Tramways Co. began operations over a single track running 1½ miles from the depot at Thornton Heath Pond south along London Road to West Croydon station in North End

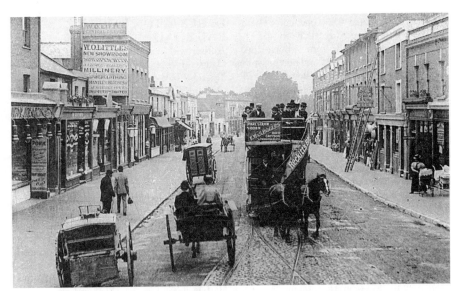

A Croydon double-deck horse car entering a passing loop in London Road. (Lens of Sutton)

with five Starbuck single-deckers. The system was expanded gradually over the next three years and on 2 August 1883 the Company amalgamated with the Norwood & District Tramways Co. which was constructing a line in South Norwood to the northeast of Croydon. The Croydon & Norwood Tramways Co.'s resulting single-track system eventually resembled a letter Y with a line from the Red Deer on Brighton Road in South Croydon running north along South End to the Crown (see below) from where the original line carried on north to Thornton Heath Pond whilst a branch to the east along George Street led to East Croydon station, and from there northeast through Addiscombe and Woodside to South Norwood. Two link lines and a short branch filled the gap between these two main arms of the network.

Two more Starbuck single-deckers (Nos 6 and 7) had been added to stock by 1883 when the first double-deckers arrived. Full details of the cars are not available though by 1897 the number series had reached 31, with probably all after No 7 double-deckers from a number of manufacturers. Steam, oil and battery-electric traction were all experimented with at different times without lasting success.

On 25 October 1887 the Company went into liquidation and the system was cut back with the closure of unprofitable routes and on the first day of 1890 a new concern, the Croydon Tramways Co., took over the line and its 14 cars. By the end of the decade though Croydon Corporation had decided to take over the line in order to electrify it and in 1900 did so under the Croydon Tramways Act of that year (see below).

Bibliography: *The Tramways of Croydon*

G. E. Baddeley (The Light Rail Transit Association, rev ed 1983) 0 900433 90 6

CROYDON CORPORATION TRAMWAYS

Authority: Croydon Corporation Tramways Order 1894
Gauge: 4ft 8½in
Traction: Horse, overhead electric
Took Over: 22 January 1900
Taken Over: 1 July 1933
System: Radial network
Length: 11.92 miles
Stock: 125 dd electric
Livery: Munich lake & ivory to 1928, then port wine & grey

Croydon Corporation began tramway ownership in a very modest way with just 286yd of track in the High Street linking the CROYDON TRAMWAYS' hitherto unconnected sections in North End and South End (see above). This opened on 6 June 1897 and was leased to the Company. Two years later, the Corporation had decided to take over the whole system as soon as it was entitled to do so and lease it to the BET. The price paid was £50,000 and the agreement signed on 22 January 1900 (though preparatory work on the electrification had already started).

The first section of the new system opened, on 26 September 1901, ran from Norbury station near the town's northern boundary south along the London Road to Thornton Heath Pond (and rebuilt depot) and then continued along the former horse route through South Croydon and on Brighton Road into Purley where it terminated at the town's southern boundary. The first cars were Nos 1-35, open-top double-deckers (as were all the cars) from Milnes with similar bogie vehicles 36-45 arriving in

1902 as more routes were opened. (These latter cars were owned directly by the BET). On 10 January 1902 the former horse link line from Thornton Heath Pond northeast to Thornton was re-opened, followed on 24 January by the former route from West Croydon to Selhurst, extended on 14 March to South Norwood. The last horse cars were sold by auction on 17 February that year. Later in 1902 Nos 46-55, Milnes bogie cars, were added to the fleet, followed by similar cars 56-60, this time from Brush (and again BET-owned). A second depot was provided in Purley to cope with the growing number of cars.

In 1905 the Corporation decided to terminate the BET's lease (it was concerned about the Company's empire-building plans for the surrounding area) with 1 July 1906 as the expiry date. The BET promptly withdrew from the Croydon operation, taking its own trams with it. To fill the gap, the Corporation purchased a series of Brush bogie cars, Nos 36-60 in 1906 and Nos 61-70 a year later, joined in 1911 by similar vehicles 71-75, the last pre-World War I purchases.

Further routes opened and, after relations with the BET's subsidiary, the SOUTH METROPOLITAN TRAMWAYS, had improved, through running began on 24 June 1907 across the boundary at South Norwood to Penge High Street and to the Crystal Palace via Anerley Road. (These two short branches had been built by the BET prior to its split with the Corporation.) On 17 February 1926, after years of negotiating, through running over LONDON COUNTY COUNCIL metals began at Norbury (where a conduit plough had to be affixed to a Croydon car going through to the Victoria Embankment). The South Met meanwhile had opened two routes from Tamworth Road, opposite West Croydon station, northwest to Mitcham and on to Tooting and southwest past Croydon Aerodrome to Sutton.

During 1927-28 a large-scale reorganization of the car fleet took place. Surviving cars of the 1-35 batch were withdrawn, Nos 46-55 were fitted with top covers and renumbered 21-30 and Nos 43, 44, 62-64, 66, 67 and 69 sold to the South Met. Nos 41 and 57 were scrapped whilst the remainder of the Brush cars 36-75 were renumbered 1-20 (though in reverse order). At the same time 25 new HN enclosed bogie double-deckers Nos 31-55 were bought.

On 28 March 1927 the short eastern Addiscombe route was closed, the trams replaced by London General Omnibus Co. buses. Early in 1933 the track-doubling programme was completed (much of the system was so treated), just in time for the 1 July takeover by LONDON TRANSPORT.

Bibliography: as above

DARLINGTON STREET RAILROAD

Authority: Local authority permission
Gauge: 4ft 8½in?
Traction: Horse
Opened: 1 January 1862
Closed: 8 January 1865
System: Branching
Length: c1 mile
Stock: 2 sd
Livery: ?
Last Car: ?

Darlington's first tramway was operated by the Darlington Street Railroad Co. Ltd in the wake of G. F. Train's pioneering street railway experiments at BIRKENHEAD and elsewhere, the authority for it being obtained from the local Board of Health. The single-track line was constructed by Charles Hathaway & Co. in 1861 and ran northwards from The Shambles by the Market Place up Northgate and North Road to Durham Road where it terminated at Whessoe Street. A short branch off North Road served the Stockton & Darlington Railway's station (later the NER's North Road station). The two cars used on the tramway were named, in Train's fashion, *Nelson* and *Wellington*.

The line was not a success, largely because of the opposition from other road users raised by its use of Train's step rails, and it was closed suddenly in 1865 by the Local Board (according to one account, because of the amount of compensation paid out when one of the cars ran over a valuable greyhound).

Bibliography: *Darlington Municipal Transport: Trams, Trolleys & Buses* Ron Howe (Darlington Corporation, 1972)

DARLINGTON: STOCKTON & DARLINGTON STEAM TRAMWAYS

Authority: Darlington Tramways Order 1880
Gauge: 3ft
Traction: Horse
Opened: 10 October 1880
Closed: 18 August 1903
System: Single line
Length: 2.13 miles
Stock: 12 sd & dd
Livery: Chocolate & white
Last Car: ?

Despite its title, the Stockton & Darlington Steam Tramways Co. Ltd's only steam tramway was in STOCKTON, the Darlington line being always horse-worked. Its single track ran across the town from the NER's Bank Top station in the southeast, via Victoria Road and Feethams to the Market

Place, and from there northwest via Bondgate and Woodland Road to Cockerton, terminating at Carmel Road on the borough boundary. The depot was in Woodland Road and the line was worked as two routes from the Market with seven cars in service at any one time.

The Bank Top station half of the tramway was closed as unprofitable in 1885 and eleven years later (following its financial collapse in 1893 when control passed to the Stockton & District Tramways Co.) the remainder was acquired by IMPERIAL TRAMWAYS who wished to electrify it but then changed its mind. Then, on 24 January 1902, they sold it for £7,600 to Darlington Corporation who leased it to C. J. O'Dowd until it was ready to convert it to electric operation. It was then closed to allow reconstruction to take place (see below), O'Dowd becoming the new Traffic Superintendent.

Bibliography: as above

DARLINGTON CORPORATION LIGHT RAILWAYS

Authority: Darlington Corporation Light Railways Order 1902
Gauge: 3ft 6in
Traction: Overhead electric
Opened: 1 June 1904
Closed: 10 April 1926*
System: Radial
Length: 4.87 miles
Stock: 16 sd, 8 dd
Livery: Dark blue & white
Last Car: ?

Darlington Corporation had built its own power station in 1900 and, when it acquired the town's horse tramway two years later (see above), sought the necessary powers to extend and electrify it. Laid by J. G. White & Co., the new system comprised four mainly double-track routes radiating from the Market Place: northwest to Forcett Street, Cockerton (an extension of the horse line), north up North Road and Durham Road to Harrowgate Hill (an extension of the 1862 route), northeast along Freemans Place past the depot and along Haughton Road to Barton Street and east along Parkgate past Bank Top station to Cobden Street in Eastbourne. (The first route opened was the Harrowgate Hill line which was followed the next day by that to Cockerton, then shortly after by the other two.)

Services were worked by single-deck combination cars Nos 1-16 from Milnes which were joined in 1913 by Nos 17 and 18, UEC top-covered cars. The only other cars added, Nos 19-24, were open-top Brush cars bought from SHEERNESS in 1918 (plus two more for their spare parts). By the end of World War I though the aging track was not so easily replaced and it was decided to switch over to trolleybuses. The Haughton Road route was converted on 16 January 1926 and the line to Cockerton on 20 February with the last day of tramcar operation over the Eastbourne–Harrowgate Hill through route officially being 10 April 1926 although the cars remained in use at peak periods for a while longer. After withdrawal, Nos 17 and 18 were sold to DOVER and the other survivors scrapped.

Bibliography: as above

DARTFORD HOSPITALS TRAMWAY

A private 4ft gauge tramway served the Long Reach, Orchard and Joyce Green isolation hospitals sited on the marshes between Dartford and the Thames estuary. It was built in 1897 by the Metropolitan Asylums Board and ran from a loading stage on the river, through Long Reach Hospital then across a causeway to serve the other two sites. The line was single-track with various branches added throughout its life, making a total track length of 3.4 miles.

The system was apparently used only for the carriage of goods, not patients, until 27 February 1902 when four second-hand LONDON single-deck horse cars (Nos 5-8) were put into service to cope with the influx of patients caused by a smallpox epidemic, followed in 1905 by a purpose-built ERTCW ambulance tram (No 1). Four further ambulance trams (Nos 3-6) were added in 1909 (from UEC).

Horse traction ceased in 1925 and from then on the cars were towed by Talbot motor ambulances. Regular services ceased in 1931 although the system saw occasional use until 1936, the rails being lifted during World War II.

Bibliography: *The Tramways of Woolwich and South East London* 'Southeastern' (The Light Railway Transport League, 1963)

DARTFORD & DISTRICT LIGHT RAILWAYS

Authority: Dartford and District Light Railways Order 1902
Gauge: 4ft 8½in
Traction: Overhead electric
Opened: 14 February 1906
Taken Over: 1 July 1933
System: Radial
Length: 6.55 miles
Stock: 1 sd, 12 dd
Livery: Maroon & cream
Last Car: ?

Although constructed and originally

Car No 10, one of Darlington Corporation's original single-deckers, at Cockerton, the system's western terminus. (Lens of Sutton)

operated by the firm of J. G. White & Co. Ltd, this system was owned by Dartford UDC which leased it out to BB from 1909. It was essentially a single-track line running from the municipal boundary with BEXLEY in the west through Crayford to Dartford where it turned northeast along the Dover Road to the district of Horns Cross. A short branch in Dartford ran northwards to the SECR station and the depot whilst a slightly longer one ran south to the village of Wilmington.

The system's original passenger fleet comprised twelve UEC open-top double-deckers (Nos 1-12) of 1905 which were joined in 1915 by an MV demi-car (No 13) purchased from ERITH. Two years later, on the Bank Holiday of 7 August 1917, the depot burnt down and all thirteen cars were destroyed. Temporary replacement vehicles were provided by Bexley UDC (the wartime importance of the local munitions industry saved the tramway from closure), which authority operated the line on behalf of BB until 1921 when the latter's lease ran out. From April 1921 the two UDCs operated both systems as a joint enterprise under the Bexley Council Tramways and Dartford Light Railways Joint Committee, with through running to Woolwich, until 1 July 1933 when both were taken over by LONDON TRANSPORT who closed them in favour of trolleybuses two years later.

Bibliography: as above

DARWEN CORPORATION TRAMWAYS

Authority: Blackburn and Over Darwen Tramways Act 1879

Gauge: 4ft
Traction: Steam/overhead electric
Took Over: 1 January 1899
Closed: 5 October 1946
System: Branching
Length: 4.36 miles
Stock: 3 locos, 3 dd steam; 3 sd, 22 dd electric
Livery: Vermillion & purple lake, later vermillion & cream
Last Car: No 3

Following its purchase of that section of the BLACKBURN & OVER DARWEN TRAMWAY within its boundaries from the start of 1899, Darwen Corporation ran it as a steam line until the electrification work was completed, re-opening it as a mainly double-track line on 17 October 1900 – the day after the last steam trams ran – with ten Milnes open-top double-deck cars. A year later, on 11 October 1901, an eastwards single-track branch of 1¼ miles across the moors to Hoddlesden was opened and the car fleet expanded by the purchase of Nos 11-14, again Milnes open-toppers. (Several of these early cars were later given top covers and/or rebuilt.)

Although a small system compared with many of the others in south Lancashire, it formed part of an extensive 4ft gauge network through its connection with BLACKBURN to the north and the car fleet was kept up to date with a series of replacement vehicle purchases. These were MV single-deck demi-cars 15-17 of 1905-06 (No 15 was later converted into a works vehicle and No 17 rebuilt as double-deck No 10), UEC open-toppers 18 and 19 of 1915 and Nos 20-22, EE open-toppers of six years later.

In 1933 the Corporation bought two ex-RAWTENSTALL double-deckers, numbering them 9 (fully enclosed) and 11 (balcony) and three years later purchased two new EE streamlined double-deckers, Nos 23 and 24, which were slimmed-down versions of that company's BLACKPOOL 'Balloon' cars.

On 13 October 1937 the Hoddlesden branch closed but the main Whitehall–Blackburn route survived intact for nearly three years until 31 March 1940 when the southernmost mile, from Whitehall to Circus, was abandoned. In 1945 the two streamliners were withdrawn, leaving only Nos 3, 7 and 10 to work the final year's services. Nos 23 and 24 were then sold to the Llandudno & Colwyn Bay Electric Railway in Wales and the other cars scrapped.

Bibliography: *The First in the Kingdom: a history of buses and trams in Blackburn and Darwen* R. P. Fergusson, G. Holden & C. Reilly (Darwen Transport Group, 1981).

DEARNE DISTRICT LIGHT RAILWAYS

Authority: Dearne District Light Railways Order 1915
Gauge: 4ft 8½in
Traction: Overhead electric
Opened: 14 July 1924
Closed: 30 September 1933
System: Branching
Length: 14.18 miles
Stock: 30 sd
Livery: Bright red & cream
Last Car: ?

This single-track tramway was a late-comer to the British scene and filled the wide gap in the south Yorkshire network between BARNSLEY to the northwest and MEXBOROUGH & SWINTON to the south. It was in fact the last system to be opened in the British Isles until SEATON in the 1970s (which is hardly comparable) and the MANCHESTER METRO in the 1990s (which is). But for the intervention of World War I the tramway would have been constructed earlier for several years of negotiations between the various local authorities affected (the Wath-under-Dearne, Wombwell, Bolton-upon-Dearne and Thurnscoe UDCs) had resulted in the 1915 LRO authorizing the project.

Construction did not begin until 1923 with the whole system opening the following year. As built, the line was unusual in that it was laid with sleepered track throughout, ballasted on the roadside sections and paved in the streets; the idea was that such track would be easier to repair or re-align than more conventional constructions as and when the mining subsidence prevalent in the area necessitated it.

The main route ran from the Alhambra Theatre in Barnsley by the Market Place (though because of mutual antagonism no physical connection was made with that town's neighbouring track) and ran out southeastwards along the Barnsley Road through Stairfoot and Wombwell, past the depot (known officially by the American term 'Car Barns') and on through West Melton to Wath-upon-Dearne. Here a branch of 1½ miles led south to the Woodman Inn at Swinton on the M&S system whilst a second branch of some 5 miles led north through Bolton-upon-Dearne to Thurnscoe. The main route itself continued eastwards from Wath for another mile to Manvers Main Colliery where it met the M&S trolleybus feeder.

Because of a low railway bridge at Wath the tramway was restricted to the use of low single-deck cars. Thirty of these (Nos 1-30) were constructed for the line by EE and, following the tramway's closure after just nine years in favour of Yorkshire Traction Co. buses, five were sold to Falkirk, four to LYTHAM ST ANNES and the trucks and other parts of the rest to HULL.

DEPTFORD see LONDON, DEPTFORD & GREENWICH

DERBY TRAMWAYS

Authority: Derby Tramways Order 1879
Gauge: 4ft
Traction: Horse
Opened: 6 March 1880
Taken Over: 1 November 1899
System: Radial
Length: 4.68 miles
Stock: 16 sd, 4 dd
Livery: Possibly by route to 1894, then crimson lake & white
Last Car: ?

Promoted and operated by the Derby Tramways Co. – after initial opposition from Derby Council and a rival private group – work on constructing Derby's horse tramway system was begun in October 1879 by Mousley & Co. of Bristol and Wolverhampton. The first route opened ran southeast for 1 mile from the Market Place up St Peter's Street, through The Spot, along London Road and Station Street (later Midland Road) to the MR station with the first batch of 16 cars being supplied by Starbuck.

On 1 October 1880 a second route (also 1 mile long), from Victoria Street just south of the Market Place northwestwards to Windmill Hill via Friargate and the Ashbourne Road, was opened, followed on 8 October by another southeastern line, this time running for 1¼ miles from The Spot down Osmaston Road to Cotton Lane.

The last two routes opened in 1881: south from The Spot for 1 mile to the Normanton Hotel via Babington Lane and Normanton Road (28 May) and on southeast down the London Road from the London Road/Station Street junction to Deadman's Lane (14 July). All routes were primarily double-track with the main depot off Friargate by the GNR station. Horse bus services were also operated.

In 1887 two double-deckers (Nos 17 and 18) were bought from Shrewsbury, followed in 1894 by two more (Nos 19 and 20) from an unknown manufacturer. By this date the Corporation was considering the idea of buying the system in order to modernize it and, on 28 December 1898, agreed a price of £32,000 with the Company and took control on 1 November of the following year.

Bibliography: *The Story of Transport in Derby* Barry Edwards (Breedon Books, Derby, 1993) 1 87362 657 6

DERBY CORPORATION TRAMWAYS

Authority: Derby Corporation Act 1899
Gauge: 4ft
Traction: Horse, overhead electric
Took Over: 1 November 1899
Closed: 2 July 1934
System: Radial network
Length: 13.96 miles
Stock: 4 sd, 22 dd horse; 4 sd, 74 dd electric
Livery: Dark olive green & cream
Last Car: No 78

Following its purchase of the city's horse tramways in 1899 (see above), the Corporation set about obtaining powers in the form of the Derby Corporation Act 1901 to enable it to construct new lines. Meanwhile the horse fleet was overhauled, No 13 converted in 1900 to an open-top single-decker, three 1894 double-deckers (Nos 21-23) purchased from Glasgow and, in 1903, three more bought (and which probably took numbers vacated by withdrawn cars).

Work on converting the system began in November 1903 (with the horse services progressively curtailed) and a new depot built on Osmaston Road. The first electric routes opened on 27 July 1904: from The Spot to the Harrington Arms in Alvaston (the extended London Road horse line), the branch to the MR station and from The Spot to Abingdon Street (the new depot). The first cars (Nos 1-25) were Brush open-toppers, followed in 1905 by

Nos 26-29, Brush top-covered vehicles.

On 4 September 1904 the system was extended back from The Spot to Victoria Street and on 18 September a short link between the London Road and Osmaston Road was provided via Bateman Street. On 24 February 1905 the Market Place was reached and on 31 July a route from there was opened up Kedleston Road to Penny Long Lane. Other routes after that served the Ashbourne Road, Uttoxeter Road and Burton Road with a loop line out along Normanton Road to the Cavendish Hotel and back along Walbrook Road and Douglas Street to the Osmaston Road line on the western side of the city, and along the Nottingham Road (where a second depot was built) to the Cemetery on the east. This last line was opened on 8 February 1908, by which time the car fleet had grown with the addition of 18 trams from MV: top-covered 30-35 and single-deckers 36-39 (to work under a low railway bridge in Friargate) in 1906 and open-toppers 40-47 over the next two years.

The last horse tram service, along the Ashbourne Road, seems to have ceased on 1 June 1907 though the horse bus service survived for another ten years!

In 1911 Brush supplied top-covered cars 48-50, after which some of the open-toppers were either fitted with top covers or enclosed, with another ten similar cars following in 1920 (Nos 51-60). The last cars bought, during 1925-27, were Nos 61-78, all enclosed double-deckers from Brush. During the 1920s the track-doubling programme continued (most of the system was eventually so treated) but, although the Corporation now operated a growing fleet of battery and motor buses, it was decided in 1930 to replace the trams with trolleybuses! The first of these entered service on 9 January 1932, that same day seeing the withdrawal of the trams on the Buxton Road and Uttoxeter Road routes. Over the next two years the other lines were soon converted, the last public service car running in 1934 from Victoria Street to Osmaston Depot.

Bibliography: as above

DERBYSHIRE see NOTTINGHAMSHIRE & DERBYSHIRE

DEVONPORT & DISTRICT TRAMWAYS

Authority: Devonport Corporation Tramway Order 1899
Gauge: 3ft 6in
Traction: Overhead electric
Opened: 26 June 1901
Taken Over: 20 October 1915
System: Network
Length: 9.2 miles

Stock: 33 dd
Livery: Chocolate & cream pre-WWI, then dark green & cream

The last of the three tramway companies to begin operations in the PLYMOUTH area, the Devonport & District Tramways Co. (registered 1898) was part of the BET group and had the advantage of starting out with an electric system. Initial authorization was for 5 miles of routes within the borough boundaries, from the town west to Morice Town, north through South Keyham, North Keyham and Keyham to Camel's Head, northeast to the depot at Milehouse and east to Victoria Park. To work the line 20 open-top double-deckers (Nos 1-20) were ordered from Brill.

In 1900 Devonport Corporation, wishing to see the system extended, obtained powers for another 4 miles of lines to Tor Lane, Peverell and Saltash Passage and, having constructed the last two, leased them to the D&D. The line from North Keyham east to Milehouse and Peverell was connected to the main system but the Saltash passage route to Camel's Head just north of Keyham was not because a wooden bridge over the Weston Mill Creek would not support the cars; this isolated section was worked for a short while by Nos 20 and 24 from a small depot at Camel's Head until a connecting embankment was built.

In 1902 five Brush open-toppers (Nos 21-25) were purchased new, followed ten years later by eight similar Brush cars obtained second-hand from BIRMINGHAM (Nos 26-29 of 1904 and 31-33 of 1902) and SHEERNESS (No 30 of 1902).

In October 1914 the Plymouth local authority area was enlarged to include Devonport and the D&D was then purchased by Plymouth Corporation, the final takeover coming twelve months later.

Bibliography: *The Trams of Plymouth: a 73 Years Story* Martin Langley & Edwina Small (Ex Libris Press, 1990) 0 948578 25 4

DEWSBURY, BATLEY & BIRSTAL TRAMWAY

Authority: Dewsbury Batley and Birstal Tramways Order 1873
Gauge: 4ft 8½in
Traction: Horse, steam
Opened: 25 July 1874
Closed: 26 September 1905?
System: Single line
Length: 4.29 miles
Stock: 11 locos, 18 dd horse & steam
Livery: Locos dark brown/black, later chrome yellow & brown; cars chrome yellow & cream
Last Car: No 6 (loco unknown)

The DBB was not only one of the first horse tramways to be built after the 1870 Act, it was one of the very first to make the switch to steam traction and was promoted by the Dewsbury, Batley & Birstal Tramway Co. (using the archaic spelling of Birstall) to serve those places in the Heavy Woollen District of the West Riding of Yorshire.

The section from Dewsbury to Batley (1½ miles) was the first opened, then the next mile to Carlington (where the depot was sited) on 25 March 1875 and the final section to Birstall on 23 June that year; the whole line was a single track laid along the highway. In 1879 powers were obtained for a 1-mile extension from Birstall to Moor Lane at Gomersal and this opened in the autumn of 1881 (exact date unknown). Original stock comprised five Starbuck open-top double-deckers but as these did not arrive until September 1874 two cars had to be borrowed from LEEDS for the opening.

In 1876 trials were undertaken on the line with Merryweather and Kitson prototype steam tramway engines and the directors were sufficiently impressed to request the BoT to sanction the regular use of this form of traction. (At the time, only the WANTAGE TRAMWAY, under rather different conditions, was using it.) Steam services began on 10 April 1880, making the line the first street tramway in England to introduce them. Horse working ceased the following year, by which time the line operated nine locos, all from Merryweather; five years later three closed double-deck bogie trailers were purchased to augment the ex-horse car fleet.

In 1902 the Company was acquired by the BET and three years later the relevant local authorities exercised their right to purchase the line and leased it back to the BET in order that it might be electrified. On the first day of 1906 the DBBT Co. went into voluntary liquidation, the refurbished line now the responsibility of a new BET subsidiary, the YORKSHIRE (WOOLLEN DISTRICT) TRAMWAYS Co. Ltd.

Bibliography: *The Tramways of Dewsbury and Wakefield* W. Pickles (The Light Railway Transit Association, 1980) 0 900433 73 6

DEWSBURY, OSSETT & SOOTHILL NETHER TRAMWAYS

Authority: Dewsbury Corporation Tramway Order 1904; Ossett Corporation Tramway Order 1904; Soothill Nether Urban District Tramways Act 1904
Gauge: 4ft 8½in
Traction: Overhead electric
Opened: 11 November 1908
Closed: 19 October 1933
System: Branching

Length: 3.14 miles
Stock: 12 dd
Livery: Dark red & off-white
Last Car: ?

The DOSNT was one of those grandly-named systems whose length of track was in inverse proportion to that of its title; not surprisingly, it was generally known as the Dewsbury & Ossett Tramways and provided a link between the YORKSHIRE (WEST RIDING) and YORKSHIRE (WOOLLEN DISTRICT) systems centred on Wakefield and Dewsbury respectively.

For such a small system its promotion and eventual authorization was complicated and protracted; after several earlier schemes at the turn of the century had come to nothing, the three local authorities within whose territory the line would pass in 1904 finally received the go-ahead to commence construction. This was carried out by the NEC who then leased the line from the three authorities for operating purposes.

As built, the line ran from Ossett Market Place, where it had an end-on connection with the WAKEFIELD & DISTRICT LIGHT RAILWAY, past the depot in Church Street and then in a roughly north-westerly direction to Dewsbury Market Place, ½ mile before which a trailing junction into High Road brought in the ½-mile branch from Earlsheaton to the south. Both main line and branch were single-track and incorporated many stiff climbs. The official opening took place on 12 November 1908, the day after the BoT inspection and public opening.

The tramway's first eight cars were Brush open-top vehicles (later fitted with top covers); in 1911 these were joined by Nos 9 and 10, two more Brush cars, this time ex-

MEXBOROUGH & SWINTON (another NEC concern). Both open-toppers, these two were also fitted with top covers. In 1928 two sister cars were acquired (Nos 11 and 12), these coming with top covers already in place.

Although the line was physically connected to the W&D, through running (though originally envisaged) was restricted to specials (eg for Wakefield Trinity v Dewsbury rugby matches). By the late 1920s the NEC was considering replacing the trams with buses or trolleybuses but the idea was overtaken by events when the BET bought out the Company in 1931 and for the last two years of its life worked the tramway through the Yorkshire (Woollen District) Electric Tramways Co. Ltd before replacing it with a bus service.

Bibliography: *as above*

DONCASTER CORPORATION TRAMWAYS

Authority: Doncaster Corporation Light
    Railways Order 1899
Gauge: 4ft 8½in
Traction: Overhead electric
Opened: 2 June 1902
Closed: 8 June 1935
System: Radial
Length: 14.7 miles
Stock: 1 sd, 46 dd
Livery: Maroon & cream
Last Car: ?

Faced with the threat of a private concern setting up an electric tramway system, Doncaster Corporation decided in the 1890s to construct its own to accompany its municipal electric street lighting (inaugurated in 1899) in this important railway town. After

an inspection visit to HULL it was decided to use centrally-grooved rails, Doncaster thus becoming the only other British electric tramway to do so.

The first two routes opened ran from Station Road in the town centre southwest to Balby High Street via St Sepulchre Gate with a parallel branch off this along Hexthorpe Road to Old Hexthorpe; these were followed on 30 June 1902 by a line southeast from the High Street via Hall Gate, South Parade and Bennetthorpe Road to the Racecourse. On 1 August a short southern branch off St Sepulchre Gate was opened to Jarratt Street (and extended two months later to Childers Street, Hyde Park) and on 27 October a northern route was opened up Bentley Road to Bentley High Street. This line remained isolated from the rest of the system until the long North Bridge was opened in 1911 to carry the Great North Road over the GNR's main line railway tracks north of the town centre.

A 1-mile branch northeast from the Station Road/High Street one-way complex was opened in 1903 up Nether Hall Road to Avenue Road (15 January), with a short branch off this along Beckett Road (17 August), whilst on 25 November a very short branch was opened off St Sepulchre Gate south into Oxford Street, only to be abandoned two years later because of poor receipts.

The tramway's first cars, Nos 1-15, were ERTCW open-toppers and were followed in 1903 by similar vehicles 16-25; after that there was a gap of ten years until the arrival of top-covered UEC cars 26-32 in 1913 and 33-36 three years later. (Many of the older cars were by now fitted with top covers as well.) Also in 1916 the Corporation purchased MV single-deck demi-car No 37 and, four years later, bought EE top-covered cars 38-47 to complete the fleet. The depot and power station were sited in Grey Friars Road by the North Bridge (prior to the opening of which a separate depot existed in Marsh Gate to serve the Bentley route).

The last routes opened were a 1½-mile extension of the Balby line southwest along Warmsworth Road to the village of that name on 5 February 1915 and a 3-mile northern route on reserved track beside the Great North Road to Brodsworth on 21 February 1916 to serve the housing development there. All routes were primarily single-track with the exception of the racecourse line (which ended in a balloon loop) on account of the large crowds it had to cope with on occasions.

Early in the 1920s the Corporation was once again under commercial pressure, this time from growing bus competition, and decided to abandon the tramways. In 1922 it began running its own motor buses, using

Postcard view of Doncaster High Street with Corporation No 2 of 1902 approaching. (Lens of Sutton)

Tramways of England 55

them to replace the trams (on 1 May 1925) on the Avenue Road route. On 19 August 1928 the last trams ran to Bentley, replaced by trolleybuses – this route had been extended just four years before to take it to Bentley Colliery – with the Hexthorpe and Beckett Road lines going the following year, the Hyde Park and racecourse routes in 1930 and the Balbey line in 1931, leaving just the Brodsworth route to survive another four years.

Bibliography: *The Story of Doncaster Corporation Transport* (Doncaster Corporation, 1952)

DOVER CORPORATION TRAMWAYS

Authority: Dover Corporation Tramways Order 1896
Gauge: 3ft 6in
Traction: Overhead electric
Opened: 6 September 1897
Closed: 31 December 1936
System: Branching
Length: 4.29 miles
Stock: 45 dd
Livery: Green and ivory, later dark red and ivory*
Last Car: ?

The Dover system formed a crooked Y in shape with its two branches meeting in the town centre from where a single line ran down to, then along beside, the harbour. It was promoted and operated by Dover Council, the actual construction being by Dick, Kerr, and originally ran from the shore end of the Admiralty Pier (Clarence Place) via the Market Place, Biggin Street, High Street and London Road northeastwards as far as Buckland Bridge (where it crossed the River Dour); a branch from Biggin Street ran southwest to Maxton. Total route length was just over 3 miles – virtually all single track – and, unusually for such a small system, had a depot sited at the end of each branch.

Ten Brush open-top cars (Nos 1-10 of which 8 and 10 ran as trailers for a few months) were ordered for the opening, the date of which made the line an electric pioneer in southern England. Six similar cars were purchased in 1898, Nos 11-14 from Milnes and Nos 15 and 16 from Brill. By this time the system had undergone its first route change with the abandonment of 200yd or so of track at the Admiralty Pier end of the line. (This section only opened at the beginning of 1898 and was closed in April of that year to avoid trams being held up by a level crossing over the pier railway line there; from then on services started from Strond Street by the LCDR's Harbour Station.) In 1902 another open-

Dover Corporation No 18 of 1905 with proudly-posed crew. (Lens of Sutton)

topper (No 17) was bought, this time from ERTCW.

In 1905 the Buckland route was extended for just over a mile up Crabble Hill, down Crabble Road and thence over a private right of way to the village of River. The opening of this new double-track section took place on 2 October and the purpose of its construction was partly to alleviate local unemployment; at the same time four further ERTCW open-toppers (Nos 18-21) were purchased, followed in 1912 by three more similar Brush cars (Nos 22-24).

In 1920 the line's last new open-toppers, from EE, were bought and numbered 25-27; thereafter second-hand vehicles were obtained as replacements for its older cars, these being Nos 8 and 9 in 1926 (formerly DARLINGTON 17 and 18 of 1913), Nos 1-5 in 1927 (WEST HARTLEPOOL 1-5 of 1913), Nos 11 and 12 in 1928 (BIRMINGHAM & MIDLAND 15 and 17 of 1915), Nos 6, 7, 10, 14 and 17 in 1930 (B&M of 1904) and Nos 19-22 in 1933 (BIRMINGHAM CORPORATION of 1905 which retained their Birmingham blue and cream livery).

In 1936 the trams gave way to bus competition after the East Kent Road Car Co. Ltd reached a financial agreement with the Corporation allowing it to operate within the town.

Bibliography: *The Tramways of Kent Vol 2: East Kent 'INVICTA'* (The Light Railway Transport League, 1975)
0 900433 45 0

DRYPOOL & MARFLEET STEAM TRAMWAY see HULL: DRYPOOL & MARFLEET STEAM TRAMWAY

DUDLEY, SEDGLEY & WOLVERHAMPTON TRAMWAYS

Authority: Dudley Sedgley and Wolverhampton Tramways Order 1880
Gauge: 4ft 8½in
Traction: Horse/steam
Opened: 7 May 1883
Closed: 21 February 1901
System: Single line
Length: 5.78 miles
Stock: 8 dd? horse; 9 locos, 5 dd steam
Livery: Maroon & yellow
Last Car: ?

Owned originally by the Dudley, Sedgley & Wolverhampton Tramways Co. Ltd (incorporated 20 December 1879), this Black Country tramway ran northwards from the Post Office in Wolverhampton Street, Dudley, through Upper Gornal and Sedgley, across the Wolverhampton boundary at the Fighting Cocks and up the Dudley Road to Snow Hill, just south of Queen Square, the focal point of the WOLVERHAMPTON TRAMWAYS system.

Although services began with seven Ashbury horse cars, the Company decided very early on to use steam because of the gradients on the undulating single-track line (the cars needing three horses in places) and this was introduced on 16 January 1886, the necessary Order having been obtained two years earlier and horse working having ceased on 8 November 1885 to allow for track relaying. (It is thought an eighth horse car was acquired in 1884, source unknown.) The depot was at Sedgley by the Upper Gornal boundary.

Five Kitson tramway locomotives (Nos 1-5) were bought to work the steam service, plus five large top-covered bogie trailers Nos

1-5 from Starbuck. A sixth loco (No 7) was bought from Kitsons in 1894 and three BH locos (Nos 6, 8 and 9) four years later from HUDDERSFIELD CORPORATION (their Nos 7-9); it is possible that an earlier No 6 was envisaged but never bought. By then the line was about to change hands for the third time: the DSWT Co. went into liquidation in March 1888 and was bought by two contractors named Oppert and Fell on 6 April 1889; they in turn sold it on 18 October that year for £44,000 to the newly-formed Midland Tramways Co. Ltd (reconstructed in 1893 as the Dudley & Wolverhampton Tramways Co. Ltd). This company fared no better – the line was difficult to work, understocked and services slow - and at the end of 1898 agreed to sell out to the BET, the tramway being bought from the Receiver on 22 April 1899 for £18,300 after the DWT Co. had gone into voluntary liquidation.

The BET set about incorporating its new line into its proposals for a grand BLACK COUNTRY system, promoting the Dudley and Wolverhampton Tramways Order 1899 to this end. The Order however gave Wolverhampton Corporation the power to purchase the mile or so of track within that town, which it did for the arbitrated sum of £4,250 later that year. (It intended to work this section with ex-WT horse cars but was unable to do so since the DSW was laid with centre-grooved rails which only accommodated stock with centre-flanged wheels.)

Work began on electrification and regauging to 3ft 6in on the Dudley–Sedgley section in late 1899 with electric services beginning on 3 October 1900 operated by the DUDLEY, STOURBRIDGE & DISTRICT, the steam services from Sedgley to the Fighting Cocks continuing into the next year before being replaced by WOLVERHAMPTON DISTRICT electric cars.

Bibliography: *Black Country Tramways Vol 1: 1872-1912* J. S. Webb (Author, Bloxwich, 1974)

DUDLEY & STOURBRIDGE STEAM TRAMWAYS

Authority: Dudley Stourbridge and
 Kingswinford Tramways Order 1881
Gauge: 3ft 6in
Traction: Steam
Opened: 31 May 1884
Closed: July 1899?
System: Single line
Length: 5.15 miles
Stock: 12 locos, 8 dd
Livery: Crimson & cream (locos later
 crimson)
Last Car: ?

This BLACK COUNTRY tramway was

promoted by the Dudley, Stourbridge & Kingswinford Tramways Co. Ltd (registered 22 December 1880), which company changed its name two years later to the Dudley & Stourbridge Steam Tramways Co. Ltd, probably in recognition of the fact that its proposed branch to Kingswinford (north of Stourbridge) was not approved.

The predominantly single-track line opened with Kitson tram locomotives Nos 1-8 and Starbuck passenger cars Nos 1-8, bogie double-deckers with top covers, and ran from the depot by the LNWR station on Tipton Road in Dudley, through the Market Place and High Street then southeast through Round Oak, Brierley Hill and Amblecote to terminate before the River Stour bridge north of Stourbridge town centre. Stourbridge and Dudley were both in Worcestershire (the latter in a detached portion of the county) and the intervening places all in Staffordshire. (The only extension made was at the Stourbridge end when, on 30 July 1887, an extra 100yd of track took the line over the river and a railway level crossing to the bottom of the High Street.)

Four more Kitson locos were bought (No 9 in 1885, No 10 by early 1892 and Nos 11 and 12 four years later) but no further passenger cars. (As with many of the Black Country lines, the route was a very hilly one – the journey time was an hour – and took its toll on the engines.)

In 1897 control of the tramway passed to the BET who had been buying up the Company's shares in order to add it to its grand Black Country scheme. Negotiations with the affected local authorities followed, with all except Dudley Corporation agreeing not to exercise their powers of compulsory purchase until 1921; Dudley insisted on purchasing its portion of the line after reconstruction, then leasing it back to the BET. On 2 April 1898 the BET purchased in full the old DSST and changed its name to the Dudley, Stourbridge & District Electric Traction Co. Ltd (see below).

It is not known exactly when steam services ceased as they continued in piecemeal fashion either side of the advancing track relaying during late 1898 and early 1899; as permission to use steam for another month was given by the BoT in June 1899 the locos might well have seen service right up to the opening of the new line on 26 July of that year. In January 1900 eight of the locos and all eight cars were sold to the BIRMINGHAM & MIDLAND TRAMWAYS (including one loco then being used during the construction of the KINVER LIGHT RAILWAY).

Bibliography: as above

DUDLEY, STOURBRIDGE & DISTRICT ELECTRIC TRAMWAYS

Authority: Dudley Stourbridge and
 Kingswinford Tramways Order 1881
Gauge: 3ft 6in
Traction: Overhead electric
Opened: 26 July 1899
Taken Over: 1 July 1904
System: Network
Length: 21.24 miles
Stock: 33 sd, 24 dd
Livery: BET mustard & ivory

The DSD began life in 1898 as the renamed DUDLEY & STOURBRIDGE STEAM TRAMWAYS (see above) which re-opened in electrified form a year later. Further lines were authorized under a succession of LROs, the first opened being a 3-mile branch from Queen's Cross in Dudley which ran south down Blowers' Green Road and Cinder Bank, through Netherton High Street and Market Place, then down Halesowen Road to Old Hill where it swung southwest to terminate at Five Ways at the far end of Cradley Heath High Street. Services began over this route on 1 October 1900 but stopped three days later as the line had not been passed by the BoT. (An official opening took place on 19 October.) On 7 December 1900 services began to Kingswinford with a 3-mile branch from Dudley running westwards along Kingswinford Road through Pensnett to the High Street where it joined a 2-mile branch running north from Amblecote on the main Stourbridge–Dudley route.

On 3 September 1901 a ¼-mile extension up Stourbridge High Street from the Town Clock opened, followed by a further 2-mile extension to Lye on 1 November 1902, running eastwards along Birmingham Street, Stourbridge Road and the length of Lye High Street to The Hayes. On 13 December of that same year a ½-mile branch from the Town Clock northeast down Enville Street and Bridgenorth Road opened, forming a second connection with the DSDET-operated KINVER LIGHT RAILWAY (the other junction being at Amblecote). The system was virtually all single-track.

The first services were operated by Brush single-deckers Nos 1-18 of which Nos 15-18 were rebuilt in 1902 as open-top double-deckers. These were joined in 1900 by Nos 19-25, ERTCW single-deckers of which four were soon sold to the BET's KIDDERMINSTER & STOURPORT line. In 1901 16 open-toppers (Nos 23-25 and 26-38) were bought from the same manufacturers, followed the same year by Nos 39-42, four Brush cars of a similar type. These were not a success however and early in 1904 they were exchanged for WOLVERHAMPTON & DISTRICT open-toppers 1-4 (which took the old DSD numbers). Finally, in 1902 eight high-capacity bogie single-deckers were bought from Brush (Nos 52-59) to work the Cradley Heath line as double-deckers were not permitted on this route.

From 1 July 1904 the system passed into the hands of the BIRMINGHAM & MIDLAND TRAMWAYS JOINT COMMITTEE.

Bibliography: as above and *Vol 2* (1976)

DULWICH *see* LONDON, CAMBERWELL & DULWICH

EAST HAM CORPORATION TRAMWAYS

Authority: East Ham Improvement Act 1898
Gauge: 4ft 8½in
Traction: Overhead electric
Opened: 22 June 1901
Taken Over: 1 July 1933
System: Branching
Length: 8.34 miles
Stock: 76 dd
Livery: Chocolate & cream

The municipally-owned tramway system of East Ham was the central one of a close group of five in southwest Essex next to London. In layout, it comprised a main north-south route from Wanstead Park Avenue (by the City of London Cemetery) running down Forest Drive through Manor Park, the High Street (North and South) through East Ham itself to Beckton and on via Manor Way to a terminus in Cyprus Place just short of the Woolwich boundary by the Royal Albert Dock. Running east from this main line were branches from Manor Park Broadway along Romford Road to Ilford Hill to connect with the ILFORD system and from East Ham Town Hall along Barking Road to connect with the BARKING tramways. Opposite branches west from Manor Park Broadway and the Town Hall formed connections with the WEST HAM system at Green Street (and through it to LEYTON in the north), as did a central, parallel branch from the Burnell Arms on the High Street North along Plashet Grove.

Services began with DK open-top cars 1-15, quickly followed by Nos 16-20, over the completed sections which were Beckton-Manor Park Broadway–Ilford and Barking boundary–Town Hall–West Ham, some 4½ route miles in all. The depot was in Nelson Street by the Town Hall and the routes were a mixture of single and double tracks (although most of the single sections were later doubled). The northern ¾ mile from Manor Park Broadway to the Cemetery opened on 24 March 1902 and that year DK

supplied cars 21-30, again open-top double-deckers. That November the Plashet Grove route opened whilst in March 1903 the main line was extended slightly past the Cemetery to Wanstead Park Avenue at the northern end and from Beckton to Cyprus Place in the south. Later that year similar DK cars 31-35 arrived, after which a top-covering programme was begun.

In 1905 top-covered cars 36-40 were bought from DK and on 17 November that year the service to Barking was extended over that Corporation's metals to Barking station. This left to be added to the system the Manor Park Broadway–West Ham section which had been worked (as a through route from Stratford to February 1905) by the NORTH METROPOLITAN TRAMWAYS as a horse line. Now only the section within East Ham remained and in 1908 the Corporation purchased it for £8,000 and re-opened it that June for electric cars. Through running with West Ham and LONDON COUNTY COUNCIL saw cars 17, 19 and 21-33 being adapted for the latter's conduits, as were DK top-covered 41-45 of 1910; 46 was ex-Barking No 9 purchased in 1915 whilst 47-52 and 37-40 were top-covered Brush cars of 1921 (when scrappings had begun). Brush 51-60 were top-covered bogie cars of 1927, also equipped for dual working, with similar Nos 61-70 joining the fleet in 1928, five years before LONDON TRANSPORT absorbed it.

Bibliography: *The Tramways of East London* 'Rodinglea' (The Tramway & Light Railway Society/The Light Railway Transport League, 1967)

ERITH URBAN DISTRICT COUNCIL TRAMWAYS

Authority: Erith Tramways and Improvement Act 1903
Gauge: 4ft 8½in
Traction: Overhead electric
Opened: 26 August 1905
Closed: 9 November 1935
System: Branching
Length: 4.7 miles
Stock: 2 sd, 19 dd
Livery: Apple green & primrose to 1917, then dark red & ivory
Last Car: ?

This system was promoted by Erith UDC to link the Thameside towns of northeast Kent with the LONDON COUNTY COUNCIL system at Plumstead some 3 miles to the west. As built though the double-track main line ran from the end of Erith High Street along West Street, Lower Road and Abbey Road only as far as the UDC boundary at Abbey Wood (which the LCC reached with

its own extension from Plumstead in 1908).

From Erith the main line continued as a mainly single-track route southwestwards down Walnut Tree Road (past the depot) and the Bexley Road to meet the BEXLEY system at Northumberland Heath (with an end-on connection to permit through running). A ½-mile mainly double-track branch from the Erith end of Bexley Road running south to North End completed the system; services to both the other termini started from here.

To work the system 14 double-deck cars were purchased from Brush in 1905: Nos 1-6 and 9 were open-topped and Nos 7, 8 and 10-14 balcony cars. It quickly transpired that it was better to work the system as a single route from Abbey Wood to Northumberland Heath with a shuttle service from Erith to North End (commencing 18 September 1905); to make further economies on this route two MV single-deck demi-cars (Nos 15 and 16) were bought in March 1906, but the route was still not profitable and services were reduced, until 31 August 1910 when they were withdrawn altogether. In 1915 No 15 was sold to DARTFORD and No 16 to DONCASTER. Before then though the local munitions industry had produced an upsurge in traffic at the start of World War I (and the tramway's first profit) and four 1902 Milnes open-top cars were hired in 1915 from LONDON UNITED TRAMWAYS to help cope. In 1919 they were purchased outright and renumbered 15-18 (LUT 187, 192, 221 and 252); in 1916 ex-HULL balcony car No 101 was bought (and later renumbered 19). This car retained its Hull livery of maroon & cream which, in 1917, was closely matched by Erith's new livery.

After the war the tramway's losses began again and bus competition became serious, leading to the demise of the system as an independent when it was taken over by LONDON TRANSPORT from 1 July 1933 for just £4,667 and for the rest of their lives the former systems of Erith, Bexley and Dartford were operated as a single entity. Only then, on 18 December 1933, was the long-awaited connection between the Erith and London tracks made at Abbey Wood when a short link was laid to facilitate stock movements. Less than two years later the whole route from Abbey Wood to Bexleyheath closed, replaced by a trolleybus service.

Bibliography: *The Tramways of Woolwich and South East London* 'Southeastern' (The Light Railway Transport League, 1963)

EXETER CORPORATION TRAMWAYS

Authority: Exeter Tramways Act 1881
Gauge: 3ft 6in
Traction: Horse/overhead electric

Commemorative postcard of Exeter Corporation's first tram, car No 1, inaugurating the new service.
(Lens of Sutton)

Opened: 6 April 1882
Closed: 19 August 1931
System: Radial
Length: 4.95 miles
Stock: 8 sd, 4 dd horse; 37 dd electric
Livery: Chocolate & yellow horse; dark
    green & cream to 1925, then light green
    & cream electric
Last Car: No 14

The Exeter system began life as a private concern with three single-deck cars operated by the Exeter Tramway Co. over a ½-mile route running eastwards from the Bude Hotel at the northern end of the High Street along Paris Street to the Diocesan Training College in Heavitree Road. In 1883 the line was extended northwards across the High Street and up New North Road to the GWR's Exeter St Davids station and eastwards from the High Street out along Sidwell Road to Pinhoe Road. All lines (totalling 2.34 route miles) were single-track and the depot was in New North Road. Three extra cars were bought to work the new routes, followed by another two a year later.

In 1896 two replacement double-deck cars were purchased for the tramway – now operated by the Tramway Purchase Syndicate – and another two in 1900 from PLYMOUTH CORPORATION TRAMWAYS, though by now the steep and winding St Davids line had been closed as too expensive to maintain. The Company was in fact having financial problems all round and in 1899 offered the system to the Corporation. After much negotiation a price of £6,749 was agreed and ownership was transferred on 1 February 1904 to the Corporation who immediately put in hand extension and electrification plans.

The last horse and the first electric trams ran on 4 April 1905. The new car fleet comprised Nos 1-12 (open-top double-deckers from ERTCW) and Nos 14 and 15 (similar cars from UEC); these were followed by another six from UEC the next year (Nos 16-21). New routes ran from St Davids station to the High Street via Queen Street (the old New North Road section having been abandoned) and from the Guildhall at the southern end of the High Street east along Heavitree Road. This latter route was extended further to the Cross Park Terrace/Fore Street junction in Heavitree and, at the other end, westwards across the River Exe on a new bridge past the GWR's Exeter St Thomas station to just past the football ground in Cowick Street.

On 22 September 1906 the system's last branch opened from just south of the river bridge out south along the Alphington Road to Stone Lane. All routes were mainly single-track with short sections of double or interlaced track.

The car fleet stayed unchanged until 1914 when four replacement cars were supplied by Brush (Nos 22-25), followed after World War I by Nos 26 and 27 in 1921, 28-30 in 1925, 31-34 in 1926 and replacement Nos 1-4 in 1929 – all open-toppers from the same firm. By this time though the inevitable bus competition was being felt and in April 1929 the Corporation entered the bus business itself and made that its transport priority. In April 1931 cars 26-34 were sold to Plymouth and Nos 1-4 to HALIFAX before the system closed later that summer.

Bibliography: *Exeter, A Century of Public Transport* R. C. Sambourne (Glasney Press, Falmouth, 1976) 0 950282 53 7

FAREHAM *see* GOSPORT & FAREHAM

FARNBOROUGH *see* ALDERSHOT & FARNBOROUGH

FARNWORTH COUNCIL TRAMWAYS
Authority: Farnworth Urban District
    Council Act 1900
Gauge: 4ft 8½in
Traction: Horse/overhead electric
Opened: 9 January 1902

The opening of Exeter's last route, to Alphington Road, on 22 September 1906 with new UEC open-toppers bearing assorted dignitaries. (Lens of Sutton)

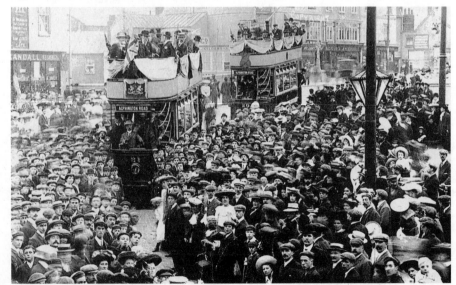

Taken Over: 1 April 1906
System: Network
Length: 4.65 miles
Stock: 13 dd
Livery: Chocolate & yellow

The Farnworth system began life as part of the horse tramway promoted by BOLTON CORPORATION and the Astley Bridge, Farnworth and Kearsley Local Boards to link those towns along the Bolton–Manchester road. The Farnworth section ran as a double-track line from Moses Gate on the edge of Bolton southeast along the Bolton Road, through Farnworth via Market Street and out to just past the Black Horse in Kearsley where there was a turning circle (though the use of Eades patent reversible cars rended this surplus to requirements and it was soon removed), a distance of almost a mile.

Although built by the different authorities, the line was worked originally on a 21-year lease by Edmund Holden & Co. Under the Bolton Tramways and Improvements Act of 1897 Holdens agreed to surrender their lease, and on 2 January 1900 electric trams began running from Bolton town centre to Moses Gate with Holdens providing a replacement horse bus service on the Farnworth and Kearsley section until 13 April 1900 when the electric service was extended to the Black Horse. That same year Farnworth UDC obtained the Farnworth Urban District Council Act to construct more than 5½ miles of its own electric tramways, intended to connect with neighbouring systems.

Construction began in May 1901 and the following year the first section opened. This ran south from Moses Gate (with no connection to the Bolton line) down Egerton Street, Albert Road and Worsley Road to Brookhouse with an eastern branch from the Albert Road/Worsley Road junction along Longcauseway to terminate just before meeting the Bolton Road south of the Black Horse by the former horse tramway terminus.

The tramway's thirteen cars were supplied by Milnes during 1901-02 and were all open-top bogie vehicles; the depot and generating station were in Albert Road. Also in 1900, Kearsley UDC had secured an Order permitting it to construct just over 1½ miles of electric line and, on 3 October 1900 agreed to lease it to Farnworth. On 20 February 1902 this single-track extension of the Bolton line from the Black Horse through Kearsley to Spindle Point was opened (together with a connection to the Farnworth line at the Black Horse), the last ¼ mile from here to the boundary at Unity Brook following on 13 March that year.

On 1 June 1902 Bolton's powers to operate the former horse line expired and, as that corporation proved unwilling to operate a joint service with Farnworth, on 2 June the electric connection at Moses Gate was broken and Farnworth took control of the its portion of the line, shortly afterwards linking it to its Egerton Street terminus at Moses Gate. Even with the addition of this main route the tramway was not a financial success and the SOUTH LANCASHIRE TRAMWAYS agreed to take over operations from 1 April 1906 on a 21-year lease. The Farnworth cars became SLT Nos 46-58, many of them to be top-covered or otherwise rebuilt in later years.

Bibliography: *South Lancashire Tramways 1900-1958* E. K. Stretch (Manchester Transport Museum Society, 1972)

FELIXSTOWE PIER TRAMWAY

This 3ft 6in gauge centre rail electric railway was opened with the ½-mile pier in August 1905 by the Coast Development Co. (see WALTON-ON-THE-NAZE PIER TRAMWAY) and closed at the outbreak of World War II; the original stock was two motor cars and one trailer, all roofed toastracks mounted on Peckham trucks. In 1926 an ex-IPSWICH double-decker was purchased (delivered minus the top deck fittings), the body of which became a waiting room at the pier head and the truck used as a replacement for one from a motor car. The other two cars were scrapped five years later. After closure the pier was irrevocably damaged by the sea and following the end of the war it was demolished completely to make way for a shorter structure.

Bibliography: *Pier Railways* (Locomotion Papers No 60) K. Turner (The Oakwood Press, 1972)

FLEETWOOD *see* BLACKPOOL & FLEETWOOD

FOLKESTONE, HYTHE & SANDGATE TRAMWAYS
Authority: Folkestone, Sandgate and Hythe Tramways Act 1884
Gauge: 4ft 8½in
Traction: Horse
Opened: 18 May 1891
Closed: 30 September 1921
System: Branching
Length: 3.36 miles
Stock: 5 sd
Livery: SER carriage lake
Last Car: ?

The idea of linking the south Kent coastal resorts of Hythe and Sandgate with a tramway was first mooted seriously in 1880 and four years later an Act was obtained for a horse-worked standard gauge line. Further Acts followed to obtain extra time and alter the route and it was not until 1889 that construction began. The first section completed ran from the Sandgate School terminus near St Paul's Church along Sandgate High Street and Esplanade to the Seabrook (now Imperial) Hotel on Hythe seafront. The short completing section into Hythe proper via South Road, Stade Street and Rampart Road to the Red Lion Square depot opened on 6 June the following year. A short spur midway along the Esplanade ran up to serve the SER's Sandgate station whilst a longer, ½-mile branch led from Princes Road up Canongate Road to Hythe station. This was never used for passenger traffic though and had in fact begun life as a standard gauge railway siding built for the construction of Princes Parade (opened 1883).

In 1893 the SER – which already had a

Folkestone, Hythe & Sandgate winter saloon No 3 of 1892. (Lens of Sutton)

financial interest in the owner, the Folkestone, Sandgate & Hythe Tramways Co. – purchased the line outright and, for some reason, rearranged the place names of its title in non-topographical order. Despite the continuing presence of 'Folkestone' in the tramway's name, the short stretch from Sandgate into that town was considered too steep to permit an extension of the line, nor was the local authority willing to countenance such an outside venture. Without the traffic a terminus in Folkestone would have generated, and with increasing competition from firstly horse brakes and then motor-buses, it was only a matter of time before the tramway was forced to close after World War I with various schemes for electrifying it having come to nothing. (It had already closed for the duration of the war and, re-opening for Whitsun 1919, made use of ex-army mules for a while until horses could be obtained. They were not a success, proving more than unusually stubborn and wilfully disobedient!) The end came in 1921, the SER bowing to the concerns of Sandgate UDC over the poor state of the track.

The tramway's first two cars were Milnes toastracks (No 1 was roofed from the start and No 2 from c1897); these were joined in 1892 by two built by the SER of which No 3 was a roofed toastrack and No 4 a winter saloon. In 1897 the SER built the line's last car, No 5, another open toastrack.

Bibliography: *The Hythe & Sandgate Railway*
Brian Hart (Wild Swan Publications, 1987) 0 906867 53 3

GATESHEAD & DISTRICT TRAMWAYS
Authority: Gateshead and District Tramways Act 1880

Gauge: 4ft 8½in
Traction: Steam/overhead electric
Opened: 22 October 1883
Closed: 4 August 1951
System: Radial network
Length: 12.47 miles
Stock: 16 locos, 16 dd steam; 50 sd, 49 dd electric
Livery: ? steam; crimson & white electric
Last Cars: No 20 (service), No 16 (official)

A smaller, mirror image of the NEWCASTLE system across the Tyne, the Gateshead tramways differed in that they were always privately-owned and went from steam to electric traction without operating any horse lines. Promoted by local business interests, the system was owned by the Gateshead & District Tramways Co. and, after a series of enabling Acts, opened in 1883 when the first two locomotives arrived.

Centred on the High Street, the mainly single-track system's three routes ran southeast along Sunderland Road through Felling to Heworth (just over 2¼ miles), south to Low Fell via the Durham Road (2½ miles) and southwest to Teams via Mulgrave Terrace and Askew Road (just over 1¼ miles). The first 15 tram locos (Nos 1-15) were all supplied by the local firm of BH (and were joined in 1885 by a 16th, heavier engine which proved unsatisfactory and was returned). Passenger cars were Falcon open-top (later enclosed) double-deck bogie trailers Nos 1-14 of 1883-84 followed in 1889 by Nos 15 and 16, enclosed Lancaster bogie vehicles. The depot was in Sunderland Road near the junction with the High Street.

On 12 November 1897 the BET took control of the Company and two years later, under the Gateshead and District Tramways Act 1899, obtained the necessary authority to extend and electrify the system. The steam

services were cut back accordingly as reconstruction work proceeded (beginning 12 June 1900) with the last steam cars running on 8 May 1901, the electric cars entering service the next day (a day after the official re-opening).

The first electric routes were the three steam lines plus another southerly route to Sheriff Hill via Brunswick Street and the Old Durham Road (1½ miles). This line was extended another mile to Wrekenton in October 1903 by which time the mixed single and double-track system was virtually complete with shorter southern branches to Saltwell Park and Benham (1901) and a western one off the Teams route to Dunston (1902) having been added.

The first cars were single-deckers 1-10 and 11-20 (these latter being bogie vehicles) plus open-toppers 21-45, all from ERTCW. These were joined in 1902 by bogie single-deckers 46-50 from Milnes. No further cars were added until 1908 when the Company built bogie single-decker 53, followed in 1913 by Nos 54 and 55, two more of the same. Similar vehicles 56-60 were supplied by Brush in 1921, the Company building at the same time four more of this type, taking the numbers 12, 13, 15 and 19 from older cars. The main depot was on the site of the former steam car one.

The only other new cars bought for the fleet were enclosed double-deckers 61-67 and bogie single-deckers 1 and 20 from Brush in 1923; between then and 1928 the Company built Nos 2-11, 14 and 16-18, all bogie single-deckers again. A number of second-hand cars were bought over the years: open-toppers 29, 30 and 38 ex-LIVERPOOL CORPORATION in 1921, top-covered 24, 25, 31, 33, 35-37 and 42 ex-SHEFFIELD CORPORATION in 1922, enclosed double-deckers 35 and 68-72 ex-OLDHAM in 1946 and bogie single-deckers 73-77 ex-Newcastle two years later.

In 1922 work took place on adapting the NER's High Level Bridge over the Tyne to take a tramway link between the Newcastle and Gateshead systems with the first through services being inaugurated on 12 January the following year. A second link was provided from 10 October 1928 when the New Tyne (road) Bridge was opened with double tram tracks in place.

In 1938 Gateshead Corporation, following Newcastle's example of four years before, obtained powers to allow it to operate trolleybuses but, after the intervention of World War II, began running (on 5 March 1950) motor buses instead. In June 1950 the (reduced) service over the Wrekenton and Heworth routes was terminated as, on 3 March 1951, were the Salthill Park and Bensham trams. The Lower Fell line closed on 7 April and the Teams route on 14 July,

Commemorative postcard of Gateshead & District No 67 of 1923 inaugurating the new road (and tramway) link across the River Tyne. (Lens of Sutton)

TRAMS LINK UP NEWCASTLE & GATESHEAD.
New Tram Service across High Level Bridge. (January 1923).

leaving just the Dunston Route as the last survivor.

After the closure bogie cars 1, 3-11, 16-18, 20 and 56-60 were sold to the GRIMSBY & IMMINGHAM line and two of these are now preserved, as is No 52 (renumbered 7 of 1901), now at the National Tramway Museum, Crich.

Bibliography: *The Tramways of Gateshead* George S. Hearse (Author, Corbridge, 1965)

GLOSSOP TRAMWAYS

Authority: Glossop Electric Tramways Order 1901
Gauge: 4ft 8½in
Traction: Overhead electric
Opened: 21 August 1903
Closed: 24 December 1927
System: Branching
Length: 4.56 miles
Stock: 2 sd, 7 dd
Livery: Dark green & primrose
Last Car: ?

The idea for this small Derbyshire system, in the extreme northwest of the county, came from local electrical engineer Charles Knowles whose employer, the Urban Electric Supply Co., promoted the scheme. As built, the single-track main line ran from close to Hadfield station on the GCR's Manchester–Barnsley line in a broad sweep northwest along Station Road then west on Wolley Bridge Road and south through Brookfield and Dinting, then through Glossop itself (passing the High Street depot and power station before it curved east to a terminus outside the Queen's Arms Hotel in Old Glossop, 4 track miles from Hadfield but less than half that as the crow flies. A ½-mile branch south to Whitfield via Victoria Street and Charlestown Road left the main line at Norfolk Square in the centre of Glossop.

The main users of the system were the local textile mill workers and their families (its long curving route was designed to pass as many mills as possible) with services operated initially by Milnes open-top double-deckers 1-7 which were joined in 1904 by No 8, a BEC single-deck demi-car to work the Whitfield route. Only one further passenger car was ever added to stock: No 9, a second-hand ERTCW single-decker (No 56 of 1899) bought in 1918 from SHEFFIELD.

Early extension schemes came to nothing – there were hopes of connecting up with the MANCHESTER system just over the border – as did the idea of goods workings to the mills as on the UES Co.'s other tramway at CAMBORNE & REDRUTH in Cornwall and after its Edwardian heyday the tramway was, by the end of World War I, badly in

Postcard of Glossop No 7 of 1904 passing typical mill-workers' houses in Dinting Vale. In the distance is Dinting railway viaduct. (Lens of Sutton)

need of a thorough overhaul (and with the Whitfield branch closed since the autumn of 1918 as an economy measure). It never received one; instead the Company offered the line to Glossop Town Council, which body prudently declined to buy it and its lingering decline was brought to an end by bus competition.

Bibliography: *Glossop Tramways 1903-1927* Barry M. Marsden (Foxline Publishing, Stockport, 1991) 1 870119 12 6

CITY OF GLOUCESTER TRAMWAYS

Authority: Gloucester Tramways Order 1878
Gauge: 4ft
Traction: Horse
Opened: 24 May 1879
Taken Over: 30 September 1902
System: Radial
Length: 6.5 miles
Stock: 16 sd
Livery: Crimson lake & cream ?

The first Gloucester tramways were promoted by the Gloucester Tramways Co. Ltd, an IMPERIAL TRAMWAYS subsidiary, and worked by six single-deck horse cars (a mixture of closed saloons and roofed summer toastracks) built by Bristol and Hughes. There were five routes radiating from the city's central Cross: north up Northgate Street, Worcester Street and Kingsholm Road to Kingsholm; northeast up Northgate Street and London Road to the Fleece Inn at Wotton; southeast along Eastgate Street and Lower Barton Street to India Road (and the depot); southwest along Southgate Street

and Bristol Road as far as Theresa Place and northwest up Westgate Street as far as St Nicholas' Church. A short branch from Eastgate Street served the neighbouring GWR and MR stations.

The tramway was not a financial success. The multiplicity of short routes could not have helped matters and in July 1881 it was sold for £8,000 to a new concern, the City of Gloucester Tramways Co. Ltd and both the very short Westgate and station branches abandoned. Six new Starbuck cars were bought and two of the old ones withdrawn. Thereafter things improved sufficiently to warrant a short extension down the Bristol Road to Tuffley Avenue which opened on 10 July 1897, and a Light Railway Order was applied for in order to extend further and electrify the whole undertaking.

The electrification proposal was approved by the City Corporation which, on 30 September 1902, purchased the concern for £26,000 in order to carry out the work itself, although the Company continued as operator until the end of the year. (See below.) By now another four cars (believed Nos 11-14) had been added to the fleet, probably all from the local Gloucester builders.

Bibliography: *Tramways of the West of England* P. W. Gentry (The Light Railway Transport League, 2nd ed 1960)

GLOUCESTER CORPORATION TRAMWAYS

Authority: Gloucester Tramways Order 1878
Gauge: 3ft 6in
Traction: Horse/overhead electric

Took Over: 30 September 1902
Closed: 11 January 1933
System: Radial network
Length: 9.75 miles
Stock: 14 sd horse; 30 dd electric
Livery: Crimson lake & cream to 1915,
    then light grey
Last Car: ?

On 9 November 1903 work began on rebuilding the Gloucester horse lines (see above) to the narrow gauge 'standard' 3ft 6in and horse services were slowly curtailed, finishing completely on 17 March the following year. The car fleet by then had risen to 14 open and closed single-deckers, including vehicles from Gloucester and Starbuck. (One survives in the local Folk Museum.)

The rebuilt system, a mixture of single and double-track routes, was officially opened on 7 May 1904 with 20 open-top Brush cars (Nos 1-20) which were joined shortly by another ten; the fleet remained unchanged until the closure. (As on many systems, the trams were painted light grey during World War I as an economy measure but, unlike elsewhere, were never repainted later.) All the former horse routes were rebuilt (the first to re-open, on 29 April 1904, was the Bristol Road line) with the exception of the stations branch and the following extensions were laid: Barton Street and Painswick Road to Cemetery Road and the Westgate Street line as far as the other side of the River Severn. In addition a branch was laid from the end of Bristol Road where it met Southgate Street along Stroud Road to Reservoir Road, Tuffley (also opened 29 April), with a link line from it to Barton

Street via Parkend Road. These new lines were authorized by the Gloucester Corporation Light Railways Order 1903 whilst the County of Gloucester (Gloucester and Brockworth) Light Railways Order of the same year authorized a 2-mile extension from the Fleece Inn across the city boundary along Barnwood Road and Ermine Street to Hucclecote. This last line opened on 3 May 1904 with the other routes following by mid-June. Although owned by the County Council, the Hucclecote line was worked by the Corporation as an integral part of the system and was extended in 1917 to serve a new aerodrome at Brockworth. This was laid as a reserved track beside the roadway and used the rails from the Westgate Bridge route which closed on 12 August that year. Although of great importance – and very busy – at the time, it was closed on 1 October 1924 when traffic no longer warranted its staying open. (A spur off the London Road to the GWR goods yard was also laid in 1917 to handle war material for the aerodrome using car No 14 modified for that purpose.)

The next sections to close were the Stroud Road–Barton Street link in 1927 and, on 8 September 1929, the Cemetery Road route. The Corporation had already decided to replace the trams with buses and that same month closed the Kingsholm and Tuffley routes as well, leaving just the Bristol Road–Hucclecote line to survive another few years while it remained profitable.

Bibliography: as above

GORLESTON *see* YARMOUTH & GORLESTON

GOSFORTH *see* NEWCASTLE & GOSFORTH

GOSPORT & FAREHAM TRAMWAYS

Authority: Gosport Street Tramways Act
    1879
Gauge: 3ft/4ft 7¾in
Traction: Horse/overhead electric
Opened: 17 July 1882
Closed: 31 December 1929
System: Branching
Length: 7.75 miles
Stock: 4sd, 1 dd horse?; 18 dd electric
Livery: Emerald green & cream
Last Car: No 8

This tramway opened as a single-track single line operated by the Gosport Street Tramways Co., a subsidiary of PROVINCIAL TRAMWAYS (who already had interests across the Harbour in PORTSMOUTH). The first section, of just over 1½ miles, ran from the beach at Gosport Hard westwards past the depot in the High Street, then in a roughly northwesterly direction up Clarence Road and Mumby Road, past the station and along Forton Road to Ann's Hill. Services were worked by four single-deck cars, shortly joined by four more. At the end of January or the beginning of February 1883 the line was extended further north for 1¼ miles up Brockhurst Road to the junction with Elson Road in Brockhurst. In June that year the first double-deck car was put into service, the intention being to replace the single-deckers eventually. Later that year the Company was amalgamated with the various Portsmouth concerns to become part of the Portsmouth Street Tramways Co.

In 1900 Gosport and Alverstoke UDC decided to buy the line but the Company raised objections – although a year later it offered to sell it to the UDC without success! In 1901 and again in 1903 Provincial obtained Parliamentary approval to electrify and extend the tramway as far as Fareham, under the name Gosport & Fareham Tramways. The first portion opened, on 20 December 1905 (it is not known when the horse trams ceased running), was basically the old line, reconstructed to the 4ft 7¾in gauge of the other Portsmouth-area lines. There was a remodelled Gosport Hard terminus and a 4-mile, mainly reserved roadside extension at the northern end up the Fareham road to Hoeford Depot and it ran on along Gosport Road to Fareham where the line swung west along West Street to terminate by the railway station.

Services began with Brush open-toppers Nos 1-12 which were joined by identical cars 13-18 in 1906 in time for the 13 October

An early shot of Gloucester Corporation No 21 of 1904, a typical Brush product of the period typifying Edwardian tramcar design. (Lens of Sutton)

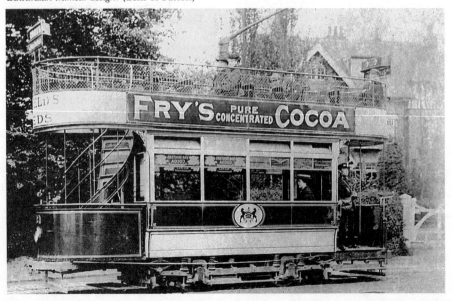

opening of a 1-mile branch westwards from the end of the High Street along Walpole Road and Stoke Road, then past Gosport Road station into Foster Road and Bury Road to terminate by the Wiltshire Lamb at Bury Cross. No further routes were opened (though more than half the track was eventually doubled) though four MV open-toppers, Nos 19-22, were later purchased.

Proposals to construct other routes – and even to link the tramway to the Portsmouth system – came to nothing and in late 1929 the Bury Cross route was closed, as was that part of the main line between Fareham and Ann's Hill; that same year saw the PST Co. change its name to the Gosport & Fareham Omnibus Co. before promptly closing the last section of the line in favour of buses. After the closure seven of the cars were transferred to the PORTSDOWN & HORNDEAN LIGHT RAILWAY and six to the GREAT GRIMSBY STREET TRAMWAYS, two other Provincial concerns.

Bibliography: *The Tramways of Portsmouth* S. E. Harrison (The Light Railway Transport League, 1963)

GRAVESEND, ROSHERVILLE & NORTHFLEET TRAMWAYS

Authority: Gravesend, Rosherville and
    Northfleet Tramways Order 1881
Gauge: 3ft 6in
Traction: Horse, conduit electric
Opened: 15 June 1883
Closed: 30 June 1901
System: Single line
Length: 2.19 miles
Stock: 5 sd, 4 dd horse; 2 sd electric
Livery: ?
Last Car: ?

The first 1½ miles of this grandly-named tramway opened in 1883 as a horse line using five single-deck cars. The operator was the Gravesend, Rosherville & Northfleet Tramways Co. Ltd and the single-track line ran from the depot by the Leather Bottle Inn in Northfleet, eastwards along the London Road past Rosherville station on the LCDR to the Church Tower in King Street, Gravesend. A westwards extension of nearly ¾ mile along Northfleet High Street was authorized in 1884 but not opened until 1889, it having been built by the contractors DK for the Series Electrical Traction Co. as a demonstration line for the Short-Nesmith system of conduit electricty supply for which it held the rights. (The system involved the use of positive and negative cables in a conduit, the entrance to which was the gap formed by a bullhead running rail and a second rail laid just inside

Postcard of Gosport & Fareham No 11 of 1905 outside Fareham Post Office. Such a location was common as a terminus or stopping place on most tramway systems. (Lens of Sutton)

it; the other running rail was of the usual grooved tramway pattern.) The line, which ran from the Leather Bottle down The Hill and along the High Street as far as Huggens College opposite Station Road, was supposed to have opened to the general public on 16 April 1889, but it appears to have been used only for trial runs with school children (possibly from March 1889) and by November 1890 the two electric saloon cars had been replaced by horse trams.

Both electric cars were built by Falcon; their subsequent disposal is unrecorded. In 1898 four double-deck horse cars were purchased (probably second-hand) to replace the five single-deckers, two of which were sold the following year to LINCOLN. That same 1899 saw the controlling interest in the Company obtained by the Drake & Gornham Electric Power and Traction Syndicate Ltd. As implied by the new owner's title, the intention was to electrify the line and also extend it on a new gauge of 4ft 8½in so as to be able to link it to the DARTFORD system. It was resold to the BET on 1 January 1901 and on 18 April of that year the Gravesend & Northfleet Electic Tramways Ltd was registered to build and operate the new line. (See below.)

Bibliography: *The Tramways of Kent Vol 1: West Kent 'INVICTA'* (The Light Railway Transport League, 1971) 1 900433 38 8

GRAVESEND & NORTHFLEET ELECTRIC TRAMWAYS

Authority: Gravesend, Rosherville and
    Northfleet Tramways Order 1899
Gauge: 4ft 8½in
Traction: Overhead electric
Opened: 2 August 1902
Closed: 28 February 1929
System: Network
Length: 6.47 miles
Stock: 4 sd, 24 dd
Livery: Maroon & cream to 1921, then
    cherry red & ivory
Last Car: ?

Construction work on the new Gravesend system commenced with the former horse line (see above), the work being carried out by William Griffiths & Co. and the Clock Tower–Leather Bottle section was the first to re-open, followed on 22 September 1902 by extensions eastwards along Milton Road to Denton, westwards along the London Road to Swanscombe and southwards down Pelham Street in Gravesend. This last line was extended on 30 January 1903, up the Dover Road past the new depot to rejoin the main route at the Leather Bottle. The final, 5-furlong section opened on 4 December 1903 ran from King Street (near the Clock Tower) southwards down Windmill Street to the Old Prince of Orange pub. (The hoped-for link to DARTFORD never materialized, the 1½-mile gap between the two systems being the result of opposition to such a connection by the SECR.)

Original stock comprised 20 ERTCW open-top double-deckers of which Nos 1-10 were bogie vehicles and Nos 11-20 shorter four-wheelers. It soon transpired though that the fleet was too large and the bogie cars too costly to run for such a small undertaking and two were sold to JARROW in 1904 (possibly Nos 5 and 6), followed by four to Swansea (probably Nos 7-10) in 1904 and the final four to the SOUTH METROPOLITAN in 1906. Two Brush one-man operated single-decker replacements for use on the Windmill Street and Dover Road routes were bought in 1904 (and took the vacated numbers 9 and 10 in the fleet list). In 1905 replacement Nos 1-4 were obtained from Brush, these being open-top double-deckers, followed in 1908 by two slightly smaller Brush cars (Nos 5 and 6) from Jarrow.

This restructed fleet ran until 1921 when Nos 9 and 10 were replaced by two ex-TAUNTON single-deckers (renumbered 7 and 8) whilst Nos 15-20 were fitted with top covers.

As an isolated system, with aging rolling stock, the Gravesend tramway was no match for the growing number of local bus companies and had indeed been running its own bus service under the title North Kent Motor Services since 1913 (merged with the BET's Maidstone & District Motor Services Ltd in 1920) and it came as no surprise when the tramway was taken over by the M&D at the beginning of 1929 as a prelude to its abandonment.

Bibliography: as above

GREAT CROSBY *see* WATERLOO & GREAT CROSBY

GREAT GRIMSBY *see* GRIMSBY

GREAT YARMOUTH *see* YARMOUTH

GREENWICH *see* LONDON, DEPTFORD & GREENWICH

GREAT GRIMSBY STREET TRAMWAYS

Authority: Great Grimsby Street Tramways Act 1879
Gauge: 4ft 8½in
Traction: Horse/overhead electric
Opened: 4 June 1881
Taken over: 15 July 1936
System: Branching
Length: 6.3 miles
Stock: 20 sd & dd horse?; 2 sd, 57 dd electric
Livery: Emerald green & cream

The tramway systems linking the twin towns of Grimsby (the port) and Cleethorpes (the seaside resort) began as a 3-mile horse line operated by the Great Grimsby Street Tramways Co., a PROVINCIAL subsidiary. The southwest terminus was at the Wheatsheaf pub in Bargate from where the single-track main line ran northwards via Deansgate and Victoria Street past the Alexandra Dock where it turned east along Cleethorpes Road to the junction with Park Street at the town boundary. A spur from here led to the depot in Carr Lane. A 1-mile single-track branch ran south from Riby Square at the start of Cleethorpes Road along Freeman Street and Hainton Street on the other side of the Manchester, Sheffield & Lincolnshire Railway from the Bargate route. (Proposals to link the two close termini never succeeded.)

The original car fleet was made up of seven small open-top double-deckers of unknown origin, followed by two more (Nos 8 and 9) in 1882; possibly they were built by another Provincial system.

In 1887 the main line was extended on 21 May for just over a mile into Cleethorpes with a single-track line along Grimsby Road to where Poplar Road joined it, bringing the route length to 4.84 miles. This section was extended again on 4 September 1898 when

The Series Electrical Traction Co.'s experimental conduit car on the Gravesend, Rosherville & Northfleet line as drawn for the Illustrated London News *of 6 April 1899.*

Tramways of England 65

just under ½ mile of double tracks took the tramway down Isaac's Hill, along the High Street and into Alexandra Road on the seafront, the new terminus being by Albert Road. Three open toastracks (No 10 of 1886 and Nos 11 and 12 of 1888) were built by the Company to help work this extension during the summer months. After that car details are sketchy though it seems certain that several more single and double-deck vehicles were built or bought by the Company as returns show 14 in 1892 and 16 a year later while photographic evidence suggests that some renumbering went on as well to confuse matters more.

By now it was clear how tramway development was going nationally and Provincial decided to electrify the system, obtaining the Great Grimsby Street Tramways Act of 1900 as the necessary authority. Reconstruction (by DK) began in 1899 and the last horse car ran on December 1901 with electric services commencing the next day from Cleethorpes, past the new depot and generating station in Pelham Road (off Grimsby Road) to Freeman Street and the Old Market Place where Victoria Street met Deansgate. (A new, one-way detour was built here.) The line from the Old Market to the Wheatsheaf, then east for some 500yd to a new terminus in Welholme Road outside the People's Park Gates opened on 15 February of the following year. A final, short extension along Alexandra Road and High Cliff in Cleethorpes was officially opened on 12 July 1906 to complete the system. The main line was now double-tracked from Cleethorpes as far as the Old Market whilst the Freeman Street branch always remained single.

The original 22 cars (Nos 1-22) were ERTCW open-top double-deckers and these were joined later in 1902 by Nos 23 and 24, an identical pair. The next four powered cars were acquired by Provincial from the defunct Alexandra Park Electric Railway which had closed in 1899 (see LONDON: ALEXANDRA PARK); these were rebuilt at Grimsby in 1903, becoming Nos 25, 26 and 28 (open-top double-deckers) and 27 (enclosed double-decker). Also purchased in 1913 were ERTCW open-toppers Nos 29 and 30 and the same firm supplied No 37 in 1906 (a 1904 top-covered car) and No 38 in 1915 (a 1900 single-decker ex-OLDHAM). Many of the open-top cars were later fitted with top covers but some were not, presumably because they were popular in the summer.

Initially, six trailers were operated in conjunction with the powered cars: Nos 31-34 were ERTCW open-toppers built for the line in 1899 as horse cars but designed to be converted into electric trailers and Nos 35 and 36 were adapted from horse cars, the latter pair being sold in 1918 to LINCOLN

and the former quartet motorized two years later by DK. The last car added to the fleet during this period was in 1922 when the Company constructed a unique, open chara-banc-style vehicle numbered 40 but generally known as the Tram Coach.

The next major change to the tramway came in 1922 when on 21 July the Corporation exercised its power to purchase that portion of the system within its boundaries, though it took until 6 April 1925 for the takeover to be finally completed and the arbitrated price of £109,848 paid (see below). Under the agreement the Company kept the depot, the Tram Coach (which in 1925 was sent to the Provincial's PORTSDOWN &

HORNDEAN line and cars Nos 1-3, 22-29, 37 and 38 whilst the Corporation took the remaining vehicles. The fleet was now aging and in 1925 the Company built open-topper (later top-covered) No 39 and in 1926 Nos 35 and 36, a pair of top-covered cars. The last cars added to the Company's fleet were twelve Brush open-toppers of 1905 vintage transferred from GOSPORT & FAREHAM in 1930 after being regauged from 4ft 7¾in; these took the numbers 1-3 and 22-30 made vacant by withdrawals.

In 1935 the Company offered to sell their line to Cleethorpes UDC and a price of £50,000 was agreed, to include the power station and the Company's bus fleet

Great Grimsby Street Tramways Co. timetable of 1 September 1903, published in Mate's guide to Cleethorpes.

Great Grimsby Street Tramways Company.

NOTICE. CARS ARE ANNOUNCED TO RUN AS FOLLOWS:

CLEETHORPES & OLD MARKET PLACE.

A Car will leave the Depot, Pelham Road, Cleethorpes, for Old Market Place at 5.15 a.m. The first Car from Cleethorpes Terminus will leave at 5.30 a.m., and Cars will run at intervals of 15 minutes until 6.30 a.m. From 6.30 until 7.30 a.m. Cars will run at intervals of 10 minutes, after which time at intervals of 5 minutes until 10.0 p.m. Supplementary Cars leave Cleethorpes for Old Market Place at 10.10, 10.20, and 10.30 p.m.

The first Car leaves Old Market Place for Cleethorpes at 6.2¼ a.m.
The last Car leaves Old Market Place for Cleethorpes at 11.2¼ p.m.

BARGATE SECTION.

On week days there is a 10 minutes service between the Old Market Place and the Park. The first Car leaves the Old Market at 8.0 a.m., and the last Car leaves the Park at 9.40 p.m.

These Cars run to and from Cleethorpes.

FREEMAN STREET & HAINTON STREET.

The first Car will leave the Depot at 5.20 a.m. for Hainton Street, and leaves that Terminus at 5.40 for Riby Square. Between 5.40 a.m. and 7.40 a.m. Cars will run at intervals of 12 minutes, and from 7.40 a.m. to 10.57 p.m. at intervals of 6 minutes. The last Car leaves Hainton Street for Cleethorpes at 11.20 p.m.

SUNDAYS.

The first Car leaves Cleethorpes for Grimsby at 9.30 a.m., and the last Car at 10.15 p.m.
The first Car leaves Grimsby for Cleethorpes at 10.0 a.m., and the last Car at 10.45 p.m.
The first Car on the Freeman Street Route leaves Hainton Street Terminus at 10.10 a.m., and the last Car at 10.50 p.m.

H. L. WHITE, Manager.

Manager's Office—Southampton House, Cleethorpes.
1st Sept., 1903.

(which had been operated since 1909); the takeover was on 15 July 1936 with the line being closed in favour of a trolleybus service the very next year. (See CLEETHORPES.)

Bibliography: *The Tramways of Grimsby, Immingham & Cleethorpes* J. H. Price (The Light Rail Transit Association, no date) 0 948106 10 7

GRIMSBY CORPORATION TRAMWAYS

Authority: Grimsby Corporation Act 1921
Gauge: 4ft 8½in
Traction: Overhead electric
Taken Over: 6 April 1925
Closed: 31 March 1937
System: Branching
Length: 4.39 miles
Stock: 38 dd
Livery: Crimson lake & ivory
Last Car: ?

With its takeover of the Grimsby portion of the Company system (see above) Grimsby Corporation acquired cars Nos 4-21 and 31-34, several of which needed replacing urgently. Consequently 16 Brush balcony cars (GC Nos 41-56) were purchased in 1925 from SUNDERLAND and by the beginning of 1927 all stock was housed in a new depot built in Victoria Street.

Meanwhile, the Corporation had decided to commence trolleybus operations as an alternative to expensive track renewal and on Sunday 2 October 1926 began a service down Freeman Street and Hainton Avenue, the last tramcars running over the route the previous day. Some of the trams were now withdrawn and on 27 November 1927 bus services were begun as well. The next section of the tramway to close was the Bargate route beyond the Old Market which gave way to buses on 3 June 1928, followed on 21 November 1936 by the section between the Old Market and Riby Square. Fourteen more trams were then sold off, leaving just No 7 and four of the ex-Sunderland cars to provide a through service to Cleethorpes. Four years later, that service too was withdrawn.

Bibliography: as above

GRIMSBY & IMMINGHAM ELECTRIC RAILWAY

Authority: Grimsby and District Light Railways Order 1906
Gauge: 4ft 8½in
Traction: Overhead electric
Opened: 15 May 1912
Closed: 1 July 1961
System: Single line*
Length: 7.75 miles
Stock: 36 sd
Livery: GCR reddish-brown, LNER teak, BR (post-1951) SR electric green
Last Car: No 4

In appearance the G&I was more akin to a North American interurban line than perhaps any other in the British Isles (the Isle of Man excluded). It began life as a hastily-contructed contractor's line laid in 1906 to move workmen and materials to the GCR's massive Immingham Docks construction project. On 3 January 1910 the (upgraded) line was opened to the public by the GCR using a 1904 steam railmotor and ran from Grimsby (Pyewipe Road) for some 4½ miles to the dock site boundary.

The GCR's authority for the line was its 1906 Light Railway Order which included provision for a second, electric tramway-type line to be constructed beside the steam one and this was completed in May 1912 in time for the grand opening of Immingham Dock by King George V on 22 July of that year. In its final form the electric line began beside the roadway in Immingham docks and ran for about a mile to Immingham town where it became a street tramway. This was the original terminus (the docks extension opening on 17 November 1913) and it had been intended to construct a branch south-west from here to serve the village of Immingham proper but only a token ½ mile down Queen's Road was ever laid; this was 'opened' in July 1915 but no public service was ever run over it, even though it would have served the railway loco shed nearby, and was gradually stripped and lifted from World War II to 1955 when the road was resurfaced.

From Immingham town (where cars reversed direction) the tramway ran parallel to the Humber estuary shoreline southeast to the depot at Pyewipe for nearly 5 miles as a single-track railway line beside the goods-only steam line (by now integrated into the GCR network) to Grimsby, reaching a terminus by Alexandra Dock by way of Gilbey Road and Corporation Road. A swing bridge over the dock provided easy pedestrian access to the town's street tramway (see above).

In January 1923 the GCR became part of the new LNER which in turn, from 1 January 1948, became part of BR. On 13 June 1956 the 1¼-mile street section in Grimsby was closed from Alexandra Dock to Cleveland Bridge (across the railway line at the end of Gilbey Road) with services replaced by Corporation buses, the rest of the line going the same way five years later. (A suggested diesel unit passenger service on the light railway failed to materialize.)

The tramway's purpose-built car fleet consisted of sturdy Brush bogie single-deckers built for safe, fast running with high seating capacity for the heavy workmen's traffic generated by the industry along this part of the Lincolnshire coast. Nos 1-4 of 1911, 9-12 of 1913 and 13-16 of 1915 all seated 72 passengers and, at nearly 44ft long, were the longest single-deckers in the British Isles, whilst the smaller Nos 5-8 of 1911 seated 48 and were intended for possible through running over the Grimsby street system. In the event the necessary connection was never made and No 5 was converted into a works car after the arrival of Nos 13-16 (this latter batch was actually built by the GCR at its Dukinfield carriage works to the Brush design). Nos 6-8 were scrapped in the early 1930s.

In 1948, to cope with increased traffic, the LNER purchased three 1901 HN single-deckers from NEWCASTLE and gave them the numbers 6-8 which were now vacant. In 1951 a further 19 second-hand Brush cars were purchased from GATESHEAD and given the numbers 17-33 (one was badly damaged in transit and scrapped and one became a works car to replace the former No 5). During the period 1951-53 Nos 2, 9, 10 and 13 were withdrawn and scrapped, the rest being scrapped after the closure with the exception of Nos 14 and 20, which are at the National Tramway Museum (the latter car restored as Gateshead 5), while No 26 (restored as Gateshead 10), can be seen at the North of England Open Air Museum (see Section 7).

Bibliography: as above

HALIFAX CORPORATION TRAMWAYS

Authority: Halifax Corporation Tramways Act 1897
Gauge: 3ft 6in
Traction: Overhead electric
Opened: 9 June 1898
Closed: 14 February 1939
System: Radial network
Length: 39.07 miles
Stock: 6 sd, 137 dd
Livery: Blue & white to 1924, bright red & yellow to 1927, then dark red & white
Last Car: No 109 (official)

At its fullest extent, Halifax's tramway system consisted of eleven hilly routes radiating from a network of inter-linked lines in the town centre plus an outer linking line to the south and west. After two unsuccessful proposals for a cable tramway system, Halifax Corporation sought the necessary powers to construct its own electric system and in 1898 opened the first three single-track routes (3½ miles in total) centred on the Post Office: east along Horton Street to the Old Railway Station, southwest to King Cross Street and west to High Road Well via Gibbet Street and the depot.

Services began with ten open-top Milnes double-deckers, followed by 48 more (Nos 11-58) over the next two years to keep pace with the succession of new routes being opened. A new depot was built to handle the enlarged fleet south of the town centre off Skircoat Lane (the old one becoming a works facility).

In 1901 Brush open-toppers 59-70 were bought, followed by another dozen (Nos 71-82) in 1902 and yet a third (Nos 83-94) a year later. In 1904 Brush supplied one-man single-deckers 95 and 96 and by the end of 1905 the system was virtually complete at 37 miles of routes. Over the next ten years many of the open-top cars were fitted with top covers and windscreens (except No 64 which was destroyed in an accident – one of many on the system – in 1907) and in 1912 six Brush top-covered cars (Nos 97-102) entered service whilst during World War I single-decker 95 was used as an Army recruiting office and 96 as a mobile kitchen.

The last wholly new route, south to Stainland, was opened on 14 May 1921 and, apart from later extensions and modifications, this completed the system. Between that year and 1927 the Corporation built a series of cars, these being single-decker 96 (later converted to an open-top double-decker), open-toppers 9, 11, 17, 64 and 80 and top-covered 71, 73, 75, 76, 81 and 92, these all taking the numbers of the withdrawn vehicles they replaced. Also constructed in 1924 were three bogie single-deckers (Nos 103, 105 and 106) and a top-covered car (No 104), introducing a new livery at the same time. These were followed in 1928-29 by Corporation-built top-covered cars 107-113 and 124-127 and by similar EE cars 114-123 two years later.

The first route closure, on 31 March 1929, was the easternmost double-track section along Bradford Road between Brighouse in the south and Bailiff Bridge 1½ miles to the north which provided an (unconnected) link between the HUDDERSFIELD and BRADFORD systems. (The Bradford system was also met with at Queensbury and Shelf in the north and the Huddersfield system at Greetland in the south, but because of gauge differences the Halifax system was always isolated from its neighbours). The following year four open-toppers (Nos 128-131) were bought from EXETER as the last car purchases.

The 1930s saw a succession of further route closures, killed and replaced by Corporation and private bus services, the last to go being the short line from the town centre to the depot.

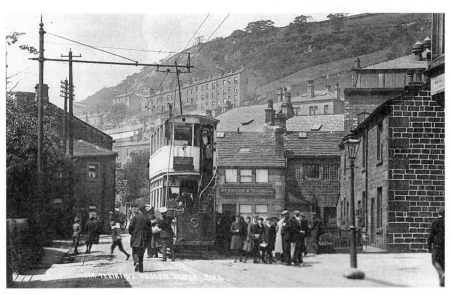

Postcard view of Halifax Corporation's westernmost route terminus, Hebden Bridge, with No 82 of 1902 (in top-covered form) unloading. (Lens of Sutton)

HANHAM see BRISTOL

HARROW ROAD & PADDINGTON see LONDON: HARROW ROAD & PADDINGTON

HARTLEPOOLS STEAM TRAMWAYS

Authority: Hartlepool Tramways Order 1883
Gauge: 3ft 6in
Traction: Steam
Opened: 2 August 1884
Closed: 21 February 1891
System: Single line
Length: 2.51 miles
Stock: 6 locos? 5 dd
Livery: ?
Last Car: ?

After several proposals in the early 1880s for tramways in the Hartlepools had come to nothing, an Order was secured in 1883 and the Hartlepools Steam Tramways Co. Ltd (registered 16 October 1883) was formed to operate a steam system. Work began that November on the first section, a single-track line running in a broad arc from Northgate in Hartlepool northwest along Milbank Crescent, west along Cleveland Road (and past the depot at the junction with Hart Road) and on south into Clarence Road before turning east into Church Street, West Hartlepool.

The first two tram locomotives were Nos 1 and 2 hauling two top-covered double-deck trailers (presumably also Nos 1 and 2), all from Falcon; these were soon joined by two further locos (Nos 3 and 4) and two more cars (presumably Nos 3 and 4), again from Falcon. In 1885 another Falcon loco and car arrived (both numbered 5) and locos 1-3

withdrawn, presumably because of unsatisfactory perfomance. One was sold to BIRMINGHAM CENTRAL and another to SOUTH STAFFORDSHIRE. No 6, a similar locomotive, is thought to have arrived then or the following year.

The tramway was not a financial success – perhaps because the other authorized routes were never constructed – and in 1891 it closed, by which time however the two local authorities affected were ready to consider approving an electric system. (See below.)

HARTLEPOOL ELECTRIC TRAMWAYS

Authority: Hartlepool Electric Tramways Order 1895
Gauge: 3ft 6in
Traction: Overhead electric
Opened: 19 May 1896
Closed: 25 March 1927
System: Branching
Length: 6.98 miles
Stock: 4 sd, 38 dd
Livery: GET green & cream, HET orange & white, Corporation dark red & white
Last Car: ?

On 28 Febrary 1895 the General Electric Tramways Co. Ltd, a subsidiary of the Electric Construction Co. Ltd, was registered to rebuild the defunct HARTLEPOOLS STEAM TRAMWAYS line (see above), services commencing the following year with five Milnes open-top double-deckers (Nos 1-5) working between Northgate in Hartlepool and the Clarence Road/Church Street junction in West Hartlepool. A new depot was built on Cleveland Road midway along the line at Greenland.

On 9 October 1897 the last section of

steam line was re-opened in Church Street (now double-tracked); that year also saw the arrival of another five cars: Nos 8 and 9 (similar to Nos 1-5), bogie open-topper No 10 (all from Milnes) and toastrack trailers Nos 6 and 7 (provenance unknown and used only when needed).

On 15 October 1896 the Hartlepool Electric Tramways Co. Ltd (a BET subsidiary) was registered to construct the 1895-authorized routes in West Hartlepool. Work began in 1897 and on 10 March 1899 the first two of these, a mile-long continuation of the GET's Clarence Road line past Church Street and along Stockton Street to Foggy Furze, plus a mile-long branch off Stockton Street along Grange Road to Ward Jackson Park, were opened. Both lines were single-track and worked as one route until the overhead was installed to allow cars to run to and from Church Street. The service was worked initially by five Brush open-toppers (Nos 11-15), joined later in 1899 by Nos 19 and 20, two ERTCW single-deckers on loan from the BET.

The next route opened, built under the West Hartlepool Light Railways Order of 1897, was a 2¼-mile extension of the Church Street line south, along Mainsforth Terrace and then Seaton Road on the seafront all the way to the village of Seaton Carew as a single reserved track. Services began on 28 March 1902, four ERTCW open-toppers (Nos 16-19) having been bought to work them. Just after the opening of the new route two Brush bogie open-toppers (Nos 20 and 21) were bought (and the single-deck 19 and 20 presumably returned to the BET). These were joined early in 1902 by four ERTCW bogie open-toppers (Nos 22-25) whilst at the same time the two trailers Nos 6 and 7 were disposed of and Nos 8 and 9 given their numbers. Then, in 1904, Nos 1-4 were rebuilt as two bogie open-toppers and given the numbers 8 and 9, the work being carried out by the Company. (The whole system was now operated by the HET Co., the BET having bought out the GET Co. in January 1899.)

After some three years of negotiations, West Hartlepool Corporation took over the system from the Company, completing the complicated arrangements as from 31 August 1912, buying the lines within its boundaries and leasing the section in Hartlepool. Two years later five new UEC open-toppers (Nos 1-5) were bought; later that year (on 16 December 1914) the tramway suffered slight damage when German warships shelled the town.

Six new cars (Nos 27-32) arrived in 1920, these being Brush bogie open-toppers but, ominously, on 17 July the Corporation commenced bus operations. Three years later Nos 8 and 9 were rebuilt with EE open-top

bodies, the last major alterations to the passenger fleet to take place. More cars were withdrawn and, on 4 October 1923, the Foggy Furze route closed, replaced by a temporary bus service until the planned trolleybuses began running the following year. The Park line closed in November 1925, the Hartlepool line on 22 February 1927 and the Seaton Carew line a month later. Earlier that year cars 1-5 had been sold to DOVER, the other vehicles being scrapped or otherwise disposed of after the closure.

HASLINGDEN CORPORATION TRAMWAYS
On 1 January 1908 Haslingden Corporation assumed full control of the 2.9 miles of single track within its boundaries which had previously been leased to the ACCRINGTON CORPORATION STEAM TRAMWAYS Co. At the same time it purchased eight locomotives and seven cars (numbers unknown) from the Company in order to work the single line itself until 5 September that same year when work began on electrifying the tramway in conjunction with Accrington Corporation who, on 28 September began services to the Commercial Hotel in the centre of the town and then, on 20 October, through to Lockgate (and on to RAWTENSTALL two years later). From then on this portion of the local network was nominally independent though in practice run by Accrington (though Haslingden Corporation kept one of the locos for use as a works engine). The line closed on 30 April 1930 as part of the abandonment of the whole Accrington–Rawtenstall route in favour of Corporation-operated motor buses.

Bibliography: *The Tramways of Accrington 1886-1932* Robert W. Rush (The Light Railway Transport League, 1961)

HASTINGS & DISTRICT ELECTRIC TRAMWAYS
Authority: Bexhill and St Leonards Light
    Railway Order 1900; Hastings Tramway
    Act 1900
Gauge: 3ft 6in
Traction: Overhead, stud electric, petrol-
    electric
Opened: 31 July 1905
Closed: 15 May 1929
System: Network
Length: 19.57 miles
Stock: 65 dd
Livery: Maroon & cream
Last Car: ?

The two main components of the Hastings tramway layout were a long, circular route inland from Hastings to Baldslow and back via Ore and a long east-west route on or close

to the seafront from Hastings through its twin town of St Leonards to beyond Bexhill. (All routes were principally double-track except for the northern half of the Circle.)

The system emerged from a number of (often conflicting) proposals, the PROVINCIAL Co. eventually winning the day with an LRO authorizing the Bexhill line plus an Act of Parliament for the whole network, both in the same year. Before construction could start however Provincial sold its interest in the scheme to the Hastings & District Electric Tramways Co., incorporated 1904, with tracklaying beginning in December that year.

The first two routes opened were the Circle which ran (clockwise) from the Albert Memorial in Hastings northwest up Bohemia Road to Silverhill (and the depot) then northeast along Sedlescombe Road to Baldslow, then southeast down London Road through St Helens to Ore, then westwards to wind behind West Hill to the Memorial and a 1-mile branch north up Battle Road from Silverhill to Hollington. Of the original order of 30 open-top ERTCW cars, 22 arrived in time for the opening and the remaining eight the next day.

A third route, from Ore southeast along Harold Road for a mile to Hastings Old Town (the terminus was by the Market Cross in the High Street), opened on 21 August 1905 and soon after another ten ERTCW open-toppers (Nos 31-40) were delivered. The next route to open, on 9 April 1906, was a separate section from St Leonards to the Metropole Hotel in Bexhill via Bexhill Road and De La Warr Road; this was extended to Cooden Beach, about 3 miles from St Leonards, on 28 July and was worked by eleven cars shedded at Bulverhythe Depot just outside St Leonards. That year another 20 open-toppers (Nos 41-60) were ordered from and delivered by UEC. Also on 28 July 1906 another route from Silverhill, this time due south down London Road to the seafront Grand Parade, was opened.

All that remained to complete the system was a seafront link between St Leonards, the Grand Parade and the Memorial. The obstacle to completing this was the refusal of Hastings Corporation, enshrined in the 1903 Act authorizing the route, to countenance overhead wires on the seafront. Accordingly, the Dolter stud system was employed on this section and the line opened on 12 January 1907 using UEC cars which had been equipped for both systems of current collection.

As experienced elsewhere, the Dolter system was not a satisfactory or reliable one and in 1913 the BoT instructed the Company to find an alternative and so the cars were fitted with Tilling-Stevens 24hp petrol engines and dynamos and operated the

*Hasting's first tram, No 10 of 1905, with an escort of small boys in this postcard marking the occasion.
(Lens of Sutton)*

seafront service until March 1921 when, the Corporation having relented, overhead wires were brought into use.

Hardly had the system been unified as regards current collection than the Company decided to deal with the problem of increasing bus competition by converting to trolley-buses. On 1 April 1928 these took over the Hollington branch, followed on 21 May by the London Road route to the Grand Parade and, on 30 July, on to Bexhill Marina and the Memorial; the Cooden extension went the same way on 18 September that year. The Circle was then so treated, in sections, with the last piece to go being the northern half from Silverhill to St Helens.

HELLINGLY HOSPITAL RAILWAY

Built to aid the construction of the East Sussex County Asylum (later Hellingly Hospital), this standard gauge railway ran for just over a mile northeast from a platform and sidings at Hellingly station on the LBSCR's Eridge-Polegate line to the hospital. The asylum opened on 20 July 1903 and it is thought that the private branch opened for passenger traffic at the same time. It is included here because the line was electrified with a tramway-style overhead after the construction work was finished. Passengers were conveyed until 1931 in a single-deck four-wheeled saloon car supplied by Robert W. Blackwell & Co. of London and freight services were worked until 1931 by a small four-wheeled steeple cab locomotive.

Bibliography: *The Hellingly Hospital Railway*
  Peter A. Harding (Author, Woking,
  1989) 0 9050941 45 X

HERNE BAY PIER TRAMWAY (1)
Authority: –
Gauge: ?
Traction: Sail, manual
Opened: 13 June 1833?
Closed: 1864
System: Single line
Length: c0.68 miles
Stock: 1 sd?
Livery: ?
Last Car: ?

Opened in June 1832 by the Herne Bay Pier Co. to serve the General Steam Navigation Co.'s steam traffic from London, the 3,640ft-long Herne Bay pier incorporated a tramway which had probably been used during the construction. When the pier opened to the

public, so did the tramway (of which no mention is made in the pier's 1831 Act) with hand-propelled four-wheeled wagons used to carry passengers' luggage to and from the boats; it is doubtful the passengers themselves were carried until 13 June of the following year when a sail-propelled carriage (grandly entitled *Old Neptune's Car*) made its maiden run. The idea for such a vehicle came from Sir Henry-Chudleigh Oxenden, the pier's local financial backer and an ice and land yacht enthusiast; when the wind was not favourable (or non-existent) the car was hand-propelled by two or three porters.

The pier closed in 1864 and with it the tramway. Its demise was brought about partly by the cessation of the steamer trade two years earlier and partly by 30 years of general decay on the part of the wooden structure; this was by no means the end of the story though (see below).

Bibliography: *Pier Railways* (Locomotion
  Papers No 60) K. Turner (The Oakwood
  Press, 1972)

HERNE BAY PIER TRAMWAY (2)
Authority: Herne Bay Pier Order 1891
Gauge: 3ft 4½in
Traction: Conduit electric/petrol-
  electric/battery
Opened: 1 April 1899
Closed: 3 November 1939
System: Single line
Length: c0.74 miles
Stock: 3 sd electric; 1 petrol railcar;
  1 battery railcar
Livery: Green & cream

After the closure of the original pier (see above), plans were made for a replacement. In 1871 the old pier was demolished and the following year work began on a new structure which was opened in August 1873; as built it

*Postcard of car No 3 on the Herne Bay Pier Tramway. The cable conduit is next to the righthand rail.
(Author's Collection)*

was just 320ft long but in 1891 authority was obtained by the Herne Bay Pier Co. to extend it and lay a tramway for both the construction work and passenger traffic. The line was built by BTH and the greatly-lengthened pier (now 3,930ft long) was opened in June 1898, the tramway opening the following year with a single Brush-bodied car (No 1) supplied with electricity via an off-centre conduit. In May 1901 this vehicle was joined by two ex-BRISTOL horse trams (Nos 2 and 3) which were converted for use as trailers to serve the (recommenced) steamer traffic.

In February 1905 the pier was placed in the hands of a Receiver and sold on 5 November 1908 to Herne Bay UDC. World War I interrupted both the steamer and tramway services and the tramway did not re-open until the 1925 August Bank Holiday, this time using a petrol-electric vehicle built locally by Strode Engineering. (The old car bodies are believed to have been used as shelters on the pier for a while before being scrapped.) The new car proved unreliable however and was converted in 1934 to serve as a trailer to accompany a new battery railcar from F. C. Hibberd & Co. of London.

The outbreak of World War II saw the suspension of the steamer service once again and following the last day of tramway operations the pier was breached as an anti-invasion measure. Although re-opened after the end of hostilities, the tramway was not reinstated and the cars sold for scrap.

Bibliography: as above

HEYWOOD CORPORATION TRAMWAYS

Authority: Heywood Corporation Tramways Order 1902
Gauge: 3ft 6in
Traction: Steam
Opened: 10 December 1904
Closed: 20 September 1905
System: Branching
Length: 4.33 miles
Stock: 13 locos, 10 dd
Livery: Locos brown, cars brown & cream?
Last Car: Loco 81

This very short-lived system (and the last municipally-owned steam tramway in Britain) was the last chapter in the MANCHESTER, BURY, ROCHDALE & OLDHAM saga. Caught midway between BURY, which had started running electric cars to the Heywood boundary in April 1904 and ROCHDALE, which had stopped its steam trams on the other side two months later, Heywood Corporation opted to buy some of the old steam tramway stock and re-open the lines within its boundaries.

Thirteen locomotives and ten trailers

(their identities not fully known) were moved by road in the middle of winter from Rochdale to Heywood (where a new depot was built in York Street) and on 10 December 1904 the old main line was re-opened. followed two days later by the Hopwood branch.

The initiative was not a great success. The stock was decrepit and Rochdale Corporation would not let Heywood run it over the mile or so of track from its boundary to Sudden where its electric service terminated. By April 1905 this gap had been closed with the extension of the electric line and that August Bury Corporation began reconstructing Heywood's main line back from the boundary in order to link up eventually with the Rochdale system and on 15 September steam services over this eastern portion of the tramway were halted altogether. Five days later, a satisfactory agreement having been reached with Rochdale, the remaining services were terminated and the rolling stock sold for scrap.

Bibliography: *The Manchester Bury Rochdale and Oldham Steam Tramway* W. G. S. Hyde (The Transport Publishing Co, 1979) 0 903839 37 7

HIGHGATE HILL TRAMWAYS see LONDON: HIGHGATE HILL TRAMWAYS

HORNDEAN see PORTSDOWN & HORNDEAN

HOYLAKE & BIRKENHEAD TRAMWAY see BIRKENHEAD: HOYLAKE & BIRKENHEAD TRAMWAY

HUDDERSFIELD CORPORATION TRAMWAYS

Authority: Huddersfield Improvement Act 1880
Gauge: 4ft 7¾in
Traction: Steam, horse, overhead electric
Opened: 11 January 1883
Closed: 29 June 1940
System: Radial network
Length: 39.12 miles
Stock: 36 locos, 37 dd horse & steam; 144 dd electric
Livery: Locos crimson, cars red/maroon & cream
Last Car: No 132 (official)

To Huddersfield Corporation goes the honour of owning the first municipally-operated tramways in the British Isles, if only because it could not find anyone who would lease them. Empowered by its 1880 Act, work began in June 1881 on track laying with a gauge of 4ft 7¾in being adopted, the

Corporation's (unrealised) intention being to allow for the running of railway wagons over the system which meant unfortunately, that connections could not be made with any of its West Riding neighbours (HALIFAX to the north and DEWSBURY to the south). Powers to work the lines themselves were granted by the Huddersfield Corporation Act 1882 and on 11 January the following year the first two lines opened, north from St George's Square in the town centre up Northgate and the Bradford Road to Fartown Bar, and the south from the Square along New Street, Buxton Road, Chapel Hill and Lockwood Road to Lockwood Bar in the district of Salford. The two lines were worked as one route with Wilkinson tram locomotives 1-6 (arriving in batches from 1882 to January 1884) hauling open-top double-deck trailers Nos 1 (an Eades patent reversible car from Ashbury – a curious choice for a steam trailer) and 2-6 (from Starbuck).

Other routes slowly followed: northwest to Lindley (9 June 1883) and Edgerton (10 January 1884) and east to Moldgreen (9 May 1885) – this last route being horse-worked on account of a narrow roadway with Ashbury cars 7 and 8 (again Eades open-toppers). On 11 October 1886 the Lindley and Edgerton routes were linked via Holly Bank to form a loop and on 15 February 1889 a southeastern line was opened to Almondbury via Kidroyd, followed on 23 May 1890 by a short western line to Crosland Moor. The Moldgreen route was extended to the Waterloo Inn on the Wakefield Road on 26 September that year and by the end of 1899 the single-track system was virtually complete, with no less than nine radial routes plus two out-and-back loops, to serve almost all areas of the town and its periphery.

The tramway's stock had meanwhile continued to grow to keep pace with the new routes and extensions. Locos 7-9 were bought from BH in 1885-86, Nos 10-18 and 21 and 22 from Kitsons in 1887-89, Nos 19, 20 and 23-30 from Greens in 1891-92 and Nos 31 and 32 from Kitsons again in 1894; the only other engines added were Nos 7-9 in 1897 and No 6 in 1898, assembled by the Corporation from Kitson parts. Open-top bogie trailer No 9 (from Lancaster) and 10 and 11 (Starbuck) and Eades four-wheeled open-toppers 12 and 13 (from Ashbury) were bought in 1885 and were followed in 1887 by bogie open-toppers 14 and 15 from Milnes – which firm supplied over the next twelve years another 21 bogie top-covered cars to take the number series up to 26 plus replacements for lower-numbered vehicles.

The depot was located just north of St George's Square in Northumberland Street until 1887 when a new one was built in Viaduct Street to the east of Northgate. On

21 May 1900 a 3-mile extension of the Marsden Road route southwest of the town was opened from the municipal boundary, out along the Manchester Road through Linthwaite to the Star Hotel in Slaithwaite. This was authorized by the Huddersfield Corporation Tramways Order and the Linthwaite Tramways Order of 1898 and, although owned by Linthwaite UDC, was worked by Huddersfield.

By 1899 the Corporation was planning the electrification of the system, with new routes authorized by the Huddersfield Corporation Act of the following year. On 14 February 1901 the first two converted routes were opened: the Lindley Circular (the loop via Edgerton) and the long western line out on the New Hey Road to Outlane. The last steam trams ran on the Far Town route on 21 June 1902, marking the end of the conversion work.

The system continued to grow until 1923 when the last route, an extension of the Far Town route northwards through Rastrick to Brighouse, was opened on 12 March that year. As completed, the system was the old steam system enlarged to some 14, mainly double-track, radial routes with a large fleet of cars based on the old steam depot site and a new depot by the Corporation's generating station in St Thomas' Road off the Manchester Road, just west of the town centre.

The first electric cars were Milnes bogie open-toppers of 1900 (Nos 1-25) which were followed by open-toppers 26-61 from BEC over the next two years (No 40 was renumbered 62 after an accident in 1902), followed in 1902 by Nos 40 and 63-66 which had top covers. No 67 of 1903 was an open-top American import and Nos 68-70 futher top-covered BEC vehicles. UEC supplied top-covered 71-75 in 1909, enclosed 76 a year later and top-covered 77-106 during 1912-14 whilst the remainder of the fleet were EE products: top-covered 107-126 of 1919-20 and enclosed 127-144 delivered during the ten years from 1923 onwards. Two powered coal trucks, supplied by MV in 1904 and numbered 71 and 72 (renumbered 1 and 2 in 1909) were employed until 1934 to make deliveries to mills on the Outlane route.

The beginning of the end for the tramway came, in the face of bus competition, in 1932 when the Almondbury route was gradually cut back as it was converted for trolleybus operation, closing altogether on 16 April of the following year. On 10 November 1935 the Waterloo, Lindley and Outlane routes were closed and by 1940 only the Brighouse line was left. All surviving cars were scrapped, the most modern ones (Nos 137-144) having been sold in 1938 to SUNDERLAND.

Bibliography: *Huddersfield Corporation*

Tramways Roy Brook (Author, Accrington, 1983) 0 950858 91 9

HULL STREET TRAMWAYS
Authority: Hull Tramways Order 1872
Gauge: 4ft 8½in
Traction: Horse
Opened: 9 January 1875
Closed: Autumn 1896
System: Radial
Length: 10.81 miles
Stock: 4 sd, 31 dd
Livery: Dark red-brown & white
Last Car: ?

The first section of Kingston-upon-Hull's first tramway system was built and operated by the Continental & General Tramway Co. Ltd. This consisted of a single-track line 1½ miles in length running northwards from Saville Street in the city centre up Beverley Road to Rose Cottage near Queen's Road. It was worked by two single-deckers of unknown manufacture (Nos 11 and 12); these were joined over the next four years by six large double-deckers (Nos 51-56) – possibly all from Belgium – four small double-deckers (Nos 5-7, 9, 10 and 14) and another single-decker (No 13). The reasoning behind the somewhat bizarre numbering system is not known.

From 1 November 1876 the tramway was owned and worked by the newly-formed Hull Street Tramways Co. Ltd, which company set about opening other routes to outlying districts thus: on 12 December 1876 north-westwards up Springbank to the Botanic Gardens and in 1877 south to the Pier on the River Humber, westwards along Hessle Road to Dairycotes, west along Anlaby Road and eastwards up Holderness Road to Mile House. Short extensions the following year completed the single-track system. Depots were sited in Hessle Road and Holderness Road and off Beverley Road.

By the end of 1882 the car fleet was complete with the 1879 purchase of another single-decker, followed by thirteen small and six medium-sized double-deckers; after the 1882 withdrawal of the four single-deckers all the double-deck cars were now renumbered 1-31 in line with more conventional thinking.

The Company failed in 1889 – largely as a result of competition from cheap and speedy waggonette competitors – and was wound up and put into receivership on 30 November that year. Thereafter the stock and track slowly fell into disrepair until being taken over by the Corporation on 15 October 1896 and leased out to a local cab proprietor. The Corporation's intention was to replace the horse trams with electric ones (see below) and services on the Hessle Road were withdrawn accordingly at the end of

May 1898, the other routes all gradually going the same way by the end of September of the following year (though one staff recollection was of a date in early November).

One feature of the system was shared with that of the BURTON-UPON-TRENT system: a number of level crossings over railway lines (seven in the case of Hull) which, as well as disrupting services frequently, had to be protected by catch points and signals.

HULL: DRYPOOL & MARFLEET STEAM TRAMWAY
Authority: Drypool and Marfleet Steam
　Tramways Order 1886
Gauge: 4ft 8½in
Traction: Steam
Opened: 21 May 1889
Closed: 13 January 1901
System: Branching
Length: 1.34 miles
Stock: 7 locos, 8 dd
Livery: Deep crimson & white
Last Car: ?

On 15 January 1886 a local company was incorporated, the Drypool & Marfleet Steam Tramway Co. Ltd, to construct and operate tramways on the eastern side of Hull, especially on a line along Hedon Road past the newly-built Alexandra Dock and out to the village of Marfleet some 2 miles distant.

Construction did not begin until July 1888 and, as laid, the line ran from the North Bridge over the River Hull, down through Drypool Square and Union Street, past Victoria Dock and out along Hedon Road only as far as its junction with Lee Smith Street by Alexandra Dock – half the projected route length. The only other portion of line was a 100yd-spur near the North Bridge terminus which ran back westwards to the Drypool Pool Bridge (opened 1888) over the Hull and was, in the early days of the tramway, also used as a terminus. When opened, not only was the line one of the last steam street tramways to be built in Great Britain (only the ST HELENS & DISTRICT in 1890 came later), it was the shortest.

Four tram locomotives (Nos 1-4) and five trailers (Nos 1-5) were supplied for the opening of the line with locos 5-7 and trailers 6-8 following by the end of the year; the engines were from Greens and the large, enclosed double-deck bogie trailers from Milnes. (The extra trailer over engine numbers is accounted for by the fact that the Company intended to run a two-car train if need be and apparently did so on occasions.) The depot was in Hotham Street, reached by a short spur off Hedon road by the terminus.

From the outset the tramway's major problem was that its western termini were some ten minutes' walk from the city centre and consequently it suffered from waggonette competition. Attempts to solve the problem by either running combined services in conjunction with the horse trams (see above) or by actually buying some of the horse lines (notably the one across North Bridge only yards from the D&M line) for steam working were strongly opposed on the grounds of the noise and pollution produced by the engines. In any event the 1896 purchase of the horse tramways by the Corporation effectively quashed any such plans and about this time the Drypool Bridge spur seems to have been abandoned as an economy measure.

The Company soon found itself bypassed by outside events – notably the electrification of the old horse system – and in 1899 it successfully negotiated the sale of the tramway to the Corporation. Completed on 31 January 1900, the price was £15,500, after which the Company went into voluntary liquidation. By the time of the sale the locos and cars were showing signs of wear and by October 1900 one loco and two trailers had been withdrawn; by the following January only two engines were in service.

CITY OF HULL TRAMWAYS

Authority: Hull Corporation Tramways
    Order 1896
Gauge: 4ft 8½in
Traction: Overhead electric
Opened: 5 July 1899
Closed: 30 June 1945
System: Radial network
Length: 20.48 miles
Stock: 182 dd
Livery: Red & white
Last Car: No 169

The first Kingston-upon-Hull electric tram services began along the former Anlaby Road

and Hessle Road routes of the old horse tramway system using centre-grooved rails with the rest of the horse lines and the steam line being similarly converted over the next few years. (See previous two entries.) Services were worked initially by Milnes open-top cars Nos 1-25 hauling open-top trailers Nos 101-125, all built 1898-99 and which were joined in 1899 by Brill Nos 26-30 and in 1900 by Brush open-toppers 31-60 plus five of the same from ERTCW (Nos 61-65). The Milnes trailers were thereupon motorized and renumbered 66-90, joined in 1901 by Nos 91-100, HN open-top cars and Milnes 101, a bogie open-topper.

As can be judged by the size of the car fleet (and the speed at which it was built up) the electric lines were spreading rapidly and eventually formed a radial network of lines on the north side of the River Humber stretching westwards to Anlaby Park and along Hessle Road, eastwards to Marfleet and along Holderness Road and northwards through Newland and up Beverley Road. In addition, a double rectangle of lines off to the west of Beverley Road, completed in 1927, served the residential area there. Virtually all the routes were double-tracked throughout with most of the extremities occupying sleepered roadside reservations. The only southerly route was a short ¼-mile double-track branch from the city centre down through the Market Place to Victoria Pier.

By the time the last section opened the car fleet (known locally as 'Kipper Boxes') was complete. In 1903 Milnes supplied top-covered cars 102-116 with similar vehicles arriving from UEC in 1909 (Nos 117-122) and being built by the Corporation in 1909-10 (Nos 123-136). Meanwhile, in 1909 bogie car 101 was sold to ERITH. In 1912 Brush supplied top-covered cars 137-160, followed by 161-180 three years later. Many of these were replacements for withdrawn older

vehicles and many were rebuilt (and often enclosed) later. The last car to be bought rather than modernized was a new No 101, an enclosed EE double-decker of 1923. This was followed in 1925 by the system's final passenger car, No 113, another enclosed double-decker this time built by the Corporation.

Cutbacks to the system began in the 1930s with the closure on 5 January 1931 of the Victoria Pier branch. The Hedon Road route to Marfleet went in 1932 and two years later an agreement was reached with the local bus operator, East Yorkshire Motor Services Ltd, one of the provisions of which was that the Corporation would cut its outermost tramways back, thus closing the Anlaby route beyond Wheeler Street Depot, the Hessle Road route beyond Dairycoats (and the Liverpool Street depot) and the northern Cottingham road route off Beverley Road (again just beyond a depot).

On 23 July 1937 trolleybus services began and they put an end to the northern part of the system leaving just the Holderness Road, Anlaby Road and Hessle Road routes to see the start of World War II, during which the first of these (on 17 February 1940) and the second (5 September 1942) both closed. Many of the surviving tramcars were thereafter sold to LEEDS, leaving just twelve to work the last route to Dairycoats until that too was abandoned.

HUNDRED OF MANHOOD & SELSEY TRAMWAY

Commonly known as the Selsey Tramway, this standard gauge West Sussex line was, despite its title, a typical light railway of the Colonel H. F. Stephens empire. Starting from its own little station next to the LBSCR's Chichester station (where there was a physical connection). It ran due south for 7¾ miles through Hunston, Chalder and Sidlesham to Selsey. It opened on 27 August 1897, was extended a further 1¼ miles to Selsey Beach and in 1924 changed its name to the West Sussex Railway. Operated with a typical motley Stephens' collection of second-hand tank engines and carriages (plus two railcar sets), it was closed on 19 January 1935 and the stock sold.

Bibliography: *The Selsey Tram* David
    Bathurst (Phillimore, 1992)
    0 850338 39 5

HYTHE PIER TRAMWAY

The present third-rail electric railway running down the south side of the 700yd-long 1881 Hythe pier in Hampshire, and opened in 1922, was the rebuild of a single-track luggage line which had opened in 1909 to serve the ferry across the Solent to Southampton. It is thought that the tramway was of 2ft gauge like its successor and operated

One of the City of Hull's first cars from a batch of open-toppers, complete with curtains in the lower saloon, built at the turn of the century. (Lens of Sutton)

with at least two small hand-propelled trucks.

Bibliography: *Pier Railways* (Locomotion Papers No 60) K. Turner (The Oakwood Press, 1972)

HYTHE *see* FOLKESTONE, HYTHE & SANDGATE

ILFORD COUNCIL TRAMWAYS
Authority: Ilford Improvement Act 1898
Gauge: 4ft 8½in
Traction: Overhead electric
Opened: 14 March 1903
Taken Over: 1 July 1933
System: Radial
Length: 7.4 miles
Stock: 57 dd
Livery: Crimson lake & cream to 1914, then green & cream

Ilford UDC operated 6.66 miles of its own tramways and 0.74 miles leased from BARKING UDC. Its four routes radiated from Ilford Broadway west to the borough boundary on Ilford Hill, south down Ilford Lane to the Barking boundary at Loxford Bridge, east along High Road to the boundary at Chadwell Heath and north up Ley Street and Horns Road through Newbury Park to Tanners Lane, Barkingside. The first and last of these were mainly single-track and opened with the Chadwell Heath route on 14 March 1903, the Loxford Bridge line following on 22 May that year.

The first cars were HN open-toppers 1-12 and bogie open-toppers 13-18, all shedded off Ley Street and joined later in 1903 by Nos 19-22, four more single-truck vehicles. All were later top-covered. These were joined in 1910 by top-covered Brush cars 23-26, by No 27 in 1914 (ex-Barking No 10) and No 28 a year later (ex-Barking No 8). During the period 1920-23 20 Brush top-covered cars were bought, partly as replacement vehicles, and took the numbers 1-20 (with surviving old cars being renumbered higher in the series). Three similar bodies were bought in 1929 for fitting with existing trucks and numbered 21-23; these were followed three years later by Nos 33-40, eight top-covered Brush cars of a new design – the last additions to the fleet before it became part of the new LONDON TRANSPORT.

The system was connected in the west to the EAST HAM CORPORATION TRAMWAYS which, from April 1905, worked the short Ilford Hill line with cars running through to the Broadway, and in the south with the Barking system at Loxford Bridge where a similar arrangement, from 6 June of that year, saw Ilford working a short, isolated route on behalf of that system.

Bibliography: *The Tramways of East London*

'Rodinglea' (The Tramway & Light Railway Society/The Light Railway Transport League, 1967)

ILKESTON CORPORATION TRAMWAYS
Authority: Ilkeston Tramways Order 1899
Gauge: 3ft 6in
Traction: Overhead electric
Opened: 16 May 1903
Closed: 15 January 1931
System: Branching
Length: 3.78 miles
Stock: 13 dd
Livery: Maroon & cream
Last Car: ?

Ilkeston Town Council decided in the 1890s to promote an electric tramway scheme to serve this Derbyshire town and, in 1899, obtained the necessary powers with the short system opening four years later with nine open-toppers from ERTCW which were joined later in 1903 by Nos 10-13, four open-toppers from Milnes.

The system comprised a main north–south single-track line from Cotmanhay, down Cotmanhay Road, through the town centre on Granby Street between the GNR's North station and the MR's Town station and out along Bath Street and South Street past the depot and then via the Nottingham Road to Hallam Fields where it terminated in Hallam Fields Road. A single-track branch of just over ½ mile ran east off Bath Street down Station Road to Ilkeston Junction station on the MR's main line (Town station being on an equally short railway branch).

The tramway quickly began losing money and was offered to the neighbouring NOTTINGHAMSHIRE & DERBYSHIRE concern who took over operation of both the Council's tramway and electricity undertakings as from 30 June 1916 with a follow-up purchase – in a reversal of the normal course of events – being agreed to on 5 September. The purchase price was £28,150 and on 31 October 1916 the Tramway Committee was wound up, the N&D assuming full ownership from the next day.

After the N&D took over it rebuilt car No 7 as a single-decker for the Station Road service and transferred five of the other cars to CARLISLE and two to Dunfermline in Scotland. Fifteen years later the tramway was closed by the N&D in favour of its motor buses (and later trolleybuses).

Bibliography: *Ilkeston as a Borough* Cyril Hargreaves (Moorley's Bible & Bookshops Ltd, Ilkeston, 1974) 0 901495 41 7

IMMINGHAM *see* GRIMSBY & IMMINGHAM

IMPERIAL TRAMWAYS
The Bristol-based Imperial Tramways Co. Ltd (1878-1930) owned, at one time or another, the tramways at BRISTOL, DARLINGTON, GLOUCESTER and READING as well as the MIDDLESBROUGH, STOCKTON & THORNABY system and the LONDON UNITED TRAMWAYS (formerly the WEST METROPOLITAN TRAMWAYS) in London; in addition it owned the Dublin Southern District Tramways in Ireland and the narrow gauge Corris Railway in Wales.

IPSWICH TRAMWAY
Authority: Ipswich Tramways Order 1879
Gauge: 3ft 6in
Traction: Horse
Opened: 13 October 1880
Closed: 6 June 1903
System: Network
Length: 4.25 miles
Stock: 3 sd, 6 dd
Livery: Maroon & cream
Last Car: ?

Although the Ipswich horse tramway system ended its days under Corporation ownership, it began as a private concern, promoted and built by S. A. Graham of Manchester. The first line opened ran for ¾ mile from the GER's station down Princes Street to Cornhill in the town centre and was worked by three single-deck Starbuck cars; the depot was in Quadling Street about ¼ mile from the station.

A second Order of 1880 led to the construction of a branch from by the depot up Portman Road and Norwich Road to Brooks Hall. A year later, under the Ipswich Tramways Act of 1881, the Ipswich Tramway Co. was formed to take over the two lines and provide a link between them from Cornhill along Westgate Street and St Matthews Street, thus producing a triangular layout. An eastwards extension from Cornhill to Derby Road station in 1884 completed the system. To work the extra lines three more cars were purchased in 1882 and another three two years later. All lines were single tracks.

Under its 1900 powers (see below) the Corporation purchased the system on 1 November 1901 to provide the basis for its planned electric tramways and, as the system was now operating at a loss, closed it down as soon as possible.

Bibliography: *The Tramways of East Anglia* R. C. Anderson (The Light Railway Transport League, 1969) 0 900433 00 0

IPSWICH CORPORATION TRAMWAYS
Authority: Ipswich Corporation Tramways Act 1900

Gauge: 3ft 6in
Traction: Overhead electric
Opened: 23 November 1903
Closed: 26 July 1926
System: Network
Length: 10.82 miles
Stock: 36 dd
Livery: Dark green & cream
Last car: ?

Under its 1900 Act the Corporation was empowered to take over the existing Ipswich horse tramways (see above), electrify and extend them. This it set about doing, more than doubling the length of the old system with seven basic routes, all primarily single-track, radiating out from Cornhill to serve most parts of the town. Services began with 26 open-top Brush cars which were quickly followed by ten more (Nos 27-36) a year later. The car shed and power station were in Constantine Road, just off Portman Road.

The first section of the system to close was the very short branch in Bath Street which was used only to link the station with the Quay when GER steamers docked there; this closed in 1917 and was followed in 1923 by the station–Cornhill and Princes Street–Mill Street routes, the original horse lines being replaced by Corporation trolleybus services. Three years later the rest of the system went the same way (with the Corporation not adopting motor buses until the 1950s). Following the closure, seven cars were sold to SCARBOROUGH and one, (No 34) to FELIXSTOWE PIER.

Bibliography: as above

ISLE OF THANET ELECTRIC TRAMWAYS

Authority: Isle of Thanet Light Railway Order 1898
Gauge: 3ft 6in
Traction: Overhead electric
Opened: 4 April 1901
Closed: 27 March 1937
System: Split single line
Length: 10.84 miles
Stock: 60 dd
Livery: Maroon & cream to 1927, then crimson & ivory
Last Car: No 20

Despite the failure of the abortive RAMSGATE & MARGATE tramway, interest remained high in the idea of a line linking the major towns on the Isle of Thanet in northeast Kent. Of the various proposals made, that of William Murphy proved the successful one. On 3 March 1896 he formed the Isle of Thanet Light Railways (Electric) Co. Ltd – the name was changed on 11 March 1899 to the Isle of Thanet Electric Tramways & Lighting Co. Ltd – and two years later obtained the necessary LRO.

The line was constructed by the Thanet Construction Co. Ltd, another Murphy company (he had interests in several British tramways, including Dublin United where he became Chairman), with some nine-tenths of it being double-track. It commenced in Canterbury Road, Westbrook on the western edge of Margate and from there ran along the sea front past the LCDR's West station and the SER's Sands station before turning inland east, then south through Cliftonville to cross the Isle of Thanet, partly on road and partly on reserved sections, to Broadstairs on

its eastern coast. Here, the main line ran through the town via the High Street and Dumpton Park Road whilst a 'top road' provided a bypass route to the west. South of Broadstairs, Ramsgate was reached where the line followed the sea front before swinging back on itself north up Grange Road then east along Park Road to terminate by the SER's Town station.

The first section to open – the bulk of the line in fact – was from the Margate stations to Ramsgate Harbour via the top road, the main line through Broadstairs and the short sections at either end opening on 6 July that year. The original car fleet comprised 20 open-toppers from the St Louis Car Co. of the USA but it quickly became clear that these would not be sufficient and another twenty of larger capacity (Nos 21-40) arrived in July 1901, followed by ten open-top Milnes cars (Nos 41-50) that same year. Finally, ten similar cars (Nos 51-60) were purchased in 1903 from BEC. The system was plagued with problems in its early years on account of the number of steep hills in the towns and accidents were frequent, culminating in car No 41 going over the cliff at Ramsgate on 3 August 1905. Amazingly, the driver was the only person seriously injured, but the car had to be scrapped. In the early 1920s Nos 42 and 45 had their stairs removed for conversion to one-man operation (although only No 45 had its top deck removed as well).

Although the Company (known as the Isle of Thanet Electric Supply Co. from June 1924) had been operating motor buses since 1913, it seems that pressure from the local councils led to the tramway's demise in 1937, to be replaced by East Kent Road Car Co. buses – which firm had purchased the tramway bus operation the previous year.

Bibliography: *The Tramways of Kent Vol 2: East Kent* 'INVICTA' (The Light Railway Transport League, 1975) 0 900433 45 0

JARROW & DISTRICT ELECTRIC TRAMWAY

Authority: Jarrow and South Shields Light Railway Order 1901
Gauge: 4ft 8½in
Traction: Overhead electric
Opened: 29 November 1906
Closed: 30 June 1929
System: Single line
Length: 2.54 miles
Stock: 12 dd
Livery: Maroon & off-white*
Last Car: ?

Promoted by the BET, this tramway was owned and operated by its subsidiary, the Jarrow & District Electric Traction Co. Ltd,

Isle of Thanet No 4 of 1900, one of the system's original cars. (Lens of Sutton)

and ran eastwards south of the River Tyne from Western Road along Ormonde Street, Staple Road, the High Street and Church Bank in Jarrow, after which it occupied a reserved right of way for ¼ mile (crossing the River Don and passing into South Shields) before joining Straker Street and its continuation Swinburne Street, then entering Jarrow Road where there was an end-on connection with the SOUTH SHIELDS CORPORATION line. Virtually all the route was single-track. (The short Western Road–Ormonde Street stretch was opened on 21 December 1906 after it had been brought up to standard.)

Services began with Brush open-top double-deckers Nos 1-8 which were joined in 1907 by No 9, a second-hand Brush car of similar type built in 1902 for display at that year's Trade Exhibition. Always known at Jarrow as the 'Show Car', it retained its own green livery. In 1908 Nos 5 and 6 were exchanged for two GRAVESEND & NORTHFLEET bogie cars which were renumbered accordingly. The last car to arrive was No 10, formerly GATESHEAD 35, which was borrowed then purchased in 1911; this was an ERTCW open-topper of 1901 vintage.

Through running between the Jarrow and South Shields lines began on 18 June 1908, much to the benefit of the shipyard and other workers who provided the bulk of the trams' passengers, but was discontinued on 17 June 1911 after a dispute over the financial arrangement between the two concerns. (The Jarrow cars were in effect hired by South Shields in return for the fares collected.) On 14 July 1922 through running recommenced, the dispute having been resolved, only to stop again on 13 July 1927, by which time bus competition was affecting the line seriously and shortly forced its closure, after which cars 5 and 6 were sold to South Shields and the remainder scrapped.

Bibliography: *The Tramways of Jarrow and South Shields* George S. Hearse (Author, Corbridge, 1971)

KEIGHLEY TRAMWAYS
Authority: Keighley Tramways Order 1888
Gauge: 4ft
Traction: Horse
Opened: 8 May 1889
Closed: 28 May 1904
System: Single line
Length: 2.28 miles
Stock: 7 dd
Livery: ?
Last Car: ?

Promoted by the Keighley Tramways Co. Ltd (a consortium of local businessmen and councillors), Keighley's first tramway was

a simple single-track line running south from the residential district of Utley down Skipton Road, North Street and South Street past the depot to industrial Ingrow. The North Street–Ingrow section was the first to open in 1889, the Utley half following on 18 December that year. Very short extensions at both ends were constructed c1897 (to the Roebuck Inn at Utley and the new bridge at Ingrow) and the two halves of the line were normally worked as separate routes. The car fleet – all probably purchased in 1889 – comprised seven open-top double-deckers by Starbuck.

The tramway was never a financial success and on 25 November 1896 the Company sold the track to Keighley Corporation for the nominal sum of £5 and leased it back for thirteen years. On 15 January 1901 the Corporation, wanting to extend and electrify the line, became the effective owner after the Company agreed to sell them the rest of the concern (although municipal operations only began on 21 September with the formal change of ownership). The Company was wound up in December of that year. The tramway continued much as before under its new owner (but with a number of minor improvements and the sale of one of the cars) until 1904 when both routes were closed to clear the way for the planned rebuilding. (See below.)

Bibliography: *Keighley Corporation Transport* J. S. King (The Advertiser Press, Huddersfield, 1964)

KEIGHLEY CORPORATION TRAMWAYS
Authority: Keighley Corporation Act 1898
Gauge: 4ft
Traction: Overhead electric
Opened: 12 October 1904
Closed: 17 December 1924
System: Radial
Length: 3.44 miles
Stock: 12 dd
Livery: Crimson & white
Last Car: No 6

Even before operating the old horse tramway (see above), Keighley Corporation was planning its electrification and, by means of a branch to Stockbridge (authorized by the Keighley Corporation Tramways Act of 1903), a link with SHIPLEY and thence BRADFORD in conjunction with the Mid-Yorkshire Tramways Co. Ltd. This company failed however and the Corporation never managed to connect its system to any other.

The horse tramway was reconstructed as a double-track line and the Stockbridge route laid as double tracks from the Institute in North Street eastwards along Cavendish Street to the MR station where it became a

single track along Bradford Road to Victoria Park (about a mile from the Institute). All three routes opened together and were worked by eight open-top Brush cars, joined by two more (Nos 9 and 10) in 1905 after the 10 February opening of a ½-mile extension of the Stockbridge line to the Dale Street/ Bradford Road junction in Stockbridge.

The arrival in 1906 of a pair of top-covered Brush cars (Nos 11 and 12) completed the fleet but soon after this the Corporation appears to have set its collective heart on introducing trolleybuses to Keighley and, in 1913, did so. The gradual expansion of the new system was interrupted by World War I but in the 1920s, faced with the prospect of having to replace all the tramway track, the Corporation decided to abandon the system. The Utley route closed on 20 August 1924, followed by the Stockbridge route in mid-November and the Ingrow line a month later, making Keighley the first local authority to close its electric tramway system and the first to replace its trams with trolleybuses – a dubious double honour indeed.

Bibliography: as above

KIDDERMINSTER & STOURPORT ELECTRIC TRAMWAY
Authority: Kidderminster and Stourport Electric Tramway Act 1896
Gauge: 3ft 6in
Traction: Overhead electric
Opened: 25 May 1898
Closed: 2 April 1929
System: Branching
Length: 4.6 miles
Stock: 21 sd?, 7 dd?
Livery: Originally BET mustard & ivory, then Munich lake & cream?
Last Car: ?

Although sometimes considered as part of the BLACK COUNTRY TRAMWAYS network for the sake of completeness, the K&S was not situated in the Black Country and was always physically isolated from its close neighbours despite early plans to link it to the KINVER LIGHT RAILWAY at Stourton. It was promoted by the private consortium which, on 7 November 1895, became the British Electric Traction (Pioneer) Co. Ltd, the forerunner of the BET, and can be regarded as that company's first tramway.

The purpose of the line's construction was to link the Worcestershire market town and carpet manufacturing centre of Kidderminster with the village of Stourport, a small port at the junction of the Stour and Severn rivers and a popular spot for day-trippers from the West Midlands. It was built by the Kidderminster contractor George Law and consisted of a 3¾-mile main route running more or less in a straight line south from the Bull Ring in the centre of Kidderminster, along New Road past the depot and power station, then on the Stourport Road through Foley Park, Upper Mitton and Newtown to terminate at the Swan Hotel in Stourport High Street, just before the bridge over the Severn. There was also a short branch from the Bull Ring running eastwards along Oxford Street and up Comberton Hill past the GWR station to a terminus at Somerleyton Avenue. Both lines were single tracks.

The tramway's entire electrical equipment, from the generating plant to the cars themselves, was supplied by Brush (the firm's first such complete tramway contract). Cars Nos 1-6 were closed single-deckers with vestibules – the first in Britain – and Nos 7-9 three open cross-bench trailers. Thereafter the rolling stock situation became increasingly complicated for such a small system with two of the cars being rebuilt as double-deckers, the trailers being motorised and several cars being acquired new or via other BET concerns at various times and with incompletely-recorded number changes.

The line was nominally owned by the Kidderminster & Stourport Electric Tramway Co. until the BET subsidiary the Kidderminster & District Electric Lighting & Traction Co. Ltd was registered on 19 December 1898 to acquire it. In 1901 a LRO was obtained for a 3-mile route west to Bewdley as part of the BET's grand design for a West Midlands network extending right out to the Severn as far as WORCESTER in the south but it was never built, the only 'link' coming in 1917 when the Company joined the BIRMINGHAM & MIDLAND TRAMWAYS JOINT COMMITTEE.

On 31 December 1923 the Comberton Hill route closed, its services replaced by motor buses (which the Company had been operating since October 1913 in the face of local competition), and the main line followed less than six years later.

Bibliography: *Black Country Tramways Vol 2* J. S. Webb (Author, Bloxwich, 1976)

KINGSTON-UPON-HULL *see* HULL

KINVER LIGHT RAILWAY
Authority: Kinver Light Railway Order 1898
Gauge: 3ft 6in
Traction: Overhead electric
Opened: 5 April 1901
Closed: 1 February 1930?
System: Single line
Length: 4.18 miles
Stock: 21 sd
Livery: BET mustard & ivory, then DSDET green & cream
Last Car: ?

The KLR occupied the extreme south-west corner of the BLACK COUNTRY TRAMWAYS network. The south Staffordshire village of Kinver, some 4 miles west of Stourbridge (just over the Worcestershire boundary), has long been a popular beauty spot for day trippers from the industrial conurbation to the east and it was this traffic that the promoters, the BET, hoped to tap. Construction began soon after the necessary LRO was obtained with the work being split between the BET itself and George Law (see above).

In appearance, the tramway too was divided. It began as a conventional street tramway by the Fish Inn in Amblecote, just to the north of Stourbridge, where there was a small depot and a connection with the DUDLEY, STOURBRIDGE & DISTRICT main line. From here it ran southwest for ½ mile along Wollaston Road to the district of that name (another outlying area of Stourbridge) where, from 13 December 1902, it connected with the DSD's Enville Street route to the town centre (passengers for which always had to change cars here). The line then swung westwards up the Bridgnorth Road for about another ½ mile to its summit at Ridge Top where it left the road to run on sleepered railway track along the lefthand grass verge. This it occupied for about 1½ miles through agricultural countryside (and passing into Staffordshire) as far as the Stewponey Hotel at Stourton where it crossed the main Wolverhampton–Kidderminster Road, the Staffordshire & Worcestershire Canal and the River Stour in quick succession before entering a private right of way across the fields and through the woods beside the canal to terminate at the eastern end of Kinver village. A second small depot was picturesquely sited midway along this section in the woods at The Hyde.

The line was an immense success from the very start, especially on Bank Holidays when huge crowds travelled from as far afield as Wolverhampton and Birmingham to sample its delights. Worked by them from the outset, it was purchased by the DSDET Co. on 29 September 1902 for £60,000 and two years later a controlling interest was bought by the BIRMINGHAM & MIDLAND TRAMWAYS Ltd.

Although visited regularly by other Birmingham and Black Country cars on excursion and other special workings, the KLR always kept its own dedicated rolling stock (including two vans for its important milk churn traffic picked up en route). It opened with Nos 1-3, ERTCW single-deckers of 1900 construction borrowed from the DSDET as its own original three cars, all 1900 ERTCW open-top bogie vehicles, were prohibited by the BoT from working the line in case they overturned on the railway-type track. These latter cars were lent accordingly to the DSDET and numbered 46-48 in that fleet but soon returned to the KLR cut-down to single-deckers to replace the borrowed cars. (Nos 46 and 47 were scrapped c1911 and No 48 at the end of World War I.)

A rush order to Brush resulted in the delivery of three summer cars in 1901: Nos 1-3 (later DSDET 49-51), bogie cross-bench vehicles with open centre sections. Replacements for Nos 46 and 47 arrived c1912; these were ex-SOUTH STAFFORD-

The coming of the tramways was often the occasion for the appropriate naming of new streets. This sign still denotes the location of the (now demolished) Kidderminster & Stourport depot. (Author)

TRAM STREET

SHIRE Brush open-toppers cut-down to single-deck and given the former cars' numbers (and trucks) and were both scrapped in the mid-1920s. In 1916 four new cars were constructed for the line by the BIRMINGHAM & MIDLAND TRAMWAYS JOINT COMMITTEE; these were Nos 6, 21, 32 and 70, all bogie single-deckers not too dissimilar to Nos 49-51 (although the centre section could be closed in for winter service). The tramway's own car fleet was completed by Nos 63-68, six 1899 bogie crossbench ex-CITY OF BIRMINGHAM Hockley Hill cable cars, electrified in 1904, which came from the CBT in 1911 and worked summers on the line until 1916 when the new semi-open cars arrived.

It is significant that all the tramway's stock was built or purchased prior to the end of World War I; during the war years track and old stock deteriorated badly and after the war the line's tripper trade was hit increasingly by the motor car and bus. By the end of the 1920s all that was left of the former DSDET system was the KLR and the Stourbridge-Dudley main line. This latter route closed on 1 March 1930 but it is thought the KLR shut down exactly a month earlier – although press reports at the time suggest some sort of service might have lingered on for a few days.

Bibliography: *The Kinver Light Railway* (Locomotion Papers No 73) S. L. Swingle & K. Turner (The Oakwood Press, 2nd ed 1987) 0 85361 333 8

LANCASTER & DISTRICT TRAMWAYS
Authority: Lancaster and District Tramways Order 1889
Gauge: 4ft 8½in
Traction: Horse
Opened: 2 August 1890
Closed: 31 December 1921
System: Single line
Length: 4.3 miles
Stock: 14 dd
Livery: ?
Last Car: ?

Despite their being linked by both the MR and the LNWR, a horse tramway between Lancaster and Morecambe was promoted and constructed at the end of the 1880s by the Lancaster & District Tramways Co. Ltd. It was a single-track line commencing by the Royalty Theatre in Market Street, Morecambe, close to the MORECAMBE TRAMWAYS terminus there (though no

connection was ever put in), from where it ran roughly southeast through Torrisholme to Stonewell in north Lancaster, the actual terminus being the triangle formed by Cable Street, North Road and Chapel Street. The double-deck stock – hardly surprisingly – was built by Lancaster and the depot was on Lancaster Road, Morecambe. (Some of the cars were converted later to single-deck form.)

As a relatively short, simple system relying heavily on summer excursion traffic to Morecambe the line was never taken over by one of the large tramway groups for electrification, nor could it find the money for modernization itself and at the end of 1921, after failing to sell out to the local authorities, it closed quietly – another victim of the motor bus and one of the last horse tramways in the British Isles.

Bibliography: *The Lancaster and Morecambe Tramways* (Locomotion Papers No 95) S. Shuttleworth (The Oakwood Press, 1976)

Trade advertisement for George Law, the Kidderminster contractor responsible for constructing the Kidderminster & Stourport Tramways and the Kinver Light Railway, as well as others in the Black Country and elsewhere.

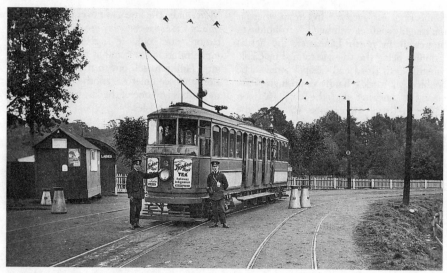

Postcard of Tividale single-decker No 6 at the Kinver terminus of the Kinver Light Railway with evidence of the line's regular milk transportation service. (Author's Collection)

LANCASTER CORPORATION TRAMWAY

Authority: Lancaster Corporation Act 1900
Gauge: 4ft 8½in
Traction: Overhead electric
Opened: 14 January 1903
Closed: 4 April 1930
System: Radial
Length: 2.99 miles
Stock: 12 dd
Livery: Chocolate & primrose
Last Car: No 8

Promoted and operated by Lancaster Corporation, the first section opened of this tiny system ran from the Boot & Shoe Inn in the southernmost district of Scotforth (then a separate village) north up Scotforth Road, Greaves Road and Thurnham Street to Dalton Square in the centre of the city whilst a second route ran back from Thurnham Street in a southeasterly direction down Quarry Road, Dale Street and Bowerham Road to the village of that name where it doubled back northwards up Golgotha Road to the Williamson Park Gates. Both lines were single-track (though part of the Bowerham route was almost immediately doubled) and the depot sited at the top of Thurnham Street. The original cars were ten Lancaster open-top double-deckers. Early in 1905 a third route was opened, this being a short line from Dalton Square westwards via Market Street and Meeting House Lane to terminate in County Street by the LNWR's Castle station; to augment the car fleet two more open-top vehicles were bought (Nos 11 and 12), this time from MV. From the beginning the tramway operated at a loss and planned lines never materialized; instead efforts were made to attract more passengers by fitting top covers to four of the cars in

1911 and to a further pair two years later while in 1917 an attempt at economy was made by converting No 11 into a one-man single-decker. The measure was judged a success and by July 1920 the remaining five open-toppers had been treated similarly. The following year the idea of purchasing the LANCASTER & DISTRICT TRAMWAYS was raised (see above) but came to nothing and in April 1922 the Castle station line was lifted. Two years later the Corporation began petrol bus operations (abandoning its electric buses first used in December 1916), in view of which it is surprising that the trams lasted as long as they did. The Bowerham route closed on 18 January 1930 and the Scotforth line that April.

Bibliography: as above

LEA BRIDGE, LEYTON & WALTHAMSTOW TRAMWAYS

Authority: Lea Bridge Leyton and Walthamstow Tramways Act 1881
Gauge: 4ft 8½in
Traction: Horse
Opened: 12 May 1883
Taken Over: 1 June 1905
System: Branching
Length: 4.8 miles
Stock: 8 sd?, 30 dd?
Livery: Brown & white to 1884? then red & white from 1889

Formed by a group of local dignitaries, the aim of the Lea Bridge, Leyton & Walthamstow Tramways Co. was to provide a means of easy access to the northern part of Epping Forest from London. The project got off to a shaky start – it was offered to the NORTH METROPOLITAN TRAMWAYS in October 1881 but turned down – but then

the financial situation seems to have improved and construction went ahead. The first section opened ran northeast as a single track from Lea Bridge, on the London/Leyton boundary, past the depot in Russell Road and along Lea Bridge Road (just inside the Leyton/Walthamstow boundary) to Whipps Cross on the edge of the forest, a distance of some 3 miles. The first cars were ten Merryweather vehicles, of which eight or nine were single-deckers, bearing the legend 'EPPING FOREST'.

A further ½ mile of line from Lea Bridge Road along Forest Rise to the Rising Sun was also built but not opened at this time, the contractors not having been paid for it, and the Company was wound up on 13 December 1884, services having ceased some months earlier (probably in October). Again it was offered unsuccessfully to the North Met and not until 1888 was it transferred to a new company, the Lea Bridge, Leyton & Walthamstow Tramways Co. Ltd (registered 19 October 1888). Twelve second-hand double-deckers were bought, possibly from the North Met and probably numbered 1-12, and housed in a new depot across Lea Bridge Road from the old one.

Services recommenced on 13 May 1889, now going all the way to the Rising Sun. Connections were however urgently needed to other systems to make the line pay and authorization was sought and obtained for these. (At the same time the Company was dissolved and the statutory Lea Bridge, Leyton & Walthamstow Tramways Co. incorporated.) On 31 March 1890 a 1½-mile branch was opened south from the Baker's Arms (by the depot) along Leyton Road to the GER station in Leyton where it terminated opposite Maud Road; about half this line was double-track. The system was completed on 21 or 22 April 1892 with the opening of a ½-mile westwards continuation (again, half double-track) of the line across Lea Bridge into London to terminate at the corner of Cornthwaite Road.

More cars were bought to cope with the increasing traffic, probably six second-hand ones numbered 37-42 (lower numbers being taken by horse buses) and a track-doubling programme started. In 1896 cars 51-54 were bought, again probably second-hand, followed in 1904 by Nos 55-60, ex-North Met double-deckers. (An associated concern, the Great Eastern London Suburban Tramways & Omnibus Co. Ltd, was set up in 1900 to take over the bus side of the business as it was illegal for the LBLWT Co. to run it as a statutory tramways company.) With the tramway's first 21 years about to be reached, complicated negotiations resulted in the 1905 takeover of the line by LEYTON DISTRICT COUNCIL, effective from 1 June. (The 748yd of line across the boundary in London was bought by the LCC for £8,040 and leased to Leyton who continued its horse service for another three years. In 1908 the lease was terminated and the line reconstructed for electric working, the horse cars finishing on 9 December and the electric cars commencing the next day.)

Bibliography: *The Tramways of East London* 'Rodinglea' (The Tramway & Light Railway Society/The Light Railway Transport League, 1967)

LEAMINGTON & WARWICK TRAMWAYS

Authority: Leamington and Warwick Tramways Order 1879
Gauge: 4ft 8½in
Traction: Horse
Opened: 21 November 1881
Closed: 16 May 1905?
System: Single line
Length: 3 miles
Stock: 16 dd
Livery: Maroon & cream
Last Car: ?

The line linking the prosperous twin towns of its title was constructed by the Leamington & Warwick Tramways & Omnibus Co. Ltd, a company registered on 18 February 1880, after the original promoters had pulled out having secured an 1872 Order. Construction began in July 1881 and the single-track tramway opened that November with two open-top BM cars followed shortly by two from Metropolitan, these all being numbered 1-4. In 1882 a second-hand BIRMINGHAM & DISTRICT car was purchased (No 5?) together with two more Metropolitan cars. (Like all the line's trams these were open-top double-deckers). In 1895 three Brush cars were ordered to replace older vehicles and another three the following year. (Whether these cars carried on the number sequence or took vacated numbers is not known.) In 1899 three more Metropolitan cars were purchased which, after scrappings, brought the fleet total to eight, where it stayed until closure.

The tramway ran from close to Lord Leicester's Hospital, straight along Warwick High Street and Jury Street (one of the town's principal thoroughfares), through the ancient Eastgate (for the Castle) and on down the slope of Smith Street into St John's (close to the GWR station) and the suburb of Coten End where the small depot was situated. From here it carried on along Emscote Road, under the railway line and over the Grand Union Canal as it continued in a straight, northeasterly direction through the intermediate district of Milverton as far as Warwick Street

in Leamington Spa where it made a sharp turn to the south to descend the length of The Parade, the town's principal thoroughfare, to reach the railway station (shared between the GWR and the LNWR) via Spencer Street. The only layout change later made was the bypassing of the narrow Eastgate archway with a short loop on the south side just after the line opened. In 1884 the Company began running horse brakes on excursions to Coventry and Stratford-on-Avon but sold them in 1894. Three years later the BET approached the Company proposing electrification and in 1899 made an amicable takeover. Two years later, after successful negotiations with the local authorities, the necessary powers had been obtained for the rebuilding.

In 1902 the LWT Co. changed its name to the Leamington & Warwick Electrical Co. Ltd (it intended to supply power to the area as well as operating the tramway) and in 1905 began reconstruction work. The actual closure date is uncertain: Company records say February but printed memorial cards give 16 May, possibly referring to a rump service provided before a temporary brake and horse-bus service took over until the new line opened. Two cars were rescued in 1984 from a local country estate where they had been built into a pair of cottages and, after being displayed at the Birmingham Railway Museum for several years, are now undergoing restoration.

Bibliography: *The Leamington & Warwick Tramways* (Locomotion Papers No 112) S. L. Swingle & K. Turner (The Oakwood Press, 1978)

LEAMINGTON & WARWICK ELECTRIC TRAMWAY

Authority: Warwick Tramways Order 1900; Leamington Tramways Order 1901
Gauge: 3ft 6in
Traction: Overhead electric
Opened: 12 July 1905
Closed: 16 August 1930
System: Single line
Length: 3 miles
Stock: 12 dd
Livery: Dark green & cream
Last Car: ?

The reconstructed LEAMINGTON & WARWICK TRAMWAYS (see above) re-opened in July 1905 with twelve open-top double-deck cars of which Nos 1-6 were new Brush vehicles and Nos 7-12 were 1901 Brush cars purchased from TAUNTON (another BET subsidiary) when that system was reconstructed; one of this latter batch – possibly No 11 – was converted to a scrubber car upon arrival. The mainly double-track line adhered faithfully to the horse tramway route though now used the West Midlands 'standard' electric tramway gauge of 3ft 6in. The depot and power station were sited to the south of Emscote Road with the neighbouring Grand Union Canal bringing in fuel and the River Avon providing cooling water.

Ominously, the summer of 1905 also saw the introduction of bus competition along the tramway's route and, although the Company fought back with its own feeder bus service, the writing was on the wall for the line right from the start. On the last day of 1912 the BET sold its interest in the Company to a BB offshoot, the Tramways,

In memoriam postcards were routinely issued during the late Victorian and Edwardian era to mourn the closure of a tramway or, in the case of this Leamington & Warwick example, to mark the changeover to electric traction. (Author's Collection)

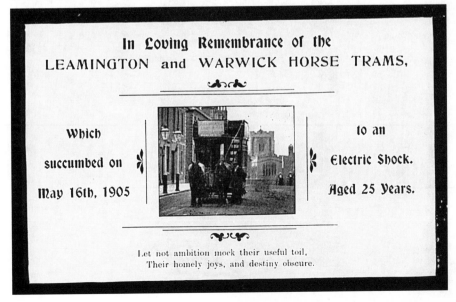

In Loving Remembrance of the
LEAMINGTON and WARWICK HORSE TRAMS,

Which succumbed on May 16th, 1905

to an Electric Shock.

Aged 25 Years.

Let not ambition mock their useful toil,
Their homely joys, and destiny obscure.

Light & Power Co. Ltd – but kept the buses.

The tramway acquired its last car in 1921: an EE open-topper ex-CHELTENHAM (another BB concern); this was numbered 14 on the L&W, the number 13 being avoided presumably for superstitious reasons. That year also saw the TLP Co. change its name to the Midland Counties Electric Supply Co. and in 1928 it began running buses, deciding shortly after to abandon the tramway side of its operations.

All the cars were broken up after the 1930 closure, with the exception of No 7 which had been scrapped following an accident in 1916. It had run down the slope of Warwick High Street unattended and being thrown off the curve round the Eastgate arch and through the wall of the Castle Arms on the corner. The works car was sold to another BB tramway, the Llandudno & Colwyn Bay Electric Railway in Wales.

Bibliography: as above

LEEDS TRAMWAYS
Authority: Leeds Tramways Order 1871
Gauge: 4ft 8½in
Traction: Horse, steam
Opened: 16 September 1871
Taken Over: 2 February 1894
System: Radial
Length: 14.16 miles
Stock: 37 sd, 40 dd horse; 32 locos, 24 dd steam
Livery: Chocolate & white/primrose

Owned by the Leeds Tramways Co. and municipalized in 1894, the Leeds system grew to be the largest in Yorkshire. The first route opened ran from Boar Lane in the town centre (Leeds did not become a city until 1893) via Park Row, Cookridge Street and Woodhouse Lane to the Oak Inn at Headingley, 3 miles away. Roughly half the line was double-track and the first cars Starbuck double-deckers Nos 1-4, each hauled by three horses.

The second route, northeast from Boar Lane up Wellington Street to the Cardigan Arms on Kirstall Road, opened on 1 April 1872 and was extended on 18 May along Commercial Road as far as Kirkstall village (3 miles), terminating by the Star & Garter. Three more routes followed in 1874 – north to Meanwood Road and Chapeltown, east to York Road via Marsh Lane and southeast across the River Aire to Hunslet via the Hunslet Road – whilst the Headingley line was extended the following year to the Three Horse Shoes with further openings in 1878-79, by which time steam traction was about to be introduced after successful trials. Three Kitson locomotives (Nos 1-3) were hired in 1880 and used to haul double-deck horse cars until 1882-83 when they were purchased together with trailers from Ashbury (Eades reversible No 55) and Starbuck (Nos 59 and 60).

During 1883-84 two Green locos (Nos 1 and 2) were hired and from then until 1890 25 more Green and Kitson locos (Nos 4-28) were bought along with another 21 Starbuck, Ashbury and Milnes trailers. Meanwhile the horse car fleet was not neglected as the system expanded again in the later 1880s and early 1890s with 77 cars (by Stephensons, Starbuck, Ashbury, Milnes and the Company itself) operating from six depots. By this time LEEDS CORPORATION was running its own electric tramcars (see below) and the Company was perfectly willing to sell out after its initial 21 years were up. The only problem was agreeing a price, this being fixed by arbitration at £112,225 in 1893 with the transfer of the whole concern taking place the following year.

Bibliography: *Leeds Transport Vol 1: 1830 to 1902* J. Soper (The Leeds Transport Historical Society, 1985) 0 951028 00 6
Leeds: a history of its tramways Noel Proudlock (J. N. D. Proudlock, Leeds, 1991) 0 951718 50 9

LEEDS CITY TRAMWAYS
Authority: Leeds Corporation Tramways Order 1888
Gauge: 4ft 8½in
Traction: Overhead electric, horse, steam
Opened: 11 November 1891
Closed: 7 November 1959
System: Radial network
Length: 72.05 miles
Stock: 31 sd, 36 dd horse; 27 locos, 24 dd steam; 10 sd, 869 dd electric
Livery: Blue & ivory to 1901, chocolate, yellow & white to 1925, blue & cream to 1950, then crimson & cream
Last Car: No 160

In 1889 Leeds Corporation constructed a line off Chapeltown Road at Sheepscar (just north of the junction with the LEEDS TRAMWAYS' Meanwood Road line) running northeast along Roundhay Road to the gates of Roundhay Park (opened 1873) and tried to interest the Leeds Tramways Co. in working it, though it was not until 15 May 1891 that a proper (steam) service was started. By then though the Company was nearing the end of its existence and the Corporation had already decided to electrify the line. This was done that same year by the Thomson-Houston International Co. of America, working the line on concession from the Corporation with six Stephenson single-deck cars, licence numbers 75-80, collecting current from an overhead wire. Its official opening on 29 October 1891 made it the first street tramway to collect its current solely in this fashion in the whole of Europe.

Public services began on 11 November 1891 and eight days later a second route opened, from midway along Roundhay Road south via Harehills Road (and depot) to Beckett Street. Three years later the Corporation took over the existing horse and steam tramways (see above) in order to electrify them. While the conversion was still being planned however more horse and steam routes were opened, to help work

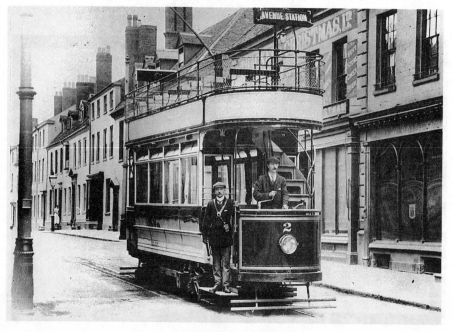

Leamington & Warwick new electric car No 2 at the Warwick terminus about to depart on its short journey to Leamington railway station. (Lens of Sutton)

which locos 29 and 30 were bought in 1897 from Greens and, between 1897 and 1899, single-deck horse cars 111-120 and double-deckers 50, 78, 93-97 and 105-110 were bought from Milnes.

On 31 July 1896 the Thomson-Houston concession ended and the electric cars stopped running, though on 2 August the following year they were re-introduced by the Corporation and now ran all the way through to Kirkstall Abbey. Other routes were similarly converted with the last horse services (on Whitehall Road) ending on 13 October 1901 and the last steam services (on Armley Road) on 1 April following. The system continued to expand during succeeding decades right up to the end of the 1940s with the completion on 28 August 1949 of a long southern loop to Middleton Park and back – much of it on a private right of way – matching the long northern loop past Roundhay Park and back via Moorstown and Chapeltown.

Inevitably, this expansion was accompanied by the occasional abandonment of unprofitable routes, the first to go (on 15 June 1922) being a short line to the Cattle Market from City Square southwest across the River Aire via Whitehall Road. The system was also well-connected with its neighbours with through running over YORKSHIRE (WEST RIDING) tracks south to Rothwell via Hunslet commencing on 1 June 1905 whilst on 9 June 1909 through running to BRADFORD began. In this latter case, where the two systems met at Stanningley a tapering section of track was laid to connect the 4ft 8½in and 4ft gauge tramways with each system equipping ten cars with specially-designed sliding axle sleeves to enable them to run on either gauge lines.

Corporation bus services began on 31 March 1906 and were joined on 21 June 1911 by trolleybuses; the Corporation kept faith with the tramways though as the long expansion and improvement programmes indicate. (The trolleybuses were replaced by motorbuses during the late 1920s after they had brought about the closure of the Whitehall Road route.)

The next route closure did not come for another ten years when, on 31 May 1932, the YWD closed its Rothwell branch, whereupon the Corporation services were cut back to Thwaite Gate, Hunslet, on the city boundary. More closures followed every year from 1934 to 1938 with only World War II temporarily halting the abandonments. In 1947 they recommenced with the very last route to go being that from the Corn Exchange in the city centre out along York Road to Crossgates, plus its branch to Templenewsam Park.

From the very beginning the Leeds car

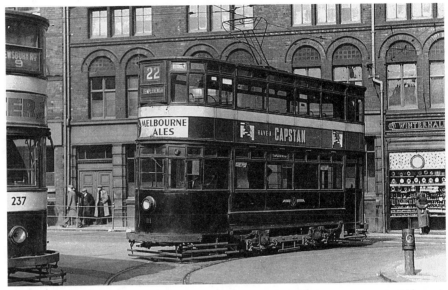

This shot of Leeds City double-deckers 111 and 237 shows just how tight a curve a tramcar could negotiate. Note also Leeds' distinctive pattern of current collector. (Lens of Sutton)

fleet reflected the latest development in tramcar design. In all, the Corporation operated nearly nine hundred electric cars, including the original six Stephenson vehicles which were bought in 1898, used as trailers and two years later converted into salt cars. The first Corporation-owned cars were Nos 1-25, Milnes open-top double-deckers of 1897 which were followed by a succession of new cars to 1953 from a number of manufacturers (including many built by the Corporation itself). These are listed below and, unless decribed otherwise, were double-deck vehicles:

Nos 85, 90, 133-182: Brush open-toppers of 1899

Nos 98-103, 128-132: ditto trailers of 1897, motorized 1900

Nos 44, 46, 55, 79, 83: Brush open-toppers of 1900 (originally built for LIVERPOOL)

No 49: Brush single-decker of 1900

No 52: Brush bogie open-topper of 1900

Nos 183-282: DK open-toppers of 1901

Nos 27-32, 34, 39, 40, 42, 43, 45, 47, 48, 50, 51, 55-58, 67-70, 74-78, 80, 82, 84, 86, 87, 91-97, 104-113: Brush open-toppers of 1902

General route map of the Leeds City Tramways, from the 1904 Manual of Electrical Undertakings.

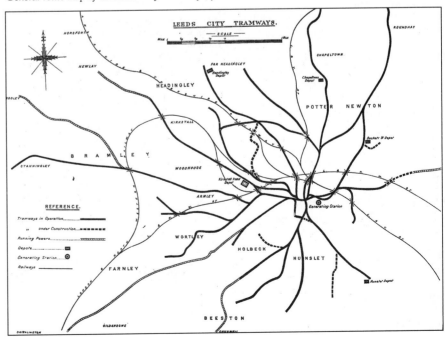

Nos 26, 33, 35, 41, 53, 54, 59-66, 71-73, 81, 88, 89, 114, 127: Brush top-covered cars of 1904

Nos 115-126, 283-369: Corporation balcony cars of 1908-23

Nos 370-405: Corporation enclosed cars of 1923-26, No 400 being the prototype for:

Nos 76-150: EE enclosed 'Chamberlains' (named after the then General Manager)

Nos 1-75: Brush ditto of 1926-27

Nos 411-445: Corporation ditto of 1926-27

Nos 406-410: Corporation enclosed cars of 1928

Nos 151-154: Corporation ditto of 1930

Nos 155-254: Brush ditto of 1931-32

No 255: Brush experimental high speed enclosed bogie car of 1933

Nos 256-271: Brush and EE ditto of 1935

Nos 272-274: Corporation streamlined cars of 1935

No 104: Corporation replacement 'Austerity' enclosed car of 1943

No 276: Corporation protoype enclosed car of 1948

Nos 601, 602: Chas. H. Roe Ltd of Leeds bogie single-deckers of 1953

Many of the above cars differed within their batches as well as being top-covered or otherwise modified and modernized during their lifetime.

Second-hand cars bought by Leeds were:

Nos 446-477: ex-HULL enclosed double-deckers bought 1942

Nos 478-487: ditto 1945

Nos 281-287: ex-MANCHESTER 'Pilchers' bought 1946-49

Nos 290-300: ex-SOUTHAMPTON enclosed double-deckers bought 1949-50

No 301: ex-LONDON TRANSPORT 'Bluebird' bought 1951

Nos 501-590: ex-LONDON TRANSPORT enclosed bogie double-deckers bought 1949-52

No 600: ex-SUNDERLAND bogie single-decker bought 1944, numbered 288 but not used in service until 1953 when it was rebuilt as a centre-exit car. It is now preserved at the National Tramway Museum, Crich, along with Nos 180, 345, 399, 602 and 301 (this last car restored as No 1 of London Transport).

Bibliography: as above

LEICESTER TRAMWAYS

Authority: Leicester Tramways Order 1873
Gauge: 4ft 8½in
Traction: Horse
Opened: 24 December 1874
Taken Over: 1 July 1901
System: Radial
Length: 12.06 miles
Stock: 46+ sd & dd?
Livery: Various, then biscuit & grey

Operated by the Leicester Tramways Co. Ltd, services in the city began with three single-deck cars working a single route northwards from the central Clock Tower out along Belgrave Gate, Belgrave Road and Loughborough Road to the Folly Inn, Belgrave, close to the depot. Two further routes were added in 1875: eastwards along Humberstone Gate and Humberstone Road as far as Ash Street and southeast along London Road to Victoria Park Road. In 1878 the London Road route was extended another mile to Knighton Drive and a southerly route opened down Aylestone Road to the Grace Road cricket ground; these were joined by a short northern route from the Clock Tower up Churchgate to Woodgate. The last section added was an extension of about a mile along Humberstone Road into Uppingham Road with the new terminus by the GNR station there. Details of the car fleet are unfortunately very sketchy but it appears that the Company operated at least 46 tramcars (the 1886 fleet maximum) of at least ten different designs including the original three single-deckers (of which two were later converted to double-deck form). At the end of the 19th century the Corporation decided to purchase, electrify and extend the horse system (see below) and in 1897 obtained the necessary authority to operate its own lines, paying £110,210 for the concern (including 39 cars and 30 horse buses) four years later.

Bibliography: *Tramcars in Leicester* M. S. W. Pearson (The National Tramway Museum, Crich 1988) 0 949007 02 1

LEICESTER CORPORATION TRAMWAYS

Authority: Leicester Corporation Act 1897
Gauge: 4ft 8½in
Traction: Horse/overhead electric
Took Over: 1 July 1901
Closed: 9 November 1949
System: Radial network
Length: 22.74 miles
Stock: 43 sd & dd horse; 178 dd electric
Livery: Dark crimson lake & cream to 1937, then maroon & cream
Last Car: No 58

After its takeover of the horse system (see above) Leicester Corporation worked it whilst the process of track relaying and installing the electric overhead went on throughout the next two years; indeed, four second-hand cars (ex-NOTTINGHAM) were purchased to augment the ageing fleet. Electric services began on 18 May 1904 over the refurbished Belgrave Road and London Road routes, plus a link from the latter via Melbourne Road to Humberstone Road and

a new route south to Clarendon Park via London Road.

Services were worked by cars 1-59, ERTCW open-toppers. On 17 July 1904 a line westwards from the Clock Tower along the High Street was opened; this divided at the end of Braunston Gate with one route carrying on along Hinckley Road to Western Park and the other turning southwards down the Narborough Road. At the same time a northern branch off Hinckley Road via Fosse Road led back to the High Street in a circle via Woodgate and Great Central Street. These routes were followed on 5 September by the substitution of electric trams for horse cars on the Aylestone route and on 1 November by the rest of the Humberstone Road route (so ending the horse car service) with another link opening from Humberstone Road to London Road, this time down East Park Road. This was followed at the end of the month by the opening of a northwestern line from the High Street via Great Central Street and Woodgate to Groby Road. The last route built during this period was opened on 8 June 1905 and continued on from the end of Belgrave Road (where Loughborough Road turned off) to run up Melton Road.

To help work the new lines another 40 ERTCW open-toppers (Nos 60-99) were bought in 1904, plus 21 balcony cars (Nos 101-121) and 21 open-toppers (Nos 122-141) a year later, all from UEC. Between 1912 and 1927 all the open cars were fitted with top covers (and most fully enclosed later). The number 100 was taken by a works car but in 1912 it was renumbered 141 with No 137 becoming No 100 and the former 141 becoming 137; then in 1913 UEC supplied another ten balcony cars (Nos 141-150) and Brush Nos 151-160 likewise a year later (which meant that works car 141 became 151 and 161 in rapid succession, finally ending its days as No 179!) On 15 September 1915 a link between Fosse Road and Branstonegate via King Richard's Road was opened, followed in September 1922 by a route from Clarendon Park back to the city centre along Welford Road to Aylestone Road. In June 1924 a link was opened between Groby Road and Belgrave Road via Blackbird Road and Abbey Park Road and, in March 1927, this was followed by a short branch off Humberstone Road near the terminus south down Coleman Road to complete the system. Meanwhile the car fleet had been completed with the 1920 construction at Leicester of six balcony cars (Nos 161-166) and the purchase of twelve similar vehicles (Nos 167-178) from UEC. Virtually the whole system was double-track (the principal exception being the Coleman Road branch) and the main depot was in Abbey Park Road.

Cutbacks began in 1933 when, on 13 December, the Melbourne Road route closed, followed on 23 October 1938 by the Coleman Road branch and on 2 April 1939 by the King Richard's Road link. World War II provided a temporary breathing space for the tramways but after it was over the closures began again: the Aylestone route on 5 January 1947 and on 15 July Fosse Road. One by one the others followed during 1948 and 1949, the last to go being the Humberstone Road route. Just one car, No 76, survives having been rescued from Yorkshire long after it was sold and can now be seen at the National Tramway Museum at Crich.

Bibliography: as above

LEYTON DISTRICT COUNCIL TRAMWAYS

Authority: Leyton Urban District Council Act 1898
Gauge: 4ft 8½in
Traction: Horse, overhead electric
Opened: 1 June 1905
Taken Over: 1 July 1921
System: Network
Length: 9.52 miles
Stock: 31? horse; 60 dd electric
Livery: Primrose and green electric

The first (horse) trams in Leyton were operated in the 1870s by the NORTH METROPOLITAN TRAMWAYS Co. of LONDON who had a standard gauge line from Stratford running north up Leytonstone High Road from West Ham into Leyton as far as the Green Man Hotel at Leytonstone. Then, in 1890-92, the LEA BRIDGE, LEYTON & WALTHAMSTOW TRAMWAYS Co. Ltd opened a standard gauge single-track line from Cornthwaite Road in Clapton, Hackney, northeastwards along Lea Bridge Road, crossing the borough boundary formed by the River Lea and on to the Baker's Arms at the junction with Leyton Green High Street. Beyond here it was already open for ¾ mile along Lea Bridge Road to its junction with Whipps Cross Road then along Forest Rise and Woodford New Road to the Rising Sun Inn in Epping Forest. A branch opened in 1890 ran from the Baker's Arms south down the High Street to Leyton station (GER).

By the end of the 19th century Leyton UDC had obtained powers to operate its own horse or mechanical tramways and in 1904, under the Leyton Urban District Council Act of that year, electric ones. On 1 June 1905 it purchased the LBLWT Co.'s lines within its boundaries, together with 28 cars and the depot by the Baker's Arms. The line was promptly rebuilt (and doubled) and a

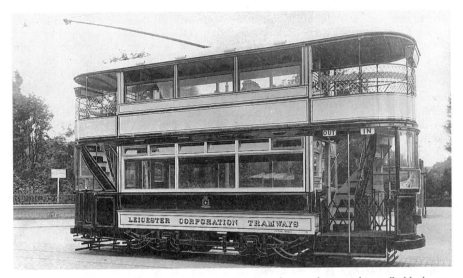
One of Leicester Corporation's balcony cars as new in pristine livery and apparently unsullied by human hand. (Author's Collection)

connection made to the WALTHAMSTOW system at the Baker's Arms.

The North Met line within the borough was taken over on 1 June 1906 as soon as its lease ran out, together with 15 cars (which the Council never used), and again promptly relaid (mainly with double tracks) and extended on north from the Green Man up Whipps Cross Road to meet the Lea Bridge Road line. At the same time the Leyton station branch was extended south down Leyton High Road, then east along Crownfield Road by the borough boundary to the Thatched House where it joined the Leytonstone High Road line. Three ex-

LONDON COUNTY COUNCIL cars were bought to work this line in the short term. Finally, an eastern extension of the branch from the Thatched House was laid along Cannhall Road and Dames Road to the boundary at Vansittart Road but this was never worked by horse cars, being without a service until 1 December 1906 when electric working started (with through running from WEST HAM).

The electric services began with MV top-covered cars Nos 11-50 based on a new depot by the Baker's Arms. (The numbers 1-10 were used for the slimmed-down fleet of horse cars used on the Hackney through

Comic Edwardian postcard of a 'tram jam' in the centre of Leicester – an ironic foretaste of today's car-dominated streets.

service, that portion of the LBLW line not having been converted.) The system was now complete with some 6 miles of former horse lines and 3 miles of new routes. Twenty similar MV cars (Nos 51-70) were ordered in 1907 to cope with demand. The last horse tram ran on 9 December 1908 and through running with the LCC commenced, followed ten days later by through running from Vansittart Road south over West Ham metals via Forest Road and Woodford Road, through Forest Gate to Woodgrange Road. Through running to Chingford via Walthamstow began on 8 October the following year and in 1910 cars 31-70 were fitted with plough carriers for conduit working over the LCC's tracks beyond Clapton. By the end of World War I though, both track and car fleet were in very poor shape and in 1921 the LCC was forced to take over the tramway.

Bibliography: *The Tramways of East London* 'Rodinglea' (The Tramway & Light Railway Society/The Light Railway Transport League, 1967)

LINCOLN TRAMWAY
Authority: Lincolnshire Tramways Order 1881
Gauge: 3ft 6in
Traction: Horse
Opened: 8 September 1882
Closed: 22 July 1905
System: Single line
Length: 1.84 miles
Stock: 10 sd
Livery: Dark red & cream?
Last Car: ?

Although authorized to construct a number of routes in the city, the Lincoln Tramway Co. Ltd built and operated just one single-track line running southwards from St Benedict's Church in the city centre down the High Street, past the Manchester Sheffield & Lincolnshire Railway (later the GCR) station, and along the Newark Road to the Gatehouse Hotel in Bracebridge (just past the depot). It seems the tramway settled down to an uneventful life but by the end of the decade modernization was already being mooted by the City Council as part of an overall improvement in the public transport facilities of a growing city. Accordingly, in the early years of the 20th century, purchase and reconstruction of the old line as part of a larger electric system was agreed upon (see below) and in July 1904 the Council paid £10,488 for the line, closing it a year later. After the closure the tramway's seven surviving cars were sold off. In all the car fleet totalled ten single-deckers with Ashbury vehicles 1 and 2 being purchased in 1882, Nos 3 and 4 in 1883, No 5 in 1884 and

No 6 in 1885; these were followed in 1899 (probably as replacement vehicles) by Nos 7 and 8 of unknown make, possibly bought from GRAVESEND. Finally, in 1900 two Falcon cars (Nos 9 and 10) were acquired, again probably as replacements for older vehicles.

CITY OF LINCOLN TRAMWAYS
Authority: Lincoln Corporation (Tramways Etc.) Act 1900
Gauge: 4ft 8½in
Traction: Stud/overhead electric
Opened: 23 November 1905
Closed: 4 March 1929
System: Single line
Length: 1.84 miles
Stock: 13 dd
Livery: Pale green & cream
Last Car: No 6

The new Lincoln line was laid by William Griffiths & Co. Ltd of Ilford, Essex, and utilized the Griffiths Bedell stud surface contact system for supplying power to the cars of which eight were ordered from Brush for the opening (Nos 1-6 being open-top vehicles and Nos 7 and 8 balcony cars). The route was the same as for the horse line (see above) and was half single-track and half (the central portion) double; the depot was situated on the site of the old horse car shed and stables and although tentative proposals were made to extend the tramway northwards and eastwards nothing ever came of them. As elsewhere, the stud system did not prove very satisfactory – gas leaking into the cable conduits linking the studs was one problem – and with proper maintenance difficult during World War I it was decided to switch to a more conventional overhead system of supply. This work was carried out at

the end of 1919 by DK but just ten years later the line was closed, the Council having built up a replacement bus fleet during that decade. By the time of the abandonment the car fleet had grown to thirteen with the purchase in 1918 of GRIMSBY horse cars Nos 32 and 33 (they retained their old numbers at Lincoln) for use as trailers (until 1921) and in 1919 of three EE balcony cars (Nos 9-11) which, in 1929, were sold to PRESTON.

LIVERPOOL: OLD SWAN TRAMWAY
Authority: Turnpike Trust permission
Gauge: 4ft 8½in*
Traction: Horse
Opened: 2 July 1861
Closed: May 1862?
System: Single line
Length: c1.5 miles
Stock: 1 dd?
Livery: ?
Last Car: ?

The British street tramway was born on Merseyside but, as with many such births, it is difficult to put a precise date on the event. Rather, a series of events marked the evolution of the railway proper into the tramway proper. One of these events was undoubtedly the construction of G. F. Train's street railway just across the Mersey from Liverpool in BIRKENHEAD in 1860, though a year earlier a significant development in the genesis of the tramway had occurred in Liverpool.

The story actually begins in 1856 when, on 7 May of that year, William Joseph Curtis of London was granted Patent number 1071 in respect of a device to be fitted to the wheels of horse-drawn vehicles and

Liverpool's Last Car, complete with parallel procession of cars and a motorcycle escort. (Author's Collection)

Liverpool 'Green Goddess' No 869 of 1936 (later Glasgow Corporation 1055) preserved at the National Tramway Museum, Crich. (Author)

controlled by the driver which enabled the wheels to run plain (on roads) or flanged (on railway tracks). In 1859 he began running horse buses thus equipped along the paved double tracks of the Line of Docks Railway in Liverpool (so called because it ran from Brunswick Dock in the south to Huskisson Dock in the north) used to move wagons in and out of the docks all along that side of the river. The only problem was that other bus operators pirated his invention, introducing rival services, and Curtis' buses lasted only a few months.

Two of Curtis' main rivals were William and Daniel Busby who, inspired by Train's pioneering line across the river, constructed their own street railway from the Old Swan westwards along the Liverpool–Prescot road to the Liverpool boundary at Fairfield, a distance of just under 1½ miles. Permission for the line was given by the Liverpool & Prescot Turnpike Trust and the single track down the centre of the road was laid with 4in-wide sleepered plate rails with a slightly convex running surface between two low flanges. The gauge was given as 4ft 8½in but exactly how this was measured is uncertain.

Services were apparently worked by an ornate open-top double-deck car built by Oldbury (at a cost of £200) housed in the Busbys' horse bus stables at the Old Swan, though possibly one or more converted buses were also used. The line was not a success though – probably because of the type of rails used and its poor construction – and at the end of May 1862 the Turnpike Trustees began to lift it, the cost of this being borne by the operators, the Liverpool Road & Railway Omnibus Co. (registered 14 May 1860). By the beginning of September the whole track had been taken up, so ending the life of the city's first genuine tramway. The Company continued in the bus business though until 1876 when it merged with the LIVERPOOL TRAMWAYS Co. (see below). As for the Line of Docks special buses, these continued to run until at least 1872 – and possibly for another 20 years after that.

Bibliography: *Liverpool Transport Vol 1: 1830-1900* J. B. Horne & T. B. Maund (The Light Railway Transport League, 1975) 0 900433 53 1

LIVERPOOL TRAMWAYS
Authority: Liverpool Tramways Act 1868
Gauge: 4ft 8½in
Traction: Horse
Opened: 1 November 1869

Taken Over: 1 January 1897
System: Radial network
Length: 42.78 miles
Stock: 300+ dd?
Livery: Maroon/crimson lake & white/cream; route colour added c1884

Following the failure of the OLD SWAN TRAMWAY (see above) a second attempt to provide Liverpool with a tramway system was made a few years later with the registration on 12 December 1865 of the Liverpool Tramways Co. Ltd. Nothing concrete happened though until 1868 when an empowering Act was obtained and a new Liverpool Tramways Co. incorporated.

The 1868 Act authorized the construction of a north–south line across the city plus a circular system in the city centre (which became known as the Inner Circle). Construction began in May 1869 with the Inner Circle and the line south to Dingle via Renshaw Street, Great George Street and Park Road (just over 3¼ miles in total) opening that November; the 2½-mile northern route to Walton via Byrom Street, Scotland Road, Kirkdale Road and Walton Road opened 1 September following. Exactly one year later the Dingle route was extended just over a mile along Aigburth Road through Toxteth Park to Aigburth Vale. (The depot had already been built on this section, in Tramway Road off Aigburth Road.)

In 1869 the Liverpool Road & Railway Omnibus Co. (see above) tried to promote a

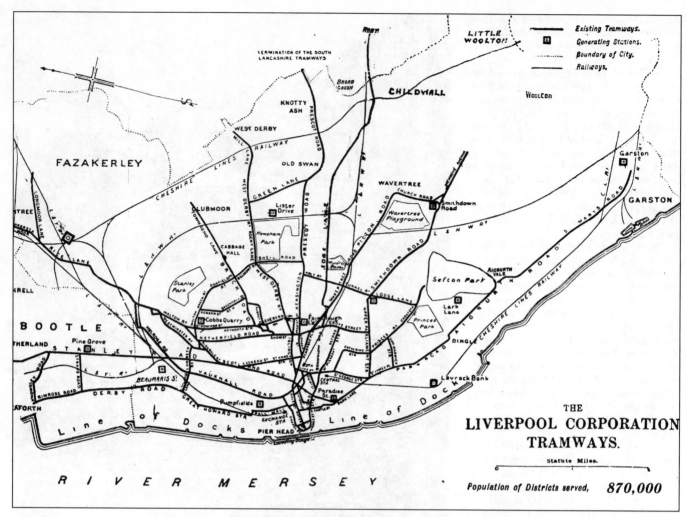

Map of Liverpool Corporation Tramways from the 1920-21 Manual of Electrical Undertakings.

tramways Bill of its own but was opposed by Liverpool Corporation. The following year it accordingly decided to try to join forces with the LT Co., and on 8 February 1871 a new concern, the Liverpool Omnibus & Tramways Co. Ltd was registered, the LRR Co. being wound up a year later. In February 1876 the two businesses merged to form the Liverpool United Tramways & Omnibus Co. in the hope of making the tramway more of financial success.

The original rails used had very wide side grooves but from 1877 onwards these were replaced with centre-grooved ones and the cars fitted gradually with centre-flanged wheels which could run on both types of track. Always concerned about the condition of the tramway, the Corporation purchased it under the provisions of the Liverpool Tramways (Purchase) Act 1872 on 1 January 1880 for the sum of £30,000 and leased it back to the Company until the end of 1896. By this time the system had expanded considerably with lines extending

north, east and south beyond the city limits to Bootle, West Derby and Wavertree and west from the centre to the Pier Head. The tramway's financial position had now improved greatly with receipts overtaking those from the buses in 1882, despite a Company programme of buying-out rival operators.

Detailed information regarding the cars is lacking. Services began with 16 open-toppers (from an initial order of 24) from Starbuck, possibly assembled from components supplied by Stephensons. By June 1880 30 cars were at work with later vehicles being supplied by Starbuck and Ashbury (Eades reversible cars). From 1883 onwards the Company built its own cars – again all double-deckers – and by the time of the Corporation's purchase of the remainder of the system in 1896 for £567,375 there were 281 in service, though how many had been withdrawn is not known. Trials were also conducted with steam (1879), cable (1883) and compressed air vehicles (1884-86).

Bibliography: as above

LIVERPOOL CORPORATION TRAMWAYS

Authority: Liverpool Tramways Transfer Act 1897
Gauge: 4ft 8½in
Traction: Horse, overhead electric
Took Over: 1 January 1897
Closed: 14 September 1957
System: Radial network
Length: 97.37 miles
Stock: 281 dd horse; 45 sd, 1,260 dd electric
Livery: Crimson lake & cream to 1933, then privet green & ivory
Last Car: No 293

In November 1895 Liverpool's boundaries were enlarged to include areas previously in neighbouring authorities served by the Liverpool United Tramways & Omnibus Co. (see above); the Corporation took over the powers of the Company in those areas (though Bootle Corporation was empowered by Liverpool's 1897 Act to convert the lines in its borough and lease them to Liverpool). In all, the Corporation acquired 281 horse cars, 69 miles of track in Liverpool, 6 in Bootle and ¾ mile in Litherland on a total of 17 routes.

The first electric route, to Dingle via Park Road, was opened on 16 November 1898 and from then on the other lines were converted quickly so that by October 1901 only one horse car was left in service (until 25 August 1903) on a shuttle working from the boundary at Linacre to Litherland Canal Bridge. The other horse cars were scrapped as they were withdrawn with the exception of seven which were sold to Aberdeen Corporation in 1900 and three which went to WALLASEY a year later.

The system continued to expand over the decades leading up to the outbreak of World War II with lines extending eventually as far as Bootle, Litherland, Aintree, Fazakerley and Kirkby in the north and Garston and Woolton in the south. Eastwards, the system was connected in 1902 with that of ST HELENS via Knotty Ash and the LIVERPOOL & PRESCOT LIGHT RAILWAY (see below) which, in 1919, was taken over by Liverpool. (This was the system's only connection with a neighbouring tramway but through it a link was made with the rest of the south Lancashire network.) Modernization came in the 1930s and 1940s when several outlying routes were opened (the final extension, to Kirkby, being on 12 April 1944), mainly on sections of reserved track which came to account for a third of Liverpool's route mileage. At the end of World War II though the Corporation decided to replace the trams – many of them of relatively modern design and construction – with buses, a programme hastened along by the destruction of 66 cars in a fire on 7 November 1947 at Green Lane Depot.

Piecemeal route closures began in June 1948 with services and cars withdrawn gradually over the next nine years, the last day of operation seeing the closing of the routes from the Pier Head to Bowring Park and from Castle Street to Page Moss Avenue.

The first electric cars introduced by the Corporation were Nos 400-429, single-deck motor cars (even numbers) and trailers (odd numbers) of 1898 from W. C. F. Busch of Eimsbuttel, Hamburg. These were all withdrawn by 1901 and broken up in 1914 (with the exception of some converted into works cars). These were joined in 1898 by Nos 432-446, Brill single-deck bogie vehicles later renumbered 6-20 of which Nos 6, 8 and 12 were rebuilt as double-deckers 1900-01 to survive until 1933 whilst the others were scrapped in the early 1920s. Thereafter the

car fleet grew as follows (with later numbers in brackets):
Nos 447-458 (21-32): Milnes open-toppers of 1899
Nos 459-463 (43-47): Brush ditto
Nos 464-468: Brush ditto but never paid for and returned (then delivered to LEEDS)
Nos 469-478 (33-42), 54-133, 141: ERTCW ditto of 1899-1900
Nos 479-484 (48-53): Corporation ditto of 1899
Nos 1-4, 134-140: Corporation open-toppers of 1899-1900 (known as 'Bellamys' after the then General Manager)
No 5: Corporation open-topper of 1901
Nos 142-441: ERTCW 'Bellamys' of 1900-01
Nos 442-447: Corporation ditto but top-covered of 1902-03
Nos 448-452: ERTCW ditto but open-topped of 1902-03
Nos 453-477: ditto but top-covered
Nos 478-483: Corporation ditto but open-topped of 1902-03
Nos 1-4, 484-570: ditto but top-covered of 1907-12
No 571: UEC top-covered car of 1912
No 572: UEC enclosed bogie car of 1912
Nos 573-576: Corporation 1st class 'Bellamys' of 1913
No 44: Corporation top-covered 'Exhibition' car of 1914
Nos 577-599: Corporation top-covered cars of 1913-15
Nos 600-605: ditto of 1919-20
Nos 609-633: EE ditto of 1919-20
Nos 606-608, 634-636: Corporation balcony 'Birdcages', 1921
Twenty-seven cars: ditto rebuilds of 'Bellamys', 1920-22
Nos 637-756 + 201 cars: Corporation new enclosed top cars and rebuilds of older cars, 1924-1933
Nos 757: EE long bogie single-decker of 1929 for possible Mersey tunnel line
Nos 758-769: EE enclosed bogie cars of 1931-32
Nos 770-781: Corporation ditto of 1933
Nos 782-817: ditto of 1933-34 (known as 'Robinsons' after the then Chief Electrical Engineer)
Nos 818-867: Corporation enclosed bogie cars of 1935-36 (known as 'Marks' after the then General Manager)
Nos 868-992, 151-200: Corporation stream-lined bogie cars of 1936-1937 (known as 'Liners' or 'Streamliners')
Nos 201-300: Corporation streamlined 'Baby Grands' of 1937-42

Many of the open-topped vehicles were later top-covered and or/rebuilt, a fact which perhaps explains why so few Liverpool's cars were ever sold to other operators, the only

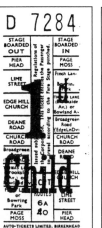 

Two souvenir tickets issued to mark the closing of Liverpool's tramways, with their common back design.

sales being of the bodies of Nos 48, 49 and 50 which were sold to TYNEMOUTH & DISTRICT in 1920 (but used on the GATESHEAD & DISTRICT system) and of 46 'Green Goddesses' (as the streamliners were collectively known) in 1953-54 to Glasgow Corporation. The only working preserved Liverpool car is No 869 (latterly Glasgow 1055), now at the National Tramway Museum, Crich.

Bibliography: as above and
– *Vol 2: 1900-1930* (The Transport Publishing Co./The Light Rail Transit Association, 1982) 0 903839 50 4
– *Vol 3: 1931-1939* (1987) 0 86317 141 9
– *Vol 4: 1939-1957* (The Transport Publishing Co., 1989) 0 86317 148 6

LIVERPOOL & PRESCOT LIGHT RAILWAY

Authority: Liverpool and Prescot Light Railway Order 1898
Gauge: 4ft 8½in
Traction: Overhead electric
Opened: 24 June 1902*
Taken Over: 1 October 1919
System: Single line
Length: 3.11 miles
Stock: 7 dd
Livery: As for ST HELENS

Owned by the Lancashire Light Railways Co. Ltd (registered 21 April 1898), the LPLR was the only part constructed of a grand scheme of some 24 miles of tramways proposed for the south Lancashire area. The Company had common board links with the SOUTH LANCASHIRE TRAMWAYS, its shares being bought by the South Lancashire Electric Traction Power Co. Ltd before construction actually began.

The tramway ran eastwards from the (then) Liverpool boundary at Berry's Bridge, Knotty Ash, along Prescot Road and Liverpool Road to Brook Bridge, Prescot (where it connected end-on with the St Helens system) as a single track in a then rural area. It was ready for opening some months before it did so as the Company was waiting for the LIVERPOOL CORPORA-TION route to Knotty Ash to be completed (and connected to the light railway); the first cars ran on 24 June 1902 to allow the crews to learn the road and passengers were carried although regular services did not begin until the following day with through running from Knotty Ash to St Helens. It is thought the line was worked by South Lancs cars for a brief period, its own BEC open-toppers not arriving until 1903; these latter vehicles were numbered 37-43 in the St Helens fleet (and shedded there). On the same day that St Helens Corporation took over the St Helens tramways (1 October 1919) the Company sold its cars to South Lancs and the light railway to Liverpool for £18,000 for incor-poration into that system.

Bibliography: *South Lancashire Tramways* E. K. Stretch (Manchester Transport Museum Society, 1972)

LONDON

The history of London's tramways is that of England's tramways in microcosm. In the early 1860s G. F. Train of BIRKEN-HEAD fame opened three experimental street railways in the capital, but such was the opposition from the local authorities that all were closed within months. After a few years' hiatus, other promoters constructed more conventional tramways to usher in a period of piecemeal horse, steam and cable systems, not helped by the fragmentary nature of the city's local government structure. Gradually though the various companies coalesced through a series of mergers and takeovers until 1933, when the entire network was taken over by the London Passenger Transport Board to become part of LONDON TRANSPORT – the largest single tramway system in the British Isles. The tramways were electrically-worked and had been in the hands of three major operators – LONDON COUNTY COUNCIL, LONDON UNITED TRAMWAYS and the METROPOLITAN ELECTRIC TRAMWAYS – who had already extended their lines well beyond the growing capital's boundaries into the surrounding counties. In chronological order of opening, the London tramways were:

LONDON: TRAIN'S TRAMWAYS

Authority: Local authority permission
Gauge: 4ft 8½in?
Traction: Horse
Opened: 23 March 1861
Closed: 20 June 1862
System: Three single lines
Length: c3 miles
Stock: 5 sd
Livery: Various?
Last Cars: ?

The first three tramways in London were all unsuccessful promotions by the flamboyant American entrepreneur George Francis Train. In 1860 he had opened a line in BIRKENHEAD (which was to fare better than his London efforts) and, turning his attention to the great metropolis, persuaded the local authorities (not without some diffi-culty) to permit him to construct three separate lines. The first of these ran from Marble Arch for 1 mile along the Bayswater Road as far as Porchester Terrace and was opened on 23 March 1861 with Charles Dickens and William Thackeray among the assembled dignitaries and onlookers. It was worked by the Marble Arch Street Rail Co. with two single-deck cars, built by Prentiss of Birkenhead, named *Princess Royal* and *Her Majesty*.

The second line, opened on 15 April 1861, ran from Victoria station up Victoria Street to Parliament Square, and was operated by the Westminster Street Rail Co. Ltd with one car named *The People*. The third tramway, opened 15 August 1861, ran from the other side of Westminster Bridge, past Lambeth Palace to Kennington Gate and was operated by the Surrey Side Street Rail Co. Ltd with two cars. All were single-track lines, each about a mile in length.

Public opinion was sharply divided over the tramways. Those who used them – several tens of thousands a week – liked them but residents and other road users (especially omnibus operators) did not. Matters were not helped by Train's use of step rails and the authorities soon ordered their removal. The Bayswater line was closed by mid-September 1861 and the Victoria Street line on 6 March 1862; the tramway south of the Thames closed on 20 June 1862 when the Sheriff's workmen lifted the rails whilst the cars were running, after Train had defied a court order to do so!

Bibliography: *The London County Council Tramways Vol 1: South London* E. R. Oakley (The London Tramways History Group, 1989) 0 951300 10 5

LONDON: NORTH METROPOLITAN TRAMWAYS

Authority: North Metropolitan Tramways Act 1869
Gauge: 4ft 8½in
Traction: Horse, battery electric
Opened: 25 April 1870
Closed: 28 April 1908
System: Network + single line
Length: 56.77 miles
Stock: 16 sd?, 730+ dd? horse; 4 locos, 6 dd battery electric
Livery: Route colour
Last Car: ?

In 1869 the North Metropolitan Tramways Co. (incorporated 12 July 1869) obtained powers to build 7 miles of horse tramways in east London. Construction began that November and the following April the first 2½ miles of double tracks between Whitechapel Church and Bow Bridge opened with five Stephenson open-top double-deckers. From this small beginning sprang a major tramway system eventually reaching Aldgate, London Docks and the West India Dock in the south, Holloway, Stamford Hill and Finsbury Park (in Middlesex) in the north, Holborn, Bloomsbury and Islington in the west and Leytonstone, Manor Park and Plaistow (all in Essex) in the east.

In 1878 the Company began production of its own cars at its Leytonstone Works, eventually becoming a major supplier of tramcars to other British lines, and by 1883 had 16 single-deckers and 225 double-deckers in service. Steam traction had been experimented with by then, a Merryweather tram locomotive having being tried at Stratford in 1878 for a month before being sent to WANTAGE. A compressed air locomotive was tested in 1881 whilst the following year a horse car was converted into a battery electric vehicle for trials. In 1883 another battery car was tested and three years later an Elieson patent electric locomo-tive from the Electric Locomotion Power Co. Ltd was put on trial. This proved more successful for, on 4 August 1887, two of these entered public duty on the Stratford–Manor Park route, each hauling a horse car trailer. Two more were added though the service lasted only a year before being abandoned. This was not the end of this form of traction for on 14 June 1889 six self-contained open-top double-deck battery cars began operating on the Canning Town–Plaistow route. (This 1.3-mile line along Barking Road, opened in September 1886, was always isolated from the rest of the system to the north and west.) The use of the battery cars, rented from the General Electric Power & Traction Co. Ltd, ceased on 27 July 1892 after a disagreement over their hire charges.

By 1891 the Company was operating nearly 400 double-deckers (the single-deckers apparently having been withdrawn). Six years later, on 14 October 1897, it took over operation of the LONDON STREET TRAMWAYS system, this having been purchased the previous day by LONDON COUNTY COUNCIL and leased to the North Met. The network remained at its greatest extent for just five years for on 26 November 1902 the METROPOLITAN ELECTRIC TRAMWAYS took over the 7 miles of line in Middlesex, whilst on 1 July following, WEST HAM bought its 4 miles of line there. On 1 April 1906 LEYTON took over its lines with the entire London network passing to the County Council that same day. All the Company was left with was its line to Manor Park in East Ham, depots in Romford Road and Barking Road, six trams and the Leytonstone car works. EAST HAM CORPORATION then successfully offered £8,000 for the Romford Road line, the last services running on 28 April and the last cars and horses being auctioned in May. The Company was liquidated on 15 February 1913 after disposing of its remaining properties.

Bibliography: *The Tramways of East London* 'Rodinglea' (The Tramway & Light Railway Society/The Light Railway Transport League, 1967)
The London County Council Tramways Vol 2: North London E. R. Oakley (The London Tramways History Group, 1991)
0 951300 11 3

LONDON TRAMWAYS

Authority: Metropolitan Street Tramways Act 1869; Pimlico Peckham and Greenwich Street Tramways Act 1869
Gauge: 4ft 8½in
Traction: Horse, cable
Opened: 2 May 1870
Taken Over: 1 January 1899
System: Network + single line
Length: 24.37 miles
Stock: 330+ sd & dd horse; 50 tractors, 29 dd cable*
Livery: Route colour*

Following the failure of Train's Surrey Side Street Rail Co.'s line (see LONDON: TRAIN'S TRAMWAYS) the first successful tramway south of the Thames was opened in 1870 by the Metropolitan Street Tramways Co., this time using grooved rails. The first section opened ran from Gresham Road in Brixton, north for 1¼ miles along Brixton Road to The Horns in Kennington. This was extended on 5 October up Kennington Road to Westminster Bridge Road (and a short extension opened from Gresham Road south to Brixton Church) and on 22 October westwards along Westminster Bridge Road to

The opening of G. F. Train's first tramway in London as portrayed by the Illustrated London News *of 20 April 1861 in this scene near Marble Arch.*

the river. On 7 December a second route was opened, as a branch heading southwest from St Mark's Church, Kennington, down Clapham Road to The Swan at Stockwell and extended on 1 May 1871 to The Plough at Clapham. On 11 September 1871 a ¼-mile branch was opened eastwards off Kennington Road to St George's Circus.

While all this expansion was going on a second concern, the Pimlico, Peckham & Greenwich Street Tramways Co., had since 13 December 1870 been running trams from Blackheath Road in Greenwich westwards along New Cross Road, followed on 4 March 1871 by the opening of a branch northeast from Blackheath Road to Christchurch in Greenwich. During 1871 this system crept further westwards, on 1 September reaching St George's Circus where it was connected ten days later with the Metropolitan line. Other lines were added over the next three years to form a network of routes centred on the Elephant & Castle and St Mark's Church with one short line (opened 20 October 1873) isolated on the north side of the river, running from Vauxhall Bridge up Vauxhall Bridge Road to the Windsor Castle by Victoria railway station. Shortly after this, under the provisions of the London Tramways Company Limited Purchase Act 1873, the two companies were bought by the London Tramways Co. Ltd (registered 12 December 1870) in order to rationalize matters.

The combined system continued to grow slowly, including an extension of the Clapham line to Tooting Bec Road (on 15 December 1888) and on to Tooting (16

December 1890). A cable line was also constructed to continue the Brixton route up Brixton Hill and Streatham Hill whereupon it was decided, in 1890, to replace the existing horse line back as far as the Kennington junction, a total distance of 2¾ miles. Accordingly a winding house was constructed at Telford Park on the top of Streatham Hill and double tracks laid with a continuously-wound cable running at 8mph in a central conduit in each. The rebuilt line opened on 11 August 1891 for struggling horse-haulage until (probably) 7 December 1892 when cable working began with 30 tractor cars hauling ordinary horse trams. These 'dummies' as they were known were small, open-sided four-wheeled vehicles fitted with driver-controlled grippers to engage the cable. Most were housed in the winding house with one or more shedded at Kennington.

The construction and equipping of the cable line was by DK who, in 1895, extended it a further ¾ mile down the other side of Streatham Hill to Streatham Village to terminate by the Tate Library. This section was inspected on 23 November that year and presumably opened shortly afterwards, again using dummies of which 50 were eventually supplied. In 1896 however work began on rebuilding some of the double-deck horse cars specifically for cable working and by 1900 29 of these had been fitted with grippers to enable them, like the dummies, to tow horse cars to Kennington whence they could be horse-hauled onwards, so doing away with the need for passengers to change cars. Presumably they proved more popular with the local residents than the dummies which, because of complaints about the noise they made, had had to be fitted with tanks for watering the track.

The MST Co.'s first horse cars, housed in the first depot at Brixton, were open-toppers supplied by Starbuck, Stephensons, Metropolitan and the Danish firm of Rowan of Randers (numbers unknown) and the original livery is thought to have been blue and white with subsequent cars taking different colour schemes as new routes opened. The PPGST cars (of which there were at least nine) were again double-deckers, probably from Messrs Drew & Burnett of Fountainbridge in Edinburgh. With the amalgamation of the two concerns a score or so of depots were built around the system to house the growing fleet of single and double-deck vehicles supplied by a range of builders. There was also a fleet of horse buses, one of their functions being to link the two portions of the system across Vauxhall Bridge.

By the early 1890s LONDON COUNTY COUNCIL had already made its intentions plain of taking over the tramways as and when their 21 years were up, much against the wishes of the Company. Not until 1898 was agreement reached on a total package deal of nearly £1m, the transfer of control being at the start of the following year.

Bibliography: *The London County Council Tramways Vol 1: South London* E. R. Oakley (The London Tramways History Group, 1989) 0 951300 10 5

LONDON STREET TRAMWAYS

Authority: London Street Tramways Act 1870
Gauge: 4ft 8½in

Traction: Horse
Opened: 27 November 1871
Taken Over: 13 October 1897
System: Network
Length: 13.45 miles
Stock: 140+ dd?
Livery: White & route colour

Until its takeover in 1897 by the LONDON COUNTY COUNCIL, the London Street Tramways Co. ran a small network of lines in north London, with routes from Holborn and Farringdon in the south meeting at King's Cross from where a branch east along the Pentonville Road led to The Angel, Islington. A line north from King's Cross went up the Caledonian Road whilst a line northwest went to Camden Town and Kentish Town. Lines from Camden Town led northeast to Hampstead and south to Euston Road whilst branches north from Kentish Town went to Parliament Hill and the Archway Tavern on Junction Road. The Hampstead Road line opened on 27 November 1871 before it had been inspected by the BoT, though the Company continued to operate services in spite of this – and despite an adverse inspection report – claiming that it was entitled to do so under its Act. Further sections followed, authorized by further Acts and Orders of the 1870s and 1880s. By the 1890s though London County Council was ready to begin taking over those parts of the system which were 21 years old. This was opposed by the Company, so forcing the dispute to go first to arbitration, then to the courts and finally to the House of Lords who found, on 30 July 1894, in favour of the Council. The 4¼ miles of line in question were thereupon leased back, as from 1 April 1895, to the Company. After this negotiations were entered into by the LCC with the

NORTH METROPOLITAN TRAMWAYS Co. with a view to that company working all the Council's lines, and on 27 May 1897 the buy-out of the LST was agreed, the purchase by the LCC becoming effective that October.

Details of the car fleet are sketchy. All were probably double-deckers from more than one manufacturer with 139 of them being transferred to the NMT in 1897 – though whether older cars had already been withdrawn is not certain. Six depots were spread around the system near the various termini to house them all. Trials were also carried out on the Caledonian Road with at least one compressed air car (built by Lancaster for the British Mekarski Improved Air Engine Co. Ltd), commencing in 1883, but for how long they continued, and how many of the open-top double-deck cars were actually put into public service (if any), is not known.

Bibliography: *The London County Council Tramways Vol 2: North London* E. R. Oakley (The London Tramways History Group, 1991) 0 951300 11 3

LONDON: WEST METROPOLITAN TRAMWAYS

Authority: Southall Tramway Order 1873
Gauge: 4ft 8½in
Traction: Horse
Opened: 1 June 1874
Taken Over: 6 August 1894
System: Branching + single line
Length: 8.74 miles
Stock: 49 sd & dd?
Livery: Yellow & ivory

The West Metropolitan Tramways Co. Ltd was the forerunner of the LONDON UNITED TRAMWAYS of west London and, in turn, had its origins in a line opened in 1874 by the Southall & Shepherds Bush Tram-Railway Co. Ltd (incorporated 12 May 1870), which ran westwards for just over a mile along Uxbridge Road between Uxbridge Road station in Shepherds Bush and Askew Crescent in Acton Vale. The two cars are thought to have been Starbuck double-deckers. The single-track line was constructed by Reid Bros of City Road and, after it closed for financial reasons on 20 February 1875, they took it over, re-opening it on 21 September and extending it another 1½ miles to Acton Lane (18 February 1878) with a third (and later fourth) car added. On 6 March 1882 the tramway was acquired by the West Metropolitan Tramways Co. Ltd (incorporated 12 August 1881) who had a number of other routes planned.

On 18 March 1882 a 1½-mile line from Shepherds Bush, worked by Falcon single-deckers, was opened along Goldhawk Road southwest to Young's Corner, extended

This unidentified North Metropolitan Tramways horse car appears on a postcard of Clapton Common at the turn of the century. (Courtesy Andrew Maxam)

westwards on 16 December through Chiswick to the Star & Garter at Kew Bridge, terminating north of the river crossing. Then, on 17 April of the following year, a 2-mile line was opened south of the Thames from Kew Bridge to Lower Mortlake Road, Richmond (the bridge itself not being crossed on account of its narrowness). Finally, on 14 July 1883, the northern route to Kew Bridge was extended back eastwards for a mile from Young's Corner to the Hammersmith boundary. (This whole route from Hammersmith to Kew Bridge was doubled over the next ten years.)

Although other routes were planned and the possibilities of electric traction investigated, the Company was failing and in 1893 a Receiver was appointed; on 13 June 1894 everything was put up for auction – only to attract no bids at all, such was the state of the assets. Rescue was at hand though for on 19 July the London United Tramways Co. Ltd was incorporated to purchase the tramway in order to rebuild it and this it did (for £30,000) on 20 August. From the auction details it would appear that the tramway was worked by at least 49 cars of which the youngest 15 were Milnes double-deckers. The main depot was off Chiswick High Street with smaller ones at Shepherds Bush and in Kew Road, Richmond.

Bibliography: *London United Tramways: A History – 1894 to 1933* Geoffrey Wilson (George Allen & Unwin, 1971) 0 0438 8001 0
London United Tramways Vol 1: Origins to 1912 C. S. Smeeton (The Light Rail Transit Association/The Tramway and Light Railway Society, 1995) 0 948106 13 1

LONDON, DEPTFORD & GREENWICH TRAMWAYS

Authority: Southwark and Deptford Tramways Act 1879
Gauge: 4ft 8½in
Traction: Horse, oil-gas
Opened: 28 October 1880?
Taken Over: 7 July 1904
System: Network
Length: 6.87 miles
Stock: 42+ sd & dd horse?; 1 loco oil-gas
Livery: Route colour

Built by the Southwark & Deptford Tramways Co., this southeast London single-track system began with a short line in Bermondsey running northeast along Spa Road, Jamaica Road, Union Road and Lower Road through Rotherhithe to the depot by the bridge carrying the LBSCR's Deptford Wharf branch line. On 5 June 1881 the track was extended along Evelyn Street to the Noah's Ark in Deptford High Street,

Edwardian postcard of London United Tramways' terminus at Hampton Court with No 296 of 1903, one of the batch bought for this route. (Author's Collection)

followed by an extension at the other end along Grange Road and Bermondsey New Road to the Bricklayers Arms, a branch west from Jamaica Road along Parker's Row to Tooley Street, a branch south from the Red Lion on Lower Road along Rotherhithe New Road to the Canal Bridge just short of the LONDON TRAMWAYS line in the Old Kent Road, and a short link line between Rotherhithe New Road and Grange Road.

Services were worked by an unknown number of single and double-deck cars, at least some of which were supplied by Metropolitan. Official returns give a total of 42 in 1904 though this figure probably includes replacements for withdrawn cars. That year saw the sale of the system by the Company – renamed the London, Deptford & Greenwich Tramways Co. in 1893 – to the LONDON COUNTY COUNCIL for £91,363 plus costs. There was also a Connelly oil-gas locomotive built by Weymann & Co. of Guildford used on the Rotherhithe New Road line from the end of 1892 to (probably) October 1895. This was a small, double-ended, four-wheeled vehicle similar in shape and size to a steam or battery electric tramway locomotive, equipped with side windows and emblazoned 'The CONNELLY MOTOR'.

Bibliography: *The London County Council Tramways Vol 1: South London* E. R. Oakley (The London Tramways History Group, 1989) 0 951300 10 5

LONDON: SOUTH LONDON TRAMWAYS

Authority: The South London Tramways Company Act 1879

Gauge: 4ft 8½in
Traction: Horse
Opened: 1 January 1881
Taken Over: 22 November 1902
System: Network
Length: 12.87 miles
Stock: 28 sd?, 67 dd?
Livery: White & route colour

The South London Tramways Co. operated a long, thin network of lines on the south bank of the River Thames in the Battersea area. The first to open ran from (probably) the Princes Head at the junction of Battersea Park Road and Falcon Lane, along Battersea Park Road and Nine Elms Lane to the Royal Rifleman. On 5 January 1881 the short stretch on from here to the Coal Wharf Gates was opened, followed on 21 March by a short section in Falcon Lane.

Within two years the single-track system was complete. The final layout consisted of a main line running southwest from London Bridge down Southwark Bridge Road, Lambeth Road, the Albert Embankment to Vauxhall station and Vauxhall Bridge, Nine Elms Lane, Battersea Road, York Road and North Street with branches off north towards the Thames, serving Southwark Bridge, Waterloo station (via Waterloo Road), Westminster Bridge (via Stangate) and Chelsea Bridge (via Queens Road). Two southern branches opposite Waterloo Road served the Elephant & Castle. A second, parallel main line left the first west of Vauxhall station to follow Wandsworth Road, Lavender Hill and St John's Hill. This was linked to the first line via Queens Road and Falcon Lane.

The tramway is recorded as opening with

28 cars – possibly all single-deck vehicles – though at the time of the takeover by the LONDON COUNTY COUNCIL in 1902 95 cars were transferred, these being mainly double-deckers based on depots at Southwark Bridge Road, Queens Road and Falcon Lane.

Horse bus feeder services began in March 1882 and in December 1884 the Company bought out the London Tramways Omnibus Co. and its thirteen buses. In 1891 the Company leased the Waterloo Road section to the LONDON TRAMWAYS Co. so when that company was taken over by the LCC on 1 January 1899 the Council negotiated to buy that line too, doing so from 11 August 1900 and paying £5,276 for it. The remaining 12.73 miles of the system were purchased two years later for £¼m as part of the LCC's tramway acquisition and electrification policy.

Bibliography: as above

LONDON: NORTH LONDON TRAMWAYS

Authority: North London Suburban
  Tramways Order 1879
Gauge: 4ft 8½in
Traction: Horse, steam
Opened: 10 April 1881
Taken Over: 1 August 1891
System: Branching
Length: 8.37 miles
Stock: 20 sd horse?; 25 locos, 27 dd steam
Livery: Dark green & white

Promoted and built by the North London Suburban Tramway Co. Ltd (registered on 14 December 1878 but dissolved and replaced in 1882 by the North London Tramways Co.), the first section of this Middlesex system opened ran south along the Hertford Road from the depot in Tramway Avenue, Ponders End, for 2 miles through Edmonton to the boundary with Tottenham. The line was continued on through Tottenham on 16 May 1881 for 1½ miles to High Cross and, on 4 June, for another mile through Seven Sisters to Stamford Hill where it made an end-on connection with the NORTH METRO-POLITAN TRAMWAYS line. On 7 January 1882 a northern extension of 1 mile took the mainly single-track tramway to close to the boundary with Hertfordshire at Waltham Cross.

Services began with twelve Eades patent reversible single-deck cars joined later in 1881 by eight more. On 1 April 1885 steam working began with Merryweather tram locomotives 1-14 and open-top bogie trailers 1-20 from Falcon (with horse working lasting until the end of May). These were joined by loco No 15 from Merryweathers in 1885 and Nos 16-25 from DK in 1886-87, plus another seven Falcon trailers.

A ½-mile branch from Seven Sisters south-

west to the Manor House opened on 24 October 1885, extended on 12 December another ½ mile to Finsbury Park. A third route, north from the Manor House to Wood Green Town Hall (again single-track), opened on Christmas Eve 1887, by which time the short Seven Sisters Corner-Stamford Hill section had fallen into disuse. The Company too was ailing – a poor service resulted from track and other mechanical problems – and in 1890 it went into receiver-ship, being purchased a year later for £22,600 by the North Metropolitan Tramways Co. who worked it with its own horse cars. The old stock was sold for scrap with two of the locos finding their way to the DEWSBURY, BATLEY & BIRSTAL line nine years later.

Bibliography: *The Metropolitan Electric Tramways Vol 1: Origins to 1920* C. S. Smeeton (The Light Rail Transit Association, 1984) 0 900433 94 9

LONDON: WOOLWICH & SOUTH EAST LONDON TRAMWAYS

Authority: Woolwich and Plumstead
  Tramways Order 1880
Gauge: 3ft 6in
Traction: Horse
Opened: 4 June 1881
Taken Over: 1 June 1905
System: Branching
Length: 4.96 miles
Stock: 35 dd
Livery: Various

The authority for this line was secured by the Woolwich & Plumstead Tramways Co., which company was then sold almost immediately to a new concern, the Woolwich & South East London Tramways Co. Ltd. As built, the original single-track line ran roughly east-west from Plumstead Church along the High Street and Plumstead Road, through Beresford Square and on along Beresford Street to Woolwich High Street where it terminated by the Free Ferry in Nile Street (1½ miles), with a branch of 328yd heading in the same direction from Beresford Square along Powis Street just south of the main line. The narrow gauge, unique for horse lines in London, was chosen on account of the narrow winding streets.

Services began with three Metropolitan double-deckers, shortly joined by three more. In 1881 an Act was obtained for an eastwards extension of 2¾ miles past the dockyards and Royal Arsenal to Greenwich by way of Church Street, George Street, Albion Road and Woolwich Road to a terminus adjacent to the LONDON TRAMWAYS line. This mainly single-track line opened on 21 November 1882 with six more Metropolitan cars having been added to stock. These were

followed by another ten two years later, another five in 1895-96, six in 1900-01 and two in 1902, all probably a mixture of new and second-hand vehicles. The depot was in Cage Lane off Plumstead High Street. The only other extension made to the line was in 1903 when the Plumstead terminus was moved a few yards further east to meet the new electric line from BEXLEY (though no connection could be made on account of the gauge difference).

By the early 1900s LONDON COUNTY COUNCIL was permitted to purchase the tramway and in 1905 it did so for the arbitrated total price of £46,667 for the assets, including the thirty-two surviving cars.

Bibliography: *The London County Council Tramways Vol 1: South London* E. R. Oakley (The London Transport History Group, 1989) 0 951300 10 5

LONDON SOUTHERN TRAMWAYS

Authority: London Southern Tramways Act
  1882
Gauge: 4ft 8½in
Traction: Horse
Opened: 7 December 1883
Taken Over: 20 December 1906*
System: Radial
Length: 5.75 miles
Stock: 33 dd?
Livery: Route colour

This small system linked Vauxhall, Camberwell Green, Brixton and West Norwood with four, mainly single-track routes radiating from 'Loughborough Junction' where Coldharbour Lane met Hinton Road and Loughborough Road. The first sections opened were the east-west line from Camberwell Green along Coldharbour Lane to Brixton Church and part of the northern route off Coldharbour Lane along Gresham Road towards Vauxhall. These were inspected by the BoT on 4 December 1883 and opened shortly afterwards. The first part of the southern route from Loughborough Junction south down Milkwood Road to Herne Hill station opened on 30 May 1884, followed on 10 July by its extension along Thurlow Lane (now Norwood Road) to Tulse Hill and, on 4 June 1885, by the remaining portion along Church Street to Thurlow Place in West Norwood.

The system was completed on 21 August 1887 with the opening of the rest of the Vauxhall line from The Swan at Stockwell, along Stockwell Road and South Lambeth Road. This route crossed the lines of the LONDON TRAMWAYS twice, in Brixton Road and Clapham Road, before connecting with those of the SOUTH LONDON TRAMWAYS on the other side of the

LSWR's Vauxhall station. Services were worked by an unconfirmed number of double-deck cars (the returns of 1902 give 33), the first batch all probably from Falcon with later ones being constructed by the Company, based at depots off Stockwell Road and Thurlow Place.

The tramway was bought by LONDON COUNTY COUNCIL for £62,085 in 1906 with the Council taking over operations on 2 October (but not ownership until 20 December that year).

Bibliography: as above

LONDON: HIGHGATE HILL TRAMWAYS

Authority: Highgate Hill Tramways Order 1882
Gauge: 3ft 6in
Traction: Cable
Opened: 29 May 1884
Closed: 23 August 1909
System: Single line
Length: 0.71 miles
Stock: 3 tractors, 8 dd
Livery: ?
Last Car: ?

Operated by the Highgate Hill Tramways Co. (a successor to the Steep Grade Tramways & Works Co. Ltd who had obtained the original authority), this short single-track line ran up the road of its title on a 1 in 11 gradient from the Archway Tavern to Highgate Village but no further. Plans to extend it another 6½ miles to Finchley, New Barnet and Chipping Barnet came to nothing. Opened by the Lord Mayor of London, Sir Robert Fowler, the line was worked in true cable tramway fashion with a constantly-moving cable in a conduit and grippers on the cars which could be engaged or disengaged by their drivers. Three types of cars were used on the line, the original fleet being made up of three passenger-carrying single-deck tractor cars Nos 4-6 hauling open-top double-deckers 1-3, plus three driver-controlled bogie open-toppers Nos 7-9 (soon joined by Nos 10 and 11), all from Falcon.

An accident on 5 December 1892 resulted in the line closing until 19 April 1897. This was but the latest in a long line of (mainly financial) problems resulting in the liquidation of the Company later that same month. On 14 August 1896 the line was sold to a new concern, the Highgate Hill Tramways Ltd, and re-opened on 19 April (Easter Monday) the following year. The Company apparently considered converting the line into a standard gauge electric tramway but got nowhere with the idea, caught as it was in the middle of London and Middlesex County Council rivalry. In 1909 it was

London County Council No 106 of 1903 in service at the National Tramway Museum, Crich. (M. Donnison)

agreed that the LCC would buy its portion of the line (for £13,099) from 24 August and the MCC its 400yd at the village end (for £6,377) and lease it back to the LCC for working. After the takeover the tramway closed for reconstruction as part of LONDON COUNTY COUNCIL TRAMWAYS, re-opening eight months later in its new guise. The cars were sold for scrap.

Bibliography: *The London County Council Tramways Vol 2: North London* E. R. Oakley (The London Tramways History Group, 1991) 0 951300 11 3

LONDON: HARROW ROAD & PADDINGTON TRAMWAYS

Authority: Harrow Road and Paddington Tramways Act 1886
Gauge: 4ft 8½in
Traction: Horse
Opened: 7 July 1888
Taken Over: 16 August 1906
System: Branching
Length: 2.85 miles
Stock: 21+ dd?
Livery: Red, later brown

This short, mainly single-track line was owned and operated by the Harrow Road and Paddington Tramways Co. A main line ran in a southeasterly direction from the Royal Oak, Harlesden Green, along the Harrow Road to Lock Bridge over the Grand Junction Canal at Amberley Road, Paddington whilst a branch to the north just before this terminus ran for a little over ½ mile up Chippenham Road into Cambridge Road. Services began with twelve Milnes

London County Council Class C car No 230 of 1904 on a postcard of the Dog Kennel Hill section of the route through East Dulwich. This class was fitted with mechanical track brakes specifically for this section. (Courtesy Andrew Maxam)

double-deckers. Details of later cars are incomplete: by 1901 21 were recorded, with some of the later additions (from Falcon) probably being replacements for older vehicles. The depot was in Trenmar Gardens off the Harrow Road about ¾ mile from the Royal Oak.

No extensions were made to the tramway, though several were planned and authorized, and during the early 1890s the Chippenham Road branch fell into disuse (but a car was occasionally run over it to preserve the Company's rights regarding it). In 1903 the Company obtained an Act permitting electrification and another the following year to authorize the sale of the line to the

METROPOLITAN ELECTRIC TRAMWAYS. This took place two years later (at a price of £36,921) with the MET running the line with the existing stock as reconstruction work went ahead, the residual horse service ceasing on 1 September.

Bibliography: *The Metropolitan Electric Tramways Vol 1: Origins to 1920* C. S. Smeeton (The Light Rail Transit Association, 1984) 0 900433 94 9

LONDON: SOUTH EASTERN METROPOLITAN TRAMWAYS
Authority: South-Eastern Metropolitan Tramways Act 1888

Gauge: 4ft 8½in
Traction: Horse
Opened: 11 October 1890
Taken Over: 1 April 1902
System: Single line
Length: 2.56 miles
Stock: 10 dd
Livery: White

After nearly 20 years of proposals a short, isolated tramway was finally built in Lewisham in southeast London as the last such private venture in the city. The one, mainly single-track line ran south from South Street in Greenwich, down Lewisham Road, Lewisham High Street and Broadway to terminate at the depot by the Black Horse in Rushey Green. After a few months delay upon completion, the South Eastern Metropolitan Tramways Co. opened the line with ten open-top cars built by the NORTH METROPOLITAN TRAMWAYS.

In 1899 the Company obtained an Act authorizing electrification of the line – on the face of it not a viable proposition considering the length of the tramway and the fact that it connected with no other system. The real purpose was probably to ensure a better price in the event of a likely LONDON COUNTY COUNCIL takeover. This came three years later, the Council paying £50,000 for the concern.

Bibliography: *The London County Council Tramways Vol 1: South London* E. R. Oakley (The London Tramways History Group, 1989) 0 951300 10 5

LONDON UNITED TRAMWAYS
Authority: London United Tramways Order 1895
Gauge: 4ft 8½in
Traction: Horse, overhead electric
Took Over: 6 August 1894
Taken Over: 1 July 1933
System: Network + single line
Length: 53.75 miles
Stock: 70+ horse?; 4 sd, 386 dd electric
Livery: Route colour to 1920, then scarlet

Formed in 1894 to take over the WEST METROPOLITAN TRAMWAYS, the London United Tramways Co. Ltd set about turning round the ailing fortunes of that concern. New cars were ordered and old ones scrapped whilst in 1895 authorization was given for new lines and the Shepherds Bush–Acton line doubled and extended ¾ mile on 31 August to the top of Acton Hill. Further Acts and LROs were obtained with a view to building a sprawling electric tramway system in west and southwest London on both sides of the Thames, stretching out as far as Uxbridge, Maidenhead, Staines, Hampton Court and Tooting.

Postcard of the Embankment entrance to the Kingsway Subway immediately after its 1908 opening with one of the London County Council single-deckers exiting. (Author's Collection)

The first electric routes, the Shepherds Bush to Acton and Shepherds Bush to Hammersmith and Kew Bridge re-opened on 4 April 1901 after the reconstruction work had been completed and inspected, followed by a formal inauguration on 10 July (and the opening of the Acton line extension through Ealing and Hanwell to Southall). Services began with 80 cars from the first order of Nos 1-100, open-top bogie double-deckers from HN, these being followed in 1902 by similar cars 101-211 and 237-300 from Milnes and 212-235 from BEC. (Some 50 of these were later top-covered). The main depot and power station were off Chiswick High Road beside the West Met horse depot, with additional depots being opened at Acton, Hanwell, Hillingdon, Isleworth and Fulwell.

An extension from Kew Bridge through Brentford and Isleworth to Hounslow opened on 6 July 1901, followed by new lines and extensions from Isleworth south to Twickenham and on via Teddington or Hampton to Hampton Wick and across the Thames to Kingston which became the focal point for lines radiating south to Surbiton, Ditton and Tolworth, north to Ham Boundary and Richmond Park Gates and east to Kingston Hill, Wimbledon, Tooting and Summerstown. (This last branch, opened on 27 June 1907, was the final part of the system opened.) The northern part of the network was completed by a long westwards extension of the Southall line through Hayes and Hillingdon to Uxbridge, together with link lines to the Hammersmith–Hounslow Heath line to the south. (The authorized lines to Staines and Maidenhead were never built.)

In 1906 UEC supplied top-covered bogie cars Nos 301-340 to meet the tramway's increasing needs, with no further vehicles being added until after World War I when, in 1924, the Company put into service four single-deck one-man cars. These were No 341 (a rebuild of METROPOLITAN ELECTRIC No 132 of 1905) and Nos 342-344 (rebuilds of double-deckers 175, 178 and 275). In 1928 the MET's experimental bogie enclosed car No 319 'Poppy' was bought (and renumbered 350), followed three years later by Nos 351-396, 'Feltham' bogie enclosed cars from the Union Construction & Finance Co. Ltd to complete the fleet.

Horse car services lasted until 20 April 1912, on the Kew Bridge–Richmond route which always remained isolated from the rest of the system and, because of local opposition, never electrified. By the time of its closure, the horse car fleet (which had grown from the 33 cars inherited from the West Met to 59 in 1899) had dwindled to single figures. Ten years later, on 2 May 1922, LONDON COUNTY COUNCIL took over those sections of the system within its boundaries (in Hammersmith and Shepherds Bush) and

The last night of London Transport tramways: appropriately – numbered car 1952 on the final Plumstead–Woolwich service.
(Author's Collection)

on 5 July that same year the Hounslow Heath route was cut back to Hounslow. On 1 October 1924 the Richmond Bridge–Twickenham line closed, and between 1931 and 1933 when LONDON TRANSPORT took over the tramway, the routes south of there centred on Kingston were converted to trolleybus operation.

Bibliography: *London United Tramways: a History – 1894 to 1933* Geoffrey Wilson (George Allen & Unwin, 1971) 0 0438 8001 0
London United Tramways Vol 1: Origins to 1912 C. S. Smeeton (The Light Rail Transit Association/The Tramway and Light Railway Society, 1995) 0 948106 13 1

LONDON: ALEXANDRA PARK ELECTRIC RAILWAY
Authority: –
Gauge: 4ft 8½in
Traction: Overhead electric
Opened: 13 May 1898
Closed: 30 September 1899
System: Single line
Length: 0.38 miles
Stock: 4 sd
Livery: Dark green?
Last Car: ?

To this short, short-lived line goes the honour of being the first electric tramway in London. Although sited wholly within Alexandra Park in North London, it was not a pleasure line as such but had a real trans-

port function in conveying visitors from the Park Gates, opposite Wood Green railway station, some 660yd to the eastern entrance to Alexandra Palace for the various events held there.

At the close of the 19th century the Palace and Park were leased to Thomas Hawkins who allowed the Berlin firm of Elektrizitäts-gesellschaft Wandruska to construct and work the tramway, a double-track line laid with grooved rails on wooden sleepers on a continuous slope (as steep as 1 in 9¾) up to the Palace, generating station and car shed. The line's four semi-open single-deck cars were by Waggonfabrik Falkenried of Hamburg.

The tramway was also intended to be a showcase for the Company and its engineer, Victor Wandruska, and it might well have lasted longer than it did (from May to 5 November and Christmas week in 1898 and 31 March to 30 September the following year) had not Hawkins gone bankrupt and the tramway seized and sold by a creditor after it closed for the winter, the cars eventually making their way to the GREAT GRIMSBY STREET TRAMWAYS.

Bibliography: *The Metropolitan Electric Tramways Vol 1: Origins to 1920* C. S. Smeeton (The Light Rail Transit Association, 1984) 0 90043 39 4

LONDON, CAMBERWELL & DULWICH TRAMWAYS
Authority: Peckham and East Dulwich Tramways Act 1882

Gauge: 4ft 8½in
Traction: Horse
Opened: Early 1896
Closed: 1900
System: Branching
Length: 2.89 miles
Stock: 4 sd
Livery: ?
Last Car: ?

Details of this small system are tantalizingly vague. A minor tramway in every sense, it was built by the Peckham & East Dulwich Tramways Co. – after a considerable delay – as the only portion of a grand scheme for a network of lines in the Peckham Rye area of south London. Construction began soon after authorization was obtained though the single-track tramway did not open until early 1896 with (probably) four roofed and curtained Midland toastracks more suited to a seaside line.

The main route ran south along Hollydale Road, west along Brayards Road and Choumert Road (to the south of Peckham Rye railway station), then south again down Maxted Road, Adys Road and Crystal Palace Road to terminate by the Plough Inn in Lordship Lane. A short branch ran east off Adys Road along East Dulwich Road to the Kings Arms (and depot) where it swung north along Peckham Rye before terminating at the Heaton Arms in Rye Lane.

No connections were made to other tramways and in 1900, after an unprofitable existence not helped by the expense of promoting four Acts of Parliament between 1882 and 1887, services ground to a halt (after running weekdays-only in the latter days). The Company – grandly renamed the London, Camberwell & Dulwich Tramways Co. in 1887 – went into receivership and the line was bought by the LONDON COUNTY COUNCIL (see below) for just £6,500 with part of it earmarked for possible incorporation into its own expanding electric system.

Bibliography: *The London County Council Tramways Vol 1: South London* E. R. Oakley (The London Tramways History Group, 1989) 0 951300 10 5

LONDON COUNTY COUNCIL TRAMWAYS

Authority: London County Tramways Act 1896
Gauge: 4ft 8½in
Traction: Horse, cable, conduit, overhead electric, petrol-electric
Took Over: 1 January 1899
Taken Over: 1 July 1933
System: Network
Length: 167.18 miles
Stock: 500+ horse?; 50 tractors, 29 dd cable;

50 sd, 2,282 dd electric; 3 dd petrol-electric
Livery: Purple lake & primrose to 1926, then crimson & cream

The London County Council's tramway system – one of the 'Big Three' in the capital during the first quarter of the 20th century – came about as a consequence of the Council's decision to buy up the independent tramways within its boundaries in order to unite, extend and electrify them. Its first takeover as an operator, as from the beginning of 1899, was of the LONDON TRAMWAYS system, thereby acquiring 24.38 miles of route, nine horse cars based on a main depot at Penrose Street, Walworth (plus numerous other small depots), 50 dummies and 29 cable cars. (The Council, formed in 1889, already owned the LONDON STREET TRAMWAYS and the NORTH METROPOLITAN TRAMWAYS' lines within its boundaries, having bought them on 24 June 1896, but these were leased back to those companies for operating purposes.)

Subsequent acquisitions were of the SOUTH LONDON (22 November 1902), the SOUTH EASTERN METROPOLITAN (1 April 1904), the LONDON, DEPTFORD & GREENWICH (7 July 1904), the LONDON, CAMBERWELL & DULWICH (15 August 1904), the WOOLWICH & SOUTH EAST LONDON (1 June 1905), the LONDON SOUTHERN (2 October 1906) and the HIGHGATE HILL cable line (24 August 1909). Also bought was the London County section of the the the LEA BRIDGE, LEYTONSTONE & WALTHAM-STOW line (1908) though this was then leased to Leyton District Council.

By the time the above purchases had been completed, the electrification programme was well under way. Electric services, using the conduit system of current supply as pioneered at BLACKPOOL, began on 15 May 1903 on the lines in the Westminster Bridge/Waterloo station/Blackfriars Bridge area, out through Kennington and Clapham to Tooting some 8½ miles away, after which the conversion work proceeded apace, firstly south of the Thames and then north of it. The resulting network spread right across London in all directions with river crossings via (from east to west) Southwark, Blackfriars, Westminster, Vauxhall, Battersea and Putney bridges. Connections were made with, or termini sited close to, other systems in the north and west (METROPOLITAN ELECTRIC), east (LONDON UNITED), south (SOUTH METROPOLITAN), south-east (BEXLEY and ERITH) and east (WEST HAM and LEYTON).

A notable feature of the system was the only underground section of tramway in the British Isles, the Kingsway Subway. Opened in stages between 1906 and 1908 to link Bloomsbury and the Victoria Embankment, this was constructed beneath Kingsway and Aldwych, new thoroughfares built after slum clearances in the area. Underground stations were provided at Holborn and Aldwych and 50 single-deckers bought to operate services through it. Rebuilt in 1930-31 to allow the passage of double-deck trams, the subway closed for good on 6 April 1952, just three months before the rest of what was left of the London network.

The last horse cars ran on 19 July 1913 in Liverpool Road, Islington (this route was not electrified) whilst the Highgate Hill cable line was not operated in that form by the LCC but closed upon takeover in 1909, re-opening on 25 March 1910 as part of the electric network. The Brixton cable line was operated as such until 5 April 1904 when it too closed for rebuilding.

The LCC's first electric car was No 101, a Milnes open-top bogie car of 1900, purchased for conduit trials after the London Tramways Exhibition of that year, but after World War I it was converted to a single-decker, renumbered 110 and withdrawn c1926 for scrapping. From 1903 onwards, with the introduction of electric services, the car fleet was assembled as follows:

Nos 1-100: ERTCW bogie open-toppers of 1903 (Class A)
Nos 102-201: ERTCW open-toppers of 1903 (Class B)
Nos 202-301: Brush open-toppers of 1903 (Class C)
Nos 302-376: Brush bogie open-toppers of 1904 (Class D)
Nos 377-401: BEC ditto
Nos 402-551, 602-751: HN top-covered bogie cars of 1906 (Class E)
Nos 552-567: UEC bogie single-deckers of 1906 (Class F)
Nos 568-601: Brush ditto (Class G)
Nos 752-1001: HN top-covered bogie cars of 1907-08 (Class E/1)
Nos 1002-1051: LCC ditto
Nos 1052-1426: HN ditto of 1908-09
Nos 1477-1676: Brush ditto of 1910-11
No 1427: LCC open-topper of 1909 (Class M)
Nos 1428-1476, 1677-1726: HN ditto of 1910
Nos 1727-1776: HN Class E/1 of 1921-22
Nos 1777-1851: Brush ditto
No 1852: LCC experimental top-covered bogie car of 1929 (Class HR/1)
No 1853: ditto (Class HR/2)
Nos 1854-1903: EE ditto of 1930
Nos 1904-2003: HN enclosed bogie cars of 1930 (Class E/3)

Nos 101-160: HN Class HR/2 of 1931
Nos 161-210: EE Class E/3 of 1931 for use
   in Leyton.

Classes F and G were rebuilt in 1929-30 as double-deckers with new EE bodies. The last car built for the system was No 1 of 1932, an experimental enclosed bogie car nicknamed 'Bluebird' on account of its royal blue and ivory livery. Sold to LEEDS in 1951, No 1 survives at the National Tramway Museum, Crich, together with Nos 106 of 1903 and 1025 of 1908 whilst No 1858 of 1930 is at the East Anglia Transport Museum, Carlton Colville.

On 1 July 1921 the LCC took over the Leyton municipal system, inheriting 60 top-covered cars (Nos 11-70) which were gradually withdrawn over the next twelve years, replaced by E/1 and later E/3 class cars. Trailer cars were also operated for a while, beginning in 1913 with eight ex-North Met double-deck horse cars suitably converted (and renumbered T1-T8). These lasted in service until 1919 and were joined in 1915 by purpose-built Brush open-top trailers T9-T158, the use of which (almost exclusively south of the Thames) lasted until 1924, after which they were broken up. During 1913 three petrol-electric cars joined the fleet (Nos P1-P3), again conversions of former horse cars with 40hp petrol engines supplied by W. A. Stevens Ltd of Maidstone, but their period of service lasted only from May to December that year.

The principal problem encountered by the LCC after the system's electrification was that the neighbouring operators all used overhead wires to supply current to their cars, not conduits, hence making through running impossible. A solution was found whereby those operators seeking through running agreements equipped some of their cars with carriers which could be fitted with conduit ploughs at special change pits where the two systems connected; the LCC likewise equipped many of its cars with trolleypoles for overhead working. In addition, some 27 miles of the Council's peripheral routes were constructed with overhead wires rather than conduits to simplify matters somewhat. (A surface-contact system of current supply via studs set into the roadway was experimented with on the Aldgate-Bow Bridge route in 1908 but the trials lasted less than a month and the studs were replaced by a mixture of overhead and conduit sections.)

In all, 22 electric car depots were used around the system, with most surviving until the 1933 incorporation of the tramways into the new LONDON TRANSPORT network. The Central Car Repair Works (opened in March 1909) was on Woolwich Road,

Charlton, and had a rail connection to the nearby SECR line and its own steam shunting locomotive.

Bibliography: *The London County Council Tramways Vol 1: South London* E. R. Oakley (The London Tramways History Group, 1989) 0 951300 10 5
– *Vol 2: North London* (1991) 0 951300 11 3

LONDON: METROPOLITAN ELECTRIC TRAMWAYS

Authority: County of Middlesex Light
   Railways Order 1901
Gauge: 4ft 8½in
Traction: Horse, overhead electric
Took Over: 26 November 1902
Taken Over: 1 July 1933
System: Network
Length: 53.51 miles
Stock: 62 horse; 20 sd, 362 dd electric
Livery: Vermillion & ivory

The Metropolitan Electric Tramways Ltd was a BET subsidiary operating lines in the north and northwest of London. It began life as the Metropolitan Tramways & Omnibus Co. Ltd (incorporated 21 November 1894) which was taken over by the BET in 1901 (and the name changed), the intention being to buy the NORTH METROPOLITAN horse lines and, working in partnership with Middlesex County Council, extend and electrify them. The North Met was purchased accordingly in 1902 and work begun on the reconstruction.

The first routes to re-open were the MET's line from Finsbury Park, northeast along Seven Sisters Road to Seven Sisters Corner and the branch north from the Manor House to Wood Green with electric services beginning on 22 July 1904. The MCC's first tramway was a new line from Wood Green east along Lordship Lane and Bruce Grove to Tottenham which opened on 20 August that year.

Thereafter, over the next six years, the system grew to form a sprawling network of double-track lines of which the Company owned nearly 9½ miles (the Wood Green route and the line to Seven Sisters which continued northwards up the High Road to Tottenham and on via Fore Street through Edmonton, and then along the Hertford Road to Ponders End). Hertford County Council owned 1½ miles (the northwestern extremity of the system from the county boundary at New Barnet to Chipping Barnet Church) and MCC the remainder of the network which stretched to Sudbury via Willesden and Wembley in the west, to Edgware and Barnet in the northwest, to Enfield and Waltham Cross (from Ponders End) in the north, to Tottenham in the east

and to Paddington and Acton in the south. The last section opened, on 20 February 1911, was a branch west from Ponders End to the GER's Enfield Town station.

The horse car services in Tottenham ceased in 1904 and the cars sold back to the North Met (which retained a nominally separate existence) for use on the lines it still leased from LONDON COUNTY COUNCIL, whilst the last horse services in Edmonton probably ceased on 18 July 1905, the day before electric cars began running there.

Electric services began with Brush open-top bogie cars Nos 1-70 which were joined in 1904-05 by similar vehicles 71-130; most of these were later top-covered. In 1905 Brush supplied single-deckers 131-150 for use on the two short branches to Alexandra Palace and a year later bogie open-top cars 151-165 (later top-covered) and Nos 166-190, four-wheeled open-toppers. In 1907 Brush open-topper 191 entered service: this had been a 1903 sample car built for LEICESTER CORPORATION (where the tender was not won) bought by the MET in 1904 and used briefly as an engineers' inspection car. In 1908 the same firm supplied bogie open-toppers 192-211 (again later top-covered) and enclosed-top bogie cars 212-216, followed a year later by bogie open-toppers 217-236 (also top-covered).

Between 1909 and 1912 Brush provided a further batch of enclosed-top bogie cars, Nos 237-316 (nicknamed 'Dreadnoughts'), after which World War I put a stop to acquisitions until 1921 when the Company built open-top bogie car No 317 (later top-covered) which had the distinction of being, before its withdrawal in 1938, the last MET car in service. Between 1924 and 1925 the Company constructed enclosed-top bogie cars 2, 12, 22, 31, 46 and 82 to replace withdrawn trams (some parts of which were incorporated into the new cars). In 1927 it produced a unique car, No 318, which was a fully-enclosed bogie vehicle with a rear entrance and front exit, and nicknamed 'Bluebell' on account of its pale blue livery. A companion car, No 319, painted dark red and white and known as 'Poppy', was constructed for the Company by the London General Omnibus Co. but sold in 1928 to London United Tramways.

In 1928 the Union Construction & Finance Co. Ltd built two enclosed bogie cars, Nos 320 ('Blossom') and 330 ('Cissie'), designated 'Experimental Felthams' after that company's works, and in 1930 No 331, which had a centre entrance and stairs. These were followed by 'Felthams' 319, 321-329 and 332-375 from 1931 onwards just before the whole system became part of LONDON TRANSPORT.

The fleet was housed in five depots: Edmonton, Finchley, Hendon (the main works), Stonebridge Park and Wood Green.

The system was connected at several of its southern termini to the LCC network and through running began on 1 August 1912, for which the Council had to fit a number of its cars with trolley poles for overhead current collection and the MET some of its with plough carriers to enable them to work over the LCC's conduit tracks.

The Company also operated buses through a subsidiary, the Tramways (MET) Omnibus Co. Ltd (registered 13 January 1912) which, later in 1912, combined with the MET and the LUT under a holding company, the London & Suburban Traction Co. Ltd, as a combine with links (through the LUT) to the Underground group. The SOUTH METROPOLITAN ELECTRIC TRAMWAYS joined the combine the following year, thus paving the way for a city-wide unified transport system 20 years before the London Passenger Transport Board came into existence and took it over as part of London Transport. Car No 331 is now at the National Tramway Museum, Crich (after seeing service as LT 2168 and SUNDERLAND 100), whilst No 335 of 1931 (latterly LT 2099 and LEEDS 501) is on display at the London Transport Museum.

Bibliography: *The Metropolitan Electric Tramways Vol 1: Origins to 1920* C. S. Smeeton (The Light Railway Transit Association, 1984) 0 900433 94 9
– *Vol 2: 1921 to 1933* (1986) 0 948106 00 X

LONDON TRANSPORT

Authority: London Passenger Transport Act 1933
Gauge: 4ft 8½in
Traction: Overhead electric
Took Over: 1 July 1933
Closed: 5 July 1952
System: Network
Length: 328.45 miles
Stock: 19 sd, 2,611 dd
Livery: Red & cream
Last Car: No 1951

The London Passenger Transport Board was established in 1933 to provide a single body responsible for the whole of the capital's public transport on and below its streets; the existing tramways were to be unified, including those systems outside the city's boundaries but connected to those of the London operators. The Board therefore assumed control of not only the LONDON COUNTY COUNCIL lines, the METROPOLITAN ELECTRIC TRAMWAYS and, as part of the Underground Electric Railway Co., LONDON UNITED TRAMWAYS, but also the systems of BEXLEY, CROYDON, EAST HAM, ERITH, ILFORD, LEYTON, WALTHAMSTOW, WEST HAM and the SOUTH METROPOLITAN TRAMWAYS.

With the lines came the operators' surviving cars – all 2,630 of them – to be merged into a single fleet. More than half were ex-LCC vehicles and these retained their old numbers, as did the ex-MET and ex-LUT cars, whilst the others were given temporary suffixes to their fleet numbers thus: Bexley – C, Erith – D, Croydon – E, Ilford – F, East Ham – G, West Ham – H, Walthamstow – K and Southmet – S. Withdrawals of unwanted vehicles began immediately and a renumbering programme begun which eventually took the number series up to 2529, the cars being lettered 'LONDON TRANSPORT'. During the next 20 years no further passenger cars were added to the stock; instead, many of the inherited cars were rebuilt and modernized as the fleet continued to shrink. Seventy trams went in the first twelve months, after which the withdrawal rate accelerated: 87, 150 and 263 went during the next three years, including all the cars inherited from Bexley, Croydon, Erith and the Southmet.

The reduction in fleet size was accompanied by a rationalization of the depot arrangements and, ominously, by an increase in the size of the Board's trolleybus fleet. During the first twelve months of the Board's operations however just 3 miles of route were trimmed from the network and no further cuts were made until 1935-36 when 40 miles were abandoned to the trolleybuses; over the next twelve months another 58 miles went. By mid-1939 the car fleet had shrunk by almost exactly half and now stood at 1,316 vehicles operating over 135 route miles – both figures comfortably exceeded by the corresponding trolleybus totals. The abandonments and withdrawals continued during World War II, hastened by the damage suffered during the Blitz, and at the end of 1946 913 cars were operating over 102 miles of route.

On January 1948 the Board's operations were nationalized with the London Transport Executive assuming control to oversee the tramways' final days, it being announced in July 1950 that the trams were to be replaced by motor buses over the next two years. So it proved, with the last service car running from Woolwich on the night of 5 July 1952, arriving at New Cross in the early hours of the following day.

Bibliography: as for above LONDON entries and
A History of London Transport Vol 1: The Nineteenth Century T. C. Barker & Michael Robbins (George Allen & Unwin, 1963)
– *Vol 2: The Twentieth Century to 1970* (1974) 0 0438 5063 4

LOWESTOFT CORPORATION TRAMWAYS

Authority: Lowestoft Corporation Act 1901
Gauge: 3ft 6in
Traction: Overhead electric
Opened: 22 July 1903
Closed: 8 May 1931
System: Branching
Length: 4.08 miles
Stock: 4 sd 15 dd
Livery: Tuscan red & primrose
Last Car: ?

The Lowestoft system was owned and worked throughout its life by the Corporation, although the local authority's original intention had been to build the tramways and then lease them to a private company. The system consisted of a single, mainly single-track route which ran, like the Suffolk town itself, in a north-south direction roughly parallel to the shore from Yarmouth Road (by the GER's Lowestoft North station), down the High Street and London Road to cross the narrow harbour entrance by way of a swing bridge and thence down London Road South (the 'touristy' hotels and Esplanade part of the town) as the southern half of the line. The southern terminus was in the district of Pakefield where Pakefield Street met London Road South. A 1-mile branch ran inland on the northern side of the harbour past Lowestoft Central railway station to the depot in Rotterdam Road. (The intention had been to continue the tramway around the back of the town from here but the idea never came to fruition.) Original stock comprised eleven open-top double-deckers (Nos 1-11) and four single-deck saloon cars, all from Milnes. These latter vehicles were numbered 21-24, presumably to begin a separate single-deck number sequence, and were followed a year after the opening by four more double-deckers (Nos 12-15) of a similar type to the first batch.

By the end of the 1920s it was time for the Corporation to face the problem of whether to modernize the tramway or replace it with a bus service. It opted for the latter course of action and the section north of the harbour bridge closed in April 1931 and the southern half the following month. The body of car No 14 survives nearby as a static exhibit at the East Anglia Transport Museum, Carlton Colville.

Bibliography: *The Tramways of East Anglia* R. C. Anderson (The Light Railway Transport League, 1969) 0 900433 00 0

LUTON CORPORATION TRAMWAYS

Authority: Luton Corporation Tramways
    Order 1905
Gauge: 4ft 8½in
Traction: Overhead electric
Opened: 21 February 1908
Closed: 16 April 1932
System: Radial
Length: 5.25 miles
Stock: 1 sd, 12 dd
Livery: Grass green & ivory
Last Car: No 7

This little system – Bedfordshire's only tramway – consisted of five mainly single-track routes (none much more than a mile in length) radiating from the Town Hall north up Manchester Street and New Bedford Road to Wardown Park, northeast along Midland Road and High Town Road to Stockingstone Lane, Round Green, southeast along George Street and Park Street to Bailey Street and the depot, south off George Street to the London Road via Chapel Street, Hibbert Street and Ashton Road and northwest along Upper George Street and the Dunstable Road. The whole system opened as one with twelve UEC open-toppers numbered 1-12 of which Nos 1-4 and 5 were later top-covered. The only other car added to the fleet was No 13 (ex-Glasgow 118), a single-deck former horse car and later passenger then parcels car bought in 1923 when Luton Corporation took over the running of the system itself, it having been operated previously on lease first by J. G. White & Co. Ltd (the constructor) and then, from 1909, by BB. The system was closed by the Corporation in 1932 in favour of its own motor buses, the London Road, Dunstable Road and Wardown Park routes closing on 28 February, leaving just the Round Green–Depot route to survive another few weeks.

LYNTON & LYNMOUTH CLIFF RAILWAY

Although not a tramway as such, this water-powered funicular railway possesses one fascinating tramway feature. Offically opened on Easter Monday, 7 April 1890, as a double-track 3ft 9in gauge line nearly 300yd long to link the twin Devon towns of its title on a gradient of 1 in 1¾, it was the brainchild of the publisher Sir George Newnes (who had a residence nearby) with George Marks (see MATLOCK) as the project's Hydraulic Engineer. The two cars had triangular under-frames holding the water tanks used to move them and upon each was mounted not an integral body but a small, locally-built tramcar on its own set of narrow-gauge L-section rails which could be run off at

A somewhat unlikely subject for a turn of the century Christmas card: a pair of Lowestoft trams on a summer's day! (Author's Collection)

either station to allow the empty platform to be used for the conveyance of goods and, especially in the early years, motor vehicles. As far as is known this ingenious arrangement, patented by Newnes and Marks in 1889, was never adopted by any other British cliff railway though it could, in theory, have been used as part of a tramway system to connect routes on two different levels (as indeed it did in Cincinnati in the USA). The cars were rebuilt in 1947 but retain their flangeless wheels.

Bibliography: *Baron Marks of Woolwich*
    Michael R. Lane (Quiller Press, 1986)
    0 907621 77 5

LYTHAM ST ANNES CORPORATION TRAMWAYS

Authority: Blackpool St Anne's Lytham
    Tramways Act 1893
Gauge: 4ft 8½in
Traction: Gas, horse/overhead electric
Opened: 11 July 1896
Closed: 28 April 1937
System: Single line
Length: 7.51 miles
Stock: 16 dd gas; 3 sd, 17 dd horse; 4 sd, 52
    dd electric
Livery: Light blue & cream to 1920, blue &
    ivory to 1933, then blue & white
Last Car: ?

This simple system on the north shore of the Ribble estuary, just south of Blackpool, had a far from simple history. It was opened in 1896 by the Blackpool, St Anne's & Lytham Tramway Co. and was built to link Lytham with Blackpool using a coastal route through the new development of St Anne's-on-the-

Sea midway between them, there being no coast road at that time. The idea was to connect the line to BLACKPOOL's Lytham Road route (opened in 1895) to permit through running but in the event the first, mainly single-track section, ran from St Anne's to close to Blackpool's Station Road terminus with the 1-mile stretch from here back to the joint boundary at Squires Gate being owned by Blackpool Corporation. The line was operated on lease from the Company by the British Gas Traction Co. Ltd using four open-top double-deck cars (Nos 1-4) built by the Woodbury Carriage Co. and fitted with German gas engines. It was extended to Lytham in February 1897 and another twelve cars put into service (these being equipped with 15hp Crossley engines).

In 1898 the tramway was bought by the Blackpool, St Anne's & Lytham Tramways Co. Ltd (registered 15 October that year) for £115,000 including the cars. It would appear that the latter did not prove entirely successful for Blackpool Corporation refused to allow them over its portion of the line from 1900 onwards and until 1902 this section was worked by horse cars (possibly obtained from BOLTON). By now though the Company had obtained the Blackpool St Anne's and Lytham Tramways Act 1900 to authorize electric working and early in 1901 was bought out by the Electric Tramways Construction & Maintenance Co. Ltd who began reconstruction work in December 1902. The gas trams were sold the following year to TRAFFORD PARK and Neath in Wales. The tramway re-opened on 28 May 1903 as a double-track line following the route of the gas and horse line along the sand

A postcard view of Luton Corporation No 9 of 1908 passing the Market Cross. (Lens of Sutton)

dunes from Blackpool to St Anne's and then via Clifton Road South to Ansdell, then along Church Road into Lytham and through the Market Square past the old gas tram depot where it turned south towards the shore, terminating in Dicconson Terrace opposite the pier. That September a 1-mile extension east from the Market Square along Clifton Street and Warton Street took the line to a new terminus by the East Beach close to the Cottage Hospital. The depot was in Squires Gate Lane by the northern terminus, housing the new cars Nos 1-30, all BEC open-toppers.

Through running to Blackpool began in July 1905 after the two systems had been connected, with ten open-sided crossbench cars (Nos 31-40) being bought from Brush for summer workings. These proved so popular that the following year Nos 21-30 were converted by UEC to a similar configuration. On 28 October 1920 the tramway was purchased for £132,279 by St Anne's UDC which, in 1922, became part of the newly-incorporated borough of Lytham St Anne's which began motor bus operations the following year. Ten new top-covered cars (Nos 41-50) were bought in 1924 from EE however but two years later, on 23 July 1926, the eastern end of the line was cut back to Lytham Market Square. The future of the rest of the tramway appeared bright though and cars and track were kept in good order with minor rebuilds of the former taking place. In 1930 No 26 was converted to a works car to sweep sand from the line –

A postcard issued shortly after the opening of the Lynton & Lynmouth Cliff Railway showing the run-off tracks for the wheeled cars – a tramway invention that literally progressed no further than this in Britain. (Author's Collection)

always a serious problem on the exposed northern section.

In 1933 four relatively new (1924) single-deck EE cars were bought from the DEARNE DISTRICT system for winter workings and numbered 51-54, followed the next year by No 55, a double deck-enclosed Brush bogie car ex-ACCRINGTON. The last car purchased, No 56 in 1934, was an ex-PRESTON enclosed vehicle (No 42 there). By now though the Corporation was looking to sell the line to Blackpool but to no avail and, as its bus fleet grew, so the tram fleet was reduced by withdrawals until 1936 when it was decided to abandon the trams entirely. The southern section to St Anne's closed on 15 December that year

The Cliff Railway, Lynton.

with the original northern section going the same way the following spring – and with it the chance of a superb scenic run the length of the Fylde coast all the way from Lytham to Fleetwood.

Bibliography: *The Tramways of Lytham St Annes* (Locomotion Papers No. 189) P. H. Abell, J. A. Garnham & I. McLoughlin (The Oakwood Press, 1995) 0 85361 475 X

MAIDSTONE CORPORATION TRAMWAYS

Authority: Maidstone Corporation Light Railways Order 1903
Gauge: 3ft 6in
Traction: Overhead electric
Opened: 14 July 1904
Closed: 11 February 1930
System: Radial
Length: 5.25 miles
Stock: 1 sd, 17 dd
Livery: Golden ochre & white
Last Car: No 2?

Maidstone's first authorized tramway was a 2-mile street line running westwards from the High Street across the River Medway and out along the Tonbridge Road to the village of Barming (where the depot was situated). To work it six open-top double-deck cars were supplied by ERTCW with identical car No 7 being bought a year later. A second route opened on 16 October 1907 running southwards from the High Street, out along Loose Road for 2 miles to the village of that name, while a third, shorter line came off the Loose route just below the High Street, running southwestwards to Tovil paper mill. Opened on 9 January 1908, it completed the mainly single-track system. (Only the two main routes in the centre of the town were double-tracked.) To work the enlarged system ten further cars were purchased from UEC in 1907 and numbered 8-17; these were similar to Nos 1-7 but slightly smaller. A single-deck UEC demi-car (No 18) bought in 1909 completed the passenger car fleet.

In 1924 the Corporation started operating motor buses, followed by trolleybuses which, on 1 May 1928, began by taking over the Barming route (though the tramway track was left in situ to enable the depot to be reached). The next closure came on 1 August 1929 when motor buses replaced the Tovil trams (one of these, No 14, being sold to CHATHAM) with the Loose service succumbing to trolleybuses the following February.

Bibliography: *The Tramways of Kent Vol 1: West Kent 'INVICTA'* (The Light Railway Transport League, 1971) 0 900433 38 8

MANCHESTER TRAMWAYS

Authority: Manchester Corporation
    Tramways Order 1875; Salford Tramways
    and Improvement Act 1875
Gauge: 4ft 8½in
Traction: Horse
Opened: 18 May 1877
Closed: 31 March 1903
System: Network
Length: 27.63 miles
Stock: 84 sd?, 431 dd?
Livery: Red & cream
Last Car: ?

Lytham St Annes Corporation No 12 of 1903 on the seaside track that comprised most of this line. (Lens of Sutton)

This extensive system grew piecemeal during the 1870s and 1880s using conventional grooved rails following the unsuccessful experiment of Haworth's patent track (see SALFORD TRAMWAYS). The history of the system is an immensely complicated one, partly because of the large number of routes and extensions involved and partly because of the number of local authorities who owned and leased track to the tramway's operator. In the beginning this was the Manchester Carriage Co. Ltd who opened the first line from the Pack Horse Inn, Pendleton, southeastwards into the city centre along the route of the original Salford tramway via Broad Street and Chapel Street as far as Bridge Street (2 miles), then back out northwards via Deansgate and the Bury New Road to the Grove Inn, Higher Broughton (another mile), the two sections being leased respectively from Salford and Manchester Corporations. The line was extended from the Grove Inn to the toll bar at Kersal on 30 July 1877 with each route being worked by 15 Starbuck open-top double-deckers (Nos 1-30) based on depots at Church Street, Pendleton and Knoll Street, Higher Broughton. At least some of these cars carried the legend 'MANCHESTER & SALFORD TRAMWAYS'.

Surrounding local authorities wished to get in on the act and a succession of Orders were obtained to expand the system, whilst the Manchester Suburban Tramways Act of 1878 authorized a new concern, the Manchester Suburban Tramways Co., to construct a string of outlying lines and which, in 1880, merged with the MC Co. to form the Manchester Carriage & Tramways Co. Two years later the system was virtually complete. The western routes converged on Deansgate and the eastern on Piccadilly, the two being connected via Market Street. The routes were a mixture of single and double tracks (with a depot on most of them) running out as far as Stockport in the southeast, Eccles in the west, Ashton-under-Lyne and Stalybridge to the east and Oldham to the northeast.

Full details of the passenger stock are not

known though it is certain that well over 500 cars were used, lettered and numbered according to their usual route, the vast majority of which were reversible cars built 1877-1890 by the Company at its Pendleton Works to the patented designs of John Eades, the Works Manager. (The basic design was that of a single-ended body which could be rotated on its truck at a terminus in order to avoid unhitching the horses.) Some idea of the scale of the Manchester operation can be gauged by the fact that at one time the Company was the biggest single purchaser of horses in the north of England, with over

5,000 in the stud in 1900, each animal having a life expectancy of only five years.

As Manchester expanded its boundaries in the 1880s and 1890s, so the Corporation turned its thoughts to running the tramway system itself. There then followed a protracted round of disputes, negotiations, 'horse-trading' and non-agreements between the Company and the various local authorities involved, resulting finally in arbitration in 1901-03 to settle the matter. As from 2 May 1901 SALFORD CORPORATION took over its portion of the system (and 94 cars) and on 30 October that same

Commemorative postcard of the official procession of cars at the opening of the Maidstone Corporation Tramways. (Author's Collection)

year the Company stopped its services in OLDHAM, the Corporation there having already begun electric services. The Manchester lines were handed over to the Corporation as and when horse-working ceased, the last such transfers being the Oldham Road and Ashton routes.

Bibliography: *The Manchester Carriage and Tramways Company* Edward Gray (Manchester Transport Museum Society, 1977)

MANCHESTER CORPORATION TRAMWAYS

Authority: Manchester Corporation Act 1897
Gauge: 4ft 8½in
Traction: Overhead electric
Opened: 6 June 1901
Closed: 10 January 1949
System: Network
Length: 119.23 miles
Stock: 73 sd, 1,028 dd
Livery: Red & cream
Last Car: No 1007

Manchester Corporation's first electric route was the Cheetham Hill Road line from Albert Square to Hightown, after which the remainder of the horse system was converted and new routes and extensions added, until by the end of the 1900s, the system was one of the largest in the country and closely linked to the surrounding tramways of SALFORD, STOCKTON, ASHTON, OLDHAM and MIDDLETON. Through running to Salford began on 31 May 1903, to Oldham on 21 January 1907 and to Ashton on 4 March that year. To the south, Altrincham was reached on 10 May 1907 and to the west the TRAFFORD PARK electric tramway had been taken over (on 31 October 1905) jointly with Salford Corporation.

World War I caused a pause in this relentless expansion but it began again in the 1920s when the end of the lease of the OLDHAM, ASHTON & HYDE system on 24 June 1921 opened the way for new through services to Ashton and Hyde. The takeover of the Middleton system on 9 August 1925 by the surrounding local authorities (including Manchester) led to a new through service to ROCHDALE commencing that same day; three years later, on 19 May 1928, through running began to BURY via Middleton and HEYWOOD. The system was now at its peak with nearly a thousand trams out on the roads, a fleet second only in size to those of LONDON and Glasgow.

The 1930s were very different. It was now the turn of the buses, the Corporation's own fleet having grown to 127 by 1930, and on

6 April that year tramway route 53 from Cheetham Hill to Stretford Road was closed and on 26 October route 25 (Bradford Road) treated likewise. The long southwestern route down Chester Road, Washway Road and Manchester Road to Altrincham (and the short branch to Sale) went the following year, and in 1932 the through service to Rochdale was another casualty.

On 1 March 1938 the Ashton Old Road line to the east was converted to trolleybus operation and on 8 February 1939 the Corporation agreed a three-year plan to abandon the tramways altogether. As elsewhere though, World War II put the plan on hold, though not before further cutbacks had occurred (and some reinstatements made during the war in order to save fuel). By the end of 1945 only the Oldham route remained to the north of the city. The abandonment programme was now resumed in earnest, the last route to go being 35 from Exchange to Hazel Grove. The story does not end there though for the city has pioneered the resurrection of the British tramway – literally in the case of Heaton Park (see Section 7) where the only preserved tramway in these islands runs. Far more importantly, the modern METROLINK system is set to serve the city's residents well into the next millenium. (See below.)

Because the car fleet was so large, only the briefest details can be given here (and ignoring later modifications). The first six cars arrived in 1899 as samples of their manufacturers' products so that the Tramways Committee could decide where to place its initial large order. No 101 was a Manchester Carriage & Tramways open-topper and No 102 the same from HN. No 103 was a bogie open-topper from Brush, No 104 an Ashbury open-topper and Nos 105 and 106 two Milnes cars, an open-topper and a single-deck saloon. After this the fleet was assembled as follows:

Nos 107-187, 238-276: Brush open-toppers of 1901-03
Nos 277-436, 487-511: Milnes ditto
Nos 437-486: Brush bogie open-toppers of 1901
Nos 188-237, 537-548: ditto of 1902-04
Nos 512-536: Milnes bogie single-deckers of 1903
Nos 549-648: Brush top-covered bogie cars of 1904-05
Nos 649-668: UEC bogie single-deckers of 1907
Nos 669-679: Corporation balcony cars of 1909
Nos 680-717, 748-762: ditto bogie cars of 1909-1914
Nos 718-747: Corporation balcony cars of 1912
Nos 763-767: Corporation bogie single-deckers of 1914
Nos 768-792: Corporation bogie balcony cars of 1914-1919
Nos 793-797: Corporation bogie enclosed cars of 1920
Nos 798-835: EE ditto of 1920
Nos 836-847: EE bogie single-deckers of 1920-21
Nos 848-897: EE bogie enclosed cars of 1920-22
Nos 898-933: Corporation ditto of 1920-22

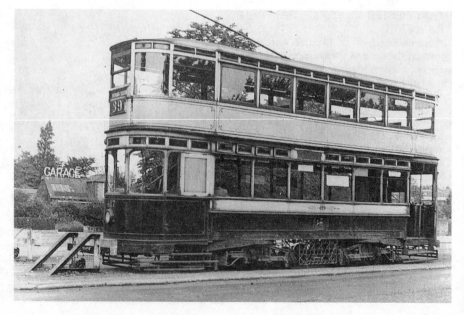

Manchester Corporation No 427, one of a 1901-03 delivery from Milnes. Note the unusual railway-type track buffers. (Lens of Sutton)

Nos 934-993: EE ditto of 1925-26

Nos 994-1003: Brush bogie single-deckers
ex-Middleton 1925

Nos 1004-1053: EE bogie enclosed cars of
1927-28

In addition, between 1924 and 1930 the Corporation built 110 bogie enclosed double-deckers which were given the numbers from withdrawn vehicles, and between 1927 and 1930 38 enclosed double-deckers (known as 'Pilchers' after the then General Manager) were similarly added to the fleet. The system's four depots were at Queens Road in Hightown, Princess Road in Moss Side, Birchfields Road in Levenshulme and Hyde Road (the main depot and works) just east of the city centre.

At the final closure 35 passenger cars still survived, only to be burnt en masse on 16 March following. Sadly, out of such a large fleet only one car – No 765 of 1914 – can be seen in working order today, on the Heaton Park line.

Bibliography: as above and

The Manchester Tramways Ian Yearsley & Philip Groves (The Transport Publishing Co., 1988) 0 86317 144 3

MANCHESTER METROLINK

Authority: Greater Manchester (Light Rapid Transit System) Act 1988

Gauge: 4ft 8½in

Traction: Overhead electric

Opened: 6 April 1992

System: Branching

Length: 19.26 miles

Stock: 26 sd

Livery: Aquamarine & pale grey

More than 40 years after the last Corporation trams ran in Manchester (see above) a new, high-technology system was opened to herald a new age of British street tramway construction. Inspired by light rail developments elsewhere in Europe and America and, closer to home, by the 1980s' successes of the Tyne & Wear Metro in Newcastle and the Docklands Light Railway in London, this historic project was promoted by a Rail Study Group made up of representatives from BR, the Greater Manchester Council and the Greater Manchester Passenger Transport Executive set up in 1982 to plan for the city's future local rail needs. Six years of analyses, planning and lobbying finally led to Parliamentary approval for the first stages of an envisaged city-wide light rail network to include purpose-built street sections in the centre and the use of existing BR lines to serve the peripheral areas.

The first, northern half of the system opened on 6 April 1992 and ran from the former BR Manchester Victoria station, along a refurbished double-track (formerly third-rail) line through Crumpsall, Prestwich, Whiteford and Radcliffe to a new interchange station at Bury, with nine intermediate stations en route. On 27 April the double-track street section from Victoria to BR's Manchester Piccadilly station opened, followed by the southern branch back out from Piccadilly to Altrincham. The city centre portion of this, from Piccadilly to the new G-MEX exhibition and conference centre, converted from the former Central station, is a street tramway occupying the High Street, Market Street, Piccadilly Gardens, Moseley Street (where the Bury branch departs), St Peter's Square and Lower Moseley Street. From G-MEX to Altrincham the cars travel over the refurbished BR line through Old Trafford, Stretford, Sale (and five other stations) to BR's Altrincham station. The official opening of the system, on 17 July 1992, was by HM the Queen.

The initial car fleet is made up of 26 articulated three-bogie vehicles built by the Firema Consortium of Italian rolling stock manufacturers. Numbered 1001-1026, each double-body unit is 30m long and can seat 86 passengers. With a top speed of 50mph they represent the latest in such vehicle design and technology.

Operated by the Greater Manchester Metro Ltd and funded largely by the Government, the total cost of the project was some £135m though the story is unlikely to stop here for further routes are planned, including east to Glossop, south to East Didsbury and west to Eccles.

Bibliography: *Manchester Metrolink* (UK Light Rail Systems No 1) David Holt (Platform 5 Publishing, 1992) 1 872524 36 2

Metrolink John Senior & Eric Ogden (The Transport Publishing Co., 1992) 0 86317 155 9

MANCHESTER, BURY, ROCHDALE & OLDHAM STEAM TRAMWAYS

Authority: Bury and District Tramways Order 1881; Rochdale Tramways Order 1881

Gauge: 4ft 8½in and 3ft 6in

Traction: Steam, horse

Opened: 12 March 1883

Closed: 30 May 1904

System: Branching

Length: 30.28 miles

Stock: 91 locos, 72 dd steam; 3 dd? horse

Livery: Locos brown, cars oak & white, later brown & cream

Last Cars: Locos 46 and 87

Despite its title, this impressive system – of which only a third of the planned lines were constructed – never served Manchester, only the other three towns of its title. Because of the number of different local authorities involved, the promotion was a complicated affair for the owner and operator, the Manchester, Bury, Rochdale & Oldham Steam Tramways Co. (a subsidiary of the City of London Contract Corporation). Matters were not helped by having the two ends of the system laid to standard gauge (with an eye on future through running with its neighbours) whilst the central portion had to employ 3ft 6in gauge track on account of the narrow roadways encountered.

The shape of things to come? Manchester Metrolink articulated two-car unit No 1001. (Courtesy Metrolink)

The first, standard gauge section opened ran northwards from Moor Lane in Broughton, just inside the SALFORD boundary north of Manchester, through Whitefield on Bury New Road and the Manchester Road to the Derby Hotel in the centre of Bury, a distance of some 6 miles (and later extended as a narrow gauge branch northwest up the Tottington Road.) The first three engines (Nos 1-3) were by Wilkinsons, hauling the first arrivals of a batch of 16 standard and narrow gauge six-wheeled open-top cars (Nos 1-16) from Starbuck.

On 20 March 1883 a second route opened: a 2½-mile continuation of the line northwards to Limefield which, until road-widening work was completed, had to be worked by horses with (probably) three Starbuck double-deckers Nos 33-35 being bought for this purpose. The third section opened, on 7 May 1883, was an isolated route in the east, parallel to the existing line, running south from the Wellington Hotel in the centre of Rochdale, down the Oldham Road to the village of Buersil with a northeastern branch from Rochdale along Entwistle Road and the Halifax Road through Smallbridge to Littleborough. Both these lines were narrow gauge and worked by tram locos from a fleet of 26 based at Rochdale and supplied by Greens (9-12, 18-20 and 27-34), Wilkinson (13-17) and BP (21-26) hauling trailers 17-26, more six-wheel open-toppers from Starbuck. These were joined in 1883-84 by Nos 31, 32 and 36-39, conventional Starbuck bogie open-toppers. Locos 4-8 and 35-38 were further Wilkinson standard gauge engines of 1883 and later that year the Tottington Road branch northwest from Bury was extended as far as the village of that name.

March 1884 saw the opening of a narrow gauge line from Bury eastwards to Heywood Depot, halfway to Rochdale (plus a ¾-mile branch south from Heywood to Hopwood) with the other half of this 7-mile section opening on 30 May. Another northern narrow gauge branch, from Rochdale to Whitworth via the Whitworth Road through Shawclough was in operation by July that year and, on 1 March 1885, services began over a southern extension from Buersil to Royton (where another depot was sited). The line from here through Oldham, opened in stages to 1 August, was standard gauge (with a branch opened on 4 July 1889 to Werneth station). Further standard gauge locos were bought in 1885: Nos 52-54 from MW and 55-59 from Falcon. Three more narrow gauge locos came that year (No 60 from Greens and 61 and 62 from Wilkinsons) plus Falcon narrow gauge cars 40-64 (of 1884-85). Thereafter the remaining stock purchases were all in 1886: standard gauge BP locos 83-88 and 91, bogie top-covered cars 65-70 from Lancaster and 71-74 from Falcon plus

narrow gauge locos 63-82 from BP and 89 and 90 from Wilkinsons with bogie top-covered cars 75-81 from Falcon.

In December 1887 the Company went into receivership and ten months later a new concern, the more appropriately-named Bury, Rochdale & Oldham Steam Tramways Co. Ltd was formed to take over the tramway which, with its lengthy, single-track, largely rural sections was at one time the longest steam-worked system in the world. The first cutbacks, in the name of economy, were not long in coming with a mile being lopped off the southern end of the Bury-Broughton route and, on 22 July 1891, the Whitworth branch was cut in half at Henley. On 19 December that year the Hopwood branch was closed (until 18 November 1892), followed by a further truncation of the standard gauge line south of Bury. These and other measures succeeded in turning the tramway's fortunes round but by now the local authorities affected were looking towards a more modern, electric future for the line. On 31 October 1901 Oldham Corporation took over the track within its boundaries (which had been leased to the Company) and on 28 June 1902 the last steam trams ran there. The closure of the rest of the system followed in stages until 30 May 1904 when the last standard gauge stretch (from Royton to Oldham boundary) and the last narrow gauge section (from Royton to Summit on the Rochdale boundary) closed. Only the Littlehampton branch survived, to be worked by ROCHDALE CORPORATION.

Bibliography: *The Manchester Bury Rochdale and Oldham Steam Tramway* W. G. S. Hyde (The Transport Publishing Co., 1979) 0 903839 37 7

MANSFIELD & DISTRICT LIGHT RAILWAY

Authority: Mansfield and District Light Railways Order 1901
Gauge: 4ft 8½in
Traction: Overhead electric
Opened: 16 July 1905
Closed: 9 October 1932
System: Radial
Length: 12.28 miles
Stock: 31 dd
Livery: Red & cream, later light green & cream
Last Car: ?

Operated by the Mansfield & District Light Railway Co. and owned through a hierarchy of companies by BB, this comparatively extensive system served the small Nottinghamshire town of its title with five radial single-track routes. Each longer than the previous one (if taken in order), they

radiated from the Market Place in the town centre, south down the Nottingham Road to Berry Hill (1 mile), east along Eakring Road to Crown Farm (1½ miles), north up Woodhouse Road Yorke Street, Sherwood Street and Station Street to Mansfield Woodhouse, just past the MR's station of that name (1¾ miles), northwest up Westgate, the Chesterfield Road and Mansfield Road to Pleasley (2¾ miles) and southwest out along Stockwell Gate and past the depot, then along Sutton Road and (another) Mansfield Road to the GNR's Sutton-in-Ashfield station. From here it continued west through Sutton and out along Hucknall Lane and Sutton Road to Hucknall-under-Huthwaite (5¼ miles).

Services began with twelve HN open-toppers which were joined in 1906 by four Brush top-covered cars (Nos 13-18). Some of the older cars were later top-covered as well and in 1912 two Brush second-hand open-toppers (Nos 19 and 20) were bought from the Cavehill & Whitewell line in Ireland. Six UEC top-covered cars (Nos 21-26) were added in 1916 and the last two new cars (Nos 27 and 28), enclosed EE double-deckers, nine years later. Finally three more second-hand cars came from NOTTINGHAMSHIRE & DERBYSHIRE c1930: balcony car No 29 and open-top Nos 30 and 31 (of which No 31 was returned to the N&D after a year).

Given its size and the essentially rural nature of much of the system it is not surprising that the tramway was a comparative early casualty of motor bus competition. After its closure in 1931 cars 27 and 28 were sold to SUNDERLAND and the other survivors scrapped.

MARBLE ARCH STREET RAILWAY
see LONDON: TRAIN'S TRAMWAYS

MARFLEET *see* HULL: DRYPOOL & MARFLEET

MARGATE *see* ISLE OF THANET; RAMSGATE & MARGATE

MATLOCK CABLE TRAMWAY
Authority: Matlock Tramway Order 1891
Gauge: 3ft 6in
Traction: Cable
Opened: 28 March 1893
Closed: 30 September 1927
System: Single line
Length: 0.5 miles
Stock: 3 dd
Livery: Royal blue & white
Last Car: ?

Matlock's tramway belonged to not only that select group of British cable tramways but also to a similarly select assembly of lines associated with the publisher and philanthropist Sir George Newnes (himself a native of this Derbyshire town). The line was the brainchild of Job Smith, sometime Chairman of the Local Board and Managing Director of the Matlock Cable Tramway Co. Ltd, who first conceived the idea after seeing the famous cable trams in San Francisco in the 1860s. The principal purpose of the line was to convey patients from the middle of Matlock (where they arrived by train) up the hillside to Matlock Bank where a flourishing growth of hydropathic establishments had begun a decade earlier. Nothing happened however until 1890 when Newnes and George Croydon Marks (Newnes' engineer on the LYNTON & LYNMOUTH CLIFF RAILWAY project) became involved, calling in as a consultant W. N. Colam who had worked on similar systems at Edinburgh, BIRMINGHAM and LONDON (Highgate Hill and Brixton). Accordingly the MCT Co. was formed and a single-track line constructed from Crown Square by Matlock Bridge up the 1 in 5 Bank Road and Rutland Street – no easy climb for those in the fittest of health – to the corner of Wellington Street and the depot and steam-driven winding gear.

The tramway was worked in classic fashion with a continuously-wound cable in a central conduit to which the line's two service cars could be attached or detached by driver-operated grippers. The line's third car was kept as a standby in case one of the others needed attention; all three were open-top bogie double-deckers from Milnes. A loop at Smedley Street allowed the two cars to pass. In 1896 Newnes bought out his fellow shareholders and presented the tramway to Matlock UDC, a not altogether welcome gift as it was losing money! The losses increased steadily until 1927 when the Council decided to close the line, replacing it with a bus service the following day.

Bibliography: *The Matlock Steep Gradient Tramway* (The Arkwright Society, Matlock, 1972)
Baron Marks of Woolwich Michael R. Lane (Quiller Press, 1986) 0 907621 77 5

METROPOLITAN ELECTRIC TRAMWAYS *see* LONDON: METROPOLITAN ELECTRIC TRAMWAYS

METROPOLITAN STREET TRAMWAYS *see* LONDON TRAMWAYS

MEXBOROUGH & SWINTON TRAMWAYS
Authority: Mexborough & Swinton Tramways Act 1902

The lower terminal loop on the Matlock Cable Tramway with the whole of the line receding into the distance. The gradient has been flattened deceptively by the postcard camera. (Author's Collection)

Gauge: 4ft 8½in
Traction: Stud/overhead electric
Opened: 6 February 1907
Closed: 9 March 1929?
System: Single line
Length: 6.48 miles
Stock: 20 dd
Livery: Bright red & cream
Last Car: ?

The short, simple M&S tramway provided the vital link between the larger systems of ROTHERHAM and SHEFFIELD to the south and DEARNE DISTRICT and BARNSLEY to the north. It was constructed by the NEC and worked by a subsidiary, the Mexborough & Swinton Tramways Co. It ran northwards from Rotherham Bridge (where it connected with that town's Effingham Street line) through Parkgate, Rawmarsh and Ryecroft to the Woodman Inn where it met (from 1924) the Wath Wood Road route of the DD. Here the M&S line swung northeast through Swinton and Mexborough to terminate at the Old Toll Bar at Denaby. The first section opened in 1907 was from Rotherham Bridge to Ryecroft with the remainder following on 3 August with the Dolter surface contact system being used to supply current to the 16 Brush open-top cars. These were also equipped for overhead current supply, presumably on the 'belt and braces' principle which in the event proved a wise choice for, as elsewhere, the Dolter system was a failure and the Company was in the process of converting the line to an overhead system when, on 30 July 1908, the BoT ordered its closure until the work was completed.

The tramway re-opened on 29 August 1908 with another four Brush double-deckers added to the stock (Nos 17-20); these were top-covered cars and over the next four years all the earlier cars were fitted with top covers with the exception of Nos 10 and 14 which in 1911 were sold to DEWSBURY & OSSETT. Also in 1908, on 20 October, through running from Rotherham began. On 31 August 1915 the Company began two short trolleybus routes as feeders to the tramway and thirteen years later, in January 1928, they replaced the Mexborough–Denaby trams entirely. The next cutback came in November that year when the stretch from Mexborough back to the Woodman Inn was closed (again replaced by a trolleybus service) with the remaining southern half of the line following the next year. After the closure two more cars (Nos 7 and 15) were sold to the D&O and the others scrapped.

MID YORKSHIRE TRAMWAYS *see* SHIPLEY: MID YORKSHIRE TRAMWAYS

MIDDLESBROUGH & STOCKTON TRAMWAYS
Authority: Middlesbrough and Stockton Tramways Order 1973
Gauge: 4ft 8½in
Traction: Horse
Opened: November 1874?
Closed: 24 December 1897
System: Radial
Length: 2.59 miles
Stock: 2 sd, 2 dd?
Livery: Red & cream
Last Car: ?

The history of the tramways of Teesside is a seemingly complicated one involving two counties, three towns, the bridging of a major river and a number of separate lines and companies. In fact, the story can be seen as the familiar one of a number of different concerns slowly coming together, with their lines passing through the common horse-steam-electric traction sequence.

The first line in the area, opened by the Middlesbrough & Stockton Tramways Co., ran from the Wellington Hotel, in Albert Road in the centre of Middlesbrough, southwest along Corporation Road and Newport Road to terminate in Calvert Street, Newport by the ferry landing stage. Two single-deck and two double-deck cars were supplied by Starbuck and the line is thought to have opened in late 1874 sometime after a trial run on 23 November. In August 1878 the line was purchased by IMPERIAL TRAMWAYS who opened a second route in 1880 running south from Albert Street along Linthorpe Road to the village of that name, terminating by the Cleveland Hotel. The third and shortest route opened two years later northwards to Clarence Ferry on the river to complete the single-track system (which therefore never reached Stockton). By this date the STOCKTON & DARLING-TON steam tramway had been opened and this too was bought by Imperial in order to pave the way for a linked electric system (see below), both tramways being closed accordingly.

MIDDLESBROUGH, STOCKTON & THORNABY ELECTRIC TRAMWAYS

Authority: Middlesbrough Stockton-on-Tees and Thornaby Tramways Order 1897
Gauge: 3ft 7in
Traction: Overhead electric
Opened: 21 May 1898*
Taken Over: 3 April 1921
System: Radial network
Length: 9.61 miles
Stock: 10 sd, 50 dd
Livery: Vermillion & white

Following the closure of its STOCKTON & DARLINGTON steam line and MIDDLES-BROUGH & STOCKTON horse line (see above), IMPERIAL TRAMWAYS set about reconstructing and linking the two tramways via the south Teesside town of Thornaby. Work began at Norton at the western end of the planned system and progressed eastwards. As inspected by the BoT on 21 May 1898 the mainly double-track system comprised a main line from Norton through Stockton-on-Tees (the former steam tramway route extended along Middlesbrough Road and Stockton Road) to Newport Road in Middlesbrough

where it picked up the former horse tramway route to the centre of that town (extended eastwards along north Ormesby Road to the district of that name), plus the refurbished Linthorpe branch. The total route length was some 8 miles. It seems that trial journeys were made over the tramway for the purposes of driver training from 21 May onwards though the official opening was not until 13 July, by which time 35 of an order of 50 Milnes open-toppers (Nos 1-50) had been delivered. Depots were provided at Norton, by the Victoria Bridge (built 1887) over the Tees in Stockton, and in Parliament Road off the Newport Road in Middlesbrough on a 1-mile link line to the Linthorpe route which, after the system's early years, was used only for special workings and stock movements.

The only other route opened, in August 1901, was the former Cleveland Street branch for which ten Milnes single-deckers (Nos 51-60) were purchased that year, there being a low bridge by the NER's station on this double-track route; in 1911 Nos 37 and 50 were cut down to single-deck form as well. In 1918 the local authorities of Middlesbrough, Stockton and Thornaby decided to exercise their right to buy the system and did so from 3 April 1921, 29 of the double-deckers being allocated to STOCKTON & THORNABY and the remainder of the passenger fleet to MIDDLESBROUGH CORPORATION (see below).

MIDDLESBROUGH CORPORATION TRAMWAYS

Authority: Middlesbrough Corporation Act 1919
Gauge: 3ft 7in

Traction: Overhead electric
Took Over: 3 April 1921
Closed: 9 June 1934
System: Cross
Length: 5.49 miles
Stock: 12 sd, 28 dd
Livery: Dark blue & cream
Last Car: No 103

Following the local authorities' takeover of the MIDDLESBROUGH, STOCKTON & THORNABY system (see above), Middlesbrough Corporation acquired the track within its boundaries and 31 passenger cars: single-deckers 51-60 which were variously renumbered 100-109 and double-deckers 37 and 50 (renumbered 110 and 111) and 1-3, 6, 10, 15, 18, 21, 24, 25, 27, 28, 34, 36, 40-42, 46 and 47 which were variously renumbered 113-131; nine HN top-covered bogie cars (Nos 132-140) were purchased at the same time.

In 1931 the STOCKTON & THORNABY tramways closed down and Middlesbrough accordingly closed the whole of its main line from the Thornaby boundary to North Ormsby (through running between the two systems had been the norm), leaving just the route between Linthorpe and the Transporter Bridge (which had replaced the old ferry in 1911) to survive less than a year and a half until that too was replaced by a bus service.

MIDDLETON ELECTRIC TRAMWAYS

Authority: Middleton Light Railways Order 1898
Gauge: 4ft 8½in
Traction: Overhead electric
Opened: 27 March 1902

Postcard of Norton Road, Norton, looking towards the High Street, with Middlesbrough, Stockton & Thornaby No 36 of 1898 about to reach the terminus. The spur to the right led to the depot. (Lens of Sutton)

Taken Over: 16 June 1925
System: Branching
Length: 8.51 miles
Stock: 32 sd, 5 dd
Livery: Crimson & primrose

Promoted by the BET and operated by the Middleton Electric Traction Co. Ltd (registered 29 December 1900), this small single-track system occupied a place in the south Lancashire network between MANCHESTER to the south, OLDHAM to the east and HEYWOOD and ROCHDALE to the north. The first route opened ran east–west from the Oldham boundary, along Middleton Road though Chadderton and on through Mills Hill on the Oldham Road, past the depot and station, through the town centre via Townley Street, Old Hall Street and the Market Place then out along Manchester Old Road to Rhodes. On 28 March 1902 (Good Friday) the system's other route, north from the Market Place up the Rochdale Road to Castleton, was opened to double the route mileage. South Middleton was served by two lines operated by Manchester Corporation. The first of these, from the Market Place south along Manchester New Road, was opened on 24 December 1902 and the second, a branch off this along Oldham Road east to the railway station, then southeast down Grimshaw Lane to Middleton Junction station, followed on 21 September 1903; no connection however was made with the Middleton system.

The first cars were Brush bogie single-deck combination cars 1-20, joined in August 1902 by Nos 22-25 of the same type but different design. (No 21 was a water car.) It would appear that these were not entirely satisfactory for in 1903 OLDHAM, ASHTON & HYDE open-top double-deckers 39 and 46 were hired and in late 1903 and early 1904 four of the single-deckers (from Nos 11, 14 and 16-18) were exchanged for Oldham, Ashton & Hyde single-deck motorized trailer cars 27-34 (which retained those numbers at Middleton), after which Nos 39 and 46 were returned. Then, in 1905, six of the original Brush cars were sold to Swansea and replaced by Brush open-top double-deckers 11-15, the tramway's last acquisitions.

The system remained unchanged until the 1920s (apart from the sale of Nos 22-25 to the POTTERIES system in 1916-20) when, in 1925, an agreement was reached whereby the Middleton, Rochdale and Chadderton local authorities would buy the tramway for £79,000 on 15 June that year. Middleton's portion of the system was then leased to Manchester Corporation and Chadderton's sold to Oldham, after which the tramway quickly became integrated into the area's larger network. As

A fine side-on shot of one of Middlesbrough Corporation's new balcony cars of 1921. (Lens of Sutton)

regards the cars, Rochdale ended up with the double-deckers (Nos 11-15), Oldham with the ex-OAH cars (Nos 27-34) and Manchester the remainder.

Bibliography: *Middleton Tramways* A. K. Kirby (Manchester Transport Museum Society, 1976)

MORECAMBE TRAMWAYS
Authority: Morecambe Tramways Act 1886
Gauge: 4ft 8½in
Traction: Horse/petrol*
Opened: 3 June 1887
Closed: 24 October 1924
System: Single line
Length: 3.59 miles
Stock: 2 sd, 15 dd horse; 4 sd petrol
Livery: Maroon, teak & white, later green
Last Car: ?

For such a short line, Morecambe's street tramway had a very complicated history. It owed its origin to the rise of the town as a Lancashire holiday resort in the second half of the 19th century and the first 1¼ miles ran from the Central Pier (opened 1869) southwards along the seafront to the Battery Hotel. On 19 May 1888 a southern continuation from the Battery, along the Heysham Road to Strawberry Gardens (in the borough of Heysham) was opened, followed on 17 June 1895 by a northwards extension from the Central Pier to East View. The depot was on the Heysham Road and the line primarily single-track though a doubling programme was soon begun. The line was owned and operated by the Morecambe Tramways Co., originally with four cars supplied by Lancaster: Nos 1 and 2 were open-top double-deckers and Nos 3 and

Postcard view of the long Castleton route of the Middleton system with No 5 of 1901 almost the only vehicle in sight. (Lens of Sutton)

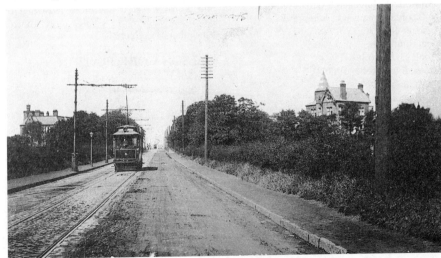

4 open single-deckers for summer use. In 1888 two similar double-deckers were added (Nos 5 and 6), followed by another (No 7) a year later.

In 1897 Morecambe Corporation received authorization for its own ¾-mile tramway and this opened the following year as a northwards single-track extension of the existing line on to Bare, leased to the MT Co. To cope with the extra workload four more open-toppers were bought from Lancaster in 1897 (Nos 8-11), followed soon after by four smaller cars (Nos 12-15), possibly secondhand vehicles. In 1901 two more open-toppers (Nos 16 and 17) completed the car fleet. On 26 July 1909 however the Corporation invoked its powers to purchase at least part of the line and bought the section from the Battery Hotel northwards for an arbitrated price of £13,391; the sale including cars 1-14 and part of the depo as well as 1.58 miles of the Company's tramway. (See below.) Although neither half of the line was ever electrified, some modernization took place when, from 15 January 1912, petrol-driven trams were operated by the Company. These were three closed cars of 1911 and one open car of 1913, all single-deckers, built for the line by Leyland Motors (with bodies by UEC) and took the numbers 1-4; the use of this type of motive power was a first for Britain. During World War I these vehicles (which had replaced the horse trams) were converted to run on town gas, a large canvas bag being fitted on the roof as a reservoir. They remained in service until the end of the 1924 summer season.

Bibliography: *The Lancaster and Morecambe Tramways* (Locomotion Papers No 95) S. Shuttleworth (The Oakwood Press, 1976)

MORECAMBE CORPORATION TRAMWAYS

Authority: Morecambe Urban District Council Tramways Order 1897
Gauge: 4ft 8½in
Traction: Horse
Took Over: 26 July 1909
Closed: 6 October 1926
System: Single line
Length: 2.4 miles
Stock: 2 sd, 16 dd
Livery: Maroon & white?
Last Car: No 13

Morecambe Corporation's tramway was made up of its own ¾-mile stretch from East View to Bare and that part of the MT Co.'s line from East View back to the Battery Hotel acquired in 1909 (see above). It remained

Postcard of unidentified Lancaster horse car on the Promenade at Morecambe about to pass the West End Pier, probably – judging by the crowds – on a Bank Holiday or similar occasion. (Lens of Sutton)

faithful to horse traction which meant that by the time of its closure in 1926 it was the last such survivor on the British mainland. Indeed, until nearly the end the Corporation was buying replacement cars: Nos 13 (of 1919) and 16 (1922) were double-deckers and Nos 14 (1919) and 15 (1922) toastracks, all from EE.

Bibliography: as above

MOUSEHOLD LIGHT RAILWAY *see* NORWICH ELECTRIC TRAMWAYS

NATIONAL ELECTRIC CONSTRUCTION CO. LTD

Established in 1897 (renamed in 1903) the NEC, among its other interests, owned at one time or another the English tramway systems of DEWSBURY, OSSETT & SOOTHILL NETHER (which it operated directly), OXFORD, MEXBOROUGH & SWINTON and TORQUAY. In addition, it owned the Rhondda system in Wales and that at Musselburgh in Scotland.

NELSON CORPORATION TRAMWAYS

Authority: Nelson Light Railways Order 1901
Gauge: 4ft
Traction: Overhead electric
Opened: 23 February 1903
Closed: 6 January 1934
System: Branching
Length: 2.74 miles
Stock: 3 sd, 17 dd
Livery: Red & white, then brown & cream
Last Car: ?

This short line formed the central portion of the BURNLEY-COLNE multiple-ownership tramway route and was the northern end of the former BURNLEY & DISTRICT steam tramway plus a short single-track branch northwards from Nelson Centre, along Scotland Road past the depot, then through Barrowford to Higherford Bridge. The old line was relaid to Burnley's 4ft gauge to allow through running (which system had opened in 1901) and the southern ¾ mile of double tracks from Nelson Centre to the Burnley boundary was in fact leased to that Corporation. In practice, Burnley cars usually terminated at Nelson Centre on account of a low bridge in Colne, whilst Nelson cars normally worked only from Higherford Bridge to Colne (after that system opened in 1903) via the Centre. Through working by Colne cars began in 1911 as part of a joint service.

The first Nelson cars were Brush open-toppers Nos 1-6 and ERTCW bogie single-deck combination cars 7 and 8 (followed in 1909 by similar car No 9). In 1912 two top-covered UEC lowbridge cars were bought and numbered 10 and 11, followed in 1916 by Nos 1-6, six more of the same which replaced the original cars of those numbers. Finally, three similar cars (Nos 7-9) were purchased in 1925, this time from Brush. From 1 April 1933 the line was run briefly by the Burnley, Colne & Nelson Joint Transport Committee (and the cars numbers given the suffix N) until it and the Colne system closed togther.

Bibliography: *Trams in the North West* Peter Hesketh (Ian Allan, 1995) 0 7110 2349 2

NEWCASTLE & GOSFORTH TRAMWAYS

Authority: Newcastle-upon-Tyne Tramways
  and Improvement Act 1877
Gauge: 4ft 8½in
Traction: Horse, steam
Opened: 1878
Closed: 13 April 1901
System: Network
Length: 12.19 miles
Stock: 4 locos, 44 horse & steam
Livery: ?
Last Car: ?

The Newcastle & Gosforth Tramways &
Carriage Co. Ltd operated its own 2-mile
line from Newcastle's northern boundary up
North Road to the centre of Gosforth, plus a
city network of lines leased from Newcastle
Corporation in 1878 for a period of 21 years.
The cars were horse-drawn (though in 1879
four Hawthorn tramway locomotives were
bought for the Gosforth to Westgate in
Newcastle route but sold to SUNDERLAND
three years later).

In 1899 the Corporation obtained the
necessary powers to extend and electrify
its own lines – and purchase compulsorily
connecting tramways outside its boundaries.
When it informed the Company of
its decision to electrify the horse lines on
expiry of the lease the Company promptly
closed the whole system, leaving the way
clear for the Corporation's own network (see
below).

Bibliography: *The Tramways of
  Northumberland* George S. Hearse
  (Author, Blanchland, 1961)

NEWCASTLE-UPON-TYNE CORPORATION TRAMWAYS

Authority: Newcastle-upon-Tyne Tramways
  and Improvement Act 1899
Gauge: 4ft 8½in
Traction: Overhead electric
Opened: 16 December 1901
Closed: 4 March 1950
System: Network
Length: 51.27 miles
Stock: 110 sd, 218 dd
Livery: Brown & orange
Last Car: ?

In 1899 Newcastle Corporation obtained
the necessary powers to construct and
operate its own electric tramways and
purchase the NEWCASTLE &
GOSFORTH routes outside its boundary
(see above), with work on the new system
commencing the following year. In its final
form this was a network of radial and cross
routes on the north bank of the Tyne extending as far as Wallsend and Walker in the east,
north on a long loop through Gosforth Park

and out on a long route along Westmorland
Road past the other western termini to
Throckley.

Some 14½ route miles opened in 1901 with
an impressively large car fleet. (Both system
and fleet grew to become the largest in the
North East.) Nos 1-20 were by HN, Nos 21-
28 by Brush and Nos 29-110 bogie cars by
HN – all single deckers. Nos 111-130 were by
HN and 131-165 by Brush – all open-toppers.

More cars soon followed: Nos 170-191
were Corporation-built open-toppers of 1904-
05 followed from 1906-14 by top-covered cars
1-28 and 192-209; Brush supplied similar cars
210-224 that last year. After that the
Corporation built top-covered cars 225-229
during 1915-18 and enclosed cars 232-236 in
1917-18, after which Brush provided
enclosed cars 240-309 from 1921-26 to
complete the fleet – surprisingly early for a
system that lasted so long (though many of
the trams were subsequently rebuilt and
modernized).

The mainly double-track system continued
to expand before, during and after World War
I with two important lines across the Tyne
opening on 12 January 1923 and 10 October
1928 to provide links with GATESHEAD.
Gosforth had been reached on 8 April 1921
and three years later the construction of the
Gosforth Park Light Railway connected with
the TYNESIDE system to form the great
northern loop. When the latter system closed
on 6 April 1930 the Corporation took over
that company's track on the Great North
Road to keep the service going (and also ran
over its line to Wallsend until 25 May when
a bus service was substituted). This was not
the first cutback though: on 3 June 1929 the
line to Denton Burn, only opened in 1926,
had been similarly treated.

From now on the Corporation's policy was
to replace the trams with buses or trolleybuses
as and when the tracks became worn out and
from 1935 to 1939 two-fifths of the system
was abandoned. After World War II this
programme was resumed with the last route –
the long one across the river and right
through Gateshead to Wrekenton – closing
in 1950 (though Gateshead trams still ran
into the city until that system closed the
following year).

Over the years the car fleet, based at Byker
Depot east of the city centre, was slimmed
down as new cars were added and in later
years several were sold to other operators: in
1941 Nos 112-114, 116-119, 122-126, 128
and 129 were sold to SHEFFIELD, in 1948
Nos 29, 42 and 77 to BR for its GRIMSBY &
IMMINGHAM line and Nos 43, 52, 54, 80
and 88 to GATESHEAD.

Car No 102 is now running at the National
Tramway Museum, Crich and No 114 at the
North of England Open Air Museum,
Beamish.

Bibliography: as above

NEWPORT PAGNELL & DISTRICT TRAMWAYS

A late 1880s tramway which almost but not
quite made it, this was to have been a steam-
worked 3ft 6in gauge line between the north
Buckinghamshire market town of Newport
Pagnell and the small town of Olney 6 miles
to the north. Some 5 miles of track were laid
by a local contractor, Charles Herbert
Wilkinson, for the Newport Pagnell &
District Tramways Co. and a new bridge over
the Great Ouse built, but the project
foundered when the BoT refused to sanction
running along the main street through the
village of Emberton just south of Olney. (The
rails were not lifted until at least 1893 so
some hopes of buying the land needed to
bypass the village were kept alive for a
while). If it had been completed, it would
have provided an interesting partner to its
close neighbour (and other Wilkinson
line) the WOLVERTON & STONY
STRATFORD TRAMWAY which opened
in 1887, the year the NPDT Co. obtained
the authority for its own line.

Bibliography: *The Wolverton & Stony
  Stratford Trams* Frank D. Simpson (The
  Omnibus Society, 1981) 0 901307 42 4

NORTH METROPOLITAN TRAMWAYS see LONDON: NORTH METROPOLITAN TRAMWAYS

NORTH SHIELDS see TYNEMOUTH

NORTH STAFFORDSHIRE TRAMWAYS see POTTERIES: NORTH STAFFORDSHIRE TRAMWAYS

NORTHAMPTON STREET TRAMWAYS

Authority: Northampton Street Tramways
  Act 1880
Gauge: 3ft 6in
Traction: Horse
Opened: 4 June 1881
Taken Over: 21 October 1901
System: Radial
Length: 5.25 miles
Stock: 4 sd, 26 dd?
Livery: ? to 1893, then route colour

The Northampton Street Tramways Co. was
formed on 9 January 1880 to operate horse
tramways in that town. The Chairman was J.
S. Balfour though the initial idea seems to
have come from J. F. Meston, a London
tramway constructor who had just built the
CAMBRIDGE system. The first route to
open ran from just west of the West Bridge
over the River Nene, eastwards past the

LNWR station, through the town centre via Gold Street and Abington Street (past the depot) then northeast up Kettering Road past the race course to the district of Kingsley Park, a total of some 2½ miles. On 30 July 1881 a short westwards extension took the line up St James's Road to the Cafe Square in the district of St James. This set the pattern for the growth of the system: first short routes were laid, then later extensions made to them.

The second route opened on 7 October 1881, from the Drapery/Gold Street junction in the town centre due north for a mile up Sheep Street and Barrack Road to St George's Terrace. Two further extensions opened on 4 January 1883: from the Cafe Square to Melbourne Gardens in St James and from St George's Terrace up Kingsthorpe Road to terminate in the district of that name at the junction with Welford Road. The last extension opened on 18 May 1893 and ran for about a mile from the end of Abington Street along Wellingborough Road to Abington Park. All routes were single-track.

The tramway's original six cars were Birmingham open-top double-deckers (Nos 1-6) which were joined in November 1881 by two more (Nos 7 and 8); in 1883 two more arrived (Nos 9 and 10) with the opening of the Kingsthorpe route. In 1886 financial problems led to the Company converting No 3 into a single-decker and the acquisition of four Birmingham single-deckers (Nos 11-14); in 1893, with the opening of the Abington Park route, two Falcon double-deckers (Nos 15 and 16) were bought. (At this time a livery change was made in that the Abington cars were painted red and the Kingsthorpe cars blue.) By 1899

several more Falcon double-deckers had been purchased (some as replacements for older vehicles) but full details do not survive. It is probable that 14 in all were bought, taking the new numbers 20-25 and earlier ones of those they replaced. (Nos 17-19 were 1894 horse buses used on a service to Far Cotton, south of the river.)

Towards the end of the 1890s the Town Council began plans to modernize the system, in 1900 deciding to purchase the concern for £37,000, and on 21 October 1901 took the tramways over (see below).

At least two other vehicles were experimented with under Company ownership. The first was a four-wheeled locomotive built at Mobbs' Vulcan Ironworks of Northampton and powered by a single-cylinder engine fuelled by a mixture of air and town gas. This was tested on the tramway in 1882-3 (possibly making it the first internal combustion-powered road vehicle) and in July 1883 a lightweight machine, built by a Mr Gabby of the local Lion Cycle Works and powered by floor-operated treadles via gearing to the wheels, succeeded in pulling a tramcar up Abington Street – the only known instance of pedal power being used on a tramway in Britain.

NORTHAMPTON CORPORATION TRAMWAYS

Authority: Northampton Corporation
   Tramways Order 1901
Gauge: 3ft 6in
Traction: Horse, overhead electric
Took Over: 21 October 1901
Closed: 15 December 1934
System: Radial
Length: 6.41 miles
Stock: 4 sd, 33 dd electric

Livery: Vermillion & white
Last Car: No 29

Following the Corporation's takeover of the old horse system (see above), it continued to work the lines much as before with reconstruction work not commencing until the end of 1903; the St James–Kingsley Park and Abington Park routes switched from horse to electric operation during 21 July of the following year. These routes were now principally double-track with the new depot sited on St James's Road west of the West Bridge and railway station.

Services on the Kingsthorpe route changed over on 19 August 1904; this was rebuilt as a single-track line again (probably because of its low traffic figures) and remained so until 1913-14 when it was doubled (except in the narrow Sheep Street). During that latter year it was decided to construct a new, southern route from the town centre down Bridge Street and over the South Bridge to St Mary's Church in Far Cotton under the provisions of the Northampton Corporation Act of 1911 to replace the tramway's existing horse bus service; this double-track line opened 23 October 1914 and completed the system.

For the opening of the new tramway 20 ERTCW open-top double-deckers were purchased, followed in 1905 by a further two as back-up vehicles (Nos 21 and 22). In 1910 two UEC open-topper (Nos 23 and 24) were bought to handle inceasing traffic demands as the town grew and another pair in 1911 (Nos 25 and 26). Seven Brush balcony cars were added in 1914 to work the Far Cotton route and numbered 27-33; these were followed in 1922 by four EE single-deckers (Nos 34-37).

After World War I the tramway suffered the usual problems caused by poor maintenance and in 1922 the Corporation began running motor buses, using them on 20 April 1929 to replace the trams on the Abington Park route. The move proved a successful one and a year later, on 31 August 1930, the same thing happened on the Kingsley route and on 27 September 1933 the Kingsthorpe line was similarly treated. On 15 December the two remaining routes – to St James and to Far Cotton – went the same way, the wheel for the latter route, in a sense, having come full circle.

NORTHFLEET *see* GRAVESEND & NORTHFLEET; GRAVESEND, ROSHERVILLE & NORTHFLEET

NORWICH ELECTRIC TRAMWAYS

Authority: Norwich Electric Tramways Act
   1897
Gauge: 3ft 6in

Postcard of Northampton Corporation Nos 16 and 2 of 1904 awaiting passengers in Kingsthorpe Road, the system's northern route. (Lens of Sutton)

Traction: Overhead electric
Opened: 30 July 1900
Closed: 10 December 1935
System: Radial network
Length: 15.16 miles
Stock: 52 dd
Livery: Maroon & ivory
Last Car: No 10

After a number of unsuccessful attempts from the 1870s onwards to provide the city with horse or cable tramways – despite the popular perception of Norfolk as being 'very flat', Norwich has its fair share of steep hills – it was not until the last year of the century that tramcars appeared in its streets. This followed unsuccessful proposals by the BET in 1896 and the New General Traction Co. Ltd in 1897, who also owned the COVENTRY and Douglas Southern (Isle of Man) tramways.

Construction began in June 1898 and routes were opened in batches, from July 1900 until the year's end, by the NGT Co.'s subsidiary, the Norwich Electric Tramways Co. Originally, all services began and ended at Orford Place in the city centre (where a magnificent circular tram shelter was constructed) but in 1901 more convenient through services were introduced. In all, eleven radial routes, with some cross-connections between them, served the suburbs, the Barracks and all three railway stations and, apart from a short connecting line laid in 1919, the passenger network was complete. As regards the carriage of goods however, a notable development came in 1918 with the construction of just over ½ mile of sleepered track across Mousehold Heath – a high point overlooking the city to the north – from the existing terminus there to a munitions factory. (The rails for this line, known as the Mousehold Light Railway, came from lifting one of the double tracks in the narrow King Street.) Two powered trucks were built by the Company to serve the factory which was now connected, via the passenger line down Gurney Road and Riverside Road, with exchange sidings beside the GER's Thorpe station.

In 1914 the Company obtained powers to operate bus services which would be less obstructive in the city's narrow, medieval streets and these began in 1915; in 1918 the first prunings of the tramway system began though improvements to the rest of it continued to be made. It was clear however that the system had now reached that critical age when wholesale track relaying and stock modernisation were needed if it was to survive, but these options were not viable on the scale needed and little-used routes were slowly shortened or abandoned altogether with the trams replaced by buses. By 1932 the City Council was in favour of buying the

A postcard view of Orford Place in the centre of Norwich shortly after the 1900 opening of the city's tramways. (Lens of Sutton)

concern but a public poll the following year swayed them against the idea. Instead, the Eastern Counties Omnibus Co. Ltd purchased the NET Co. in 1933 and set about closing the tramways, the last route to go being Newmarket Road–Cavalry Barracks.

The original fleet of rolling stock comprised 40 Brush cars (Nos 1-40) and ten trailers (Nos 41-50), all open-top double-deckers. In 1901 two similar motor cars (Nos 41 and 42) were transferred from Coventry to Norwich and in 1910 five Norwich cars (motorised Nos 43-47) made the return journey. In 1923 Nos 7 and 9 were built by EE – again open-toppers – using the electrical equipment and trucks from the former Mousehold Light Railway freight cars, and between then and 1930, 32 of the original motor cars were rebuilt by the same company.

Bibliography: *The Tramways of East Anglia* R. C. Anderson (The Light Railway Transport League, 1969) 0 900433 00 0

NOTTINGHAM & DISTRICT TRAMWAYS

Authority: Nottingham and District Tramways Order 1877
Gauge: 4ft 8½in
Traction: Horse, steam
Opened: 17 September 1878
Taken Over: 16 October 1897
System: Branching + radial network
Length: 7.5 miles
Stock: 27 sd, 15 dd horse; 1 loco, 1 dd steam
Livery: Route colour*

Nottingham's first tramway system was owned and operated by the Nottingham &

District Tramways Co. Ltd, a local company, which began with a 1-mile route from St Peters Square south along Carrington Street and Arkwright Street past the MR station to Trent Bridge, stopping just before the river crossing; a short branch east, midway along this down Station Street served the GNR station. A third, unconnected route opened on 11 August 1879 from the Market Place (just north of St Peters Square) running north up Mansfield Road to Carrington, with a northeasterly route from the Market Place following on 5 June 1881 up Derby Road, Alfreton Road and Radford Road to Basford Gas Works. A short link line along Forest Road was opened in September 1881 between the two.

The original cars were single-deck Starbuck saloons 1-8, joined in 1879 by open-toppers 9-11 and another single-deck saloon (No 12) from Stevensons. These were followed in 1880 by five more Starbuck saloons (Nos 13-17), in 1881 by another five (Nos 18-22) then in 1883 by two more (Nos 23 and 24). In 1884 Starbuck supplied a pair of low-slung single-deck summer cars (Nos 25 and 26) and the next year a pair of more conventional saloons (Nos 27 and 28). That same year (1885) a Wilkinson steam tram locomotive was introduced on the Basford route (which included a 1 in 17 ascent on Derby Road) pulling a bogie top-covered Starbuck car (No 29); this service lasted until 1889, whereupon the car was rebuilt as a four-wheeled open-topper for horse haulage.

The cars were housed in three depots: one by the Carrington terminus, one in Isandula Road near the Basford terminus and one in Muskham Street by Trent Bridge. The Company also operated horse bus feeder services to its routes and in 1888 bought four open-top horse buses from one of its competitors (a Mr Andrews of Carrington) who had gone bankrupt and converted them into tramcars Nos 31-34 (No 30 being an ex-MANCHESTER open-topper on an Eades reversible truck bought the year before).

In 1891 two summer toastracks (Nos 19 and 34) were acquired from an unknown source and a programme of withdrawals and renumbering started. The last new cars bought were Milnes open-toppers 31-34 of 1891-92 and similar cars 36-38 three years later. The cars were painted according to the routes they worked (with the toastracks green) and the whole undertaking bought by Nottingham Corporation in 1897 as a prelude to extension and electrification (see below).

Bibliography: *Nottingham City Transport* F. P. Groves (The Transport Publishing Co., 1978) 0 903839 25 3

NOTTINGHAM CORPORATION TRAMWAYS

Authority: Nottingham Corporation Act 1899
Gauge: 4ft 8½in
Traction: Horse, overhead electric
Took Over: 16 October 1897
Closed: 5 September 1936
System: Radial network
Length: 25.39 miles
Stock: 26 sd, 11 dd horse; 200 dd electric
Livery: Maroon & cream
Last Car: No 190

Following its takeover of the city's horse tramways in 1897 (see above), Nottingham Corporation obtained the necessary Act two years later to enable it to proceed with its modernization plans. The contract for the work was awarded to DK who, during 1900-01, supplied ERTCW open-top cars Nos 1-57; the first of the horse lines re-opened, on 1 January 1901, was the Carrington route. On 15 October that year the Trent Bridge line (plus the Station Street branch) followed, now extended back to the Market Place to connect the two halves of the system. Also in 1901 a new main depot and works was built at Trent Bridge, ten open-toppers (Nos 58-67) and ten bogie open-toppers (Nos 68-77) arrived from Milnes and, on 23 July, the Basford route re-opened with an extension up Highbury Road to Bulwell Market.

More cars arrived in 1902: Nos 78-83 (Milnes), Nos 84-89 (Milnes bogie) and Nos 90-105 (ERTCW). These were the last of the open-top cars and virtually the entire fleet was later fitted with top covers. That year saw the opening of five new radial routes and, on 30 April, the abandonment of the Forest

Road link and the end of the horse cars.

The system continued to expand until 1915, by which time all areas of the city were served by the mainly double-track network centred on the Market Place plus a connection made in 1914 with the NOTTINGHAMSHIRE & DERBYSHIRE tramway (see below). This had opened its line to Cinderhill on the city's northwestern boundary, the 1.34 miles of track from there to the Church Street/Radford Road junction at Basford being laid by the Corporation and leased to the N&D with running powers over the rest of the line to the Market Place. The car fleet had also grown with the addition of top-covered cars 106-115 in 1907 from Milnes, 116-145 during 1908-14 from UEC and 146-155 in 1914 from Brush. Thereafter the only other cars purchased were (in 1920) top-covered vehicles Nos 156-180 and (in 1926) enclosed cars 181-200, all from EE.

In 1926 and 1927 the last two short extensions were made to the system – but by then its future had already been settled for in 1924 the Corporation had decided to begin a trolleybus substitution programme. On 10 April 1927 the Nottingham Road line (which linked the Basford and Carrington routes) was converted, so beginning a gradual series of abandonments in favour of motor and trolleybuses. The N&D regular service ceased in 1932 and the last Corporation route (the Carrington line which had been extended as far as the village of Arnold) went four years later. After the closure, cars 181-184 and 186-199 were sold to Aberdeen and the remaining survivors scrapped.

Bibliography: as above

NOTTINGHAMSHIRE & DERBYSHIRE TRAMWAYS

Authority: Nottinghamshire and Derbyshire Tramways Act 1903
Gauge: 4ft 8½in
Traction: Overhead electric
Opened: 4 July 1913?
Closed: 5 October 1932?
System: Single line
Length: 12.72 miles
Stock: 24 dd
Livery: Light green & cream
Last Car: ?

As built, the Notts & Derbys single line tramway was little more than one-tenth of a planned grand network first proposed in the 1900s to cover the coal mining and industrial area of the East Midlands bounded by Derby in the west, Nottingham in the east and Mansfield in the north. By the time the necessary authority had been secured, it was for some 47 miles of route – roughly half the original proposal – on account of opposition from the MR and those urban authorities wishing to construct or expand their own tramway systems. All that was then built was just a quarter of that as a single-track link between Nottingham and Ripley – again, the result of local authority pressure to take over sections of the planned routes which delayed the opening by another decade.

Prior to the opening of the line 24 double-deckers were ordered from UEC: Nos 1-12 were open-toppers whilst Nos 13-24 were top-covered. These remained the tramway's sole passenger stock throughout its life though by the time closure came (brought about by bus competition) twelve had been scrapped as worn-out and two sold to

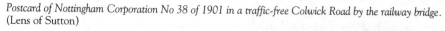

Postcard of Nottingham Corporation No 38 of 1901 in a traffic-free Colwick Road by the railway bridge. (Lens of Sutton)

MANSFIELD. Since 1912 the Nottinghamshire & Derbyshire Tramways Co., along with the Mansfield and Llanelly operating companies, had been part of the Tramways, Light & Power Co., a BB subsidiary and driving force behind the line's opening. (The NDT Co. also owned the neighbouring ILKESTON system, having purchased it in 1916 from the local authority there.)

The tramway ran northwestwards from Upper Parliament Street in the centre of Nottingham, out along the roads through the villages of Basford, Cinderhill, Nuthall, Kimberley, Giltbrook, Eastwood, Langley Mill (where the depot was located), Loscoe and Codnor before entering Ripley where it terminated near the Ebenezer Chapel, a total of some 15 miles. Of this, 11.36 miles from Ripley were actually owned by the N&D, 1.36 miles on the outskirts of NOTTINGHAM were leased from Nottingham Corporation and the last 2.3 miles into the city centre were run over the Corporation's metals.

The first section opened appears to have been from Kimberley to Loscoe on 4 July 1913 (a definitive record of the date is lacking) with the remainder following in stages by 15 January 1914. The closure date is similarly ill-defined – it was intended to be 3 September 1932 but it seems a workmen's car was run for another month until the Company's replacement trolleybus overhead was completed. (This latter service lasted as long as the tramway had done – until 1953 in fact – before it too succumbed to its internal combustion-engined rivals.)

Nottinghamshire & Derbyshire Tramways No 22 of 1913, one of the line's twelve balcony cars, apparently on a busy summer working with a companion car following. (Lens of Sutton)

OLDHAM CORPORATION TRAMWAYS

Authority: Oldham Corporation Act 1899
Gauge: 4ft 8½in
Traction: Overhead electric
Opened: 15 December 1900
Closed: 3 August 1946
System: Network
Length: 25.18 miles
Stock: 33 sd, 117 dd
Livery: Maroon & white
Last Car: No 4

The first tramway in Oldham, although built by the Corporation under the Oldham Borough Tramways Order of 1878 and opened 16 September 1880, was operated on lease by the Manchester Carriage & Tramways Co. (see MANCHESTER TRAMWAYS) and ran from Waterhead west along the Huddersfield Road and Manchester Road through the town to Hollinwood on the boundary with Manchester to the southwest. This was followed in 1885 by two lines of the MANCHESTER, BURY, ROCHDALE & OLDHAM steam system.

The first line operated by the Corporation opened on 15 December 1900 and ran east from Chadderton along Middleton Road to Rochdale Road (and the MBRO line). Other routes followed though these were separated by the horse and steam lines until the horse cars ceased to run on 31 October 1901 with the expiry of the lease; at the same time the Corporation took over the steam routes by agreement and began converting them all to electric traction. The Waterhead–Hollinwood line re-opened on 17 May 1902 with the steam routes re-opening in stages that year.

The last route of the mainly single-track system to be constructed was a northeasterly branch off the Huddersfield Road along the Ripponden Road through Moorside to Grains Bar. This opened on 4 June 1914 with the last extension to the tramways, in August 1925, coming with the purchase of the stretch of 1.55 miles from Chadderton to Mills Hill Bridge from MIDDLETON. (Other connections for through running were made, at one time or another, with ROCHDALE in the north, Manchester to the southwest and Ashton-under-Lyne to the south via the OLDHAM, ASHTON & HYDE ELECTRIC TRAMWAY (see below).

Services began with single-deckers Nos 1 and 4 and open-top double-deckers 2 and 3, all from ERTCW, of which Nos 3 and 4 were bogie vehicles. These were followed in 1901 by bogie single-deckers 5-16 and in 1902-03 by single-deckers 17-26 and open-toppers 27-80, again all from ERTCW. No further cars were bought until 1911 when UEC supplied

balcony cars 81-92, followed by similar vehicles 93-111 over the next four years. EE balcony cars 4-12 and 14-16 were bought in 1921 as replacements for those-numbered vehicles sold to ROTHERHAM in 1916, with enclosed cars 17-20, 22 and 24 coming from the same firm three years later. In 1925 Brush single-deckers 113-120 were bought from Middleton and enclosed cars 121-132 from EE a year later.

The only other passenger car in the fleet was No 112, built by the Corporation in 1921 from the body of No 3 as a balcony car. The two depots were at Hollinwood and Wallshaw (just east of the town centre).

The eastern route along Lees Road to Lees closed on 2 May 1928 and the Grains Bar route that 24 December. In 1934 the Corporation decided to abandon the remaining routes over the next five years but, as elsewhere, World War II delayed the closure programme with the last line – the original horse route from Waterhead to Hollinwood – surviving until 1946, after which cars 17, 18, 24, 122, 125 and 128 were sold to GATESHEAD.

OLDHAM, ASHTON & HYDE ELECTRIC TRAMWAYS

Authority: Oldham Ashton-under-Lyne Hyde and District Electric Tramways Order 1896
Gauge: 4ft 8½in
Traction: Overhead electric
Opened: 12 June 1899
Taken Over: 2 July 1921
System: Single line

Length: 9.1 miles
Stock: 56 sd, 12 dd
Livery: Dark green & white
Last Car: ?

After a steam tramway proposal of the 1880s had failed, the early 1890s saw the promotion of an electric tramway linking the southeast Lancashire towns of its title, this time by the Oldham, Ashton-under-Lyne & Hyde Tramways Co. Ltd. This scheme too failed (after ¼ mile of track had been laid in Ashton), only to be revived in 1896 by the BET through its subsidiary, the Oldham, Ashton-under-Lyne & Hyde Electric Tramways Ltd. Construction began in early 1898 with services commencing the following year using 16 small Brush single-deckers (possibly Nos 1-16). These proved inadequate to cope with the traffic and eight open-toppers built by Brush for LEEDS CORPORATION were bought instead. Later numbered 39-46, these arrived with Leeds fleet numbers and had their staircases and top seats removed to work as single-deckers on account of a low bridge in Hyde (though restored from 1902-04 onwards).

By the middle of 1900 Brush had supplied single-deckers 1-26 and single-deck trailers 27-38, which were also no great success, with Nos 35-38 being motorized in 1900 and Nos 27-34 sold to MIDDLETON three years later. The tramway's other passenger cars were Nos 47-50, Brush open-toppers supplied in 1903 and Nos 27-30, ERTCW single-deck combination cars bought from Middleton a year later (and which ran for a while with the suffix B added to their Middleton numbers 11, 14, 17 and 18).

Power was supplied by Ashton Corporation.

In layout the tramway's northern section was a single-track north-south line running from Hathershaw at the Oldham boundary in a straight line south down the Oldham Road through Waterloo to Ashton Market Place. From the terminal stub here (connected to the ASHTON CORPORATION system) the tramway's second route ran southwest along Katherine Street and the Stockport Road to Audenshaw, then out south along Denton Road (past the depot) and Ashton Road to Denton where it turned east to reach Hyde via Hyde Road and Manchester Road. In Hyde the line swung south again along Market Street, Lumb Street and Back Lane through Gee Cross to terminate at Pole Bank on the boundary with Bredbury. This last 1-mile section was leased from Hyde Corporation and opened on 1 January 1903, connecting with STOCKPORT CORPORATION TRAMWAYS; that authority's cars immediately began running into Hyde from here and the Company cut its own services back to the Grapes Hotel at Gee Cross shortly after. The system's only other section of line, a short connecting link between the two routes in Ashton just west of the Market, was never used for passenger workings.

By 1910 it was clear that the relevant local authorities were wanting to purchase the tramway at the end of the 21 years and in 1921 they did so, by which time the Company had allowed cars and track to become decrepit. After arbitration Ashton paid £62,875 for its tracks and acquired cars 1-9, 18, 21, 26-28, 35-39 and 44-48 whilst Hyde paid £26,600 and received cars 19, 20, 22-25, 29, 30, 49 and 50 to be operated by

the STALYBRIDGE, HYDE, MOSSLEY & DUKINFIELD TRAMWAYS. Audenshaw paid £13,550 and got cars 14-17 and 40 whilst Denton paid £21,975 and received Nos 10-13 and 41-43, their lines in both cases to be worked by MANCHESTER CORPORATION (with four of the cars being sold to Ayr in Scotland and the remainder scrapped).

Bibliography: *A History of Public Transport in Ashton-under-Lyne* W. G. S. Hyde (Manchester Transport Museum Society, 1980)

OSSETT *see* DEWSBURY, OSSETT & SOOTHILL NETHER

OVER DARWEN *see* BLACKBURN & OVER DARWEN

CITY OF OXFORD & DISTRICT TRAMWAYS
Authority: Oxford Tramways Order 1879
Gauge: 4ft
Traction: Horse
Opened: 1 December 1881
Closed: Summer 1914
System: Radial
Length: 5.25 miles
Stock: 12 sd? & 20 dd?
Livery: Dark red & white
Last Car: ?

Like its CAMBRIDGE counterpart (which also closed in 1914), this small 4ft gauge horse tramway system was never electrified although for the last half-dozen years of its life such a move was proposed by various interested bodies. It was promoted by the Oxford Tramways Co. Ltd (incorporated 20 November 1879) but opened by the City of Oxford & District Tramways Co. Ltd (incorporated 14 December 1880), the latter company having taken over the powers of the former. Starting with just a single line from the twin GWR and LNWR stations running eastwards through Carfax in the city centre to Cowley Road, by 1898 three branches had been added: south from Carfax via St Aldates and Abingdon Road to Lake Street, New Hinksey (15 March 1887), northeast from Carfax to Kingston Road via Beaumont Street and Walton Street (15 July 1884) and, thirdly, north from Carfax via St Giles and Banbury Road to South Parade, Summertown (opened to Rackham's Lane on 28 January 1882 and to South Parade on 5 November 1898).

Rolling stock details are sketchy. Services commenced with four single-deck cars which were soon joined by several more, after which a number of double-deckers were bought, some new from

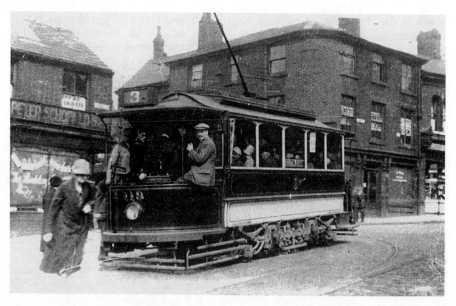

Oldham Corporation No 119 of 1903 acquired in 1925 from Middleton. Before that it was an Oldham, Ashton & Hyde trailer. (Lens of Sutton)

Milnes and a dozen or so second-hand from various LONDON operators.

With electrification proposals never coming to fruition, the tramway was soon killed off by motor bus competition – competition in which the City of Oxford Electric Tramways Ltd, an NEC subsidiary and the 1908 successor to the City of Oxford & District Tramways Co. Ltd, itself joined. Services to Walton Street and New Hinksey were withdrawn on 27 January 1914 though the closing dates for the other lines are not known.

PADDINGTON see LONDON: HARROW ROAD & PADDINGTON

PETERBOROUGH TRAMWAYS
Authority: Peterborough and District Light
    Railway Order 1900
Gauge: 3ft 6in
Traction: Overhead electric
Opened: 24 January 1903
Closed: 15 November 1930
System: Radial
Length: 5.31 miles
Stock: 14 dd
Livery: Lake-brown & cream pre-World
    War I, then holly green & cream
Last Car: No 12

Huntingdonshire's only tramway was operated by the BET-owned Peterborough Electric Traction Co. Ltd after the failure of a number of proposed horse tramway schemes. It was an urban street tramway with three long, single-track branches to the northern outlying areas of Walton, Dogsthorpe and Newark from a short stem leading south to the Market Place. The line's first twelve cars (Nos 1-12) were open-top double-deckers built in 1902 by Brush, followed two years later by two more (Nos 14 and 15). The depot was in Lincoln Road on the Walton route.

From 1913 onwards the PET Co. supplemented the trams with motor buses; these inevitably complemented then replaced the tram services entirely, the Company becoming a co-founder of the Eastern Counties Omnibus Co. Ltd in 1931. Although the last public services ran on 15 November 1930, all routes had been abandoned to the buses in all but name from the Bank Holiday Monday, 4 August of that year and, until the closure proper, car No 12 – nicknamed the 'Ghost Tram' – toured each route in turn throughout the day until the necessary authority to dispense with the service completely had been obtained.

Bibliography: *Peterborough Tramways*
    (Peterborough Papers No 1) G. D. Austin
    (Greater Peterborough Arts Council,
    1975)

PIMLICO, PECKHAM & GREENWICH STREET TRAMWAYS
see LONDON TRAMWAYS

PLYMOUTH, STONEHOUSE & DEVONPORT TRAMWAYS
Authority: Plymouth Stonehouse and
    Devonport Tramways Act 1870
Gauge: 4ft 8½in/3ft 6in
Traction: Horse/overhead electric
Opened: 18 March 1872
Taken Over: 1 July 1922
System: Single line
Length: 2.93 miles
Stock: 20 dd horse; 15 dd electric
Livery: Emerald green & cream

The tramway history of Plymouth is a complicated one in relation to the size of the town and is partly due to the fact that until 1914 it was, municipally, the 'Three Towns' of Plymouth, Stonehouse and Devonport. All three were connected by Plymouth's first tramway – the first in Britain to open after the 1870 Tramway Act – which ran for about 2 miles from Derry's Clock in Plymouth westwards along Union Street (past the depot) and over Stonehouse Bridge (where passengers had to pay a ½d toll) to terminate at Cumberland Gardens, Devonport. Originally owned by the Plymouth, Stonehouse & Devonport Tramways Co., it was taken over by PROVINCIAL TRAMWAYS within a year.

In 1874 the tramway was extended slightly in Devonport to the junction of Marlborough Street and Fore Street (including a one-way system around Chapel Street and St Aubyn Street); the line was a single track except for a double section on the 1 in 11 Devonport Hill.

Originally eight double-deck cars worked the line but these were later replaced by twelve larger versions (makers unknown). Any hope of connecting with the later PLYMOUTH, DEVONPORT & DISTRICT and DEVONPORT & DISTRICT tramways was a non-starter because of the gauge difference so, when the Company decided to electrify the line at the beginning of the 20th century, it adopted the narrower 3ft 6in gauge of the others.

The rebuilt line opened on 18 November 1901 with ERTCW open-top double-deckers 1-12 (joined by similar cars 14 and 15 in 1903 and 1904); no further additions were made to the fleet until 1916 when a similar but more modern UEC No 16 was acquired. Some minor alterations to the old line had been made during the reconstruction including the building of a new depot in Market Street in Stonehouse and the doubling of the track within the Plymouth and Devonport boundaries, those portions of the line having been sold to those two local authorities and leased back for 21 years. This left the Company owning just over 1½ route miles of its own. The system accordingly stayed independent until 1 July 1922 when it was bought to become an integral part of PLYMOUTH CORPORATION TRAMWAYS.

Bibliography: *The Trams of Plymouth: a 73
    Years Story* Martin Langley & Edwina
    Small (Ex Libris Press, Bradford on Avon,
    1990) 0 948578 25 4

PLYMOUTH, DEVONPORT & DISTRICT TRAMWAYS
Authority: Plymouth Devonport and
    District Tramways Act 1882

One of Peterborough's original cars, No 11 of 1902, on a postcard of the Long Causeway terminus in the city centre. (Lens of Sutton)

Gauge: 3ft 6in
Traction: Steam/horse
Opened: 1884
Taken Over: 28 September 1892
System: Branching + single line
Length: 2.44 miles
Stock: 5 locos, 8 sd & dd steam, 12 dd horse
Livery: Locos brown, trailers brown &
   white; horse cars red & cream

Plymouth's second tramway, unusually, reversed the normal pattern of events and replaced steam traction with horses. For the first year of its life Wilkinson tram locomotives were operated over a winding route from the GWR's Millbay station in South Plymouth, along Millbay Road, Princess Square, Westwell Street, Russell Street, Richmond Street, North Road, Houndiscombe Road and Mutley Plain to the district of Mannamead, a distance of some 2½ miles – a far cry from the 10½-mile radial network planned by its owners, the Plymouth, Devonport & District Tramways Co. Ltd. A ½-mile branch from Princess Square ran eastwards via Notte Street and Southside Street to the Yarmouth Inn, Barbican.

Even this short, single-track line had its operating problems: the BoT would not permit trams to run through the steep and narrow Richmond Street so a two-section service had to be operated. There were also complaints about the noise and smoke of the engines and in 1885 the Company went into liquidation after Devonport Corporation obtained an injunction in December 1884 stopping it from running trams until its planned Devonport lines had beeen constructed – for which the Company had no money! Accordingly, in 1886 a new company, the Plymouth Tramways Co. Ltd, was authorized under the Plymouth & Devonport (Extension) Transport Act to take over the existing line and construct the Devonport routes.

It is not known exactly when steam traction finished – the five Wilkinson locos were sold to a colliery in Kent – but it seems likely that the Company began operations with horse traction from the outset using double-deck cars and, far from extending the system as authorized, actually abandoned the Barbican branch! It was not a satisfactory situation and in 1892 Plymouth Corporation set up its own Tramways Department to run the line after paying £12,500 for it, it then forming the nucleus of the PLYMOUTH CORPORATION TRAMWAYS (see below).

Bibliography: as above

PLYMOUTH CORPORATION TRAMWAYS

Authority: Plymouth Tramways Act 1892

Gauge: 3ft 6in
Traction: Horse, overhead electric
Took Over: 28 September 1892
Closed: 29 September 1945
System: Network
Length: 17.57 miles
Stock: 47 horse?; 6 sd, 171 dd electric
Livery: Vermilion & white horse; red &
   yellow to 1922, yellow & cream to 1927,
   varnished teak to 1930, then maroon &
   ivory electric
Last Car: No 158

As described above, Plymouth Corporation took over the two sections of the Plymouth Tramways Co.'s line in 1892 and by early the following year had extended it in the north from Mannamead to Compton Lane End and, in the south, from Millbay station along West Hoe Road (past the depot) and the seafront to Pier Street, West Hoe.

In 1895 a second, more direct route to Mutley Plain was opened up with a line leaving the old one at the Guild Hall in the centre of the city and going northwards up Tavistock Road and over North Hill before rejoining it (thus bypassing Russell Street, Richmond Street, North Road and Houndiscombe Road) and in 1896 a branch from Drake Circus just north of the Guild Hall was opened to Prince Rock to serve the hitherto neglected eastern side of the town. To work the extended system – now 5.15 miles in length – three open-toppers and two single-deckers (Nos 13-17) were bought from Milnes in 1894 and a further two double-deckers (Nos 18 and 19) a year later. Further details of the horse car fleet are incomplete.

In the last years of the 19th century the Corporation decided to electrify its system and on 22 September 1899 the first such service began from Prince Rock to Market Avenue with six Milnes open-toppers equipped to tow converted horse-car trailers; the service was extended very soon after as far as the Theatre Royal at the west end of George Street (shortly before Millbay Road was reached). In 1901 14 open-top Brush cars were bought (Nos 7-20) to work the Compton route which opened on 4 April that year, followed by ten more in 1902 (Nos 21-30), six in 1905 (Nos 31-36) and six single-deckers (Nos 37-42) a year later, all from Brush. In 1915 twelve more Brush open-toppers were acquired (Nos 43-54) and the DEVONPORT & DISTRICT system taken over and through services begun with the PLYMOUTH, STONEHOUSE & DEVONPORT following suit seven years later. (The cars from these two systems were renumbered and incorporated into the Corporation's fleet.) That year also saw, in May 1922, the opening of a new route along Alma Road to link Milehouse (where the central depot was) on the former D&D with

Plymouth centre to complete the system. (This utilized part of the old horse route to Mutley Plain.)

In 1924 20 open-top EE cars (Nos 131-150) were added to the fleet, followed the next year by No 151, a home-built bogie open-topper. In 1927 and 1928 15 more were contructed (Nos 152-166), the last new cars on the system.

Serious bus competition began in the 1930s and the Corporation decided to join it, cutting back or closing routes entirely to replace them with bus services, though it did purchase another 21 second-hand Brush open-toppers from EXETER (Nos 1-9 in 1931) and TORQUAY (Nos 10-21 in 1934) to replace some of its ageing fleet. Only the intervention of World War II prolonged the tramway's existence until the Corporation's buses were able to take over completely, making it the last West Country system to close.

Bibliography: as above

POOLE & DISTRICT ELECTRIC TRAMWAYS

Authority: Poole and District Light Railway
   Order 1899
Gauge: 3ft 6in
Traction: Overhead electric
Opened: 6 April 1901
Taken Over: 22 June 1905
System: Single line
Length: 3.75 miles
Stock: 17 dd
Livery: Cambridge blue & white

Whilst its counterpart in neighbouring BOURNEMOUTH was, throughout the 19th century, resolutely opposed to the whole idea of tramways, Poole Corporation was not and in April 1899 a BET subsidiary, the Poole & District Electric Traction Co., was registered to construct a line from Poole railway station out through the town via the district of Upper Parkstone to the Poole/Bournemouth boundary at County Gates (which also, as the name suggests, marked the Dorset/Hampshire border).

Construction began in May 1900 and the line was ready less than a year later. On 22 July 1905 however the Company was purchased for £112,000 by Poole Corporation who then leased the tramway to Bournemouth for 30 years. (Bournemouth Corporation had by this time undergone a sea-change in its opinion of this new form of public transport and was already operating tramways of its own.) From now on the Poole line was operated as an integral part of the Bournemouth system and the taken-over cars were withdrawn slowly; these were Milnes 1-4 and ERTCW 5-11 of 1901 and Brush 12-17 of 1901-02, all open-top double-deckers shedded at Ashley Road Depot in Upper Parkstone.

Bibliography: *The Tramways of Bournemouth and Poole* R. C. Anderson (The Light Railway Transport League, 1964)

PORTSDOWN & HORNDEAN LIGHT RAILWAY

Authority: Portsdown and Horndean Light Railway Order 1898
Gauge: 4ft 7¾in
Traction: Overhead electric
Opened: 3 March 1903
Closed: 9 January 1935
System: Single line
Length: 5.98 miles
Stock: 1 sd, 23 dd
Livery: Emerald green & cream
Last Car: No 6

Operated by a PROVINCIAL TRAMWAYS subsidiary, the Hampshire Light Railways Electric Co. Ltd (incorporated 17 May 1897), this line had its origin in the intention of Portsmouth Corporation in the 1890s to municipalize the PORTSMOUTH STREET TRAMWAYS – also owned by Provincial. This would have meant that the PST Co. would have been left with just a short stretch of line from the borough boundary at Hilsea north to Cosham plus a horse bus service from there on north to Horndean; consequently it was decided to extend and electrify the line, in effect as an extension of the Corporation's system.

Formally opened on 2 March 1902, the mainly single-track line ran across the fields and beside the London Road over Portsdown Hill and through the villages of Widley, Purbrook, Waterlooville and Cowplain (the site of the depot opposite Park Lane) to Horndean.

Although the Corporation had running powers over the first mile of the tramway, the arrangement was not reciprocated until 1 August 1924 when Company cars began running into Portsmouth (first to the Town Hall and then, from 1927, all the way through to South Parade Pier). Despite the Company offering to sell the line to its neighbour on more than one occasion – the last time in 1934 – the offer was never taken up and the trams were killed off by motor and trolleybus competition.

Services began with BEC open-top double-deckers Nos 1-9, joined later in 1903 by Nos 10-14, five similar cars; in 1905 two more of the same configuration, Nos 15 and 16, were bought from Brush. No further stock was added until 1925 when No 17, an open toastrack ex-GRIMSBY was put into service for a short while. Following the closure of the Provincial's nearby GOSPORT & FAREHAM line, seven of that tramway's

open-toppers were transferred in 1930 to the P&H. Nos 8, 20 and 21 entered service with their old numbers whilst Nos 2, 10, 14 and 22 were mounted on the trucks from withdrawn P&H cars 2, 8, 10 and 14 and were (re)numbered 2, 17, 10 and 14 respectively.

Bibliography: *The Tramways of Portsmouth* S. E. Harrison (The Light Railway Transport League, 1963)

PORTSMOUTH STREET TRAMWAYS

Authority: Landport and Southsea Tramways Act 1863
Gauge: 4ft 7¾in
Traction: Horse, steam
Opened: 15 May 1865
Taken Over: 1 January 1901
System: Network
Length: 13.41 miles
Stock: ? horse; 1 dd steam
Livery: Route colour

To Portsmouth goes the honour of having Britain's first statutory street tramway when, in 1865, the Landport & Southsea Tramways Co. opened a single-track line (using step rails) from the joint LSWR and LBSCR station at Landport (later Portsmouth Town Station) south through the town centre and onto Clarence Pier, Southsea, just a mile away. The line was intended to meet the needs of passengers to and from the Isle of Wight ferries and for that reason the gauge was chosen to permit the through working of railway wagons. This appears never to have come about however though pairs of luggage trucks (of railway origin?) were towed behind the (two?) two-horse single-deck tramcars; the gauge determined

though that of the later tramways in the area.

The LST Co. was joined in 1873 by a second concern, the Portsmouth Street Tramways Co. (a PROVINCIAL TRAMWAYS subsidiary) who opened the following year a much longer single-track north-south route from a depot at North End on the London Road via Kingston Crescent and Commercial Road to Landport station. There it paralleled the L&S line to Cambridge Street, which it then followed southwestwards into the High Street and then along Broad Street to a second depot at Point (where a floating bridge across the mouth of Portsmouth Harbour connected Portsea Island to Gosport). The line was approved by the BoT on 11 September 1874 and presumably opened then or shortly afterwards and was better received than the LST Co.'s tramway which was relaid in 1875 with grooved rails.

A third company appeared on the scene in 1875, the General Tramways Co. of Portsmouth Ltd, though its first line did not open until 18 March 1878. This ran from the PST line at the end of the High Street, southeast along Alexandra Road to the L&S line which it then shared for Kings Terrace and Jubilee Terrace as far as the Pier Hotel where it turned east along Southsea Terrace and Castle Road to Queens Hotel in Osbourne Road. The GT single-deckers ran through to Point on what was now in effect its own line since Provincial had, in February of that year, bought up both the other companies (and amalgamated them all into the PST Co. in 1883).

A succession of routes (and some abandonments), and the opening of several new depots to service the growing network, now followed. By the end of the 1890s the system extended to the Hard by the Harbour

Postcard view of Portsdown & Horndean Light Railway No 6 of 1903 capturing the essentially rustic nature of this line. (Lens of Sutton)

TO THE TRADESMEN
or
Landport & Southsea.

WHAT ARE THE

TRAMWAY
COMPANY

DOING FOR US ?

1.—They are monopolizing a considerable portion of some of our most important thoroughfares, without payment of rent or compensation !

2. - They are conveying the Passengers to the Isle of Wight, direct from the Railway Station to the Southsea Pier, to the loss and injury of Tradesmen, Cab and Omnibus proprietors and drivers, and everybody else, excepting the Pier and Steam Packet Companies and themselves !

3.—They are causing a most dangerous nuisance—imperilling the safety of persons, horses, and vehicles, and seriously impeding the public traffic !

Shall we silently submit any longer ? Let us all unite in getting rid of so erving an evil ! No half measures ! It is "NOW OR NEVER !"

A TRADESMAN.

Commercial Road, Landport.
September 16th, 1867.

Not everyone welcomed the coming of the tramways, as is shown by this 1867 notice against Portsmouth's first such line.

to the west, East Southsea to the southeast, Fratton and Buckland to the east and as far as Cosham to the north. By now Portsmouth Corporation was desirous of purchasing the tramways in order to electrify them and did so under the Portsmouth Corporation Tramways Act 1898 though the compensation agreement was complicated and slow to be reached, the Corporation eventually taking possession at midnight on the very last day of the century.

Details of the stock are unfortunately sparse. Both single-deck and double-deck horse cars were used and in 1894 the series number 69 was reached, though whether there was any duplication of numbers is not known. The Company also operated a double-deck steamcar in regular service. This was constructed by an Isle of Wight firm of steam yacht builders, the Liquid Fuel Engineering Co. of East Cowes, and was a large, top-covered vehicle (but with no glazing to the upper deck) powered by an oil-fired boiler and engine. Known as 'Lifu' (after the firm's trademark), it operated from 1896 to Whit Monday 1901, always under Provincial ownership, and ended its days as an office at the Park Lane Depot of that company's PORTSDOWN & HORNDEAN LIGHT RAILWAY (see above).

Bibliography: as above

PORTSMOUTH CORPORATION TRAMWAYS

Authority: Portsmouth Corporation
   Tramway Act 1898
Gauge: 4ft 7¾in
Traction: Horse, overhead electric
Took Over: 1 January 1901
Closed: 10 November 1936
System: Network
Length: 17.7 miles
Stock: 1 sd, 113 dd electric
Livery: Crimson lake & cream
Last Car: No 106 (official)

Having decided to exercise its option to purchase the PORTSMOUTH STREET TRAMWAYS (see above), the Corporation did so on the first day of the 20th century, paying the arbitrated price of £185,633 for the tramway side of the business. Reconstruction work was then put in hand with the official inauguration of the new system taking place on 24 September 1901 with 80 DK open-top double-deckers based at a new depot under construction in Gladys Avenue just off the London Road in North End. In essence, the mainly double-track system was the horse tramway one with minor alterations and the short Hilsea-Cosham section retaining horse traction until May 1903 when the Portsbridge had been strengthened.

Four more cars (Nos 81-84) were added to stock in 1902, these being 1896 Milnes open-top horse cars ex-NORTH METROLPOLITAN TRAMWAYS, the bodies of which were mounted on new electric trucks; in 1906-07 another 16 DK open-toppers were bought (Nos 85-100), the last additions to the fleet until after World War I. Their purchase was followed

in 1909 by the opening of an eastwards extension from Fratton along Goldsmith Avenue to the White House, Milton; four years later this line was extended south down Eastney Road to meet the Eastney route at the Highland Chief. Also in July 1913 the former horse line linking the South Parade Pier with Highland Road via Festing Road was reinstated and a new extension opened from Stamshaw north, up Twyford Road and Northern Parade to Alexandra Park.

In 1919 an open toastrack (No 104) was bought from SOUTHAMPTON (and later roofed) whilst in 1920 twelve EE enclosed double-deckers (Nos 105-116) were purchased, the last cars to join the fleet until 1930 when the Corporation built a new No 1, a modern enclosed car of its own design. By this time though the tramways had not long to go for six years later the Corporation closed the system down, replacing the trams with trolleybuses. On the tramway's final night car No 106 led a procession of three others back to the depot on the last run. After the closure all the surviving trams were scrapped (though No 1 escaped by virtue of having been sold to SUNDERLAND) with the exception of No 84, one of the converted horse cars, which was saved for official preservation (though is not currently on display).

Bibliography: as above and
Portsmouth Corporation Tramways 1896-1936 (Portsmouth Papers No 45) Edwin Course (Portsmouth City Council, 1986) 0 901559 66 0
Fares Please: The History of Passenger Transport in Portsmouth Eric Watts (Milestone Publications, Portsmouth, 1987) 0 903852 98 5

Many tramways operated a route to a local park, common or other beauty spot for the benefit of day-trippers. In this postcard Portsmouth Corporation Nos 16 and 47 of 1901 await passengers on Southsea Common. (Courtesy Andrew Maxam)

POTTERIES: STAFFORDSHIRE POTTERIES STREET RAILWAY

Authority: Local authority permission
Gauge: 4ft 8½in
Traction: Horse
Opened: 11 January 1862
Taken Over: 8 November 1879
System: Single line
Length: c1.5 miles
Stock: 2 sd?
Livery: ?

The first tramway in the Potteries was another of G. F. Train's street railways (see BIRKENHEAD and LONDON) of the early 1860s. It was operated by the Staffordshire Potteries Street Railway Co. Ltd and the original scheme was for 8 miles of line from Longton, running in a northwesterly direction through Fenton, Hanley, Burslem and Tunstall to Goldenhill. In the event less than a quarter of that total was laid beside Waterloo Road between Foundry Street, Hanley and Burlsem Market Place using Train's customary step rails. There was just one passing loop at the halfway point. Further details of the line and its history are sketchy. Soon after its opening the tramway was leased to a succession of local operators and, c1865, relaid with grooved rails which, unlike with most of Train's other promotions, ensured its survival. The one-track depot was in Foundry Street and housed the entire car fleet – probably two single-deckers, one of which was numbered 15 and named *Queen*.

It appears that the tramway was a success for it paid regular dividends to shareholders and by the end of the 1870s was carrying 300,000 passengers a year. Indeed, such was the traffic potential of this industrial area that in 1878 the North Staffordshire Tramways Co. Ltd was formed to exploit it and, from 8 November 1879, took over the working of the tramway until its new, parallel line was ready to open. (See below.)

POTTERIES: NORTH STAFFORDSHIRE TRAMWAYS

Authority: Stoke-upon-Trent Fenton
    Longton and District Tramways Order
    1879
Gauge: 4ft 8½in, 4ft
Traction: Horse, steam
Took Over: 8 November 1879
Taken Over: 28 June 1898
System: Branching
Length: 6.64 miles
Stock: *
Livery: Dark green

On 4 December 1878 the North Staffordshire Tramways Co. Ltd was formed to construct tramways in the Potteries area of its title, and a year later obtained authority for a number of lines to be worked by horse or steam power. Also in 1879, on 8

November, it purchased the STAFFORD-SHIRE POTTERIES STREET RAILWAY (see above) for £2,388 and continued to operate it for another three years until its own line opened between Hanley and Burslem.

The first section of 4ft gauge line opened (soon after the BoT inspection of 22 April 1881) ran southeast from the centre of Stoke-upon-Trent, out along the High Street to Fenton Road and on via King Street and Church Street to Longton Market Place. Here the tramway divided with one line continuing on along the High Street and the other turning south down Stafford Street and Trentham Road as far as Rosslyn Street. Two short branches in Stoke are thought to have been opened at the same time: south down London Road and north up Glebe Street, the two worked as one route (and, until 1884, by horse cars). None of the branches was more than 300yd long and, like the main line, single-track.

The tramway's first two locomotives (Nos 1 and 2) were 1880 MW products, joined in 1881 by Nos 3 and 4 from Merryweather. That same year saw the arrival of a top-covered double-deck steam car (No 5) from BP (with an Ashbury body) and Nos 6-9, four more MW locos. In 1882 the last six locos, Nos 10 and 11 from Merryweather and 12-15 from MW, were added as the system expanded. It is thought the next extension was opened in February 1882 when the main line was extended north from Stoke along Stoke Road, Snow Hill and Broad Street into Hanley and later that year (possibly in June) it was extended (again as a single track) to replace the old street railway along Waterloo Road to Burslem where it terminated on Newcastle Street west of the Market Place.

About this time serious consideration was given to the use of cable traction but a decade later the Company had decided to use electricity instead, entering into an agreement whereby the BET (which had acquired control of the NST Co.) would construct and work a new, enlarged system on its behalf through the Potteries Electric Traction Co. Ltd (see below).

Details of the passenger stock are incomplete. It seems likely that there were no more than half a dozen single-deck horse cars plus 20 or so bogie single-deck steam trailers which replaced earlier double-deck bogie vehicles. The depot was off Church Street in Stoke.

POTTERIES ELECTRIC TRAMWAYS

Authority: Potteries Light Railway Order
    1897
Gauge: 4ft
Traction: Steam, overhead electric
Took Over: 28 June 1898

Closed: 11 July 1928
System: Network
Length: 31.73 miles
Stock: ? steam; 121 sd electric
Livery: Deep red & cream
Last Car: ?

Registered on 28 June 1898, the Potteries Electric Traction Co. Ltd was set up by the BET to electrify and extend the NORTH STAFFORDSHIRE TRAMWAYS (see above). The official opening of the first rebuilt section, from Hanley to Burslem, extended on north via Tunstall to Goldenhill, was on 15 May 1899 with steam working withdrawn the next day (and from the rest of the system shortly afterwards); southwards extensions of the main line down Longton High Street to Meir and the Stafford Street branch down Trentham Road to Dresden were opened at the same time. The first electric cars, Nos 1-17 and trailers 18-27, were Brush single-deckers shedded at Goldenhill.

New lines followed quickly: branches from Burslem east to Smallthorne and west to Longport in 1899 and, in 1900, a route west from Hanley to Newcastle-under-Lyme via Etruria. To work the enlarged system (now three times the length of the steam line) more cars were bought: Nos 28-40 in 1899 from Brush and in 1900 Nos 41-70 from ERTCW plus bogie cars 71-85 from Midland and 86-106 from Brush; No 64 was rebuilt by the Company as a bogie combination car soon after it was delivered.

By the end of 1905 the single-track system (parts of which were later doubled) was complete as a straggling collection of routes with no single focus connecting the principal pottery towns and districts with each other in a roughly triangular shape. Longton and Meir were in the southeast corner, Newcastle and Silverdale in the west and Tunstall and Goldenhill in the north; Stoke-upon-Trent, where the main depot and works were situated, was somewhere in the middle.

In 1906 Brush supplied bogie cars 113-117 which were followed by Brush cars 99, 100, 119 and 120 transferred by the BET from MIDDLETON. In 1907 the original trailers were motorized, never having seen much use in their original form, with Nos 18 and 19 being fairly straightforward conversions and Nos 20-27 rebuilds as bogie cars 20-23 using pairs of bodies for each car; the vacated numbers 24-27 were taken in 1908 by four new Brush bogie vehicles. No further stock was added to the fleet until after World War I when three 1899 ex-SHEFFIELD cars were bought in 1920 and numbered 121 (ERTCW), 122 and 123 (Brush).

In 1922 No 125, an ex-DUDLEY & STOURBRIDGE car, was bought to

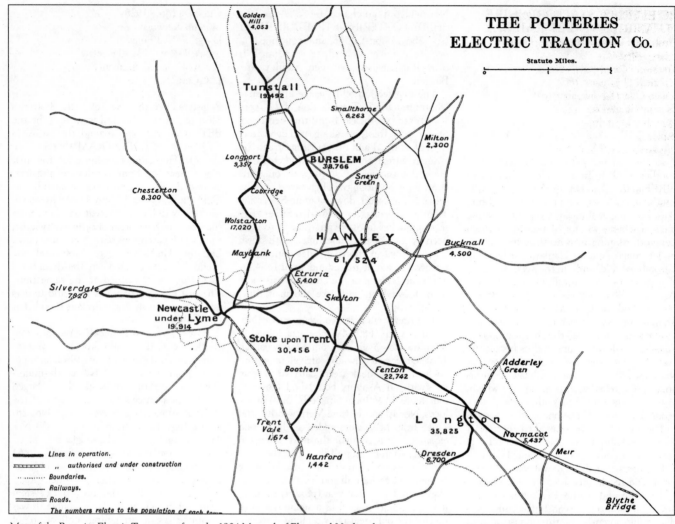

Map of the Potteries Electric Tramways, from the 1904 Manual of Electrical Undertakings.

round off the small second-hand acquisition programme for bus competition was already hurting this sprawling, vunerable system. The western branch from Newcastle to Chesterton and Silverdale (both opened 1901) closed on 30 September 1926 whilst the northern branch from Tunstall to Goldenhill went the following year, leaving the remainder of the network to be abandoned a whole year later. After the closure the car fleet (which included a number of parcel trailers and goods wagons) was scrapped with two of the bodies finding their way to the Wemyss line in Scotland for a short extension of life there.

PRESCOT see LIVERPOOL & PRESCOT

PRESTON TRAMWAYS

Authority: Preston Tramways Act 1876
Gauge: 3ft 6in
Traction: Horse
Opened: 20 March 1879

Closed: 31 December 1903
System: Radial
Length: 7.01 miles
Stock: 6 sd, 8 dd
Livery: Yellow & cream
Last Car: ?

Preston's first tramway was opened by the Preston Tramways Co. and ran for nearly 2½ miles from the Town Hall, northwards up Lancaster Road, North Road and Garstang Road, then eastwards along Victoria Road and Watling Street Road to Fulwood Barracks where the depot was sited. It was a single-track line worked by six single-deckers and was joined in 1882 by two more routes, this time built by Preston Corporation and leased to a local horse bus operator by the name of Harding. The first of these (2 miles of single track) ran northwest from the Town Hall up Friargate, Fylde Street, Fylde Road and Tulketh Road to a terminus in Newton Road in Ashton-on-Ribble whilst the second (nearly 3 miles of

single track) ran eastwards up Fishergate Hill from the Ribble, along Fishergate past the Corporation's depot and the main railway station, past the Town Hall and out along Church Street, Newhall Lane and Blackburn Road to Farringdon Park. The new routes were worked by eight open-top double-deckers.

In 1886 the Corporation bought the Company's line and this too was worked by W. Harding & Co. Ltd from 1 January 1887 until the lease expired at the end of 1903 whereupon Harding substituted horse buses for the trams whilst the Corporation pressed ahead with plans for an electric system. (See below.)

Further details of the horse tramways are tantalisingly sketchy, especially as regards the stock. It is known though that in later years the depot was sited off Lancaster Road.

Bibliography: *Trams in the North West*
  Peter Hesketh (Ian Allan, 1995)
  0 7110 2349 2

PRESTON CORPORATION TRAMWAYS

Authority: Preston Corporation Act 1900
Gauge: 4ft 8½in
Traction: Overhead electric
Opened: 7 June 1904
Closed: 15 December 1934
System: Radial network
Length: 10.53 miles
Stock: 12 sd, 42 dd
Livery: Maroon & yellow*
Last Car: No 4?

Constructed under its 1900 and 1902 Acts, the first two electric routes to open in Preston were conversions of the horse lines from the Town Hall to Fulwood Barracks and to Farringdon Park (see above), the former being modified slightly by using a longer stretch of Watling Street Road to avoid Victoria Road. Shortly after the opening, on 30 June 1904, a southern link between Fulwood and Church Street was opened along Deepdale Road off which, in Holmbrook Road, the depot and generating station had been built. From the Town Hall this line followed the old horse tramway route down Fishergate Hill, then turned south along the river bank (Broadgate) to Penwortham Bridge. All three routes were mainly double-track with services worked by open-toppers 1-30 (the last four being bogie vehicles) built by ERTCW and supplied by DK who constructed the tramways.

The penultimate route opened – on 1 July 1904 – was the reconstructed Ashton horse route (again modified slightly at its extremity to terminate in Long Lane) with the final line, a new, northeast route to Ribbleton via Ribbleton Road and Ribbleton Avenue opening on 26 June the following year to serve the district between the Fulwood and Farringdon Park lines. Both these later lines were mainly single-track.

Three new cars, bogie single-deckers 31-33, were bought in 1912 from UEC, followed two years later by Nos 34-39, six UEC balcony cars. The only other passenger cars purchased were single-deckers 40-48, bought from SHEFFIELD CORPORATION (and retaining their blue livery) just after World War I to replace some of the older cars, and balcony cars 13, 18 and 22 bought in 1929 from LINCOLN; at the same time the Corporation constructed three enclosed double-deckers of its own (Nos 30, 40 and 42) from parts of withdrawn vehicles.

On 4 July 1932 the Farringdon Park and Penwortham Bridge routes closed, replaced by Corporation bus services. The Ashton route went on 6 August 1934 whilst the Ribbleton services had withered away earlier that summer. All that remained was the circular route from the Town Hall to Fulwood and back and that too had gone by the end of the

year. The surviving cars were sold off with one – the rebuilt No 42 – gaining a new lease of life at LYTHAM ST ANNES.

Bibliography: as above

PROVINCIAL TRAMWAYS

The Provincial Tramways Co. Ltd, established in London in 1872, was a tramway-owning concern which began with horse lines, made the transition to electric tramways and power supply and ended with motor bus operations. Its main focus of tramway interests was in the PORTSMOUTH area where it owned, through nominally-independent companies, the GOSPORT & FAREHAM and PORTSDOWN & HORNDEAN lines as well as the city's tramways, though at one time or another it also owned the GRIMSBY system, the LONDON SOUTHERN TRAMWAYS and the PLYMOUTH, STONEHOUSE & DEVONPORT line in England and the Cardiff Tramways in Wales.

RAMSGATE & MARGATE TRAMWAY

This was an example of a tramway which almost made it but failed, for financial reasons, at the very last hurdle. In 1879 the Ramsgate and Margate Tramways Act authorized the construction of 6.44 miles of 2ft 6½in gauge horse tramway between the Kentish towns of its title, via St Peters and Broadstairs. In 1880 the Ramsgate & Margate Tramways Co. Ltd was empowered to use steam traction and two years later was empowered to use a wider (and more conventional) gauge of 3ft 6in. About a mile of track was then laid from Broadstairs station on the LCDR northwards along St Peters Road to St Peter's Church in the district of that name. By 1884 however

the Company appears to have had no reserves left to draw upon – promoting three Acts of Parliament in as many years could scarcely have helped matters – and the Company accordingly was wound up on 1 August 1893 by a High Court order.

The unsolved mystery is this: did the tramway ever operate a public service? It seems not, though it is believed that one double-deck car from the initial order of six (possibly from Metropolitan) was actually delivered to the line – probably then going the length of the country to SOUTH SHIELDS in 1882 and five years later to Douglas Bay in the Isle of Man where it became that fleet's No 18 (see Section 5). The value of the scheme was proved however nearly 20 years later with the opening of the ISLE OF THANET tramway.

Bibliography: *The Tramways of Kent Vol 2: East Kent 'INVICTA'* (The Light Railway Transport League, 1975) 0 900433 45 0

RAWTENSTALL CORPORATION TRAMWAYS

Authority: Rawtenstall Corporation Act 1907
Gauge: 4ft
Traction: Steam/overhead electric
Took Over: 1 October 1908
Closed: 31 March 1932
System: Radial
Length: 11.75 miles
Stock: 12 locos, 12 dd steam; 6 sd, 26 dd electric
Livery: Maroon & cream
Last Car: ?

Following the 1908 takeover of the ROSSENDALE VALLEY TRAMWAYS, Rawtenstall Corporation set about refurbishing and extending the system with 16 UEC

Postcard of Preston Corporation No 20 1904 in Fishergate, shortly after the opening of the system, complete with attendant policeman. (Author's Collection)

top-covered cars entering service the following year. The single-track system, focussed on Queen's Square in the town centre, was made up of four routes: west to Lockgate where it connected end-on with HASLINGDEN CORPORATION's portion of ACCRINGTON's route from Baxenden, north up the former steam line to Crawshawbooth and on to Loveclough and east along the former steam line to Bacup with a branch off this at Waterfoot, running north through Lumb to Water. The steam service ended on 22 July 1909 after which the routes were switched over to electric working and the old rolling stock disposed of, with the exception of two locos which were kept for use as snowploughs.

In 1912 another two UEC top-covered cars (Nos 17 and 18) were bought, together with UEC single-deckers 19-24 for use on the Water route. The last cars were Nos 25-32 in 1921, eight Brush enclosed double-deckers. The depot was in the centre of Rawtenstall off the Bacup Road. The system died eleven years later, killed by bus competition, with an official closing ceremony on 7 April 1932, a week after public services ceased.

Bibliography: *The Tramways of Accrington 1886-1932* Robert W. Rush (The Light Railway Transport League, 1961)

READING TRAMWAYS

Authority: Reading Tramways Order 1878
Gauge: 4ft
Traction: Horse
Opened: 5 April 1879
Taken Over: 1 November 1901
System: Single line
Length: 2.37 miles
Stock: 7 sd, 6 dd?
Livery: ?

Reading's first tramway was a simple east–west line though the town centre. The western half from the Barracks down Oxford Road to the Bull Hotel in Broad Street opened first, followed on 31 May 1879 by the eastern half from the Bull out along King Street and Kings Road to the London Road junction at the Cemetery Gates in the district spelt variously as Early, Earley and Erleigh. The line was single-track except for a short central double section and operated by the Reading Tramways Co., an IMPERIAL TRAMWAYS subsidiary; the original rolling stock comprised four single-deck cars with two more added for the opening of the whole line. The depot and stables were in Oxford Road. Later in 1879 another single-decker was added, this time from Hughes, which had a reversible body (possibly an Eades patent car). It is likely that the single-deckers were numbered 1-7 and were followed during the 1880s by double-deckers 8-10 (and later others to replace the older cars) but full details are lacking. The Company also operated horse buses.

In 1899 Reading Town Council decided to exercise its powers of compulsory purchase and a price of £11,394 was fixed, the last day of Company ownership being 31 October 1901 by which time the Corporation had already obtained authority to extend the system as a prelude to electrification. (See below.)

Bibliography: *The Tramways of Reading* H. E. Jackson (Adam Gordon, Chetwode, 2nd ed 1990)

READING CORPORATION TRAMWAYS

Authority: Reading Tramways Order 1899
Gauge: 4ft

Traction: Horse/overhead electric
Took Over: 1 November 1901
Closed: 20 May 1939
System: Radial
Length: 7.45 miles
Stock: 10 horse; 36 dd electric
Livery: Claret & cream
Last Car: No 13

Reading Corporation began work on extending and electrifying the horse line (see above) in April 1902 with the new lines completed by mid-December, after which the original tramway was converted (and doubled) with the work being completed by the following July. The new routes, as authorized by the 1899 Order, were a 3-furlong extension west along Oxford Road from the Barracks to the Pond House, a 6-furlong extension east along Wokingham Road from the Cemetery Gates and a 3-furlong branch northeast from the former terminus along London Road. The last horse car ran on 21 July in readiness for the electric cars' assumption of services the next day. Two of the old cars (both double-deckers) were sold to the nearby WANTAGE TRAMWAY and the others disposed of.

Before reconstruction had begun, powers for further lines had been granted under the Reading Corporation (Tramways) Act 1900; these comprised a northern branch along Caversham Road from the Oxford Road/ Broad Street junction, a branch south from there along Bridge Street, Southampton Street and Whitley Street with a south-western branch along Castle Street and Castle Hill to the start of Bath Road, and a southeastern branch off King Street along London Street and part of London Road, then into Erleigh Road. The new system was principally double-track with the new branches being in the order of a mile or so each (the Bath Road line being half that).

The initial order of cars was for 30 ERTCW open-toppers (Nos 1-30) based on a new depot by the power station in Mill Lane off London Street; these were joined a year later by Nos 31-36, more of the same only this time mounted on bogies.

The Corporation began running motor buses in 1919 though this does not seem to have threatened the tramway which continued to be kept in good order (with minor track adjustments made to several of the termini in the late 1920s and early 1930s). The car fleet, somewhat surprisingly, was never added to during the rest of the tramway's life though Nos 1-9, 11-30 and 36 were all rebodied in the 1920s at Mill Lane.

The system's gradual abandonment, when it came, was brought about by a combination of increased Corporation and private bus operations, increased private car use and its conccommitant road congestion.

Postcard view of Broad Street, Reading, with Corporation open-toppers 11 and 24 the only motorized vehicles visible. (Lens of Sutton)

The short Bath Road route went on 31 March 1930, the Erleigh Road route on 7 August 1932 and on 15 July 1936 the Caversham–Whitley through route was closed (to be converted to trolleybus operation). This left just the original horse tramway route (and its extensions) to survive another three years; after the final closure the 24 cars still in service were sold for scrap.

Bibliography: as above

REDRUTH see CAMBORNE & REDRUTH

ROCHDALE CORPORATION TRAMWAYS
Authority: Rochdale Corporation Act 1900
Gauge: 4ft 8½in
Traction: Overhead electric, steam
Opened: 22 May 1902
Closed: 12 November 1932
System: Network
Length: 28.71 miles
Stock: 35 sd, 64 dd electric
Livery: Dark brown & yellow
Last Car: No 80

As with many of the components of the Lancashire tramway network centred on Manchester, the history of Rochdale's system is a complicated one. Briefly, what happened was that at the end of the 19th century Rochdale Corporation decided to purchase the MANCHESTER, BURY, ROCHDALE & OLDHAM routes within its boundaries, electrify and extend them as a standard gauge system linked to its neighbours. In the event the latter part of the scheme came first when, in May 1902, it opened a short route from the end of Manchester Road on the west of the town centre westwards along Bury Road to the Cemetery, followed on 17 June by another westwards branch, this time to Norden via Spotland Road and Edenfield Road, and on 21 July by a short northern branch off this to Spotland. (All these routes passed close to the main depot in Mellor Street before diverging.)

As did a number of other operators, the Corporation ordered six sample cars initially with follow-up orders to be placed in the light of their performance. These were bogie single-decker No 1, bogie open-topper No 2 and single-truck open-topper No 3 from DK and bogie open-toppers Nos 4-6 from Milnes.

On 10 July 1904 the Corporation purchased the MBRO routes it wanted for the (arbitrated) price of £74,769 and thereafter set about converting them to electric working as well as continuing its new routes programme. The last steam tram ran on 8 May 1905 on the Littleborough route during its reconstruction.

By 1 August 1925 when the Corporation took over the northern portion of the MIDDLETON route through Castleton to Sudden, it had built up a network of routes within the town centre and a number of radial routes in all directions including connections into OLDHAM and Middleton to the south and HEYWOOD to the west; in addition it operated the 1½-mile BACUP LIGHT RAILWAY.

The first cutback came just five years later when, on 18 October 1930, the long and exposed mainly single-track route northeast through Littleborough and along the Todmorden Road to an isolated terminus by the Summit Inn, was abandoned. More closures came in 1931 and by mid-1932 only a through, jointly-operated service to MANCHESTER remained; this too went on 12 November of that year as Manchester in turn cut back its routes. Once again, the buses were the victors.

Arriving after cars 1-6, the following electric trams made up the Rochdale fleet:

Nos 7-9: ERTCW open-toppers of 1902
Nos 10-29: Brush open-toppers of 1903-05
Nos 30-43: Brush bogie single-deckers of 1905
Nos 44-40: Brush bogie open-toppers of 1905
Nos 50-59: Brush single-deckers of 1906
Nos 60-69: Brush single-deckers of 1912
Nos 70-79: EE top-covered double-deckers of 1920
Nos 80-92: EE enclosed double-deckers of 1925-26
Nos 93, 94: EE/Corporation enclosed double-deckers of 1927-28

In addition, Middleton cars 12-15 were taken into the fleet in 1925 but probably never used in service in view of their poor condition.

Bibliography: *Rochdale's Tramways* Clifford Taylor (The Manchester Transport Museum Society, 1987) 0 900857 26 9

ROSHERVILLE see GRAVESEND, ROSHERVILLE & NORTHFLEET

ROSSENDALE VALLEY TRAMWAYS
Authority: Rossendale Valley Tramways Act 1888
Gauge: 4ft
Traction: Steam
Opened: 31 January 1889
Taken Over: 1 October 1908
System: Single line
Length: 6.35 miles
Stock: 12 locos, 12 dd
Livery: ?

One of the last of Britain's urban steam tramways to open, this was a single-track line owned and operated by the Rossendale Valley Tramways Co., running south from Crawshawbooth south of Burnley down the Burnley Road to Rawtenstall where it connected with the ACCRINGTON CORPORATION steam line coming in from the northwest, then swinging east to follow the River Irwell, road and railway in the valley of its title for 4½ miles to Bacup. This latter section opened first, followed in 1891 by the extension to Crawshawbooth.

Services began with Green locomotives Nos 1-9 hauling bogie double-deck trailers

Commemorative postcard of the opening of Rochdale's northeastern route towards Todmorden, terminating at the Summit Inn; Brush open-topper 19 of 1903 does the honours. (Lens of Sutton)

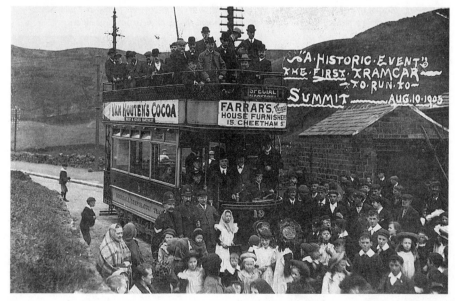

Nos 1-10 from Milnes. Additions to the stock made after that were three more Green locos (No 10 in 1893, 11 in 1894 and 12 ex-BLACKBURN in 1901) and two more trailers (No 11 in 1901 and 12 in 1903), both probably also ex-Blackburn.

In 1900 the concern was acquired by the BET who wished to electrify it but co-operation was not forthcoming from the two local authorities involved, Bacup and Rawtenstall (or even between each other), until 1 October 1908 when they purchased the line jointly in preparation for their building an electric tramway between the two towns (to be worked by RAWTENSTALL CORPORATION).

ROTHERHAM CORPORATION TRAMWAYS

Authority: Rotherham Corporation Act 1900
Gauge: 4ft 8½in
Traction: Overhead electric
Opened: 31 January 1903
Closed: 13 November 1949
System: Radial
Length: 11.55 miles
Stock: 15 sd, 68 dd
Livery: Chocolate & yellow
Last Car: No 11

The Rotherham system formed part of the south Yorkshire tramway network, being connected to SHEFFIELD to the southwest and MEXBOROUGH & SWINTON to the north. After early horse tramway proposals had come to nothing Rotherham Corporation successfully promoted an electric line which opened with twelve open-toppers (Nos 1-12) and three single-deckers (Nos 13-15) from ERTCW.

The first two routes opened ran from College Square in the town centre, north up Effingham Street for just over 1 mile to the local authority boundary (and depot in Rawmarsh Road) and northeast along Fitzwilliam Road from the start of Effingham Street to the Pumping Station, a distance of about 1½ miles. A third, westerly route from College Square along the High Street, Main Street and Masbrough Street to Kimberworth was opened on 8 April 1903, followed on 6 June by a southern route down Cranklow Road to Canklow (1½ miles) and on 8 June by a southwestern line of about the same length to Templeborough (extended on 21 July another mile to Tinsley where the rails stopped just short of those of the Sheffield system). That year also saw the arrival of cars 16-30, more ERTCW open-toppers.

A connection between the two systems having been put in, through running with Sheffield began in September 1905 whilst in the following year, on 1 October, the Fitzwilliam Road line was extended for ¾ mile to Dalton and, on 6 February 1907, through running with Mexborough & Swinton began via Effingham Street. The system was proving a success and a programme of fitting top covers to the cars was well under way; in 1908 the three single-deckers were rebuilt as roofed balcony cars and in 1909 six UEC balcony cars (Nos 32-37) were bought and a track-doubling programme begun on the single-track system. A new, 1-mile route from the High Street southeast along Wellgate was opened on 2 March 1910; in 1912 this was extended along Broom Road and Wickersley Road whilst in the same year the Dalton route was extended another mile up the Doncaster Road to Thrybergh to complete the system. That year also saw the introduction of trolleybus feeder services.

By World War I more cars were needed and the Corporation was forced to shop around for second-hand vehicles, eventually buying twelve ERTCW single-deckers (Nos 38-49) from OLDHAM in 1916 and ten ERTCW enclosed cars (Nos 50-59) from LONDON COUNTY COUNCIL a year later. The war also brought an unexpected disruption to services: in 1912 Tinsley had become part of Sheffield and disputes between Rotherham and Sheffield Corporations over the affected portion of track meant that on 30 September 1914 through running ceased, not to be reinstated until 15 May 1915 (Sheffield finally taking over that piece of track from 1 January 1926).

After the war the car fleet was increased by the 1920 purchase of thirteen EE top-covered cars (Nos 1-4 and 60-68); no further vehicles were bought until 1934-35 when Nos 1-11, enclosed EE cars, were added to stock, followed in 1942 by the hire and subsequent purchase of No 14, formerly enclosed car 125 of LEEDS. By this latter date much of the system had been abandoned, the closures beginning with the Broom Road route – always a loss-maker – on 10 June 1929 (replaced by trolleybuses), followed on 16 May 1931 by the Kimberworth–Thrybergh cross-town route. The last trams to Canklow ran on 9 July 1934 leaving just the Templeborough (and Sheffield) service to survive World War II; the through service ceased on 11 December 1948 with the Rotherham section of the route closing less than a year later.

ROTTINGDEAN *see* BRIGHTON & ROTTINGDEAN

RYDE PIER TRAMWAY

Authority: Ryde Pier and Tramways Act 1865*
Gauge: 4ft 8½in
Traction: Horse/steam/horse
Opened: 29 August 1864
Closed: March 1886?
System: Single line
Length: c1.51 miles
Stock: 2 locos, 3 sd, 6 dd steam & horse
Livery: Various
Last Car: ?

The Ryde Pier Tramway was not only the Isle of Wight's sole tramway, it was the only British pier tramway that actually managed to progress more than a few yards inland. The original pier was opened in 1814 in response to the growing popularity of the island as a holiday resort and was gradually extended to 2,250ft to serve the Southampton ferries. In 1862 work began on a new pier on the eastern side of the original; also of timber construction, it sported two standard gauge tracks linked by a crossover

Rotherham Corporation No 26 of 1903, in post-World War 1 top-covered form, in Main Street – a postcard street scene typical of many northern towns between the wars. (Author's Collection)

at the shore end (but apparently worked as two separate lines). The rails were laid in 1863 and were of railway rather than tramway type and in order that other vehicles might use the pier it was asphalted to rail level. Two cars (a 1st class open-top double-decker and a 2nd class single-decker) were delivered in September that year and the following March trials began with an MW steam locomotive. This proved to create excessive vibration in the structure and was returned to the makers, the tramway opening with horse traction and a new, lighter single-deck car from T. B. Ayshford of Walham Green in London. (There appears to have been no authority for the tramway other than the original 1812 Ryde Pier Act.)

The intention was to extend the tramway southwards through the town to the Isle of Wight (Eastern Section) Railway's terminus at St John's Road, about a mile away, and on 28 January 1870 a section 1,180ft long to Ryde Castle on a widened Esplanade opened (authorized by the Ryde Pier and Tramways Act 1865). The remaining section south through (literally!) Holywell House into Cornwall Street, then beside the culverted Monkton Road Brook, across Link Road and Park Road to the station, opened on 7 August 1871, the whole line now being known as the Ryde Pier Railway. Two years later a parallel goods branch was laid on the Esplanade to serve the shorter Victoria Pier.

Passenger trams were horse-worked from St John's to the pier head (where they were turned on a turntable) with a horse-drawn luggage van following behind. More stock was added at this time, including five Starbuck open-toppers and a locally-built ornate single-decker (later fitted with roof seats) known as the 'Grapes' car on account of its carved embellishments. Some through running of railway vans and wagons occurred but the only section used by railway engines was that just north of St John's in order for them to run round their trains.

The double transhipment of ferry passengers and their luggage was not a satisfactory arrangement and on 5 April 1880 the railway was extended (via a tunnel) onto the Esplanade where a station (Ryde Esplanade) was built at the pier gates; on 12 July it was extended all the way along a new railway pier (owned jointly by the LSWR and LBSCR but worked by IoWR and Isle of Wight Central Railway trains) beside the tramway one. From then on the town tram service ceased and the rails were lifted about five years later.

Two coke-fired steam locos were supplied by F. Bradley of Kidderminster to work the pier line from February 1881 to October 1884 (and then sold to the Ryde Gas Co.); in 1885 Messrs Siemens of Chorlton were

Pre-1871 view of Ryde Pier with the pier head turntable and car shed siding to the fore. (Author's Collection)

contracted to electrify the line on the third-rail system and the tramway was fenced off from the rest of the pier to become an electric railway which began working on 6 March 1886 (with regular services starting a week later). Some continuity was provided with the past with at least two of the horse cars (including the 'Grapes' car) being converted for use on the new railway. Electric working lasted until 1927 when the then owners, the SR, abandoned it in favour of two new Drewry petrol railcars. In 1969 BR withdrew services completely – as over much of the island – replacing the railcars with an ex-London Underground stock shuttle service on the adjoining railway pier. Happily the 'Grapes' car, which survived as a railcar trailer until an accident in 1935 led to its withdrawal (by which date it must have been the oldest working tramcar in the British Isles), is now restored and on display in the Hull Transport Museum.

Bibliography: *The Railways and Tramways of Ryde* A. Blackburn & J. Mackett (Town & Country Press, 1971)

RYE & CAMBER TRAMWAY

A 3ft gauge railway which ran through open country and sand dunes close to the north bank of the River Rother from Rye in East Sussex to close to the beach at Camber Sands. The line was constructed by local businessmen on private land, thus obviating the need for Parliamentary approval. The engineer was Holman F. (later Colonel) Stephens of light railway fame and the first 1½ miles to the Rye Golf Club opened on 13 July 1895; a ½-mile extension to Camber

Sands opened thirteen years to the day later.

Stock consisted of two small Bagnall tank engines, a four-wheeled petrol locomotive (from 1925), two saloon coaches and a handful of goods wagons. The line closed in 1939 at the outbreak of World War II and was requisitioned by the Admiralty, never to re-open to the public.

Bibliography: *The Rye & Camber Tramway: A Centenary History* Laurie A. Cooksey (Plateway Press, 1995) 1 871980 26 7

ST GEORGE & HANHAM LIGHT RAILWAY *see* BRISTOL TRAMWAYS

ST HELENS & DISTRICT TRAMWAYS

Authority: St Helens and District Tramways Act 1879
Gauge: 4ft 8½in
Traction: Horse, steam, overhead electric
Opened: 5 November 1881
Closed: 31 March 1936
System: Radial network
Length: 21.96 miles
Stock: 4 sd?, 9 dd horse; 9 locos, 10 dd steam; 2 sd, 48 dd electric
Livery: ? & cream horse & steam; dark red & white to 1913, green & white to 1919, then red & white electric
Last Car: No 26 (official)

Armed with its empowering Act, the St Helens & District Tramways Co. began construction in October 1880, opening its first horse route just over twelve months later. This ran southwest for 3½ miles from the town centre along Prescot Road and St Helens Road to the King's Arms at the junction of Warrington Road and Prescot High Street. In May or June 1882 a second cross-town route opened from Denton's Green, southeast for just over a mile along Denton's Green Lane and Duke Street to the town centre, then onwards for another ½ mile to Peasley Cross to terminate at the junction of Peasley Cross Lane and Sutton Road. A one-way system in the town centre linked the Town Hall, the depot in Hall Street, Coronation Street, Church Street and the railway station. A route to the north-east later ran for 3¾ miles along Park Road, West End Road and Clipsley Lane to Holly Bank Road, just past Haydock railway station.

Services were worked by open-top Eades reversible cars from Ashbury of which six were bought in 1881 (Nos 1-6?), three Oldbury single-deckers of c1882, three Metropolitan open-toppers of 1882 and, possibly, a single-decker purchased between 1886 and 1890 from Milnes.

The tramway was not an immediate financial success and in 1883 the Company obtained powers to use steam traction in order to expand the system along other (hilly) routes. The money for this expansion was presumably not forthcoming as nothing happened for another six years. Then, on 22 October 1889, the St Helens & District Tramways Co. Ltd was registered to take over the old company, buying it for £39,000 on 1 February 1890 and commencing steam trials later that month. Public steam services began on 3 April over the whole system with the exception of the last half of the Haydock line from the Ship Inn, Blackbrook, which was not converted until 12 May. That April three of the Ashbury cars and the

three Oldbury cars were sold to the Birkdale & Southport Tramways Co. at SOUTH-PORT and two of the Metropolitan cars (and the Milnes single-decker?) to the MORECAMBE TRAMWAYS.

The steam services were worked by Green tramway locomotives 1-6 hauling top-covered Milnes bogie trailers of which seven had been bought by July 1890 (with the fleet increasing to ten over the next three years). Green loco 7 followed in May 1890 and Nos 8 and 9 the next year.

In March 1897 St Helens Corporation agreed to purchase the 9½-mile single-track system for £23,000 from 1 April, leasing it back to the Company which, on 4 November 1898, became the New St Helens & District Tramways Co. Ltd. That year the Corporation obtained an Act enabling it to double the size of the system and electrify it, entering into a new lease with the Company for 21 years from 1 October.

On 20 July 1899 electric working began over the Denton's Green route and part of the line to Prescot (which was reached two days later); the official opening was on 3 August. The Peasley Cross line was inspected on 8 December (and presumably opened shortly afterwards) and was extended on 19 September 1900 south along Marshalls Cross Road, then east along Rodins Lane and Station Road to just short of St Helens Junction railway station. (The 111-yard gap to the station was not bridged until 1927.) Other extensions included a ½-mile branch south from the Toll Bar on the Prescot line along Lugsmore Lane to Thatto Heath station, extended another ½ mile down Nutgrove Road to Nutgrove, and a ¾-mile extension of the Haydock line

to the Rams Head in Church Road.

A 1½-mile branch east along Parr Stocks Road and Oak Road to the Horse Shoe in Parr opened on 2 June 1900 with a 1-mile branch north up North Road and City Road to Windle following on 19 September. The last route opened (sometime after its inspection on 8 January 1901) continued the Nutgrove line south along Rainhill Road to near Rainhill station, then northwest along Warrington Road to meet the Prescot line at its terminus (2¾ miles); this was later extended ½ mile southwest to Derby Street, Brook Bridge where, on 25 June 1902, it connected with the LIVERPOOL & PRESCOT LIGHT RAILWAY. Earlier, on 4 April 1902, through running to Hindley and beyond had begun when a connection was made with the SOUTH LANCASHIRE TRAMWAYS at Haydock (in which concern the Company bought a controlling interest four years later).

Relations betwen the Company and the Corporation were never good and the latter refused to renew the lease, taking over the tramway on 1 October 1919, thereafter refurbishing the car fleet which had become much neglected. On 1 April 1921 LIVER-POOL CORPORATION began operating through to the King's Arms in Prescot (having taken over the LPLR two years earlier), purchasing for £8,000 the 946 yards of track between there and Brook Bridge. On 17 August 1923 the Corporation began its own regular bus services and used them from March 1927 to replace the trams on the Nutgrove and Prescot section of the tramway. On 8 December 1923 the Parr route closed, again replaced by a bus service (in preparation for the introduction of trolleybuses) whilst on 21 June 1931 trolley-buses took over on the Haydock route. Buses took over on the Windle line on 12 July 1932 and, on 1 May 1935, the St Helens Junction line went.

The original electric car fleet comprised Brush open-toppers taking the odd numbers between 1 and 15 with Brush bogie open-toppers taking the even ones. (One theory is that the shorter, odd-numbered cars were intended originally to be trailers.) Brush bogie cars 17-36 were bought 1899-1900, some of which were cannabalized during World War I (and No 24 rebuilt as a works car in 1923) and the others renumbered when EE open-toppers (top-covered 1920-21) were bought in 1918 and numbered 33-36; these were followed the next year by Nos 37-44, top-covered vehicles from Brush (renumbered 21-28 in 1929). In 1927 two ex-WIGAN single-deckers were bought, these being DK 1904 cars 68 and 77 which were renumbered (order unknown) 30 and 31 (and 13 and 14 two years later at a time of wholesale scrapping and renumbering).

St Helens & District bogie car No 18 of 1899 in immaculate livery, probably soon after delivery, its decency boards still untainted by advertisements. (Lens of Sutton)

Between 1910 and at least 1919 various South Lancs cars were borrowed or hired to help out on the tramway, some of which were given the temporary numbers 44-46 whilst the numbers 37-43 were taken originally by the LPLR's fleet of seven cars shedded by St Helens even though they were never actually owned by the St Helens company.

Bibliography: *St Helens Tramways* E. K. Stretch (St Helens Town Council, 1968)

SALFORD TRAMWAY

Authority: Local authority permission
Gauge: c5ft?
Traction: Horse
Opened: Late 1861
Closed: Early 1872?
System: Single line
Length: c1 mile
Stock: *
Livery: Red & white?
Last Car: ?

Salford's first tramway was a unique affair and one of the handful of early 1860s pioneering lines. It was laid by John Greenwood, a local bus operator, and used a single, three-rail track of a type patented by Greenwood's brother-in-law John Haworth under the title 'Haworth's Patent Perambulating System'. Unlike other tramways of the time such as G. F. Train's in BIRKENHEAD, the Haworth track did not use step rails but two flat rails or plates some 3in wide set flush into the surface of the road and upon which ran the flangeless wheels of the tramway vehicles. Guidance was provided by a third rail laid down the centre of the track which had a slot in it to accommodate a small guide wheel (the 'perambulator') attached to the front of the tramcar (or rather converted horse omnibus).

Permission was given from Salford Council and the Pendleton Turnpike Trustees for the line from Pendleton (to the northwest of Manchester) down Broad Street, the Crescent and Chapel Street to a terminus at Albert's Bridge on the Salford/Manchester boundary. Other details of the line are sketchy but it is thought that the line opened in stages during 1861-62 and was initially well-regarded as being smooth, reliable and no hinderance to other road users. The gauge used is not known but must have been sufficient to accommodate the outside wheels of Greenwood's buses, some of which were fitted with the guide wheels (which could be raised at the end of the tramway section to allow the bus to continue along the road).

On 1 March 1865 Greenwood, Haworth and other local businessmen came together to form the Manchester Carriage Co. Ltd, later to play an important role in the development of horse tramways in MANCHESTER and the surrounding district. By the late 1860s though it appears that maintenance of the tramway had been let slip – possibly because the MC Co. was now expressing an interest in laying conventionally-railed lines – and in February 1870 the Council ordered the removal of the rails though this was not in fact done for another two years.

Bibliography: *The Manchester Carriage and Tramways Company* Edward Gray (Manchester Transport Museum Society, 1977)

SALFORD CORPORATION TRAMWAYS

Authority: Salford Corporation Act 1897
Gauge: 4ft 8½in
Traction: Horse, overhead electric
Took Over: 28 April 1901
Closed: 31 March 1947
System: Network
Length: 38.8 miles
Stock: 77 horse?; 10 sd, 231 dd electric
Livery: Chocolate/maroon/red & cream
Last Car: No 350

With its 1901 takeover of part of the MANCHESTER TRAMWAYS for £42,500 Salford Corporation found itself the owner of 77 cars, some 50 miles of track within its boundaries and the depots at Weaste, Pendleton and Broughton. It thereupon set about converting the system to electric working with the first route, from Kersal Bar down Bury New Road to Blackfriars Bridge in Manchester re-opening on 4 October with the others following quickly. The last horse trams ran in October 1903, by which time the new services were being worked by Milnes open-toppers 1-100 (1901-02), Milnes bogie open-toppers 101-130 (1903) and similar BEC cars 131-150 (also 1903) with a new depot constructed on Frederick Road in the town centre to house them. (Most of these cars were later top-covered and/or rebuilt.)

Three years later, on 2 October 1906, the last route opened, northwest to Worsley, to produce a sprawling network of lines connected to those of Manchester to the east, TRAFFORD PARK to the south, SOUTH LANCASHIRE to the west and BURY to the north – though through running agreements were not fully exploited until the 1920s when bus competition was beginning to pose a serious threat. The Corporation introduced its own bus services in 1920, by which time the tramcar fleet had grown with the purchase of the following vehicles:

Nos 151-160: ERTCW single-deck combination cars of 1905
Nos 161, 162, 173-177: ex-Trafford Park cars bought 1905
Nos 163-172: UEC balcony cars of 1906
Nos 177-196: ditto of 1908
Nos 197-200: HN balcony cars of 1908
Nos 151-160: Brush open-toppers of 1913-14
Nos 201-212: Brush bogie balcony cars of 1915

John Haworth's guided tram mechanism used on Salford's first tramway, as depicted in the Illustrated London News *of 16 November 1861.*

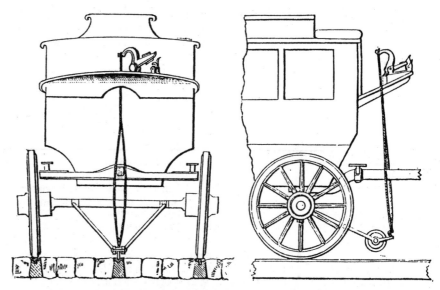

NEW STREET RAILWAY AT MANCHESTER, WITH OMNIBUS PERAMBULATOR.

Postcard of Salford Corporation Nos 30 and 63 of 1901-02 with the almost inevitable crowd of fascinated small boys. (Lens of Sutton)

Nos 213-224: Brush bogie open-toppers of 1915-16

These were followed in 1923-24 by enclosed Brush cars Nos 225-230, the Corporation's last purchases, and eight years later, on 19 March 1932, the through service northeast to MIDDLETON up the Middleton Road to Rhodes and then on via Manchester tracks, was withdrawn. This was followed on 9 March 1935 by the closure of the two northwestern branches from Irlams O'Th'Height to Swinton and Pendlebury. Other closures followed, accompanied by car withdrawals; by 1938 the Corporation was operating more buses than trams and complete closure was planned for the following year. World War II however saw this postponed (though cutbacks continued) and it was not until 1947 that the last three routes went, the final service being on the Deansgate and Docks circular.

Bibliography: *Salford City Transport* Edward Gray (The Transport Publishing Co., 1975) 0 903839 06 7

SANDGATE *see* FOLKESTONE, HYTHE & SANDGATE

SCARBOROUGH TRAMWAYS
Authority: Scarborough Tramways Act 1902
Gauge: 3ft 6in
Traction: Overhead electric
Opened: 6 May 1904
Closed: 30 September 1931
System: Network
Length: 4.78 miles
Stock: 29 dd
Livery: Dark red & cream
Last Car: No 12?

Owned and operated by the Scarborough Tramways Co., a subsidiary of Edmundson's Electricity Corporation Ltd (although promoted by the Corporation), this compact little system was surprisingly short-lived for so popular a seaside resort. As opened on 6 and 7 May 1904 the route layout resembled a figure 8 on its side with West Pier and Foreshore Road on the South Bay seafront to the east, Vernon Place at the central crossroads and Scalby Road Depot on the western edge. In addition, a ¼-mile branch northwards from the western loop led via Castle Road and North Marine Road to the entrance to Alexandra Park in the area known as North Side whilst a ¼-mile southern branch continued the Foreshore Road line southwards past the Aquarium and along the private toll road to the Spa; a link via Barwick Street and Hanover Road provided a shortcut across the western loop. Route length was just over 4½ miles of which roughly half was double-tracked.

Services were worked by a fleet of open-top double-deckers, Nos 1-15 being from Brush and Nos 16-18 from BEC; these were joined in 1905 by Nos 19-22, four similar Brush vehicles.

A ¼-mile extension eastwards from the West Pier along Sand Side to the Marine Drive toll gate, opened at the start of the 1906 summer season, completed the system which remained intact until receipts were hard-hit by World War I and immediately afterwards minor trimmings of the network began. In 1925 though six Brush open-toppers were bought from IPSWICH and renumbered 21 and 23-28, the first of these taking an Ipswich body and the truck from Scarborough No 21 after that car had been damaged in a serious accident on 16 September that year.

In March 1931 the Corporation decided to buy the tramways (for £20,000) in order to close them and, under the Scarborough Corporation Act of that year, took them over on 30 September in order to do just that, immediately scrapping the trams in favour of a profit-sharing bus service operated by United Automobile Services Ltd.

SEATON & DISTRICT TRAMWAY
Authority: British Railways Board (Seaton and Beer) Light Railway Order 1969
Gauge: 2ft 9in
Traction: Battery/overhead electric
Opened: 28 August 1970
System: Single line
Length: 3.23 miles
Stock: 4 sd, 5 dd
Livery: Various

The previous incarnations of this tramway are described in Section 7 under Rhyl and Eastbourne. With the closure of the latter line imminent in the mid-1960s, a search was made for a new site that would permit a longer run, a wider track gauge and long-term security. The site chosen was the former British Railways branch from Seaton Junction to Seaton, on Devon's Lyme Bay coast, which had closed in 1966; Modern Electric Tramways Ltd took an option on the final 3 miles from Colyton to Seaton (and later changed its name to the more appropriate Seaton & District Tramway Co.).

Transfer of stock and equipment from Eastbourne began in February 1970 (the necessary Transfer Order for the new use of the trackbed having been obtained the previous June) with tracklaying commencing shortly afterwards. A limited service began later that summer over the first mile from Seaton, beside the River Axe to Bobsworth Bridge, using open-top car No 8 and a battery trailer; on 9 April the following year the battery-powered service was extended another mile as far as Colyford.

The overhead was brought into use on 7 June 1974 and the final third of the line to Colyton opened on 3 April 1980, since when the line has operated as a genuine tramway rather than a pleasure line – though it must be the only one to run bird watchers' specials on a regular basis!

All stock is Company-built and a feature is the use of parts from scrapped trams from other systems. Nos 2, 4, 6-8 and 12 were transferred from Eastbourne, all being regauged except No 8 which had been constructed in 1968 to the new gauge. In addition, single-deck saloon cars Nos 14 (1984) and 16 (1992) are rebuilds of METROPOLITAN 94 of 1904 and BOURNEMOUTH 106 of 1921 respectively whilst No 16 is a 1988 covered toastrack; there is also a small fleet of fully-functional works cars, those often-ignored but vital components of a working tramway.

Bibliography: *Seaton Branch and Seaton Tramway* (Locomotion Papers No 182) C. G. Maggs (The Oakwood Press, 1992) 0 85361 425 3

SEDGLEY *see* DUDLEY, SEDGLEY & WOLVERHAMPTON

SELSEY TRAMWAY *see* HUNDRED OF MANHOOD & SELSEY TRAMWAY

SHEERNESS & DISTRICT TRAMWAYS

Authority: Sheerness and District Light Railway Order 1903
Gauge: 3ft 6in
Traction: Overhead electric
Opened: 9 April 1903
Closed: 7 July 1917
System: Radial
Length: 2.47 miles
Stock: 12 dd
Livery: Chocolate & cream
Last Car: ?

Although short in route miles and short-lived in years, the only tramway on Kent's Isle of Sheppey possessed a number of interesting features. Owned by the Sheerness & District Power & Traction Co. Ltd (a member of the BET group), it operated no less than three single-track routes radiating from the town's central Clock Tower: westwards along the High Street past the SECR's Town station to terminate by that railway's Dockyard station; eastwards to the Marine Parade in the direction of Cheyney Rock and southeast along the High Street to Sheerness East station on the Sheppey Light Railway. Here were sited the tramway's power station and car sheds – the latter served, most unusually for Britain, by a turntable rather than the customary track fan or even traverser. The promoters had planned a grander system with branches out to the village of Minster and the port of Queensborough but the SLR opposed these on account of the level crossings they would have made over its metals.

A grand total of twelve open-top double-deckers were ordered from Brush for the opening but, hardly surprisingly, this number was found to be far too large for the needs of the system and Nos 9-12 were promptly sold to the CITY OF BIRMINGHAM TRAMWAYS (where they became Nos 189-192). The cars were equipped with enormous Siemens bow collectors unique on British tramways (as were any bow collectors on

Seaton Tramway No 17, specially equipped to carry wheelchair passengers. (Courtesy Seaton Tramway)

open-top cars) whilst the overhead, installed by Siemens & Halske of Berlin, was suspended from distinctive German-style bow-shaped brackets. The line's Continental appearance was enhanced further by the practice of running the line close to the kerb (with passing loops in the centre of the road) in the narrow part of the High Street, West Street and in front of the Town station.

The system had the dubious honour of becoming Britain's first electric tramway to close, its demise caused partly by the non-availability of spare parts from Germany during World War I, after which the eight

cars were sold to DARLINGTON. Bus competition had also appeared in 1913 and both Sheerness UDC and RDC had declined to buy the system when offered it.

Bibliography: *The Tramways of Kent Vol 1: West Kent 'INVICTA'* (The Light Railway Transport League, 1971) 0 900433 38 8

SHEFFIELD TRAMWAYS

Authority: Sheffield Tramways Act 1872
Gauge: 4ft 8½in
Traction: Horse

Car No 4 of 1903 on the short-lived Sheerness & District system. The unusual bow current collectors and bowstring bracket arms for the overhead can just be made out on this postcard. (Lens of Sutton)

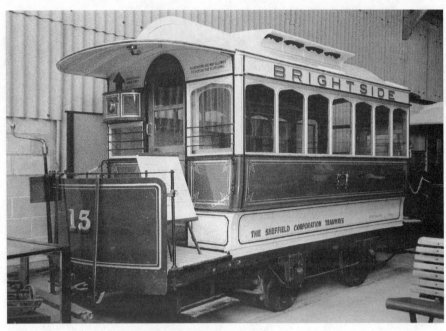

Sheffield horse car No 15 of 1874, now immaculately restored at the National Tramway Museum, Crich – where it was the first tram to operate. (M. Donnison)

Opened: 7 October 1873
Taken Over: 11 July 1896
System: Branching + branching
Length: 9.43 miles
Stock: 18 sd, 35 dd
Livery: Route colour

Built by Thomas Lightfoot, a local contractor, the first Sheffield horse tramway was owned by the Corporation but leased to its promoters, the Sheffield Tramways Co. The official opening of the mainly double-track route, from the Wicker on the edge of the city centre northeast up Savile Street and the Attercliffe Road to the Golden Ball in Attercliffe (about 2¼ miles), was on 6 October 1873 with public services beginning the next day with double-deck Starbuck cars Nos 1-12. On 7 May 1874 the line was extended another mile to Carbrook (where Tinsley Depot was built). A year later, on 26 May 1875, a parallel route was opened to the north of the first line, off Savile Street and up Brightside lane to the district of that name (where a second depot was later built). To work the enlarged system cars 13-20 were purchased, all Starbuck single-deckers.

On 19 May 1877 a third route was opened west of the Wicker running northwest along Infirmary Road and Langsett Road to Hillsborough (2½ miles) and to work this ten more Starbuck double-deckers (Nos 22-31) were bought; No 21 is thought to have been a Falcon single-decker used on trials with a Hughes steam tramway locomotive and subsequently kept.

In 1877 the last two Company-operated routes were opened. Running south down

The Moor from the Moorhead (south of and unconnected to the Wicker terminus), the line then divided with one branch (opened 29 October) continuing south down the London Road to Heeley and the other (opened 24 December) veering southwest down Washington Road and Wostenhome Road to Nether Edge. Depots were provided at both these southern termini with the Heeley line worked by (probably) Starbuck double-deckers 32-40 with (probably) Starbuck single-deckers 41-45 on the Nether Edge route.

In 1878 further steam trials were carried out, this time with a Yorkshire Engine Co. locomotive, but again nothing came of them. By now Company-Corporation relations were not very good and the Company was operating horse bus services as well as the trams. In 1882-83 car No 16 was rebuilt as a double-decker and in 1884 (probably) Ashbury single-deck saloons 46-49 were added to stock (and converted to double-deckers five years later). In 1886 two Ashbury double-decks on Eades reversible trucks were bought (Nos 1 and 50), followed a year later by Nos 2 and 12, more conventional Ashbury double-deckers. (As the numbers suggest, some of the older cars were by now being withdrawn.)

By the 1890s the Corporation was ready to terminate its lease and run the tramways itself and, in 1896, secured the necessary Act to enable it to do so. (See below.)

Bibliography: *Sheffield Transport* Chas C. Hall (The Transport Publishing Co., 1977) 0 903839 04 0

Sheffield Corporation Tramways Kenneth Gandy (Sheffield City Libraries, 1986?) 0 86321 032 5

SHEFFIELD CORPORATION TRAMWAYS

Authority: Sheffield Corporation Tramways Act 1896
Gauge: 4ft 8½in
Traction: Horse, overhead electric
Took Over: 11 July 1896
Closed: 8 October 1960
System: Radial network
Length: 52.05 miles
Stock: 68 horse; 69 sd, 820 dd electric
Livery: Route colour horse; royal (later azure) blue & cream electric
Last Car: No 510

Following its 1896 takeover of the SHEFFIELD TRAMWAYS (see above) Sheffield Corporation gained possession of 44 tramcars and four horse buses and, far more importantly in historical terms, the first clear Parliamentary mandate for a municipality to both own and operate a tramway system. A number of the old cars were quickly withdrawn and 24 new ones purchased, these being double-deck vehicles 6-9, 14, 30 and 51-56 and roofed toastracks 27 and 57-67, all from Milnes.

The intention from the outset was to extend and electrify the tramways but before this could take place three new routes were opened: northwest to Walkley via West Street and Crookes Valley Road from a terminus in Church Street sited between the other two, southwest from the Nether Edge/Heeley routes junction along Ecclesall Road to Hunter's Bar and southwest from a point midway along the Heeley route down Abbeydale Road. Conversion work on the original horse lines was also put in hand, including the linking of the three central termini.

The first converted routes to re-open, on 6 September 1899, were to Nether Edge, Heeley and Tinsley (a short extension beyond Carbrook). The first electric cars were short, open-top double-deckers 1-25 and single-deckers 39-52, all from Milnes. More conversions (and new routes) followed, the last horse trams running on 11 November 1902 on the (cutback) Hillingsborough route; by then the car fleet had been increased by the addition of Milnes open-toppers 26-38, ERTCW single-deckers 53-58, ERTCW open-toppers 59-88, Brush single-deckers 89-103, Brush open-toppers 104-123, Corporation single-deckers 124-129, Milnes open-toppers 131-155 plus single-deckers 156-165 and open-toppers 167-186 from Cravens of Sheffield. A number of horse trams were converted into works cars, one of which – No 15 of 1874

Sheffield Corporation-built No 213 of 1904 in pre-World War I service on a postcard of Nethergreen terminus. The F denotes the route. (Lens of Sutton)

renumbered 166 as a breakdown car – can now be seen restored to its original state at the National Tramway Museum, Crich (and was the first car to run there). Two others were sold to CHESTERFIELD and the remainder scrapped.

As the system continued to grow so more cars were bought or built: Milnes single-deckers 187-192, Corporation open-toppers 193-198, Corporation single-deckers 200-211 (1903), Corporation open-toppers 213-218, Brush open-toppers 219-243 and original horse cars 6 and 7 motorized by the Corporation using Brush trucks (1903-04). These were followed in 1905-06 by Corporation open-toppers 246-257 and, in 1907, by UEC 258-272, the first top-covered cars. (Many of the open-toppers were later top-covered or fully enclosed.) The main depot was originally at Tinsley and then, from 1911 onwards, in Queens Road south of the city centre; there were several other smaller depots scattered around the system.

No new cars were added until 1912 when the Corporation built top-covered cars 281-295; these were followed in 1913-14 by similar Brush vehicles 296-345 and, in 1913-15, similar Nos 346-355 from the Corporation. The systems's other new cars added after World War I (all double-deckers) were:

Nos 367-369, 401-500: Corporation
enclosed cars of 1918-21
Nos 376-400: Brush ditto of 1921-22
Nos 1, 451-500: Cravens ditto of 1926-27
Nos 36-60: Brush ditto of 1924-25
Nos 2-35, 61-130; Corporation ditto of
1924-33
Nos 131-155: W. E. Hill Ltd of South
Shields ditto of 1929-30
No 370: Corporation ditto of 1931
Nos 156-303: ditto of 1933-39

Between 1941 and 1944 the Corporation built 14 enclosed double-deckers to replace ones lost as a result of German bombing. These took the numbers 83, 85, 100, 112, 119, 129, 133, 192, 201, 227, 261, 274, 430 and 483 and were appropriately termed 'Blitz' class cars. A number of second-hand vehicles were also bought: 20 ex-LONDON COUNTY COUNCIL ERTCW enclosed double-deckers of 1903 vintage bought 1917-18 which took the numbers 356-365 and vacated earlier numbers; eight similar balcony cars which came via ROTHERHAM in 1926 of which six were put into service; 14 ex-NEWCASTLE HN double-deckers of 1901 which were bought in 1941 and numbered 311-324 and ten EE double-

deckers of 1920-21 bought in 1943 from BRADFORD (Nos 325-334).

The only passenger cars bought or constructed after the war were the 'Jubilee' class of streamlined enclosed double-deckers Nos 501-536 of which the first was built by

the Corporation in 1946 and the remainder between 1950-52 by Charles Roberts & Co. of Wakefield.

The system continued to expand during the 1920s and 1930s – including the 1926 takeover of 1.28 miles of line from

Map of Sheffield Corporation's developing system, from the 1904 Manual of Electrical Undertakings.

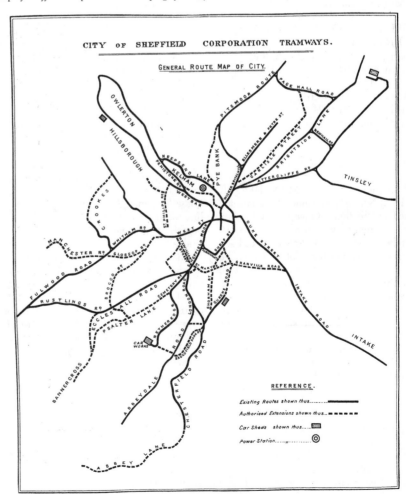

Rotherham (the only connecting system) between Tinsley and Templeborough when Sheffield's boundaries were enlarged – though by now the tramway was being trimmed elsewhere. It was hit badly by bombing raids during World War II and replacement vehicles had to be built or bought (as listed earlier) though in the late 1940s its future seemed bright – but things were soon to change. Through running to Rotherham ceased on 11 December 1948 when a railway bridge needed to be rebuilt and that route's services were terminated at Tinsley; three years later the Corporation decided to abandon the other routes over the next 15 years, though in the event it took only nine.

Because of the late closure of the tramway, several of its electric cars have been saved for preservation. Currently on view at the National Tramway Museum, Crich, are Nos 46 of 1899, 189 and 264 of 1934, 510 of 1950 and ex-Bradford car 330 which was converted to a rail grinder in 1951, whilst Nos 264 of 1907 and 513 of 1950 are at the North of England Open Air Museum, Beamish.

Bibliography: as above

SHEFFIELD: SOUTH YORKSHIRE SUPERTRAM

Authority: South Yorkshire Light Rail
    Transit Act 1988
Gauge: 4ft 8½in
Traction: Overhead electric
Opened: 21 March 1994
System: Branching
Length: 17.68 miles
Stock: 25 sd
Livery: Grey & blue

Hard on the heels of the MANCHESTER METROLINK project came a similar one centred on Sheffield. Government funding for the scheme was announced on 11 December 1990 although the idea dated back more than 20 years when, not long after the 1960 closure of the city's tramways (see above), proposals were explored for a brand-new system costing some £230m. Planning and evaluation studies continued up until 1985 when the South Yorkshire Passenger Transport Executive successfully promoted a Bill for a route running northwest–southeast across the city. This was followed by a second Bill (which became the South Yorkshire Light Rail Transit Act 1989) for a route northeast from the city centre past the World Student Games arena to the Meadowhall Shopping Centre as part of the area's regeneration plan, giving the proposed system the shape of a tilted Y. This line was in fact the first to be constructed.

Work began immediately after the closing

of the World Student Games at the end of July 1991 with the public opening less than three years later (the official opening by HRH The Princess Royal being on 23 May 1994), the main contractors being BB. The double-track line begins at Meadowhall Interchange station, at the junction with BR's lines from Sheffield to Barnsley and Rotherham (and actually just over the Sheffield/Rotherham boundary), then circles the shopping centre before running south-west along the trackbed of the former GCR branch to Barnsley. It then passes the Sheffield Arena and the Don Valley International Stadium before leaving the old trackbed on its own alignment past the Woodbourne Athletics Stadium, to reach Nunnery Depot by Sheffield Parkway which it crosses via a bridge (the number of new bridges is a feature of the route) and then follows to a city centre terminus in Commercial Street by Haymarket some 4½ miles from Meadowhall.

A triangular junction just before the terminus feeds the Phase 2 route to a second Interchange, this time behind Sheffield Midland station in Granville Street. The section south from here (Phases 2 and 5) opened on 5 December 1994 and takes the line on street and reserved sections over Norfolk Park Viaduct, along Park Grange Road, City Road and Ridgeway Road to Gleadless Townend. Here, Phase 5 veers west as a short branch to Castelayn and Herdings (opened 3 April 1995) whilst the main line carries on as Phase 6 and 7 to Halfway (opened 27 March 1995) some 8¼ miles from the city centre. The northwestern branch of the Y opened westwards from Commercial Street/Fitzalan Square to Cathedral (Phase 3) on 20 February 1995 and on to the University of Sheffield where it swung north to Shalesmoor (Phase 4) on 27 February. Phase 8 opened 23 October, continues this line, northwest to Middlewood with a short branch west from Hillsborough to Malin Bridge.

The initial 25 cars (single-deck, eight-axle articulated two-car units Nos 1-25) were built by Siemens in Düsseldorf, delivered by mid-1994 and finished in a modern version of the city's old blue and cream tramcar livery, the light silver-grey bodywork finished off with a blue-grey skirting. The operator is South Yorkshire Supertram Ltd, a subsidiary of the SYPTE.

Bibliography: *Tram to Supertram* Peter Fox,
    Paul Jackson & Roger Benton (Platform
    5 Publishing, 1995) 1 872524 61 3

SHIPLEY TRAMWAYS

Authority: Shipley Tramways Order 1881
Gauge: 4ft?
Traction: Horse

Opened: 3 August 1882?
Closed: 9 October 1891
System: Branching
Length: 2.31 miles
Stock: 6 sd?, 1 dd?
Livery: Varnished wood?
Last Car: ?

The first tramway in Shipley, immediately to the north of Bradford, was a short, unsuccessful single-track horse line running from the Fox & Hounds at Briggate in the town centre westwards along Commercial Street and Saltaire Road to its junction with Bingley Road (where the depot was sited in Moorhead Lane behind the Rosse Hotel). It was promoted by the tramway contractor Joseph Speight of Eccleston Park near Prescot who, after the failure of an 1873 scheme, obtained authorization in 1881 for 1.39 miles of line, of which only 0.8 miles was laid. The line's one single and one double-deck car were both from Oldbury. The BoT inspection was on 2 August 1882 and the line possibly opened to the public the following day. Some uncertainty also surrounds the tramway's gauge. It was planned as a 3ft 6in gauge line but believed to have been constructed to a gauge of 4ft at the request of Shipley Local Board who had an eye on a possible connection to the new system at Bradford. (The official returns are of no help in resolving the matter as they give both gauges at different times.)

By 1883 the tramway (and/or Speight) was in financial difficulties and on 10 May that year the horses and cars were auctioned (though the latter apparently failed to find buyers) and later that year ownership of the line passed to a Maurice Jones of Liverpool who, in February 1884, re-opened the line with two new, lighter cars. Jones' operation was no more successful than Speight's for, on 13 February 1885 (reportedly), the tramway shut once more. Jones then offered it to the Local Board, who declined to buy it. Attempts to re-open it as a steam tramway by Bradford District Steam Tramways Ltd (who took over the line later that year) came to nothing and horse working resumed, albeit very intermittently, until mid-1887, after which the Company went into liquidation. Rescue was at hand though for the following March saw the line bought by Bradford & District Tramways Ltd, which concern opened a second single-track line on 26 August 1888, this running southeast from the Rosse Hotel along the Bradford Road to the Shipley boundary at Frizinghall where it met but did not connect with the steam tramway line from Bradford. Two further cars were obtained to help work the enlarged system, followed by another some months later – presumably all single-deckers again.

Plans for additional routes came to

nothing and in February 1891 the Company went into receivership, services ceasing nine months later. It is thought that two of the cars found their way south to Bradford to join the fleet there and, two years after the tramway closed, the Bradford Road line reopened as part of Bradford's Keighley Road steam route into Shipley. Ten years later though a new, electric system began operations in the town (see below).

Bibliography: *Bradford City Tramways 1882-1950* D. M. Coates (Wyvern Publications, Skipton, 1984)

SHIPLEY: MID-YORKSHIRE TRAMWAYS

Authority: Shipley Improvement Act 1901
Gauge: 4ft
Traction: Overhead electric
Opened: 23 July 1903
Taken Over: 30 April 1904
System: Cross
Length: 3.43 miles
Stock: 10 dd
Livery: Royal red & ivory

Following the failure of Shipley's horse tramway (see above), early in the 20th century proposals were made for a grand tramway network to link all the major towns of central Yorkshire but all that came of them was the opening by the Mid-Yorkshire Tramways Co. (on behalf of Shipley UDC) of two short routes through the centre of Shipley just north of Bradford. The first ran east-west from the Bradford boundary at Thackley via the Leeds Road, Briggate, Saltaire Road and Bingley Road to Nab Wood Cemetery and the second, shorter north-south from Baildon Bridge through Briggate to the Branch Hotel on the Keighley Road (opened 14 November 1903); at both Saltaire and the Branch the lines connected with the BRADFORD CITY TRAMWAYS' new electric line in Bradford Road.

Ten HN open-top double-deckers (Nos 1-10) were ordered for the tramway, of which four arrived in time for the opening with trials and (probably) some early services being worked by cars borrowed from Bradford. The depot was in Exhibition Road off Saltaire Road. Traffic on the system did not live up to expectations – the Council would not agree to through running with Bradford – and less than a year after it opened the whole concern was sold to Bradford Corporation to become integrated into the larger system. The cars, renumbered 230-239, were thereafter used mainly on Shipley services.

Bibliography: as above

SHIPLEY GLEN TRAMWAY

Not a tramway but a funicular railway (with a maximum gradient of 1 in 12, far less steep than its cliff railway counterparts) that serves visitors to the beauty spot of its name near Bradford. Opened 18 May 1895, it is a double line of 1ft 8in gauge tracks, 386yd long. The pair of small open cars on each track were built by S. Halliday of Baildon using parts from the companion cars to the Shipley Glen Pond Pleasure Tramway (see Section 7); these were heavily rebuilt 1955-56 though it is thought that some of the original parts (including one underframe) were incorporated into the 'new' cars. The railway runs from Coach Road at the bottom of the Glen to Glen Top where the cable winding-house is situated in standard funicular fashion.

Bibliography: *1d.Up – ½ d.Down: the Story of Shipley Glen and its Tramway* Alan Whitrick & Michael J. Leak (Michael Bentley, Pudsey, for the Bradford Trolleybus Association, 1982) 0 86275 014 8

SHOREHAM *see* BRIGHTON & SHOREHAM

SKEGNESS TRAMWAY

Authority: Local authority permission?
Gauge: ?
Traction: Horse
Opened: c1880
Closed: c1882
System: Single line
Length: c0.25 miles
Stock: 2 sd?
Livery: ?
Last Car: ?

This short-lived, little-known line was almost unique in the British Isles in that it was built to meet the needs of bathers, the only comparable example being the similarly short-lived line at Harlech in Wales. It ran as a single track from the seafront (near the site of the Clock Tower) across the lawns of the promenade then straight out across the sand towards the sea. It is thought to have been operated, presumably at low tide only, with a pair of open toastracks equipped with canvas roofs.

SOOTHILL NETHER *see* DEWSBURY, OSSETT & SOOTHILL NETHER

SOUTH EASTERN METROPOLITAN TRAMWAYS *see* LONDON: SOUTH EASTERN METROPOLITAN TRAMWAYS

SOUTH LANCASHIRE TRAMWAYS

Authority: South Lancashire Tramways Act 1900
Gauge: 4ft 8½in
Traction: Overhead electric
Opened: 20 October 1902
Closed: 16 December 1933
System: Network
Length: 39.1 miles
Stock: 91 dd
Livery: Red & white/cream
Last Car: No 7

Part of the large, standard gauge network of tramways stretching across south Lancashire from LIVERPOOL to MANCHESTER, this system was promoted by the brothers Jacob and James Atherton who had a number of other tramway interests, including the ST HELENS system and who, after a number of false starts, obtained the necessary empowering Act.

Built by the South Lancashire Electric Traction & Power Co. Ltd (registered 29 November 1900), the first section opened ran for 6½ miles from the Lowton St Mary's boundary, northeast through Leigh and Atherton (with the main depot and power station midway between the two) and on to Four Lane Ends where it connected with the BOLTON system. This was followed on 25 October 1902 by a southeastern branch of some 2 miles from Atherton to Tyldesley, which route on 7 February 1903 was extended northwestwards 3¾ miles from Atherton through Hindley Green to Hindley, followed on 4 April by a route southwest from Hindley for 6 miles through Platt Bridge and Ashton (where it passed close to the WIGAN terminus) to Haydock and a connection with St Helens to complete the northern half of the system.

The first cars were Nos 1-45, Milnes open-top double-deckers of 1902 (many of which were later top-covered). There was also a private director's single-deck saloon car, possibly by Milnes of 1897, painted white and used briefly on private hire services such as weddings or funerals. There were plans to operate an extensive night-time freight service with special goods trains but these never materialized.

The first eastern extension, from Tyldesley through Mosley Common to Boothtown (2 miles) opened on 20 April 1905; by this time though (from July 1904) the Company was in receivership and on 29 December 1905 a new concern, the Lancashire United Tramways Ltd, was registered to take over the tramway (which it did on 2 January 1906) and on 1 April 1906 it took over the FARNWORTH UDC system as well, opening on 29 June a 1-mile southern extension of this from Brookhouse to Walkden Memorial, the thirteen Farnworth cars becoming Nos 46-58 in the South Lancs fleet. The network continued to expand with a ½-mile extension from the Lowton/Leigh boundary to the

South Lancashire No 2 of 1902 before its top cover was fitted. (Lens of Sutton)

GCR station in Lowton St Mary's opening on 6 July 1906 and, on 27 September 1906, a 4-mile eastern extension from Boothstown was opened to Swinton Church via Leigh Road through Worsley. That year also saw the arrival of 24 Brush and UEC top-covered double-deckers (Nos 59-82) whilst 1907 saw the opening of two further lines: a 1½-mile extension of the former Farnworth line from Unity Brook to the Oddfellows Arms on the Kearsley/Pendlebury boundary (28 February) and a ½-mile branch from Worsley south to Winton (29 March). Like the rest of the system, these lines were principally single-track.

On 14 June 1909 through running to Bolton commenced and that October St Helens (which had been controlled by the South Lancs since October 1906) took over operation of the Haydock–Ashton section. The last extension opened on 28 August 1913 running as a single track northwest from Walkden Memorial up Manchester Road East to Little Hutton where it swung

Map of the South Lancashire system and connections, from the 1909 Manual of Electrical Undertakings.

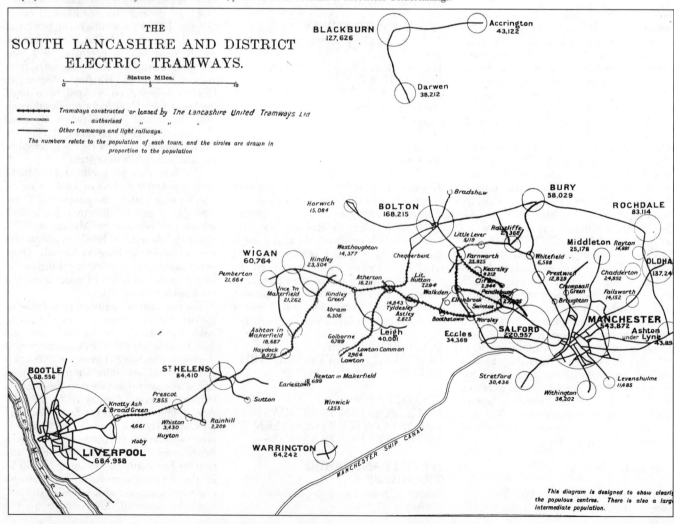

northwards up Cleggs Lane to meet the Buckley Lane route in Farnworth.

In 1919 the Company bought seven BEC open-top cars (Nos 83-89) from the LIVER-POOL & PRESCOT LIGHT RAILWAY with the fleet being completed in 1927 by the purchase of EE top-covered bogie cars 44 and 45, a year after a connection to the SALFORD system had been put in at Swinton and one to WIGAN at Ashton.

In 1929 the Company obtained an Act to abandon the tramways in favour of trolleybuses (it was already operating motor buses) and changed its name to South Lancashire Transport in anticipation of this event. On 3 August 1930 the Atherton–Ashton route was switched over, followed on 21 June 1931 by the isolated, St Helens-worked Ashton–Haydock section at the same time as the rest of the route to St Helens was similarly converted by that Corporation. Other changeovers came quickly with the last tram route, Leigh–Four Lane Ends, being closed two years later. After the abandonment, eight of the surviving bogie cars (Nos 44, 45, 47, 48, 50, 54, 55 and 58) were sold to Bolton and the remainder scrapped.

Bibliography: *South Lancashire Tramways*
    E. K. Stretch (Manchester Transport Museum Society, 1972)

SOUTH METROPOLITAN ELECTRIC TRAMWAYS
Authority: Mitcham Light Railway Order 1901
Gauge: 4ft 8½in
Traction: Overhead electric
Opened: 14 February 1906?
Taken Over: 1 July 1933
System: Branching + branching
Length: 13.36 miles
Stock: 55 dd
Livery: Brunswick green & ivory to 1921, then Underground red & white

The South Metropolitan Electric Tramways & Lighting Co. Ltd, registered on 3 August 1904 as a BET subsidiary, operated tramways either side of the Surrey town of CROYDON (which Corporation's tramways the BET worked on lease from 1902-06). Work began in 1905 on a continuation of Croydon Corporation's line to South Norwood across the town and county boundary along Croydon Road into Kent, then northwest into Penge High Street (1¾ miles) as authorized by the 1902 Croydon and District Electric Tramways Act. This opened shortly after the BoT's inspection of 13 February 1906 as far as the Pawleyne Arms (1 mile) at the Croydon Road/High Street junction and was worked by the BET as a through route from Croydon until the end of May, there-

after becoming the nucleus of the South Met system. On 12 April 1906 the rest of the line along the High Street and west into Thicket Road was opened, as was a branch off Croydon Road at the Robin Hood (opposite Penge Depot in Oak Grove Road) northwest along Anerley Road to the Low Level station (extended up Anerley Hill to Crystal Palace on 28 May).

UEC open-top double-deckers 1-16 of 1906 took over the working of the Penge lines after Croydon Corporation withdrew its cars. Meanwhile work on the other half of the system was progressing and on 26 May 1906 2¾ miles of double-track line from Tooting Junction, south to Mitcham, then southeast over Mitcham Common to the Croydon boundary was opened, together with a ½-mile branch south from Mitcham to the Cricket Green. (These were the lines authorized by the 1901 Mitcham LRO.) Also opened was a continuation of the light railway along Mitcham Road past the Company's Aurelia Road Depot to Canterbury Road (authorized by the 1902 Act), extended on 14 July to Lower Church Street and on 9 October into Tamworth Road opposite West Croydon station. This was also the terminus for the Company's double-track route westwards along Epsom Road and Stafford Road (past what was to become Croydon Aerodrome) through Wallington and Carshalton to Benhill Street, Sutton, where it terminated by the Grapes. (The Company's third depot was sited in Westmead Road just before the terminus.) This route opened in stages from August to December 1906 to complete the two-part system.

The new lines were worked by Milnes 17-26 (Nos 36-45 at Croydon), Brush 27-29, 31 and 35 (Croydon's 56-60) and new Brush open-toppers 36-51; also acquired in 1906 were two ERTCW bogie open-toppers of 1902 built for GRAVESEND & NORTH-FLEET which were renumbered 30 and 32 by the South Met and joined by similar cars 33 and 34 a year later.

On 13 October 1907 LONDON COUNTY COUNCIL opened a branch to Tooting Junction which connected end-on with the Company's line but because the LCC used a conduit current supply through running did not take place. On 14 June 1913 ownership of the Company was transferred to the London & Suburban Traction Co. Ltd, a holding company registered on 20 November 1912 and owned jointly by the BET and the Underground Electric Railways Co. of London Ltd (the Underground group), to become part of a massive Greater London tramway, bus and railway empire.

On 4 November 1926 the LCC began through working from Victoria to the Cricket Green and the Company ceased

its own services over this part of the system. In 1927 it purchased twelve cars from Croydon Corporation as replacements for older vehicles (its No 13 was sold to LONDON UNITED TRAMWAYS for conversion to a rail grinder) but put only four into service as Nos 17, 21, 47 and 52, all Brush vehicles of 1906-07 vintage. Two years later the legend 'SouthmeT' began to appear on the cars, which were joined in 1931 by ten LUT top-covered cars on loan. Two years later, as at Croydon, the system was absorbed into the new LONDON TRANSPORT network.

Bibliography: *The Tramways of Croydon*
    G. E. Baddeley (The Light Rail Transit Association, rev ed 1983) 0 900433 90 6

SOUTH SHIELDS TRAMWAYS
Authority: South Shields Corporation Tramways Order 1881
Gauge: 3ft 6in
Traction: Horse
Opened: 1 August 1883
Closed: 31 January 1906
System: Single line
Length: 2.53 miles
Stock: 12 sd, 17 dd?
Livery: ?
Last Car: ?

Owned by South Shields Corporation, this line was leased originally to the South Shields Tramways Co. which began services with five MRCW open-top double-deckers, plus a similar number of vehicles borrowed in 1882 from the aborted RAMSGATE & MARGATE line for the offical inspection. It was constructed by James Gowans of Edinburgh – but to the unauthorized gauge of 3ft 6in which meant that a second Order had to be secured in 1883 to permit the use of the narrower gauge. The portion built of the authorized (mainly single-track) line ran from the South Pier on the sea coast along Ocean Road and King Street to the Market Place from where it continued in a zig-zag fashion beside the River Tyne to Slake Terrace at Tyne Dock. A short midway branch down Victoria Road led to the depot.

The tramway was not a financial success and at midnight on 30 April 1886 the cars were driven off the end of the line and along the roadway to a timber yard in East Jarrow – presumably to prevent their seizure by the Corporation or creditors – and promptly sold by auction, going to Douglas in the Isle of Man where they took the numbers 13-18 (of which No 14 is preserved in the Manx Museum). In 1887 the line was rented to a new concern, the South Shields Tramways & Carriage Co. Ltd, and re-opened on 28 March. The new car fleet eventually comprised Nos 1-6, Milnes single-deckers on Eades patent reversible trucks, Nos 7-10 (Milnes open-top double-deckers), another similar but longer No 8, six Ashbury open toastracks (Nos 11-16?) and possibly six more Milnes open-toppers. At least some of the cars bore names.

In July 1899 the tramway was taken over by the BET but not electrified, presumably because of uncertainty over the lease. In the event the Corporation decided to terminate it from 1 February 1906 and the line closed the day before, the 19 cars and eleven buses being sold by auction. The Company itself was wound up later that year.

Bibliography: *The Tramways of Jarrow and South Shields* George S. Hearse (Author, Corbridge, 1971)

SOUTH SHIELDS CORPORATION TRAMWAYS

Authority: South Shields Corporation Act 1903
Gauge: 4ft 8½in
Traction: Overhead electric
Opened: 30 March 1906
Closed: 31 March 1946
System: Network
Length: 7.51 miles
Stock: 59 dd
Livery: Crimson lake & ivory to 1935, then royal blue & primrose
Last Car: No 39 (official)*

Well before the closing of the horse tramway (see above), South Shields Corporation had been planning the extension and electrification of the line with work commencing in June 1905 on the new routes. The heart of the new system was a figure-8 track plan, the western side of which was formed by the northern part of the former horse route from Tyne Dock up to King Street (though with a more direct route from Green Street down Frederick Street and South Eldon Street) and the eastern side by a line from there down Fowler Street past the Town Hall, Westhoe Road, Dean Road and Stanhope Road, where it swung westwards via Boldon Lane and Hudson Street to Tyne Dock (and a connection with the JARROW system). The two sides of the '8' were connected midway along Laygate, near the junction of which with Dean Road was the depot.

The first section opened was the stretch from Fowler Street to Stanhope Road with the rest following in stages over the next twelve months, including a short extension of the Fowler Street line at the King Street junction up Mile End Road and a longer extension of the King Street line from the same junction down Ocean Road to the South Pier (the last portion of the old horse tramway in fact). This junction was one of

the few 'Grand Union' junctions in Britain (where two double tracks cross with double-track connections in each quadrant). All routes were totally or predominantly double-track. The original car fleet was made up of HN open-toppers 1-10 and similar UEC vehicles 11-20; these were joined in 1907 by UEC Nos 21-25 (virtually identical to the earlier cars) and 26-35 (with top covers).

In 1913 the Corporation began operating battery electric buses (mainly to counter the threat of competition from neighbouring BET subsidiaries) and the following year purchased five Brush top-covered cars (Nos 36-40). Improvement and expansion were very much in the Corporation's mind and suggestions were made to Jarrow Corporation that it should buy the Jarrow line so as to make for a more unified system (through running had ceased in 1911) but nothing came of the plan. Instead, in 1920 the Corporation obtained the South Shields Corporation LRO authorizing 1¼ miles of reserved section line from Dean Road south down King George Road to its new, large housing estate at Cleadon. This double-track line down the centre of a dual carriageway opened on 1 June 1922 for two-thirds of its length, the final portion to the Ridgeway opening that December. Five 1921 EE enclosed bogie double-deckers (Nos 41-45) were bought to cope with the extra traffic. Plans to continue the line on to link with SUNDERLAND just 2 miles away sadly never bore fruit.

All further stock acquisitions (with one exception) were of second-hand vehicles thus: Nos 29 and 48 in 1929 ex-Jarrow, Nos 46 and 47 in 1930 ex-TYNESIDE, Nos 23, 33, 50 and 51 in 1931 ex-WIGAN, Nos 16 and 34 ex-Ayr and Nos 18 and 20 ex-YORKSHIRE (WEST RIDING) in 1932; the sole exception was the purchase in 1936 of No 52, a new Brush enclosed car. (Many of these cars carried temporary numbers as rebuilding and withdrawal programmes progressed.) Of special interest is that in 1929 the Corporation revived the horse tramway practice of naming cars and did so with an odd mixture in honour of local dignitaries, Roman Emperors and ocean liners. It is thought that 18 in all were so treated before the practice ceased in 1934 (and the existing names painted out).

Whilst many other systems were succumbing in the 1930s to a combination of bus competition and maintenance costs, the South Shields system stayed open as a result of investment in its cars and track. In 1936 however the Corporation began trolleybus operations with the intention of their eventually replacing the trams, which on 3 May 1937 they did from the Market Place to Stanhope Road. On 1 April 1946 they took over the last route, that to the Ridgeway,

with a 'Last Car' ceremony the day after public services ceased. All surviving cars were then broken up with the exception of No 52, the fast streamlined Brush car of 1936, which was sold to Sunderland for £250 – a tenth of its purchase price.

Bibliography: as above

SOUTH STAFFORDSHIRE TRAMWAYS

Authority: Staffordshire Tramways Order 1879
Gauge: 3ft 6in
Traction: Steam, overhead electric
Opened: 16 July 1883
Taken Over: 1 July 1904
System: Network
Length: 23.07 miles
Stock: 38 locos, 34 dd steam; 46 dd electric
Livery: Locos oak brown, later red-brown, then BET Munich lake, cars ditto + cream

This BLACK COUNTRY system occupied a central position in the network with links northwards to Walsall and Wolverhampton and southwards to Dudley and Birmingham. The first routes were constructed when a number of different promoters came together on 28 March 1882 as the South Staffordshire & Birmingham District Steam Tramways Co. Ltd, pooling their various Tramway Orders. Construction began in July 1882 and twelve months later the first route opened from the New Inns, Handsworth (the BIRMINGHAM & DISTRICT TRAMWAY terminus) running as a double-track line along the Holyhead Road over the BT's abandoned horse tramway route, through West Bromwich and Carter's Green to Wednesbury where it looped around the GWR station before carrying on as a single track via High Bullen (Darlaston Road) to the centre of Darlaston and the principal King's Hill Depot (actually just over the boundary in Wednesbury).

Original stock comprised 21 tramway locomotives from Wilkinsons (Nos 1, 2 and 17-21), BP (Nos 3-12) and Greens (Nos 13-16) plus 28 double-deck bogie trailers with canopy top covers from Starbuck (Nos 1-12) and Falcon (Nos 13-28), thought to have been the first bogie tramcars in England.

On 14 January 1884 a short branch was opened from Carter's Green northwest to Great Bridge, followed a week later by a southwesterly route from Wednesbury through Tipton to Dudley (where it shared DUDLEY & STOURBRIDGE metals from Tipton Road to the Market Place). At the same time a short branch westwards from Darlaston was opened to Moxley where it met the WOLVERHAMPTON TRAMWAYS' (standard gauge) line. Nearly a year later, on

4 December, another major route was opened, northwards from Wednesbury through Walsall to Bloxwich, followed within a few days by a linking line from Darlaston to Walsall (meeting the former route at Pleck); services on this route ran out through Walsall to a terminus in Mellish Road. During this year another 16 locos were bought (BP 22-29 and Green 30-37) and six more Falcon canopied cars (29-34). The only further item of rolling stock added to the steam fleet was a Falcon loco, No 38, bought from HARTLEPOOLS (to replace No 37 which was sold to the MANCHESTER, BURY, ROCHDALE & OLDHAM line) in 1885, during which year the system was completed with opening of a Great Bridge–Dudley link (12 October) and a short extension of the line at Bloxwich (21 November). Two years later No 38 was in turn sold to the COVENTRY & DISTRICT; at the same time the Company began operating regular goods trains using Dickinson patent wagons equipped with both road and rail wheels. Some 20 of these were in operation by 1890, by which date the Company (which had changed its name the previous year to the simpler South Staffordshire Tramways Co.) was investigating the possibility of electrifying the system.

In the event only 7½ miles of the network were converted to electric traction, the Wednesbury–Walsall–Bloxwich and Darlaston–Pleck–Walsall–Mellish Road routes both re-opening on 1 January 1893, worked by the Electric Construction Corporation who had converted them. This Wolverhampton firm (later the Electric Construction Co. Ltd) also built the electrical gear for the 16 open-top cars used, Nos 40-47 having bodies by BM and Nos 48-55 bodies by Lancaster. Relations between the two companies soon deteriorated though with the EC Co. having to go to court to obtain payments due from the tramways company and, on 29 July 1897, it sold its interest in the tramway to the BET who took over the electric operation.

On 31 July 1899 the BET subsidiary, the South Staffordshire Tramways (Lessee) Co. Ltd, was registered to work the electric lines and on 23 June 1900 leased the steam lines from the old South Staffs Company as a prelude to electrifying them. On 31 December that same year WALSALL CORPORATION bought the 5½ miles of line within its boundaries from the South Staffs for £18,500 and leased them to the Lessee Company the next day for three years whilst it built its own system; on 31 December 1901 West Bromwich Corporation bought the 5 miles of South Staffs lines within its boundaries in order to electrify them before leasing them back whilst Handsworth, Dudley and Wednesbury similarly purchased their portions to lease

back for electrification and working. Steam working ended on 15 June 1904, on the Wednesbury–Dudley and Wednesbury–Darlaston routes, just a few days before the system and its neighbours came under the control of the BIRMINGHAM & MIDLAND TRAMWAYS JOINT COMMITTEE.

Cars added to the fleet by the BET during this period were (all open-top double-deckers) Nos 1-4 in 1901 from ERTCW, Nos 5-7 in 1902 from the same firm, Nos 8 and 9 in 1902 from Brush as part of an original order for the BET's POOLE & DISTRICT line, Nos 10-27 in 1902-03 from the same firm (bogie vehicles) and Nos 28-30 in 1903, from Brush again. There was also an ornate, unnumbered single-deck directors' saloon bought in 1903 from that company. (Owned by the BET, not the Lessee Company, it was not used for public workings in pre-BMTJC days.)

Bibliography: *Black Country Tramways Vol 1: 1872-1912* J. S. Webb (Author, Bloxwich, 1974)
– *Vol 2* (1976)

SOUTH YORKSHIRE SUPERTRAM see SHEFFIELD: SOUTH YORKSHIRE SUPERTRAM

SOUTHALL, EALING & SHEPHERDS BUSH TRAMWAY see LONDON: WEST METROPOLITAN TRAMWAYS

SOUTHAMPTON TRAMWAYS
Authority: Southampton Street Tramways Act 1877
Gauge: 4ft 8½in
Traction: Horse
Opened: 5 May 1879
Taken Over: 1 July 1898
System: Branching
Length: 4.86 miles
Stock: c40 sd & dd
Livery: ?

Built by the Southampton Tramways Co. (incorporated 1876) after an earlier proposal by the British & Foreign Tramway Co. had failed because of Corporation opposition, the first route opened was a simple north-south line running from Alma Road north of the town centre, down The Avenue and London Road to Above Bar Street. From here it continued south through the Bargate in the city wall and down the High Street to Holy Rood at the junction with Bridge Street. On 6 May 1879 the line was extended at both ends: east and north from Stag Gates just south of Alma Road via Lodge Road and Portswood Road to Portswood and east along Bridge Street, Oxford Street and Canute

Road to the floating bridge across the River Itchen.

A second route opened on 9 June 1879 from the end of Above Bar Street ('the Junction') west along Commercial Road and northwest up Shirley Road to Shirley High Street. Like the first route, this was a single-track line.

Services began with six single-deckers and nine double-deckers (Nos 1-15), probably from Starbuck; the double-deckers proved so heavy that many later had their upper super-structures removed (whilst the single-deckers had seats added to their roofs!). These were joined in 1881 by four Starbuck double-deckers and later by more vehicles, including some from the NORTH METROPOLITAN. The two depots were at the Shirley and Portswood termini. From 1887 the Company also operated horse buses, housed in a separate depot off The Avenue north of the old Alma Road terminus. (The short stretch from Alma Road back to Stag Gates was abandoned c1890.)

On 30 June 1898 Southampton Corporation exercised its right to buy the tramway (the arbitrated figure being £51,000) in order to electrify it. (See below.)

Bibliography: *100 Years of Southampton Transport* John B. Horne (Southampton City Transport and Southampton City Museums, 1979)

SOUTHAMPTON CORPORATION TRAMWAYS
Authority: Southampton Corporation Tramways Act 1897
Gauge: 4ft 8½in
Traction: Horse, overhead electric
Took Over: 1 July 1898
Closed: 31 December 1949
System: Network
Length: 13.7 miles
Stock: 142 dd electric
Livery: Red & white
Last Car: No 9

After its purchase of the horse tramway (see above), Southampton Corporation set about electrifying the line, cutting back services as work progressed. On 22 June 1900 the line from Shirley to the Junction was opened to the new cars, followed on 29 May by the Holy Rood–Stag Gates main line. On 12 September the line from Holy Rood was re-opened as far as the dock (the Canute Street section being abandoned), followed on 4 October by Stag Gates to Portswood to complete the conversion of the horse system. The routes were mainly double-track with a short stretch of single through the Bargate. This was not quite the end of the horse trams though for a second north–south route was laid at this time from the Ordnance College

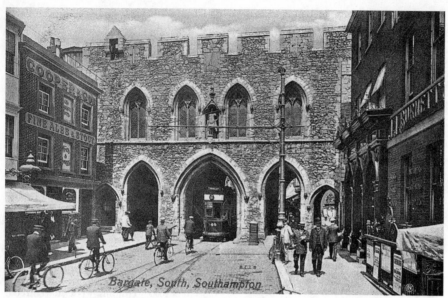

Postcard of Southampton Corporation No 40 threading the Bargate before it was bypassed. (Author's Collection)

on London Road down Bellevue Terrace, St Mary's Street, Marsh Lane and Terminus Terrace to meet the other main line at the docks on which horse cars were used until 3 August 1901 when work was completed to enable the new trams to run.

The first electric cars were special low bridge open-toppers with knifeboard seating on the upper decks (ie one long back-to-back seat down the centre of the car) to enable them to pass under the Bargate safely (even though the roadway had been lowered). Numbered 1-39, these were supplied by Milnes in 1899-1902 and joined in 1903 by twelve HN cars (Nos 40-51) of a similar but not so satisfactory design. In 1908 the Corporation began constructing its own cars at the main Portswood Depot (the old Shirley Depot was also retained) and between then and 1915 produced 21 similar vehicles, Nos 52-62 and 64-73 (No 63 was a 1911 version from UEC) with No 74 of 1917 having conventional seating on top.

After World War I new cars were bought from ERTCW (Nos 75-80 in 1918-19) and EE (Nos 82-91 in 1919-20) while the Corporation built No 81 in 1919 and Nos 92-109 in 1925-30 to complete the original number series. Over a similar period (1923-31) another 33 double-deckers were constructed and given numbers of withdrawn older cars. All cars from No 74 of 1917 onwards had cross seating on the upper deck and all from No 12 of 1923 had enclosed tops of a special section, a low floor and very small wheels to enable them to negotiate the Bargate.

All this time the system had been expanding slowly until 10 July 1930 when the last route opened from Bassett

Crossroads (at the northern end of the extended Avenue route) eastwards along Burgess Road to Swaythling (to meet the extended Portswood Road line), the resulting system being a complicated network of routes covering the whole of the town peninsula with one route crossing the Itchen, via Cobden Bridge east of Portswood, to Bitterne. The only major alterations to the track layout before the closures began in earnest came on 24 April 1932 and 5 June 1938 when, after decades of discussion, first the east and then the west side of the Bargate were bypassed.

The first abandonment of a line came on 4 June 1936 when the short eastern route to Northam on the Itchen was closed, after which World War II gave the system a respite until 1948 when the closures resumed with a vengeance, all routes going within two years. After the final closure 22 cars were sold to LEEDS but only eleven – Nos 23, 25, 32, 35, 50 and 104-109 – entered service there. (All were final-period Southampton-built vehicles.) Car No 45 of 1903 HN construction was sold in 1948 to a group of enthusiasts to provide the inspiration for what became the National Tramway Museum at Crich (see Section 7).

Bibliography: as above

SOUTHEND-ON-SEA CORPORATION TRAMWAYS

Authority: Southend-on-Sea and District Light Railways Order 1899
Gauge: 3ft 6in
Traction: Overhead electric
Opened: 19 July 1901
Closed: 8 April 1942

System: Network
Length: 9.22 miles
Stock: 6 sd, 65 dd
Livery: Cream & green (1907-25 sage & olive green)
Last Car: ?

Built and extended by Southend-on-Sea Corporation under a succession of Light Railway Orders, the Southend system was intended to serve residents and holiday-makers alike in this increasingly-popular Thames estuary resort. The system was centred on Victoria Circus just south of the GER's Victoria station and the first two lines opened ran from here north up Victoria Avenue to Prittlewell then back in a loop via North Road and London Road, and east then south along Southchurch Road and Southchurch Avenue to the beach.

On 9 August 1901 (after the necessary road works had been completed) a third, longer route westwards along London Road through Chalkwell to Leigh-on-Sea was opened. Original cars were ten small open-top double-deckers (Nos 1-10), two large open-top bogie cars (Nos 11 and 12) and two single-deckers (Nos 13 and 14), all from Brush. A further three open-top bogie cars (Nos 15-17) followed a year later. Route length was 6¼ miles of mainly single track and the depot was in London Road, about ¼ mile from Victoria Circus.

Another five open-top bogie cars (Nos 18-22) were bought in 1904, this time from Milnes, and after this some of the older cars were renumbered thus: the single-deckers became Nos 1 and 2, the old 1 and 2 became 11 and 12 and the old 11 and 12 became 13 and 14, thus giving consecutive numbers for the three different types of car.

On 10 August 1908 an extension of the line to the beach was opened along Southchurch Beach Road (Eastern Esplanade) as far as Bryant Avenue (about ½ mile) and on 16 November for another ¼ mile to The Halfway House; the whole extension was single-track but now a track-doubling programme was begun, starting at Victoria Circus and working outwards.

The car fleet grew steadily with another 20 open-toppers being added by the end of 1912 and numbered either at the end of the sequence or given the numbers of withdrawn vehicles. These were: 23-25 (UEC 1909), 26-31 (Brush 1910), 33-39 (Brush 1912) and 3, 5, 8, and 11 (Brush 1911). The former No 11 was rebuilt at Southend in 1911 and renumbered 32 whilst in 1914 three open toastracks, Nos 40-42, were bought from Brush. The reason for their purchase was that the eastern routes had been extended further, firstly on 10 February 1912 from The Halfway House to Thorpe Bay, secondly from the High Street eastwards along

Southchurch Road and Southchurch Boulevard to Bournes Green on 30 July 1913 and, lastly, on 16 July 1914 the link southwards from Bournes Green to Thorpe Bay was opened along Thorpe Boulevard. This completed a large out-and-back loop from the town centre, the eastern half of which was on a reserved, tree-lined double-track section known as the Boulevards route, the whole being worked by the toastracks as a circular pleasure tour. That same year, on 1 April, Southend became a county borough. The system was now complete, the only previous change being the closure on 22 January 1912 of the North Road section of the loss-making Prittlewell route.

The Corporation had its own loading pier opposite the gas works where East Parade met Eastern Esplanade and in 1914 this was rebuilt and a tramway spur laid onto it to enable coal to be moved to the municipal power station next to the tramway depot. Early in 1915 three powered open coal cars were supplied by the firm of Grenshaw & Piers of Bolton and numbered 1A-3A; these were used until 1931 when the coal traffic ceased with the Council's decision to stop generating electricity and take it instead from the National Grid.

After World War I Southend's popularity soared as a cheap, accessible seaside resort close to London and the tramway, with its ageing fleet, desperately needed new stock. In 1921 a Brush bogie roofed toastrack was purchased (No 43), followed by a dozen top-covered cars from the same manufacturer (Nos 44-55); these were joined in 1924 by six similar cars (Nos 56-62) from EE. The Corporation however was now considering the introduction of trolleybuses and in 1925 hired two for tests and driver training on the Prittlewell route. The trials were judged a success, the Corporation committed itself to this new mode of transport and on 18 December 1928 the last tramcars ran on the Prittlewell–High Street route.

During the next decade more trolleybuses were bought and their routes extended; in contrast, the car fleet was cut down slowly with withdrawals and scrappings. No further stock was added to the fleet until the 1934 purchase (as replacement vehicles) of Nos 62-65, four ex-MIDDLESBROUGH balcony cars and Nos 66-68, three enclosed-top ex-ACCRINGTON trams.

The next major happening came in 1938 when, in the face of the cost of renewing its deteriorating track, the Boulevards section was closed on 6 July, making Southchurch and Thorpe Bay termini again. (The trams were replaced by motorbuses.) The Esplanade route was cut back to the end of Southchurch Avenue (the Kursaal) on 3 June 1939, to be replaced by a trolleybus service. Ageing track elsewhere on the system meant that the last routes could not survive the war years and the Southchurch line closed on 7 January 1942, just three months before the Leigh-Victoria Circus-Kursaal route.

Bibliography: *The Tramways of Southend-on-Sea* V. E. Burrows (The Advertiser Press, Huddersfield, 1965)

SOUTHEND PIER TRAMWAY

Authority: –
Gauge: c3ft 6in
Traction: Horse
Opened: 1850s?
Closed: 1881
System: Single line
Length: c1.25 miles
Stock: 2 sd
Livery: ?
Last Car: ?

As the longest such structure in the world, Southend Pier is justly famous and, since 1890, has operated (with some interruptions) an electric railway along its 1¼ mile length. Prior to this date though the site had been occupied since June 1830 by a wooden pier which, by 1846, had grown to a comparable length and sported a baggage line laid in that year down the eastern side which was worked by three hand-propelled trucks on wooden rails. At an unknown date the tramway was relaid with iron rails and two small enclosed carriages provided for passenger transport (possibly rebuilds of the luggage trucks) running coupled as a train with a flat driver's truck at the seaward end. The whole rake was pulled by two horses in tandem. A notable feature of the line was that it ran through the middle of the pier's entertainment tent – even during shows!

In 1875 the pier was purchased by the local authority under the Southend Local Board Act of that year and ten years later it was decided to replace the ageing wooden structure with a new, cast iron one (opened 1889) though the tramway did not last even that long. The weight of the train, the light rails spiked directly to the decking and the wear and tear of the horses' hooves meant that by 1881 the line had been closed as unfit for use.

Bibliography: as above and
Pier Railways (Locomotion Papers No 60) K. Turner (The Oakwood Press, 1972)
Southend Pier Railway K. A. Frost & D. J. Carson (Ian Henry Publications, Romford, 2nd ed 1990) 0 86025 431 3

SOUTHPORT TRAMWAYS

Authority: Southport Tramways Order 1872
Gauge: 4ft 8½in
Traction: Horse, overhead electric
Opened: 31 May 1873
Closed: 31 December 1934
System: Network
Length: 17.4 miles
Stock: 25 horse?; 17 sd, 37 dd electric
Livery: ST Co. green & white, Corporation maroon & cream
Last Car: ?

Unlike the majority of the Lancashire tramways, Southport's compact network of criss-crossing routes was never connected to any others; as if to make up for this it had an extremely complicated history all of its own. The first (horse) line, operated by the Southport Tramways Co., ran southwest from Churchtown station in the north via Mill Lane and Roe Lane to Lord Street, thence on to Birkdale station on the LYR. This was soon followed by a second route, closer to the shore, which headed back up Lord Street and Cambridge Road to rejoin the first line by Churchtown station before continuing east a short distance to the Botanic Gardens. The length of the single-track system was 6¼ miles, worked by a fleet of (eventually) thirteen trams, all probably open-top double-deckers.

The ST Co.'s monopoly lasted for ten years until 12 May 1883 when the Birkdale & Southport Tramways Co. opened a separate line to the east of the ST system, running

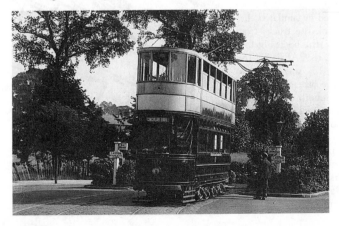

Southend-on-Sea Corporation No 20 of 1904 (with top cover added in 1925) on the Boulevards circular working. (Lens of Sutton)

from London Square on Lord Street, southeast to Kew Gardens via Scarisbrook Road, with a short southern branch down Sefton Street to the Crown Hotel opening on 5 November 1884 (the only part of this company's system actually in Birkdale). A probable total of twelve cars worked this tramway.

In 1896 Southport Corporation and Birkdale UDC purchased those portions of the lines within their respective boroughs and leased them back to the ST Co. for 21 years (the B&S lines only until electrification, these being taken back on 1 January 1900), Southport Corporation having obtained an Order to electrify its lines (and lay new ones) the year before. Three new electric routes were opened on 18 July 1900 with nine open-top double-deckers (many of which were later top-covered) numbered 2, 4, 6, 8, 10, 12, 14, 16 and 18, six combination single-deckers Nos 1, 3, 5, 7, 9 and 11 and single-deck saloon No 13 from ERTCW. These were joined in 1901 by Nos 15 and 17, two more combination cars, all based at Crowland Depot on the east side of the town.

Other routes soon followed with the final horse trams running on 13 December 1902, by which time eight more electric open-toppers had been bought (even numbers 20-34). Meanwhile the ST Co. had been busy electrifying its leased lines, beginning services on 11 August 1901 on the Botanic Gardens route via Cambridge Street and Lord Street to the Southport/Birkdale boundary using 20 Brush open-toppers (Nos 1-20) based at the former horse depot at Churchtown. A single-decker, No 21, was added two years later, by which time conversion of the Company's 5½-mile system was complete.

In 1912 Birkdale was absorbed into Southport and five years later, from 1 January 1918, the Corporation took ownership of the Company's effects for £35,000 with the expiry of its lease, taking over operations from 1 March that year. Of the newly-acquired cars, No 21 was scrapped and the double-deckers renumbered 35-44 plus the odd numbers 1-19, the Corporation's single-deckers having been withdrawn. In 1914 ERTCW supplied open toastrack 21 for use on a circular tour, followed by similar bodies 23, 25 and 27 which took the trucks from withdrawn single-deckers (the bodies of four of which had been sold to BARROW-IN-FURNESS). Car No 13 was sold to GRIMSBY and one of the others withdrawn until 1927 when its was rebuilt as an illuminated car. Three new toastrack bodies (Nos 29, 31 and 33) were bought in 1919 and a top-covering programme begun for the double-deckers. This make do and mend policy kept the ageing trams running through the 1920s with the first route closure not coming until March 1931 when most of the former ST lines were abandoned, followed

Postcard of the Corporation's No 12 of 1900 in Lord Street, Southport. (Lens of Sutton)

three years later by the rest of the system in favour of buses.

SOUTHPORT PIER TRAMWAY
Authority: –
Gauge: ?
Traction: Manual
Opened: 7 May 1863
Closed: 1863?
System: Single line
Length: c0.8 mile
Stock: 1 sd
Livery: ?

Opened in 1860 by the Southport Pier Co., the 1,465-yard long pier was the first such iron structure in the British Isles. With such a length the need for a tramway or railway of some kind soon became apparent and three years later a single-track line of unknown gauge was laid down the centre of the decking from shore to pier head; along this was hand-propelled the tramway's single carriage. The line was an immediate success and caused such a rise in numbers of people using the pier that the Company decided in December of the same year to widen the pier,

Map of Southport's tramways, from the 1909 Manual of Electrical Undertakings, showing the complicated ownership pattern.

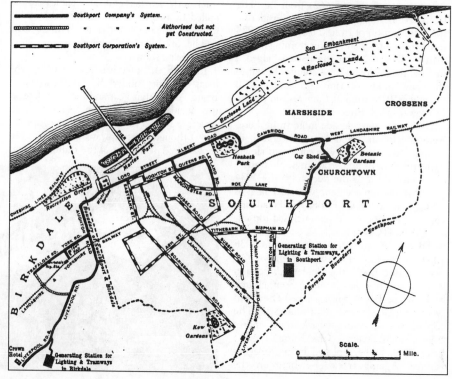

move the tramway to the south side and adopt cable traction. The line accordingly re-opened in 1865 as a railway, fenced-off from the rest of the decking and worked on the funicular system. Several reincarnations later it is currently a 60cm gauge diesel-worked railway (future uncertain).

Bibliography: *Pier Railways* (Locomotion Papers No 60) K. Turner (The Oakwood Press, 1972)

SPEN VALLEY LIGHT RAILWAY *see* YORKSHIRE (WOOLLEN DISTRICT) ELECTRIC TRAMWAYS

STAFFORDSHIRE POTTERIES STREET RAILWAY *see* POTTERIES: STAFFORDSHIRE POTTERIES STREET RAILWAY

STALYBRIDGE, HYDE, MOSSLEY & DUKINFIELD TRAMWAYS

Authority: Stalybridge Hyde Mossley and Dukinfield Tramways and Electricity Board Act 1900
Gauge: 4ft 8½in
Traction: Overhead electric
Opened: 15 October 1903
Closed: 12 May 1945*
System: Network
Length: 21.19 miles
Stock: 20 sd, 44 dd*
Livery: Dark green & white
Last Car: No 18* (official)

This cumbersomely-named tramway, operated by the Stalybridge, Hyde, Mossley & Dukinfield Tramways & Electricity Board, was built to serve the towns of its title immediately to the east of the Lancashire/Cheshire border systems of ASHTON CORPORATION and OLDHAM, ASHTON & HYDE. The Board was set up as a joint venture by the relevant local authorities on 23 October 1899 and between 1902 and 1905 it constructed an intricate network of long and short single-track lines along a north–south axis from Roaches and Haddens in the north down through Mossley, Stalybridge, Ashton-under-Lyne and Dukinfield to Hyde.

Services from Stalybridge west to Ashton began in October 1903, using cars borrowed from Ashton, over the former horse tramway route operated by the Manchester Carriage & Tramways Co. (see MANCHESTER TRAMWAYS); on 22 May 1904 the Board's own cars were introduced with the opening of the next route from Stalybridge to Hyde. These were open-toppers 1-20, single-deck 21-30 and single-deck combination cars 31-40, all from BEC and joined in 1905 by Nos 41-55, open-toppers from HN who also

supplied open-top bogie cars 56-60 two years later. No further trams were added until 1924-25 when the Board constructed balcony cars 61-64 using equipment from four of the single-deckers. Most of the open-toppers were fitted later with top covers, No 24 was rebuilt as a balcony car in 1911 and, following the break-up of the OAH system in 1921, ten cars were acquired and scrapped after seeing little if any service with the Board. Several small depots were scattered around the system to supply cars for the many different routes operated.

After the break-up of the OAH through services began to STOCKPORT via Hyde and to Manchester via Denton. In 1923 though the Board obtained powers to operate buses and, as that fleet grew, so the tram services were slowly run down – on many routes to holidays and peak hours only. On 12 January 1928 the Ashton–Hyde service was withdrawn completely, initiating a series of abandonments which left, by 1939, only the Hyde–Manchester and Hyde–Stockport routes in the hands of half a dozen cars (Nos 18, 42 and 61-64). On 12 May 1945 the last Board cars ran from Hyde to Gee Cross on the Stockport route though No 18 was brought out on 29 May for an official farewell ceremony. This was not quite the end of the story though for Stockport cars continued to run to Hyde Market Place until 2 March 1947 and Manchester trams until 30 December that year.

STOCKPORT CORPORATION TRAMWAYS

Authority: Stockport Corporation Act 1899
Gauge: 4ft 8½in
Traction: Overhead electric, horse
Opened: 26 August 1901
Closed: 25 August 1951
System: Radial network
Length: 19.46 miles
Stock: 4 sd, 16 dd horse?; 87 dd electric
Livery: Red & cream
Last Car: Nos 82 (service) and 53 (official)

Stockport's first tramway, promoted by the Manchester Suburban Tramways Co. (see MANCHESTER TRAMWAYS), was a 2¼-mile double-track line opened 7 May 1880 running south from Levenshulme, down the Stockport Road and Wellington Road North to the George Hotel on Mersey Square by the river. The Stockport end of the line was extended by early 1881 to the start of Wellington Road South where it turned sharply northeast up St Petersgate to St Peter's Square. Services operated through from the Manchester Royal Infirmary, Piccadilly, using cars from a stock of some 60 double-deckers based at Longsight Depot on the corner of Stockport Road and Grey Street. (In the same year as the line opened the MST Co. became a constituent part of the Manchester Carriage & Tramways Co.)

Under the Stockport Corporation Act 1899 the Corporation obtained the authority to buy the line, electrify it and lease it back to the Company and, under the Stockport Corporation Act 1900, it obtained powers to construct further tramways, the first of which opened the following year. This ran from Lancashire Bridge north of St Peter's Square in a northeast direction along Warren Street, Great Portwood Street, Carrington Road, Stockport Road (West and East) to Ashton Street, Woodley. On

Postcard of Hyde Market Place sited towards the southern end of the sprawling Stalybridge, Hyde, Mossley & Dukenfield system. The nearest car is BEC-built combination car 36 of 1904. (Lens of Sutton)

MARKET PLACE, HYDE.

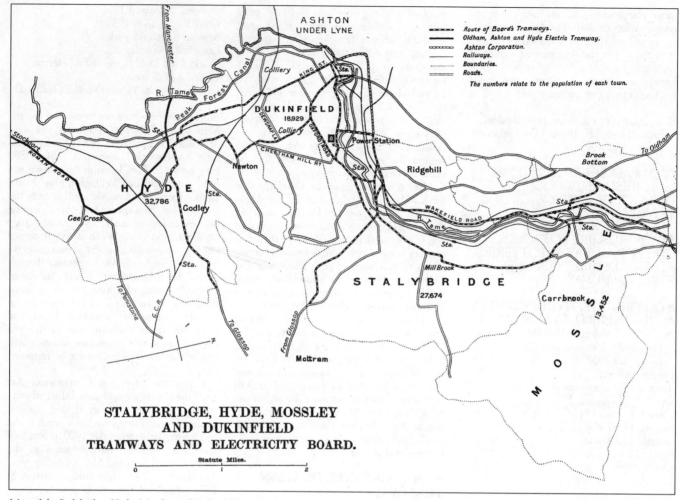

STALYBRIDGE, HYDE, MOSSLEY
AND DUKINFIELD
TRAMWAYS AND ELECTRICITY BOARD.

Statute Miles.

Map of the Stalybridge, Hyde, Mossley and Dukinfield system, from the 1909 Manual of Electrical Undertakings.

31 August 1901 a short, ½-mile branch north from Lancashire Bridge was opened up Lancashire Hill to Sandy Lane and by the end of the year ten open-top double-deckers (Nos 1-10) had been supplied by DK and housed in a new depot in Mersey Square.

Further lines soon followed. On 1 June 1902 a route was opened along Prince's Street to connect Mersey Square with Lancashire Bridge, followed some six months later by a connection between St Peter's Square and Mersey Square via Daw Bank. At the end of January 1902 a 1-mile double-track western branch along Chestergate and Brinksway was opened to the then town boundary, extended on 1 August 1903 as a single-track line another 2 miles along Stockport Road to the railway bridge at Cheadle Heath, on 26 January 1904 to Cheadle Church and finally, on 25 March, to the Horse & Farrier at Gatley. Meanwhile other extensions were being opened. The terminus at Sandy Lane was moved northwards in stages along Reddish Road, through Reddish and up Gorton Road (25 November 1903) to the

Old Bull's Head Inn where it was connected five years later to MANCHESTER CORPORATION's Hyde Road route and on 18 July 1902 the Woodley line was extended to the Hyde boundary with through running to Hyde Town Hall beginning 1 January 1903 over the OLDHAM, ASHTON & HYDE TRAMWAY.

The car fleet grew to keep pace with the expanding system with DK supplying cars 11-30 in 1902-03, similar vehicles to the first batch. The purchase of the STOCKPORT & HAZEL GROVE TRAMWAY (see below) was completed on 24 January 1905; reconstruction started in April and the single-track line re-opened on 5 July and the horse cars sold off (but two years later bought back for conversion to salt cars). UEC top-covered cars 41-45 were bought in 1906 and 46-50 a year later (after which several of the open-toppers were similarly equipped). On 2 October 1906 a short double-track extension from Torkington Road to the Rising Sun Hotel completed the system.

In 1919 five of the older cars were rebodied and renumbered 61-65 whilst EE enclosed

cars 51-60 were bought in 1920, the same year that the Corporation' trolleybus operations which had begun in 1913 finished. More ominously, 1920 also saw the start of Corporation bus services though the tram fleet continued to grow with the addition in 1923 of enclosed cars 66-75 from Cravens and, a year later, similar cars 76-85 from the same firm; in 1928-29 the Corporation constructed enclosed cars 6 and 26 to complete the fleet. To help accommodate them all a new depot was opened in Heaton Lane just north of the river.

On 19 September 1931 the Gatley line was cut back to the boundary though the rest of the system survived until 14 January 1950 when the Crossley Road–Hazel Grove through route was closed, followed on 3 March 1951 by that from Edgeley to Vernon Park. On 10 April the Cheadle route closed entirely, leaving just the Reddish line as the last to go that August.

Bibliography: *Stockport Corporation Tramways* Maurice Marshall (Manchester Transport Museum Society, 1975)

STOCKPORT & HAZEL GROVE TRAMWAY

Authority: Stockport and Hazel Grove
  Tramways Order 1889
Gauge: 4ft 8½in
Traction: Horse
Opened: 4 April 1890
Taken Over: 24 January 1905
System: Branching
Length: 3.45 miles
Stock: 4 sd?, 16 dd?
Livery: ?

The second tramway to be built in Stockport, after the MANCHESTER TRAMWAYS' line from the north (see above), was a southerly route from St Peter's Square (where it shared a terminus with the MT line) back to Wellington Road South and thence via Buxton Road and the London Road to the Bull's Head Hotel in Torkington Road, Hazel Grove, some 3 miles away. A ½-mile branch running southwest off Wellington Road South served Edgeley, terminating at Grenville Street. Both lines were single-track, owned and operated by the Stockport & Hazel Grove Carriage & Tramway Co. Ltd. Details of the rolling stock are patchy, though at least one of the single-deck cars was a roofed toastrack, and the depot was at Dialstone Lane behind the Crown Inn on Wellington Road South.

In 1899 the Stockport Corporation Act empowered that body to purchase the tramway (and the MT line) but this was not done – for a price of £24,000 – until six years later, by which time the municipal electric system was in operation. (See above.)

Bibliography: as above

STOCKTON & DARLINGTON STEAM TRAMWAYS

Authority: Stockton-on-Tees and District
  Tramways Order 1880
Gauge: 4ft
Traction: Steam
Opened: November 1881
Closed: November 1897
System: Branching
Length: 3.25 miles
Stock: 8 locos, 15 dd?
Livery: Chocolate & white
Last Car: ?

The Stockton & Darlington Steam Tramways Co. Ltd operated two separate tramways, one in each town of its title, of which only the Stockton system was worked by steam. (The DARLINGTON line, opened in 1880, was horse-worked.) It began as a single line running south from the Green in Norton along Norton Road and Stockton High Street where it swung east past the depot to cross the River Tees via

Stockport Corporation No 70 of 1923, built by Cravens of Sheffield, on a Cheadle Heath working. (Lens of Sutton)

Victoria Bridge into Mandale Road, terminating by the Harewood Arms. Later extensions were a ½-mile branch from the northern end of the High Street, west along Bishopton Lane to the NER station and a 1-mile branch from the southern end of the High Street west and south along Yarm Lane and Yarm Road to St Peter's Church.

Services were worked by Merryweather steam locomotives 1-6 joined in 1883 by Nos 7 and 8, ex-NORTH STAFFORDSHIRE TRAMWAYS, hauling an unknown number of trailers (possibly by Starbuck).

In 1893 the Company went into liquidation and was succeeded by the Stockton & District Tramways Co. until 1896 when the tramway was bought by IMPERIAL TRAMWAYS and closed the following year to make way for reconstruction and electrification. (See MIDDLESBROUGH, STOCKTON & THORNABY.)

STOCKTON & THORNABY JOINT CORPORATION TRAMWAYS

Authority: Stockton-on-Tees Corporation
  Act 1919; Thornaby-on-Tees
  Corporation Tramways Order 1919
Gauge: 3ft 7in
Traction: Overhead electric
Took Over: 3 April 1921
Closed: 31 December 1931
System: Single line
Length: 3.76 miles
Stock: 29 dd
Livery: Vermillion & white
Last Car: MIDDLESBROUGH 113

This short line straddling the Durham/Yorkshire boundary was made up of the two sections of the longest route of the former

MIDDLESBROUGH, STOCKTON & THORNABY system which lay within the Stockton and Thornaby local authorities' areas. When Middlesbrough Corporation took over its part of the system, the other two Corporations did likewise, working the line through a Joint Committee with cars 4, 7, 9, 11, 14, 17, 19, 20, 22, 23, 26, 29-32, 38, 39 and 43-45 owned by Stockton and Nos 5, 8, 12, 13, 16, 33, 35, 48 and 49 owned by Thornaby. Several of these were then renumbered to make a single sequence of 1-29 thus: 30-32 became 1-3, 33 (24), 35 (10), 38 and 39 (27 and 28), 43-45 (18, 25 and 15) and 48 and 49 (6 and 21).

No further cars were added under the new ownership (solely by Stockton from 1 August 1930 onwards) with the line closing at the end of 1931, the trams displaced by Stockton's buses.

STONEHOUSE see PLYMOUTH, STONEHOUSE & DEVONPORT

STONY STRATFORD see WOLVERTON & STONY STRATFORD

STOURBRIDGE see DUDLEY & STOURBRIDGE; DUDLEY, STOURBRIDGE & DISTRICT

STOURPORT see KIDDERMINSTER & STOURPORT

STRATFORD AND MORETON TRAMROAD

Authority: [Stratford and Moreton Railway
  or Tramroad Act 1821]
Gauge: c4ft 8½in*
Traction: Horse

Pro bono Publico!!!

Notice is hereby given,

THAT ON

TUESDAY, the 5th of SEPTEMBER next,

MORETON RAIL--WAY

Will be opened for Public use;

ON WHICH DAY,

A GREAT Market

WILL BE HELD,

And continued Weekly, agreeable to the Charter,

**For the Sale of Corn, Seeds, and all kinds of Grain;
also, for Cattle, Sheep, Pigs, Poultry, Meat Butter,
Eggs, and Merchandise of every description.**

At the particular desire of the many highly respectable Farmers, Dealers, and others, who intend giving this Market their Support, the following Regulations have been determined on, and will be strictly adhered to.--Viz. That all Corn shall be bought and Sold by a *pitched Sample or Bulk* ; and that the hours for holding the same, shall commence *precisely at Eleven o'Clock in the Forenoon*, and end at *Two in the Afternoon.*

N.B. A large Wharehouse, nearly in the centre of the Town, will be gratuitously provided by Mr. Hooper, and every accommodation afforded therein for the pitching of Samples, until a more commodious Market House can be erected.

Moreton-in-Marsh, July 24, 1826.

F. W. LANE, PRINTER, STOW

Poster proclamation of the opening on 5 September 1826 of the Stratford & Moreton Tramroad.

opening. From 1 May 1847 the line was leased by the Oxford, Worcester & Wolverhampton Railway (incorporated 1845) and taken over outright on 1 January 1852; on 4 June 1853 the OWWR's connecting line from Oxford to Worcester via Moreton was opened. Passengers were still carried as before though from 1 August 1853 until about September 1858 a regular service of one or two round trips a day was operated by a Mr Bull of the George Hotel, Shipston, using a horse-hauled railway carriage.

In 1886 the GWR (which had taken over the OWWR's successor, the West Midland Railway, in 1863) began converting the southern section from Moreton to Darlingscott and on to Shipston into a railway branch line. This opened on 1 July 1889; railway passenger services ceased in July 1929 and on 3 May 1960 the line closed altogether. The Stratford end of the tramway ceased operations c1904 and the track was lifted in 1918, ideas of converting it into a railway branch as well having come to nothing.

The route of the mainly roadside line can be traced easily today. The Stratford end is clearly defined with its impressive bridge over the Avon by the canal basins and a long embankment leading out of the town. Here too can be seen displayed a restored goods waggon once used on this historic line. A second waggon, in almost original condition, was presented by a local farmer in 1994 to the National Railway Museum at York.

Bibliography: *The Stratford & Moreton Tramway* John Norris (The Railway and Canal Historical Society, 1987)
0 901461 40 7

SUNDERLAND TRAMWAYS

Authority: Sunderland Tramways Order 1878
Gauge: 4ft 8½in
Traction: Horse
Opened: 28 April 1879
Closed: 19 February 1901
System: Network
Length: 6.41 miles
Stock: 5 sd, 28 dd?
Livery: ? & white?
Last Car: ?

The Sunderland Tramways Co. operated horse tramways both sides of the mouth of the River Wear in this major Durham town, beginning in April 1879 with a short line from the Royal Hotel in Monkwearmouth on the north bank of the river, northeast up Roker Avenue to the district of

Opened: 1833?
Closed: c1904
System: Branching
Length: 19 miles
Stock: *
Livery: ?
Last Car: ?

Like its Welsh counterpart the Oystermouth Tramroad (see Section 3), the S&M belongs to that phase of British tramway history when tramroads were evolving into railways prior to the widespread introduction of the steam locomotive. It was promoted by William James, a Warwickshire land agent, as part of a grand scheme to link Stratford-on-Avon with London by way of a Central Junction Railway in order to carry manufactured goods from Birmingham and the Midlands (to be brought to Stratford by canal) on to the capital. The 1821 empowering Act led to the formation of the Stratford & Moreton Railway Co. to construct a line

between those two places, plus a short branch to Shipston-on-Stour. The single-track line was laid with fish-bellied iron rails mounted on a mixture of wooden sleepers and stone blocks; the original gauge was probably the tramroad 'standard' 4ft 8in which later spread up to an inch.

A grand opening of the 17 miles of main line on 5 September 1826 meant the Company was in business – not by operating as a common carrier though but by charging local carriers (who supplied their own waggons and horses) for the use of the line. Licence fees for the conveyance of passengers were set in December 1834 though it seems certain that passengers were being carried on a regular basis at least a year before this (especially on market days).

The 2½-mile Shipston branch opened on 11 February 1836, running northeast from Darlingscott, a place 9½ miles south of Stratford. Passenger traffic was permitted over this line and probably began with its that name. The first cars were three single-deckers, joined by two double-deckers when, on 11 June, two southern routes opened. The first of these continued the original line south across the river via North Bridge Street, Bridge Street, Fawcett Street and Burdon Road to Christ Church before swinging east along Gray Road to Tatham Street then back north to rejoin Fawcett Street; the second was a northwards continuation of the line in Tatham Street along Nicholson Street and Cousin Street to form a short branch to the docks, terminating at Adelaide Street. The 3½ miles of routes were principally single-track.

While the above lines were being constructed, Sunderland Corporation was planning to build lines of its own and in 1880-81 added a northern (North Bridge Street west to Southwick via Southwick Road) and two southern (High Street East and New Durham Road) branches to the system, leasing them to the Company. (During this period steam traction was experimented with but not adopted.)

By 1894 the car fleet had grown to a total of 33 (of which details are sketchy though several of them were Eades patent reversible cars) and the Corporation was planning to take the system over in 1899 when the Company's lease expired; in that year it obtained the necessary Act of Parliament to enable it to operate its own tramways. The purchase – for £35,000 – of the horse system was completed on 26 March 1900 with the Corporation assuming control of operations as from 30 March, shutting down routes as reconstruction work progressed. (See below.)

Bibliography: *The Tramways of Sunderland* S. A. Staddon (The Advertiser Press, Huddersfield, 1964)

SUNDERLAND CORPORATION TRAMWAYS

Authority: Sunderland Corporation Act 1899
Gauge: 4ft 8½in
Traction: Overhead electric
Opened: 15 August 1900
Closed: 1 October 1954
System: Radial network
Length: 12.24 miles
Stock: 13 sd, 127 dd
Livery: Light maroon & cream
Last Car: No 86

One of the longer-lasting of the English tramways, Sunderland's municipal system was a compact network of three routes north of the River Wear and five south of it worked by a fleet of new and second-hand cars bought as other tramways closed down. Immediately after taking possession of its

leased lines and the Company-owned lines in 1900 (see above), the Corporation set about relaying and electrifying the system with the first route (Roker to Christ Church) opening that August with other routes following. Services were worked by open-toppers 1-12 and bogie open-toppers 13-18 from ERTCW (1900) and single-deckers 19-26 of 1901, again from ERTCW. Later in 1901 ERTCW open-toppers 27-50 were added as further routes were opened (including north from Roker along the coast via Whitburn road to Seaburn and south along Ryhope Road to Grangetown), all mainly double-track.

By the end of January 1904 the first flurry of construction was over with the three northern routes (northwest via Southwick Road and Sunderland Road to Southwick, north via Gladstone Road and Fulwell Lane plus the Seaburn line) all open. South of the river, via Bridge Street, a line ran south to Grangetown with a loop along Villette Road, Suffolk Street and Tatham Street, a new branch led to the docks and a western circular route occupied Hylton Road and Chester Road. The former horse lines to the docks and High Street East were abandoned.

For the next 20 years the only major changes to the tramway were the additions of new batches of cars. In 1902 ERTCW supplied single-deck combination cars 52-55 and open-toppers 56-65; in 1906 Brush provided balcony cars 66-71 (nicknamed 'Dreadnoughts') and in 1918 UEC supplied top-covered car No 10, a replacement for the original of that number destroyed in an air raid two years before. (Virtually all these cars were later fitted with top covers and/or fully enclosed.) The trams were based at the Wheatsheaf Depot where Roker Avenue met North Bridge Street at the works on Hylton Road.

On 3 January 1921 through running with the SUNDERLAND DISTRICT line via Grangetown began (see below) and during that year and the next a dozen EE enclosed double-deckers (Nos 72-83) were added to stock; on 2 December 1925 a new route, southwest along the Durham Road to Barnes Park, was opened. This was extended on 4 August 1929 over Humbledon Hill to serve the residential development there. By this date though the first cutback had occured with the abandonment on 6 February 1928 of the Barrack Street (Docks) branch – though for legal reasons a token car was run over it occasionally for another year.

In 1925 enclosed double-deck cars Nos 22, 23 and 25 emerged from the Corporation's works, followed a year later by No 84, a rebuild of the SD's former parcel car. In 1931 Brush supplied bogie single-decker 85, the Corporation-built enclosed cars 86 in 1932 and 96-98 in 1933 whilst EE supplied enclosed cars 87-95 (1933) and 99 (1934), the latter a streamlined bogie vehicle. The other new cars added were Corporation-built 26-28 (1935) and 49-54 (1936-40) and Brush 55 (1935), all enclosed vehicles. These were joined by second-hand enclosed double-deckers 19 and 20 (ex-ACCRINGTON in 1931), 52 (ex-PORTSMOUTH in 1936), 100 (ex-LONDON TRANSPORT in 1937), 2-9 (ex-ILFORD in 1938), 29-36 (ex-HUDDERSFIELD in 1938), 48 (ex-SOUTH SHIELDS in 1946), 37-42 (ex-MANCHESTER in 1947) and 85 (ex-BURY in 1948); in 1933 the Corporation produced enclosed cars 21 and 24, rebuilds of MANSFIELD cars 27 and 28 (EE of 1925).

Further route extensions took place before and after World War II: on 10 May 1937 the Fulwell Lane Route was extended east along Dykelands Road to Seaburn (where it termi-

Sunderland Corporation balcony car 68 of 1906 (after it was top-covered in 1923) on the system's Circle route. (Lens of Sutton)

nated close to the Whitburn Road route) and, on 21 February 1948, the Durham Road line was extended on a central reservation first to Grindon Lane and then, on 7 February 1949, to Thorney Close Road to serve new housing estates. The decision though had already been taken to close the system in favour of buses. On 5 November 1950 the Villette Road-Suffolk Street loop was closed, followed on 2 September 1951 by the Southwick route. The Grangetown line went on 30 November 1952 with the remaining services going in 1954 (the Chester Road Circle and the Roker line on 3 January, Durham Road on 28 March and the Seaburn via Fullwell route at the beginning of October). After the closure those trams not already scrapped met that fate with the exception of No 100, which can be seen operating on museum lines around the country. No 85 of 1931 was sold to LEEDS in 1944 and as No 600 is now at the National Tramway Museum, Crich.

Bibliography: as above

SUNDERLAND DISTRICT ELECTRIC TRAMWAYS

Authority: Houghton-le-Spring and District
    Tramways Order 1900
Gauge: 4ft 8½in
Traction: Overhead electric
Opened: 10 June 1905
Closed: 12 July 1925
System: Branching
Length: 14.28 miles
Stock: 57 dd

Livery: Blue & white
Last Car: ?

Built to serve the mining villages southwest of Sunderland, this strung-out single-track system had a main line like a letter Z on its side, plus two short branches, laid along rural roads. Promoted by the United Kingdom Tramways, Light Railways & Electrical Syndicate Ltd, the Company was reformed in November 1903 as the Sunderland District Electric Tramways Ltd with construction by BP commencing in January 1904 and the opening the following year.

The main line began near the coast at Grangetown (where it connected with the SUNDERLAND CORPORATION TRAMWAYS route) and ran south to Ryhope before turning westwards for a long run through Tunstall, Silksworth, East Herrington and West Herrington to New Herrington where it swung south through Philadelphia (where the depot was sited) and Newbottle to Houghton-le-Spring. The two branches – northwest from New Herrington to New Penshaw via Shiney Row and west from Houghton to Fencehouses – opened at the same time with services worked by open-top Brush cars Nos 1-15 together with Nos 16-30, top-covered cars from Etablissements Arbel of Paris. Just two days after the opening, on Whit Monday 1908, No 8 was involved in a fatal accident and rebuilt as No 31 some two years later.

On 20 October 1905 the main line was extended further south by 2 miles to Hetton-le-Hole and, in August 1906, by another

mile to Easington Lane to complete the system. Two years later Brush top-covered cars 32-34 were added to stock, followed in 1913 by similar cars 8 and 16-30 to replace the worn-out French vehicles. Finally, eight more were bought in 1920 and it is thought these took the numbers 35-38 plus four from withdrawn older cars.

By now the tramway was nearing the end of its relatively short life for it was particularly vulnerable to bus competition, and on 13 May 1921 the Company replaced the New Penshaw branch service with its own buses. In June 1924 the line south of Houghton was abandoned and later that year the 1920 cars were sold to BOLTON. In January 1925 the Fencehouses branch was closed and the Company changed its name to the Sunderland District Transport Co. Ltd.

The next closure came on 12 March 1925 when the Grangetown–New Herrington section was abandoned with the last stretch closing four months later. The 1913 cars were sold to GRIMSBY and the remainder scrapped with the exception of No 33 which, after an accident in 1922, had been converted to a single-deck parcels car. This was sold to Sunderland Corporation and rebuilt as a passenger car (see above).

Bibliography: as above

SURREY SIDE STREET RAILWAY *see* LONDON: TRAIN'S TRAMWAYS

SUTTON-ON-SEA *see* ALFORD & SUTTON

SWINDON CORPORATION TRAMWAYS

Authority: Swindon Corporation Tramways
    Order 1901
Gauge: 3ft 6in
Traction: Overhead electric
Opened: 22 September 1904
Closed: 11 July 1929
System: Radial
Length: 3.7 miles
Stock: 13 dd
Livery: Maroon & cream
Last Car: ?

Apart from being Wiltshire's only tramway, the Swindon system had little of distinction about it. Corporation-owned from the outset, it had its centre in New Town at the junction of Bridge Street and Fleet Street; from here two lines radiated out to the outlying districts of Gorse Hill and Rodbourne to the north of the GWR's main line and works, whilst a third ran south through the Old Town to the Market Square. A short spur from Mill Street on the Gorse Hill route, down Wellington Street to the railway

Sunderland District balcony car 32 of 1908 as new. (Lens of Sutton)

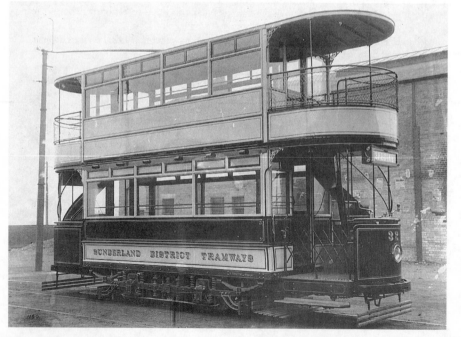

station, completed the system. All lines were primarily single-track.

Services began with seven open-top double-deckers from ERTCW which were joined by two more (Nos 8 and 9) the following year. In 1906 similar Brush cars 10 and 12 were acquired, followed by a similar EE car (No 13) in 1921 to complete the fleet. The depot was in Mill Street, nearly opposite the spur to the station. The system's early demise and replacement by the inevitable bus services was hastened by the deteriorating state of the track, condemned in 1928 by the Borough Surveyor.

Bibliography: *The Swindon Tramways* (Locomotion Papers No 65) L. J. Dalby (The Oakwood Press, 1973)

SWINTON *see* MEXBOROUGH & SWINTON

TAUNTON ELECTRIC TRAMWAYS

Authority: Taunton Tramways Order 1900
Gauge: 3ft 6in
Traction: Overhead electric
Opened: 21 August 1901
Closed: 28 May 1921
System: Single line
Length: 1.66 miles
Stock: 6 sd, 6 dd
Livery: Crimson lake & cream
Last Car: ?

The Taunton tramway – it could hardly be called a system – is generally noted for two main claims to fame: possessing the shortest route of any British electric street tramway and one of the longest operators' titles: the Taunton & West Somerset Electric Railways & Tramways Co. Ltd, taken over in 1903 by the Taunton Electric Traction Co. Ltd, a BET subsidiary.

Swindon Corporation No 3 of 1904 in an Edwardian postcard view of the town's bustling Bridge Street. (Lens of Sutton)

The first section of the single-track line to be opened ran from the depot in East Reach via East Street, North Street and Station Road to the GWR's station, a distance of just a mile; an extension from here up Kingston Road to terminate opposite Salisbury Street in Rowbarton was opened on 13 August 1909 to complete the undertaking.

The tramway's original fleet comprised six Brush open-top double-deckers (with No 6 arriving in 1902). In 1905 however services were temporarily suspended for two months whilst the track was relaid (a move necessitated by its poor construction) and the cars sold to LEAMINGTON & WARWICK to be replaced by a similar number of Brush single-deckers (also numbered 1-6) more in keeping with a realistic assessment of the line's volume of traffic. Two of these latter vehicles were sold to GRAVESEND and three to TORQUAY following the closure, an event brought about by the Company's refusal to

agree to new, higher charges for its electricity which it purchased from Taunton Corporation.

Bibliography: *The Tramways of the West of England* P. W. Gentry (The Light Railway Transport League, 2nd ed 1960)

THANET *see* ISLE OF THANET

TORQUAY TRAMWAYS

Authority: Torquay Tramways Act 1904
Gauge: 3ft 6in
Traction: Stud/overhead electric
Opened: 4 April 1907
Closed: 31 January 1934
System: Network
Length: 9.24 miles
Stock: 3 sd, 39 dd
Livery: Maroon/brown & cream/yellow
Last Car: No 3

Built by the Torquay Tramway Construction Co. Ltd, a subsidiary of the NEC, the first-opened section of the system used the Dolter system of stud electricity supply on a triangle of nearly 4 miles of mainly single-track routes. This linked Torre station on the GWR to the west, St Marychurch (and depot) to the east and Beacon Quay on Torbay to the south. The original cars (Nos 1-18) were open-top Brush double-deckers. A fourth route of just over 2 miles from St Marychurch to Beacon Quay via Babbacombe opened on 11 November 1907 having been delayed by road-widening work.

The system's first extension opened on 16 April 1908 with 2 miles of double-track line skirting the shore from Beacon Quay, along Torbay Road to the Grand Hotel by Torquay station on the railway line from Torre to Paignton. The Company wanted to push the tramway on to Paignton but with the Dolter

Taunton's original No 2 seen on a postcard, running through the town centre before its 1905 replacement by a single-decker. (Courtesy Andrew Maxam)

Torquay Tramways Nos 13 and 4 on the opening day of the system, 4 April 1907. (Lens of Sutton)

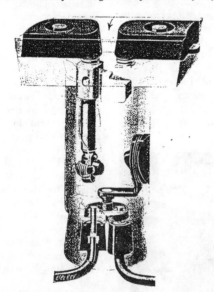
studs increasingly prone to failure, decided that a more conventional system would have to be used – which meant that the rest of the studs in Torquay would have to go. This Torquay Council refused to countenance on the grounds that overhead wires and standards would be unsightly in the resort; the dispute went to arbitration which found in favour of the Company and on 6 March 1911 the conversion was completed as far as the Grand Hotel. The double-track extension from here along Torbay Road and Torquay Road to Paignton station opened on 17 July that year with the car fleet increased by a further 15 Brush open-top cars (Nos 19-33). Three Brush single-deckers (Nos 34-36) for winter one-man operation were bought in 1921 from TAUNTON and over the next seven years six open-top bogie cars (Nos 37-42) were bought from Brush. By 1928 (when the last two arrived) bus competition was making the tramway's position precarious in streets becoming increasingly traffic-filled and the Paignton line closed on 14 January 1934, followed by the rest of the system at the end of the month.

In an unusual reversal of the normal situation, the tramway was also in the railway operating business as it ran the Babbacombe Cliff Railway from when it opened on 1 April 1926 until 13 March 1935 when it was sold to the Council.

Bibliography: *Torbay Transport* Fisher
    Barham (Glasney Press, Falmouth, 1979)
    0 950282 54 5

TRAFFORD PARK TRAMWAYS
Authority: –
Gauge: 4ft 8½in
Traction: Gas, overhead electric
Opened: 23 July 1897
Closed: 1 May 1908
System: Single line + loop
Length: c4 miles
Stock: 4 dd gas; 1 sd, 6 dd electric
Livery: Green & cream gas, blue electric
Last Car: ?

For a short line, this tramway system had an astonishingly varied history. Situated in Trafford Park immediately to the south of the Manchester Ship Canal (opened 1894) to the west of Manchester, its function was to help in the conversion of the park from a rural haven to an industrial estate.

The park was purchased in 1896 by the Trafford Park Estates Ltd who invited the British Gas Traction Co. Ltd (see LYTHAM ST ANNES) to lay and operate a tramway of just under 3 miles in length along its east-

Trade advertisement for the (unsuccessful) Dolter surface contact system of current supply, as used at Torquay and elsewhere.

west axis. The single-track line (with no passing loops) opened the following year and was laid along the existing roadways between Barton in the west and the show ground near the eastern end of the park. Services began with car No 1, an open-top double-decker built by Gas Motorenfabrik Deutz of Cologne and powered by a two-cylinder gas engine complete with large flywheel in the lower saloon. Three cylindrical tanks stored the town gas used.

On 28 July 1897 however a slight accident led to the suspension of services – and a long dispute between the two companies over the state of the track – until 8 April of the following year when the line re-opened to coincide with a visit by Barnum & Bailey's Circus. By now the line had been extended ½ mile east to the Trafford Road entrance to the park, a car shed erected at Barton, passing loops added and three cars (Nos 2-4), identical to No 1, provided. The tramway was now also connected to the park's industrial railway system and used by goods trains as well.

As more business moved to the park, so more workmen were carried on the tramway on weekdays and the idea was mooted of linking it to the MANCHESTER CORPORATION system at Old Trafford. Before this could be done, the BGT Co. went into liquidation at the end of 1899 with the cars stopping on 3 November after the gas supply was cut off. The equipment was bought by the Estates Co. for £2,000 and services resumed. In 1902 it was decided to construct a new, electric tramway in the form of an out-and-back loop from the Trafford Road entrance along Trafford Park Road, then along Westinghouse Road to the southwest past the BEC works and the car shed, north up Third Avenue and then east on Ashburton Road back to the old Post Office at Hatton's Wood where it rejoined the Trafford Park Road to run as a double track back to the terminus. Total length of this 'Westinghouse Loop' was 2.55 miles and included no less than 34 railway level crossings! The gas line now terminated at the old Post Office, with no connection to the new line.

The new stock was built by BEC and comprised Nos 5-9 and bogie car No 10, all open-top double-deckers (though No 8 was immediately top-covered), and No 11, a single-deck bogie trailer converted in 1904 to a roofed, double-deck motor car known as the 'Cattle Truck' seating 132 passengers (plus standing room) and which, at 16ft 7in high, was Britain's tallest tramcar.

On 31 October 1905 the line was finally connected to the SALFORD and Manchester tramways in Trafford Road. Salford Corporation bought the seven electric cars and took over the running of the

Tynemouth & District No 10 of 1900 at the Whitley Bay terminus. (Lens of Sutton)

tramway with both Salford and Manchester running alternate trams into the park. Cars 10 and 11 became Salford 161 and 162 and Nos 5-9 became 173-177 respectively. The Estates Co. retained and operated the gas trams – now increasingly decrepit – until 1 May 1908, replacing them the next day with a Hudswell, Clarke saddle tank locomotive and two small carriages from the CLC, whereupon the gas trams were sold for scrap. The original tramway was now just another part of the estate's railway network and workmen's trains were run until 1921 when they were replaced by three motor buses.

Bibliography: *Trafford Park Tramways 1897 to 1946* (Locomotion Papers No 26) Edward Gray (The Oakwood Press, 1964)

TRAWDEN *see* COLNE & TRAWDEN

TYNEMOUTH & DISTRICT TRAMWAYS

Authority: Tynemouth and District Tramways Order 1879
Gauge: 3ft
Traction: Horse/steam
Opened: 1883
Closed: 1900
System: Single line
Length: 2.58 miles
Stock: ? horse; 5 locos, 5 sd steam
Livery: ?
Last Car: ?

This short line at the mouth of the River Tyne in Northumberland, linking Prudhoe Street in North Shields with Percy Park in Tynemouth, had a very complicated history. It was opened as a horse line by the Tynemouth & District Tramways Ltd, then sold in 1884 to the North Shields & District

Tramways Co. Ltd. That same year the Company began steam working with five Wilkinson patent design locomotives (Nos 1-3 from BH and Nos 4 and 5 from Greens) with the same number of bogie passenger trailers from Lancaster. The depot was in Suez Street off Northumberland Square in the centre of North Shields.

In 1890 the line was sold to the North Shields & Tynemouth District Tramways Ltd, which Company was bought by the BET in 1897, changing its name two years later to the Tynemouth & District Electric Traction Co. Ltd in readiness for the planned electrification of the line (see below).

Bibliography: *The Tramways of Northumberland* George S. Hearse (Author, Blanchland, 1961)

TYNEMOUTH & DISTRICT ELECTRIC TRAMWAYS

Authority: Tynemouth and District Tramways Order 1879
Gauge: 3ft 6in
Traction: Overhead electric
Opened: 18 March 1901
Closed: 4 August 1931
System: Single line
Length: 4.23 miles
Stock: 1 sd, 23 dd
Livery: Crimson lake & cream
Last Car: ?

Following the closure of the TYNEMOUTH & DISTRICT steam line (see above), the Company set about relaying, extending and electrifying it, the contractor for the work being George Law of Kidderminster. As re-opened, it ran from New Quay in North Shields up the 1 in 10 Borough Road to the junction of Prudhoe Street and Saville Street, turning east down the latter to follow the former steam line along Tynemouth

Road and Percy Park Road with an extension along the Grand Parade, through Cullercoats and past the depot in John Street to a terminus in Whitley Road, Whitley Bay.

The tramway's original car fleet was a very mixed bag indeed. The first ten trams were ERTCW open-toppers, No 11 was a Midland single-decker (possibly ordered by the BET-owned Merthyr Tydfil system in Wales but transferred north) which was used as a Borough Road shuttle until Nos 12-18, more ERTCW open-toppers, arrived in October 1901 after which it was rebuilt as a works car whilst Nos 19-22, Milnes open-toppers, were again built for another line (probably POOLE) but transferred to Tynemouth.

No further cars were added to stock from 1901 to 1927 when ten Brush open-toppers were bought from the BURTON & ASHBY LIGHT RAILWAYS, but only four (Nos 21-24) put into service to replace some of the older cars.

In 1902 the TYNESIDE system was opened as far east as Prudhoe Street (see below) though no physical connection could be made on account of the two tramways' different gauges. Two years later, under the Tynemouth and District Tramways Act 1903, a short northern extension was made from Whitley Road further on up the coast via Park Avenue and Park Road, terminating by the bandstand on Whitley Bay Links to complete the mainly single-track system, to which no further major changes were made until bus competition, and the age of its track and rolling stock, brought about its demise.

Bibliography: as above

TYNESIDE TRAMWAYS

Authority: Tyneside Tramways and Tramroad Act 1901
Gauge: 4ft 8½in
Traction: Overhead electric
Opened: 4 September 1902
Closed: 6 April 1930
System: Branching
Length: 10.99 miles

Stock: 29 dd
Livery: Dark green & cream
Last Car: ?

The gap between the north Tyneside electric systems of NEWCASTLE and TYNEMOUTH was bridged by the Tyneside Tramways & Tramroad Co., the first section of whose system opened from Prudhoe Street in North Shields westwards to the boundary of Wallsend with Newcastle. From here a stretch northeast to Gosforth opened on 18 October 1902 (although the official opening had been on 29 September). The last 2 miles ran north from Gosforth to Gosforth Park Gates and was opened on 18 June 1904 with a ½-mile branch from Wallsend to Neptune Bank completing the system.

Original stock comprised bogie cars Nos 1-4 and single-truck cars Nos 5-18, all open-top double-deckers from Milnes. These were joined in 1903-04 by four single-truck cars (Nos 19-22) and two bogie vehicles (Nos 23 and 24) from Brush and in 1910 by single-

Map of the tramways of north Tyneside, from the 1909 Manual of Electrical Undertakings.

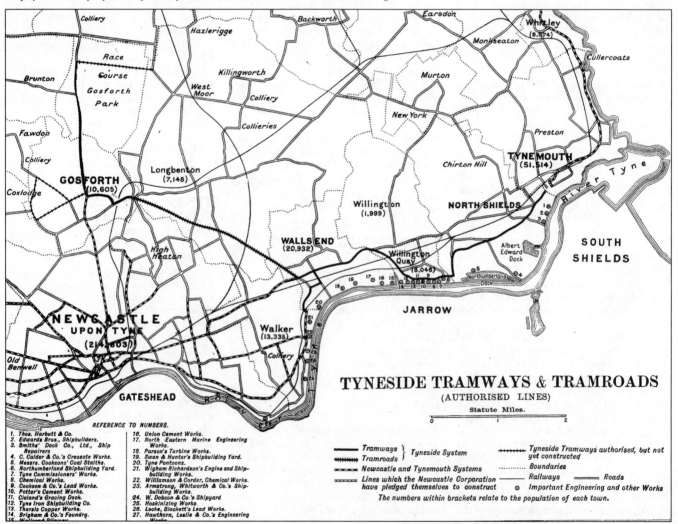

truck Nos 25 and 26 from UEC. Again, all these cars were open-toppers. The last arrivals, Nos 29 and 30 in 1919, were similar EE vehicles.

Although the tramway abutted the Tynemouth system no through running was possible because of the different gauges; where the two lines met in Prudhoe Street, however, there was some 300yd of overlapping mixed gauge track (the only other example of this in the British Isles being on the Blackrock & Kingstown line in Ireland). Leaving North Shields, the single-track line ran southwestwards along Howdon Road to the Howdon Ferry across the Tyne to Jarrow, then swung westwards along Ropery Lane into Wallsend where the branch to Neptune Bank (and the depot) left it. Here the track was doubled along the High Street before singling again for some 3 miles of reserved sleeper track to Gosforth. Here it zig-zagged (and doubled again) before a second stretch of reserved sleeper track of some 2 miles took it up to Gosforth Park Gates. (This section was soon metalled over to form part of the Great North Road) where for some 350yd before the single terminal stub a third track was laid to cater for traffic to the racecourse there.

Three links with the Newcastle system were made at Wallsend, Neptune Bank and Henry Street, Gosforth. Through running to Gosforth Park began on 6 August 1904 and to Park Road, Wallsend, on 29 August that same year.

Although several extensions were planned, none were ever built and when the great depression of the 1920s hit the region it was just at the time when much of the track and car fleet needed renewing. Newcastle Corporation declined to buy the undertaking and the Company had very little option but to close it down. All the cars were scrapped with the exception of Nos 3 and 4 which were sold to SOUTH SHIELDS.

Bibliography: as above

UPWELL *see* WISBECH & UPWELL

WAKEFIELD & DISTRICT LIGHT RAILWAY
Authority: Wakefield and District Light
   Railway Order 1901
Gauge: 4ft 8½in
Traction: Overhead electric
Opened: 15 August 1904
Closed: 25 July 1932
System: Network
Length: 16.95 miles
Stock: 55 dd
Livery: Crimson lake & cream
Last Car: ?

Several tramway schemes were proposed

for the county town of the West Riding of Yorkshire from the late 1870s onwards, to use a variety of traction methods. The one which eventually succeeded was a promotion by a group of businessmen which resulted in a 1901 LRO for 10 miles of line and the incorporation of the Wakefield & District Light Railway Co. Ltd. Two further extension LROs brought the length authorized by 1902 to 22 miles.

The situation was complicated by the fact that 25 April 1903 saw the registration of the Yorkshire Electric Tramways Construction Syndicate Ltd to actually build the W&D system (and others in the area) and then take it over completely through a subsidiary set up in 1905, the Yorkshire (West Riding) Electric Tramways Co. Ltd.

As built, the W&D comprised three routes. The longest ran some 9 miles from the Castle Inn, Sandal, north through Wakefield to the Leeds boundary where it made an end-on junction with the LEEDS system at Thwaite Gate, Hunslet. The second route ran east-west from Agbrigg to Ossett where it made another end-on connection, this time with the DEWSBURY, OSSETT & SOOTHILL NETHER line, where it crossed the Sandal–Leeds route south of Wakefield the two lines sharing a mile of double track. Both routes were originally single-track but later doubled for the most part and both opened on the same day in 1904 with through running into Leeds commencing 1 June the following year. The W&D's third route was a 1½-mile single-track branch from Rothwell Haigh (1½ miles south of the Leeds boundary), eastwards to the village of Rothwell; this opened about the second week of December 1904 (the exact day is uncertain) and was worked as a service from Thwaite Gate.

To work the line 55 open-top double-deckers were ordered from DK in 1903; the first batch of these (Nos 1-30) were delivered during 1904 from the summer onwards whilst Nos 31-55 arrived during the first half of 1905 with top covers fitted (the first batch later being similarly equipped). By this time the tramway had become part of the YORKSHIRE (WEST RIDING) system although it was not until August 1911 that the Company was wound up.

Bibliography: *The Tramways of Dewsbury
   and Wakefield* W. Pickles (The Light Rail
   Transit Association, 1980) 0 900433 73 6

WALLASEY TRAMWAYS
Authority: Wallasey Tramways Act 1878
Gauge: 4ft 8½in
Traction: Horse
Opened: 28 June 1879
Closed: 19 March 1902
System: Single line

Length: 3.33 miles
Stock: 7 sd, 15 dd
Livery: Red & ivory, later maroon & cream
Last Car: ?

After a number of unsuccessful proposals to provide a tramway link between at least some of the towns and villages on the northern part of the Wirral peninsula, the Wallasey Tramways Co. was ultimately successful in doing so. Its line ran from close to the ferry landing stage on the Mersey at Seacombe, northwards along Brighton Street to Egremont (from where there was another ferry service to Liverpool), then northwest along Liscard Road to Liscard then north along Rake Lane to Upper Brighton and the depot in Field Road just south of New Brighton (whose residents did not wish anything so common as a tramway to despoil their streets). Virtually all the line was single-track with a long one-way loop in Egremont.

Services began with Starbuck single-deckers Nos 1-7 – possibly transfers from the neighbouring WIRRAL TRAMWAY (see BIRKENHEAD) – with services commencing from Church Road in Seacombe in June 1879, the 150-yard extension to the ferry not being opened until the autumn. In 1880 five Eades reversible double-deckers (Nos 8-14) were added to the fleet.

On 8 May 1891 the Company became part of the Wallasey United Tramway and Omnibus Co. Ltd (incorporated 20 April 1888 to bring together the directors' interests of its title) and in 1893 seven Milnes double-deckers were purchased; these took the numbers 13 onwards with some later taking numbers vacated by withdrawn cars so that they had become Nos 6, 7, and 10-14 by 1901 when Wallasey UDC purchased the line. The takeover was effective from 1 April 1901 and the arbitrated price paid was £20,500; on 26 April three ex-LIVERPOOL double-deckers were added to the fleet, presumably as replacement vehicles.

The Council's intention was to replace the line with a larger, electric system (see below) though the horse cars continued to operate amidst the reconstruction work, often on diverted sections of track. Following the line's total closure the stock was auctioned off though one of the Milnes cars survived to become a Corporation works vehicle.

Bibliography: *The Tramways of Birkenhead
   and Wallasey* T. B. Maund & Martin
   Jenkins (The Light Rail Transit
   Association, 1987) 0 948106 03 4

WALLASEY CORPORATION TRAMWAYS
Authority: Wallasey Tramways and
   Improvements Act 1899
Gauge: 4ft 8½in

[Ch. ccxxxviii.]   *Wallasey Tramways*   **[41 & 42 Vict.]**
Act, 1878.

A.D. 1878.

`SCHEDULE referred to in the foregoing Act.`

Tolls to be charged on Tramways.

d.

1. From Seacombe to Upper Brighton, or vice versâ, a sum
   not exceeding   -   -   -   -   -   3

2. From Seacombe to Liscard, or vice versâ, a sum not
   exceeding   -   -   -   -   -   2

3. From Liscard to Upper Brighton, or vice versâ, a sum
   not exceeding   -   -   -   -   -   2

Beyond the above distances (2) and (3), for every mile or
part of a mile a sum not exceeding   -   -   1

For any distance less than two miles, any sum not exceeding   2

Between 9 p.m. and 5 a.m. double the above rates.   Children in
arms under three years of age free.

LONDON : Printed by George Edward Eyre and William Spottiswoode,
Printers to the Queen's most Excellent Majesty.   1878.

*Tramway Acts of Parliament normally laid down a strict scale of charges, this example being the passenger
fare structure imposed by the 1878 Wallasey Tramways Act.*

Traction: Overhead electric
Opened: 17 March 1902
Closed: 30 November 1933
System: Network
Length: 12.06 miles
Stock: 77 dd
Livery: Green & cream to 1924, then
   greenish-yellow & cream
Last Car: No 68

Under its empowering Act of 1899 Wallasey
UDC was authorized to construct 8½ miles of
mainly single-track lines based on the old
horse line (see above) which was the first
route to re-open (extended into New
Brighton), followed on 19 March 1902 – the
system's official opening – by a second, 2½-
mile line to Upper Brighton from Egremont,
along Seabank Road much closer to the
shore. A third, 3¾-mile linking route to the
west, from Liscard to New Brighton via
Wallasey, opened on 17 May the same year.
The depot was sited on this route, off
Seaview Road between Liscard and Wallasey,
and a one-way loop at New Brighton served
the ferry pier there. The landscape traversed
was a mixture of residential, industrial and
rural areas and traffic was very mixed with
trippers to the northern beaches and

commuters to Liverpool using the three
ferries; the short crossing from Seacombe was
the most popular and the trams even
carried warning flags when the two more
exposed northern Mersey crossings were
affected by inclement weather (usually fog).

The system's original 25 cars (Nos 1-25)
were ERTCW open-toppers and were joined
in 1903 by five more, Nos 27-31 (No 26 was
a works car). All 30 had been fitted with top
covers by mid-1905, which year saw the
arrival of Nos 32-36, top-covered UEC
vehicles. From then on all Wallasey's new
cars – Nos 37-41 (UEC of 1907) and 42-78
(Brush of 1910-20) – were of this type. After
the town became a Municipal Borough in
1910 the 'WALLASEY COUNCIL
TRAMWAYS' legend on the cars was
changed to 'WALLASEY CORPORATION
TRAMWAYS'.

A fourth, even more westerly route from
Seacombe to New Brighton was added in
1910-11, beginning with a 1-mile section
westwards from Seacombe along Poulton
Road to St Luke's Church in Poulton
opened on 8 July 1910, followed on 7
February 1911 by the remaining 2¼ miles
northwards up Marlowe Road and St
George's Road through Wallasey Village,

then eastwards along Grove Road to join the
Liscard-New Brighton route in Wallasey. All
this route (nicknamed the 'Switchback') was
double-track and, coupled with a track-
doubling programme on the other routes,
meant that nearly three-quarters of the
system was eventually so laid.

After World War I the tramway entered a
boom period – especially as regards the
holidaymaker traffic – but much of the track
had reached that critical point in its life
when renewal was necessary and, ominously,
on 3 April 1920 the Corporation began its
first motor bus service. By the end of
November 1929 no less than 56 buses were
being operated and it was only a matter of
time before the tramways were abandoned as
worn out. (The Seabank Road route had in
fact closed on 19 June that year.) The last
Rake Lane trams ran on 4 February 1933 and
those on the remaining routes at the end of
November, after which they were sold for
scrap (with some bodies retained to become
bus shelters).

Bibliography: as above

WALSALL CORPORATION TRAMWAYS
Authority: Walsall Corporation Act 1900
Gauge: 3ft 6in
Traction: Overhead electric
Took Over: 1 January 1901*
Closed: 30 September 1933
System: Radial
Length: 13.51 miles
Stock: 49 dd
Livery: Dark red & cream
Last Car: No 44

Following its 1899 agreement with the
BET, the SOUTH STAFFORDSHIRE
TRAMWAYS Co. and the South
Staffordshire Tramways (Lessee) Co. Ltd,
Walsall Corporation assumed ownership of
the 1.37 miles of track and overhead within
its boundaries for a cost of £18,500 and
leased them back to the Lessee Co. from 1
January 1901 for three years. Meanwhile it
pressed ahead with its own extensions, as
authorized by its 1900 Act, opening the first
of these, a single-track northwards continuation of the Bloxwich line for two-thirds of a
mile to Bell Lane, on 13 December 1902
(with working by the SST). A year later, on
31 December 1903, this whole line and the
other completed new routes – westwards
along the Wolverhampton Road to
Willenhall (2½ miles), southeast along the
Birmingham Road to the boundary at the
Bell Inn (2 miles) and northeast up the
Lichfield Road through Rushall to Walsall
Wood (3¾ miles) – were officially opened.

Corporation working began the next day,
the SST cars replaced by Corporation Nos 1-

28, Brush open-top double-deckers (later top-covered) based on a new depot at Birchills, halfway along the Bloxwich route. On 1 May 1907 through working began to Wednesbury and Darlaston over SST tracks whilst in 1908 Nos 29-32, UEC top-covered cars, were added to the fleet followed in 1912 by Nos 33-39, more modern UEC top-covered vehicles. The last stock purchases, Nos 40-49 in 1919, were similar Brush cars.

On 1 April 1929 the first route – the Walsall Wood line – was closed (replaced by a bus service), followed on 30 September by the Birmingham Road line. On 4 February 1929 the Willenhall line went, by which time the car fleet had been slimmed down. A year later however, on 1 October 1930, the Corporation took over the whole of the routes to Darlaston and Wednesbury (from the BIRMINGHAM & MIDLAND TRAMWAYS JOINT COMMITTEE and Wednesbury Corporation), replacing them with bus services on 5 March following. Two years later the Bloxwich trams ceased to run, this time replaced by trolleybuses.

WALTHAMSTOW COUNCIL LIGHT RAILWAYS
Authority: Walthamstow and District Light Railway Order 1903
Gauge: 4ft 8½in
Traction: Overhead electric
Opened: 3 June 1905
Taken Over: 1 July 1933
System: Branching
Length: 9.14 miles
Stock: 8 sd, 64 dd
Livery: Brown & primrose

Owned and operated by Walthamstow UDC, this southwest Essex single-track system opened with Brush open-toppers Nos 1-32 working an east-west main line and a succession of branches to the north and south. The main line began at the Napier Arms on Woodford New Road on the edge of Epping Forest, then joined Forest Road after ½ mile to run right across the borough whilst a ½-mile branch south down Woodford New Road led to the Rising Sun (the eastern terminus of LEYTON COUNCIL TRAMWAYS) which, for most of its life, was worked summer weekends only (and never connected with the Leyton system until 5 March 1931 to permit a year-round service of through running).

After 1¼ miles along Forest Road the Bell was reached in the centre of the town and here a branch north up Chingford Road past the depot led to Chingford Mount and a branch south down Hoe Street led to the Baker's Arms, just across the boundary in Leyton, where it later connected with that system's Lea Bridge Road line. The main line continued for another mile to

Blackhorse Road station where a short northern branch led up Blackhorse Lane to Higham Hill and a longer one south down Blackhorse Lane and Markhouse Road led to (but again stopped just short of) Lea Bridge Road. The last ¾ mile of the Forest Road line terminated by the Ferry Boat Inn in Ferry Lane on the bank of the River Lea.

A track-doubling programme was commenced in 1912 with much of the system being so treated over the next thirteen years; a year later six HN top-covered cars (Nos 33-38) were purchased. As elsewhere though the tramway was plagued by maintenance problems during World War I and in 1919 was forced to hire six LONDON UNITED open-toppers and in 1920 eight ERTCW bogie single-deckers (Nos 37-46) were bought from ROTHERHAM; the next year the hired cars were bought and numbered 47-52 (from LUT 226, 230, 232, 280, 289 and 298 variously).

Twelve new cars were bought in 1927, these being HN enclosed bogie vehicles 53-64, after which the open-top cars were fitted with top covers (except the ex-LUT cars which were gradually withdrawn). In 1932 eight Brush enclosed bogie cars were purchased and numbered 39-46 as more cars were scrapped, the last acquisitions before the system became part of LONDON TRANSPORT.

See also LEA BRIDGE, LEYTON & WALTHAMSTOW TRAMWAYS.

Bibliography: *The Tramways of East London* 'Rodinglea' (The Tramway & Light Railway Society/The Light Railway Transport League, 1967)

WALTON-ON-THE-NAZE PIER TRAMWAY
Not a tramway but a 3ft 6in gauge centre-rail electric railway running the length of the 2,600-ft long 1898 pier owned by the Coast Development Co. Ltd (who later opened a similar line further up the coast at FELIXSTOWE). The one motor car and two trailers – all roofed toastracks – were by Ashbury on Peckham trucks and ran coupled together as a train. The line closed in 1935 to be replaced by a battery-powered carriage running in a 6-ft wide wooden trough – a primitive forerunner of modern guided bus systems and about as long-lived. In 1942 the pier was destroyed by fire but was rebuilt and in 1948 re-opened with a 2ft gauge contractor's line adapted as a miniature railway.

Bibliography: *Pier Railways* (Locomotion Papers No 60) K. Turner (The Oakwood Press, 1972)

WANTAGE TRAMWAY
Authority: Wantage Tramways Order 1874
Gauge: 4ft 8½in
Traction: Horse, steam
Opened: 11 October 1875
Closed: 31 July 1925
System: Single line
Length: 2.48 miles
Stock: 1 sd, 1 dd horse; 6 locos, 1 steamcar, 7 sd steam
Livery: Locos green, cars brown
Last Train: ?

Each English roadside steam tramway had its own unique character and the historic Wantage line was perhaps the most appealing of them all. Like many of its kind it was built to link a community with a railway which had passed it by: in this instance the north Berkshire market town of Wantage with Wantage Road station on the GWR's main line to Swindon and the west through the Vale of the White Horse.

After an 1860s scheme to build a railway branch to Wantage had failed, the opening afforded by the 1870 Tramways Act led to the promotion of a roadside tramway by the Wantage Tramway Co. Ltd (incorporated 10 November 1873). Services began with Starbuck open-top double-deck horse car No 1 in October 1875 which was joined in December by a single-decker (No 2) from the same manufacturer. Even before the line had opened though, in the summer of 1875, a primitive open-top double-deck steamcar had been brought to the line for trials. Designed by John Grantham (and thereafter known as the 'Grantham Car'), this had been constructed in 1872 by Oldbury and was powered by a Merryweather steam engine. The intention was to use it on the line if the trials proved successful and to this end the Company obtained an Act of Parliament on 27 June 1876, amending its original Order, to permit the use of mechanical traction; on 1 August 1876 regular steam passenger working began – the first such in the British Isles. Later that year the car was purchased outright for the sum of £250, the Company having calculated that it was considerably cheaper to run than horses. It lasted in service until about 1890 when it was withdrawn and broken up (after possibly running in its final years as an engineless trailer).

In 1877 a more orthodox, Hughes tram loco was purchased (No 4) and from this date the use of horses gradually decreased and had probably been abandoned by 1888 when engine No 6, a Matthews tram loco, was bought as a replacement for the 'Grantham Car'. Two years later car No 3, a Milnes single-deck saloon vehicle arrived and worked the passenger services with Nos 1 and 2 until 1903 when Nos 4 and 5, a pair of

Wantage Tramway Co., (Ltd.)

Monday day of Dec 7th 1885

Train.	First No. in Book.	Last No. in Book.	No. of Passengers. Intermediate.		Luggage. s.	d.	£	s.	d.
Down 7.35	11	11	1st						
	161	169	2nd	8				4	6
Up 7.35	11	11	1st						
	169	172	2nd	2				1	0
Down 9.20	11	14	1st	3			2	6	3
	171	184	2nd	13	6			6	6
Up 9.20	14	14	1st					2	6
	184	189	2nd	5					
Down 12.5	14	15	1st	1				3	9
	189	196	2nd	7					
Up 12.5	15	15	1st					4	6
	196	205	2nd	9					
Down 12.40			1st						
			2nd						
Up 12.40			1st						
			2nd						
Down 2.0	15	15	1st					2	0
	205	209	2nd	4 4		2			
Up 2.0	15	15	1st					2	6
	209	214	2nd	5					
Down 5.25	15	15	1st						6
	214	215	2nd	1					
Up 5.25	15	17	1st	2			1	6	
	215	225	2nd	10 5			5	0	
Down 6.5	17	17	1st					2	6
	225	230	2nd	5 4					
Up 6.5	17	18	1st	1					9
	230	234	2nd	4 6					
Down 8.20	18	18	1st				1		0
	234	236	2nd	2 2					
Up 8.20	18	18	1st				4		6
	236	205	2nd	9 4					

Conductor

Signed _____   Total...£ 2 - 10 8

Wantage Tramway conductor's way bill of 7 December 1885 recording the number of passengers carried and fares taken.

goods workings but outlasted them all and can now be seen at Didcot Railway Centre. Passenger services ceased in 1925, primarily because the GWR had started a competing bus service the year before; goods services continued until 21 December 1946, the line independent to the last.

The tramway was a simple, single-track line laid with bridge rails on longitudinal wooden sleepers – a hangover from the GWR's old broad gauge practice. It ran in a southwesterly direction from beside the goods yard at Wantage Road station (a physical connection allowed the through running of goods wagons), out along the eastern side of what is now the A338 to its terminus, depot and yard just past the Gas Works off Mill Street. (Plans for a short extension into the Market Place were never realised.) The only major alteration to this layout came in 1905 when a second goods yard (the Lower Yard) was opened on the west side of the Gas Works close to the Wantage Arm of the Berkshire & Wiltshire Canal.

Bibliography: *The Wantage Tramway* S. H. Pearce Higgins (The Abbey Press, Abingdon, 1958)
The Wantage Tramway 1875-1945 Nicholas de Courtais (Wild Swan Publications, 1981) 0 906867 06 1

WARRINGTON CORPORATION TRAMWAYS

Authority: Warrington Tramways Act 1900
Gauge: 4ft 8½in
Traction: Overhead electric
Opened: 21 April 1902
Closed: 28 August 1935
System: Radial
Length: 6.84 miles
Stock: 27 dd
Livery: Munich lake & cream
Last Car: No 1

Planned and operated by Warrington Corporation to serve this large industrial south Lancashire town, this system grew to form a starfish-shaped layout of five routes of roughly equal length radiating from the town centre. The first 1½ miles opened ran east from Rylands Street across the River Mersey via Warrington Bridge and down Knutsford Road to Latchford, terminating on the northern bank of the Manchester Ship Canal. This was double-track throughout though the second route opened, from Rylands Street west along Sankey Street and Liverpool Road to Sankey Bridges with a terminus close to Sankey station, was mainly single-track. This half of the original one

ex-READING single-deck horse cars were purchased. All trailers (except No 3) lasted in service until about 1912 (with No 1 converted to single-deck form about 1900) when two HN cars were bought. The first of these (No 4) was a 1900 bogie double-deck electric exhibition car which was cut down to single-deck form for Wantage, and No 5, a single-decker begun some ten years earlier for BRADFORD but never delivered.

The tramway also operated a goods service, taking all manner of wagons from Wantage Road down to the town and back again. This began about the end of 1878 when the Company purchased from the LNWR a George England 0-4-0 tank engine built in 1857 for the Sandy & Potton Railway in Bedfordshire. Numbered 5 (and unofficially known as *Jane*), she was followed by a succession of other engines for through route, another 1½ miles in length, was opened on 23 April 1902 with services operated by open-top double-deckers Nos 1-8 from Milnes, quickly joined by Nos 9 and 10, a similar pair. The depot was in Mersey Street, off Rylands Street.

On 4 October 1902 a southern, double-track line to Wilderspool was opened. This left the Latchford line just south of Warrington Bridge and ran south for 1¼ miles along Wilderspool Causeway to terminate by Stafford Road, again just short of the Ship Canal. (This route was extended a few hundred yards on 7 July 1905 over the canal on the Northwich Road Swing Bridge to Victoria Square in Stockton Heath, Cheshire, the canal forming the county boundary.)

The last of the five radial routes were northeast to the Cemetery (mainly double-track, opened 22 November 1902) and north up the Winwick Road past the CLC's Central station to Longford (mainly single-track, opened 29 October 1902), the car fleet being increased accordingly with the purchase of Nos 11-21, another eleven Milnes open-toppers. Between 1904 and 1905 18 of the cars were fitted with top covers and in 1909 No 18 (one of those not so equipped) was cut down to single-deck status to become a one-man car for the financially unrewarding and sparsely-populated Longford route.

In 1919-20 six new Brush cars were delivered to the tramway. These were Nos 21-27, all top-covered double-deckers, and were a sign that the system was enjoying a ten-year period of capital expenditure after the war years: new cars were bought, track relayed and doubled, the town centre layout remodelled and new, enclosed top covers fitted to some of the cars.

The beginning of the end came on 17 September 1931 when the Stockton Heath line closed, followed by that to Longford on

31 December. Six of the cars were then withdrawn, followed by a further five some time later. On 27 March 1935 the Cemetery and Sankey Bridges routes closed and seven more cars withdrawn, leaving the last nine to work the Latchford route for the tramway's final summer.

Bibliography: *75 Years of Municipal Transport in Warrington* Warrington Transport Dept (Warrington Borough Council, 1977)

WARWICK *see* LEAMINGTON & WARWICK

WATERLOO & GREAT CROSBY TRAMWAYS

Authority: Great Crosby Tramways Order 1898; Waterloo-with-Seaforth Tramways Order 1898
Gauge: 4ft 8½in
Traction: Overhead electric
Opened: 19 June 1900
Closed: 31 December 1925
System: Single line
Length: 2.53 miles
Stock: 2 sd, 14 dd
Livery: Green & cream
Last Car: ?

Situated immediately to the north of Bootle, the neighbouring UDCs of Waterloo-with-Seaforth and Great Crosby (both created in 1894) promoted jointly a single-track tramway which ran inland from Seaforth Sands at the mouth of the River Mersey along Crosby Road South through Seaforth to Waterloo, then continued on along Liverpool Road to Great Crosby to terminate in Cook's Road by the police station.

Construction began in 1899 and the southern half of the line, from Seaforth Sands to Five Lamps, Waterloo, opened in June 1900

with the northern half following some time that September. The main feature of this otherwise undistinguished tramway was that although built by the two UDCs, it was stocked and worked by the Liverpool Overhead Railway. It is possible that the UDCs hoped that LIVERPOOL CORPORATION would operate the line for them but in the event the LOR (which had reached Seaforth Sands on 30 April 1894) agreed to lease the line for 26 years from 1 January 1900, stocking it with DK open-toppers 1-8 and 11-14 plus open-sided single-deckers 9 and 10 for summer use. The cars were lettered 'LIVERPOOL OVERHEAD RAILWAY CO' and housed in the depot beside the Seaford Sands terminus under the LOR station (with passenger transference by means of one of the very first escalators in England).

In 1903 DK open-toppers 15 and 16 were added to the fleet and nine years later two of the older cars (possibly Nos 5 and 7) were rebodied; some of the cars were later top-covered and the single-deckers withdrawn.

After World War I the LOR, fearing its lease would not be renewed, allowed the tramway to run down and the two Councils entered into negotiations with Liverpool Corporation who expressed an interest in buying the line and connecting it to its neighbouring terminus in Bootle. It was not to be though and from 1 January 1926 the trams were replaced by buses.

Bibliography: *Liverpool Transport Vol 2: 1900-1930* J. B. Horne & T. B. Maund (Transport Publishing Co./LRTA, 1982) 0 903839 50 4

WEST HAM CORPORATION TRAMWAYS

Authority: West Ham Corporation Act 1898
Gauge: 4ft 8½in
Traction: Overhead electric
Opened: 27 February 1904
Taken Over: 1 July 1933
System: Network
Length: 16.8 miles
Stock: 162 dd
Livery: Maroon/chocolate & cream

The first tramways in the borough of West Ham (created 1886) were horse lines operated by the NORTH METROPOLITAN TRAMWAYS Co. of LONDON. The first of these, running from Aldgate in London northeast along the Mile End Road and Bow Road to Bow Bridge (where it crossed into Essex) and continuing up the High Street to Stratford Church, opened on 9 November 1870; it was extended later as two branches from here, northeast to Manor Park and north to Leytonstone. A parallel line to the south, linking Canning town and

Waterloo & Great Crosby cars 1 and 14 of 1899 in Waterloo in an early postcard view. (Lens of Sutton)

Plaistow via Barking Road, opened in 1886 to make a 1¼-mile route isolated from the rest of the system.

In February 1903 West Ham Corporation agreed to buy the horse lines in stages in order to convert them as part of its planned electric system, paying £108,386 in all. Construction work on the new lines began that July and early the following year the first route opened. This ran from Stratford Broadway, southeast down West Ham Lane, Plaistow Road, Plaistow High Street and Balaam Street to the Abbey Arms on Barking Road (thus linking the two horse routes). This was followed, on 31 March 1904, by a separate line along Barking Road from the Greengate (to the northeast of the Abbey Arms) on up Barking Road to the Boleyn.

Other routes followed, with the last section of the horse tramway being converted in February 1905; the last section of electric line opened, on 1 May 1912, ran south from the Greengate down Prince Regent's Road to Connaught Road by the Victoria & Albert Docks. This completed the compact, mainly double-track network of lines connected at three points in the west to the LONDON COUNTY COUNCIL system, at two points in the north to LEYTON and at three points in the east to EAST HAM (and beyond that to ILFORD and BARKING). Through running arrangements meant that West Ham cars worked over as many miles of track outside their boundary as inside.

The first cars (Nos 1-50) were Milnes open-toppers, followed in 1905 by similar vehicles 51-85 and, in 1906, by similar type Nos 86-93 from MV. (Most of these were later top-covered and some were cannibalized during World War I to keep the others running.) There then came a succession of top covered cars:

Nos 94-100: MV of 1906
Nos 101-106: UEC of 1910
Nos 107-118: bogie HN cars of 1911
No 119: Corporation of 1923, renumbered 64
Nos 60-63, 65: ditto of 1924
Nos 119-124: bogie EE cars of 1925
Nos 125-137: ditto Corporation and Brush of 1926
No 138: ditto Corporation of 1928
Nos 76-85: ditto Brush of 1929
Nos 69-75: ditto Corporation and Brush of 1930
No 68: enclosed bogie Corporation car of 1931

Twenty-five of the cars were fitted in 1909 with plough gear for working over the LCC's conduit tramways (commencing in 1910); thereafter new cars came with this equipment as standard. The first, temporary depot was in Stratford, replaced in 1906 by a purpose-built one in Greengate Street, between the Greengate and Plaistow High Street and connected to both the original routes.

As can be seen from the above list, the car buying/building programme continued after World War I and, perhaps more importantly for the future of the system, all the track was relaid between 1920 and 1925 (apart from a short stretch in Beckton Road in Canning Town which had been abandoned during the war) so that when, in 1933, the tramway became part of the new LONDON TRANSPORT, it did so virtually in its entirety along with 134 tramcars which became LT Nos 211-344 (West Ham 1-26, 28-43, 45-65, 86-106, 68-85 and 107-138). LT No 290 (formerly West Ham 102 of 1910) is now preserved in the London Transport Museum, Covent Garden.

Bibliography: *The Tramways of East London* 'Rodinglea' (The Tramway & Light Railway Society/The Light Railway Transport League, 1967)

WEST METROPOLITAN TRAMWAYS *see* LONDON: WEST METROPOLITAN TRAMWAYS

WEST RIDING *see* YORKSHIRE (WEST RIDING)

WEST SUSSEX RAILWAY *see* HUNDRED OF MANHOOD & SELSEY TRAMWAY

WESTMINSTER STREET RAILWAY *see* LONDON: TRAIN'S TRAMWAYS

WESTON-SUPER-MARE & DISTRICT TRAMWAYS

Authority: Weston-super-Mare Tramways Order 1900
Gauge: 4ft 8½in
Traction: Overhead electric
Opened: 12 May 1902
Closed: 17 April 1937
System: Branching
Length: 2.92 miles
Stock: 6 sd, 12 dd
Livery: Crimson lake & cream
Last Car: No 8

This small system, operated by the Weston-super-Mare & District Electric Supply Co. Ltd as part of the BET group, relied heavily on holidaymaker traffic for its revenue and was well positioned to do so since its principal route ran the length of the seafront from the Old Pier in the north to the West of England Sanatorium in the south; a branch mid-way led through the town via Oxford Street and Locking Road to the depot. The line's official opening was held the day after public services began on the Old Pier–depot section with the southern half of the seafront line along Beach Road opening on 17 May.

Despite an early setback when, on 10 September 1903, four of its cars were flooded by high seas on the promenade and had to be withdrawn from service (the BET subsequently moved them to Swansea) the tramway survived on its largely seasonal receipts until 1 June 1936 when the Company and Weston UDC agreed – for a price – to its closure on behalf of the Bristol Tramways & Carriage Co. Ltd, which

Weston-super-Mare Brush toastrack No 16 of 1902 en route to the Sanatorium, followed closely by one of the Brush double-deckers. (Lens of Sutton)

concern then set about replacing the trams with its own motor buses.

Services began with eight open-top cars (Nos 1-8) and four roofed toastracks (Nos 13-16) from Brush; these were joined by four open-toppers in 1903 (Nos 9-12) to complete the order. After four went to Swansea the remainder of the double-deckers were renumbered 1-8; the only other cars added were two more roofed toastracks (Nos 17 and 18) in 1927, again from Brush.

Bibliography: *Weston-super-Mare Tramways* (Locomotion Papers No 78) C. G. Maggs (The Oakwood Press, 1974)

WESTON, CLEVEDON & PORTISHEAD RAILWAY

Although operated as a standard gauge light railway, this north Somerset line was intended originally to include nearly ½ mile of steam tramway through the streets of Weston-super-Mare as authorized by the 1885 Weston-super-Mare, Clevedon, and Portishead Tramways Act. Progress on building the line was exceedingly slow and it was not until 1897 that the first 8 miles from Weston to Clevedon were completed; Weston-super-Mare UDC however objected to the rails used on the street section (they apparently protruded above the road surface) and, indeed, to the whole notion of steam trains running through the town and the Company was forced accordingly to lift this section. At the same time it tried unsuccessfully to persuade the BET to buy the line for electrification.

Public services began on 1 December 1897 though the final 6 miles to Portishead did not open until ten years later, by which time the line had become known officially as the Weston, Clevedon & Portishead Railway. Its financial problems persisted, attempts to link up with the WESTON-SUPER-MARE electric tramway via Locking Road (see above) came to nothing after looking promising and from 1909 it was in the hands of a Receiver until the final train ran on 18 May 1940, after which its assets – including a motley collection of second-hand locomotives – were sold to the GWR.

Bibliography: *The Weston, Clevedon and Portishead Railway* Christopher Redwood (Sequoia Publishing, 1981) 0 905466 42 X
The Weston, Clevedon & Portishead Light Railway (Locomotion Papers No 25) C. G. Maggs (The Oakwood Press, 2nd rev ed 1990) 0 853613 88 5

WESTWOOD HO! *see* BIDEFORD, WESTWARD HO! & APPLEDORE

WEYMOUTH HARBOUR TRAMWAY

Opened on 16 October 1865, the Weymouth & Portland Railway connected the Channel port of Weymouth with the national railway network, being worked from the outset by the GWR as a mixed gauge line. Also authorized by the WPR Co.'s 1862 Act was a goods tramway from Weymouth station, south and east to the harbour. Also of mixed broad and standard gauge but laid with some form of tramroad rails, this opened for horse-worked goods traffic the same day as the railway line.

The tramway, which ran for 1 mile along the edge of the docks, was relaid with more orthodox rails in 1869, converted to standard gauge five years later and, from 1880 onwards, saw the use of steam locomotives as well as horses (the use of the latter lasting into the 20th century). The principal traffic of the line was generated by the Channel Island steamers. On 4 August 1889 – after extensive reconstruction of the line – passenger traffic began with a through boat train from Paddington. Since then further modifications have been made, usually to accommodate longer carriages, and new landing stages built.

The last goods trains ran on 28 February 1972 following the withdrawal of freight shipments through the port but passenger traffic has continued to the present time, if somewhat erratically with closure threatened yearly and services often suspended.

Bibliography: *The Weymouth Harbour Tramway* J. H. Lucking (Oxford Publishing Co., 1986) 0 86093 304 0

WIGAN & DISTRICT TRAMWAYS

Authority: Wigan Tramways Order 1879
Gauge: 3ft 6in
Traction: Horse, steam
Opened: 2 August 1880
Taken Over: 30 September 1902
System: Single line + branching
Length: 5.49 miles
Stock: 8 dd horse & steam; 23 locos, 20 dd steam
Livery: Locos dark brown, cars dark red & cream

Wigan's first tramway system was certainly unusual. Not only did it chop and change between horse and steam traction, it did so on two physically separated lines. It was operated by the Wigan Tramways Co. Ltd and constructed by the contractors Holme & King of the town; the first route ran west from Queen Street by the LNWR bridge in Wallgate in the town centre for just over 2 miles to the Black Bull at Lamberhead Green, Pemberton and was worked by Eades patent reversible double-deck horse cars 1-8

built by Ashbury. On 23 September 1880 a short extension taking the line along Wallgate to the Market Place was opened. The small depot was in Smethurst Street, Pemberton, near the terminus.

Steam trials were held on the line in 1881 and on 11 February 1882 the BoT authorized the use of steam locomotives. By the summer of that year Wilkinson tram locos Nos 1-4 were in service (Works Nos 1-4) pulling Starbuck top-covered cars Nos 9-12 as well as the Eades cars which had been fitted with canvas roofs.

On 13 January 1883 the system's second line opened; this ran eastwards for 2½ miles from King Street in the centre of Wigan via Darlington Street and Manchester Road through Ince, and from there via the Wigan road to Market Street, Hindley, terminating by the corner of Bridge Street. Here a small depot was sited off Market Street in Albert Street. To work the new line another four Wilkinson locos (Nos 5-8) were purchased, hauling some of the existing cars (which were horse-drawn for about six months until the locos had arrived).

In February 1884 the locos were withdrawn from the Pemberton route and horses reinstated, the direct result of a fatal accident the previous December, but brought back that August; horse services ceased for good the following spring. In 1886-87 the tramway's last four Wilkinson locos, Nos 9-12, were added to the fleet. The Company's financial problems resulted in a Receiver being appointed in 1890 and three years later it was taken over by a new concern, the Wigan & District Tramways Co. All the passenger cars and locos Nos 1-4 and 9 were scrapped, replaced by 16 large, enclosed bogie double-deckers of unknown origin, two Wilkinson locos (Nos 5 and 6) of 1884 vintage ex-BRIGHTON & SHOREHAM and five new Kitson engines (Nos 10-14). The remaining Wilkinson locos were renumbered 1-4 (the former 5-8) and 7-9 (the former 10-12). Kitson locos 15 and 16 were added in 1895 and 17 and 18 a year later.

By the early 1890s Wigan Corporation was planning its own tramway system, obtaining in 1893 the Wigan Corporation Act which empowered it to construct two separate lines from the town centre, one northeast to Martland Mill and the other southeast off the Company's line in Darlington Street to Platt Bridge, a total of nearly 4 miles of route. Two years later, before construction had begun, the WDT Co. obtained the Wigan and District Tramways Order to authorize a short link between the proposed Corporation lines and its own, plus a short extension at Platt Bridge. In the event only the line down the Warrington Road to Platt Bridge was constructed, opening on 2 September 1896 with the Company leasing the main

Corporation-owned section of the route. A third depot was then necessary and one built in Tram Street off Walthew Lane at the Platt Bridge terminus. Soon the Corporation was planning further lines and electric traction was now envisaged on a wider gauge (see below). For a short while the two systems co-existed until 30 September 1902 when the Corporation took over its independent rival.

Bibliography: *The Tramways of Wigan* E. K. Stretch (Manchester Transport Museum Society, 1978)

WIGAN CORPORATION TRAMWAYS

Authority: Wigan Corporation Act 1898
Gauge: 3ft 6in, 4ft 8½in
Traction: Overhead electric
Opened: 25 January 1901
Closed: 28 March 1931
System: Radial network
Length: 24.83 miles
Stock: 54 sd, 49 dd
Livery: Crimson lake & cream to 1913,
   then carmine red & white
Last Car: ?

As mentioned above, Wigan Corporation entered the tramway fray in 1893 when it obtained powers to construct two lines though it was not until 1898 that it was empowered to operate its own tramways, the first of which ran northeast from the town centre to Maitland Bridge (on a 3ft 6in gauge) and opened in January 1901 with cars 1-12, ERTCW open-toppers. A second route, north up Wigan Lane to the Boar's

Head, opened on 7 June that same year. More lines followed and the car fleet grew to keep pace with the addition in 1901 of open-toppers 13-24 and, in 1902, of open-top bogie car 26, all from ERTCW again. (No 25 was a works car.)

In 1902 the Corporation bought out its independent steam rival (see above) and, on 29 May 1903, the reconstructed Platt Bridge line re-opened though no more narrow gauge cars were bought for it as the decision had been taken to construct all future routes to standard gauge and regauge existing ones. The following year cars 1-12 were sold accordingly to COVENTRY.

The Pemberton line closed on 10 April 1904, re-opening on 26 July with electric trams on the new gauge (bogie single-deckers 27-50 from HN). On 2 September that year the regauged Platt Bridge line re-opened with the very last steam trams running on 26 September, to Hindley. (The steam services were worked on lease by the Wigan & District Tramways Co.) As the system continued to enlarge, so did the car fleet. In 1904-05 ERTCW supplied bogie combination cars 51-80 which met the tramway's needs until 1914 when UEC top-covered bogie vehicles 1-6 were bought, followed in 1920 by EE top-covered cars 7-12 whilst in 1921-22 the local firm of Massey Brothers constructed identical cars 81-92, using EE electrics, in Pemberton Depot. (No 80, with a unique cream livery, could be hired for weddings.)

It appears that the tramway, from the start, was not a financial success and a thorough overhaul of working practices was attempted and economy measures introduced. By the

time of World War I the narrow gauge track and cars were in an especially bad way and on 15 July 1923 the northeasterly route to Aspull via New Springs was closed for regauging with only the Wigan–New Springs section (inside the borough boundary) re-opening in stages to 23 December. (The outlying section was replaced by a bus service.) On 7 May 1925 the northwesterly route to Maitland Mill – the last narrow gauge line left – was closed with trolleybuses taking over that same day. On 22 August 1927 the Platt Bridge service was cut down to just workmen's cars (the others replaced by buses), followed on 30 November 1930 by the closure of the Ashton route entirely. On 28 February 1931 the Platt Bridge line closed for good, as did the Hindley route, leaving just the routes north to Standish (the extended Boar's Head line) and west to Abbey Lakes (the extended Pemberton line) to last another four weeks.

In many respects, the story of Wigan's tramways is one of lost opportunities. Not only was the town saddled with operating two differently-gauged systems but it failed to take full advantage of the proximity of its southern neighbour the SOUTH LANCASHIRE TRAMWAYS with connections at Ashton and Hindley only being made in 1926 and 1927 respectively.

Bibliography: as above

WIMBLEDON COMMON TRAMWAY

From 1864 to 1889 the National Rifle Association operated a seasonal tramway on Wimbledon Common to serve its summer Annual Meetings (begun in 1860). Relaid every year with very light (14lb/yd) sleepered rails on the turf, it ran to the various firing points and grew over the years to about a mile in length. The intial cost of installation, in time for the July 1864 event, was £400 and until 1876 the open four-wheeled cars (originally four, later at least six) were towed by horses ridden by soldiers beside the single standard gauge track. In 1877 however a Merryweather tram locomotive was borrowed from the manufacturers, named *Alexandra* in honour of the Princess of Wales and the line formally opened by her husband, the future King Edward VII (who even tried his hand at driving the loco himself).

The engine was obviously a success – it could haul six cars at once – for in 1878 it was bought and named *Wharncliffe* in honour of the Chairman of the NRA, Lord Wharncliffe,

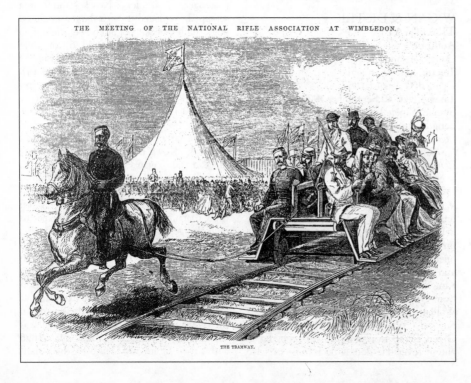

THE MEETING OF THE NATIONAL RIFLE ASSOCIATION AT WIMBLEDON.

THE TRAMWAY.

The Wimbledon Common temporary tramway as depicted in the Illustrated London News *of 23 July 1864.*

and worked the line until the 1883 season when one of the cars was fitted with an electric motor, taking and returning current via two copper strips laid between the rails, and put into service from 27 July. This experiment (in the very early days of electric traction) was not a success and *Wharncliffe* continued to work the line until 1889, its last summer operation.

In 1890 the Annual Meeting decamped to Bisley Common in western Surrey (where it thrives to this day) and the loco and portable line went with it, apparently being used until at least the summer of 1914 though further details are sadly lacking. The reconstruction of the tramway here as a 1.21-mile line was authorized by the National Rifle Association (Bisley Common Tramway) Order 1890 though it is thought that at both locations the route varied from year to year and members of the public – presumably interested spectators – as well as officials and competitors were carried from range to range.

Bibliography: *The London United Tramways Vol 1: Origins to 1912* C. S. Smeeton (The Light Rail Transit Association/The Tramway and Light Railway Society, 1995) 0 948106 13 1

WIRRAL TRAMWAY(S) *see* BIRKENHEAD: WIRRAL TRAMWAY (1) *and* (2)

WISBECH & UPWELL TRAMWAY

Authority: Great Eastern Railway Act 1881
Gauge: 4ft 8½in
Traction: Steam
Opened: 20 August 1883
Closed: 31 December 1927
System: Single line
Length: 5.9 miles
Stock: Locos*, 12 sd
Livery: Locos painted teak pre-1918, dark red to 1923 then brown; coaches painted teak pre-1918, then dark red
Last Train: ?

This roadside steam tramway was promoted, built and operated by the GER for the dual purpose of carrying passengers and agricultural produce from the villages southeast of the Cambridgeshire market town of Wisbech to its railway station there (Wisbech East). To avoid freight transhipment problems, the line was laid to standard railway gauge with bullhead rails to permit through running of goods wagons.

The line was built under the provisions of the Tramway Acts in order to keep costs down and its success helped pave the way for the 1896 Light Railway Act which was to facilitate greatly the construction of such rural lines. For virtually all its length it ran on a roadside reservation beside the moribund Wisbech Canal until it reached the twin villages of Outwell and Upwell on the border with Norfolk (which county it entered twice during its length). The last 1½ miles from Outwell Basin to Upwell Depot opened 8 September 1884.

Mixed goods and passenger trains were the norm though whilst the freight wagons travelled on from Wisbech, the passenger vehicles did not. The line's first four coaches were Starbuck ex-Millwall Extension Railway carriages, Nos 1 and 2 dating from 1871 and Nos 3 and 4 from a year later. In 1884 however the GER built four new, low carriages for the line: Nos 5 and 6 being four-wheeled vehicles and Nos 6 and 7 longer bogie coaches, all with ornate end balconies. A purpose-built luggage van (No 9) and a 1875 brake van (No 16) were added to the tramway's 'own' stock at the same time. In 1890 the original Nos 1-4 were withdrawn when the GER built another

The first passenger timetable for the opening of the final section of the Wisbech & Upwell Tramway.

GREAT EASTERN RAILWAY

OPENING

OF THE

WISBECH & UPWELL TRAMWAY

THROUGHOUT TO UPWELL

On MONDAY, 8th SEPTEMBER, 1884, the WISBECH & UPWELL TRAMWAY will be Open throughout to Upwell, and Tram Cars will run as under:—WEEK DAYS.

	a.m.	a.m.	a.m.	p.m.	p.m.	p.m.
Wisbech Station	6 45	9 15	11 40	2 15	5 10	7 50
Elm Bridge	7 3	9 35	12 0	2 33	5 28	8 8
Boyce's Bridge	7 17	9 50	12 15	2 47	5 42	8 22
Outwell Basin	7 25	10 0	12 25	2 55	5 50	8 30
Outwell Village	7 35	10 10	12 35	3 5	6 0	8 40
Upwell	7 45	10 20	12 45	3 15	6 10	8 50

	a.m.	a.m.	p.m.	p.m.	p.m.	p.m.
Upwell	7 55	10 30	12 55	3 40	6 25	9 0
Outwell Village	8 5	10 40	1 5	3 50	6 35	9 10
Outwell Basin	8 15	10 50	1 15	4 0	6 45	9 20
Boyce's Bridge	8 23	10 58	1 25	4 10	6 53	9 28
Elm Bridge	8 37	11 12	1 40	4 25	7 7	9 42
Wisbech Station	8 55	11 30	2 0	4 45	7 25	10 0

The Tram Cars will stop for the purpose of setting down or taking up Passengers at any point along the line of route.

FARES:—

	Wisbech 1st Class	2nd Cl.	Elm Bridge 1st Class	2nd Cl.	Boyce's Bridge 1st Class	2nd Cl.	Outwell Basin 1st Class	2nd Cl.	Outwell Village 1st Class	2nd Cl.	
Elm Bridge	3d.	2d.									
Boyce's Bridge	3d.	2d.	3d.	2d.							
Outwell Basin	3d.	2d.	3d.	2d.	2d.	1d.					
Outwell Village	4d.	3d.	3d.	2d.	3d.	2d.	2d.	1d.			
Upwell	4d.	3d.	4d.	3d.	3d.	2d.	2d.	1d.	2d.	1d.	Upwell

Personal Luggage not exceeding 28 lbs. in weight will be allowed to be taken by each Adult Passenger free of charge if carried by hand.

MERCHANDISE TRAFFIC

Will be dealt with at the following Sidings or Depots —

ELM BRIDGE, BOYCE'S BRIDGE, OUTWELL BASIN, OUTWELL BRIDGE, UPWELL.

Moderate charges for haulage will be made, particulars of these and other information can be obtained from the Company's Inspectors at the Depots, from the Station Agent at Wisbech, the District Goods Manager at Cambridge, or the Goods Manager, London, September, 1884. at Liverpool Street.

WILLIAM BIRT, General Manager.

Printed at the Stratford.

GER tram locomotive No 134 of 1897 and train at the Wisbech & Upwell Tramway's Upwell terminus. (Author's Collection)

four four-wheelers (which took their numbers).

To haul the trains the GER used its own distinctive steam tram locomotives taken from a fleet of ten 0-4-0s (Class G15) and, from 1903, twelve 0-6-0s (Class C53); those used on the line were shedded at March whilst the others of the fleet were employed on the GER's freight-only quayside lines at YARMOUTH, Colchester and Ipswich.

At the time of the 1923 Grouping the tramway passed, along with the rest of the GER, into the control of the LNER, which company terminated passenger services over the line at the end of 1927 in the face of the growing road competition. The tramway was subject to a 12mph speed restriction and frequent shunting stops. Goods traffic however continued until 20 May 1966, latterly operated by BR with trains hauled by specially-adapted diesel shunters (and for a brief period in 1930 before they went to the Yarmouth Quay line, a pair of 0-4-0 Sentinel locos). After the withdrawal of passenger services carriages 2-4 and 6-8 were transferred to the Kelvedon & Tollesbury Light Railway in Essex. No 8 was set aside for preservation after that line closed in 1951 and appeared in the Ealing comedy *The Titfield Thunderbolt* but was wantonly scrapped some time afterwards; the former No 7 however, rescued after many years in a field, can be seen undergoing restoration at the Rutland Railway Museum, Cottesmore.

Bibliography: *The Wisbech & Upwell Tramway* Chris Hawkins & George Reeve

(Wild Swan Publications, 1982) 0 906867 09 6

WOLVERHAMPTON TRAMWAYS
Authority: Wolverhampton Tramways Order 1877
Gauge: 4ft 8½in
Traction: Horse, steam
Opened: 1 May 1878
Taken Over: 1 May 1900
System: Radial
Length: 8.69 miles
Stock: 1 loco, 28 sd & dd horse & steam?
Livery: Maroon/nut brown & cream?

The Wolverhampton Tramways Co. Ltd (incorporated 14 December 1876) operated three routes radiating from the town centre. The first opened ran from Queen Square westwards to Newbridge on the Tettenhall Road; the second, opened 6 June 1878, ran eastwards from Queen Street (adjacent to Queen Square) along the Willenhall Road to the village of that name and the third (and longest) opened at the end of August 1879 and ran southwards from Queen Street down Bilston Road and Wellington Street, through Bilston and on to the village of Moxley.

The main depot was in Darlington Street by Queen Square, with later ones added in Newbridge and Moxley. The first route was operated by one-horse single-deck cars from Stephensons and Hughes and the other two by Hughes two-horse double-deckers; a Hughes tram locomotive was also used on the Tettenhall route from May to November 1881, hauling a pair of the double-deck cars

adapted for the purpose. Apparently unpopular with the travelling public, the use of steam ceased when the Town Council refused to allow the experimental licence period to be extended.

Further details of the rolling stock are patchy; by 1890 though the fleet numbers had reached 20 with new cars Nos 21-24 arriving from Falcon in 1892 and one from Milnes (No 25) three years later, all open-top double-deckers.

From 1896 onwards Wolverhampton Corporation was in protracted negotiations with the BET who wished to buy the line as part of its grand plan for a south Staffordshire network of electric tramways, but in the end the Corporation decided to go it alone and from 1 May 1900 became the owner of the three portions of the Company's routes which lay within the borough (some 6 miles in total). The price of £22,500 was fixed by arbitration and the portions of the routes outside the boundary (in Willenhall and Bilston) were purchased by the BET as from the same date. The Company was wound up after its last Annual General Meeting on 1 March the following year.

Bibliography: *Black Country Tramways Vol 1: 1872-1912* J. S. Webb (Author, Bloxwich, 1974)
A History of Wolverhampton Transport Vol 1: 1833 to 1930 Stanley Webb & Paul Addenbrooke (Birmingham Transport Historical Group/Uralia Press, Wolverhampton) 0 905103 07 6

WOLVERHAMPTON CORPORATION TRAMWAYS
Authority: Wolverhampton Corporation Act 1899
Gauge: 4ft 8½in, 3ft 6in
Traction: Horse, stud, overhead electric
Took Over: 1 May 1900
Closed: 30 November 1928
System: Network
Length: 13.85 miles
Stock: 20 dd horse; 25 sd, 44 dd electric
Livery: Dark green & gamboge
Last Car: ?

Included in the Corporation's purchase of the town's horse tramway (see above) were the Darlington Street and Newbridge depots and 17 cars (of which only twelve were serviceable). The Corporation promptly purchased three open-top double-deckers from the NORTH METROPOLTAN TRAMWAYS of LONDON (which retained their NMT numbers 285, 286 and 288) to help operate an increased-frequency service to Newbridge, along Willenhall Road as far as Coventry Street and on Bilston Road as far as Ettingshall Road.

Work on the new electric system began in May 1901 and on 17 September the Bilston Road horse car service was withdrawn. On 8 March 1902 the (latterly shortened) Tettenhall route closed with horse car services on the Willenhall route surviving another two years. The first mile of (narrow gauge) electrified track, in the Bilston Road from Cleveland Road to Ettingshall Road, was opened on 6 February 1902 using the Brown surface contact system of current supply manufactured by the Lorain Steel Co. of Ohio. (This system utilized magnetic skates under the cars to move contact switches within a series of metal boxes laid flush between the rails as they passed over them, so making the box covers live and thus supplying current to the cars.)

On 30 April 1902 the electric service was extended back from Cleveland Road to Victoria Square, with further routes following later that year north up Waterloo Road to the Molineux Football Ground and northwest to Newbridge (via both the Tettenhall Road and New Hampton Road). The initial car fleet was made up of single-deckers Nos 1 and 2 and open-top double-deckers Nos 3 and 19-24 from ERTCW plus single-deckers 4, 5, 7, 8, 10 and 12 and open-toppers 6, 9, 11 and 13-18 from Milnes; Nos 10-12 were the first three arrivals to inaugurate the electric service.

The fleet was joined in 1904 by Milnes open-toppers 25-30, in 1905 by UEC open-toppers 31-36 and single-deck combination cars 37-40 and in 1906 by Nos 41-43, three more of the same but equipped for both surface and overhead current collection. In 1908-09 UEC supplied open-toppers 44-49 and in 1913 Nos 50-52, top-covered cars. No further vehicles were bought until the early 1920s when EE supplied top-covered cars 53-56 (also dual-equipped) and single-deckers 57 and 58 in 1920 and top-covered 59-61 the following year (equipped for overhead current collection only) whilst in 1922 single-deckers 62-69 (also overhead-only) were bought from Brush to complete the fleet. Seveal of the open-toppers were later top-covered. The depot was in Cleveland Road (between the Fighting Cocks and Bilston routes) in the town centre.

Further routes were opened in 1904, these being the Dudley Road route to the Fighting Cocks, along the Willenhall Road east to the boundary at Deans Road, northeast along Wednesfield Road and Wolverhampton Road to Wednesfield and an extension of the Waterloo Road line to Bushbury Lane. In 1905 cars 1, 5, 7, 10, 19-28 and 37-40 were equipped for overhead as well as surface current collection so they could work through to Bilston Town Hall and Willenhall Market Place over WOLVERHAMPTON DISTRICT metals

Postcard of Wolverhampton Corporation No 44 of 1908 traversing the centre of the town in original open-top form and using the surface contact system of current supply. (Lens of Sutton)

(see below). That year also saw the introduction of Corporation motor bus services. On 10 September 1909 the last, short branch southwest along Lea Road to Stubbs Road, Penn Fields, was opened.

After World War I the idea was mooted of converting the tramways to overhead current supply and in 1921 the necessary work was undertaken, permitting through working from Dudley – though scarcely had this been done than it was decided to switch to trolleybus operation and on 23 July 1923 the Wednesfield route was closed for this reason whilst the Bushbury line went on 19 August

August 1924 (though football specials were run over it for another year). The last route to close was the Bilston line on 26 August 1928 though on 15 August 1925 the WD's Dudley–Fighting Cocks line (and Sedgley Depot) had been purchased by the Corporation and on 1 September 1928 it bought the remainder of the system (with the exception of the Willenhall–Darlaston line which had been worked by WALSALL cars since 1 October 1925); on 25 November 1928 the Fighting Cocks–Bilston line was closed with the remainder (including the Willenhall–Darlaston line) closing on the

Another Wolverhampton postcard, this time of dual-equipped No 22 outside Bilston Town Hall. (Lens of Sutton)

Postcard of one of the Wolverhampton & Stony Stratford's Green locomotives with two of the line's giant trailers in Wolverton Road, Stony Stratford. (Lens of Sutton)

last day of the month when the trolleybus conversion was complete.

Bibliography: as above

WOLVERHAMPTON DISTRICT ELECTRIC TRAMWAYS

Authority: Dudley and Wolverhampton
 Tramways Order 1899
Gauge: 3ft 6in
Traction: Overhead electric
Opened: 9 January 1902
Taken Over: 1 July 1904
System: Radial
Length: 14.67 miles
Stock: 38 dd
Livery: BET mustard & ivory, later Munich
 lake & cream

The Wolverhampton District Electric Tramways Ltd was registered on 17 December 1900 as a subsidiary set up by the BET to reconstruct and work its portion of the DUDLEY, SEDGLEY & WOLVERHAMPTON TRAMWAYS and WOLVERHAMPTON TRAMWAYS horse and steam systems recently purchased. Steam working on the Dudley–Wolverhampton line north of Sedgley ceased on 21 February 1901 to allow for electrification, the Dudley–Sedgley Depot section having been opened (and operated) by the DUDLEY, STOURBRIDGE & DISTRICT ELECTRIC TRAMWAYS for the BET from the previous October (and to Sedgley Bull Ring from 24 August 1901). On 9 January 1902 the northern portion to the Fighting Cocks (where it met the WOLVERHAMPTON CORPORATION TRAMWAYS' Dudley Road route – see above) was opened; from here an east-

eastwards line along Parkfield Road to Ettingshall and on via Millfields Road to Bilston Town Hall was opened on 14 July. The Corporation line to here was opened on 24 September with the rest of the system – southeast from Bilston to Moxley High Street with a short branch south to Bank Street, Bradley and northeast along Willenhall Road and Bilston Road to Willenhall then west from there back along (another) Willenhall Road to the Wolverhampton boundary at Deans Road – following later that year. No through running was possible with the Corporation on

on account of that system's use of a surface contact method of current supply. All routes were primarily single-track.

Services from Dudley were worked by DSD cars until early 1901 when the first WD cars arrived. These were of the batch Nos 1-13, ERTCW open-toppers followed in 1902 by open-toppers 14-30 from Brush. In 1904 cars 1-4 were exchanged with DSD cars 39-42 (and the numbers exchanged as well) though four years later two were returned and renumbered 31 and 32 by the WD. About 1914 the 'new' Nos 1-4 were cut down to single-deck form, along with No 18 (and possibly others), by which time an ex-BIRMINGHAM & MIDLAND open-topper had arrived on the line, taking the number 33, followed c1923 by No 34, another ex-B&M car. No 33 is thought to have been scrapped after this for in 1925 DSD 41 – another open-topper – was transferred as No 33 to the line. The only other addition to the fleet was ex-SOUTH STAFFORDSHIRE 34, an enclosed double-decker, transferred in 1924 and renumbered 18 (probably as the single-decker of that number had been withdrawn).

The depots were at Sedgley (the former steam depot) and at Mount Pleasant in Bilston at the start of Willenhall Road. From 1 July 1904 the system, along with the other Black Country lines of the BET, was controlled by the BIRMINGHAM & MIDLAND TRAMWAYS JOINT COMMITTEE.

Bibliography: as above and *Black Country Tramways Vol 2* J. S. Webb (Author, Bloxwich, 1976)

Another Wolverton & Stony Stratford postcard, this time of Bagnall locomotive No 5, supplied by the LNER, and 100-seater trailer outside the Foresters Arms, Stony Stratford. (Lens of Sutton)

WOLVERTON & STONY STRATFORD TRAMWAY

Authority: Wolverton and Stony Stratford
    Tramways Order 1883
Gauge: 3ft 6in
Traction: Steam
Opened: 27 May 1887
Closed: 3 May 1926
System: Single line
Length: 4.72 miles
Stock: 7 locos, 1 sd, 5 dd
Livery: Tawny-brown to 1920, then
    chocolate & white
Last Car: ?

This rural line was built to serve the LNWR's works in the Buckinghamshire village of Wolverton (chosen because it was halfway along the LNWR's predecessor, the London & Birmingham Railway) by linking it with the town of Stony Stratford, just over 2 miles to the west, where many of the railway workers lived. It had a very chequered history, despite the apparent obvious value of such a line, and it took no less than two Tramway Orders (1883 and 1884), two changes of proposed gauge (4ft 8½in to 4ft to 3ft 6in) and three different promoting companies before it commenced operations. It was built by a local contractor, Charles Herbert Wilkinson (who at the time was also constructing the NEWPORT PAGNELL & DISTRICT tramway), who formed the grand-sounding Wolverton & Stony Stratford District Light Railways Co. Ltd (incorporated 5 October 1886) to operate it.

Laid as a single track using grooved rails on the street sections and sleepered bullhead rails on the roadside stretches, the line as opened ran for nearly 2¾ miles from a reversing triangle on the east side of the main railway line at Wolverton which it then crossed by means of a bridge before travelling westwards along Stratford Road through the town (for so it became) and out beside the Wolverton Road to Stony Stratford. Here, a little way past the depot, it turned northwest at the Foresters Arms to run up the High Street for ½ mile to terminate outside the Barley Mow. The only 'branch' was a short spur at the Wolverton terminus into the railway goods yard.

The original stock comprised Krauss tram locomotives Nos 1 and 2 and four double-deck bogie cars from Midland. Three of these were enormous, 44ft-long vehicles with roofs and end glazing on the upper decks and a seating capacity of 100; the fourth car was similar but only seated 80, being shorter. It soon became clear that the Krauss locos were not up to the job of pulling two (!) of these trailers – some of the largest tramcars ever in Britain – and two more powerful, Green engines (Nos 1 and 2) were bought soon after the opening to replace them.

Later in 1887 a further Order authorized the construction of a 2.04-miles extension up the High Street to Old Stratford, then south-west to the Fox & Hounds in the village of Deanshanger. The extension opened sometime in 1888 and to work it a third Krauss loco (No 3), similar to the first pair, was bought together with a 20-seater four-wheeled roofed toastrack from Midland whilst the main route's stock was augmented by a 50-seater Midland trailer similar in type to the earlier four. The purpose of the extension was really to carry freight rather than passengers (a number of goods wagon were also bought) but the amount of traffic hoped for failed to materialize; matters were not helped by the Company (the Wolverton & Stony Stratford Tramroads Co. Ltd since 26 July 1889) going into liquidation and the line being closed by the Official Receiver on 17 December that year.

On 20 November 1891 the Barley Mow-Wolverton section was re-opened, backed by a private syndicate until 15 September 1893 when a new concern, the Wolverton & Stony Stratford & District New Tramway Co. Ltd(!) took over. In 1904 a sixth loco (No 4) was purchased, this time from Brush, and in 1910 the Stony Stratford High Street section was abandoned, partly because of the growing traffic on what was in fact a major trunk road (the A5) and partly because of deteriorating track. This second factor applied to the rest of the line as well and on 17 July 1919 the Company went into liquidation.

In February 1920 the LNWR took control, anxious to maintain the line as a transport facility for its workers, and immediately put to work a small Bagnall saddle tank (No 5) fitted with side skirts and extended chimney, at the same time relaying the track. Increasing bus competition however would almost certainly have soon killed off the line had not the General Strike of 4 May 1926 pre-empted any such decision by the then owner, the LMS.

Some confusion exists regarding the stock details. It is possible that the Green locos were briefly numbered 4 and 5 until the Krauss 1 and 2 were withdrawn in 1887; also, it is not known how the trailers were numbered as only one of the 100-seaters is known to have carried a number (2) and that in later years.

Bibliography: *The Wolverton & Stony
    Stratford Trams* Frank D. Simpson (The
    Omnibus Society, 1981) 0 901307 42 4

WOOLLEN DISTRICT see YORKSHIRE (WOOLLEN DISTRICT)

WOOLWICH & SOUTH EAST LONDON TRAMWAYS see LONDON: WOOLWICH & SOUTH

LONDON: WOOLWICH & SOUTH EAST LONDON TRAMWAYS

WOOTTON TRAMWAY see BRILL TRAMWAY

WORCESTER TRAMWAYS

Authority: Worcester Tramways Order 1881
Gauge: 3ft
Traction: Horse
Opened: 18 February 1884
Closed: 28 June 1903
System: Radial
Length: 3.28 miles
Stock: 2 sd?, 10 dd?
Livery: ?
Last Car: ?

This small city system's principal claim to fame is that it had no less than five different owners during its short life. It was built by the Tramways Trust Co. Ltd, who operated three short single-track routes radiating from The Cross in the city centre: northwards along the Barbourne Road to the Vine Hotel in Barbourne, eastwards to the GWR's Shrub Hill station and westwards across the River Severn and past the depot at the Bull Ring, St Johns, to the Portobello pub in Bransford Road in the district of that name. The original cars were six Falcon double-deckers, numbered according to their licences, joined by 1900 by another double-decker and two single-deckers.

The Company was not a financial success and went into liquidation until 1889 when it was sold to the City of Worcester Tramways Co. Ltd. Three years later though this company too went into liquidation and on 13th August 1893 it was sold to a Birmingham firm of consulting engineers, Pritchard Green & Co., passing on 27 February 1894 to a new company, Worcester Tramways Ltd, who also operated horse bus feeder services. Within a few years thoughts of electrification were being expressed and in 1898 the BET bought an interest in the Company, registering a subsidiary, the Worcester Electric Traction Co., on 22 August 1902 to work the line (which it did from 31 October of that year with the purchase of the WT Ltd completed). An unknown number of cars was then added to the fleet. Authority had already been granted the previous year for electrification and in 1903 the tramway closed to enable extensive reconstruction to take place (see below).

Bibliography: *A Short History of the Worcester
    Tramways 1881-1928* H. H. Grundy
    (Author)
Tramways of the West Country P. W. Gentry
    (The Light Railway Transport League, 2nd
    ed 1960)

WORCESTER ELECTRIC

One of a series of postcards issued at the time of the 1903 reconstruction of the Worcester Tramways.
(Author's Collection)

WORCESTER ELECTRIC TRAMWAYS

Authority: Worcester Tramways Act 1901;
    Worcester and District Light Railways
    Order 1901
Gauge: 3ft 6in
Traction: Overhead electric
Opened: 6 February 1904
Closed: 31 May 1928
System: Radial
Length: 5.86 miles
Stock: 17 dd
Livery: Holly green & cream
Last Car: ?

The reconstruction of the Worcester horse tramway (see above) – an event of some inconvenience known locally as 'the Worcester Tramway Siege' – occupied the remainder of 1903; the old depot was converted to house the new fleet of 15 Brush open-top cars and the horse lines lifted and replaced.

The new routes corresponded almost exactly to the old, the essential differences being that the final Bransford Road section was abandoned, replaced by a southerly ½-mile stretch (opened 25 August 1906) down Malvern Road to the Brunswick Arms, and

a northern branch left the Shrub Hill line to head on up Rainbow Hill to Astwood Cemetery. The system was mainly single track though a long double-track section southwards down the High Street led to single-track branches along the London Road (opened 30 April 1904) and Bath Road (opened 2 July 1904). As the new cars were supplied in batches, temporary assistance was provided by cars loaned by the BIRMINGHAM & MIDLAND TRAMWAYS JOINT COMMITTEE.

In 1921 two new cars (Nos 16 and 17) were supplied to the line, built by the BMTJC as slighter smaller versions of the older Brush cars. Five years later Worcester Corporation obtained an Act to authorize it to purchase the system, did so for £58,000 then promptly closed it in favour of an all-bus service to be operated by the Birmingham & Midland Omnibus Co. (later Midland Red). After the closure Nos 16 and 17 were sold to CHEL-TENHAM and the remainder of the fleet scrapped.

Bibliography: as above

YARMOUTH & GORLESTON TRAMWAYS

Authority: East Anglian Tramway Order
    1871
Gauge: 4ft 8in/3ft 6in
Traction: Horse
Opened: 25 March 1875
Taken Over: 12 March 1905
System: Single line
Length: 3.25 miles
Stock: 10 dd?
Livery: ?

The first passenger street tramway in East Anglia (the earliest goods tramway being YARMOUTH QUAY and earliest passenger tramway SOUTHEND PIER) was a 3-mile line from the GER's Southtown station in Gorleston, just across the River Yare from the main part of Great Yarmouth, down Southtown Road to the bottom of Gorleston High Street where the depot was sited. It was a single-track line originally promoted by the East Anglian Tramway Co., which concern transferred its powers in 1872 to the East Suffolk Tramway Co. who eventually built the line. It was laid to the not uncommon early 'standard' railway gauge of 4ft 8in.

In 1878 the line was purchased by the Yarmouth & Gorleston Tramways Co. Ltd and in 1882 extended from the depot down Lowestoft Road and Englands Lane to the quayside; at the same time it was relaid to a gauge of 3ft 6in. The new line was worked by ten Midland open-top double-deckers; whether these were rebuilds of the original stock or new cars is not known. The Company also operated seven horse buses in conjunction with the tramway and had an interest in the Yarmouth & Gorleston Steamboat Co. Ltd.

In 1905 the concern was bought by Great Yarmouth Corporation for £13,211 with the takeover taking place from 12 March that year; consequently the Corporation became a horse tramway as well as an electric tramway operator (see below) for a brief period while work progressed on electrifying and extending its acquisition.

Bibliography: *The Tramways of East Anglia* R. C. Anderson (The Light Railway Transport League, 1969) 0 900433 00 0
Transport in Great Yarmouth Vol 1: Electric Tramways 1902-1918 T. Baker (Author, Chipping Sodbury, 1980) 0 950688 90 8

GREAT YARMOUTH CORPORATION TRAMWAYS

Authority: Great Yarmouth Corporation Act 1899
Gauge: 3ft 6in
Traction: Overhead electric, horse
Opened: 19 June 1902
Closed: 14 December 1933
System: Network + branching
Length: 9.94 miles
Stock: 35 dd electric; 3 dd horse
Livery: Maroon & cream
Last Car: No 6 (official)*

Great Yarmouth Corporation was one of the handful of operators who ran a tramway system made up of two discrete sections. This was a result of the distinctive topography of the town: a long, thin development on a spit of land between the River Yare and the sea to the east and the riverside suburb of Gorleston-on-Sea across the Yare to the west. A link between the two was provided high up the river by the lifting Haven Bridge opposite Southtown station but this was not suitable for trams until rebuilt in 1930, by which time it was too late.

The western section was the rebuilt YARMOUTH & GORLESTON horse tramway (see above) which was worked by the Corporation with three of the Y&G horse cars for some three months before electric services began on 4 July 1905 (horse services ceased the same day); this ran over the same route but with a ¼-mile extension along Lowestoft Road to Springfield Road close to Gorleston-on-Sea railway station, plus a ¼-mile branch from the depot down Pier Plain to meet the (abandoned) former horse line in England Lane and on via Brush Quay to the beach.

The first section of the eastern two-thirds of the system was opened on 19 June 1902; this consisted of two main routes,

Postcard of Great Yarmouth Corporation No 16 of 1905 on the rural Caister Road route before, as elsewhere, suburban sprawl began. (Lens of Sutton)

the first being from Wellington Pier northwards along Marine Parade, then inland up St Peters Road and King Street, through the Market Place and out along Northgate Street to the district of Newtown (and the depot in Caister Road). The second cross-town route ran from Vauxhall station in the west, across the River Bure, then southwards along North Quay and Hall Quay, up Regent Street to the Market Place (where it joined and left the first route), thence via Regent Road to the northern end of Marine Parade, then south to Wellington Pier.

The first services were worked by open-top Brush cars Nos 1-14 which were joined in 1905 by another twelve (Nos 15-26), the bulk of which worked the Gorleston section (which had its own depot by the old horse sheds). Lines were a mixture of single and double tracks.

On 14 October 1904 a short branch from St Peters Road along Blackfriars Road to Camden Road was opened as an extension of the Kings Street line and shortly after this the short section in St Peters Road down to the Marine Parade was abandoned. On 19 August 1905 the Camden Road branch was extended to the Fish Wharf on the Yare and on 16 May 1907 the Newtown route was extended northwards across the town boundary as a single-track line along the main road for some 1½ miles past the Racecourse to Caister-on-Sea. To work the new routes – which completed the system – another nine Brush open-toppers (Nos 27-35) were brought during 1906 and 1907, completing the car fleet.

In the years immediately following World War I poor financial returns from the tramways led the Corporation to take reme-

Postcard of the quayside at Great Yarmouth showing the passenger and goods tramway lines. The opening Haven Bridge (right) over the River Yare prevented connection to the Gorleston portion of the Corporation system. (Author's Collection)

remedial action. In 1920 it started its own motor bus services and the cost of track renewal led, on 14 May 1924, to the closure of the Fish Wharf route. The remainder of the system was then refurbished – but only as a temporary expedient whilst the bus fleet was built up – with the next closure coming at the end of the summer season in September 1928 when the Vauxhall station branch closed for the last time – though some reports give a date a year later. (Several sections of the Yarmouth system, as in other seaside resorts, were always or often worked summers only.)

The last Gorleston tram (No 17) ran on 25 September 1930 (Nos 15-28 were currently in the depot there) and the last service car over the surviving Wellington Pier–Caister route ran on Thursday 14 December 1933, both services replaced by motor buses. The next day car No 6 was brought out for a ceremonial 'last trip'. The trams were then all scrapped, with 20 of the bodies going to become chalets at Caister Holiday Camp where they joined five bought earlier from the Gorleston stock.

Bibliography: as above and *Transport in Great Yarmouth Vol 2: 1919-1933 Electric Tramways & Petrol Omnibuses* T. Baker (Author, Chipping Sodbury, 1983) 0 950688 91 6

YARMOUTH QUAY TRAMWAY

Until December 1975 Great Yarmouth had another working tramway, though for goods only. When the town's first station – Vauxhall – was opened in 1844 by the Yarmouth & Norwich Railway, there was no convenient bridge across the River Bure to provide a speedy link with both the residential area and the quays on the River Yare. One was opened in 1848 however to allow horse-drawn vehicles to reach the station and this carried a single-track standard gauge tramway from the railway down the North Quay, Hall Quay and South Quay (a route later shared by the Corporation's trams); in 1867 it was extended down Southgates Road to the Fish Wharf, some 1½ miles from Vauxhall.

In May 1882 an extension northwards from the North Quay bypassing Vauxhall station was built by the Yarmouth Union Railway to link its Beach station, to the north of the town, with the quays. This line was just over a mile in length, though only the first 200yd or so was a street tramway, the rest being constructed as a railway branch. (The YNR and the YUR later became parts of the GER and the Midland & Great Northern Joint Railway respectively.)

Various sidings were added to the system over the years to serve neighbouring commercial premises, the longest one being some 300yd of double track laid in 1882 down Southgates Road behind the Fish Wharf.

Horses were used on the tramway until 1875 when two G15 class tram locos (identical to those used on the GER's WISBECH & UPWELL line) were introduced. These were replaced in 1908 by a pair of the more powerful C53 class locos (again as on the W&U) with a third arriving later. In 1931 the W&U's two Sentinels were transferred to the line to replace two of these (the third C53 was kept in reserve); one was withdrawn in 1948 and the other replaced in 1952 by two British Railways Class 04 Drewry 0-6-0 diesel shunters (again as on the W&U). Declining traffic during the 1960s and early 1970s led to the gradual cutback of the tramway and its eventual closure. Odd sections of the track can still be seen though, notably on the quayside and on the Bure bridge to Vauxhall (once more the town's only station); the Corporation tramways' rails which occupied the other side of the bridge after crossing the Quay Tramway in North Quay have long since been lifted.

CITY OF YORK TRAMWAYS

Authority: York Tramways Order 1879
Gauge: 4ft
Traction: Steam, horse
Opened: 27 October 1880
Taken Over: 27 February 1909
System: Branching
Length: 2.75 miles
Stock: 1 dd steam; 10 sd, 5 dd horse
Livery: Chocolate & white

The first serious proposals for tramways in York were made in the late 1870s and came rapidly to fruition with an 1879 Order authorizing the construction of two lines on the south and east sides of the city. Only the first of these was eventually built though, running northwards along the Fulford Road from the Plough Inn to Fishergate just over the River Foss from the Castle. Services began with three single-deck Starbuck horse trams and a Perrett pattern double-deck steam car. Complaints were received from residents about the latter vehicle and it was returned to its Nottingham makers Manlove, Alliott & Fryer in the December after the opening. (A similar car worked on the Dublin & Lucan tramway in Ireland – see Section 4.)

On 29 July 1882 a westwards extension of the line was opened through the city centre via Tower Street, Clifford Street, Micklegate, Blossom Street and The Mount to Mount Vale, Knavesmire. A short branch (under 3 furlongs) from the end of Bridge Street round into Station Road to serve the NER's station completed the tiny system (though this branch closed just four years later). Both lines were single-track, except for a short section in Clifford Street.

Following the opening of the extension and station branch, two further cars were ordered but later disposed of and five others – all single-deckers – were purchased, possibly from Starbuck again. In 1885 the line's owners, the York Tramways Co., was taken over by IMPERIAL TRAMWAYS and from 1 January 1886 the system was operated by a subsidiary, the City of York Tramways Co.

In 1890 seven of the eight cars had upper deck seating added, which made for a very real hazard for passengers when negotiating the Micklegate Bar archway through the city walls! In 1903 five second-hand cars, all double-deckers, were acquired to replace the same number from the ageing fleet.

The opening years of the 20th century were marred by disputes between the Company and the Corporation over the state of the track; by now the Corporation was entitled to purchase the system and in 1909 exercised this right, the actual takeover day being 27 February. Thereafter the Corporation operated the line itself until work on its expansion and electrification scheme necessitated its closure later that year (see below).

Bibliography: *The Horse Tramways of York* Hugh Murray (The Light Rail Transit Association, 1980) 0 900433 81 7

YORK CORPORATION TRAMWAYS

Authority: York Corporation Light Railways Order 1908
Gauge: 3ft 6in
Traction: Horse/overhead electric
Took Over: 27 February 1909
Closed: 16 November 1935
System: Radial
Length: 8.49 miles
Stock: 8 dd horse?; 5 sd, 45 dd electric
Livery: Royal blue & cream to 1931, then bright blue & white
Last Car: No 1 (official)

Work began on converting the horse tramway (see above) on 1 September 1909 just before it closed (on 7 September) and the first route opened (on 20 January 1910) was the rebuilt 2-mile Fulford–Nessgate portion of the old line with the (enlarged) depot at Fulford Cross housing Brush open-toppers 1-18 delivered in batches before and after the re-opening.

The next line opened ran for 1¾ miles from Nessgate across the River Ouse and along the route of the horse line branch to the station and on via Queen Street to Blossom Street to rejoin the old main line which it followed southwest to Knavesmire, continuing on to Dringhouses on the Tadcaster Road. This extension opened on 17 March 1910 (with the whole line being worked as one route) together with a short spur west off Blossom Street to the railway bridge in Holgate Road. This line was then extended along Acomb Road to the district of that name on 9 June using two cars based at a temporary depot at Acomb, passengers having to cross Holgate Bridge on foot until 1 August 1911 while it was being rebuilt. Also opened on 9 June 1910 was a northern line from the railway station (the natural hub of the system) across Lendal Bridge and out through Bootham Bar (½ mile) and Clarence Street to Haxby Road which it followed for another mile to Rose Street (extended in January 1916 a couple of hundred yards to the Rowntree Cocoa Works). To cope with the increased traffic, Brush open-toppers 20-23 were added to the fleet, followed in 1911 by Nos 24-27, four more of the same.

On 30 July 1913 a southern route was opened, from the Queen Street/Blossom Street junction along Nunnery Lane, New York Street, Bishopthorpe Road, Balmoral Terrace and Queen Victoria Street to South Bank. Four more Brush open-toppers (Nos 28-31) were purchased but these were apparently not sufficient and the following year single-deck trailers 32-35 were also bought from that company (who had unsuccessfully offered the Corporation its ex-CANVEY ISLAND cars) for use at peak periods; these were joined in 1916-17 by open-toppers 36-41 from the same firm.

On 14 June 1916 the mainly double-track system was completed with the opening of an eastern branch from Nessgate along Walmgate and Lawrence Street to the Bee's Wing Hotel on the Hull Road. In 1925 EE single-deck one-man car 37 entered service after a fleet renumbering: Nos 20-31 became 19-30, Nos 36-41 became 31-36 and the water car (No 19) and the trailers lost their numbers (the latter presumably being withdrawn).

In 1929 the Corporation built itself open-toppers 37 and 38 using two trailer car bodies, a spare truck and the truck from the water car (the former No 37 was cut down to serve as a salt/sand wagon) and these were joined that same year by ex-WOLVERHAMPTON open-toppers Nos 39-41 and in 1930 by Nos 42-45, ex-BURTON top-covered cars. By now though the trams were running at a loss and the Corporation decided to replace them (and the feeder trolleybuses which it had been operating since 1920) with motor buses, setting up on 1 April 1934 a Joint Committee with the West Yorkshire Road Car Co. to carry out this policy with their shared bus fleets. On 6 January 1935 the Dringhouses route was abandoned and less than a year later the remainder of the system followed suit, the official Last Car ironically being the very one that had opened

~~that had opened~~ it a quarter of a century before.

YORKSHIRE (WEST RIDING) ELECTRIC TRAMWAYS

Authority: The West Riding Tramways Act 1904
Gauge: 4ft 8½in
Traction: Overhead electric
Opened: *
Closed: 25 July 1932*
System: Divided network
Length: 24.13 miles
Stock: 83 dd
Livery: Crimson lake & cream pre-WWI, then green & cream
Last Car: ?

The Yorkshire (West Riding) Electric Tramways Co. Ltd was registered on 4 April 1905 to acquire, construct and operate a network of some 50 route miles of tramways in the West Riding area; half of these however were never constructed and the final grand scheme comprised only the WAKEFIELD & DISTRICT system (which had opened in 1904) and a second, separate line linking the towns of Normanton and Pontefract via Castleford. This latter tramway, a single-track, single line route 7.18 miles long, opened 29 October 1906 using half-a-dozen ex-W&D cars; by the time the route closed on 1 November 1925 a total of 16 were housed at Castleford Depot (of which ten were left for later sale). The route was never a financial success – partly because its planned branches were never built but primarily because neither were its planned connections with the Wakefield portion of the system – and the inevitable motorbus competition of the 1920s quickly killed it off. The last car was No 13, one of the ex-W&D vehicles.

As for the Wakefield network, this lasted until the 1930s before the buses won out. The main route from Leeds to Sandal (and the associated Rothwell branch) closed on 31 May 1932 whilst the Agbrigg–Ossett line followed suit just two months later.

The two systems were worked by 83 passenger cars in all: the 55 ex-W&D vehicles, six UEC top-covered double-deckers of 1906 (Nos 56-61), six UEC open-toppers of the same date (Nos 62-67), eight top-covered double-deckers built by Brush in 1899 for Leeds, covered in 1913, hired in 1913 and purchased in 1919 (Nos 68-75) and eight EE top-covered double-deckers of 1920 and numbered in 21-28 to replace eight cars destroyed in a 1917 fire in Castleford Depot. The system also employed amongst its fleet of works cars four unnumbered salt trailers rebuilt from ex-DEWSBURY, BATLEY & BIRSTAL steam trailers.

Bibliography: *The Tramways of Dewsbury & Wakefield* W. Pickles (The Light Rail Transit Association, 1980)
0 900433 73 6

YORKSHIRE (WOOLLEN DISTRICT) ELECTRIC TRAMWAYS

Authority: Spen Valley Light Railways Order 1901
Gauge: 4ft 8½in
Traction: Overhead electric
Opened: 18 February 1903?
Closed: 31 October 1934
System: Network
Length: 22.92 miles
Stock: 31 sd, 50 dd
Livery: Crimson lake & cream pre-WWI, then maroon & primrose
Last Car: No 11

The Yorkshire (Woollen District) Electric

Local photographers were never slow to issue postcards to mark tramway accidents and other disasters. Here Yorkshire (Woollen District) cars are held up by a flood at Batley Carr on 25 May 1925. (Lens of Sutton)

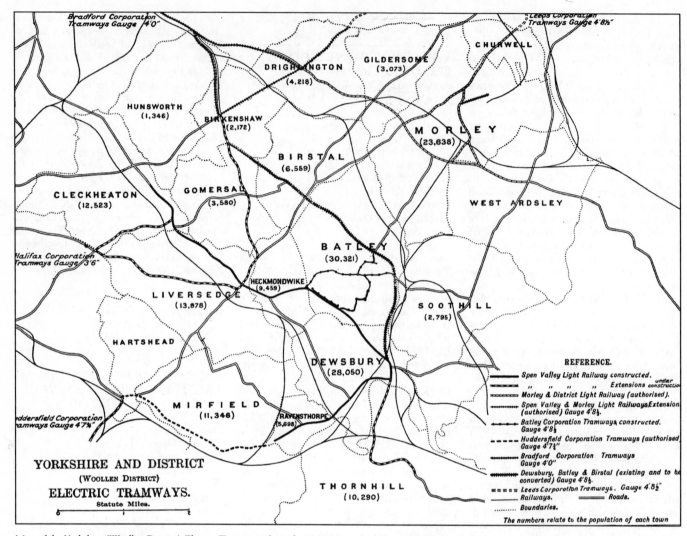

Map of the Yorkshire (Woollen District) Electric Tramways, from the 1904 Manual of Electrical Undertakings.

The Yorkshire (Woollen District) Electric Tramways Co. Ltd, a BET subsidiary, was registered on 19 November 1901 to build and operate tramways in what was known (on account of the type of goods manufactured there) as the Heavy Woollen District of the West Riding of Yorkshire. The bulk of these lines had been authorized by a LRO of 1901, radiating from the towns of Thornhill in the south, Ravensthorpe in the southwest, Dewsbury and Cleckheaton in the northeast and Birkenshaw in the north (to connect with the BRADFORD system though the latter's gauge of 4ft prevented through running).

The first section to open was the 2½-mile southerly branch from Combs Hill through Thornhill to Dewsbury, followed on 15 March by the joining Ravensthorpe to Dewsbury branch; an isolated section from the Moorhead terminus through Cleakheaton to Heckmondwike Market Place opened on 24 April of the same year. The reason for

opening separate sections was that the Company was in dispute with Batley Corporation over the use of part of the section linking them north of Dewsbury; with the resolution of the disagreement that same year however the rest of the Spen Valley system, with one exception, was open by 13 October. The only portion to be added to the network was the former DEWSBURY, BATLEY & BIRSTAL line (now electrified); this opened to the public on 23 November 1905, together with its short connection from the former terminus at Gomersal to the main route to Bradford.

Generally speaking, the lines started out from their termini as single tracks, doubling when they neared Dewsbury. Like its neighbours though – DEWSBURY & OSSETT, BATLEY and the YORKSHIRE (WEST RIDING) systems – the tramway was killed by bus competition in the 1930s, the only difference being that the Company itself became a bus operator, closing the system in

quick stages between 19 March 1932 (Liversedge–Hightown and Birstall-Birkenshaw) and 31 October 1934 (Dewsbury–Cleckheaton).

The tramway operated a fleet of 81 passengers cars in all, made up as follows:

Nos 1-6: Brush single-deckers of 1902
Nos 7-48: Brush open-top double-deckers of 1902-03
Nos 49-56: BEC open-toppers of 1903 (Batley's cars)
Nos 57, 58: Brush single-deckers of 1903
No 59: BEC single-decker of 1904
Nos 60-69: Brush single-deckers of 1904-05
Nos 70-73: Brush single-deckers of 1900 bought from SHEFFIELD CORPORATION in 1919
Nos 74-81: a mixed lot of ex-Sheffield single-deckers bought in 1920

Bibliography: as above

Section 2

Tramways of Wales

(Including Monmouthshire)

The tramways of Wales fall neatly into three geographical groupings, each with its own distinctive characteristics: the South, the North West and the North East. The earliest were those of the South, found in the towns and industrial areas of the coast and the coal-mining valleys immediately inland. As such they fulfilled predominantly the same purpose as those of their English urban counterparts (and were subject to the same promotional and operating procedures and regulations): to provide a public transport service for the working masses. As in England, they moved rapidly from horse to electric traction with mainly standard gauge lines spreading outwards to produce local systems serving housing developments, shopping centres and industrial areas alike well into the 1930s and 1940s.

The five tramways of the North West were of a totally different type altogether: short, narrow gauge, single-track horse-worked lines built on the sandy coast to cater for summer holidaymakers. They followed in the wake of the late-19th century development of this part of Wales as a holiday region – some were even there from the beginning in a previous existence as contractors' tram-roads servicing the building plots. Their size and seasonal operation meant that they could not justify the capital investment needed to make the transition from horse to mechanical traction and, victims of changing fashions, they failed to last beyond the 1920s. Ironically, had they survived until the 1960s or 1970s, they probably would have enjoyed a new lease of life as tourist attractions in their own right.

Stretching in a narrow arc from Llandudno eastwards along the coast to the Dee estuary then south to the English border at Chirk, the North East group of four systems, despite their close proximity to each other, had nothing in common other than their sheer diversity. Gauges ranged from 2ft 4¼in to 3ft 6in; traction could be steam,

horse, cable or electricity; passengers were holidaymakers and coalminers – even mineral freight and corpses were carried. Despite their astonishing diversity – or perhaps because of it – these lines proved to be the hardiest of all the Welsh tramways. Excluding the special case of modern pleasure lines (see Section 7), of the original five North East systems one – up the GREAT ORME at Llandudno – survives as Wales' only operational tramway and two – the LLANDUDNO & COLWYN BAY and GLYN VALLEY tramways – are central to the long-term aspirations of their associated preservation groups.

Coupled with on-going attempts to reinstate at least part of the SWANSEA & MUMBLES line, the construction of a replica horse tram on the Fairbourne Railway to honour its tramway origins and the regular use of two former Glyn Valley carriages on the Talyllyn Railway, in one form or another the tramway heritage of Wales is still kept very much alive.

ABERDARE URBAN DISTRICT COUNCIL TRAMWAYS

Authority: Aberdare Urban District
   Council Act 1911
Gauge: 3ft 6in
Traction: Overhead electric
Opened: 9 October 1913
Closed: 1 April 1935
System: Branching
Length: 5.77 miles
Stock: 10 sd, 16 dd
Livery: Maroon & white
Last Car: No 7

Following an unsuccessful 1899 LRO application by the BET to construct an electric tramway in the town, Aberdare UDC applied for its own powers to lay just over 4 miles of line from Trecynon in the northwest to Abercwmboi in the southeast (where it would meet a proposed Mountain

Ash UDC system). After several false starts, authority was acquired in 1911 for just 2¾ miles, the shortened line being from Trecynon into the town to terminate in Clarence Street in the district of Aberaman; the tramway was single-track and the first ten cars (Nos 11-20) were single-deck Brush vehicles. The UDC bought eight Cedes Stoll trolleybuses to work four feeder routes at the same time for it was the first (and only) example of the inauguration of a joint tram/trolleybus system in the British Isles. The depot was on the site of the former Gadlys Ironworks.

In 1914 four Brush open-toppers were purchased and numbered 6-9; at the same time it became clear that the trolleybuses were not a success and it would be better to lengthen the tramway. In the years following World War I there was talk of extending the system to link up with those of RHONDDA and PONTYPRIDD but out of all the talk only short single-track lines southeast to Abercwmboi and southwest to Cwmaman from Aberaman were constructed; the former opened in the spring of 1922 and the latter in the autumn. To work these extra routes another twelve Brush double-deckers (Nos 1-5, 10 and 21-26) were ordered.

It was however a case of too little, too late. Collieries were shutting and the popu-lation declining with the result that workmen's and other traffic decreased steadily. In 1934 the Council decided to close the tramway and substitute motor bus services. The Trecynon line closed on 30 September and the other two routes the following April. They had however outlasted the trolleybuses in no uncertain fashion – the last one oper-ational had broken down ignominiously on 23 July 1925, bringing what was left of the service to an abrupt and unlamented halt.

SOLOMON ANDREWS

Solomon Andrews was a Cardiff businessman who, in the second half of the 19th century, built up a sizeable commercial empire in the retail, coachbuilding, removal and transportation fields. Beginning as a baker and confectioner, he moved into the horse cab business in Cardiff in 1863, then into horse buses. From 1884 onwards he traded as S. Andrews & Son, which firm is still in existence. He had property interests throughout Wales, notably around Pwllheli and Barmouth, and later constructed the BARMOUTH JUNCTION & ARTHOG and PWLLHELI & LLANBEDROG tramways to help develop them.

By the 1870s Andrews was building his own buses and in 1882 patented a design which enabled a horse bus to run on tramway rails, an invention not at all popular with the tramway companies! Not content with being a major horse bus builder (and operator in several British towns and cities), he also operated street tramways in CARDIFF, PONTYPRIDD and NEWPORT.

Bibliography: *Keep Moving: The Story of Solomon Andrews and His Family* John F. Andrews (Stewart Williams, Barry, 1976) 0 900807 23 7

ARTHOG see BARMOUTH JUNCTION & ARTHOG

BANGOR PIER TRAMWAY

A manually-worked 3ft gauge luggage line was operated on the 1,550ft Bangor Pier (opened 14 May 1896) before World War I and was basically the contractor's grooved rail line down the centre of the decking. The pier was used by steamers from Liverpool and the North Wales coast and the tramway actually ran onto the floating boarding stage at the end via a flexible bridge. Although a scheme was promoted in 1898 to extend the line through the city to the railway station and electrify it, the proposal came to nothing. The pier was damaged during World War I by a cargo steamer which broke free from its nearby moorings and it is believed that the track was removed during subsequent repairs. Even if it had been repaired, it would probably have not survived in use any longer than its counterpart at BEAUMARIS directly across the Menai Straits.

Bibliography: *North Wales Tramways* Keith Turner (David & Charles, 1979) 0 7153 7769 8

BARMOUTH JUNCTION & ARTHOG TRAMWAYS

Authority: –
Gauge: 3ft
Traction: Horse
Opened: August 1899
Closed: 1903?
System: Single line
Length: c2 miles
Stock: *
Livery: Dark red & white
Last car: ?

Unfortunately little in the way of recorded facts survive regarding this grandly-titled line situated immediately to the east of the Barmouth Viaduct on the southern shore of the Mawddach estuary. Here Solomon ANDREWS had, in 1894, purchased land with the aim of developing a holiday resort. The land involved was mainly agricultural, stretching from the shore to the hill farms behind and formed part of the hamlet of Arthog. Also included were the remains of tramroads built in the 1860s for bringing stone down from hillside quarries for the construction of the viaduct; these were pressed into service to help in the construction of three short terraces of houses, including one (Mawddach Crescent) on a new promenade and sea wall.

For various reasons – including flooding and erosion affecting the rest of the proposed development – the envisaged resort never grew beyond this small beginning. For a short while though part of the tramroad network was used for passenger traffic, apparently using a car borrowed from Andrews' PWLLHELI & LLANBEDROG line, the part in question being a short spur from the Cambrian Railway's Barmouth Junction station to the main quarry line. This was laid along an embankment across the marshes to Mawddach Crescent, thence westwards along the sea wall to the southern end of the viaduct. (A planned extension eastwards from the Crescent to Arthog railway station was never built.)

The tramway's intended passengers were primarily prospective house buyers and lettees; with Andrews' abandonment of the development scheme the tramway was closed, probably at the end of the 1903 summer season, unlike its more successful neighbouring counterpart at FAIRBOURNE.

Bibliography: *Keep Moving: The Story of Solomon Andrews and His Family* John F. Andrews (Stewart Williams, Barry, 1976) 0 900807 23 7

BEAUMARIS PIER TRAMWAY

The island of Anglesey's only tramway, this was a 2ft 6in gauge grooved rail manually-operated luggage line laid on the west side of the pier, probably in 1895 when the structure (opened in 1846 and rebuilt in 1872) was extended. It fell out of use after World War I with the decline of the North Wales coastal steamer traffic.

Bibliography: *North Wales Tramways* Keith Turner (David & Charles, 1979) 0 7153 7769 8

CARDIFF TRAMWAYS

Authority: Cardiff Tramways Order 1871
Gauge: 4ft 8½in
Traction: Horse
Opened: 12 July 1872
Taken Over: 1 January 1902
System: Radial
Length: 6.31 miles
Stock: 52 dd
Livery: Route colour

Odd lengths of tramway track can still be found around the British Isles. This example is the remains of the Beaumaris Pier hand-worked luggage-line on Anglesey. (Author)

The first trams in Wales' capital city were operated by the Cardiff Tramways Co. Ltd, a member of the Provincial group (see Section 1), who opened a line from the Bute Docks Pier Head northwards up Bute Street to the Bute Monument in the High Street in 1872; later that same year (probably 10 September) a second route was opened which left the High Street line at the Hayes Bridge and went via The Hayes, St John Street and Queen Street out to the eastern suburb of Roath on the Newport Road, terminating near its junction with Castle Road. This latter line was extended in April 1879 for another ½ mile along Newport Road as far as Oakfield Street and in July of that year a 1½-mile extension from the High Street westwards via Cowbridge Road to Victoria Park in the suburb of Canton was opened. Two further routes followed: south to Clarence Road via Corporation Road (with a terminus close to the Pier Head line) and north to Cathays via Salisbury Road from Queen Street. By the end of the century the Company was operating more than 50 cars (all open-top double-deckers) based on three depots.

By the 1890s Cardiff Corporation was ready to run its own tramway system and accordingly obtained the necessary Act to enable it to do so (see below). Under the Act it purchased the Company's tracks (for £50,000) and stock (for £15,000) as from the first day of 1902 and immediately set about reconstruction and electrification. Car No 21, a Falcon double-decker of c1886, can be seen on display at the local Welsh Industrial & Maritime Museum.

Bibliography: *Keep Moving: The Story of Solomon Andrews and His Family* John F. Andrews (Stewart Williams, Barry, 1976) 0 900807 23 7

CARDIFF DISTRICT & PENARTH HARBOUR TRAMWAYS

Authority: Cardiff District and Penarth Harbour Tramways Order 1880
Gauge: 4ft 8½in
Traction: Horse
Opened: 28 November 1881
Taken Over: 10 February 1903
System: Single line
Length: 2.41 miles
Stock: 11 dd
Livery: ?

The second tramway company to commence operations in Cardiff was the Cardiff District & Penarth Harbour Tramways Co. Ltd who opened an east–west line across the city from Clifton Street, Roath to Clive Street in Lower Grangetown. (It never reached the Penarth of its title some 4 miles

further down the coast.) Of necessity, in Bute Street it crossed the metals of the CARDIFF TRAMWAYS Co. on the level.

The CDPHT Co. was an owning company only, the line being leased to and operated by Solomon ANDREWS (who also built the original five cars). Work on the line began in April 1881 and the official opening took place on 29 November (although it seems that while the tramway had been passed for traffic and was open for business, the drivers and conductors were not licensed, nor the cars passed, until some days later).

Almost immediately after the opening of the line the Company toyed with the idea of introducing mechanical traction but dropped it on the grounds of cost and in 1884 Andrews was asked to supply another two cars; by 1887 it seems that eleven open-top double-deckers were at work on the line and in the following year Andrews sold part of his interests to the owners of the CT Co., the Provincial group, including in the deal the operating contract for the tramway as from 1 April. (For some time Andrews had been in bitter conflict with Provincial over the 'poaching' tactics of his horse buses along the CT's routes.)

The line was not taken over at the same time as the CT lines as a price could not be agreed with the Corporation (the tramway was losing some £500 a month) until early 1903 when the sum of £12,000 was fixed upon. It was taken over from 10 February of that year and reconstruction began the next day (see below).

Bibliography: as above

CARDIFF CORPORATION TRAMWAYS

Authority: Cardiff Corporation Act 1898
Gauge: 4ft 8½in
Traction: Horse, overhead electric
Opened: 1 May 1902
Closed: 19 February 1950
System: Network
Length: 19.51 miles
Stock: 50 dd horse; 61 sd, 181 dd electric
Livery: Crimson lake & cream
Last Cars: No 112 (service) and No 11 (official, 20 February)

Construction of the Corporation's own routes began in December 1900 with the official opening taking place on 1 May 1902 and a limited service beginning that afternoon from Wood Street (and depot) in the city centre, westwards along Tudor Street with one route turning north up Clare Road and Cathedral Road and a second going south along the former horse line to Clarence Road via Clare Road (and another depot) and Corporation Road. The next day services began via The Hayes, Queen Street, Castle Road and Albany Road to Roath Park (the former horse route) and, on 3 May, further along Newport Road to the main Roath Depot and power station.

During 1902 the electric car fleet grew to 94 in total, all from ERTCW, Nos 41-54 being single-deckers and the rest open-top double-deckers constructed low enough to pass under certain of the city's railway bridges. (Nos 21-40 and 75-94 were bogie vehicles.) As more routes were opened (to Canton in May and and a High Street–Castle Street link and the Bute Pier Head and Cathays horse routes in June), so

Cardiff Corporation No 88 of 1925, one of a fleet of lowbridge cars, on a special working. (Lens of Sutton)

the horse car fleet was quickly run down from 40 in service on 1 May to just four by mid-July.

Further routes were opened over the next two years: the extended CARDIFF DISTRICT & PENARTH HARBOUR line from The Hayes southwest along Penarth Road and Clive Street to Grangetown and northeast via Bute Terrace, Adams Street, Moira Place and Constellation Street then southeast through Splott via Splott Road and Portmanmoor Road to Roath Dock, plus extensions of the Canton and Cathys routes. These, together with some later minor track alterations and link lines, and the extension of the Cathedral Road route and the Cathys route through Gabalfa on the Whitchurch Road in the 1920s, completed the mainly double-track system which, somewhat surprisingly, was not the longest in Wales, being pipped to that distinction by the strung-out RHONDDA system.

During 1903 20 Brush open-toppers were bought (Nos 95-114) and in 1903-04 16 Milnes single-deck bogie combination cars (Nos 115-130). Cardiff's next new car (No 101) did not arrive until 1923 when Brush built a low, enclosed double-decker which, after satisfactory bridge clearance tests, was followed by another 80 such vehicles during 1923-25 (like No 101, taking numbers vacated by withdrawn stock). In 1926 Brush supplied bogie single-decker No 53, followed in 1927 by 30 similar cars numbered 116-124 and 126-137 with the rest taking vacated numbers again. (These were sold in 1940 to Para in Brazil.)

By the 1930s track deterioration led to the consideration of replacing the trams though

the first route closure, the Salisbury Road section of the Cathays route on 4 July 1930, was brought about by operating difficulties with a low railway bridge. (The trams were replaced by buses although a link from the Roath Park route provided an alternative tram service.)

In 1934 the Corporation obtained powers to operate trolleybuses (but the next two abandonments, the Grangetown and Splott routes from 11 October 1936, were in favour of motor buses) and began running them on 1 March 1942 on the Clarence Road route. In 1948 the Pier Head–Canton service was withdrawn (6 June), as was Newport Road–Cathedral Road (4 July) and Newport Road–Pier Head (17 October). On 5 December 1949 the Roath Park route was closed, leaving just the Whitchurch Road line to survive into the following year.

Only one restored car survives: water car No 131 now at the National Tramway Museum, Crich.

Bibliography: *Cardiff's Electric Tramways* (Locomotion Papers No 81) D. Gould (The Oakwood Press, 1974)

COLWYN BAY *see* LLANDUDNO & COLWYN BAY

FAIRBOURNE TRAMWAY
Authority: –
Gauge: 2ft
Traction: Horse
Opened: 1890?
Closed: Pre-1916
System: Single line
Length: c1.75 miles

Stock: 2 sd
Livery: ?
Last car: ?

The Fairbourne Tramway began life as a single-track goods line built in 1890 by Arthur McDougall (of flour fame) and ran from a brickworks just to the north of the present Fairbourne BR station southwards onto Beach Road and then westwards to the sea – a distance of about ½ mile. From there it swung northwards beside or among the shifting sand dunes which extend out into the Mawddach estuary as a mile-long peninsula. From the tip of this sand spit – Penrhyn Point – a ferry has long existed to the town of Barmouth directly opposite across the river mouth.

The purpose of the original line was to carry bricks and other building materials from the brickyard and the Cambrian Railways for the construction of houses along the southern portion of the tramway before the sand spit proper. As soon as the resort (for that was the purpose of the development) was established a pair of one-horse passenger cars were put to work on the line; both were bogie toastracks and both later roofed.

The tramway was sold by McDougall in 1911, along with the rest of the development, but it is not known if it ceased to run then; services had certainly finished by 1916 when a 15in gauge miniature railway was opened on the route by Narrow Gauge Railways Ltd. This line was regauged to 12¼in in the 1980s and, since 1990, has actually operated a 'replica' horse car on special occasions.

Bibliography: *Narrow Gauge Railways in Mid-Wales* (The British Narrow Gauge Railway No 3) J. I. C. Boyd (The Oakwood Press, 2nd ed 1970)

GLYN VALLEY TRAMWAY (1)
Authority: Glyn Valley Tramway Act 1870
Gauge: 2ft 4¼in
Traction: Horse
Opened: 1 April 1874
Closed: 31 March 1886
System: Single line
Length: 5.25 miles
Stock: 3 sd
Livery: ?
Last Car: ?

The GVT was built primarily as a roadside mineral tramroad, its purpose being to bring down slate from the upper reaches of the Ceiriog Valley in east Denbighshire to the Shropshire Union Canal and GWR at Chirk on the border with England. It opened in April 1873 and the line's unusual gauge (believed to have been unique in the British Isles) is thought to have been the result of

Postcard of one of the Fairbourne Tramway's two cars at the railway station terminus before setting off towards the sea. (Author's Collection)

simply halving railway standard gauge. The roadside track was of flat-bottomed rails on sleepers ballasted flush with the road surface. Although owned by the Gyn Valley Tramway Co., half of the £10,000 capital was put up by the Shropshire Union Railway & Canal Co. in return for sole operating rights.

Passenger traffic was very much a secondary consideration with services beginning officially on 1 April 1874 using a single covered toastrack car built by Ashbury, though passengers had no doubt been carried on the line before this date by riding in the wagons. This first car was soon followed by two four-wheeled railway-type closed compartment carriages from the same firm and these three vehicles appear to have been the line's total passenger stock.

The line ran for some 7 miles from the Cambrian Slate Quarries above Glynceiriog, down the valley to Chirk with slate trains being worked by gravity in this direction. Passenger traffic was limited to the section between Glynceiriog and Pontfaen on the edge of Chirk where the line reversed grades for the steep haul up to the railway siding and across the line to the canal wharf. Normal passenger services consisted of three cars in each direction a day (except Sundays). Journey times were 1 hour up and ¾ hour down the valley.

The line was not a commercial success and was soon in financial trouble. In 1881 the Ceiriog Granite Co. took over the working of the line but that same year saw the closure of the slate quarries. A fittingly apt form of help however was at hand for granite had been quarried above Glynceiriog since 1875, and the market in setts of this stone to pave the new tramway tracks in the streets of Britain was just beginning to boom. Transport patterns were changing closer to home as well and the decision was taken to modernize the line with locomotive haulage, in readiness for which passenger services ceased in 1886 though the granite trains continued whilst the reconstruction went on.

Bibliography: *The Glyn Valley Tramway* W. J. Milner (Oxford Publishing Co, 1984) 0 86093 286 9

GLYN VALLEY TRAMWAY (2)
Authority: Glyn Valley Tramway Act 1885
Gauge: 2ft 4½in
Traction: Steam
Opened: 15 March 1891
Closed: 6 April 1933
System: Single line
Length: 6.19 miles
Stock: 4 locos, 16 sd
Livery: Locos medium green pre-1920s, then black; carriages medium green & cream
Last Train: ?

With authorization obtained in 1885 to convert the horse line to steam traction (see above), work began in 1887 using two locomotives from the Snailbeach District Railway, a Shropshire mineral line which had a nominal gauge of 2ft 4in; it is thought that their wheel flanges opened out the rails of the winding horse line to 2ft 4½in, another unique gauge in the British Isles.

The refurbished line opened for goods traffic in July 1888 and for passengers (still a secondary consideration) three years later. The new, single-track tramway followed virtually the identical route as the old one, the principal differences being a 2-mile extension to the Hendre and Pandy quarries above Glynceiriog (never worked by passenger trains other than quarrymen's specials) and a 1-mile deviation from Pontfaen to the railway station at Chirk. (The horse tramway from Pontfaen to the railway and canal was abandoned.)

Often regarded as another of the Welsh narrow gauge railways, the GVT was a genuine roadside tramway which just happened to be primarily concerned with freight traffic. Although the wagons and coaches were typical narrow gauge railway vehicles (and often ran in mixed trains), the line's original three locomotives were constructed in accordance with tramway legislation. These were 0-4-2 side tanks from Beyer-Peacock of Manchester with full side skirts, steam condensing apparatus and (at first) were fired by coke. Unlike their city counterparts, they had only the one cab and were consequently required to be driven with that leading so as to afford the crew the best visibility. The first to arrive was *Sir Theodore* (named after Sir Theodore Martin, the Company Chairman) in 1888; this was joined the following year by *Dennis* (named

after Henry Dennis, a fellow-director and Engineer of the horse line). A third, slightly modified sister engine was purchased in 1892 and named *Glyn*. After World War I the engines were beginning to show their age and they were supplemented accordingly by a 4-6-0 side tank loco purchased from the Ministry of Munitions. She had been built in 1917 by the Baldwin Locomotive Co. of Philadelphia for use on the light railways laid to serve the British front in France and was now surplus to requirements. On the GVT she was known simply as 'Baldwin'.

Passenger services began with the two closed horse coaches plus two closed saloon coaches from Midland which were followed later in 1891 by a roofed open coach from the same manufacturers. In 1893 Midland supplied six more open roofed coaches and three closed saloons (one of which was for 1st class passengers) and, in 1901, two more closed saloons. All were small, four-wheeled box-like vehicles of great charm.

In 1932 a motor bus service started in the valley, going on to Oswestry, and that was the end of the tramway as far as passengers were concerned. Road transport was now also biting hard into the freight traffic and on 6 July 1935 that too ended. In 1936 rails, engines and surviving rolling stock were all sold for scrap, although two closed coach bodies (including the 1st class saloon) have since been rescued and restored and put into service on the 2ft 3in gauge preserved Talyllyn Railway.

Bibliography: as above

GREAT ORME TRAMWAY see LLANDUDNO: GREAT ORME TRAMWAY

Glyn Valley Tramway Sir Theodore of 1888, crew and mixed rake of carriages pose for the postcard photographer in the yard at Chirk c1911. (Author's Collection)

The covered lower terminus of the Great Orme Tramway, 1974 (when called Great Orme Railway), with No 5 waiting to depart. (Author)

HAFAN *see* PLYNLIMON & HAFAN

HARLECH TRAMWAY

Authority: –
Gauge: 2ft?
Traction: Horse
Opened: June 1878?
Closed: 1880s
System: Single line
Length: c0.34 miles
Stock: 1 sd?

Livery: ?
Last car: ?

The most minor of the Welsh tramways – apart from the miniature line at Rhyl (see Section 7) – was laid between April and June 1878 from the Cambrian Railways station in Harlech, across the sand dunes to the beach some 600 yards away for the benefit of holidaymakers. It was a private venture, the owner being Samuel Holland,

Great Orme Tramway No 5 in 1974 in Old Road – now the only street, rather than roadside or moorland, section of the line. (Author)

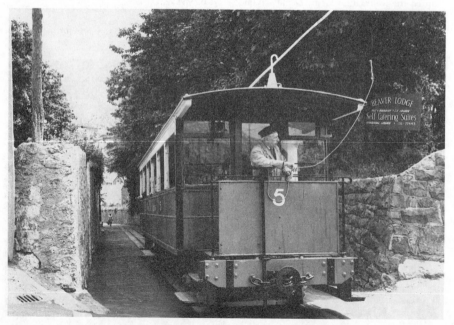

MP for Merionethshire, a man more famous for his Festiniog Railway and slate quarry interests. The stock was built locally: contempor-aneous accounts refer to both 'tramcar' and 'carriages' though it would seem unlikely that more than one car was provided.

The tramway closed sometime during the 1880s; the reasons for its demise are unknown, as is any technical information relating to it and no photographs of it are known to exist.

Bibliography: *North Wales Tramways* Keith Turner (David & Charles, 1979) 0 7153 7769 8

LLANBEDROG *see* PWLLHELI & LLANBEDROG

LLANDUDNO: GREAT ORME TRAMWAY

Authority: Great Orme Tramways Act 1898
Gauge: 3ft 6in
Traction: Cable
Opened: 31 July 1902
System: Two single lines
Length: 1.11 miles
Stock: 4 sd
Livery: Originally yellow, then royal blue to 1977, then trafalgar blue & ivory to 1991, then orient blue & ivory

The Great Orme Tramway (or Railway as it was known from 1935 to 1977) possesses many features which set it apart from other British tramways. To begin with, it is worked as two separate sections: lower (872yd) and upper (827yd) with the cable winding house sited at Halfway station between the two. The lower section (opened 1902) commences at Victoria station in Church Walks, Llandudno, and climbs at an average gradient of 1 in 6.5 with a steepest point of 1 in 3.6; it is worked on the funicular system with a car attached to each end of a cable running in a conduit down the centre of the track. The lower, street half of this section is single-track, then comes a passing loop and above that the track is interlaced, all on a roadside reservation.

The upper section – average gradient 1 in 15.5 with the steepest stretch 1 in 10.3 – was opened 8 July 1903 and runs over the rough grassland of the upper slopes of the Great Orme headland, unfenced in true tramway fashion, to Summit station, 650ft above sea level. This section too is worked on the funicular system but in a manner unique in the British Isles: the cable runs from the winding house up the single track to the first car, then on through the passing loop to the Summit, round an idler there, back down the single track to the second car, through the other side of the passing loop and back down to the winding house. Thus one car is wound *down* to the winding house, rather than *up* in the usual funicular fashion, pulling up the other car in the process. (A car going through a passing loop sets the points behind it so as to ensure its return along the same path, thus preventing fouling of the cables.) An overhead wire, connected to the cars by trolley poles, was used for tele-graphic communication with the winding house until 1990 when it was replaced by a radio link.

Promoted and opened by the Great Orme Tramways Co. Ltd, ownership of the line passed to the Great Orme Railway Ltd in 1935 following a fatal accident three years earlier and the subsequent liquidation of the GOT Co. In 1949 it was acquired by Llandudno UDC (now Aberconwy DC), which body's former Direct Labour Division, Grwp Aberconwy, has since 1991 operated it. Since 1903, a summer-only service has been run.

All four bogie saloon cars were built by HN with Nos 4 and 5 on the lower section and 6 and 7 on the upper. (The Nos 1-3 were allocated to three small vans used to carry coke up to the winding house and fuel and other supplies to the summit hotel. Known as 'jockey cars', they were propelled up the line by one of the passenger vehicles and man-handled round the winding house if need be on the short connecting track that originally existed there. They were also used to trans-port coffins up to the summit for burial in St Tudno's churchyard. They were withdrawn by 1911, presumably to be broken up. Since 1991 the passenger cars have carried the names *St Tudno* (No 4), *St Silio* (No 5), *St Seiriol* (No 6) and *St Trillo* (No 7), all names of former North Wales coastal steamers.

Bibliography: *North Wales Tramways* Keith
  Turner (David & Charles, 1979)
  0 7153 7769 8
*Narrow Gauge Railways in North
  Caernarvonshire Vol 3* (The British
  Narrow Gauge Railway No 5) J. I. C.
  Boyd (The Oakwood Press, 1986)
  0 85361 328 1

LLANDUDNO & COLWYN BAY ELECTRIC RAILWAY
Authority: Llandudno and Colwyn Bay
  Light Railway Order 1898
Gauge: 3ft 6in
Traction: Overhead electric
Opened: 19 October 1907
Closed: 24 March 1956
System: Single line
Length: 8.38 miles
Stock: 27 sd, 12 dd
Livery: Maroon & cream to 1933, then
  green & cream

The cable guidance mechanism on the upper section of the Great Orme Tramway. On the lower section, and on other cable lines, all this would be hidden in a conduit. (Author)

Last Car: No 8

After several false starts (and several years' stop-go construction) the neighbouring seaside resorts of Llandudno and Colwyn Bay were linked by a tramway in 1908 (a longer rail link had existed since 1858), the operator at the time of opening being the Llandudno & District Electric Tramway Construction Co. Ltd (which concern changed its name two years later to the Llandudno & Colwyn Bay Electric Railway

Ltd). In 1910 Balfour, Beatty (see Section 1) purchased an interest.

The first portion opened ran from the West Shore, Llandudno (on the Conwy estuary), through the centre of the town via the main thoroughfares of Gloddaeth Avenue and Mostyn Street (and their extensions) out into the country on a long reserved section over Penrhyn Hill, down onto the Company's toll road beside Penrhyn Bay at Rhos-on-Sea and thence inland to the depot; on 7 June 1908 the next stretch to the main Conway

Llandudno & Colwyn Bay No 9 of 1921 (ex-Bournemouth 108) passing two ex-Accrington single-deckers in the Penrhyn Avenue depot. (Author's Collection)

Road in Colwyn Bay was opened. As built the tramway was single-track though eventually nearly all was doubled; on 26 March 1915 the last, single-track mile along Abergele Road to Old Colwyn was opened to complete the line (though this was cut back on 22 September 1930 because of traffic congestion). Curiously, in view of its heavy reliance on holidaymakers, the tramway served neither town's railway station nor traversed their main promenades.

The original stock comprised 14 Midland bogie single-deck cars which were joined in 1909 by four single-deckers from UEC (Nos 15-18) and in 1920 four EE open bogie toast-racks were purchased (Nos 19-22). In 1932-33 five second-hand Accrington Brush bogie single-deck saloons (Nos 1-5) were bought as replacement vehicles, followed in 1936 by a second-hand UEC bogie open-topper from Bournemouth (No 6) and nine similar Brush cars from the same source (Nos 7-15). Finally, in 1936 two ex-Darwen enclosed EE double-deckers (Nos 23 and 24) were purchased.

The line's demise was brought about by growing bus competition, with the Company following suit for five years (until it sold out to Crosville). When it closed the line was the last 3ft 6in gauge electric tramway in Britain.

Bibliography: *The Llandudno & Colwyn Bay Electric Railway* (Locomotion Papers No 187) Keith Turner (The Oakwood Press, 1993) 0 85361 450 4

LLANELLY TRAMWAYS
Authority: Llanelly Tramways Order 1880
Gauge: 3ft
Traction: Horse
Opened: 28 September 1882
Closed: April 1908?
System: Single line
Length: 0.97 miles
Stock: 5 sd
Livery: ?
Last Car: ?

Llanelly's first tramway was a short and simple single-track affair. It was operated by the Llanelly Tramways Co. Ltd and ran from the GWR station northwestwards down Station Road before turning sharp right along Murray Street and past the depot, then left along Cowell Street and right again along Stepney Street to terminate at Woodend. (It should be noted here that although the Welsh spelling Llanelli has been the accepted form of the town's name since 1967, during the period of the tramways Llanelly was the official version.)

Rolling stock details are sketchy but it appears that services began with three small single-deck saloons of unknown origin which were joined later in the tramway's life by two more.

The tramway's gauge of 3ft was unusual in Great Britain and was possibly chosen as being too narrow to allow horse buses (which nor-

---

LIGHT RAILWAYS ACT, 1896.

LLANDUDNO AND COLWYN BAY LIGHT RAILWAY ORDER, 1898.

ORDER

MADE BY THE

LIGHT RAILWAY COMMISSIONERS,

AND MODIFIED AND CONFIRMED BY THE

BOARD OF TRADE,

AUTHORISING THE CONSTRUCTION OF

LIGHT RAILWAYS FROM COLWYN BAY TO LLANDUDNO IN THE COUNTIES OF DENBIGH AND CARNARVON.

Presented to both Houses of Parliament by Command of Her Majesty.

LONDON:
PRINTED FOR HER MAJESTY'S STATIONERY OFFICE,
BY DARLING & SON, LTD., 1-3, GREAT ST. THOMAS APOSTLE, E.C.

And to be purchased, either directly or through any Bookseller, from
EYRE & SPOTTISWOODE, EAST HARDING STREET, FLEET STREET, E.C., and
32, ABINGDON STREET, WESTMINSTER, S.W.; or
JOHN MENZIES & CO., 12, HANOVER STREET, EDINBURGH, and
90, WEST NILE STREET, GLASGOW; or
HODGES, FIGGIS, & CO., LIMITED, 104, GRAFTON STREET, DUBLIN.

1899.

[C. 9395.]   *Price 3d.*

Many tramway promoters took advantage of the 1896 Light Railways Act to promote their tramways, the Llandudno & Colwyn Bay Electric Railway being one such example.

too narrow to allow horse buses (which normally had large wheels outside the body) to use the rail tops for an easier run. If this was so, the plan was foiled when James Andrews (one of the local horse bus operators and brother of Solomon ANDREWS) began running one of the Andrews' 'Patent Omnibuses' over the route; in 1883 the Company took him to court for doing so but lost the case.

In 1905 the Company was purchased for £6,000 by the British Power Co. Ltd (for-merly the South Wales Electrical Power Distribution Co. Ltd), which concern bought at the same time the semi-defunct Llanelly & District Electric Lighting & Traction Co. Ltd which had been registered in 1900 in a bid to provide Carmarthenshire's largest town with an electric tramway system. In November 1905 an LRO was applied for to this end and obtained two years later.

Work on converting and extending the tramways began early in 1908 with the firm of J. G. White & Co. Ltd as the contractors. Two of White's employees at this time were George Balfour and Andrew Beatty who became LT Co. directors in January 1908 (and twelve months later founded the firm of Balfour, Beatty – see Section 1). It is not certain when the horse line closed; it seems to have operated through March 1908 but during April it was lifted in stages prior to relaying to a wider gauge (see below) with an increasingly-curtailed service being run for a short while.

Bibliography: *Llanelly Trolleybuses* Geoff Griffiths (Trolleybooks, 1992)
0 904235 15 7

LLANELLY & DISTRICT ELECTRIC TRAMWAYS

Authority: Llanelly and District Light Railway Order 1907
Gauge: 4ft 8½in
Traction: Horse/overhead electric
Opened: April 1908?
Closed: 16 February 1933
System: Radial
Length: 6.23 miles
Stock: 3 dd horse; 16 dd electric
Livery: Green & cream/ivory
Last Car: ?

In 1909 Balfour, Beatty revived the Llanelly & District Electric Lighting & Traction Co. Ltd (see above) with financial support and it became the operator of the new electric system. Although the new cars did not begin working until 1911, three ex-London County Council horse double-deckers were bought to provide an interim service along the former LLANELLY TRAMWAYS route.

Three new routes were constructed from the (slightly realigned) northern end of the old line: to Pwll in the west via Sandy Road and Pwll Road, north along Felinfoel Road to the district of that name and east along Park Street and Swansea Road to Bynea. All lines were single-track, to be worked by ten UEC open-top cars; these entered service on 12 June 1911 from the station to Felinfoel and Bynea with the Pwll line opening on 31 July. (The official inauguration of the system was on 16 July of that year.) In 1912 four similar cars (Nos 11-14) were purchased.

In 1920 two EE open-toppers (Nos 15 & 16) were bought, presumably to replace two cars which had been borrowed during World War I from another BB subsidiary, the Mansfield & District Light Railway. Although the system was still comparatively young, a sign of the coming times occurred in 1924 when the LDELT Co. changed its name slightly but significantly to the Llanelly & District Electric Supply Co. Ltd and before the decade was out plans had been made to replace the trams with trolleybuses. Powers to do so were obtained in the Llanelly & District Traction Act of 1930 and the first of the new vehicles ran over the Bynea route on 26 December 1932, the tram service presumably finishing two days beforehand. Conversion of the other two routes took place the following February without ceremony, after which the cars were scrapped.

Bibliography: as above

MERTHYR TYDFIL ELECTRIC TRAMWAYS

Authority: Merthyr Tydfil Light Railways Order 1899
Gauge: 3ft 6in
Traction: Overhead electric
Opened: 6 April 1901
Closed: 23 August 1939
System: Branching
Length: 3.5 miles
Stock: 13 sd, 17 dd
Livery: Dark red & ivory?, later bright green & ivory
Last Car: ?

During the 19th century Merthyr Tydfil grew to become a major industrial town and by the end of the 1890s it was clear that a modern public transport system was badly needed. Owned and operated by the Merthyr Tydfil Electric Traction & Lighting Co. Ltd (a BET subsidiary), the system consisted originally of a main line some 2½ miles long running southeast from Cefn Bridge on the Brecon Road, through Williamstown to Pontmorlais Circus, where it swung northeast along Penydarren Road, the High Street and Penydarren New Road to Dowlais High Street where it terminated at the Bush Inn outside the famous Dowlais Ironworks. A branch of ½ mile ran south from the Owain Glyndwr public house in Pontmorlais Circus, along Pontmorlais High Street and past the GWR's Merthyr station to a terminus in Graham Road.

Services began with thirteen Midland single-deckers (Nos 1-13) and three ERTCW open-top double-deckers (Nos 14-16). In 1903 No 10 was damaged in an accident and withdrawn though its electrical and running gear was fitted to a new open-top double-deck Brush body in 1909 (which took the old number); over the next six years Nos 2, 4, 6-9 and 11-13 were all rebuilt to a similar configuration. The depot and power station were in Trevithick Road behind Penydarren High Street on the site of the historic Penydarren Ironworks.

In 1914 the system's only extension was opened: a ½-mile continuation of the western end of the main line over Cefn Bridge and along Cefn High Street.

Further car rebuilds took place in 1929-30 – obviously the very steep gradients (as much as 1 in 11 in places) and the Welsh weather had taken their toll – when nine of the cars (Nos 2, 7-9, 11 and 14-16) were given second-hand open-top bodies ex-Birmingham & Midland Tramways Joint Committee. Finally, four complete cars were bought from Birmingham Corporation in 1933; these were UEC open-toppers of 1905-08 and were given the vacated numbers 3, 4, 6 and 12 (and some of the equipment from the older cars).

Faced with the problem of large trams blocking the growing motor traffic on its very narrow streets, Merthyr Corporation eventually paid the Company to close the tramway so that it could operate its own buses instead (it being prevented by the provisions of the Merthyr Tydfil Corporation Act of 1920 from running them whilst the tramway still provided a public service).

MUMBLES *see* SWANSEA & MUMBLES

NEATH CORPORATION TRAMWAYS

Authority: Neath and District Tramways Order 1873
Gauge: 4ft 8½in
Traction: Horse/gas
Opened: 1875
Closed: 8 August 1920
System: Single line
Length: 3.96 miles
Stock: ? horse; 23 dd gas
Livery: ?
Last car: ?

The Neath tramway ran from the appropriately named Terminus Hotel in Skewen on the western side of the town, eastwards for

Postcard of Stow Hill, Newport, with Corporation No 38 of 1904 arriving. (Lens of Sutton)

about 1½ miles into the town centre, where it turned southwards on the Neath Road to end opposite Villiers Street in Briton Ferry. It began as a horse-worked operation by the Neath & District Tramways Co. on a single track line.

In 1897 Neath Town Council acquired the line by Act of Parliament and set about modernizing it – but with gas trams rather than electric ones. In March 1898 track relaying commenced (with the installation of several more passing places) and was completed by the October of that year. In April 1898 the Corporation leased the line to the British Gas Traction Co. Ltd (a subsidiary of the Germany pioneering gas tram company Luhrig) but until 31 August 1899 when the gas cars were ready to enter service, the horse trams continued to work the line.

Almost immediately, the operating company got into financial trouble and was wound up at the end of 1899; after exploring various options the Town Council leased the line to the Neath Gas Traction Co. Ltd, a company formed by the then manager Matthew Whittington at the beginning of 1902 (and which changed its name to the Provincial Gas Traction Co. Ltd later that same year). By 1916 this concern too was bankrupt and the Council took over operations itself; by then however the line was in a bad way with only three trams operational. Again, options were explored: electrification (including linking-up with the SWANSEA system less than 4 miles beyond Skewen) or replacement by trolleybuses. The Council's hand was forced however when the South Wales Transport Co. announced that it would inaugurate a competing motor bus service on Monday 9 August 1920; the tramway was accordingly closed the preceding day.

NEWPORT TRAMWAYS

Authority: Newport (Monmouthshire) Tramways Order 1873
Gauge: 4ft 8½in
Traction: Horse, overhead electric
Opened: 1 February 1875
Closed: 5 September 1937
System: Radial
Length: 8.55 miles
Stock: 29? sd & dd horse; 57 dd electric
Livery: Green & cream horse; vermillion & primrose to WWI, then crimson/dark brown/maroon & cream electric
Last Cars: Nos 51 and 53

After a false start in 1870, authorization was obtained in 1873 for a short horse tramway from Tredegar Place, through Westgate Square, down Commercial Street and Commercial Road to terminate near the mass of railway lines serving the docks at Pillgwenlly. Construction took place in 1874 with the opening the following year; a short extension to Pill Gates opened in December 1880, bringing the total length of the line to 1.16 miles, virtually all single track. The operator was the Newport Tramways Co. Ltd.

Services began with two single-deck Starbuck cars but details of later stock are very sketchy. It is thought that in all, 29 cars were operated during the horse years, mainly double-deckers, including three (possibly reversible cars) bought in 1901 from Liverpool.

In 1892 the Corporation obtained the necessary Parliamentary powers to purchase the tramway (and build extensions) under the Newport Corporation Act and did so two years later, taking over on 30 July 1894; subsequently an additional line was opened on 7 December from Westgate Square (the northern terminus since

December 1888) up the High Street from where branches radiated out along Malpas Road, Caerleon Road, Church Road, Chepstow Road and Corporation Road. From 1881 operation of the tramway had been leased out by the Company (to Edmund Perry) and in 1894 the Corporation continued the practice by leasing it to Solomon ANDREWS (who had supplied three of his patent buses in 1886 to the NT Co.), for seven years.

In 1900 the Corporation decided to electrify the tramway, with work starting in November 1902, and on 9 April of the following year the first section (to Pill) opened. As conversion work progressed, so the other horse services were withdrawn, the last being along Church Road which ceased on 3 November 1903 (this short line never in fact being electrified). Subsequently the Malpas Road, Caerleon Road, Chepstow Road and Corporation Road lines were all extended to the borough boundary (the last named being along Alexandra Road in 1917) and a westwards branch up Stow Hill (1904) added. Lines were now mostly double track.

The first 30 electric cars were Milnes open-top vehicles; these were followed in 1904 by ten similar ERTCW cars (Nos 31-40) and another three (Nos 42-44) five years later. Nos 45-50 were purchased in 1917 as second-hand ex-London County Council open-top cars and in 1921 four Brush bogie top-covered vehicles (Nos 51-54) were bought. The last arrivals were Nos 55-58 in 1922, these being HN top-covered cars.

The beginning of the end for the tramway came on 1 February 1928 when the Westgate-Malpas Road service ceased and on 18 August 1930 the Chepstow Road service followed suit, both replaced by buses. By 1937 only the Corporation Road–Westgate–Alexander Road route was left and this closed on Sunday 5 September when No 51 made the last full trip from the Docks and No 53 the last journey along Corporation Road to the depot there.

Bibliography: *Trams and Buses of Newport 1845 to 1981* D. B. Thomas & E. A. Thomas (The Starling Press, Newport, 1982) 0 903434 48 2

OYSTERMOUTH TRAMROAD

Authority: [Swansea & Oystermouth Railway or Tramroad Act 1804]
Gauge: c4ft
Traction: Horse
Opened: 25 March 1807
Closed: 1827?
System: Single line
Length: c4.5 miles
Stock: 1 dd?
Livery: ?
Last Car: ?

If not for anything else, the Oystermouth Tramroad will always be famous for having the first rail-borne passenger service in the world. It began life as a horse-worked tramroad (or tramway, the terms then being interchangeable) running from the bottom of the Cwm in Swansea (by the old pottery works) to the seashore and thence westwards via Black Pill to the village of Oystermouth some 4½ miles distant. A short branch from Black Pill ran up the Clyne Valley to Ynys. Its function was to act as a feeder from the mineral workings to the east of the Gower Peninsula to the Swansea Canal; as such it had no real competition as the absence of a road in the vicinity meant carts had to use the beach. Much of the line was close to the high water mark and the trackbed has long since been washed away. It is known however that it was a plateway in construction with short L-section rails spiked to granite blocks upon which the flangeless wheels of the waggons could run. It appears to have opened for freight traffic – or at least part of it did – in April 1806 as the Oystermouth Railway or Tramroad.

In 1807 a regular – and historic – passenger service began on the main line operated by one Benjamin French who supplied his own four-wheeled stagecoach-like vehicle, paying the Oystermouth Railway or Tramroad Co. £20 per annum in lieu of tolls for the privilege.

Just how long the service operated by French and his partners lasted is uncertain. In 1826 a turnpike was constructed between Swansea and Oystermouth and a horse bus service introduced along it and it is thought that the tram service ceased soon afterwards. The story was by no means finished though for the line was later reconstructed as the SWANSEA & MUMBLES RAILWAY.

Bibliography: *The Swansea & Mumbles Railway* (Locomotion Papers No 50) Charles E. Lee (The Oakwood Press, 1977 ed) 0 85361 381 8
Rock & Roll to Paradise: the History of the Mumbles Railway Rob Gittens (Gower Press, 1982) 0 85088 638 4

PENARTH *see* CARDIFF DISTRICT & PENARTH HARBOUR

PLYNLIMON & HAFAN TRAMWAY

A 2ft 3in gauge steam-worked railway which ran for nearly 9 miles inland from Llanfihangel north of Aberystwyth. Its main traffic was stone (though there was one passenger carriage) and the line was open only from 1897 to 1899 before the whole enterprise was abandoned as unprofitable.

Bibliography: *The Plynlimon & Hafan Tramway* E. A. Wade (Gemini Publishing, 1976)

PONTYPRIDD & RHONDDA VALLEY TRAMWAY

Authority: Pontypridd and Rhondda Valley Tramways Order 1882
Gauge: 3ft 6in
Traction: Horse
Opened: November 1887?
Closed: February 1902?
System: Single line
Length: 3.06 miles
Stock: 8? sd & dd
Livery: ?
Last Car: ?

Incorporated in 1882 to link the Glamorgan towns of Pontypridd and Treherbert – some 12 miles apart – this tramway as built only ever reached from the edge of Pontypridd as far as the village of Porth just a quarter of the way along the planned route. Whether this curtailment of the line was the cause or the result, the Pontypridd & Rhondda Valley Tramway Co. was soon in financial difficulties and in October 1887 Solomon ANDREWS agreed to take over operations for three years after completing the line. (The rescue package came too late for the line to open as planned on 2 November of that year but services began shortly afterwards.)

The tramway's money problems refused to go away and in 1890 the Company went into liquidation and was purchased by one of Andrews' concerns, the South Wales Property, Machinery & Carriage Co. In 1898 Andrews sold the line to the BET who, in accordance with its usual policy in such matters, sought the local authority's agreement to extend and electrify the line. This agreement however was not forthcoming and when, in February 1902, an attack of glanders killed off most of the tramway's horses, services were terminated. (Like that of the opening, the exact date is unrecorded.) During the next two years the concern was purchased by Pontypridd and Rhondda Councils to extend, electrify and operate themselves (see below).

As built, the tramway was single track and ran from The Square at Porth along what is now the A4058 to the Taff Vale Railway's viaduct on its Rhondda line at Pontypridd, which structure effectively barred the Company's double-deck cars – and the tramway itself – from progressing further into the town.

Bibliography: *Passenger Tramways of Pontypridd* (Locomotion Papers No 106) R. Large (The Oakwood Press, 1977)

PONTYPRIDD URBAN DISTRICT COUNCIL TRAMWAYS

Authority: Pontypridd Urban District Council Tramways Order 1901
Gauge: 3ft 6in
Traction: Overhead electric
Opened: 5 March 1905
Closed: 30 August 1931
System: Branching
Length: 5.34 miles
Stock: 6 sd, 25 dd
Livery: Maroon & cream
Last Car: ?

Even before the purchase of the PONTYPRIDD & RHONDDA VALLEY horse tramway (see above) by the two local authorities concerned, their intentions to construct and operate electric lines were being put into practice. Work on the reconstruction began in Pontypridd in July 1903, a month before the UDC was able to invoke its statutory powers to purchase the horse line (the sale was completed on 31 October 1904 at a cost of £5,750) and the first trial trip made on 12 February 1905; the official opening was set for the following month.

The route was that of the rebuilt horse tramway extended through the town centre to Treforest railway station with a branch of roughly equal length running northeast from the High Street along Market Street and Taff Street, over the river and via Coed Pen Maen Road to Cilfynydd. The new lines were worked as a single route until the reconstructed horse tramway section was ready; this opened on 4 April 1907, still unconnected to the rest of the system.

Although the tramway was connected to the RHONDDA system following the latter's re-opening in 1908, through passengers were required to change cars at the Trehafod boundary until 14 July 1919 when through running finally commenced (and a four-minute discrepancy in the timetables was eliminated by adopting Greenwich Mean rather than local time!) The arrangement however was plagued by disagreements between Pontypridd UDC and the Rhondda company and it was finally abandoned in December 1927, by which time both systems were experiencing more serious difficulties.

In 1929 Pontypridd UDC obtained powers to operate buses and trolleybuses and in September 1930 the Treforest–Cilfynydd route was converted to trolleybus operation (although in peak periods motorbuses and trams provided a back-up service). The Trehafod route was turned over to the buses the following year and the whole system closed.

The car fleet comprised Brush Nos 1-6 (single-deck combination cars) and 7-12 (open-toppers) of 1904, Nos 13-20 (open-

Postcard of a Pwllheli & Llanbedrog open car running to the West End from the town in the 1920s.
(Author's Collection)

WEST END TRAMWAYS, PWLLHELI.

2½ MILES ALONG THE "UNRIVALLED SOUTH BEACH."

On and after August 1st, 1896, the above Trams will leave the West End Hotel and Careg-y-defaid as under, weather permitting, until further notice :---

Leaves West End Hotel.		Leaves Carreg-y-Defaid.	
9 0 a.m.	4 0 p.m.	9 20 a.m.	4 20 p.m.
9 40 a.m.	4 20 p.m.	10 0 a.m.	4 40 p.m.
10 20 a.m.	4 40 p.m.	10 40 a.m.	5 0 p.m.
11 0 a.m.	5 0 p.m.	11 20 a.m.	5 20 p.m.
11 40 a.m.	5 20 p.m.	12 0 n'n.	5 40 p.m.
12 20 p.m.	5 40 p.m.	12 40 p.m.	6 0 p.m.
1 0 p.m.	6 0 p.m.	1 20 p.m.	6 20 p.m.
1 40 p.m.	6 20 p.m.	2 0 p.m.	6 40 p.m.
2 0 p.m.	6 40 p.m.	2 20 p.m.	7 0 p.m.
2 20 p.m.	7 0 p.m.	2 40 p.m.	7 20 p.m.
2 40 p.m.	7 20 p.m.	3 0 p.m.	7 40 p.m.
3 0 p.m.	7 40 p.m.	3 20 p.m.	8 0 p.m.
3 20 p.m.	8 0 p.m.	3 40 p.m.	8 20 p.m.
3 40 p.m.	8 20 p.m.	4 0 p.m.	8 40 p.m.

Fares : 2d. each way.

Omnibuses, in connection with the above Tramways, will run from West End Hotel to Town and Station, and vice versa.

Fares :-- { West End Hotel to Town, 1d.
Town to Station, 1d. } and vice versa.

S. ANDREWS & SON, PROPRIETORS.

Office :--CARDIFF ROAD.

— TO LET, —
For Concerts, &c., West End Assembly Rooms.
Seat, 450. Terms : Apply--T. CUNNINGHAM, Cardiff Road.

Printed by Owen Humphreys, 47, High Street, Pwllheli.

Pwllheli & Llanbedrog 1896 timetable, before the line was extended into the town.

toppers of 1907) and 27-31 (top-covered cars of 1920) plus UEC Nos 21-26 (open-toppers of 1908).

Bibliography: as above

PWLLHELI CORPORATION TRAMWAYS
Authority: –
Gauge: 2ft 6in
Traction: Horse
Opened: 24 July 1899
Closed: September 1919
System: Single line
Length: 0.51 miles
Stock: 3 sd
Livery: Varnished wood?
Last Car: ?

Despite its grandiose title, this was only ever a short, single-track line from the Cambrian Railways station, along the Embankment beside the harbour to Victoria Parade (South Beach Promenade), thus connecting the old town with the beach and the houses and hotels then being built there. Running summer seasons only, it was owned and operated by Pwllheli Borough Council (apparently without proper legal authority!) although for the 1917 and 1918 seasons it was let out on lease to T. J. Williams of Bodawen.

Stock comprised small, four-wheeled single-deckers from Midland: one open and one closed were bought in 1899 followed by another open car two years later. The tiny depot was at the northern (station) end of the line.

Attempts in 1908 to link up with the PWLLHELI & LLANBEDROG line came to nothing and low receipts and next-to-nothing profits led to its demise when new track was needed.

Bibliography: *North Wales Tramways*
K. Turner (David & Charles, 1979)
0 7153 7769 8
Narrow Gauge Railways in North Caernarvonshire Vol 1: the West (The British Narrow Gauge Railway No 5)
J. I. C. Boyd (The Oakwood Press, 1981) 0 85761 273 0

PWLLHELI & LLANBEDROG TRAMWAY
Authority: –
Gauge: 3ft
Traction: Horse
Opened: Summer 1894
Closed: September 1928?
System: Single line
Length: 3.88 miles
Stock: 18 sd
Livery: Dark red & cream
Last Car: ?

The P&L was a Solomon ANDREWS

venture and arose as the direct result of his 1890s scheme to construct a promenade at Pwllheli in the sand dunes on Cardigan Bay, the beach being about ¼ mile from the town which was focussed on the old harbour. This promenade with its terrace of villas and hotels became the West End and stone for its construction came from Andrews' quarry at Carreg y Defaid, a rock outcrop 1¼ miles along the shore to the west; the stone was transported over a horse-worked tramroad of 3ft gauge. Behind the buildings on the promenade a recreation ground was laid out, served by a short spur from the tramroad.

Even while the building work was going on the tramroad was 'converted' (ie generally tidied-up) for passenger traffic; between the West End and the town itself Andrews ran a connecting horse bus service along his newly-constructed thoroughfare, Cardiff Road, though by the summer of 1897 the tramway had been extended to bridge this gap. At the same time it was extended in the opposite direction from Carreg y Defaid to the seaside village of Llanbedrog where Andrews had an art gallery, pleasure garden, roller skating rink and tea rooms at Plas Glyn y Weddw. Like the rest of the tramway, this was a single-track line with passing loops added or lifted as was thought fit. About 1906 the town section – the 'West End Tramway' – was doubled.

Cheaply built with flat-bottomed rails spiked to wooden sleepers and cheaply operated with 14 small open cars and four closed ones of various designs (all presumably built by Andrews at various times), there is no knowing how long the line might have survived if an exceptionally violent gale on the night of 28 October 1927 had not washed away ¼ mile of track and foreshore between the West End and Carreg y Defaid; the remaining track on this unprotected and unpaved section was either flooded, buried or torn up. (A similar but less damaging occurrence in October 1896 had led to the line being moved from the beach itself into the dunes.) Reconstruction was judged too expensive and so ended not only the summer holidaymakers' excursions along the bay but also the Llanbedrog villagers' winter service to Pwllheli. The ubiquitous motorbus was on hand however to meet their needs, a fact which contributed to the decision to close the town section at the end of the 1928 summer season, Pwllheli Corporation being unwilling to take it over. What could be salvaged was lifted that same year. One of the closed car bodies was rescued from a nearby farm in 1969, restored and displayed outside Pwllheli station. It has been renovated recently but its future home is at present undecided.

Bibliography: as above and *Keep Moving: the Story of Solomon Andrews and His Family*

John F. Andrews (Stewart Williams, Barry, 1976) 0 900807 23 7

RHONDDA TRAMWAYS

Authority: Rhondda Tramways Act 1902
Gauge: 3ft 6in
Traction: Overhead electric
Opened: 11 July 1908
Closed: 1 February 1934
System: Network
Length: 20.92 miles
Stock: 54 dd
Livery: Maroon & yellow
Last Car: ?

After the purchase of the Rhondda portion of the PONTYPRIDD & RHONDDA VALLEY line in February 1903, Rhondda UDC entered into an agreement with the National Electric Construction Co. to build the line on behalf of the Rhondda Tramways Co. Ltd (registered 14 April 1906) as it was specifically prohibited by its 1902 empowering Act from operating the tramway itself. Instead, it was leased to the RT Co. (a subsidiary of the NEC) for £2,250 per annum.

Services began with a fleet of 50 open-top Brush cars working two routes from Trehafod (diverging just up the line at Porth), on the municipal boundary with Pontypridd. The first route ran west and north up the Rhondda Fawr Valley as far as Partridge Road and the second north and west up the parallel Rhondda Fach Valley to Pont-y-Gwaith (later extended a mile to Ferndale), each line being about 4 miles of single track. On 2 September 1908 the Rhondda Fawr line was extended another 3 miles or so further up the valley to Pentre whilst on 5 November of the same year a third route was opened, from Porth west and north through Pen-y-Graig and Tonypandy to

rejoin the Rhondda Fawr line at Partridge Road. Total route length was now 18¼ miles and the overall appearance of the system dominated by the routes' adherence to the steep-sided valleys which they threaded on the narrow roads linking the strung-out mining communities. Current was supplied by another NEC subsidiary, the Rhondda Tramways Electric Supply Co. Ltd.

The last three short extensions opened on 30 March 1912: from Treherbert to Tynewydd and from Ferndale to Maerdy at the heads of their valleys while a 1-mile branch south from Pen-y-Graig to Williamstown completed the system. To help cope with the extra mileage four more Brush double-deckers (Nos 51-54) were bought in 1913; these were built with top covers and, following their not unsurprising popularity in the wet Welsh valleys, most of the earlier cars were similarly equipped.

Through running with the PONTY-PRIDD system began in July 1919 and in August 1920 the Company began a motor bus service. (It had already experimented with trolleybuses in 1914-15 on a feeder route to Williamstown.) The bus fleet grew over the next decade and on the last day of 1933 all the Rhondda Fawr routes closed with the Rhondaa Fach line going the same way shortly after, the Company changing its name in June 1934 to the Rhondda Transport Co. Ltd.

Bibliography: *The Rhondda Valleys* E. D. Lewis (Phoenix House, 1959)

SWANSEA TRAMWAYS

Authority: Swansea Improvements and Tramways Act 1874
Gauge: 4ft 8½in
Traction: Horse, steam/overhead electric

Rhondda Tramways No 50 of 1908 attracts a crowd of small admirers in De Winton Street, Tonypandy. (Lens of Sutton)

Opened: 12 April 1878
Closed: 29 June 1937*
System: Network
Length: 13.36 miles
Stock: 2 locos, 25? sd & dd horse & steam;
  56 sd, 51 dd electric
Livery: Maroon & cream
Last Car: No 35?

In its final form, this system consisted of a dense network of lines criss-crossing the town centre with longer routes out to the north, east and west. Originally promoted in 1874 by the Swansea Tramways Co., it was owned and operated by the Swansea Improvements & Tramways Co. Ltd (though just over 7 miles of the track was leased from Swansea Corporation) who began with a 1-mile horse line from Gower Street in the town centre southwest via St Helens Road to St Helens on the shore of Swansea Bay. Here, a connection was made beyond the depot with the SWANSEA & MUMBLES line over which, until 1896, the Company ran its horse cars (see below). A second, 2¾-miles line ran northwards along the High Street and Neath Road up the Tawe Valley to Morriston where it terminated outside the Duke's Arms, just south of the metalworking village. A third line opened in 1882 and continued up Swansea High Street northwestwards to Cwmbwrla (where a second depot was built).

For the first two years the Cwmbwrla branch was worked by two Hughes steam tram locomotives but in 1884 the horses took over. The starting point for the two northerly routes was at the end of the High Street close to but not directly connected to the Gower Street terminus though in 1882 a short, circuitous link was made off the High Street opposite the GWR's High Street station westwards along Alexandra Road, south across the Gower Street/St Helens

Road junction then southeast to the Docks via Greenfield Street and Rutland Street where it terminated close to the LNWR's Victoria station. This brought the total route length to 5½ miles.

In 1897 control of the Company was bought by the BET who wished to expand and electrify the tramways. The horse services continued to operate whilst the conversion work went on (with some accompanying track-doubling) and on 30 June 1900 the new cars took over on all four routes.

The first electric trams (shedded at a new depot and power station on the site of the old one at St Helens) were Brush single-deckers Nos 1-30 of 1900 (Nos 16-30 were bogie vehicles) which were joined later in 1900 by Brush cars 31-41 which had been built for Leeds in 1899 as single-deckers but then resold to Swansea and converted to open-top double-deckers (which meant that they were restricted to the St Helens route because of low railway bridges on all the others).

Eight second-hand cars were added to stock in 1904, all open-top double-deckers: Nos 42-45 were ex-Gravesend ERTCW cars of 1902 and Nos 46-49 Brush cars of the same date ex-Weston-super-Mare. Both the Leeds and Weston cars were later fitted with top covers.

The reason for the extra cars was that extensions were being planned, notably by the Corporation who on 22 April 1905 opened four sections of line: a ½-mile extension in Morriston to the Midland Hotel, a 1½-mile northern route between the Morriston and Cwmbwrla routes up Llangyfelach Street and Eaton Road to Brynhyfryd, a western route off the Alexandra Road line along Mabsel Street, Walters Road and Sketty Road to the district of that name, and a second western route to the south of this route from a new Wind Street terminus along

Temple Street, Oxford Street, King Edward's Road and Bryn Road to Brynmill some 2 miles away on the coast (crossing both the Docks and St Helens routes in the process).

In January 1905 Glamorgan County Council extended the Morriston line by 0.63 miles to Ynysforgan further up the valley and on 19 August that same year a fifth Corporation line, eastwards from Wind Street across the North Dock Cut and the River Tawe on newly-built swing bridges, was opened, running for a mile to Port Tennant. Apart from some later minor alterations in the town centre, the mixed single and double-track system was now complete. The enlargement generated increased traffic and more cars had to be bought. These were 1901 ERTCW bogie single-deck combination cars ex-Middleton bought in 1905 (Nos 50-55), similar new Brush cars 56-61 bought in 1906 together with open-top double-deckers 62-65, also from Brush.

In 1911 Brush single-deck combination bogie car 66 was added, together with 67, a similar Company-built vehicle. That same year saw the arrival of Brush open-topper 68 (hired until 1914 then replaced by a bogie single-decker) whilst in 1912-13 six more Brush bogie single-deckers (Nos 69-74) were purchased. After this the picture is complicated by the fact that the Company started building replacement bogie single-deckers which took the numbers of withdrawn cars, ending up (eventually) as Nos 16-21 and 50-54, all built between 1912 and 1921. These were joined in 1921 by Nos 75-79, further similar cars from Brush.

During the 1920s the system was improved greatly by a track-doubling programme and many of the older cars were rebuilt by the Company. The last new arrivals were Nos 5-15, Brush enclosed double-deckers of 1923, followed in 1925 by similar cars 3 and 4 and then, from 1926 to 1933, by similar vehicles 22-35 built by the Company.

In 1933 the first major cutback occurred when the Ynysforgan extension was closed; in April 1937 all three northern routes were abandoned, swiftly followed two months later by the eastern and western ones, the trams replaced by South Wales Transport Co. buses. The final day of normal services was 28 June 1937 although a volunteer service, in aid of the local hospital, was operated the next day using car No 35 (and possibly others).

Bibliography: *Swansea's Street Tramways* David H. Beynon (Swansea Maritime and Industrial Museum, 1994) 1 873524 04 8

Swansea single-decker 20 of 1912, built there as a replacement for an older Brush vehicle. (Lens of Sutton)

SWANSEA CONSTITUTION HILL INCLINE TRAMWAY

Authority: Swansea (Constitution-hill) Tramway Order 1896
Gauge: 3ft 6in?
Traction: Cable
Opened: 27 August 1898
Closed: 1902?
System: Single line
Length 0.19 miles
Stock: 2 sd
Livery: ?

This short-lived tramway has to be a prime contender for the title of the most unsuccessful line in the British Isles. It was constructed to serve the residents of the villas then being built on the slopes of Mount Pleasant overlooking the older town and port. The promoter was the Swansea Constitution Hill Incline Tramway Co. Ltd with G. Croydon Marks (see Matlock in Section 1) as the consulting engineer and the immediate problem was how to provide a line up the 1 in 5 gradient of the direct thoroughfare of the Company's title. The solution adopted was to use cable traction with two cars permanently attached to a cable in funicular fashion; the cable ran in a central conduit between the rails and was wound by two gas engines at the top of the hill.

The single-track line was completed by early 1898 but failed its initial BoT inspection on safety grounds and had to be rebuilt, presumably with the interlaced track specified in the 1896 Order. Unfortunately, several details of the line's specifications have vanished from the record and the exact form of the track layout – including its gauge – is now uncertain though there was definitely a mid-way passing loop to allow standard funicular working.

Even the opening of the tramway in August 1898 was marred by technical problems and it closed for a week or so before re-opening. When it did, it soon became apparent that it was not going to be a financial success with its flat 1d fare (up or down) set against staff costs of two men per car and the winding house engineer. Closure soon followed in late 1901 or early 1902; in 1903 it was offered for sale – but this move too proved unsuccessful. In 1905 the Company was wound up after the track, cars and winding gear had been disposed of.

The two Brush cars are thought to have been unique in design on British tramways in that their reversible seats were mounted at an angle to the floor so as to stop passengers sliding off them on the steep slope!

SWANSEA & MUMBLES RAILWAY

Authority: [Swansea and Oystermouth Railway or Tramroad Act 1804]
Gauge: 4ft 8½in
Traction: Horse, steam, battery/overhead electric
Opened: 27 July 1860
Closed: 5 January 1960
System: Single line
Length: 5.38 miles
Stock: 2 sd, 2 dd horse; 12 locos, 16 sd, 24 dd steam; 13 dd electric
Livery: Brown to 1893, then 1st class cars crimson lake & cream, 2nd class brown or brown & cream
Last Car: No 7

After the OYSTERMOUTH TRAMROAD had been in abeyance for several years, part of it was relaid with edge rails in 1855, again for coal traffic, and five years later a horse car passenger service was introduced between the Swansea Royal Institution and Black Pill by the line's owners, the Morris family. The section from Black Pill to Oystermouth was relaid that same year and the passenger service extended on 10 November. It is thought that the four cars used were two open toastracks and two railway-type (ex-railway?) coaches fitted with roof seats. (Fuller details of the tramway's complicated and incomplete rolling stock history are contained in the publications cited below.)

From 1 July 1877 the single-track line was worked by the Swansea Improvements & Tramways Co., the owners of the SWANSEA TRAMWAYS (see above) and, on 31 October that year, sold to a local consortium; the SIT Co. meanwhile set about introducing steam traction (which, very conveniently, was permitted by the vague wording of the 1804 Act) with two Starbuck double-deck trailers and a Hughes tram engine aptly named *Pioneer* which entered regular service on 17 August that same year. From then on the SIT Co. was in constant conflict with the line's owners (incorporated on 31 March 1879 as the Swansea & Mumbles Railway Co. Ltd), resulting in a series of court cases the upshot of which was that while the SIT Co. had running powers over the line (including operating through services from its Swansea system), its cars could only follow on after the S&M's steam trains!

In 1884 the Company leased the line to Sir John Jones Jenkins and Robert Capper who then invited the SIT Co. to run steam trams! This arrangement lasted from 1 July 1885 to the end of 1891, after which the timetable reverted to S&M steam, SIT horse.

On 26 July 1893 the Company was re-incorporated as the Swansea & Mumbles Railways Ltd, the plural form reflecting the intention to construct an extension of 1¼ miles from Oystermouth to Mumbles Head (where a deep-water pier was to be built by the Mumbles Railway & Pier Co.). Part of the extension opened on 6 May 1893 and the remainder on 10 May 1898; the new, flat-bottomed track was then continued back 1½ miles from Oystermouth to Black Pill (opening the same year), the old, bypassed section then being abandoned in favour of the new line closer to the sea. From 1 July 1899 both the S&M and the MRP were leased by the SIT Co. for 999 years; the SIT meanwhile had been acquired by the BET and, although its street lines were promptly electrified, the Mumbles line relied on steam until the South Wales Transport Co. Ltd (who had taken over the lease from 1 January 1927) introduced electric trams on

Edwardian postcard of the Swansea & Mumbles' bustling western terminus with one of the tramway's saddle tanks, a single-deck and at least two double-deck trailers arriving. (Author's Collection)

Two of the massive Swansea & Mumbles electric double-deckers of 1928-29 running as a train. (Author's Collection)

2 March 1929 with thirteen Brush 106-seater bogie cars (Nos 1-13) – some of the largest electric trams in the British Isles. Before then steam working had been the order of the day with double-deck cars (including adapted horse cars) and open cattle trucks coupled in trains behind a railway-type tank engine (although two Brush double-deck battery cars had been experimented with in 1902). One such train of 20 cars once carried 1,800 people – believed to be a world tramway record! The line now relied heavily on day-trippers and other excursionists for its traffic; goods traffic was rapidly dwindling away (hauled after electrification by Nos 14 and 15, four-wheeled Hardy petrol and Fowler diesel shunters of 1929 and 1936 respectively).

Electrification brought other improvements in its wake. Journey time from Rutland Street to Mumbles was shortened from 35 minutes to 19 whilst more passing places enabled a more frequent service to be operated, with eight stopping places between the termini (and cars often running in pairs).

In 1954 the line played host to a programme of 150th anniversary celebrations – including journeys made by replica horse and steam cars – but just four years later moves were being made to prepare this historic line for closure and replace the trams with buses. First, in 1958, the SWTC bought out the still-existing owners, the S&M and the MRP companies and then, almost immediately, applied to Parliament for the authority to close the tramway. Despite local, national and even international protests, the SWTC won the day, unopposed by Swansea Corporation – which had been promised the tramway's land for free. So, in shabby fashion, the world's oldest passenger-carrying line was closed.

The story does not quite end there. In 1975 the Mumbles Railway Society was formed which has since campaigned for the relaying of at least part of the old line as a tourist attraction. Whether it will succeed or not is another matter.

Bibliography: as for OYSTERMOUTH TRAMROAD

WREXHAM DISTRICT TRAMWAYS

Authority: Wrexham District Tramways Act 1873
Gauge: 3ft
Traction: Horse

Opened: 1 November 1876
Closed: 26 April 1901
System: Single line
Length: 2.78 miles
Stock: 1 sd, 2 dd
Livery: Brown & cream?
Last Car: No 3?

This line was constructed to serve the coal mining district immediately south of Wrexham by linking it, via the Ruabon Road, with the east Denbighshire town itself. It was promoted and owned by the Wrexham District Tramways Co. but was hardly in keeping with its grand title as authorized extensions at either end – from the southern Johnstown terminus to the village of Rhos and, more importantly, from the northern Ruabon Road terminus on the edge of Wrexham through the town centre – were never built (though a month after the opening the line was extended another ¼ mile along Ruabon Road to its junction with Ruthin Road after the removal of a toll gate).

It is likely that the Company's capital of £10,000 had all been spent on the portion of line actually laid and with only two cars (an original single-decker and one double-decker, both from Starbuck and housed at Johnstown) a high return on the investment was unlikely, even after the single-decker was rebuilt with seats on the roof. In keeping with the reality of the situation, the Company changed its name to Wrexham Tramways Ltd and c1880 leased the line for £3 a week to a local coal merchant, Frederick Jones. In 1884 Jones bought the tramway's two cars and six horses and promptly built another double-decker

The spartan Johnstown depot of the Wrexham & District with four of the line's ten cars, all of 1903, shortly after delivery. (Author's Collection)

in his Wrexham yard – and then had to remove the top deck to enable it to pass out under his archway!

In December 1898 the Company gave notice that it intended to rebuild the line and introduce electric traction and, the following year, closed the tramway down.

Bibliography: *North Wales Tramways* Keith Turner (David & Charles, 1979)
0 7153 7769 8

WREXHAM & DISTRICT ELECTRIC TRAMWAYS

Authority: Wrexham District Tramways
   Order 1899
Gauge: 3ft 6in
Traction: Overhead electric
Opened: 4 April 1903
Closed: 31 March 1927
System: Branching
Length: 4.44 miles

Stock: 10 dd
Livery: Deep red & cream
Last Car: No 9

The reconstructed Wrexham horse tramway (see above) was operated by the Wrexham & District Electric Tramways Co. Ltd, a subsidiary of the BET who had taken control of the enterprise in December 1900 after Wrexham Tramways Ltd had obtained the authority for the reconstruction. The track was relaid to a more suitable gauge, the line electrified and extended at each end as had been planned originally for the horse line; the southern terminus was in the district of Ponciau between Johnstown and Rhos (this ½-mile westwards extension opened 1904) and the northern terminus outside the Turf Hotel by the racecourse, now a football ground (this town section opening in mid-May 1903). The line was, like its predeces-sor, single-track, the only double stretch being a few hundred yards through the centre of Wrexham where the 1 in 12 of Vicarage Hill was the steepest point on the line.

Open-top double-deck cars 1-10 were supplied by Brush for the opening and no others were ever bought.

Hopes of extensions to Llangollen and elsewhere came to nothing – even an authorized branch into Rhos proper was never completed – and in 1912 the Company began motor bus operations, changing its name two years later to the Wrexham & District Transport Co. Ltd. After the hiatus of World War I the bus services increasingly dominated the trams and in 1927 the line closed completely, the two depots at Johnstown and Wrexham becoming bus garages.

Bibliography: as above

Section 3

Tramways of Scotland

The development, history and location of tramways in Scotland were influenced by the same factors that applied south of the border. The three main concentrations of systems were centred on the three great firths of the Clyde, Forth and Tay; not surprisingly this was where, for historical and geographical reasons, the main centres of population and industry were sited. Unlike in England and Wales though, the number of isolated systems outside these main concentrations was extremely small and almost without exception sited in towns along either the east or the west coast.

One feature of the Clyde network deserves special mention: the whole inter-connected network of different systems used the unusual (elsewhere) gauge of 4ft 7¾in as it was envisaged from the start that railway goods wagons would be run over tramway lines in GLASGOW and the surrounding connurbation. (See Introduction.) So it proved, with private industrial operators moving their own freight trains hauled by their own steam and electric locomotives over the street lines between railway sidings, factories and ship yards in this major area of heavy industry.

The last portion of the Clyde tramways was abandoned in 1962, closing a chapter not only in Scottish transport history but also in that of the whole British Isles for it was the last tramway abandonment to take place, leaving just a handful of surviving lines. None, alas, are in Scotland.

ABERDEEN DISTRICT TRAMWAYS

Authority: Aberdeen District Tramways Act 1872
Gauge: 4ft 8½in
Traction: Horse
Opened: 31 August 1874
Taken Over: 27 August 1898
System: Network
Length: 11.87 miles

Stock: 3 sd, 37 dd?
Livery: Route colour & cream

Aberdeen's first tramways were promoted and operated by the Aberdeen District Tramways Co., not without some initial financial difficulties which meant that track-laying did not start until April 1874, three years after fund raising began. The first routes opened were an east–west line from North Church via Castle Street, Union Street and Albyn Place to near the depot at Queens Cross (1¼ miles), and a north–south line from Causewayend down George Street and St Nicholas Street to meet the other route in Union Street (1 mile). Two single-deckers and four double-deckers were supplied for the opening, possibly by Starbuck, and were joined at the end of 1875 by another pair of double-deckers.

On 12 June 1876 the system's first extension opened: a stretch of about 200yd from the Causewayend terminus to the GNSR's station at Kittybrewster; at the same time another double-decker was bought. On 1 September 1880 three further extensions opened. The first ran southwest from the Union Street/Albyn Place junction ('Holborn Junction') down Holborn Street and Great Western Road to the district of Mannofield (1¼ miles) whilst the second was a short extension of the North Church route up King Street to the Cattle Market; the third extended the line from Kittybrewster up the Great Northern Road to Woodside (again about 1¼ miles) where a small depot was constructed. The following year the Company began running horse buses as feeders to the tramway and in 1882 added two double-deckers to the car fleet, followed by another a year later. (The last car was built by R. & J. Shinnie of Aberdeen.) All routes were single-track originally though several central sections were later doubled as routes lengthened and traffic increased.

After a shocking financial start it seems that the enlarged system was a success (helped by the growth of the city) and further extensions and new routes were planned. During late December 1883 a length of just over ¼ mile continued the Holborn Street line down to Bloomfield Road and on 30 November 1888 a circular route from Queens Cross north and east through Rosemount then south to Union Street was opened, to work which four more Shinnie double-deckers were bought.

In 1889 three more Shinnie double-deckers were added to the fleet, plus a Company-built toastrack for summer workings, followed in 1891 by (probably) five more double-deckers from Shinnies. Some of these were intended to work the lengthened King Street route which was extended in July 1892 to University Road and on 24 August that year as far as Bridge of Don where it terminated just short of the bridge on the southern bank of the river; three more Shinnie cars were bought after this line's opening.

The next new route ran in the opposite direction, south from Bloomfield Road to Bridge of Dee where the line again terminated just short of the river crossing, this time on the northern bank. This opened on 24 August 1894, by which time another nine (probably) Shinnie double-deckers had been added to stock, followed two years later by three more. The system's last extension, opened on 22 August 1896, was a ½-mile branch west from Queens Cross along Queens Road to Bayview. By now Aberdeen Corporation was expressing an interest in taking over the system (as a prelude to electrifying it) – as was the GNSR – and after obtaining the necessary authority, did so from midnight of 26 August 1898 (see below).

No mention has been made of car numbers. This is because, unusually, the trams carried route numbers only which were interchangeable; they also, not so

Aberdeen District horse car No 1, later converted to electric working by the Corporation, now restored at the Grampian Transport Museum, Alford. (Grampian Transport Museum)

unusually, were painted in distinguishing colours to denote additionally which route they worked. (One of the cars, converted to electric working by the Corporation and numbered 1, can now be seen at the Grampian Transport Museum, Alford.)

The Company was unique amongst British tramways in that, from December 1878 onwards for some years, it operated a public sledge service over the tramway routes when the Scottish winters prevented the horse cars from running. Pulled by a team of four horses, each sledge seated 20 passengers on a wooden frame mounted on iron runners.

Bibliography: *The Aberdeen District Tramways* (Public Transport in Aberdeen Vol 1) M. J. Mitchell & I. A. Souter (NB Traction, Dundee, 1983) 0 905069 20 X

ABERDEEN CORPORATION TRAMWAYS

Authority: Aberdeen Corporation
   Tramways Act 1898
Gauge: 4ft 8½in
Traction: Horse, overhead electric
Took Over: 27 August 1898
Closed: 3 May 1958
System: Network
Length: 16.12 miles
Stock: 39 sd & dd horse; 168 dd electric?
Livery: Route colour & cream horse; route
   colour, dark green & white electric
Last Car: No 36

Following its takeover of the the ABERDEEN DISTRICT TRAMWAYS (see above), Aberdeen Corporation set about modernizing the system with the first refurbished route, St Nicholas Street to Woodside, re-opening on 23 December 1899 and the remainder following within the next two years. Also built at this time was a new easterly branch from Castle Street to Sea Beach (opened 4 July 1901) and two south-easterly routes to Torry and Duthie Park via Ferry Hill to complete the system for the present.

As well as the lines, the Corporation took over a total of 39 of the District's horse cars and most of these – probably 32 double-deckers – were rebuilt as electric cars as they were needed. These were joined in 1903 by 24 DK open-top (later top-covered) double-deckers (Nos 33-56). The old Queens Cross Depot was rebuilt as the main electric car depot and the two smaller sheds at Mannofield and Woodside also converted.

Ten years later, in 1913, top-covered cars 72-77 were built by J. T. Clark and these were joined the next year by similar Brush vehicles 78-83 and in 1915 by Nos 84-86, Corporation-built vehicles. Another twelve Corporation cars, top-covered 87-98, were added five years later. Although Corporation bus services were begun at this time, the tramways were by no means neglected and during the period 1919-31 the

Corporation constructed another 26 cars (Nos 57-63, 66-67, 99-106 and 116-124); Nos 107-115 were 1925 Brush vehicles. On 16 July 1924 a 2-mile westerly branch to the residential area of Hazelhead (with a short branch off it to Woodend) was opened.

The system's first closure came in 1931 when, on 28 February, the Torry route closed, followed on 30 May by the Duthie Park line. This did not signal the end of the

Two of Aberdeen Corporation's early trams, converted horse car 27 and purpose-built 36 of 1903, both in top-covered form, on a Union Street postcard. (Lens of Sutton)

tramways however but was rather a way of making the system more efficient. Indeed, in 1937 a short new line – an out-and-back loop off the Bridge of Don route to serve the football ground at Pittodrie – was opened, followed by an extension of the Woodside line to Scatterburn, formerly part of the ABERDEEN SUBURBAN TRAMWAYS route (see below).

Meanwhile, 18 ex-Nottingham enclosed double-deckers had been bought in 1936 and numbered 1-18 to replace ageing original vehicles, and four years later modern EE streamlined double-deckers Nos 138-141 were added to the fleet. (The first two of these were bogie vehicles.)

After World War II the Corporation retained its faith in tramways whilst many others in Britain were losing theirs and continued to upgrade the system in all departments. In 1948 it purchased 14 ex-Manchester Corporation 'Pilcher' enclosed cars, Nos 39-52, and the next year bought 20 new streamlined bogie vehicles from Pickerings (Nos 19-38). It was a last, valiant gesture for as older cars were withdrawn, so were more of the services. On 3 March 1951 the Mannofield route closed, on 2 October 1954 Rosemount circle and, on 26 November 1955, the Woodside line. In 1956 the Hazelhead and Woodend lines went (7 October and 17 November respectively) and on 13 March 1957 the Sea Beach line, leaving the main north–south Bridge of Don–Bridge of Dee to be the last to go.

ABERDEEN SUBURBAN TRAMWAYS

Authority: Aberdeen Tramways Order 1902
Gauge: 4ft 8½in
Traction: Overhead electric

Opened: 23 June 1904
Closed: 9 June 1927?
System: Two single lines
Length: 4.59 miles
Stock: 11 dd
Livery: Red & white
Last Car: No 11

The Aberdeen Suburban Tramways Co. was one of that small group of tramways owners who operated a system made up of two separate sections. The first ran for some 2½ miles from the ABERDEEN CORPORATION terminus at Mannofield (see above), being in effect a single-track continuation of the Great Western Road route through Pitfodels

and Cults to Bieldside Church on northern Deeside; the second, the Donside route, was a single-track continuation of the Corporation's Great Northern Road route from Woodside out through Scatterburn and Bucksburn to Bankhead, terminating at Stoneywood Church.

The system's first six cars were Brush double-deckers of which Nos 1 and 5 were open and Nos 2-4 and 6 top-covered. These were joined in 1905 by Nos 7-9, UEC top-covered cars, in 1911 by No 10 and in 1914 by No 11, two similar cars from the same firm. Small depots were sited at Mannofield and Bankside.

Through running over the Corporation's lines had been agreed before the opening with the Deeside trams starting from Castle Street and the Donside ones from St Nicholas Street. Each line was worked by three cars on regular services with the extra cars (as they arrived) providing extra cover as required, usually on Sundays and Bank Holidays on the Deeside route which was very popular with day-trippers.

In 1914 the Company began running three Tilling-Stevens petrol-electric buses as feeders to the tramways but now the Corporation, unhappy about its arrangement with the Company, began exploring the possiblitiy of taking the two lines over, only to baulk at the asking price. It seems the Company missed its chance for by the end of World War I track and stock were in a bad way – and getting rapidly worse – and because of this, effective from 9 June 1926, the Corporation terminated through running from both routes. It was then just a year before the Company went under with the last Deeside 'Subbies' running on Saturday 2

Aberdeen Corporation streamliner No 37 of 1949, one of a batch of 20 bought after World War II to help modernize the system. (Lens of Sutton)

June 1927, the Donside service ceasing a few days (possibly one week) later. The track was lifted the following year though part of the Donside route was relaid ten years later by the Corporation (see above).

Bibliography: *The Aberdeen Suburban Tramways* M. J. Mitchell & I. A. Souter (NB Traction, Dundee, 1980) 0 905069 14 5

AIRDRIE & COATBRIDGE TRAMWAYS
Authority: Airdrie and Coatbridge Tramways Act 1900
Gauge: 4ft 7¾in

Traction: Overhead electric
Opened: 8 February 1904
Taken Over: 1 January 1922
System: Single line
Length: 3.63 miles
Stock: 15 dd
Livery: Maroon & cream

A dozen miles to the east of Glasgow, the Lanarkshire towns of Airdrie and Coatbridge prospered as iron-working centres in the 19th century but, although schemes to link them by tramway to Glasgow had been proposed since the 1870s, it was not until the next century that one was actually constructed – and another 20 years after that

before the Glasgow link was made. The line was built by the BET (who had succeeded the promoters, the Scottish House-to-House Electricity Supply Co.), and operated through a subsidiary, the Airdrie & Coatbridge Tramways Co.

The first section of the single-track line opened ran from Motherwell Street in Airdrie, westwards along the main road through Airdrie Cross and Coatdyke to the burgh boundary at Kirkwood Street, Coatbridge, a distance of 3½ miles. Twelve open-top double-deck cars were supplied by Brush and a depot erected for them on Main Street midway between Coatbridge and Coatdyke. The following year three more

The Airdrie & Coatbridge Tramways Coy.

NOTICE
RE
ALTERATION OF FARES AND STAGES.

The public are respectfully informed that the undermentioned Alterations in Fares and Sections will be introduced on 1st January, 1911, namely :--

SECTIONS.
Airdrie Cross will be a Section Point instead of Airdrie Station.
Biggar Road will be a Section Point instead of Knox Street.
Dunbeth Road Section Point discontinued.

FARES.
The route from Woodside Street Terminus to Motherwell Street Terminus will be divided into 13 Sections, as below :---

0 1 2 3 4 5 6 7 8 9 10 11 12 13

The fares will be as follows :---

Any 2 Consecutive Sections,	. . .	½d.
„ 4 „ „	. . .	1d.
„ 7 „ „	. . .	1½d.
„ 10 „ „	. . .	2d.
Through Fare,	. . . . .	2½d.

The Fare Stages, with the above exceptions, will remain as at present, except that the 1¼d, 1¾d, and 2¼d Fares will be discontinued.

ARCHD. ROBERTSON,
General Manager.

Tramway Depot, Coatbridge, December, 1910.

The Airdrie & Coatbridge Tramways 1911 new fare structure.

Brush double-deckers were purchased (No 14 with a top cover and Nos 12 and 15 so equipped soon after arrival) and, on 16 August 1905, an extension of 368yd took the western terminus to Woodside Street.

By the end of World War I the track was in need of major repair work, if not outright replacement, and on 20 September 1920 the line was purchased jointly by Airdrie and Coatbridge Town Councils for £77,550 before being passed on for working, as from the first day of 1922, to GLASGOW CORPORATION. In May of that year a start was made on connecting the two systems via a short link line from Coatbridge to Baillieston and on 28 December this was completed with a formal opening two days later.

Although through running was now possible, this did not occur until the old track had been replaced (and doubled), the line being closed on 3 June 1924 to allow the work to be done; it re-opened on 23 May following. The Company's trams were absorbed into the Glasgow fleet, taking the numbers 1073-1087, and withdrawn for scrapping in the early 1930s though former Nos 1 and 4 became briefly a decorated car and an overhead inspection works car respectively.

Bibliography: *Lanarkshire's Trams* A. W. Brotchie (ed) (NB Traction, Dundee, 1993) 0 905069 29 3

AYR CORPORATION TRAMWAYS
Authority: Ayr Burgh Act 1899
Gauge: 4ft 8½in
Traction: Overhead electric
Opened: 26 September 1901
Closed: 31 December 1931
System: Branching
Length: 6.39 miles
Stock: 4 sd, 25 dd
Livery: Dark chocolate & primrose
Last Car: No 9

Spurred into action by a private promotion, Ayr Town Council rapidly sought powers in 1898 for its own tramway operation, securing them the following year. It seems that electric traction was envisaged from the outset, making the town one of the first users of that mode of traction in Scotland. (Only GLASGOW and ABERDEEN had by then adopted it.) The Council was also one of the first to ask to operate lines beyond its boundaries, an innovation later picked up by other corporations.

The first 4 miles opened ran from Prestwick Cross north of the town southwards along the Ayr Road for 1¼ miles to the municipal boundary, then on past the depot at Newton Park, through the town centre (where the track was double for a mile) to a temporary terminus at the start of Monument Road by St Leonard's Church.

Services were operated by a fleet of HN open-top double-deckers (Nos 1-10) and electricity supplied by the Council's own generating station.

The line was an immediate success and the Council quickly pushed ahead with the remaining, rural 1½ miles authorized down Monument Road to the village of Alloway for the benefit of visitors to the twin attractions of the Burns Cottage and the Monument to the poet at Brig o' Doon. This section (again single-track) opened on 29 May 1902 and necessitated the purchase of a further six open-toppers (Nos 11-16) from HN. Car No 18, which arrived from the same firm in 1904, was a luxurious open-top vehicle built for the 1902 Tramways Exhibition in London and was used on special occasions as well as working normal services whilst Nos 19 and 20 were 1907 HN open-toppers. (No 17 was a works car.)

The only further section built (authorized in 1908) was the double-track Hawkhill branch which ran due east from the town centre for a mile along George Street and Whitletts Road to serve the Racecourse; this opened on 18 August 1913 and added two more HN open-toppers (Nos 21 and 22) to the car fleet. Nos 23 and 24 were HN top-covered vehicles of 1915, Nos 25-28 ex-Manchester Corporation single-deckers built by Brush in 1899, bought in 1922 and converted to one-man operation for the Hawkhill branch whilst Nos 29 and 30, bought six years later, were formerly DUMBARTON Nos 31 and 32, large EE top-covered cars of 1921 vintage. These last two survived the post-closure scrapping of the trams by being sold to South Shields.

Although the tramway served well both residents and visitors to this popular holiday coast, it succumbed inevitably to the competition offered by the motor bus when the Council faced a choice between serious expenditure on the track and rolling stock or curtailing the routes and withdrawing many of the cars. In December 1931 the concern was sold to the Scottish Motor Traction Co. Ltd of Edinburgh who promptly killed it off by the simple expedient of not re-opening it the day after the takeover.

Bibliography: *The Tramways of Ayr* Ronald W. Brash (NB Traction, Dundee, 1983) 0 905069 19 6

BLACKDOG see STRABATHIE & BLACKDOG

BRIDGE OF ALLAN see STIRLING & BRIDGE OF ALLAN

BROUGHTY FERRY see DUNDEE, BROUGHTY FERRY & DISTRICT

CARSTAIRS HOUSE TRAMWAY
Carstairs has been an important railway junction in the Scottish Lowlands since 1884 when the Caledonian Railway opened its lines from there to Glasgow, Edinburgh and Carlisle. During the 1880s Joseph Monteith, an amateur engineer, built a small water turbine and generator to light his residence, Carstairs House, south of the village. Then, probably in 1888, work began on the construction of an electric tramway to link the House with the railway station. The 2ft 6in gauge line was 1,890yd long and was possibly inspired by a demonstration line at the 1886 Edinburgh International Exhibition. It was laid wholly on estate land and commenced by the East Lodge just over the road from the station and followed the main driveway, then a farm boundary, to (and through!) the estate sawmill before reaching the House. Several short branches came off the single-track line, including one at the station to interchange sidings (used mainly for coal for the House) and, at the other end, to the boiler house and to a small rustic car shed.

As with all such early electric lines the distinction between 'railway' and 'tramway' was a blurred one with the current being supplied and returned by means of raised conductor strips either side of the line (except at level crossings which were coasted over).

Details of the stock are annoyingly sketchy. The principal car is thought to have been constructed locally and was a four-wheeled saloon seating six passengers. There were in addition at least two goods or luggage trucks – possibly conversions of the two North Metropolitan cars used at the Edinburgh International Exhibition which are rumoured to have passed to the line.

Electric working seems to have ceased c1895 (possibly it came to be regarded as dangerous) and the line was then horse-operated, apparently for goods traffic only. In 1924 the House was purchased by the Diocese of Glasgow for use as a children's institution; extensive alterations were made to the property and probably the tramway was abandoned then. What remained was sold for scrap c1932, thus ending the life of Scotland's first permanent, if private, electric tramway.

Bibliography: *Lanarkshire's Trams* A. W. Brotchie (ed) (NB Traction, Dundee, 1993) 0 905069 29 3

COATBRIDGE see AIRDRIE & COATBRIDGE

CRUDEN BAY HOTEL TRAMWAY
Authority: –
Gauge: 3ft 6½in
Traction: Overhead electric
Opened: June 1899?

Closed: 31 October 1932
System: Single line
Length: 0.66 miles
Stock: 2 sd
Livery: GNSR purple lake & cream, then
    LNER teak
Last Car: ?

Constructed by the GNSR to link its Cruden Bay Hotel (opened March 1899) on the Aberdeenshire coast with Cruden Bay station on its Ellon–Boddam branch (opened 1896), this short line carried both passengers (to the front door of the Hotel) and goods (via a short spur to the tradesmen's entrance). Perhaps more importantly, all the GNSR's laundry was done at the Hotel and the tramway was built as much to carry this as to carry passengers.

The Hotel was constructed under the Great North of Scotland Railway (Various Powers) Act 1893 but this makes no mention of a tramway which was presumably constructed wholly on Company-owned land. It is thought to have opened three months after the Hotel did and commenced with a paved section in the station forecourt, then crossed the roadway onto a rural reserved section where the track was laid with bullhead rails and ballasted; at the front of the Hotel a triangular junction marked the point where the goods siding diverged. Two ornate closed combination cars were built for the tramway by the GNSR at its Kittybrewster Works in Aberdeen, each with a passenger saloon and an end platform for luggage and laundry baskets. All in all they were rather sumptuous vehicles with ornate ironwork, etched and bevelled window glass, GNSR coach livery and velvet curtains and upholstery of a gold colour. In 1901 the Hotel Manager apparently proposed that they be used as staff sleeping quarters, thus making more room for guests, but it is not known if this ever came about. There was also a small number of goods vehicles.

After the 1923 Grouping control of the tramway and Hotel passed to the LNER who repainted the cars in its own passenger stock livery and numbered them 1 and 2; when the railway branch closed at the end of October 1932 (replaced by a bus service) the cars were withdrawn from passenger service and the line ran as goods-only. (The passenger service had been free to Hotel guests though non-residents could use it for a fee.) In March 1941 the Hotel was requisitioned by the Army, the tramway closed and the cars sold locally for use as summer houses – a common fate for obsolete trams though none was probably as ever as luxurious as this pair. Happily, both have been rescued for restoration as one car at the Grampian Transport Museum, Alford.

DUMBARTON BURGH & COUNTY TRAMWAYS

Authority: Dumbarton Tramways Order
    1904
Gauge: 4ft 7¾in
Traction: Overhead electric
Opened: 20 February 1907
Closed: 3 March 1928
System: Branching
Length: 13.1 miles
Stock: 4 sd*, 28 dd
Livery: Chocolate & cream to 1908, then
    green & cream
Last Car: ?

Although the envisaged through running between the two systems never came about, the Dumbarton main route formed an end-on connection with the GLASGOW network and provided a convenient escape route for the inhabitants of that city to the shores of Loch Lomond and its surrounding countryside.

The line was constructed by DK and operated initially by the Electric Supply Corporation Ltd as the sole tramway amongst its power generation concerns, but shortly after the opening the undertaking was transferred, under the provisions of the Dumbarton Burgh and County Tramways Order 1907 to a subsidiary, the Dumbarton Burgh & County Tramways Co. Ltd (though power was still supplied by the ESC from its generating station).

The line as opened consisted of a main line running northwest from Dumbuck via Dumbarton High Street to Dalreoch Quarry (some 3 miles) plus a branch from the High Street northwards to Barloan Toll (about ½ mile). In February 1908 construction began again and the main line was extended northwards beyond the burgh boundary to Alexandria. This section opened on 7 May of the same year and was followed on 25 June by two further extensions: northwards to Balloch at the southern tip of Loch Lomond and, at the other end of the line, along the northern bank of the River Clyde to Dalmuir West where the aforementioned connection with the Glasgow system was made.

The final route to open (on 24 January 1909) was a second short branch, this time from Alexandria to Jamestown. All routes were single-track in what were then principally country roads.

The original car fleet was made up of Brush open-canopied double-deckers 1-6; these were augmented in 1908 by UEC open-toppers 7-26 and in 1909 by four ex-horse cars from GLASGOW CORPORATION (Nos 27-30). These latter vehicles were used on the Jamestown branch with the upper seats and superstructure removed and the stairs boarded up on account of a low bridge in Bank Street,

Alexandria. In 1920 the line's last two cars, EE open-toppers 31 and 32, were purchased.

After initial success the tramway was soon hit by motor bus competition on this major route from Glasgow to the Highlands and no dividend was paid to shareholders after 1922; matters were not helped by the fact that Glasgow's trolley heads and Dumbarton's swivels were not compatible, thus preventing through running. After closure, all the cars were scrapped except the two youngest – Nos 31 and 32 – which went to AYR.

Bibliography: *Dumbarton's Trams and Buses*
    A. W. Brotchie & R. L. Grieves (NB
    Traction, Dundee, 1985) 0 905069 24 2

DUNDEE & DISTRICT TRAMWAY

Authority: Dundee Tramways Act 1872
Gauge: 4ft 8½in
Traction: Horse, steam
Opened: 30 August 1877
Taken Over: 31 May 1899
System: Radial network
Length: 5.66 miles
Stock: 2 sd, 20 dd horse; 13 locos, 11 dd
    steam
Livery: Polished mahogany to 1879, then
    dark red & yellow to 1894, then dark
    green & cream

Dundee's first tramway was a double-track line just over 1¼ miles in length – the first part of a grander authorized scheme – running eastwards from Windsor Street off Perth Road, down Perth Road, Nethergate, the High Street and Reform Street to the main Post Office in Euclid Crescent. It was promoted by the Dundee Tramway & Omnibus Co. Ltd, constructed by the Police Commissioners, then leased to the Dundee & District Tramway Co. Ltd (incorporated August 1877)! All in all it seems to have been a rush job in order to prevent the powers of its Act lapsing, so much so in fact that two cars from the EDINBURGH STREET TRAMWAYS and three from the GLASGOW TRAMWAY had to be hired for the opening. These were open-top double-deckers numbered 1A-5A respectively and were quickly joined by similar vehicles 6A and 7A which were purchased rather than hired from Glasgow (whereupon 4A and 5A were returned). In December 1877 the line received its first new cars, three open-toppers built by the Glasgow Tramway & Omnibus Co. and numbered 3A-5A (the Edinburgh cars now having been returned as well).

In 1878 work began on expanding the system and on 24 December 1879 a ½-mile single-track extension of the Perth Road route to West Park Road and a 1¼ mile double-track branch from the other end of

Two of Dundee City Tramways' new electric cars passing in the High Street. A typical Edwardian postcard view. (Lens of Sutton)

the line northwards up Lochee Road to the village of that name (and the site of the tramway's permanent depot) were opened. Five more double-deckers were bought, these being constructed by the local firm of T. Swinton & Sons, mounted on Eades patent reversible trucks and numbered – bizarrely and uniquely on British tramways – in Roman fashion: CI, CVIII, CIX, CX and CXI.

Two further 'East End' branches were opened on 19 June 1880 eastwards from the Post Office to Baxter Park and Morgan Hospital, both via Victoria Road. Two smaller, conventional cars (Nos CXII and CXIII) were built by Swintons to help work these lines with another of unknown origin, No 2 (!) added two years later, followed in 1883 by two open-top single-deck summer cars (Nos 14 and 15).

In 1884 the Company began serious use of steam traction (a Dickinson combined car had been experimented with four years earlier) when tram locomotives 1 and 2 were supplied by Greens and a covered double-deck bogie car (No 16) bought, probably from Lancaster, for use on the Lochee route. Two further locos (Nos 3 and 4) followed in 1885 and, with only one purpose-built trailer available, towed pairs of horse cars behind them. Public services with the new motive power began on 20 June 1885 and, from 8 July 1886, on the East End routes as well with two more Green locos. By 1894 the loco stock numbered thirteen and, unusually, they carried names as well as numbers; double-deck trailers were also purchased from a variety of builders as well as being constructed from pairs of surplus horse cars.

The last new routes opened on 17 July 1894 were a short single-track branch off Victoria

Road northwards through the aptly-named Hilltown to the village of Fairmuir, and a short single-track line along Morgan Street to link the two East End routes. (The system's final two horse cars, Nos 22 and 24, were added at this time.)

The tramway now seemed so attractive to Dundee Corporation that it decided to buy it outright and pay the Company £2,100 pa until the lease ran out in 1907, and from 1 June 1899 the Corporation became both owner and operator (see below). The Company was left with the bus side of the business (which it had maintained and expanded) and remained in existence until 1922 when it went into voluntary liquidation.

Bibliography: *Tramways of the Tay Valley*
Alan W. Brotchie (Dundee Museum and Art Gallery, 1965)

DUNDEE CITY TRAMWAYS

Authority: Dundee Corporation (Tramways) Act 1898
Gauge: 4ft 8½in
Traction: Horse, steam, overhead electric
Took Over: 1 June 1899
Closed: 20 October 1956
System: Radial network
Length: 15.51 miles
Stock: 10 dd horse; 13 locos, 10 dd steam; 6 sd, 103 dd electric
Livery: Indian red (dark red-brown) & white
Last Car: No 25

Work began on electrifying the Dundee system shortly after the Corporation takeover (see above), beginning with the

Perth Road and Lochee lines. Public services with the new cars began over the first of these on 12 July 1900 (the horse cars stopping the same day) and on the second on 22 October. Thereafter the remainder of the old system was electrified and extended (with some short central sections abandoned) with the last steam trams running on 14 May 1902 on the Fairmuir route. (The Baxter Park steam line was abandoned until eventually re-opened on 20 August 1906 with electric working).

The first ten electric cars (Nos 1-10) were ERTCW open-top bogie double-deckers (later top-covered) based on the old Lochee Depot. In 1902 eight Milnes open-toppers (Nos 41-48, renumbered 11-27 in 1927), again later top-covered, were bought together with HN bogie combination cars 49-54, the tramway's only single-deckers. On 20 November that year a new route, off the Fairmuir line, was opened to Hilltown and, in 1903, a new depot was built at Maryfield. Further short extensions followed in 1907 and, on 12 November 1908, a short southern branch to Craig Pier on the River Tay was opened. By this time five new top-covered cars had been purchased: Nos 55 and 60 (1907 Brush) and Nos 61-63 (1908 MV).

In 1912 the Corporation began trolleybus operations but abandoned them two years later (the first such services to go in Britain) and further short tramway extensions followed though, on 1 June 1919, the loss-making Craig Pier branch closed.

Four HN cars top-covered cars (Nos 75-78) were bought in 1916, followed by similar vehicles 67, 68 and 79-90 during the period 1920-21 (and which, like many of the Dundee cars, were later renumbered or even renumbered again). Corporation motor bus services began in 1922 and on 26 February 1928 the Constitution Road route was closed, though not before the Corporation had built nine totally enclosed cars (Nos 91-99 of 1923-25), followed in 1930 by ten wide-bodied Brush enclosed cars cars (Nos 19-28) for the Lochee route. The next closure came on 16 May 1931 with the abandonment of the easterly route to Belsize Road where it connected with the DUNDEE, BROUGHTY FERRY & DISTRICT line, after the Corporation had purchased that concern and closed it (see below). On 2 October 1932 the Baxter Park route closed.

The tramway survived World War II comparatively unscathed – compared with many other systems – with 56 serviceable cars and traffic heavy. Also heavy was general road traffic though and on 26 April 1952 the Moncur Crescent route closed (except to football specials). The Blackness route followed on 26 November 1955 and the Downfield route in the early hours of the next morning. The last routes closed less than a year later, on 20 October 1956, with a special farewell procession from Maryfield Depot to Lochee in the early hours of the next day.

Bibliography: as above

DUNDEE, BROUGHTY FERRY & DISTRICT TRAMWAYS
Authority: Dundee Broughty Ferry and
   District Tramways Order 1904
Gauge: 4ft 8½in
Traction: Overhead electric
Opened: 27 December 1905
Closed: 15 May 1931
System: Single line
Length: 5.1 miles
Stock: 16 dd
Livery: Lake & cream
Last Car: ?

After several false starts, the idea of an electric tramway along the north shore of the Firth of Tay became a reality when George Balfour (see Balfour, Beatty in Section 1) successfully promoted its authorizing Act. The line, almost all double-track, was quickly laid and ran for some 4 miles from Craigie Terrace (where it made an end-on connection with the DUNDEE CITY line) eastwards on a mixture of road and reserved sections, all predominantly rural in character and roughly parallel to the Dundee & Arbroath Joint Railway line between those two places, through various settlements (the principal one being Broughty Ferry) to the village of Monifieth where it terminated in the High Street by Union Street. (This section was extended in 1908 by some 300yd to Tay Street.)

Twelve Brush open-top double-deckers were bought for the opening and a depot constructed at Milton, nearly a mile from the terminus. Two more Brush cars (Nos 13 and 14) followed in 1907; these were top-covered vehicles similar to those supplied to Dundee Corporation that same year – a similarity all the more confusing to casual observers as through running was operated.

A second increase in route mileage came in 1914 when the operator, the Dundee, Broughty Ferry & District Tramways Co. Ltd, bought from the Corporation nearly a mile of track and overhead from Craigie Terrace back to the burgh boundary at Belsize Road; at the same time it purchased two of the Corporation's worn-out 1900 ERTCW cars which became Nos 15 and 16 in its fleet. It appears that relations between the two operators later began to deteriorate – the Corporation ran a rival bus service during the period 1921-22 for example – but they united in 1930 against the threat from private bus operators by inaugurating their

own joint bus service. After that it became clear that the future lay with the buses and the last trams ran at the end of the following financial year, the line having been purchased for £25,000 by the Corporation who immediately closed it.

Bibliography: as above

DUNFERMLINE & DISTRICT TRAMWAYS
Authority: Dunfermline and District
   Tramways Order 1906
Gauge: 3ft 6in
Traction: Overhead electric
Opened: 2 November 1909
Closed: 5 July 1937
System: Branching
Length: 18.36 miles
Stock: 2 sd, 45 dd
Livery: Bright green & cream
Last Car: ?

This, by far the largest of Fife's three tramway systems, was built and operated by the Dunfermline & District Tramways Co., a subsidiary of the Fife Electric Power Co. (itself a member of the BET group). The first 4 miles from Dunfermline eastwards to Cowdenbeath were followed on 3 November 1909 by a mile-long branch northwards from Dunfermline to Townshill; on 23 December of that same year the Cowdenbeath line was extended another mile to Lochgelly.

On 17 November 1910 a branch northwards of about 2 miles from Cowdenbeath was opened to Kelty, followed on 5 December 1912 by another 2-mile extension of the main line from Lochgelly to Lochore. A mile-long branch west from Dunfermline to Rumblingwell opened

27 December 1913 and a 3-mile branch south from Dunfermline to Rosyth Dockyard (17 May 1918) completed the system, although hopes were long entertained of extending even further east to link up with KIRKCALDY half a dozen miles away. All lines were single-track and the Rosyth route mainly reserved.

The car fleet was built up over the years to keep pace with the expanding system and by the time the last route opened the Company operated 43 UEC open-top double-deckers (Nos 1-20 of 1909, 21-24 of 1910, 25-28 of 1912 and 29-43 of 1917), supplemented in 1919 by Nos 44 and 45, two similar ERTCW vehicles of 1902 vintage acquired in 1919 from the Nottinghamshire & Derbyshire Tramways and replaced in 1932 by two Brush single-deckers of 1925 bought from WEMYSS & DISTRICT (and given the same numbers).

During the decade after World War I a multiplicity of motor bus operators appeared on the scene in Fife and in 1924 the Company joined the fray with five Tilling-Stevens petrol-electric buses and a track-doubling programme to speed up its tram services. This was at best a stop-gap measure and on 26 October 1931 the Kelty branch closed, leaving the remainder of the system to soldier on for another six years.

Bibliography: *Fife's Trams and Buses* A. W. Brotchie (NB Traction, Dundee, 1990) 0 905069 27 7

EDINBURGH STREET TRAMWAYS
Authority: Edinburgh Tramways Act 1871
Gauge: 4ft 8½in

Original Dunfermline open-topper in Port Street, Dunfermline, on a postcard perhaps purchased in the shop on the left. (Lens of Sutton)

Traction: Horse, steam
Opened: 6 November 1871
Taken Over: 23 October 1904*
System: Network
Length: 18.53 miles
Stock: 160+ sd & dd horse; 2 locos steam
Livery: Red-brown & cream, later various

Scotland's first street tramway – and the fore-runner of the country's second-largest system after GLASGOW – was a short line running from Haymarket west of the city centre northeast to Bernard Street in Leith via West Maitland Street, West End and Princes Street to the Post Office then up Leith Walk and Leith Street. This was joined on 29 May 1872 by a line south from the Post Office via North Bridge, South Bridge, Nicholson Street and Clerk Street to Powburn, Newington. The lines were a mixture of single and double tracks and services were worked by (probably) twelve open-top double-deckers constructed by the British & Foreign Tramways Co. Ltd of Greenwich. These were found to be too heavy for the job and in 1872-73 16 similar but much lighter vehicles were built by John Croall & Sons and Drew & Burnett of Edinburgh, and R. J. Boyall of Grantham.

After 1873 the use of fleet numbers was discontinued in favour of route numbers and as the system grew so the stud was increased by the purchase, during 1876-77, of at least ten open toastracks and eleven double-deckers from Starbuck, Boyall and Stephensons of New York. Between 1879 and 1882 some 14 double-deckers were built by the Edinburgh Street Tramways Co., the system's owner and operator, whilst BM supplied at least five double-deckers. After that all new additions were constructed by the Company, including ten long single-deckers numbered 90-99, up to 1893 when the car fleet, after several withdrawals, stood at 100. On 9 December that year though Edinburgh Corporation exercised its powers to purchase the bulk of the system within its boundaries (see EDINBURGH & DISTRICT), leaving the Company to operate just 30 cars in Leith. This it did until October 1904 when the lines there were purchased by LEITH CORPORATION.

After trials in early 1881 the Company had introduced steam traction on 23 April that year using a Kitson tram locomotive (No 1) on the Portobello route. This was joined in March 1882 by loco No 2, also from Kitsons, though their use was discontinued after 27 October that year, their licences not having been renewed in the face of local authority and public opposition.

Bibliography: *Edinburgh's Transport Vol 1: the early years* D. L. G. Hunter (Mercat Press, Edinburgh, 1992) 1 873644 02 7

EDINBURGH NORTHERN TRAMWAYS

Authority: Edinburgh Northern Tramways Act 1884
Gauge: 4ft 8½in
Traction: Cable
Opened: 28 January 1888
Taken Over: 1 January 1897
System: Two single lines
Length: 2.61 miles
Stock: 2 sd, 16 dd
Livery: Blue & cream

The origins of Edinburgh's extensive cable tramway system – by far the largest and most complicated in the British Isles – lay with the Edinburgh Northern Tramways Co. who, in 1888, opened a line northwards up Hanover Street and Dundas Street in the New Town part of the city to Ferry Road, Goldenacre, a distance of some 1½ miles. The first eight cars (Nos 1-8) were Metropolitan open-top bogie double-deckers housed in the depot in Henderson Row off to the west of Dundas Street. This was also the site of the winding house for the cable which was hauled continually through a conduit in the centre of each of the line's two tracks and to which the cars could be attached or released by means of driver-operated grippers.

A second, 1¼-mile route was opened on 17 February 1890 from George Street just west of Hanover Street northwards up Frederick Street and Howe Street, then northwest through Stockbridge to Comely Bank. Between 1890 and 1892 eight more bogie open-toppers (Nos 9-16) were bought to work the new route, this time from Falcon, and to enable them to reach the line the spur to the depot was extended along Hamilton Place to meet it midway.

In 1894, following the new local authority licensing policy, the tramway's 16 cars were renumbered 121-136 and were joined in 1894 by No 137 and in 1895 by No 138, long single-deckers of unknown origin, which only saw service for a few years. Although further routes had been planned from the outset, no more had been constructed by the end of 1896 when the Company relinquished operation of the system to the EDINBURGH & DISTRICT TRAMWAYS (see below) before, on 1 July 1897, it was sold for £110,000 to EDINBURGH CORPORATION for leasing to the EDT Co. under the Edinburgh Corporation Act of that year to become the nucleus of the municipally-owned cable network.

Bibliography: as above

EDINBURGH & DISTRICT TRAMWAYS

Authority: Edinburgh Corporation Tramways Act 1893

Gauge: 4ft 8½in
Traction: Horse, cable, overhead electric
Took Over: 9 December 1893
Taken Over: 1 July 1919
System: Radial network
Length: 18.65 miles
System: 2 sd, 96 dd horse; 2 sd, 227 dd cable; 4 dd electric
Livery: Various horse; madder & white cable & electric

By 1890 Edinburgh Corporation had decided that it wished to see a unified tramway system within the city and accordingly, with 21 years having passed, announced that it would take control of that part of the system within its boundaries. On 9 December 1893 it became the owner of the bulk of the EDINBURGH STREET TRAMWAYS, the price of £185,000 including 70 cars which were then resold to DK who had leased the tramways from the Corporation for another 21 years and who, on 6 March 1894, incorporated the Edinburgh & District Tramways Co. Ltd as its operating subsidiary. On 31 January 1896 the EST Co.'s line from Waterloo Place to Meadowbank was purchased by the Corporation for £13,615 upon expiry of its lease, the last stretch of the line to Portobello following two years later.

The decision was made in 1895 to convert the tramways to cable traction in order to cope with the many hills an expanded system would encounter and this work was carried out by DK, commencing the following year. Before operations could begin the EDINBURGH NORTHERN TRAMWAYS' two lines had been taken over from 1 January 1897 and it was in fact one of that company's cars, No 142, which was used on 1 June 1899 to officially open the new system with a trip from the winding-house at Shrubhill to St Andrew Street and back. Public services began on 26 October between Pilrig on the Leith boundary and Braid Hills Road with the rest of the system being converted over the next three years and new routes opened in the 1900s. The last horse cars ran on 24 August 1907 on the southwestern route to Craiglockhart.

The horse car fleet inherited at the end of 1893 was made up of 61 cars (Nos 1-13, 16-19, 22, 24, 25, 27, 40-43, 48, 55-62, 64-78, 86, 88, 89, 91-94 and 96-100), all open-top double-deckers with the exception of the last vehicle which was an open toastrack. This was not enough but help was close at hand for in July 1894 the Glasgow Tramway & Omnibus Co., the displaced operator of the GLASGOW TRAMWAY, had its own fleet to dispose of and the Company purchased thirteen double-deckers, numbering them 101-105 in its series and 25, 60, 61, 66, 73, 74, 76 and 94 to replace existing cars of those numbers. In

1895 Metropolitan supplied double-deckers 106-109 and that year the Company constructed double-decker 110 which was followed by similar cars 55, 71, 72, 75, 88, 89 and 111 a year later.

In 1896, with the purchase of the EST Co.'s line to Meadowbank, came cars 23, 44, 49, 52, 53 and 85, again all double-deckers except the last which was another open-toastrack. A year later double-deckers 113 and 114 were built by the Company and in 1898 it acquired double-deckers 47, 50, 51 and 80 from the EST Co. With the advent of cable traction the horse car fleet then began to shrink with five cars being sold back to the EST Co. in 1900 and three more the next year; in 1900 six (including the two toastracks) were sold to the STIRLING & BRIDGE OF ALLAN TRAMWAYS as well. By 1903 the horse car fleet had been reduced by further sales and scrappings to 20 and by 1905 to just seven – though two were then bought back from the EST Co.! By the end of horse traction just Nos 5, 47 and 72 were in service.

The Company's first cable car, No 112, was a prototype bogie open-top double-decker, longer than the ENT Co.'s cars which had been renumbered 121-138 (with single-deckers 137 and 138 being renumbered 7 and 13 later), constructed in 1897 at its Shrubhill Works. This was joined that year by similar cars 139-144 from Milnes. By 1901 another 25 had been ordered from Milnes and 120 from BM. (Some of these took lower horse car numbers whilst others continued the series – with some gaps – up to 208.) By the time services began, 24 had been delivered. In 1903 ERTCW supplied 20 more (Nos 209-228) and in 1906 the Company constructed Nos 25 and 27, followed by Nos 37 and 48 a year later. These last two cars were roofed (37 enclosed and 48 top-covered), after which the earlier cars (except the four listed below converted to electric traction) were top-covered as well. By this time former horse cars 15, 17, 19, 53 and 113 had been rebuilt as cable cars. The Company built a further dozen cars (Nos 5, 13, 35, 47, 49-52, 54, 59, 66 and 72) between 1908 and 1911 to complete the cable car fleet which was housed in depots at Shrubhill, Tollcross, Henderson Row and Portobello.

Although the myriad mechanical problems of operating a network of tramway routes using cable traction were ingeniously overcome, the system was not a total success and before the advent of World War I the Corporation was already considering other methods of propulsion. The neighbouring burghs of MUSSELBURGH (1904) and LEITH (1905) had already put electric tramcars onto their streets and, on 8 June 1910, Edinburgh followed suit with the

Corporation opening a branch off the southwestern cable route to Georgie from Ardmillan Terrace in a roughly parallel direction to Slateford. This was leased to the Company who worked it with open-top cable cars 28, 38, 64 and 74 converted to electric traction for the purpose. The coming war years put a temporary halt to the modernization programme and, when the Company's lease of the cable lines expired on the last day of June 1919, the Corporation assumed operating responsibility (see below).

Bibliography: as above

EDINBURGH CORPORATION TRAMWAYS

Authority: Edinburgh Corporation
   Tramways Order 1919
Gauge: 4ft 8½in
Traction: Cable, overhead electric
Took Over: 1 July 1919
Closed: 16 November 1956
System: Network
Length: 47.25 miles
Stock: 205 dd cable; 597 dd electric
Livery: Madder & white
Last Car: No 217

With the Corporation's takeover in 1919 of the EDINBURGH & DISTRICT TRAMWAYS (see above) it became the owner of 205 cable cars and four electric conversions; when it acquired the LEITH CORPORATION system the following year it added a further 37 double-deck passenger cars to its fleet, numbering them 231-267 to fill the gap created by the renumbering of the ex-EDT electric cars which became 229

(No 28), 230 (No 30), 268 (No 64) and 269 (No 74).

In 1921 work began on preparing the conversion of the cable lines to electric working and by 23 June 1923, when the eastern route to Portobello re-opened, the task had been completed and extensions and new routes planned to produce eventually an extensive network focussed on Edinburgh in the centre (and to a lesser degree Leith) stretching out to Costorphine in the west, Colinton, Fairmilehead and Liberton to the south and Levenhall in the east after the Corporation's 1928 takeover of the surviving portion of the MUSSELBURGH & DISTRICT line. (No connections were made to other systems, the only near neighbour being unreachable across the Firth of Forth at DUNFERMLINE.)

With the conversion of the cable system came a corresponding conversion of the cable cars, 184 being so treated during the early 1920s. At the same time a batch of top-covered cars were supplied by McHardy & Elliott of Edinburgh (16 cars), Leeds Forge (14 cars) and the Corporation itself (14 cars) which, with some renumbering, completed the 1-269 series. These were joined during 1923-29 by similar vehicles 270-311 (Leeds Forge), 312-331 (EE) and 332-366 (the Corporation again), plus another 40 from the Corporation which took on numbers of replaced older cars.

Between 1930 and 1934 the Corporation built another 53 double-deckers, enclosed ones this time, to take the number series to 371 (and replace older vehicles) whilst Pickerings supplied Nos 250-259 and Metro-Cammell Nos 260 and 265 – all similar-type vehicles. The last new cars of this period, all

Edinburgh Corporation 402 and 364 in suburban service: a study in changing tramcar design between the 1920s and 1930s. (Lens of Sutton)

varieties of double-deckers built 1934-35, were Nos 11-18, 231, 239 and 240 from HN, Nos 25-30, 241, 242, 244-246 and 249 from Metro-Cammell and Nos 19-24, 262, 263 and 267 from EE.

The last extension to the system was opened on 14 February 1937 (to Maybury on the Costorphine route) with World War II putting paid to any further expansion plans. The car-building programme continued however with 84 replacement enclosed double-deckers being built by the Corporation between 1934 and 1950, after which the only addition to the fleet was the purchase between 1947 and 1949 of Nos 401-411, enclosed double-deckers of early 1930s vintage, from Manchester Corporation. In 1950 though the Corporation decided to partially abandon the tramways with buses replacing the first route (Waverley to Comely Bank) on 1 June 1952 – the same year that the decision was taken to abandon the trams altogether.

The last route to go, Granton Road station–Morningside, went on 16 November 1956, after which the remaining trams were quickly scrapped, there being virtually no second-hand market left for them. Only one car survives in preserved form at present: No 35 (Corporation 1948) which is currently on loan to the National Tramway Museum at Crich after operating for several years at Blackpool.

Bibliography: *Edinburgh's Transport* D. L. G. Hunter (The Advertiser Press, Huddersfield, 1964)

ERROL TRAMWAY

In 1847 the Dundee & Perth Railway opened its main line between those two places along the northern bank of the Firth of Tay. In order to serve the district immediately inland it constructed two short branches to INCHTURE and North Inchmichael; the second of these ran from the village of Errol northwest for some 2 miles and was to have been worked (for passengers at least) as a horse tramway. Earthworks were constructed and some track laid but, in 1850 however, it was decided that the branches were costing too much and would not both be profitable, so the Errol project was abandoned in favour of the other and the rails lifted.

Bibliography: *Tramways of the Tay Valley* Alan W. Brotchie (Dundee Museum and Art Gallery, 1965)

FALKIRK & DISTRICT TRAMWAYS

Authority: Falkirk and District Tramways Order 1901
Gauge: 4ft
Traction: Overhead electric
Opened: 21 October 1905
Closed: 21 July 1936
System: Branching circle
Length: 7.8 miles
Stock: 19 sd, 18 dd
Livery: Prussian blue & cream to 1929, then red & white
Last Car: ?

This Stirlingshire system began as a circular route linking the town of Falkirk with (in clockwise order) the villages of Camelon, Larbert, Stenhousemuir, Carron and Bainsford and, having added then lost a branch, ended as a circle once more. Originally to have been built by the Falkirk & District Tramways Co., nothing happened until 24 October 1904 when BP set up the Falkirk Electric Construction Syndicate Ltd to take over the FDT Co., after which construction began.

At first the line was worked in two halves, owing to problems with the two bridges over the Forth & Clyde Canal which bisected the circle, but round working began on 12 March 1906 using the original fleet of 15 open-top double-deckers from the Compagnie Générale de Construction of St Denis in France (Nos 1-15) and three of a similar type but different design (Nos 16-18) from Brush. (These last three ran top-covered between 1908 and 1913.)

On 3 September 1909 a 1½-mile branch from Falkirk (at the bottom of the circle) due east to Mary Square, Laurieston, was opened to complete the system (the only 4ft gauge one in Scotland); like the main line this was primarily single-track. In 1913 the Company began motor bus operations (a turn of events ignored in its 1914 change of name to the Falkirk & District Tramways Co. Ltd) and in 1920 was taken over by the Balfour, Beatty company (see Section 1), the Fife Tramway, Light & Power Co. (see DUNFERMLINE & DISTRICT). By now the track and stock were in bad shape but the new owners set to tackling these problems with a relaying and partial doubling of the circle route, the closing on 20 July 1924 of the Laurieston branch and, in 1929-30, the purchase of ten modern Brush single-deckers (Nos 1-10) after which the double-deckers were gradually scrapped. Four similar cars were added in 1931 (Nos 13-16), followed in 1934 by five single-deckers (numbers 11, 12 and 17-19) which came from the Dearne District system in Yorkshire.

Despite the fortunes of the Company being now much improved, in 1935 the Scottish Motor Traction Co. succeeded in buying up enough of the Company's shares to close the tramway down the following year to make way for its bus services.

Bibliography: *The Tramways of Falkirk* (Tramways of Fife and the Forth Valley Part 1) Alan W. Brotchie (NB Traction Group, Dundee, 1975)

GLASGOW TRAMWAY

Authority: Glasgow Street Tramways Act 1870
Gauge: 4ft 7¾in
Traction: Horse
Opened: 19 August 1872
Taken Over: 1 July 1894*
System: Radial network
Length: 30.21 miles
Stock: c300 sd & dd
Livery: Menzies tartan & white/cream, later route colour

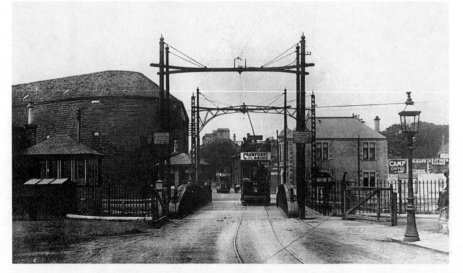

Postcard of French-built Falkirk & District No 14 of 1905 negotiating the swing bridge over the Forth & Clyde Canal at Camelon. (Lens of Sutton)

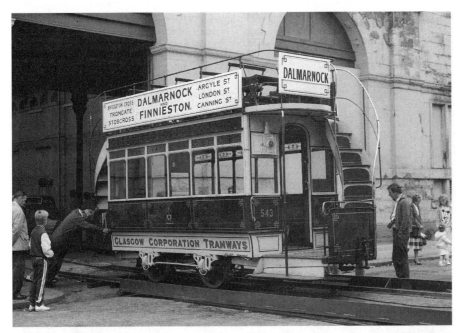

Glasgow Corporation horse car No 543 being moved out of the former Museum of Transport in Albert Drive. (Glasgow Museums & Art Galleries: Museum of Transport)

Glasgow's electric tramway system (the largest in Scotland) began with the horse tramways operated by the Glasgow Tramway & Omnibus Co. which were leased from Glasgow Corporation. The first route ran from St George's Cross to Eglinton Toll, through the city centre via Cambridge Street, Sauchiehall Street and Renfield Street and was followed by a succession of other radial routes over the next two decades. It was the second street tramway to open in Scotland – less than a year behind the EDINBURGH STREET TRAMWAYS – and from the outset used a gauge slightly narrower than standard (as used in Edinburgh) to allow for the working of railway wagons over its tracks in the dockside area; this set the gauge for later tramways in the area. It also pioneered the practice of painting its cars in different colours to denote which routes they worked, an idea taken up elsewhere (and retained in Glasgow into the electric era).

Many details of the car fleet are currently lacking. The first cars, Nos 201-314, were open-top double-deckers built by the Tramway Car & Works Co. of Greenwich and Glasgow during the first four years of the tramway's life. After that (1875-76), Stephensons supplied two single-deckers and fifty-four double-deckers (numbers unknown), following which many of the earlier cars were rebuilt or replaced by new cars (given vacated numbers) built by the Company at its Crownpoint Works, all double-deckers (including some for mule-haulage) except for two single-deck vehicles. Twenty more double-deckers were bought in 1884 and a

similar number two years later, from Metropolitan.

In 1893 westward expansion was aided by the leasing from Govan of the GLASGOW & IBROX and VALE OF CLYDE tramways (the latter having been worked during 1873-74 by the Company) but this arrangement was not to last very long. The Company's lease had been for 21 years from July 1871 and, in 1891, the Corporation obtained authority to modernize its lines and began negotiating with the Company over terms. The latter body was reluctant to let go of the

business and the dispute dragged on until it relinquished control of its Glasgow lines on the last day of June 1894 (though it continued to operate the Govan lines until 10 November 1896). Thereupon the Company sold or scrapped its cars rather than sell them to the Corporation, such was the ill-feeling between them. (See below.)

GLASGOW CORPORATION TRAMWAYS

Authority: Glasgow Street Tramways Act 1870
Gauge: 4ft 7¾in
Traction: Horse, overhead electric
Took Over: 1 July 1894
Closed: 4 September 1962
System: Network
Length: 141.37 miles
Stock: 384 dd horse; 22 sd, 1,205 dd electric
Livery: Crimson lake & cream + route colour horse; cadmium yellow & cream + route colour, later orange, green & cream electric
Last Car: No 1174

Following its takeover of the tracks of the GLASGOW TRAMWAY (see above), the Corporation inaugurated its own service the next day with its own fleet of horse cars, starting with Nos 302-541, double-deckers built by Metropolitan, BM and Midland (1894) and Nos 542-545 (built 1893), specimen double-deckers ordered from the North Metropolitan Tramways of London (two cars), Milnes and Falcon. There was also a driver training car (possibly No 301) thought to have come from the VALE OF CLYDE TRAMWAYS. These were joined between 1894 and 1897 by Nos 546-664 from

Postcard of Glasgow Corporation No 1050 of 1923 at Paisley Cross just after entering service following the takeover of the Paisley District system. (Lens of Sutton)

Glasgow Corporation No 617 of 1901-02 on red route 13 (Mount Florida–Govanhill), probably in the late 1940s. (Lens of Sutton)

Glasgow Corporation No 1392 of 1952, the last full-sized double-deck car built in Britain, in the city's new Museum of Transport, Kelvin Hall. To the left is No 1173 of 1938. (Glasgow Museums & Art Galleries: Museum of Transport)

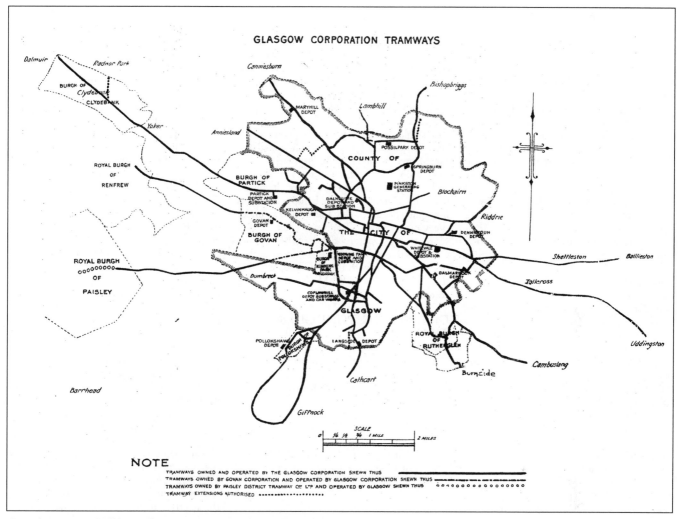

GLASGOW CORPORATION TRAMWAYS

General route map of Glasgow Corporation Tramways from the 1909 Manual of Electrical Undertakings.

Metropolitan, BM, Midland and the Corporation's works at Coplawhill. The only other additions to the fleet, in 1896, were Nos 280-300, ex-Glasgow Tramway & Omnibus Co. cars taken over with the Govan lines on 11 November that year (see above).

The first electric services began on 13 October 1898 from Mitchell Street, just off Argyle Street in the city centre, northwards up West Nile Street and Parliamentary Road to Springburn Road; the first electric cars, Nos 665-685, were Corporation-built bogie single-deckers nicknamed 'Room and Kitchen' cars on account of their two (smoking and non-smoking) compartments. These were followed by a batch of open-top double-deckers (fitted with top covers after 1904 and later fully enclosed) numbered 686-1000, all constructed between 1898 and 1900 by the Corporation with the exception of Nos 901-980 which were from Gloucester.

During 1900-01 the Corporation converted a third of its horse cars to electric

traction as they became redundant (as Nos 1-120), in which guise most of them saw service for another 20 years. (No 92 was cut down to a single deck in 1906, four sold to DUMBARTON in 1909 and one to Luton in 1923). These were followed in 1901-02 by more open-toppers (Nos 440-664) built by the Corporation and later treated similarly to the first batch.

Meanwhile the system was continuing to expand – hence the demand for new cars – across the Clyde and beyond the burgh boundaries. After the GTO Co.'s lease of the Govan lines to the west had expired in 1896 these were taken over by the Corporation and electrified; Rutherglen to the southeast was reached in 1902 and in 1923 both the PAISLEY and the AIRDRIE & COATBRIDGE systems were bought by the Corporation to form the western and eastern extremities of the system. To the northwest was a connection with the DUMBARTON system and to the southeast one with the LANARKSHIRE TRAMWAYS, though in

both these cases through running did not operate.

With the 1923 purchases came 68 Paisley double-deckers which the Corporation numbered 1001-1038, 1041-1049 and 1052-1072 and, where needed, fitted with top covers, and 15 A&C double-deckers which were renumbered 1073-1087, all open-toppers except the last three. Additions to the car fleet after that were as follows:

No 1089: Corporation bogie single-decker of 1926

Nos 1090-1140: enclosed double-deckers of 1927-29 by the Corporation, HN, Pickerings and Brush

Nos 1141-1292: Corporation streamlined bogie double-deckers of 1936-40

Nos 6, 1001-1004: Corporation streamlined double-deckers of 1940-43

Nos 1005, 1293-1398: Corporation stream-lined bogie double-deckers of 1947-54

Nos 1006-1016, 1018-1038, 1041-1049, 1052-1056: streamlined bogie double-deckers of 1936-37 bought from Liverpool 1953-54.

There was also, as would be expected in a system of this size, an extensive fleet of works vehicles, many of which were conversions of former passenger cars.

The Corporation commenced its first bus service towards the end of 1924 but, as can be seen from the above stock list, they posed no threat to the trams for three decades with only two routes closing in the 1930s. The first was the western portion of the Paisley line through Johnstone to Kilbarchan on 30 April 1932 and the second, on 25 March 1933, was the short branch north from Paisley to Abbotsinch.

New routes continued to be opened with the system reaching its greatest extent in 1948 with 1,208 cars in service on a network (with less than 1 mile of single track) nearly half of which was outside the city boundaries. That year though saw the closures start again (the southeastern line to Uddingston was cut back to Broomhouse on 29 August), after which buses and trolleybuses began nibbling away at the other outlying routes. It was not until early 1956 however that the Corporation decided to abandon those routes left outside its boundaries. The last tram (No 1277) ran in Paisley in the early hours of 12 May 1957 and on 6 February of the following year the Corporation voted to close the system altogether, the last route to go being that from Dalmuir West eastwards to Auchenshuggle in September 1962.

As might be expected from the size of its fleet and the late date of its closing, several Glasgow trams have been preserved. Horse car 543 is in the city's Transport Museum, as are electric cars 672 of 1898, 779 of 1900, 1088, 1089, 1173 and 1392 whilst No 585 of 1901 is in the London Science Museum. Nos 22 of 1922, 812 of 1900, 1100, 1115, 1282, 1297 and a works car are at the National Tramway Museum, Crich and No 1245 at the East Anglia Transport Museum, Carlton Colville.

GLASGOW & IBROX TRAMWAY

Authority: Glasgow and Ibrox Tramway Act 1877
Gauge: 4ft 7¾in
Traction: Horse
Opened: 18 July 1879
Closed: 25 May 1891
System: Single line
Length: 1.55 miles
Stock: 1 sd, 3 dd?
Livery: Blue & cream?
Last Car: ?

This single-track line, owned by the Glasgow & Ibrox Tramway Co., ran from Whitefield

Road in Ibrox eastwards along the Paisley Road to the Paisley Road Toll on the Govan boundary with Glasgow (thus traversing the whole of the burgh of Govan), where it connected with the eastern end of the VALE OF CLYDE line coming in from Fairfield to the northwest. It is thought to have been worked by just four Ashbury reversible cars, double-deckers 1 and 2 of 1879, 3 of 1880 and single-decker 4 (probably constructed between 1880 and 1884), which shared the VoC's depot in Great Wellington Street.

The line was not a commercial success and closed after just twelve years' operation with the Company going bankrupt. It was not quite dead though for in 1893, under the Govan Burgh (Tramways) Act of that year, it was purchased by the Govan Commissioners of Police – the local authority – and, along with the VoC line, leased to the GLASGOW TRAMWAY operating company.

GREENOCK & PORT GLASGOW TRAMWAYS

Authority: Greenock Street Tramways Act 1871; Vale of Clyde Tramways Act 1871
Gauge: 4ft 7¾in
Traction: Horse, overhead electric
Opened: 7 July 1873
Closed: 15 July 1929
System: Branching
Length: 7.42 miles
Stock: 25 dd horse?; 7 sd, 39 dd electric
Livery: Red & cream horse?; dark red & white electric
Last Car: No 10

Built on the south bank of the mouth of the Clyde to serve an ancient area of fishing, shipbuilding and allied industries, this line had a somewhat complicated history for so simple a system. The western half of the original single-track horse tramway from Ashton up Albert Street and through Gourock via Shore Street, Chapel Street and Cardwell Street to the Gourock/Greenock boundary (about 2 miles) was built and owned by the VALE OF CLYDE TRAMWAYS Co., whilst the rest of the line through Greenock via Eldon Street, Brougham Street, Grey Place, West Blackhall Street, Hamilton Street and Cathcart Street to Rue–End Street (another 2 miles) was promoted and owned by the then local authority, the Greenock Police Board, and leased to the VoCT Co. Services began over the Greenock section on 7 July 1873 with ten open-top double deckers (Nos 1-10) built by the Tramway Car & Works Co. Ltd of Greenwich and Glasgow and shedded off Chapel Street in Gourock. Half the Gourock section opened on 18 July that day (to Princes Pier, served by a short spur) and the final Albert Street stretch along the

seafront on 1 November. Another two open-toppers were purchased in 1875 and during 1878-79 the Company conducted steam locomotive trials on the line but nothing came of them.

In 1886 an eastwards continuation of the line was promoted by what became the Greenock & Port Glasgow Tramways Co. who secured the Greenock and Port Glasgow Tramways Act in 1887 to construct about 2½ miles of line along Main Street and Great Hamilton Street, through the district of Ladyburn and into Port Glasgow by way of the Port Glasgow Road, Ardgowan Street, Shore Street, Scarlow Street and Fore Street. Opened on 29 November 1889 the double-track line was worked by eleven Milnes open-top double-deckers (Nos 1-11) as a separate service until 15 May 1893 when the GPGT Co. took over the VoCT Co.'s lease and began operating through to the Gourock boundary. The following year the Gourock Police Commissioners bought out the VoCT Co. and, from 12 February, leased that last portion of the line to the GPGT Co. who operated it all with its own cars and (probably) six of the former VoC cars (renumbered 12-17). The last three cars acquired, Nos 18-20, were added in 1900 and were presumably double-deckers again.

In 1900 the line was double-tracked throughout (except for the Albert Street section) and electrified by the BET (see Section 1) who had taken control of the Company; the western half re-opened on 3 October 1901 with ten Brush cars. (The Princes Pier spur was abandoned.) On 7 November 1901 the electric cars took over from the horses on the Rue-End Street to Port Glasgow half of the tramway and by the end of the year the initial order of 30 Brush bogie open-toppers (Nos 1-30) had arrived, and in July 1902 a new depot was opened for them at Ladyburn.

In 1904 six Brush single-deck combination cars (Nos 31-36) were purchased (and rebuilt two years later as open-top double-deckers); in 1906 another three Brush open-toppers were bought (Nos 37-39), followed in 1908 by UEC No 40, a single-deck demi-car. The last new cars purchased were again from Brush, these being Nos 41-43 in 1911 (top-covered double-deckers) and 44-46 in 1916 (open-top double-deckers). That year also saw the arrival on loan of ROTHESAY single-deckers 11 and 12 (renumbered 47 and 48), to which system No 40 was sent three years later when these two cars were returned.

By the end of the 1920s the tramway was running at a steady loss and, with Greenock Corporation refusing to take it over, the Company obtained the necessary Act in 1928 to abandon it and replace the trams with motor buses, which it did the following year.

Bibliography: *Tramways of Greenock, Gourock and Port Glasgow* Ian L. Cormack (The Scottish Tramway Museum Society, 1975)

HAMILTON, MOTHERWELL & WISHAW TRAMWAYS *see* LANARKSHIRE TRAMWAYS

IBROX *see* GLASGOW & IBROX

INCHTURE TRAMWAY

This was a 2-mile branch of the Caledonian Railway built in 1849, like its ERROL counterpart immediately to the west, to serve a village on the northern side of the Firth of Tay. The junction with the main Perth–Dundee line was at Inchture station in Perthshire and from there it ran northwest in a straight line beside the road to the village of Inchture itself where it terminated at the crossroads known as Crossgates on the edge of the village. (Later mineral branches from here served a clay pit and brickworks and carried wagons of horse manure from Dundee for local farmers.)

The line was a single track with one passing loop, very lightly laid with wrought iron rails, and was originally built by the Dundee & Perth Railway (from 1863 the Scottish Central Railway and from 1865 part of the CR). Its closest relative in the British Isles was the Fintona branch in Ireland (see Section 4). Goods trains were steam-hauled but passenger services were provided by an old horse-drawn four-wheeled coach, replaced in 1895 by a CR-built closed single-deck four-wheeled tramcar numbered 1 and painted CR crimson lake and white.

The line was closed as a wartime measure in 1916 (possibly 31 December) and the rails lifted for use in France (though the ship carrying them is reputed to have been sunk). The fate of the car is unknown.

Bibliography: *Tramways of the Tay Valley* Alan W. Brotchie (Dundee Museum and Art Gallery, 1965)

KILMARNOCK CORPORATION TRAMWAYS

Authority: Kilmarnock Corporation Act 1904
Gauge: 4ft 8½in
Traction: Overhead electric
Opened: 10 December 1904
Closed: 3 May 1926
System: Branching
Length: 4.24 miles
Stock: 14 dd
Livery: Olive green & cream
Last Car: ?

Hard on the heels of Kilmarnock Town Council setting up its own electricity and gas

Postcard of Greenock & Port Glasgow No 18 of 1901 skirting the mouth of the Clyde at Ashton. (Lens of Sutton)

supply undertakings came its proposals to operate its own trams; these were to be electrically-powered from the start, there being no existing horse tramways to take over or modernize.

As built, the system resembled a letter T laid on its side with a north-south main line from the burgh boundary at Beansburn, running straight down through the town to its southern boundary at Riccarton. The line was single-track throughout except for a ½-mile section from the railway station southwards through the town centre to the King Street Church near Fowlds Street. (This double track was extended another ¼ mile in 1905 as far as the depot in Greenholm Street.) The one, single-track branch ran for 1¾ miles from the Cross in the town centre (close to the Tramways Office) eastwards along the London Road and through the village of Crookedholm to Hurlford Cross.

Original stock comprised eleven HN open-top double-deckers (Nos 1-11) which were joined in 1905 by one similar car (No 12) and two top-covered cars (Nos 13 and 14), all from HN again.

Despite a promising start, very soon after the system's opening it became apparent that it was not going to be a roaring financial success, probably due to a combination of poor management, Council policies and a fluctuating employment situation in this industrial northern Ayrshire town (and hence fluctuating revenues); the situation was not improved by constant permanent way problems and the general neglect occasioned by World War I. After the end of the war an easy solution to the tramway's problems was offered by the increasingly-reliable motor bus and in 1923 the Council decided to replace the Hurlford route (the part of the system in worst shape) with a bus

service and the last cars ran on 15 December of the following year; the replacement buses introduced that same afternoon established Kilmarnock as the first Scottish local authority to replace its own electric trams with such vehicles.

The line's end came by default when the tramway staff joined the 1926 General Strike and services were brought to an abrupt halt. The Council decided not to resume them and one of Britain's later-built electric tramways of the period became one of its earlier closures.

Bibliography: *Green Cars to Hurlford* Brian T. Deans (Scottish Tramway Museum Society, 1986) 0 900648 22 8

KIRKCALDY CORPORATION TRAMWAYS

Authority: Kirkcaldy Corporation and Tramways Act 1899
Gauge: 3ft 6in
Traction: Overhead electric
Opened: 28 February 1903
Closed: 15 May 1931
System: Branching circle
Length: 6.11 miles
Stock: 26 dd
Livery: Dark bronze-green & cream
Last Car: ?

The first section of the municipally-owned tramways in Kirkcaldy on the northern shore of the Firth of Forth was the single-track 'Lower Route' from the Turret Tavern, past the Gallatown Depot in Oswald Road to the West End of Linktown (Links Street) by way of The Path and the High Street (passing the end of Whytecauseway). This was followed on 28 September 1903 by the double-track 'Upper Route' from Junction Road by the railway station to Whytescauseway (with a short branch to the Beveridge Park Gates). To cope with the increased traffic the new lines generated, another twelve Milnes open-top double-deckers (Nos 11-22) were bought 1903-4 to add to the original ten similar cars. From 27 September 1906 through cars began running to the railway station via the Upper Route from Leven at the far end of the WEMYSS line (though when Kirkcaldy cars were used as opposed to the Wemyss single-deckers, passengers were not permitted to ride on the upper decks).

On 26 February 1911 a 1-mile branch southeast from Junction Road to the parish church in Dysart (a separate burgh until 1930) was opened to complete the system and four HN open-toppers were added to the fleet in 1914 and given the numbers 23-26; these were the last to be bought for burgeoning bus competition after World War I effectively killed the tramway. When the end came eight of the cars (including Nos 23-26) were acquired by Wemyss but only lasted there a matter of months before that system too closed down.

Bibliography: *The Tramways of Kirkcaldy* (Tramways of Fife and the Forth Valley Part 4) Alan W. Brotchie (The NB Traction Group, Dundee, 1978) 0 905069 00 9

Fife's Trams and Buses A. W. Brotchie (NB Traction, Dundee, 1990) 0 905069 27 7

LANARKSHIRE TRAMWAYS

Authority: Hamilton Motherwell and Wishaw Tramways Act 1900
Gauge: 4ft 7¾in
Traction: Overhead electric
Opened: 22 July 1903
Closed: 14 February 1931

System: Branching circle
Length: 28.43 miles
Stock: 92 dd
Livery: Briefly light blue & cream, then green & cream
Last Car: No 86

Situated immediately to the southeast of Glasgow, the Lanarkshire system was built up over the years before World War I to serve the towns of this industrial area and link them to the GLASGOW network. The first stretch to be opened ran from Low Blantyre eastwards through Hamilton and Motherwell to Wishaw, and was promoted by the Hamilton, Motherwell & Wishaw Tramways Co. which, in 1903, changed its name to the more succinct Lanarkshire Tramways Co. On 15 July 1905 a 1-mile branch from Hamilton Old Cross was opened to Ferniegair station on the Caledonian Railway; this was extended on 23 July a further 3 miles to Larkhill.

On 20 January 1907 a westwards extension from Blantyre to Cambuslang was opened, providing the envisaged physical connection with the Glasgow tramways (though through running never took place). The next addition to the system came on 7 August 1908 when a short line was opened from Motherwell Cross to the burgh boundary at Coursington Bridge; at the same time a short branch was opened from Hamilton to the burgh boundary at Bothwell Road by the racecourse. This latter line was extended to Uddingston Cross in June 1909, the same time as the original line was extended another 2 miles to Newmains. In August 1911 the Coursington Bridge line was extended a further 1½ miles to New Stevenston. (All lines were single-

track though a limited doubling programme in the Motherwell and Hamilton areas had been embarked upon.)

As some 7 miles of the various authorized lines had still not been constructed, Lanark County Council decided to intervene and in 1912 obtained powers to link New Stevenston via Mossend and Bellshill (opened September 1913) with Uddingston (opened 11 February 1914); a 1½-mile branch from Mossend doubling back to Holytown (opened 24 October 1913) completed the system. These lines (6.11 miles in total) were leased to the LT Co. which could now operate a grand circular route linking Motherwell, Hamilton, Bellshill, Uddingston and Bothwell in addition to the main Cambuslang–Newmains line and the Larkhill and Holytown branches.

In May 1921 the leased County Council lines were purchased for £60,981 by the Company but by now the writing was on the wall for the tramway as regards the growing bus competition – not least from the Company's own fleet. The first sections of the system to close were the Hamilton–Larkhall and Hamilton–Uddingston lines (both officially on 14 September 1928 though the latter remained in use for race-course traffic), followed on 6 October 1930 by the whole of the Newmain–Motherwell–Hamilton–Cambuslang main line, leaving the last remnants to close the following year, replaced by Company buses. (On 1 October 1930 the Company changed its name to the Lanarkshire Traction Co.)

As would be expected, the Lanarkshire fleet grew to keep pace with the expanding system, the first 76 cars all being open-top double-deckers numbered as follows: Nos 1-25 (BEC 1903), 26-35 (Brush 1904), 36-40 (Brush 1905), 41-46 (Brush 1906), 47-53 (UEC 1908), 54-60 (Brush 1909), 61-64 (Brush 1911) and 65-76 (Brush 1913). In 1923 the Company built a prototype low-level, top-covered car (No 77) and two years later HN supplied twelve similar vehicles (Nos 78-89); these were joined that same year by three more built by the Company (Nos 45, 56 and 88) which took the numbers of withdrawn vehicles. By the time of the closure only 16 cars survived (or were considered fit enough) to be put up for sale – but there were no takers for them.

Bibliography: *Lanarkshire's Trams* A. W. Brotchie (ed) (NB Traction, Dundee, 1993) 0 905069 29 3

LEITH CORPORATION TRAMWAYS

Authority: Leith Corporation Tramways Order 1904
Gauge: 4ft 8½in
Traction: Horse, overhead electric

Postcard of Lanarkshire Tramways No 28 of 1904 in Cadzow Street, Hamilton. (Lens of Sutton)

Took Over: 23 October 1904
Taken Over: 20 November 1920
System: Network
Length: 9.09 miles
Stock: 29 horse; 37 dd electric
Livery: Munich lake & white electric

After taking over part of the EDINBURGH STREET TRAMWAYS in 1904, Leith Corporation set about reconstructing and extending the tramways for electric working. Tracklaying began early in 1905, on a new route from Pilrig along Pilrig Street (and the burgh boundary) to Bonnington, followed by the conversion of the rest of the system. The first electric services began on 18 August that same year on the Pilrig–Foot of Leith Walk–Stanley Road route with the bulk of the system re-opening on 16 September. The official inauguration took place on 3 November, the day after the Seafield Place horse services ended; this was the last route to be worked by the last surviving horse cars (which had operated services as well as pos-sible during the reconstruction of each route). Electric services to Seafield Place began on 21 November, the new system com-prising the old horse routes (now double-tracked) plus the Pilrig Street line (also doubled).

Thirty-six open-top cars were bought for the opening: Nos 1-15 and 31-33 were from BTH and Nos 16-30 and 34-36 from Brush. (Many of these were later top-covered.) The only other passenger car added to the fleet was No 37 which had started life as BTH single-decker No 61 used for driver training before the opening, then fitted with an open upper deck in 1906 (and renum-bered) for passenger use. The depot was con-structed on the site of the former horse depot.

The system's only extensions came in 1909 when, under the provisions of the Leith Burgh Act of 1908 another 1.9 miles of double-track were built. The first section opened (11 May) ran westwards from Newhaven along the coastal St Arbank Road and Lower Granton Road to Granton, the second section (opened 2 July) ran south from here to Goldenacre via Granton Road, whilst the third (opened 3 August) ran east-wards along Ferry Road (and past the EDINGBURGH & DISTRICT's terminus in Inverleith Row) to Bonnington Terrace, thus making a large circular route.

Following the 1920 local government absorption of Leith by its larger neigh-bour, control of the system passed to EDINBURGH CORPORATION TRAM-WAYS with the cars being renumbered 231-267 (Leith 1-37) in that fleet.

MURCAR RAILWAY *see* STRABATHIE & BLACKDOG LIGHT RAILWAY

Two of Leith Corporation's 1905 cars appear on this early postcard of Main Street, Newhaven, on the system's northernmost route. (Lens of Sutton)

MUSSELBURGH & DISTRICT TRAMWAY

Authority: Portobello and Musselburgh Tramways Order 1900
Gauge: 4ft 8½in
Traction: Overhead electric
Opened: 12 December 1904
Closed: 25 February 1928*
System: Single line
Length: 6.62 miles
Stock: 6 sd, 16 dd
Livery: Red & ivory to 1923, then dark & light green
Last Car: ?

Six miles east of Edinburgh on the southern shore of the Firth of Forth lies the town of Musselburgh. Here, at the end of the 19th century, the idea of a tramway link to the Scottish capital was promoted, but it was not until 1903 (and after at least one false start), that any physical progress was made. It was built by the NEC and, when opened, was a double-track line from the EDIN-BURGH easterly terminus at Joppa to Bridge Street (roughly halfway), then single-track along the High Street past the Town Hall and depot to the terminus at Levenhall, a distance of some 3 miles in all.

In August 1905 another company was formed to operate the line, the Musselburgh & District Electric Light & Traction Co. Ltd, and extensions planned: on 5 August 1909 the single-track line was extended eastwards to Tranent Road in Cockenzie and on 31 December to Port Seton, its final ter-minus.

The original car fleet comprised ten open-top double-deckers from BEC (Nos 1-10), followed by four closed-top cars (Nos 11-14) in 1905 from Brush. Two similar cars (Nos 15 and 16) were purchased in 1909 to meet the demands of the Port Seton extension.

During World War I the stock suffered badly from lack of maintenance – and acci-dents – and in 1918 three single-deckers (Nos 17-19) were acquired from Sheffield.

On 24 June 1923 through running from Edinburgh commenced, that Corporation's Portobello route having been electrified from cable operation and a further three single-deckers (Nos 20-22) were purchased from Sheffield. The line was not a financial success and it closed to the general public in February 1928, although it is believed that miners' specials continued to run through to Prestongrange Colliery, midway along the line, for another month or so; thereafter operation of the Joppa-Levenhall section was taken over by Edinburgh Corporation from 1 March. However, the line itself was not acquired until 1932 when ownership was assumed under the Edinburgh Corporation Act of that year.

Bibliography: *Edinburgh's Transport Vol 1: the early years* D. L. G. Hunter (The Mercat Press, Edinburgh, 1992) 1 873644 02 7

PAISLEY TRAMWAYS

Authority: Paisley Tramways Order 1885
Gauge: 4ft 7¾in
Traction: Horse
Opened: 30 December 1885
Closed: 21 November 1903
System: Single line
Length: 2.44 miles
Stock: 4 sd, 7 dd
Livery: Red & white
Last Car: ?

Some 7 miles west of Glasgow on the south bank of the River Clyde, the Renfrewshire town of Paisley grew greatly during the 19th century, notably because of the weaving industry centred there, and during the 1870s proposals were made for a local tramway. None were successful however until 1885 when the Paisley Tramways Co. Ltd (incorporated 24 December 1884) was empowered to build a short line through the town. Construction began in December 1885 with the first mile of route, from Garthland Place in the east to Broomlands in the west, via the High Street and Paisley Cross, opening later that month.

On 20 April 1886 extensions were opened at both ends of the line: east to Greenlaw Road at the end of Garthland Street and west to Thomas Street with the final extension, from Greenlaw Road along Williamburgh to Hawkhead Road (East Toll) opening on 29 October 1888 to complete the single-track line.

Services began with three open-top double-deckers licensed by Paisley Town Council as Nos 35-37, shortly followed by two more (probably Nos 38 and 39), maker unknown. They were joined in 1887 by Nos 47 and 48, a pair of single-deckers built by the Glasgow Tramway & Omnibus Co. (That same year one of the double-deckers was rebuilt as an experimental battery car by a local millowner, James Gibson, but the experiment was discontinued some five months later and the car never apparently returned to the horse car fleet.) The depot was at Incle Street by the original Garthland Place terminus.

Initially successful, the line soon began to make a loss as the novelty of the (short and slow) trips wore off – hence the purchase of the lighter single-deckers, two more of which (probably Nos 36 and 37) were bought in 1890; four years later two of the double-deckers were hired to GLASGOW CORPORATION for driver training on its new system and then sold to it, leaving just two double-deckers (which had been rebuilt in 1893, presumably to make them lighter). The only other cars added to the fleet were ex-GC double-deckers 360 and 630, bought in 1901, probably as replacements for older cars.

At the end of the 1890s the BET tried to acquire the line but no agreement could be reached and on 17 September 1903 the tramway was bought for £15,797 by William M. Murphy, an Irish contractor with numerous tramway interests including Chairman-ship of the Dublin United Tramways, and the Company wound up two months later. Murphy had already obtained the necessary powers to electrify the line (see below) and began reconstruction work at the eastern end of the line, the horse car service being cut back accordingly over the next two months.

Bibliography: *Paisley's Trams and Buses: Eighties to Twenties* A. W. Brotchie & R. L. Grieves (NB Traction, Dundee, 1986) 0 905069 25 0

PAISLEY DISTRICT TRAMWAYS

Authority: Paisley District Tramways Act 1901
Gauge: 4ft 7¾in
Traction: Overhead electric
Opened: 13 June 1904
Taken Over: 1 August 1923
System: Radial
Length: 18.25 miles
Stock: 1 sd, 76 dd
Livery: Scarlet & cream

Although the horse tramway service ceased in November 1903 (see above), electric services did not begin for another six months, though on 26 November 1903 GLASGOW CORPORATION began operating electric cars over its new route from Crookston to Hawkhead Road, the last ½ mile of which was actually inside Paisley's boundary. Murphy's first route was from Paisley Cross to Hawkhead Road where an end-on connection was made with the GC line, both being double-track. After that, expansion was rapid with a double-track line over the rest of the old horse route extended westwards through Fergulie Mills, past Elderslie Depot and on to Houston Square at the end of Johnstone High Street opening on 12 July, a single-track branch south from the Cross to Potterhill following on 29 July and a double-track line northeast to Renfrew on 22 September, terminating at Renfrew Ferry on the Clyde. A second depot was built midway along this 3-mile route at Newmains Road off the Paisley Road. The last of these early routes, opened on 9 November, was a mirror image of the Potterhill line, running north for 1½ miles up Love Street and Inchinnan Road to Abbotsinch.

The tramway's first cars, Nos 1-39, were open-toppers from the BEC works in Manchester (another of Murphy's interests) and were followed in 1905 by Nos 40-49, ten similar vehicles. That same year saw the through running of GC cars to the Cross (from 20 March 1905), a service which reached its apogee that Spring Holiday (24 April) when the Glasgow public houses were forced to remain closed and so cars were run at the rate of one a minute to its 'wet' neighbour!

On 4 July 1905 a 1-mile extension westwards from Johnstone to the beauty spot village of Kilbarchan was opened, together with a 2-mile southwards extension from Potterhill through the residential areas of Glenfield and Cross Stobs to Barrhead; both lines were single-track. The latter route was extended eastwards on 31 December 1910

through Parkhouse and from there on reserved sleepered track to Spiersbridge where it met (but did not connect with) Glasgow's Rouken Glen route. This last double-track line completed the Paisley system (apart from a 300-yard extension at Kilbrachan on 25 June 1913 to take the tramway into the village).

In 1907 an HN open-topper was bought and numbered 52 (Nos 50 and 51 being works cars) and was followed in 1911 by Nos 53-58, top-covered cars from the same firm. These did not prove satisfactory however and were sold to DUNDEE CORPORATION TRAMWAYS just three years later. In 1912 Brush supplied open-toppers 59-62 and 53-58 in 1915, the last double-deckers being HN 63-67 of 1916 and 68-72 of 1920 (again top-covered vehicles). The tramway's only single-decker was ex-Sheffield 202 which was purchased, regauged and sent to Paisley in 1920 though it is not certain if it ever actually saw service there.

In 1921 Glasgow Corporation began to negotiate the purchase of the system, the two sides agreeing on 21 June 1922 to a price of £25,000 to take effect the year following.

Bibliography: as above

PERTH & DISTRICT TRAMWAYS

Authority: Perth and District Tramways Order 1892
Gauge: 3ft 6in
Traction: Horse
Opened: 17 September 1895
Taken Over: 7 October 1903
System: Branching
Length: 4.85 miles
Stock: 1 sd, 8 dd
Livery: Dark crimson & cream to 1898, then dark red-brown & yellow

The purpose of this tramway system was to link the town of Perth on the west bank of the River Tay with the dormitory village of Scone some 3 miles to the northeast. It was promoted by the Perth & District Tramways Co. Ltd which, on 8 May 1894, bought out the Scone & Perth Omnibus Co. before starting work on the tramway. Construction was by Alex Brunton & Sons of Inverkeithing, the result being a single-track line, commencing in Glasgow Road near Rose Crescent, running eastwards through Perth via York Place (near the Caledonian Railway's General station), County Place, the High Street and George Street before crossing the river on the Perth Bridge to the district of Bridgend. From here it followed Strathmore Street and Perth Road to Scone, terminating at the depot there. Original stock comprised four open-top double-deckers (Nos 1-4) and one single-deck toastrack (No 5), all from BM.

In 1897 authority was obtained for extending the line, first with a ½-mile branch south from County Place down King Street, Kings Place and St Leonard's Bank to terminate in Priory Place, Craigie. (This line crossed the railway at the other end of the station to the first route.) The second extension was down Glasgow Road from the former terminus for another ½ mile to Cherrybank. The new lines opened in April and December 1898 respectively and the car fleet increased to cope by addition of four new double-deckers Nos 6-9 (though possibly the last two were second-hand cars). It is believed that for a short time mules were used on the line, a rare event on a British tramway. (See also Folkestone, Hythe & Sandgate in Section 1.)

Proposals for the electrification of the system came at the end of the century but before the Company could put these into effect it sold the line to the Town Council for £21,800 and the cars ran under their new ownership from 7 October 1903 as Perth Corporation Tramways (see below).

Bibliography: *Tramways of the Tay Valley* Alan W. Brotchie (Dundee Museum and Art Gallery, 1965)

PERTH CORPORATION TRAMWAYS

Authority: Perth Corporation (Tramways) Order 1903
Gauge: 3ft 6in
Traction: Horse/overhead electric
Took Over: 7 October 1903
Closed: 19 January 1929
System: Branching
Length: 5.01 miles
Stock: 12 dd electric
Livery: Lake & cream*
Last Car: ?

The Perth horse line was electrified under the Corporation's Order of 1904, the same year that saw (unsuccessful) trials with a petrol tram, a converted double-deck horse car, from the Stirling Motor Construction Co. of Granton, Edinburgh. The electric trams took over during the afternoon of 31 October 1905 covering the whole system (which now included a ½-mile branch from the High Street north along Dunkeld Road), all routes still being largely single-track.

Twelve open-top double-deckers were supplied by HN: Nos 1-9 were painted lake and cream whilst Nos 10-12 were olive green and cream – and were 3in lower to enable them to work under a railway bridge on the Craigie route. (When the King Street bridge was raised in 1907 all cars could work the route and the green livery disappeared.) Horse car No 5 was converted into a water car and the others scrapped or used as passenger shel-

ters whilst the old depot was rebuilt for the new trams.

As elsewhere, World War I saw a neglect of track and other maintenance and during the following decade the Corporation came to the decision to replace the trams with buses. When, in 1927, the Perth General Omnibus Co. began running buses over the main tram route the Corporation's hand was forced. In an ironic reversal of the events of the 1890s, on 3 April 1928 it bought out the PGO Co. in order to operate its buses itself. By September of that year only two trams were fit to run and they staggered on – often empty – until early the following year.

Bibliography: as above

PORT GLASGOW see GREENOCK & PORT GLASGOW

ROTHESAY TRAMWAYS (1)

Authority: Rothesay Tramways Order 1880
Gauge: 4ft/3ft 6in
Traction: Horse
Opened: 1 June 1882
Closed: 19 August 1902?
System: Single line
Length: 2.37 miles
Stock: 19 sd
Livery: Maroon & cream
Last Car: ?

The only island tramway in Scotland, the Rothesay tramway on the popular holiday resort of Bute served the town's residents and visitors alike for some 70 years. It began as a horse tramway, promoted and operated by the Rothesay Tramways Co. Ltd (registered in Edinburgh on 25 November 1879), running from Guildford Square in Rothesay, close to the pier, northwards beside

Rothesay Bay and then eastwards along Ardbeg Road past Pointhouse Depot to Port Bannatyne, a total distance of just over 2 miles of which the first half was double-tracked.

Construction began in early 1882 and the line was ready by June; the public opening preceded the obligatory BoT inspection, resulting in its closure until 10 June. The original eight toastracks with canvas roofs (Nos 1-8) and four closed single-deck saloons (Nos 9-12) were all built by the Saville Street Foundry & Engineering Co. Ltd of Sheffield and were joined at the end of July by two roofed toastracks (Nos 13 and 14) constructed by a local joiner, James McBride. In 1891 two more toastracks (Nos 15 and 16) were supplied by William Lauder of Rothesay and the same builder probably supplied the tramways final three similar cars, Nos 17 and 18 in 1894 and 19 three years later. By then thoughts of electrification were in the air, and following repeated overtures, the Company sold out to the BET in 1901 after obtaining an Order for the reconstruction; the tramway was closed in preparation for this on 2 March 1902 (the work being carried out by Dick, Kerr & Co). Ten of the cars were however regauged and put back into service on the relaid line on 17 May and it is thought a horse service was operated until the electric cars began running (see below).

Bibliography: *The Rothesay Tramways Company 1879-1949* Ian L.Cormack (Scottish Tramway and Transport Society, 1986) 0 900648 23 6

ROTHESAY TRAMWAYS (2)

Authority: Rothesay Tramways Order 1900
Gauge: 3ft 6in

Rothesay 1902 open cross-bench car heading north along Argyle Street on the shores of Rothesay Bay, one of many postcards issued for this popular Scottish resort. (Lens of Sutton)

Argyle and Victoria Streets, Rothesay.

Traction: Overhead electric
Opened: 19 August 1902
Closed: 30 September 1936
System: Single line
Length: 4.87 miles
Stock: 24 sd
Livery: Maroon & cream to 1932, then blue & white
Last Cars: No 14 (service), No 9 (official)

With the horse tramway closed (see above), the rails were lifted and sold prior to new track being laid to the more common electric tramway gauge of 3ft 6in; this work was done by early June 1902 and the whole line was ready for re-opening that August. The official inauguration was on 13 August, again before the BoT inspection, the consequence of which was that public services could not commence for another week.

In 1905 a 2½-mile extension on a reserved right of way across the island from the old tramway terminus at Port Bannatyne to Ettrick Bay on the west coast was constructed, opening on 13 July to complete the system. On 1 January 1914 control of the line passed to the Scottish General Transport Co. (incorporated 24 September 1913), a subsidiary of the BET. The beginning of the end came in the 1920s when motor bus operators began to compete with the tramway. In 1925 the Company began operating its own three charabancs between Port Bannatyne and Port Ettrick; as they proved profitable the writing was on the wall for the tramway. In 1931 the line was acquired by the Scottish Motor Traction Group (the Western Scottish Motor Traction Co. Ltd from 1 June 1932), a company moving into bus operation in a big way. Four years later the tramway closed for good.

The tramway's first cars were ten roofed toastracks (Nos 1-10) and five single-deck combination saloons (Nos 11-15), all from ERTCW. One of these – usually No 14 – worked as an illuminated car during the late summer Rothesay illuminations season. Five roofed toastracks from Brush (Nos 16-20) were bought in 1903 to complete the original fleet. In 1916 the bodies of Nos 11 and 12 were sent to GREENOCK & PORT GLASGOW to help cope with the increased traffic produced by the war effort there and three years later the Company equipped the freed trucks with open toastrack bodies (which retained the old car numbers). In return, Greenock sent Rothesay a 1908 UEC demi-car which, with its truck regauged, ran as No 21 until 1920 when it was rebodied as an open toastrack No 22 – the seaside nature of the line being reflected in the predominance of open cars. Whilst the official Last Car was No 9, the final service was worked by No 14, illuminated and decorated for the last time.

Bibliography: as above

STIRLING & BRIDGE OF ALLAN TRAMWAYS

Authority: Stirling and Bridge of Allan
    Tramways Order 1872
Gauge: 4ft 8½in
Traction: Horse, petrol
Opened: 27 July 1874
Closed: 20 May 1920
System: Single line
Length: 4.35 miles
Stock: 8 sd, 11 dd horse?; 1 dd petrol
Livery: Various, finally red-brown & cream
Last Car: No 22

The purpose behind the construction of this tramway, as indicated by its name, was to link the town of Stirling on the River Forth with the village of Bridge of Allan some 3 miles to the north which, during the first half of the 19th century, had developed as a spa. Although the Caledonian Railway already linked the two places, at least two groups of promoters believed the potential traffic for a tramway was there and in 1872 an Order was obtained for a simple single-track line.

Construction began in May 1874 and was completed in time for the annual Strathallan Games which were held every August in Bridge of Allan. The 3¼-mile line ran southeast from that village for 1½ miles until it approached the hamlet of Causewayhead where it swung southwestwards to pass the NBR's station on the Alloa line and the tramway depot. It then paralleled the railway until it reached the Forth which it crossed after passing under the aforementioned CR line to run south through the centre of Stirling to a terminus on Port Street at the junction with Melville Terrace (though the last 100yd or so from the King Street junction with Port Street were only used when specials were run in connection with Public Hall functions).

Precise details of the tramway's car fleet (and their numbers) are tantalizingly sketchy. Originally there were two double-deckers (possibly Nos 1 and 2) and a single-deck saloon car (possibly No 3), all supplied by the Tramway Car & Works Co. Ltd of Glasgow. Later during 1874 the single-decker was rebuilt as a double-decker and all three cars ran until 1877 when the depot caught fire and one was destroyed, along with the Company's horse bus. Replacements for both were bought, the new double-decker (possibly No 1) coming from an unknown source in Glasgow. The following year a Dickinson double-deck steam car was tested on the line but permission was granted for one day of public service only (during the Strathallan Games).

In 1885 three open toastracks (Nos 4-6) were purchased cheaply from somewhere in England – they were possibly an unfinished order for the aborted Ramsgate & Margate tramway (see Section 1) – and two years later a reversible-body double-decker was acquired, possibly from EDINBURGH & DISTRICT, followed over the next 18 years by a succession of second-hand cars from other Scottish systems (including EDINBURGH, GLASGOW and LEITH) as they abandoned horse haulage.

In 1897 authority was obtained for a southwards extension of just over a mile to Weaver Row in the village of St Ninians; this opened on 29 January 1898 and was

A common 'last car of the day' postcard by 'Cynicus', issued in many tramway towns with the appropriate name added, in this case Govan in Glasgow.

The Last Car
to Govan

normally worked from King Street as a separate route. As elsewhere, by this time prospects of electrification were in the air but the three main interested parties – the BET, the NEC and Stirling Council – all backed out at the last minute.

Modernization, when it came, was in the form of double-deck car No 22 which was rebuilt in 1913, with a 25hp petrol engine and mechanical drive, by the Lanarkshire Motor Co. of Glasgow. It began regular duty on 9 December that year and gave sterling service, mainly on the St Ninians route, until the very last day of the tramway. By the end of World War I there were only three cars (No 22 and ex-Leith double-deckers Nos 47 and 48) in regular use. The last horse car ran on 5 February 1920, the trams' final year of service, displaced by the Corporation's own

motor buses which had been operating for the past two years.

Bibliography: *Stirling's Trams and Buses* A. W. Brotchie (NB Traction, Dundee, 1991) 0 905069 28 5

STRABATHIE & BLACKDOG LIGHT RAILWAY

Authority: –
Gauge: 3ft
Traction: Horse/petrol
Opened: February 1900
Closed: 1949
System: Single line
Length: c1.75 miles
Stock: 4 sd horse; 2 railcars
Livery: Red & grey
Last Car: Wickham railcar

This isolated line started out as an industrial tramroad, turned into a tramway and ended its life as a light railway – or rather, because of its rough and ready nature, an inexact semblance of these three types of line. It was built by the Seaton Brick & Tile Co. Ltd (incorporated in Edinburgh in 1884) in order to link its Blackdog Brickworks (opened 1898) close to the coast with Aberdeen about 5 miles to the south. The intention was to provide a physical link with the ABERDEEN CORPORATION TRAMWAYS but the idea came to nothing and the line as built stopped some 2 miles short of the city (and utilized a narrower gauge into the bargain).

It appears that the horse-worked line (its single track laid with light flat-bottom rails) carried passengers from the outset

[5 EDW. 7.]   *Wemyss Tramways Order Confirmation*   [Ch. cxci.]
Act, 1905.

CHAPTER cxci.

An Act to confirm a Provisional Order under the Private   A.D. 1905.
Legislation Procedure (Scotland) Act 1899 relating to
Wemyss Tramways.   [11th August 1905.]

WHEREAS His Majesty's Secretary for Scotland has after inquiry held before Commissioners made the Provisional Order set forth in the schedule hereunto annexed under the provisions of the Private Legislation Procedure (Scotland) Act 1899   62 & 63 Vict. and it is requisite that the said Order should be confirmed by   c. 47. Parliament:

Be it therefore enacted by the King's most Excellent Majesty by and with the advice and consent of the Lords Spiritual and Temporal and Commons in this present Parliament assembled and by the authority of the same as follows:—

1. The Provisional Order contained in the schedule hereunto   Confirmation annexed shall be and the same is hereby confirmed.   of Order in   schedule.

2. This Act may be cited as the Wemyss Tramways Order   Short title. Confirmation Act 1905.

Usually, several Tramway Orders would be confirmed within one Act; occasionally, as with this Wemyss Tramways Order, one would have an Act to itself if no others were waiting at the time.

(November 1899) with an unofficial workers' service being operated, but a public service was launched in February 1900 with the purchase of four ex-Aberdeen cars. However, this service was limited to the southern 1¼ miles and ran principally for the benefit of members of the Murcar Golf Club situated that distance up the tramway. (A steam tank locomotive worked the goods trains.)

Mechanization came in 1909 when J. B. Duff & Co. of Aberdeen built a petrol railcar for the line and in 1932 a Wickham railcar was purchased. By this time the line was owned and operated by the golf club itself, the brick company having gone into liquidation in July 1924 after which the northern section was lifted (and part of the trackbed incorporated into an enlarged gold course).

The line, which ran through rough grass sandwiched between the golf links to the east and farmland to the west (and only fenced on the latter side), closed in 1949 though the Wickham railcar was kept operational for emergency use until October 1951 when the track was lifted and the railcar body – now in extremely poor condition – became a caddy cart shed.

The tramway's alternative title (though neither was official since it was built without any formal authorization) was the Murcar Railway from the name of the club it served; no doubt for reasons of Scottish sporting rivalry trams passed but did not stop at the neighbouring Balgownie golf course!

VALE OF CLYDE TRAMWAYS

Authority: Vale of Clyde Tramways Act 1871
Gauge: 4ft 7¾in
Traction: Horse/steam
Opened: 1 January 1873
Taken Over: 10 July 1893
System: Single line
Length: 4.14 miles
Stock: 14 dd horse*; 20 locos, 22 dd steam
Livery: Brown & cream?

The Vale of Clyde Tramways Co. operated two widely-separated systems in the region west of Glasgow. Both were opened in 1873, the first being in Govan, midway between Glasgow and Paisley and the second at Gourock on the Firth of Clyde (see GREENOCK & PORT GLASGOW TRAMWAYS). The first line was a horse-worked single-track tramway which ran for some 4 miles from the Park House Toll House on Paisley Road at the Glasgow/Govan boundary, northwest along the Govan Road beside the Clyde dockyards to Linthouse Ship Yard in Fairfield. This was worked by open-top cars from the batch Nos 1-12 built by Starbuck and the Tramway Car & Works Co. of Greenwich and Glasgow with the operation of the line leased until 1 July 1874 to the Glasgow Tramway & Omnibus Co. (with through working to St Vincent Place in the centre of that city). The depot was in Great Wellington Street (later Admiral Street) immediately south of the Paisley Road Toll. Probably not all the Company's cars worked the Govan tramway, some of them being used on the GPG line as well.

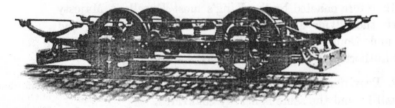
Edwardian trade advertisement for Hurst, Nelson & Co. Ltd, a major supplier of tramway rolling stock to Scotland and elsewhere.

In 1874 two more cars (Nos 13 and 14) were bought to complete the horse car fleet for in 1876, under the provisions of the Vale of Clyde Tramways Act of that year, mechanical traction was authorized to help facilitate the working of railway wagons (hitherto horse-hauled) from Govan railway sidings to the Fairfield Shipbuilding & Engineering Co. Ltd's dockside premises. Between 1877 and 1880 Hughes tramway locomotives Nos 1-10 were bought to pull open-top double-deck trailers Nos 1-12, after the arrival of the first of which three of the horse cars were sold and the remainder transferred to Gourock. Half of the original steam trailers were sold in 1881 and eight Metropolitan double-deck bogie cars bought and numbered 1-8, followed by Nos 9 and 10 two years later. During that same period a new batch of locos (Nos 1-9) were bought from Kitsons, to be joined in 1892 by Kitson No 10, bought from the Cavehill & Whitewell Tramway in Ireland.

In 1893 the line was purchased for £60,000 by the Govan local authority, the Commissioners of Police, under the Govan Burgh (Tramways) Act of that year and leased to the Glasgow Tramway & Omnibus Co. (See GLASGOW TRAMWAY.)

WEMYSS & DISTRICT TRAMWAYS

Authority: Wemyss Tramways Order 1905
Gauge: 3ft 6in
Traction: Overhead electric
Opened: 25 August 1906
Closed: 30 January 1932
System: Single line
Length: 7.45 miles
Stock: 29 sd
Livery: Wemyss yellow (mustard) to 1913, then maroon & cream
Last Car: ?

The Wemyss tramway came into being as a direct result of the early success of the KIRKALDY system. It was promoted and built by Randolph G. E. Wemyss, the local laird, and ran for the most part across his own estates from Gallatown in Kirkaldy, eastwards and roughly parallel to the coast, through the villages of West and East Wemyss and Buckhaven, then along Wellesley Road through Methil to Leven where it terminated in Durie Street. This was a coalmining area and the single-track line was financed by the laird's Wemyss Coal Co. (and operated by the Wemyss & District Tramways Co. Ltd). Where the line served the villages it did so as a street tramway but on the frequent rural stretches it was more akin to a light railway running on sleepered track on a fenced-off right of way.

Construction began in July 1905 and the line opened the following year with nine Brush single-deckers (Nos 1-9); services were soon extended from 27 September 1906 when agreement was reached for running powers over the 2½ miles of Kirkaldy's Upper Route metals from Gallatown to Whytecauseway in the town centre. (This arrangement lasted until 15 January 1917). Four more identical cars (Nos 10-13) were added to meet the increased demand, followed in 1907 by four MV long bogie cars (Nos 14-17) to serve specifically as miners' transport. (The line was restricted to using single-deck vehicles on account of the narrow gauge and railway-type sections.) The depot was at Aberhill in Leven.

The inevitable bus competition appeared on the scene shortly before World War I and expanded dramatically in the 1920s. The 'poaching' of waiting passengers by the motor buses led the Company to invest in three petrol-electric buses in 1922; for the last ten years the line had been controlled by the BB group and in 1926 it bought up its principal rival, the General Motor Carrying Co, a year after it had added bogie cars 18 and 19 to its fleet, this time from Brush. (These were sold in January 1932, just before the line closed, to DUNFERMLINE.)

In 1928 two bogie cars from the Potteries Electric Tramways were bought and numbered 20 and 21 and, following the closure of the Kirkcaldy system in 1931, eight of its double-deckers were purchased and numbered 22-29 (and the top decks and stairs removed) to augment briefly its existing fleet.

Bibliography: *The Wemyss and District Tramways Company Ltd* (Tramways of Fife and the Forth Valley Part 3) Alan W. Brotchie (The NB Traction Group, Dundee, 1976)
The Tramways of Kirkcaldy (Tramways of Fife and the Forth Valley Part 4) Alan W. Brotchie (The NB Traction Group, Dundee, 1978) 0 905069 00 9
Fife's Trams and Buses Alan W. Brotchie (NB Traction, Dundee, 1990) 0 905069 27 7

Section 4

Tramways of Ireland

The railways and tramways of Ireland had much in common with their counterparts in Great Britain, a not very surprising state of affairs considering the close political and economic ties between the two islands at the time of their construction. Capital often came from the same sources, the same engineers would be employed and the same worksplates could be seen on similar-looking locomotives, carriages and tramcars in London, Glasgow or Dublin.

There were however several major differences between the islands' tramways. To begin with, Ireland did not possess the large concentrations of industry and settlement Great Britain did with the result that, apart from BELFAST and DUBLIN, no networks of linked tramways emerged. Not only were all the other systems isolated from each other, they also tended to be small, often single line affairs.

In Ireland – more so than anywhere else in the British Isles – the dividing line between light railway and tramway was a very blurred one. Whilst the urban horse and electric tramways were easily recognisable as such, rural steam tramways were often only distinguishable from the island's narrow gauge railways in that they occupied the roadway or roadside for most of their route whereas light railways, such as the Cork & Muskerry or the Tralee & Dingle, incorporated stretches of roadway or roadside track for all but a small proportion of their overall length. For this reason, and the fact that their primary traffic was usually freight and not passengers, such railways have been excluded from this book. (Details of them can be found in Thomas Middlemass's companion *Encyclopaedia of Narrow Gauge Railways of Great Britain and Ireland*.) The rough rule of thumb adopted is that if a line had stations with railway-style platforms and locomotives without enclosed motions or skirts, then it has not been included here even if it did, in part, run along or beside a public highway.

The construction of tramways in Ireland was authorized under a mixture of general British and specifically Irish legislation. The latter was often ahead of the former and included an 1860 Tramways Act permitting the use of animal power (amended in 1871 to allow mechanical traction), the Tramways and Public Companies (Ireland) Act of 1883 and the 1889 Light Railways (Ireland) Act, under which an appropriate Order in Council could be issued by the Lord Lieutenant in the Privy Council. A system of Baronial Guarantees peculiar to southern Ireland meant that local authorities could be made to underwrite any losses made by lines within their domain; whilst this often had a detrimental effect on the local economy, without such subsidies many of the country's unique and fascinating lines would never have been built.

ARIGNA TRAMWAY
Authority: Order in Council 1885
Gauge: 3ft
Traction: Steam
Opened: 24 October 1887
Closed: 31 March 1959
System: Single line
Length: 14.75 miles
Stock: *
Livery: Locos dark green, coaches reddish-
   brown
Last Train: ?

The Arigna Tramway represented the tramway element in the title of its operating company, the Cavan, Leitrim & Roscommon Light Railway & Tramway Co. Ltd (registered 3 December 1883) which had promoted and built a 33¾-mile 3ft gauge steam railway between Belturbet on the GNR(I) in Cavan to Dromond on the MGWR in Leitrim; the Company shortened its name in 1895 to the Cavan & Leitrim Railway Co. when it became clear that it was unlikely ever to reach Roscommon.

The purpose of the C&L was to open up this sparsely-populated region of western Ireland; the Arigna Tramway in particular was intended to exploit the coal and iron deposits near that town. Laid with flat-bottom rails spiked to sleepers, the single-track line began at Ballinamore in Leitrim, midway along the C&L's main line, and followed a roughly westerly course beside the old Ballinamore & Ballyconnell Canal, twisting and winding for 3 miles to Ballyduff where it joined the public highway for the equally-twisting but now also up-and-down remainder of its course to Arigna where there was a station house, platform, goods shed and turntable to allow the tramway engines (in theory at least) to make the return journey cab-first. The very last 1½ miles of the tramway were actually in County Roscommon, a brief reminder of the Company's original aims. The C&L opened for goods traffic on 17 October 1887 and for passengers a week later.

As a tramway the line was governed by the usual BoT regulations which meant that of the original stock of eight 4-4-0 tank engines ordered by the C&L from Robert Stephenson & Sons of Newcastle-upon-Tyne, four were fitted with skirts, condensing gear and warning bells. Under the regulations they were required to run cab-first (so as to give the driver a clearer view of the road ahead) but this was found to be damaging to the track so the BoT insisted that the driver's controls be moved to the front end to allow normal running and Nos 7 *Olive* and 8 *Queen Victoria* (the regular tramway engines) were so treated. Although this modification was carried out, the regulations were, in the manner of such remote lines, quietly forgotten and well before the end of the century the main line engines were working the tramway on a regular basis. Passenger coaches – there were eventually twelve bogie vehicles – were shared between the main line and the tramway and mixed workings with goods wagons were the norm with services over the tramway fluctuating betwen two and three trains a day.

Plans to link the C&L with the CLOGHER VALLEY TRAMWAY in the 1900s came to nothing but a goods-only extension of the Arigna line, using an old tramroad formation, opened on 2 June 1920 and, although worked by the C&L, was built by the GNR(I) under Government sponsorship in order to exploit the local mineral deposits to the full.

The tramway saw action during the Civil War with trains being commandeered by both sides and from 1 January 1925 it was amalgamated along with the rest of the C&L into the GSR; from 1 January 1945 it passed into the control of the CIE. The end, when it came 14 years later, was brought about by a number of factors: fast-dwindling passenger figures, road competition, outstanding maintenance and a new power station by Lough Allen which absorbed the Arigna output, so killing the coal traffic at a stroke.

Bibliography: *The Cavan & Leitrim Railway* Patrick J. Flanagan (David & Charles, 1966)

BELFAST STREET TRAMWAYS
Authority: Order in Council 1871
Gauge: 5ft 3in/4ft 8½in
Traction: Horse
Opened: 28 August 1872
Taken Over: 1 January 1905
System: Network
Length: 24.95 miles
Stock: 3 sd, 171 dd?
Livery: Red & cream

Belfast's extensive horse tramway system started with a single-track 1½-mile route promoted and built by the Belfast Tramways Co. Ltd which ran southwards from Castle Place in the city centre along Wellington Place, Great Victoria Street and University Road to the Botanical Gardens with services provided by three German-built single-deckers.

Even before the line opened however the BT Co. was taken over by a rival concern, the Belfast Street Tramways Co. who, over the next two years, completed the first stage of a radial system with lines along the High Street, Donegall Street and York Street to the BNCR's York Road station in the north (with a short branch up Clifton Street), and from the end of the High Street northwards up Corporation Street and southwards down Victoria Street, Cromac Street and Ormeau Road to Ormeau Bridge over the River Lagan. Route length was 5½ miles of which slightly more than half was single-track and over which 14 cars now operated.

Further extensions followed to cover virtually all parts of the city under a succession of Acts, perhaps the most important of which was that of 1878 which permitted the Company to use a gauge of 4ft 8½in in the future; existing routes were subsequently converted accordingly.

The car fleet had grown to keep pace with the expanding system: by the end of 1890 there were 81 trams in use and by 1897 a total of 114 based on a number of depots scattered around the system. Most of the cars were Company-built though 16 were by Starbuck, presumably those bought immediately after the three original German cars (which were later converted to double-deckers).

By the mid-1890s the Company was considering electrification but in 1899, under its Act of that year, Belfast Corporation stepped in and built 7.95 miles of extensions of its own to the system (which the Company worked), later announcing its intention of seeking Parliamentary powers to buy the whole undertaking. This it did, taking over on 1 January 1905 after paying £356,984 for the concern. (See BELFAST CORPORATION TRAMWAYS.)

Bibliography: *Belfast Corporation Tramways 1905-1954* J. M. Maybin (The Light Rail Transit Association, no date) 0 900433 83 3

BELFAST: SYDENHAM DISTRICT, BELFAST, TRAMWAY
The SDBT was one of three short peripheral tramways connected to the BELFAST STREET TRAMWAYS system which, whilst nominally independent, were worked by the BST with BST stock and staff on a rental basis. (The other two lines were the BELFAST & LIGONIEL TRAMWAY and the BELFAST & COUNTY DOWN

RAILWAY's short spur.) Authorized by Orders in Council of 1885, 1887 and 1889 the mainly single-track line left the BST system at Holywood Arches on Newtownards Road and ran eastwards for 1½ miles along Holywood Road and Belmont Road to its Old Holywood Road terminus. It was purchased by the BST in 1902 and, like its two above-mentioned counterparts, was electrified following the Corporation's 1905 takeover.

In 1923 the line was extended just over ½ mile along Kileen (later Massey) Avenue to bring it to the gates of Stormont (later to house the Northern Ireland Parliament).

Bibliography: as above

BELFAST & LIGONIEL TRAMWAY
The B&L was to all intents and purposes a 1½-mile extension of the Belfast system running northwestwards from the BST's Crumlin Road terminus along that road to the village of Ligoniel. Constructed under an Order in Council of 1892 and opened on 24 April 1893, it was purchased by the BST Co. in 1902 and electrified in 1905 along with the BST system following the Corporation's takeover. (See BELFAST CORPORATION TRAMWAYS.)

The line was later extended a third of a mile in 1913 to a new, Mill Avenue terminus and became one of the city's last two routes to close.

Bibliography: as above

BELFAST & COUNTY DOWN RAILWAY
In 1894, under an Order in Council of that

Belfast Street Tramways No 65 on an Antrim Road working, plus two others, in a (probably) 1880s photograph of Castle Junction. (Lens of Sutton)

year, the BCDR built 111yd of single-track tramway to link its Queen's Quay station in east Belfast with the BELFAST STREET TRAMWAYS' line over Queen's Bridge, on the River Lagan, to the High Street. Worked from the outset by the BST as an integral part of its own system, unlike the BELFAST SYDENHAM DISTRICT and the BELFAST & LIGONIEL lines which it also ran, it was not purchased by the BST in 1902 but by BELFAST CORPORATION for £1,616 at the time of its purchase of the BST.

Bibliography: as above

BELFAST CORPORATION TRAMWAYS

Authority: Belfast Corporation (Tramways) Act 1904
Gauge: 4ft 8½in
Traction: Horse, overhead electric
Took Over: 1 January 1905
Closed: 10 February 1954
System: Radial network
Length: 51.45 miles
Stock: 170 dd horse; 441 dd electric
Livery: Red & cream to 1929, then blue & cream
Last Car: No 389 (official)*

At its greatest extent the Belfast system was the second largest in Ireland. Quickly electrifying the BELFAST STREET SYSTEM after its 1905 takeover, the Corporation's first reconstructed routes (Stranmillis Road, Malone Road and Ormeau Road in the south and Springfield Road in the west) opened on 30 November 1905 and the remainder of the horse lines on 5 December.

The first totally new route (Queen's Road to the northeast) opened on 11 August 1908

and, on 2 June 1911, the Corporation took control of the CAVEHILL & WHITEWELL TRAMWAY to the north to form the longest of its routes. The pattern was now set of constructing new, often short routes of only a couple of miles length and extending existing ones to 18 outlying termini to produce a double-tracked network of radial routes (with links between many of them) centred on what became known as Castle Junction where Royal Avenue, Castle Place, Castle Street and Donegall Place met in the city centre. The last section opened, to Ballygomartin in the west, opened on 23 July 1925, just a year before the Corporation began running feeder bus services.

Twelve years later, on 28 March 1938, Corporation trolleybus services began along the Falls Road, replacing the trams there. The experiment was judged a success and it was decided to convert the rest of the tramway system (which, apart from two relatively minor cutbacks, had remained complete until then) though in the event World War II slowed the process down markedly. The Ravenhill Road route to Ormeau Road was replaced by a bus service on 5 September 1940 and the southeastern route to Cregagh (13 February) and to Castlereagh (5 June) closed the next year, followed in 1942 by the two longest eastern routes to Stormont (26 March) and Dundonald via Queen's Bridge (16 November) and, on 8 March 1943, by the Dundonald via Albert Bridge route – all displaced by trolleybuses.

After this closures came thick and fast (although latterly giving way to motor buses rather than trolleybuses) until 1954, by which time only rush-hour services on the Ligoniel and Queen's Road routes were being operated. Although these services were

withdrawn on 10 February of that year, an official 'Last Car' procession was held 18 days later.

For such a large system the history of the electric car fleet is surprisingly straightforward. In number order, the cars (all double-deckers) were as follows:

Nos 1-170: Brush open-toppers of 1905
Nos 171-192: Corporation-built open-toppers of 1908-10
Nos 193-200: ex-C&W cars acquired 1911
Nos 201-250: ex-BST open-top cars rebuilt 1905
Nos 251-291: Corporation-built, mostly top-covered, 1913-19
(Many of the above cars were later top-covered.)
Nos 292-341: Brush enclosed cars of 1920-21 and known as 'Moffetts' after the then General Manager
Nos 342-381: Brush enclosed cars of 1931 and known as 'Chamberlains' for the same reason
Nos 382-392: enclosed cars built by the Service Motor Works Ltd of Belfast in 1930
Nos 392-441: streamlined cars built by EE (392 and 423-441) and Service 1935-36 and known as 'McCrearys' after the then General Manager

As new cars arrived older ones were withdrawn and scrapped with none being sold to other systems. After the closure the surviving cars were scrapped at the central Mountpottinger Depot – except for No 357, reportedly the last car to arrive there, which together with the rebuilt horse car 249 is in store awaiting the opening of the new Road Transport Gallery at the Ulster Folk & Transport Museum at Cultra, Co. Down.

Bibliography: as above

BESSBROOK & NEWRY TRAMWAY

Despite its title (and the fact that it is often written of as one of the earliest British tramways) the B&N cannot really be regarded as anything other than an electric railway. It was built to connect the Armagh town of Bessbrook's flax mills with the GNR(I) at Newry, 3 miles away. Originally planned as a steam tramway, it was constructed as a centre-rail electric railway by the Bessbrook & Newry Tramway Co. (incorporated 26 May 1884) under the 1883 Tramways and Public Companies Act and opened in October 1885, just two years after the pioneering GIANT'S CAUSEWAY line. It did however possess two tramway-like features. The first was that it used bogie passenger cars (powered and trailer) similar in design to those later used on the Manx Electric Railway in the Isle of

Postcard of Belfast Corporation double-decker No 222, rebuilt from a horse car, running in the Shankhill Road. (Lens of Sutton)

Man (see Section 5) whilst the second was that for a 50-yard stretch across the road near Bessbrook overhead current collection was used for obvious safety reasons – the first regular use of such a system in the British Isles.

One other, unique feature of the railway deserves mention: the line's goods wagons (hauled by the motor cars) had flangeless wheels so they could be road-hauled as well; on the railway they ran on flat rails laid below and outside the 3ft gauge running rails, making the line in effect a modern plateway.

Traffic – mill workers, raw materials and finished products – was heavy enough to keep the line working when many of its contemporaries had succumbed to the rival motor buses and lorries. Inevitably, on 10 January 1948, it was finally forced to close. (See also CLOGHER VALLEY TRAMWAY.)

Bibliography: *The Bessbrook & Newry Tramway* (Locomotion Papers No 115) Alan T. Newham (The Oakwood Press, 1979)

BLACKROCK & KINGSTOWN TRAMWAYS
Authority: Blackrock and Kingstown Tramways Act 1883
Gauge: 5ft 3in
Traction: Horse
Opened: 9 July 1885
Taken Over: 1893
System: Single line
Length: 2.54 miles
Stock: 6 dd
Livery: Dark green & cream?

The purpose of this short line, owned and operated by the Blackrock & Kingstown Tramway Co. Ltd (incorporated March 1883) was to provide a link between the two separated sections of the DUBLIN SOUTHERN DISTRICT TRAMWAYS. It ran from Newtown Avenue in Blackrock by the Town Hall, southeast via Monkstown Road to Kingstown (now Dun Laoghaire) where it met the southern portion of the DSD in Royal Marine Road to share interlaced double tracks to the terminus by the railway station. A difference in gauge here meant that through running was impossible; although connected at the Blackrock end to the northern portion of the DSD, no through running took place from here either as the Kingstown Township Commissioners refused to allow steam working over the line.

Construction of the mixed single and double-track line began in the spring of 1885 and the tramway was ready by the summer; the depot in Newtown Avenue housed the line's six cars. Within a year of the opening the DSD was expressing an interest in

purchasing it as a prelude to electrifying the whole system though it was not until 1893 that it obtained the necessary Parliamentary authority, paying £7,000 for the B&K line.

BLESSINGTON & POULAPHOUCA STEAM TRAMWAY
Authorized by an Order in Council of 1889 and owned by the Blessington & Poulaphouca Steam Tramway Co., incorporated in 1889 to continue the DUBLIN & BLESSINGTON tramway for 4.67 miles on to the popular beauty spot of its title on the Kildare/Wicklow boundary, this was a single-track 5ft 3in gauge roadside line running in the same southwesterly direction as the D&B to its Poulaphouca terminus close to the Liffey river bridge, gorge and waterfall.

From its opening on 1 May 1895 the line was worked by the D&B (with D&B stock), first as a separate service then, from 1896, with through trains from Terenure on the outskirts of Dublin. From then on its fortunes were inextricably linked with those of the D&B and during the 1920s took the same down turn. In the event, the Company decided in 1927 to close the line (on 30 September), leaving its bigger brother to struggle on – without the benefit of the tripper trade to Poulaphouca – for another five years.

Bibliography: *The Dublin & Blessington Steam Tramway* (Locomotion Papers No 20) H. Fayle & A. T. Newham (The Oakwood Press, 1963)

BRAY & ENNISKERRY LIGHT RAILWAY
This was Ireland's only example of a type of line more common on the British mainland: a tramway built – at least in part – but never opened. Constructed by the Bray & Enniskerry Light Railway Co. under an 1886 Act of Parliament, it was to have run for 3½ miles between the two places of its title in County Wicklow on a mixture of road and reserved sections. Much of the (extensive) civil engineering work was completed and some track for the electric line laid but local opponents of the scheme won the day and in 1893 the County Council succeeded in having the track taken up. Later attempts to reinstate it came to nothing.

BUSH VALLEY see GIANT'S CAUSEWAY, PORTRUSH & BUSH VALLEY

CASTLEDERG & VICTORIA BRIDGE TRAMWAY
Authority: Castlederg and Victoria Bridge Tramway Act 1883
Gauge: 3ft

Traction: Steam, paraffin
Opened: 4 July 1884
Closed: 31 January 1933
System: Single line
Length: 7.15 miles
Stock: 6 locos, 5 sd steam; 1 railmotor
Livery: Red
Last Car: ?

This County Tyrone steam tramway was built for the common reason of a small town, having been bypassed by the local railway company, wishing to have a connection with the nearest station more modern than that afforded by a horse and cart. In this instance the town was Castlederg, the railway was the Londonderry–Enniskillen section of the GNR(I) and the station Victoria Bridge.

The line was laid quickly, the speed of construction no doubt aided by the fact that the single track was lightly laid with flat-bottom rails entirely without passing loops and alongside the public highway with no major earthworks and gradients of up to 1 in 30 as it followed the dips in the road! The depot and offices were at Castlederg whilst the Victoria Bridge terminus was by the railway station; three official stopping places were at the villages of Fyfin, Crew and Spamount but in practice the tramway train halted to pick up or set down anywhere en route. Because of the lack of passsing loops, the line was worked on the 'one engine in steam' principle.

The line's two original steam locomotives were both Kitson tramway engines, Nos 1 *Mourne* and 2 *Derg* (named after local rivers), which were joined in 1892 by No 3 from the same makers (but not totally enclosed). In 1904 and 1912 replacement locos for the original two were purchased from Hudswell, Clarke; these (Nos 4 and 5) were conventional railway tank engines but with tramway-style side skirts. (Interestingly, these were fitted only on the nearside as the tramway occupied the same side of the road for its entire length.) The coaches were small, four-wheel affairs and there were a number of goods wagons.

After World War I the line was, in common with others like it, badly hit by the rise of motor bus competition and in 1925 a serious attempt was made to cut costs with the construction of a small 20hp railmotor (seating 24) by the tramway's Locomotive Superintendent. It was not a great success and in 1928 an ex-Ballymena & Larne Railway tank engine was purchased as a replacement (and fitted with a side skirt on the nearside).

The last trains ran on 31 January 1933 when employees joined a Northern Ireland railway strike and, before services could be resumed, the Castlederg & Victoria Bridge Tramway Co. (incorporated 16 July 1883) officially closed the line on 3 October that year. After that the stock was sold with loco No 4 making its way to the CLOGHER VALLEY line. One of the coaches is now on show in the Ulster Folk & Transport Museum at Cultra.

Bibliography: *The Narrow Gauge Railways of Ireland* H. Fayle (Greenlake Publications, 1946)

CAVEHILL & WHITEWELL TRAMWAY

Authority: Order in Council 1881
Gauge: 4ft 8in/4ft 8½in
Traction: Steam, horse/overhead electric
Opened: 1 July 1882
Taken Over: 1 June 1911
System: Single line
Length: 3.29 miles
Stock: 3 locos, 1 sd, 8 dd steam & horse;
    10 dd electric
Livery: Green & white

One of the four peripheral tramways connected to the BELFAST STREET TRAMWAYS system, the C&W – unlike the other three – was actually worked as an independent concern by its owner, the Cavehill & Whitewell Tramway Co. Its other noteworthy feature was that although short, it employed no less than three different modes of traction during its independent life: steam, then horse (a reversal of the normal sequence) and finally electricity.

The single-track line ran in a northerly direction along the Antrim Road from the BST's terminus at Chichester Park on the northern edge of the city, through Cavehill to the Glengormley Arms. It was worked at first

by two Kitson tramway locos (Nos 1 and 2) and open-top bogie double-decker No 1 and open-sided toastrack No 2, both from Metropolitan; these were joined in 1884 by another open-top bogie car, No 3, and in 1887 by Kitson loco No 3 (possibly assembled in Belfast). Car No 4, a four-wheeled open-topper, arrived in 1888, followed by similar vehicles 5-7 three years later (No 6 being possibly an ex-BST car). The depot was in Glengormley by the old Bellevue Gardens.

Early in 1892 regular steam traction was replaced by the use of horses in order to cut costs and provide a more reliable service, with loco No 1 sold to the Vale of Clyde line in Scotland, though the other two were used when demand necessitated for another three years. At the same time another open-topper (No 8) was bought, followed by No 9 in 1899 to complete the fleet. In 1892 the Company obtained an Act to permit the electrification of the line (on a 4ft 8½in gauge) though work on this did not begin until June 1905 (by J. G. White & Co.) with the BET the prime mover of this as one of the Company's shareholders. The new service began on 12 February 1906 with ten open-top Brush cars (of two designs) based on a new depot midway along the line by what were to become the New Bellevue Gardens.

There was no love lost between the Company and Belfast Corporation (now owners of the former BST system) and the latter was eager to buy up the C&W, by now the only independent line abutting the Belfast system. The Company was having none of it however and instead sought permission to run over its big brother's line. Since this was not forthcoming (there was never a connection between the two any-

way), it was perhaps inevitable that, in the circumstances, the Company should seek the best price it could get for its line (£56,155) and the formal handing-over took place on 1 June 1911 with the Corporation becoming the new owner under the provisions of the Belfast Corporation Tramways Act of the previous year. Through services began the next day, making this the longest of the city's routes (services 3 and 5), and lasted until 24 January 1949 when its trams were replaced by trolleybuses. (See BELFAST CORPORATION TRAMWAYS.)

Bibliography: *Belfast Corporation Tramways 1905-1954* J. M. Maybin (The Light Rail Transit Association, no date)

CLOGHER VALLEY TRAMWAY

Authority: Order in Council 1884
Gauge: 3ft
Traction: Steam, diesel
Opened: 3 May 1887
Closed: 31 December 1941
System: Single line
Length: 37 miles
Stock: 9 locos, 13 sd steam; 1 loco, 1 railcar
    diesel
Livery: Locos various, carriages crimson
    lake/reddish brown
Last Car: Railcar

Promoted by the Clogher Valley Tramway Co. Ltd (incorporated 1883), the purpose of the CVT was to open up the Clogher Valley region of southern Tyrone in the centre of the province of Ulster. As built, it formed the eastern and northern sides of a rough rectangle some 25 miles across with the other two sides made up of the GNR(I) lines from Tynan to Clones and Maguire's Bridge.

It was a single-track roadside tramway with numerous halts and stations, the latter (from east to west) being at Tynan (on the River Blackwater), Aughnacloy (where the workshops were), Ballygawley, Augher, Clogher, Fivemiletown (just beyond which the line left Tyrone and entered Fermanagh), Brookeborough and Maguire's Bridge on the Colebrooke River. Although a genuine roadside tramway, it nevertheless exhibited in true Irish fashion a strong railway influence: the first six engines were proper tramway locomotives built by Sharp, Stewart whilst the passenger vehicles were railway-type bogie carriages.

The locomotives were Nos 1 *Caledon*, 2 *Errigal*, 3 *Blackwater*, 4 *Fury*, 5 *Colebrooke* and 6 *Erne* and were joined later by No 7 *Blessingbourne*, a Hudswell, Clarke tank engine with side skirts and cowcatchers bought new in 1910 (but little liked or used), an Atkinson-Walker steam tractor bought new in 1929 (even less popular), and ex-CASTLEDERG & VICTORIA BRIDGE

Postcard of a typical Clogher Valley Tramway train threading its way along Main Street in Fivemiletown in the 1930s. (Author's Collection)

MAIN ST., FIVEMILETOWN.

No 4 swapped by a scrap merchant in 1934 for Nos 1 and 7 (and which retained its old number as *Fury* had been scrapped in the 1920s). Other rolling stock included some 100 goods vehicles of various types, a diesel railcar (No 1) bought new from Walker Bros of Wigan in 1932, and a diesel tractor (No 2) acquired from the same firm the following year.

The railway influence was reflected in the Company's change of name to the Clogher Valley Railway Co. Ltd in 1894 – a move made to allow the line to benefit from being in the Railway Clearing House system to facilitate through bookings and generally, in the modern parlance, 'to raise the profile' of the line.

During the last two decades of the 19th century various schemes were proposed to link the tramway with the BESSBROOK & NEWRY and the ARIGNA tramways (and through the latter the whole of the Cavan & Leitrim Railway) but nothing came of these grandiose ideas which, with the planned extensions, would have provided no less than 234 miles of narrow gauge railway and tramway from the east to the west coast of Ireland. In fact, the CVT went from one financial crisis to another throughout its life and in 1928 the Government appointed a Committee of Management (drawn principally from the County Councils of Tyrone and Fermanagh) to operate the line. This it did until 1941 when it was forced finally to give up the struggle – although the last train did not arrive until the early hours of the next year!

Bibliography: *The Clogher Valley Railway* Edward M. Patterson (David & Charles, 1972) 0 7153 5604 6

CLONTARF & HILL OF HOWTH TRAMROAD

Authority: Clontarf and Hill of Howth Tramroad Act 1898
Gauge: 5ft 3in
Traction: Overhead electric
Opened: 26 July 1900
Taken Over: 1 January 1907
System: Single line
Length: 5.48 miles
Stock: 12 dd
Livery: Terracotta

As suggested by its title, the Clontarf & Hill of Howth Tramroad Co. Ltd (incorporated 2 August 1898) was formed to construct a line from the edge of the DUBLIN UNITED system at Clontarf, out along the Howth peninsula to the northeast and up to the summit of the headland, a popular tourist attraction. It would also serve the needs of Dublin commuters and other residents in the villages of Sutton and Howth en route. The

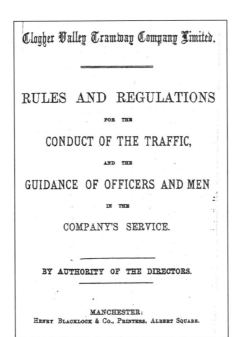

Tramways operators normally issued rule books to their staff, this being the title page of that of the Clogher Valley Tramway.

Company's first proposal in 1890 was for 9 miles of 3ft gauge horse line but, following the DUT's electrification, changed its plans to allow through running. This proposal was not looked upon kindly by the GNR(I) who owned the railway branch from Howth to Dublin and was considering extending it around the headland (and possibly electrifying it). Accordingly, the railway company successfully opposed the tramway company's full plan and the latter had to make do with a line from the DUT depot at Dollymount to Howth Harbour, partly double-track street section and partly single-track private right-of-way (at the Dollymount end).

When the GNR(I) opened its own tramway over the HILL OF HOWTH in 1901, it had of necessity to cross the CHH line at each end in order to reach its railway stations there; the crossing at Sutton was on the level and that at Howth on a viaduct.

For six years the line operated as an independent concern (with a joint through service from Nelson's Pillar on the DUT system) but from 1 January 1907 operation of the line was taken over by the DUT completely and became route 31 with its twelve ERTCW open-top bogie double-deckers absorbed into the larger fleet as Nos 301-312, although the concern remained nominally independent.

CORK TRAMWAYS

Authority: Local authority permission
Gauge: 5ft 3in
Traction: Horse

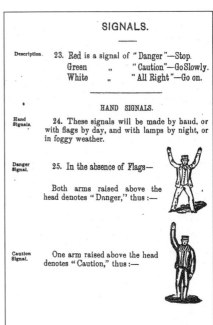

The first page of signalling regulations from the Clogher Valley Tramway rule book.

Opened: 12 September 1872
Closed: October 1875?
System: Split line
Length: c2.45 miles
Stock: 6 dd
Livery: Blue & white
Last Car: ?

Although surveyed originally in 1860 by George Francis Train of Birkenhead and London fame (see Section 1), this short-lived line was not built until 1872, the owner being the Cork Tramways Co. Ltd. Its purpose was to link as many of the city's railway termini as possible (there being six of them at one time) with a line covering the north and south banks of the River Lee and the central island between its two channels. (The Company directors were also on the boards of the Cork railway companies and had hopes of running through freight wagons over the tramway.)

As built, the single-track line began at Victoria Road Depot by the Cork, Blackrock & Passage Railway station on the south bank, and ran westwards along Albert Quay to the Bandon Railway station before turning north over Anglesea Bridge to the central district, then along South Mall, Grand Parade and Patrick Street to St Patrick's Bridge to the north bank. (A second link between the two bridges was provided by a shorter line through Warren Place and along Merchant's Quay.) At St Patrick's Bridge it turned eastwards along King Street to the GSWR station. Services were worked by a small fleet of Starbuck double-deckers. The only extension constructed ran east for ½ mile from Victoria Quay along Navigation Walk as far as the Marina (a popular spot for Sunday outings).

Relations between the (London-based) Company and Cork Corporation were not good however and in addition, after an initial welcome from the people of the city, the tramway soon came to be regarded as more of an inconvenience than a useful mode of transport and within two years it had virtually ceased to operate. In 1875 the Company sold the line for just £510 – it had cost some £10,000 – to a local resident, Stephen O'Hea-Cussen, who formed the Cork Citizens' Tramway Co. Ltd to provide investment backing, but to no avail. On 22 October 1875 the Corporation instructed the City Surveyor to take up the track and early the following year this was done (the cars already having been sold to the DUBLIN UNITED TRAMWAYS).

Bibliography: *Tram Tracks Through Cork*
Walter McGrath (Tower Books of Cork, 1981)

CORK ELECTRIC TRAMWAYS

Authority: Order in Council 1897
Gauge: 2ft 11½in
Traction: Overhead electric
Opened: 22 December 1898
Closed: 30 September 1931
System: Radial network
Length: 9.89 miles
Stock: 35 dd
Livery: Green & cream
Last Car: ?

Nearly a quarter of a century after the Cork horse tramway had ceased to run (see above), a new company began operations with electric cars. This was the Cork Electric Tramways & Lighting Co. Ltd, a BTH subsidiary, which worked a system of six radiating lines from the city centre, three north of the River Lee and three south of it, as a trio of cross-city routes.

The northern lines began at the Father Mathew Statue in Patrick Street and went north to Blackpool and east to Summerfield and Tivoli; all were less than 1½ miles long. A single line south along Grand Parade and South Mall then over the river via Anglesea Bridge led to the three longer southern lines: west to Sunday's Well, south to Douglas and east to Ballintemple (extended April 1901 by two-thirds of a mile to Blackrock). Two short, single-track cut-off links between Patrick Street and South Mall down the narrow Robert Street and Morgan Street, and the parallel Marlboro' Street, were removed by 1901 as too troublesome. The rest of the central portion of the system and the Summerhill branch were double-tracked and the remainder of the system single.

The routes were so arranged that they ran past all the city's railway stations – a fact not unconnected with its unusual gauge. This had been chosen to allow the passage of 3ft gauge railway stock (running on its flanges in the grooved rails) between the Western Road terminus of the Cork & Muskerry Light Railway on the Sunday's Well route, and the Albert Street terminus of the Cork, Blackrock & Passage Railway on the Blackrock route. In the event the plan was never proceeded with but the gauge remained.

The original cars were Brush open-toppers Nos 1-18 shedded in a depot beside the

power station in Albert Street; these were joined in 1900 by Nos 19-28 and in 1901 by Nos 39-35, all of a similar type but with minor design differences. (Many were rebuilt over the years as newer cars were never purchased.)

In 1930 the Company's operations were split when the electricity generation side of the business was taken over by the Irish Electricity Supply Board, leaving just the tramways which, from 1 April 1931, were taken over by their main competition, the Irish Omnibus Co., and closed shortly afterwards. (The abandonment was meant to be immediate but a shortage of buses and public demand resulted in a six-month reprieve.)

Bibliography: as above

CITY OF DERRY TRAMWAYS

Authority: Order in Council 1893
Gauge: 4ft 8½in
Traction: Horse
Opened: 31 March 1897
Closed: January 1919
System: Single line
Length: 1.51 miles
Stock: 9 dd
Livery: Red
Last Car: ?

This short line, built to link the Graving Dock terminus of the narrow gauge Londonderry & Lough Swilly Railway with the Foyle Road terminus of the broad gauge GNR(I), followed closely the west bank of the River Foyle for all its length. (An older, mixed gauge – 3ft and 5ft 3in – quayside tramway even closer to the river and owned by the Londonderry Port & Harbour Commissioners physically linked the two railways for the use of freight and – illegally – passenger trains.)

The tramway was constructed in two stages: from the LLSR station south to Shipquay Place and, opening 3 December 1897, through to the end of Carlisle Bridge via Foyle Street and John Street. Built and operated by Messrs McCrea & McFarland, Irish railway contractors, though owned by the City of Derry Tramways Co. Ltd (incorporated 3 September 1892) the line was laid with flat-bottom rails on concrete and the original car fleet comprised two open-top double-deckers of unknown origin. This number had doubled by 1901 and by the end of 1904 two more had been added. In 1905 three ex-BELFAST double-deckers were purchased to complete the car fleet.

Several proposals to electrify the line came to nothing and by the end of World War I it was losing money rapidly; in addition Derry Corporation wished to see the horse cars replaced by motor or trolleybuses. When a staff strike in mid-January 1919

Postcard of the Grand Parade in Cork with two of that system's double-deckers at work on the very narrow (2ft 11½in) track. (Lens of Sutton)

brought services to a halt, the Corporation moved in to provide a bus replacement. The horses and cars were sold (many of the latter to become platelayers' huts on the LLSR) and in 1925 the Company was formally wound up.

Bibliography: *The Lough Swilly Railway* Edward M. Patterson (David & Charles, 1964)

DUBLIN CENTRAL TRAMWAYS *see* DUBLIN UNITED TRAMWAYS

NORTH DUBLIN STREET TRAMWAYS *see* DUBLIN UNITED TRAMWAYS

DUBLIN TRAMWAYS *see* DUBLIN UNITED TRAMWAYS

DUBLIN UNITED TRAMWAYS
Authority: Dublin Tramways Act 1871
Gauge: 5ft 3in, 5ft 2¼in*
Traction: Horse, overhead electric
Opened: 1 February 1872
Closed: 9 July 1949?
System: Radial network
Length: 61.15 miles
Stock: 300+ sd & dd horse; 3 sd, 667 dd electric
Livery: Ultramarine & white to 1935, then green & cream
Last Car: No 252

By far the largest tramway system in what is now the Republic of Ireland grew out of a consolidation and acquisition process involving a number of different concerns which, as elsewhere in large towns and cities, went through the horse-steam-electric stage of development.

The first company on the scene was the City of Dublin Tramways Co. which, in 1867, obtained the necessary authority to construct a line along the south bank of the River Liffey to connect the termini of the Dublin, Wicklow & Wexford Railway and the GSWR. Although a start was made on track-laying, the project was halted, apparently – shades of early English tramway schemes – because of the rails used.

The first tramway opened, by the Dublin Tramways Co., ran from Nelson's Pillar in the centre of the city just north of the river, southwards down Rathgar Road to Terenure whilst its second route ran from the GSWR's terminus at Kingsbridge on the west side along the South Quay (and across the first route) eastwards to Earlsfort Terrace (opened 3 June 1872). This second route was later extended southeast to Sandymount on 1 October with later routes opened east along the Clontarf Road to Dollymount, southeast to Donnybrook via Morehampton

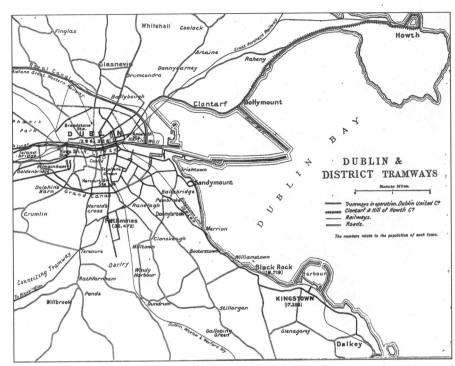

Map of the tramways in the Dublin area (though omitting the Hill of Howth line), from the 1909 Manual of Electrical Undertakings.

Road and from the O'Connell Bridge westwards along the North Quay to Parkgate Street, a total of 17¼ miles of Irish standard gauge lines.

The second tramway company to operate in the city was the North Dublin Street Tramways Co., formed by one of the DT directors to build lines in the area of the city suggested by its title. The constructed routes ran northwest from Nelson's Pillar to Phoenix Park via the North Circular Road with a northern branch up Botanic Road to

Glasnevin, another northwards branch to Drumcondra and a route south of the Liffey westwards along the High Street and James's Street to Inchicore, a total of 7½ miles, also on the 5ft 3in gauge.

On 1 January 1882 the DT Co. and NDST Co. amalgamated to form the Dublin United Tramways Co., the third party to the merger being the Dublin Central Tramways Co. which, from 1878, had operated 6½ miles of horse lines (also on the 5ft 3in gauge) in the south and central areas of the

Postcard of the Bank of Ireland building in Dublin with a Dublin United open-topper and a top-covered car passing. (Lens of Sutton)

Dublin United No 253 of 1928, formerly used on the Lucan line, now at the National Transport Museum, Howth Castle. (Dave Dunne, courtesy J. Kilroy, National Transport Museum)

city with routes radiating from College Green to (from west to east) Terenure and Rathfarnham via Harold Cross Road and Rathfarnham Road, Palmerston Park via Ranelagh and Clonskea via Ranelagh.

In 1896 the Company, reformed as the Dublin United Tramways (1896) Ltd, absorbed the DUBLIN SOUTHERN DISTRICT (see below) which had just converted its line to electric working and from the following year to 1901 treated its own horse lines in similar fashion. The first electric services began on 11 November 1897 along the Clontarf Road from Annersley Bridge to Dollymount, extended back on 20 March 1898 to Nelson's Pillar and out southeast to Haddington Road to meet the former DSD line to Dalkey on 12 July. At the other end of this route a through service was operated over the CLONTARF & HILL OF HOWTH TRAMROAD, which concern was eventually absorbed by the DUT at the beginning of 1907 to become part of the expanding system.

As the old lines were converted, so the horse services were abandoned, the last one to end, on 14 July 1901, being to Sandymount. The resulting electric system was a compact network of lines straddling the Liffey and focussed on Nelson's Pillar, with routes radiating to Kingsbridge, Phoenix Park, Glasnevin, Whitehall, Ballybough and Dollymount (then on to Howth) in the north and (continuing the clockwise listing) to Sandymount, Dalkey, the Showground, Donnybrook, Clonskea,

Palmerston Park, Dartry Road, Terenure and Rathfarnham, Rialto and Inchicore to the south.

The last major addition to the system was on 14 May 1928 when the Company began a service westwards on from Kingsbridge to Lucan to replace the defunct DUBLIN & LUCAN line's trams which had stopped running three years before. The system had now reached its greatest extent and remained so for another four years until 30 July 1932 when the Sandymount route became the first to be closed, its trams replaced by the buses the Company had been operating for the past seven years.

On 31 March 1938 it was announced that all the other routes would be abandoned over the next four years, the programme beginning that April with the Ballybough route and the line along the North Quay to Kingsbridge, the first of a series of closures within the city. Outside the boundaries, the Lucan service was withdrawn on 13 April 1940 and on 29 March 1941 that to Howth. During the World War II years services were affected severely by electricity shortages and many were suspended, some never to be reinstated. No further abandonments took place after 1941 however until 1948, by which time (since 1945) the Company had been taken over by the CIE. The last three routes to go were to Terenure and to Dartry Road on 31 October 1948 and to Dalkey the following July.

Details of the horse fleet are incomplete with over 300 cars being operated by the Company and its predecessors over nearly

30 years (the DUT alone built 181). The electric fleet is better documented though its numbering sequence complicated. The DSD ordered 60 open-top cars from Milnes for its line and these were all taken into service by the DUT. Powered cars 1-20 of 1896 and 56-60 (subcontracted to North Metropolitan of London in 1898) went into the fleet with unchanged numbers whilst trailers 21-55 of 1896-97 were motorized during the next three years and partly renumbered, Nos 41-45 staying unchanged and the others becoming Nos 84, 189, 192, 194-199, 206-208, 210-212, 215, 216, 219, 220, 223-225, 229, 232, 233, and 239-243 in unknown order.

The DUT's own original orders resulted in the delivery of Milnes 21-32 (1897), Nos 121-170 from the American Car Co. of St Louis (1900) and from Brownes of Dublin Nos 61-63 (1898) and 86-90, 92-95, 171-180, 200-205 and 269-274 (1900), all open-top double-deckers. At the same time, from 1897-1902, the Company built similar cars 33-35, 38, 39, 46, 47, 50-52, 99-108, 191, 257-268 and 275-293 plus the following conversions of its former double-deck horse cars: 36, 37, 40, 48, 49, 54, 55, 64-85, 91, 96-98, 109-120, 181-188, 190, 193,209, 213, 214, 217, 218, 221, 222, 226-228, 230, 231, 234-238, 244-251, 255 and 256; Nos 252-254 were horse double-deckers converted to motorized single-deckers, the Company's only original electric vehicles of this type (though some double-deckers were cut down in later years).

During 1906 and 1907 ERTCW bogie open-toppers 294-300, 316 and 317 were

Restoration work proceeding at the National Transport Museum, Howth Castle, on London County Council trailer T24 of 1915 to convert it to Dublin United 224; behind is the 1900 Dublin Directors' saloon. (Dave Dunne, courtesy J. Kilroy, National Transport Museum)

bought and in that latter year similar CHH cars were added to the fleet as Nos 301-312 (again in unknown order). From then on all further cars were built by the Company, these being open-top bogie cars 324 of 1907 and top- covered bogie cars 313-315, 318-323 and 325-330 of 1906-08 to complete the original number series. After that new cars took the numbers of withdrawn vehicles (with several cars being renumbered and/or rebuilt later), these being top-covered bogie cars Nos 3, 64, 70-72, 79, 81-83, 85, 91, 112, 113, 117, 183, 185, 214, 220, 221, 228 and 231 (1910-24) and enclosed bogie cars 224 (1925) and 218 (1926) to complete the passenger fleet.

The Company also built its own Directors' Car (a luxurious open-top double-decker of 1903) and operated a large fleet of works and goods vehicles with its own number series, including fish and ash wagons to serve industrial and Corporation premises on the system. The stock was based on a number of depots (many routes retained terminal depots from the horse days) with the main works being at Inchicore.

The gauge of the Dublin system has previously been given as 5ft 3in, the Irish standard railway gauge, but recent research has questioned this. Newly-discovered evidence points to a slightly narrower gauge of about 5ft 2¼in (in the case of actual track measurement) or ¹⁄₁₆in less than this (in the case of rolling stock drawings) for the electric lines. Such a gauge would explain the planned intention of running railway vehicles over the tramway tracks and which, in the case of the DUBLIN & BLESSINGTON line, is thought to have occasionally happened.

DUBLIN SOUTHERN DISTRICT TRAMWAYS

Authority: Dublin Southern District
  Tramways Act 1878
Gauge: 4ft, 5ft 3in
Traction: Horse, steam/overhead electric
Opened: 17 March 1879
Taken Over: 28 September 1896
System: Single line
Length: 7.98 miles
Stock: 4 locos? 2 sd, 26 dd horse & steam;
  14 dd electric
Livery: Bright green horse; green & yellow
  electric

The Dublin Southern District Tramways Co., formed in 1877 and taken over by Imperial Tramways (see Section 1) a year later, was one of that small group of operators with two physically separated lines; in the case of the DSD these were also of different gauges. Construction began in August 1878 with the northern, longer half of the system (4 miles) laid to a 5ft 3in gauge and opened on 16 June 1879, running southeast

from Haddington Road, where it met the DUBLIN UNITED line (see above), along Merrion Road to Blackrock on the shore of Dublin Bay whilst the second section (2 miles), opened on St Patrick's Day that same year, continued in the same direction to Dalkey but from 2 miles further down the coast at Kingstown (now Dun Laoghaire) and used a gauge of 4ft. The gap between the two sections was later bridged by the BLACKROCK & KINGSTOWN TRAMWAY. Through running powers over DUT metals were obtained in 1883 – but only using DUT horses to pull the DSD's cars.

On 9 August 1881 the BoT licensed the use of two Kitson tram locomotives (Nos 1 and 2) on the northern section to haul the horse cars (open-top double-deckers of unknown origin, all built by 1883) though steam working was short-lived however and appears to have been abandoned by mid-1884, by which time (according to one source) two Wilkinson locos (Nos 3 and 4 of 1883) had been put into service, though possibly only for trials. The two depots were on the Shelbourne Road in Ballsbridge near the Dublin terminus and off Castle Street in Dalkey.

By 1892 two open-sided single-deck cars are thought to have been added to the fleet – possibly ex-North Dublin Street Tramways vehicles (see DUBLIN UNITED) – though by now Imperial had far bigger plans for the lines. The intention was to buy the B&D, convert the southern portion of the DSD to Irish standard gauge and electrify the whole. In 1893 it obtained the necessary Parliamentary authority and the following year built a generating station by Ballsbridge Depot. In March 1895 reconstruction work began on the southern portion and on 30 November that year the first trial run was made over the whole double-track line. Public services commenced on 16 May 1986 using 14 powered cars and trailers, all Milnes open-top vehicles emblazoned, for some reason, 'DUBLIN ELECTRIC TRAMWAYS'.

Relations between the Company and the DUT had never been good but matters were resolved in 1896 when the larger concern bought control of the smaller (which retained a nominal independent existence until 1904) and began to electrify its own system (see above).

DUBLIN & BLESSINGTON STEAM TRAMWAY

Authority: Order in Council 1880
Gauge: 5ft 3in
Traction: Steam, petrol-electric, petrol
Opened: 1 August 1888
Closed: 31 December 1932
System: Single line
Length: 15.91 miles

Stock: 12 locos, 10 dd steam; 2 dd petrol-
  electric; 3 petrol railcars
Livery: Dark green & cream
Last Car: Loco No 9

The aim of the Dublin & Blessington Steam Tramway Co. was to link Dublin with the small town of Blessington some 20 miles to the south in Wicklow. The link was to be a roadside steam tramway which, somewhat unusually for this type of line in Ireland, was to be of Irish standard gauge and not the more common 3ft narrow gauge. The reason for the choice was that the Company wished to connect with the main DUBLIN UNITED system and so provide through running.

Since the area through which it was to run was sparsely populated (Blessington itself had a population of only 350 in 1901), the main traffic was seen to be goods from the local farms plus some stone traffic from a number of quarries along the route. To this end the line's original fleet of rolling stock included six goods wagons, four cattle wagons and two brake vans along with Falcon top-covered bogie passenger cars 1-10 and tramway engines 1-6 of which No 1 was scrapped in 1912, No 2 in 1906, No 3 in 1927, No 5 c1911 and No 4 withdrawn in 1894 to become a stationary engine in the Templeogue Depot near Terenure. (There was also a depot at Blessington.)

In the event the single-track line (laid with flat-bottomed rails) never reached the centre of Dublin but instead made a connection with the DUT horse line 3¼ miles away on the outskirts of the city at Terenure and though the hoped-for through passenger workings never materialized, through goods workings did. A boost to passenger revenues however came in 1895 with the opening of the BLESSINGTON & POULAPHOUCA STEAM TRAMWAY which effectively extended the D&B to the popular excursionists' destination of its title; this line was worked by the D&B from the outset and from 1896 through running from Terenure to the terminus became the norm. Business was obviously good for during the next twenty-odd years both the locomotive and passenger stock increased while the goods stock more than trebled in total. In 1892 loco No 7, a double-cabbed 2-4-2 tank engine, was supplied by Greens, followed by No 8, a smaller 0-4-2 version, four years later. In 1899 No 9, a similar 2-4-2 engine was bought from Brush, followed in 1906 by No 2, a similar one from Greens again (renumbered 10 in 1915).

Normal services were mixed trains of passenger and goods vehicles, often double-headed, though excursion traffic was passenger-only with up to five cars in a train.

In 1915 two petrol-electric open-top double-deck trams (Nos 1 and 2) were built locally to augment the ailing locomotives but were not a success; they were followed in 1916 by an 0-4-0 tank engine from the Dublin & South Eastern Railway (DSER No 70) which was swopped in 1918 for one (*Cambria*) from the GSR. Finally, in 1925 one double-ended Drewry and two single-ended Ford railcars were added to stock (the latter pair thought to have been constructed by the Company using parts of the former petrol-electric cars).

During World War I the Government laid a 1-mile branch for military traffic northwards from the Clodalkin Road passing place (3½ miles from Tenure) to serve a new airport; it is believed to have closed at the end of the War. Taken over in 1927 by a Joint Committee of the Dublin Corporation and the Dublin and Wicklow County Councils, the whole line closed in 1932, killed by financial losses, the 1927 closure of the B&P and the 1929 introduction of serious competition between Dublin and Poulaphouca in the shape of the Paragon Omnibus Co.

Bibliography: *The Dublin & Blessington Steam Tramway* (Locomotion Papers No 20) H. Fayle & A. T. Newham (The Oakwood Press, 1963)

DUBLIN & LUCAN STEAM TRAMWAY

Authority: Order in Council 1880
Gauge: 3ft/3ft 6in
Traction: Steam
Opened: 1 June 1881
Closed: March 1900?
System: Single line
Length: 8.5 miles
Stock: 6 locos, 16 sd
Livery: Dark brown
Last Car: ?

The history of the tramway between Dublin and Lucan, a small town some 7 miles to the west of the capital, is notable for the fact that the line was regauged not once but twice in its lifetime (whilst only changing traction systems once). It began as a typical Irish 3ft gauge single-track roadside steam tramway to meet the transport needs of the area's populace and to serve the growing flour and cloth industries in Lucan.

The Dublin terminus of the tramway was in Conyngham Road where a 12-yard gap separated it from the DUBLIN UNITED line, the latter's gauge of 5ft 3in ruling out a physical connection. The first section from here to Chapelizod (2 miles) opened 1 June 1881 with a single Perret Patent car that the Dublin & Lucan Steam Tramway Co. had borrowed for trials: this was a double-deck vehicle built by Manlove, Alliott, Fryer & Co. of Nottingham with a steam locomotive unit occupying the lower deck 'saloon' and

seats for nearly 50 passengers on top. Services to Palmerstown (3½ miles) commenced November 1881, by which time the line had two Kitson tramway engines (Nos 1 and 2) and four bogie single-deckers (Nos 1-4) plus a growing number of wagons for the important goods traffic.

The final section of the tramway into Lucan (7 miles) opened 20 February 1883 and by 1889 the line was carrying up to 200 tons of goods per week and over 135,000 passengers a year with its six locos (Kitson Nos 3-6 having been added by 1887) and trains of three to five cars. (The passenger car fleet eventually totalled 16.) The following year saw the opening of the LEIXLIP, LUCAN & CELBRIDGE STEAM TRAMWAY to serve the Spa Hotel at Dodsboro' and the village of Leixlip which, although nominally an independent line, was worked from the outset by the D&L (though with some stock of its own).

By the mid-1890s it was clear that the tramway's original grooved rails needed to be changed, whereupon the shareholders decided to convert the line to electric traction. It was decided to do this under the provisions of the Irish Light Railways Act which necessitated a change of name to the DUBLIN & LUCAN ELECTRIC RAILWAY (see below); as well as the new name, a new gauge of 3ft 6in was chosen – besides being a more common electric tramway gauge, it also prevented the DUT from seeking through running powers over the line!

Work on the conversion began in 1897 but – unconventionally – apart from a brief break in November and December of that year for the actual regauging, passenger sevices were maintained using most of the old cars and three of the locos regauged for the purpose. The locos were also employed to work coal trains to the new power station at Fonthill.

Bibliography: *The Dublin & Lucan Tramway* (Locomotion Papers No 29) A. T. Newham (The Oakwood Press, 1965)

DUBLIN & LUCAN ELECTRIC RAILWAY

Authority: Order in Council 1897
Gauge: 3ft 6in
Traction: Overhead electric
Opened: 8 March 1900
Closed: 29 January 1925
System: Single line
Length: 7 miles
Stock: *
Livery: Green & cream
Last Car: ?

The reconstruction of the former D&L

steam line complete (see above), the new tramway opened with five Milnes open-top double-deckers, the first electric double-deckers in Ireland. With the rebuilding, the Spa Hotel at Dodsboro' was left without the tramway access provided by the former LUCAN, LEIXLIP & CELBRIDGE line and although non-stop 'Spa Hotel Express' cars were still run from Dublin, passengers from Lucan to the Hotel were conveyed in free jaunting cars until 1912 when the LUCAN & LEIXLIP ELECTRIC RAILWAY opened.

In 1905 one of the former steam trailers was motorized as a special Royal Mail car (with room for 20 passengers as well) and a year later a new double-decker was bought from MV; in 1911 a motor car and trailer (both open single-deckers) were acquired from the 'All-Red' Railway at the British Empire Exhibition at the Crystal Palace, London.

Official returns for 1923 list eight motor cars, six trailers, one electric loco (for goods traffic), 14 open and five closed wagons and one rail and timber truck. By this time the tramway was facing severe bus competition and the Company tried to interest the DUBLIN UNITED TRAMWAYS in taking over the line but to no avail, the DUT realizing that too much money needed to be spent on it. With no saviour to hand the Company went bankrupt in January 1925, the morning papers of the 29th giving notice of the withdrawal of passenger services that night (though the mail service continued).

For once the buses did not get things all their own way. They were accused – with some justification – of damaging the road surface and were generally regarded as providing a poor service and, after protracted three-way negotiations, the DUT and Dublin Corporation signed an agreement whereby the former would take over the tramway (and the associated (LLER) and relay it to its own 5ft 3in gauge, so making it part of its system. In return, the Corporation would postpone until the end of 1966 its right to take over the DUT. The takeover of the D&L was effected on 7 July 1925, the remaining history of the line becoming part of that of the DUT (which see).

Bibliography: as above

ENNISKERRY *see* BRAY & ENNISKERRY

FINTONA BRANCH

One of the most famous photographic images of Irish tramcars is a picture of one which, curiously, ran not on a tramway but on a railway. The railway was the ¾-mile County Tyrone branch line from Fintona to Fintona Junction on the 5ft 3in gauge Londonderry & Enniskillen Railway – later the Irish North Western Railway, then the GNR(I). The line opened from Omagh to Fintona on 15 June 1853 but the town was bypassed from 16 January of the following year when the track from the junction (an easier route) was extended to Romore Road (and later Enniskillen).

After this part of the railway became a branch line, rather than part of the main line, passengers services being worked by a horse-drawn carriage with seats on the roof (though goods trains were steam-hauled). In 1883 the carriage was replaced by a new, open-top double-deck tramcar which – probably uniquely in the British Isles – boasted 1st, 2nd and 3rd class accommodation in the one vehicle, the latter being on top! (In 1950 2nd class was abolished on the railway.) The car was built especially for the GNR(I) by Midland and took the coaching stock number 74 (later changed to 381), but was always known locally as 'the van' (and is now preserved in the Ulster Folk & Transport Museum).

The passenger service lasted until 30 September 1957 when both branch and main line closed; by then it was believed to be one of the last two public railed horse services left in Europe (the other being at Douglas on the Isle of Man).

Bibliography: *The Fintona Horse Tram* Norman Johnston (West Tyrone Historical Society, 1992) 0 951717 51 0

GALWAY & SALTHILL TRAMWAY

Authority: Galway and Salthill Tramways Act 1877
Gauge: 3ft
Traction: Horse
Opened: 1 October 1879
Closed: May 1918?
System: Single line
Length: 2.13 miles
Stock: 2 sd, 11 dd
Livery: Olive green & white
Last Car: ?

Built to link the city of Galway with the resort of Salthill on the shore of Galway Bay to the southwest, this single-track line was privately promoted with share subscriptions for the Galway & Salthill Tramway Co. not invited until the line had actually opened. It ran from the depot in Forster Street, Galway, in a roughly southwest direction past the MGWR station, round two sides of Eyre Square and along William Street, Shop Street and Bridge Street to the River Corrib which it crossed into Dominick Street (Lower and Upper), thence out along the Salthill Road to a terminus on the seafront there.

Services began with four Starbuck two-horse double-deckers (soon joined by the

other two of the original order of six); in 1880 a new No 5 was bought for reasons unknown – possibly the original No 5 had been involved in an accident. Two single-deckers (possibly numbered 7 and 8) arrived in 1888 – probably from Starbuck again – for winter workings, followed in 1908-11T by five MV double-deckers to replace older double-deckers (and possibly taking their numbers).

The tramway was never a great financial success – its fortunes depended too much on the weather for that – and by 1918 the Company was in a parlous state. On 19 January that year the shareholders voted to wind up the Company and by 12 May the tramway had stopped running.

GIANT'S CAUSEWAY, PORTRUSH & BUSH VALLEY TRAMWAY

Authority: Giant's Causeway, Portrush, and Bush Valley Railway and Tramways Act 1880
Gauge: 3ft
Traction: Steam, third rail electric/steam, overhead electric
Opened: 29 January 1883
Closed: 30 September 1949
System: Single line
Length: 8.75 miles
Stock: 4 locos, 24 sd*
Livery: Red & cream
Last Car: ?

The Giant's Causeway Tramway (as it is generally known) is justly famous in tramway history for the pioneering role it played in proving the viability of electric traction. The idea of the two prime movers of the scheme, the Antrim brothers Anthony and William Traill, who set up the Giant's Causeway, Portrush & Bush Valley

Railway & Tramway Co. on 26 August 1880, was to link the seaside resort of Portrush with Bushmills 6 miles to the east and a little way inland, by way of an electric tramway; from Bushmills a light railway was to link with the famous Giant's Causeway in the north (2 miles) and Dervock and the 3ft gauge Ballycastle Railway then under construction to the south (7 miles). Both tramway and light railway were to be of 3ft gauge. During the passage of the enabling Bill through Parliament though the Bushmills–Giant's Causeway section was dropped in the face of opposition from the local landowner.

Construction began in late 1881 and it was intended that the line should be worked by electricity – a mode of railway traction then still very much in its experimental stage – with a steam-driven dynamo in the depot at Portrush supplying current to the line on the two-rail system. (Iron-tyred wooden wheels on the stock would keep the rails insulated from each other.) In practice, current was found to leak during wet weather so the third-rail system was substituted with a raised conductor rail outside the track. Because of the street sections at either end of the line however it was planned to use steam traction there. Accordingly, when the line opened, services were operated by Wilkinson tram locomotives Nos 1 and 2 (one of which was named *Wartrail*) with two 1st class closed carriages (Nos 1 and 2) and three 3rd class open toastracks (Nos 5-7), all by Midland.

It had still been hoped to work the central roadside portion of the single-tracked line by electricity from the start using a pair of Midland open 1st class power cars (Nos 3 and 4) towing the others but delays in completing the hydro-electric plant at Bushmills, which was to replace the original generator,

Early postcard of Giant's Causeway motor car No 9 with two trailers passing Dunluce Castle. (Author's Collection)

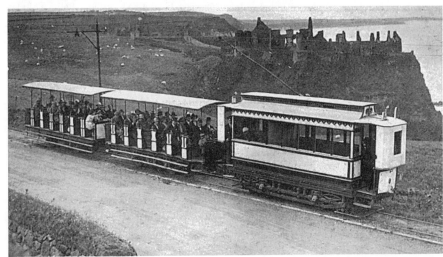

The Giant's Causeway depot at Portrush with Nos 20 and 21 of 1899 (bought to work on on the new overhead system) to the fore. (Lens of Sutton)

meant that no public electric service was run until 16 April 1883 (when one of the steam locos broke down). However, regular services were not instituted until 5 November (after the official opening on 28 September) by which time one of the other cars (believed to have been No 7) had also been fitted with a motor, thus making for an unresolvable dispute as to whether this line or the Volk's Electric Railway in Brighton (opened 4 August 1883) had been the first in the British Isles to use electric traction. A third Wilkinson loco (No 3 *Dunluce Castle*) arrived in 1886 and a fourth, (No 4 *Brian Boroihme*), in 1897.

Although the branch to Dervock was never proceeded with, on 1 July 1887 the extension to the Giant's Causeway was opened but by now the idea of using a live third rail on a public tramway (even though it was mounted on the other side of the track from the roadway) was becoming not only less acceptable but also outmoded by developments elsewhere and the electrocution of a cyclist in 1895 settled the matter. The decision was then taken to switch to overhead current supply and the changeover took place on 26 July 1899 without any interruption to services. Although the steam locos were now theoretically superfluous, Nos 3 and 4 were apparently still used – at least on occasions – until the mid-1920s (and certainly maintained until then), Nos 1 and 2 having been scrapped in 1908 and 1898 respectively.

By the mid-1920s the line was being affected by growing motor bus and coach competition (now running summers only, the tramway was heavily reliant on tourist traffic) and a long, slow decline in its fortunes led to its closure a quarter of a century later. Fortunes can rise as well as fall though and there is a powerful move at the present

time to re-open part of this historic line to enable a new generation of holidaymakers to sample the delights of a cliff-top ride along one of Ireland's most spectacular coasts.

As with many early tramways, details of the stock are not as complete as the historian would like. Locos 3 and 4 appear to have been withdrawn about 1930 whilst the passenger stock grew over the years. During the 1880s the car fleet was increased by the addition of toastracks 8 and 10, saloon car 9 and five open trailers (Nos 11-15) converted from goods wagons. Several of the earlier cars had also been rebuilt and one – No 3 or 4 – had been motorized.

In 1891 two more wagons were converted into open trailers (Nos 16 and 17) and in 1898 two more trailers (Nos 18 and 19) were bought, followed by powered toastracks 20 and 21 in 1899 and 22 three years later; No 23 of 1908 was a similar vehicle and, like the earlier ones, built by the Company. The last car was the second-hand purchase in 1937 of Dunfermline double-decker No 18 which was renumbered 24, regauged from 3ft 6in and cut down to a single deck.

Nos 2 and 5 are now preserved at the Ulster Folk & Transport Museum at Cultra.

Bibliography: *The Giant's Causeway Tramway* J. H. McGuigan (The Oakwood Press, 1983 ed) 0 8536 129 4

GLENANNE & LOUGHGILLY TRAMWAY
Authority: Local authority permission
Gauge: 1ft 10in
Traction: Horse
Opened: 1897
Closed: 1918?
System: Single line
Length: c2.5 miles

Stock: 1 sd
Livery: ?

This line, like its close neighbour the BESS-BROOK & NEWRY TRAMWAY to the south, was built as a consequence of the local linen industry. It linked the GNR(I) station at Loughgilly in County Armagh with the linen mills at Glenanne a short way to the northeast and was owned by the firm of George Gray & Sons Ltd, the mill owners.

Several features made the tramway of especial interest. Its gauge appears to have been unique amongst British tramways (and was possibly influenced by the cable and manually-operated railway network serving the mill complex) and the line was laid with flat-bottom rails bolted to iron sleepers which, on account of their raised centres, necessitated the hauling horse walking in the roadway beside the track.

The tramway's main function was to bring coal and other freight to the mill and take finished linen goods out for transhipment, but it did operate a single passenger car as part of a mixed train. This was a four-wheeled, open-sided vehicle with a knife-board seat running its length with room for seven adults on each side and was named *Carew* after a local family.

The line ran along the west side of the road from Loughgilly station (later renamed Glenanne) on the Armagh–Newry line to the main factory gates at Glenanne (the line beyond being for goods only), with intermediate halts at Barbour's Cross Roads and Tullyallen Cross Roads. At the end of World War I the Company bought a lorry to handle the goods traffic, the line was abandoned and, in 1919, the rails were lifted.

Bibliography: *Railways around County Armagh* Eddie McKee (Author, Bessbrook, 1990)

HILL OF HOWTH TRAMWAY
Authority: Great Northern Railway (Ireland) Act 1897
Gauge: 5ft 3in
Traction: Overhead electric
Opened: 17 June 1901
Closed: 31 May 1959
System: Single line
Length: 5.19 miles
Stock: 10 dd
Livery: GNR(I) teak to 1929, then GNR(I) dark blue & ivory*
Last Car: No 9

The Hill of Howth line was the closest thing Ireland ever had to a mountain railway or tramway and was somewhat comparable in function to the Great Orme Tramway in Wales. The Howth peninsula, 8 miles to the east of Dublin – and particularly the harbour at Howth on its northern shore – had been served by a branch of the Dublin & Drogheda Railway since 1847 and the summit by a horse bus service from 1867 though it was nearly 30 years before serious plans were made for a tramway up the hill.

The first proposal for such a line was made by the CLONTARF & HILL OF HOWTH TRAMROAD Co. in 1890 but in the end it was beaten to the top by the GNR(I) who secured permission for a long, U-shaped loop of a line from Howth station, up and over the 560ft summit of Slievemartin, then back down to rejoin the former DDR branch (part of the GNR(I)) since 1876) at Sutton station.

The Sutton–Summit section was the first to be opened in 1901, followed by the Summit–Howth descent on 1 August that year. The line was double-tracked throughout with mainly bullhead rails chaired to sleepers on a private right-of-way, connected to the railway branches at both ends and worked from the outset by eight Brush open-top double-deckers (Nos 1-8) which were joined in 1902 by Nos 9 and 10 of a similar design from Milnes.

The highest point of the line was 407ft above sea level and the ruling gradient 1 in 20 (including 1 in 16½ for ½ mile).

Although the tramway made an operating profit for much of its life it never repaid its capital costs and relied heavily on the seasonal tourist trade for its passengers (though a few Dublin commuters did use the line). After World War II it seemed only a matter of time before the trams would be replaced by buses (a bus with special wheels was actually experimented with on the line in the 1930s) and, following the 1953 nationalization of the railway system, it was announced in 1954 that the line was to close – though it somehow managed to hang on for another five years, by which time it was

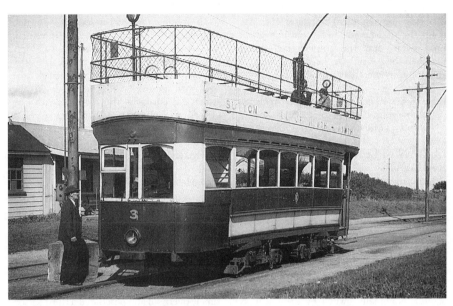

Hill of Howth No 3 of 1901 in post-1929 blue and ivory livery. (Lens of Sutton)

Ireland's last working tramway. One wonders how few years it would have needed to have survived before it became a valuable tourist attraction in its own right, especially if modernized with ex-DUBLIN UNITED equipment? As it was, out of a fleet of ten passenger cars, no less than six were set aside for preservation (though two of these were subsequently scrapped). No 2 is in a Californian museum, No 4 is currently in store at the Ulster Folk & Transport Museum at Cultra, No 9 is in the Transport Museum at Castleruddery, County Wicklow and No 10 (regauged to 4ft 8½in) is at the National Tramway Museum in Crich, England. (These last two cars were found not to be good runners on the line and were rarely used and never repainted in the post-1929 livery.)

Bibliography: *The Hill of Howth Tramway* R. C. Flewitt (Transport Research Associates, Dublin, 1968)

KINGSTOWN *see* BLACKROCK & KINGSTOWN

LEIXLIP *see* LUCAN, LEIXLIP & CELBRIDGE; LUCAN & LEIXLIP

LIGONIEL *see* BELFAST & LIGONIEL

LONDONDERRY *see* DERRY

LOUGHGILLY *see* GLENANNE & LOUGHGILLY

LUCAN, LEIXLIP & CELBRIDGE STEAM TRAMWAY

In the mid-1880s plans were put forward by an independent concern to construct single-track extensions from the DUBLIN & LUCAN STEAM TRAMWAY to the villages of Leixlip and Celbridge, these to be roadside branches from Lucan of 1½ and 3½ miles respectively. The second was never built – despite the title of the owning Lucan, Leixlip & Celbridge Steam Tramway Co. – but the first, under an 1889 Order in Council, was open by June 1890 (exact date unknown). It was worked from the outset by the D&L (some reports say it had its own stock lettered LL&C though this was never mentioned in its official returns) with the D&L operating a shuttle service between Leixlip and Lucan until August 1890 when a new agreement (a 50-50 split of the receipts) led to through workings, making the whole line in effect one tramway.

When the D&L decided to electrify its line, so did the Company (and revive the

Hill of Howth No 9 in the teak livery it retained until the very end as the Last Car on Ireland's last passenger tramway. (Lens of Sutton)

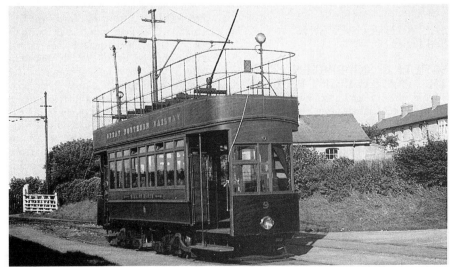

Celbridge branch idea) but after consideration the scheme was not thought a viable proposition and the tramway closed in October 1897 – only to be rebuilt some 15 years later in exactly that guise! (See below.)

Bibliography: *The Dublin & Lucan Tramway* (Locomotion Papers No 29) A. T. Newham (The Oakwood Press, 1965)

LUCAN & LEIXLIP ELECTRIC RAILWAY

Another twist was added to the DUBLIN & LUCAN saga when what was in effect a ½-mile extension to that line (by then converted from steam to electric working) was added at the Lucan end in 1912 to serve the Spa Hotel at Dodsboro' at the junction of the Leixlip and Celbridge roads, the roadside route using the same formation as the former LUCAN, LEIXLIP & CELBRIDGE line (see above). Nominally owned by the Lucan & Leixlip Electric Railway Co. – a concern financed by John Scallan, a Dublin solicitor and debenture holder in the Spa Hotel – the line was worked by the DLET under lease. (Authority for its construction was an Order in Council of 1908 while another of 1910 gave the DLET the necessary operating powers.)

From 1912 to 1925 the fortunes of the line were those of the DLET and it was closed along with its parent in that year; unlike its parent, it was not rebuilt by DUBLIN UNITED TRAMWAYS two years later but abandoned.

Bibliography: as above

NEWRY *see* BESSBROOK & NEWRY

PORTRUSH *see* GIANT'S CAUSEWAY, PORTRUSH & BUSH VALLEY

PORTSTEWART TRAMWAY
Authority: Order in Council 1880
Gauge: 3ft
Traction: Steam
Opened: 2 June 1882
Closed: 30 January 1926
System: Single line
Length: 1.85 miles
Stock: 3 locos, 4 sd, 2 dd
Livery: Connaught green
Last Cars: All stock

During the latter part of the 19th century the development of the small County Londonderry town of Portstewart as a seaside resort was hindered by the fact that the BNCR's station, named after it on its Coleraine–Portrush branch (opened 1855), had been sited nearly 2 miles outside the town in deference to a local landowner. Consequently a group of local businessmen, as the Portstewart Tramway Co., built a short steam tramway to bridge the gap. As constructed, it was a single-track line laid with grooved rails partly down the street and partly by the roadside with one central passing loop at Victoria Terrace, worked by two Kitson tramway locomotives (Nos 1 of 1882 and 2 of 1883). Original passenger cars were three Metropolitan single-deckers (Nos 1-3) and a toastrack (No 4). Together with a small luggage van various combinations of vehicles were worked as a train.

The tramway was not a financial success (out of season traffic, by virtue of the shortness of the line, was very small) and in 1897 the Company went into liquidation. On 1 June that year the line was purchased for £2,100 by the BNCR who gave it a timely overhaul and purchased a third Kitson engine (No 3 of 1901, believed to have been the last tramway engine constructed by that firm) and two Milnes bogie open-toppers (Nos 1 and 4 of 1899). Somehow the line managed to survive for nearly three more decades (passing in turn on 1 July 1903 to the MR (NCC) and on 1 January 1923 to the LMS (NCC) before its age and increasing road traffic brought about its demise and replacement by a bus service. Loco No 1 is currently preserved in the Hull Transport Museum in England whilst No 2 is on show at the Ulster Folk & Transport Museum at Cultra.

Bibliography: *The Portstewart Tramway* (Locomotion Papers No 41) J. R. L. Currie (The Oakwood Press, 1968)

POULAPHOUCA *see* BLESSINGTON & POULAPHOUCA

ROSTREVOR *see* WARRENPOINT & ROSTREVOR

SALTHILL *see* GALWAY & SALTHILL

SCHULL & SKIBBEREEN TRAMWAYS & LIGHT RAILWAY
The S&S was a 3ft gauge steam railway incorporating long roadside stretches constructed under the 1883 Tramways & Public Companies Act and was intended to open up a remote corner of southwest Ireland. Opened in 1886, it ran for 15½ miles between the two Cork towns of its title in the districts of West and East Carbery – a name reflected in the operator's original title of the West Carbery Tramways & Light Railway Company (Schull & Skibbereen Branch); no other lines were in fact ever built.

The line's first three Dick, Kerr tank engines were equipped for tramway working but were soon rebuilt, though all the line's locos sported cowcatchers. Services were suspended in 1944, victims of the wartime fuel shortage (by which date the railway was part of the GSR), and after their resumption in 1945 they ceased for good in January 1947, replaced by buses.

Bibliography: *The Schull and Skibbereen Tramway and Light Railway* (Locomotion Papers No 24) A. T. Newham (The Oakwood Press, 1964)

SYDENHAM *see* BELFAST: SYDENHAM

VICTORIA BRIDGE *see* CASTLEDERG & VICTORIA BRIDGE

WARRENPOINT & ROSTREVOR TRAMWAYS
Authority: ?
Gauge: 3ft
Traction: Horse
Opened: July 1877
Closed: February 1915
System: Single line
Length: 3.3 miles
Stock: 13 sd
Livery: Various
Last Car: ?

This seaside tramway ran along the road from its own canopied platform at the GNR(I) station at Warrenpoint (opened in 1849 by the Newry, Warrenpoint & Rostrevor Railway) along the seafront of this small County Down resort to the quayside at Rostrevor, an even smaller resort some 3 miles further along the north shore of Carlingford Lough, where it terminated outside the Great Northern Hotel.

The single-track line was operated by the Warrenpoint & Rostrevor Tramways Co. (incorporated 6 September 1875) with a stock of thirteen passenger cars added gradually through its life (which was comparatively long for a horse tramway). The cars were a mixture of closed single-deck saloons (Nos 2, 6 and 7) and open toastracks, painted in a wide range of colours.

An 1894 proposal to extend the line another 5 miles down the coast to Greencastle came to nothing and no alterations were made to the system until it closed early in 1915 after a gale washed away part of the track, the cars being auctioned that June.

WHITEWELL *see* CAVEHILL & WHITEWELL

Section 5

Tramways of the
Isle of Man

The Isle of Man has long been a railway and tramway enthusiasts' paradise. In just 221 square miles it has managed to accommodate – at more or less the same time – a narrow gauge steam railway system (part of which still operates), a narrow gauge steam pleasure railway (recently rebuilt and re-opened), a narrow gauge horse tramway (still working), a narrow gauge cable tramway, a narrow gauge electric tramway (still working), a narrow gauge electric mountain railway (still working), a standard gauge electric tramway, four funicular railways and a pier tramway – not to mention sundry contractors', mine and other industrial lines!

Whilst the gauge of the above lines ranged from 1ft 7in (Laxey mine) to 7ft 0¼in (Port Erin harbour), thus adding further to their astonishing variety, the 'standard' gauge for the island was 3ft, a figure arrived at by a combination of chance, traffic and other financial considerations, Irish narrow gauge influence and the relatively short distances involved. Man being a self-governing Crown dependency, authority for the construction of tramways had normally to be obtained from the island's ancient legislature, the Tynwald.

Although many of the island's lines have closed, victims of much the same pressures felt on the mainland, the tramways have in terms of mileage fared far better than their railway counterparts. Of an original five tramways, two have survived – and these two are probably the most important ones.

Given its position as the island's modern capital, largest town and principal port and resort, it is not surprising that the Isle of Man's tramways were centred on Douglas. Two of the five served Douglas only: the cable tramway the town and the horse line the long promenade. Another two were scenic lines running south (the DOUGLAS SOUTHERN) and north (the MANX ELECTRIC RAILWAY) from the capital whilst the fifth, the RAMSEY PIER TRAMWAY, was sited at the other end of the MER.

This concentration on the island's east coast was the result of the occupation by the narrow gauge railway system (also naturally centred on Douglas) of the southern region beyond Port Soderick to Castletown and Port Erin, the central region across through St Johns to Peel, and the west coast northwards from there to Ramsey. Thus, by the time the electric tramways arrived all but one of the major settlements outside Douglas were already served by rail. The one exception was Laxey – and so to Laxey the tramway went, and from there visitors could travel by mountain railway to the top of Snaefell, the island's highest point. Much to the delight of countless thousands of visitors each year, they still can.

DOUGLAS BAY TRAMWAY
Authority: Douglas Bay Tramway Act 1876
Gauge: 3ft
Traction: Horse
Opened: 7 August 1876
System: Single line
Length: 1.76 miles
Stock: 38 sd, 13 dd
Livery: Nos 1-8 dark blue & cream, others brown & red pre-1894, then red or teak & ivory or white, saloons cream for awhile

The driving force behind the Douglas Bay Tramway was Thomas Lightfoot, a retired civil engineering contractor, who promoted the idea of a horse tramway along the grand sweep of the bay with its fast-growing villa and hotel development and associated promenade construction. As opened in 1876, the single-track line ran from Burnt Mill Hill in the north to the Iron Pier (demolished 1894) in the south where the Promenade proper began; the stretch from here to the Victoria Pier – where the steamers arrived – opened on 31 January of the following year.

In January 1882 Lightfoot sold the tramway to the Isle of Man Tramway Ltd who added further stock; four years later a new northern terminus and depot was opened at Derby Castle at the end of the bay just on from Burnt Mill Hill and a track-doubling programme (completed in 1897) put in hand.

In 1894 the line was sold to the Douglas & Laxey Coast Electric Tramway Co. (see MANX ELECTRIC RAILWAY) who took over on 1 May but requests by that Company to electrify the line were turned down by Douglas Corporation, who in turn took control of the line in 1901 after the Isle of Man Tramways & Electric Power Co. Ltd (the renamed DLCET Co.) had gone into liquidation, its offer of £50,00 being accepted on 25 September for the horse tramway and the UPPER DOUGLAS TRAMWAY (see below). Since then the line has managed to survive – but sometimes only just. Fluctuations in the numbers of day-trippers and holiday visitors to the island, and the two World Wars, all had their effect on the tramway. In 1927 it closed for the winter, re-opening the next year as a summer-only service, as it remains today. Its survival as the only horse tramway in the British Isles is perhaps best explained by recognizing that it is very much a pleasure line now, rather than a public transport system, and as such ideally situated. But often, especially in the 1950s and 1960s, it has been a very close-run thing.

Services began with three Starbuck cars: single-decker No 1 and double-deckers Nos 2 and 3; No 1 was converted to a double-decker in 1885 and disappeared at the end of the 1890s whilst the other two lasted until the winter of 1948/9 when they were scrapped. These were joined in 1882 by No 4, in 1883 by Nos 5 and 6 and in 1884 by Nos 7 and 8, all Starbuck double-deck cars. No 7 was scrapped in 1924 and the others in 1948/9 again. All later orders for new cars

The stables at Douglas near the Derby Castle terminus in 1993, complete with horsebox. (Author)

were for single-deckers, these being Starbuck open toastracks 9 (scrapped 1952) and 10 of 1884, Starbuck/Milnes open toastrack 11 of 1886, Milnes open toastrack 12 of 1888, ditto 19 and 20 of 1889 (both withdrawn 1949 and scrapped 1952), ditto 21 and 22 of 1890 and 23-26 of 1891 (of which Nos 23-25 were scrapped in 1952 as well). Milnes supplied three closed saloons (Nos 27-29) in 1892, open toastracks 30 (scrapped 1952) and 31 in 1894, six roofed toastracks (32-37) in 1896 and three open toastracks (38-40) in 1902, these being followed in 1905 by Nos

41-42, a pair of MV open toastracks. Nos 43 and 44 were 1907 UEC roofed toastracks, Nos 45 and 46 MV roofed toastracks of 1908 and 1909, No 47 a similar vehicle of 1911; in 1913 the latter firm supplied a new No 1, a closed winter saloon. The last new cars were purchased in 1935 from the Vulcan Motor & Engineering Co. Ltd: numbered 48-50, these were roofed toastracks with folding wooden sidescreens for protection against the weather.

Nos 13-18 were six second-hand double-deckers from South Shields which were

purchased in 1887; in 1903 Nos 17 and 18 were converted into single-deckers though No 17 was withdrawn soon after. No 14 was scrapped in 1908, whereupon No 13 took its number (for superstitious reasons?) and survives to this day, being preserved in the Manx Museum at Douglas. No 16 was scrapped in 1915 and in 1949 No 15 likewise.

Bibliography: *Isle of Man Tramways* F. K. Pearson (David & Charles, 1970) 7 15347 40 3

UPPER DOUGLAS TRAMWAY

Authority: Upper Douglas Tramway Act 1895
Gauge: 3ft
Traction: Cable
Opened: 15 August 1896
Closed: 19 August 1929
System: Single line
Length: 1.57 miles
Stock: 15 sd
Livery; Red or teak & ivory or white

Following the success of the horse tramway (see above) the idea naturally arose for a line to serve at least some of the hotels and shops of the town behind the seafront. Because of the steepness of some of the streets involved it became clear that a mechanically-assisted form of traction would be called for and accordingly the promoters – the Isle of Man Tramways & Electric Power Co. – decided upon cable haulage. The route authorized by its enabling Act was from a terminus at the bottom of Victoria Street close to the end of the horse tramway (with a link between the two), up Victoria Street and Prospect Hill, along Buck's Road and Woodbourne Road, down into Ballaquayle Road (where the depot and winding house were built) and Broadway to meet the horse tramway again. (The authorized link at this end of the line was never laid.)

The mainly double-track line had a steepest gradient of 1 in 10.6 and was worked in true cable fashion, ie the cable was wound continuously in a central conduit between the rails and the cars attached or detached by means of the driver-controlled grippers. The original car fleet was made up of eight cross-bench cars (Nos 71-78) and three saloons (Nos 79-81), all bogie single-deckers from Milnes.

In 1900 the IOMTEP Co. collapsed and the line, together with the horse tramway, was purchased the following year by Douglas Corporation (see above). Although the steep and narrow depot-Broadway section was abandoned at the start of 1901 and the track lifted, plans were made to electrify the remainder of the line but these came to nothing and in 1907 a pair of cross-bench

Postcard of the Upper Douglas/Douglas Bay junction at the turn of the century with cable car 81 left and horse car 35 centre. (Author's Collection)

cars (Nos 69 and 70) were bought from UEC, followed by a similar Milnes car (No 68) in 1909 and another (No 67) two years later, again all bogie vehicles.

By the 1920s the accumulated effects of wear and tear to virtually every part of the tramway meant the Corporation faced a choice between heavy expenditure on the line or abandoning it in favour of its own growing fleet of buses. For a while (from 1921 onwards) a compromise was effected by which the buses replaced the trams in the winter months but by the end of the decade even this solution no longer made financial sense. After the last, four-week season of the 1920s, the line closed for the last time. The cars were sold to become holiday bungalows, Nos 72 and 73 surviving in this form until 1968 when they were rescued and slowly restored as a single car which can be seen in the Derby Castle Museum.

Bibliography: as above

DOUGLAS SOUTHERN ELECTRIC TRAMWAYS

Authority: –
Gauge: 4ft 8½in
Traction: Overhead electric
Opened: 7 August 1896
Closed: 15 September 1939
System: Single line
Length: 3.25 miles
Stock: 16 dd
Livery: Crimson & white
Last Car: No 7?

The stretch of coast immediately south from Douglas is one of the most dramatic on the whole island and it is not surprising that, during the late 19th century, many schemes were suggested or promoted to improve tourists' access to view its rugged grandeur. In 1890 work began on the construction of a coastal toll road southwards from Douglas Head at the southern limit of Douglas Bay; by November 1893 the builders – the Douglas Head Marine Drive Co. Ltd – had reached Keristal, nearly 3 miles away.

It had already been agreed that an electric tramway should be built along the Drive and in November 1894 two of the DHMD Co.'s major shareholders secured the concession for the line. This passed quickly through a number of hands until February 1896 when it ended up with the Douglas Southern Electric Tramways Ltd (incorporated 21 October 1895).

The first 2 miles of line to Whing were opened on 7 August 1896, the next ¾ mile to Keristal not having been passed by the BoT. During the next winter (the line had closed on 26 September at the end of the summer season) the final ¾ mile to the southern terminus at Port Soderick was completed,

Postcard view looking up Victoria Street, Douglas, with an Upper Douglas cable car being boarded centre and open and closed Douglas Bay horse cars right. (Author's Collection)

the whole line opening on 1 April 1897 in its final form.

As built, the single-track tramway was an undulating, winding affair with gradients steeper than 1 in 11 and curves as tight as 45ft radius and laid for the most part on the landward side of the Drive. The choice of standard gauge was somewhat surprising though it was probably chosen for increased stability in view of the line's exposed position. It commenced on Douglas Head itself, more than 180ft above sea level, and followed the Drive all the way to Port Soderick (the terminus above the beach here being at a similar altitude with a cliff railway connection between the two); a notable feature which added greatly to the thrill of the ride was the use of several girder bridges thrown across deep gullies and clefts in the cliffs. Current was supplied from the tramway's own power station at Pigeon Stream, ½ mile from the Head.

Original stock comprised six motor cars (Nos 1-6) and six trailers (Nos 7-12), all open-top, open-sided Brush vehicles; these were followed in 1897 by four similar but lighter trailers (Nos 13-16) whereupon Nos 7 and 8 were converted to motor cars. The depot was at Little Ness, midway along the line, where there was a suitable patch of flat land perched on the cliff edge.

In 1926, at the end of the tramway's oper-

Douglas Southern advertisement from a 1908 Isle of Man guide.

Postcard of Derby Castle in the 1920s showing the Manx Electric Railway climbing Onchan Head in the distance and the Douglas Bay Tramway in the foreground. The canopy over the tracks was demolished in 1980. (Author's Collection)

ating concession, it merged with the DHMD Co., the cars being relettered accordingly. Thirteen years later it closed for the duration of World War II (as it had for World War I) but this time it was never to re-open. Lifting took place in 1946-47 with all cars (with the exception of No 1, now preserved at the National Tramway Museum, Crich), being broken up five years later. A particularly severe rockfall closed the Drive to vehicular traffic in 1976 though it remains open for pedestrians to savour the atmosphere of this unique tramway route.

Bibliography: *Douglas Head Marine Drive & Electric Tramway* A. M. Goodwyn (Manx Electric Railway Society, Douglas, rev ed 1993)

MANX ELECTRIC RAILWAY
Authority: Howstrake Estate Act 1892
Gauge: 3ft
Traction: Overhead electric
Opened: 7 September 1893
System: Single line
Length: 17.75 miles
Stock: 64 sd
Livery: Red, cream & teak

Linking Douglas and the northern town of Ramsey with a double-track roadside line along the more sheltered eastern side of the island, the MER began as part of an 1880s development scheme centred on the Howstrake Estate just north of Douglas. This first section was promoted by the Douglas Bay Estate Ltd as a single-track electric line from Derby Castle in Douglas (the northern terminus of the DOUGLAS BAY TRAMWAY) to Groudle Glen, a noted beauty spot just 2 miles away. Before it could open though a new concern appeared on the scene with greater plans (as evinced by its title): the Douglas & Laxey Coast Electric Tramway Co., registered on 7 March 1893 and empowered by the Douglas & Laxey Electric Tramway Act of that year to take over the Howstrake tramway when completed and extend it to Laxey, 7 miles from Douglas. The extended line opened to the public on 28 July 1894, by which time the Company had purchased the Douglas Bay tramway and changed its name to the Isle of Man Tramways & Electric Power Co. Ltd. (In 1896 it purchased the SNAEFELL MOUNTAIN RAILWAY as well.)

Authority to extend the line further up the coast to Ramsey was obtained in 1897 and this northern section opened on 24 July 1899; hard on the heels of the tramway's completion though came a succession of financial scandals – and trials – in which the Company was involved, the upshot being that it went into liquidation and was purchased in 1902 by a new consortium, the Manx Electric Railway Co. A more prosperous existence lasted until after World War II when, in the 1950s, the holiday trade upon which the now double-tracked line was heavily reliant began to decline, and in 1956 the concern was nationalized by the Manx Government in whose ownership it has remained – occasional abandonment scares aside – safely ever since. Today, as a much-publicized (and much-loved) tourist attraction its closure would be unthinkable, especially after the immense success of its 1993 'Year of Railways' centenary celebrations in bringing visitors to this delightful island.

All the MER's passenger cars (with one exception) have been single-deck bogie vehicles, beginning with Milnes saloons 1-3 and open toastrack trailers 49-54 (later roofed), followed in 1894 by similar powered cars 4-9 and roofed trailers 34-39 and in 1895 by powered cars 10-13 of a slightly different design, again all from Milnes. Car 60 of 1896 was another roofed trailer. In 1898 Milnes supplied open-sided cross-bench cars 14-18 and in 1899 saloon cars 19-22 and open-sided trailers 44-48, all for use on the Ramsey extension.

In 1899 Milnes supplied four sister cars to Nos 14-18 which ran without motors as Nos 40-43 until 1903 when they were motorized as Nos 24-27 upon the arrival of trailers Nos 40-43; a year later the Company bought

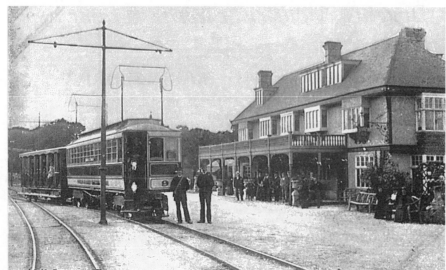

Postcard of the Groudle Glen Hotel (opened 1893), the Manx Electric Railway's first terminus. Winter saloon 9 of 1899 (with trailer) sports the troublesome Hopkinson bow collectors replaced in 1898. (Author's Collection)

ERTCW open-sided powered cars 28-31 and trailers 55-58 (the last two vehicles being saloons). The final powered cars bought were UEC 32 and 33 in 1906 (similar to Nos 28-31) together with open-sided trailers 61 and 62; no further cars were purchased until 1930 when EE supplied open-sided trailers 40, 41 and 44 to partly replace eleven cars destroyed in a fire at Laxey on 5 April that year.

The line's only four-wheeled passenger car (though fitted with bogies five years later) was directors' saloon 59 built in 1895 by Milnes and which still sees occasional service, especially for private parties. Indeed, at the time of writing no less than 24 powered cars (including Nos 1 and 2, thought to be the world's oldest working electric cars) and the same number of trailers are still in passenger service, living proof of the standard of care and attention they regularly receive.

Bibliography: *Manx Electric* Mike Goodwyn (Platform 5 Publishing, 1993)
1 872524 52 4

RAMSEY HARBOUR TRAMWAY

Not a passenger tramway but a goods-only

A number of British tramways conveyed freight on a regular basis. This is the Manx Electric Railway's mail van 16 of 1908 after losing its end platforms but before its 1977 conversion to a works vehicle. (Author)

Many tramways operated unique vehicles: this is the Manx Electric Railway's only locomotive, No 23 of 1900, seen here at Laxey in rebuilt form after restoration, and named for the line's centenary celebrations. (M. Donnison)

branch of the Manx Northern Railway which ran from the MNR's station (opened 1879) along the quayside, a distance of some 1,000yd. It was in use from early 1883 with latterly declining traffic until c1951 and was lifted shortly thereafter; the rest of the MNR closed in 1968 (by which date it was part of the Isle of Man Railway).

Bibliography: *The Manx Northern Railway* Dr R. Preston Hendry & R. Powell Hendry (Hillside Publishing Co, Rugby, 1980) 0 950593 32 X

RAMSEY PIER TRAMWAY

Authority: –
Gauge: 3ft
Traction: Manual/ic
Opened: August 1899
Closed: 9 September 1981
System: Single line
Length: 0.39 miles
Stock: 1 sd manual; 1 loco, 1 railcar, 1 sd ic
Livery: Various
Last car: ?

Like many such tramways, the line at Ramsey was built originally for the contractor's use during construction of the Queen's Pier (formally opened on 22 July 1886). For the next three decades the line, running for 693yd down the centre of the decking, was used to convey passengers' luggage on small, hand-propelled trollies from the various pleasure steamers which called there.

In 1899, at the same time as a new landing stage was opened at the pier head, an enclosed passenger van was added to the tramway's stock; this remained in service until 1937 when the owners of the pier and tramway, the Isle of Man Harbour Board, purchased a small Hibberd petrol locomotive and roofed bogie toastrack trailer from Park Royal, adding a tiny

Wickham petrol railcar thirteen years later.

The line failed to re-open after the 1981 season when it was discovered that extensive (and expensive) replacement of the wooden track beams would be needed. The loco and trailer however are preserved at Ramsey with the Hibberd loco being operated on special occasions.

Bibliography: *Pier Railways* (Locomotion Papers No 60) K. Turner (The Oakwood Press, 1972)

SNAEFELL MOUNTAIN RAILWAY

Although often described as a tramway, this is actually an electric mountain railway of a type unique in the British Isles. Hard on the heels of the initial success of the MANX ELECTRIC RAILWAY came the proposal by the Isle of Man Tramways & Electric Power Co. to construct a similar line from Laxey to the summit of Snaefell, at 2,034ft above sea level the island's highest point. It was built on land acquired without the need for compulsory purchase, so avoiding delays occasioned by seeking the necessary authority from the Tynwald, and was finished in just seven months. (It was built by the Snaefell Mountain Railway Association with the intention of selling it to the IOMTEP Co., which it did in 1896.)

The railway opened on 21 August 1895 with six Milnes single-deck saloon cars similar to those on the MER and operates summers only. Because of the more or less constant gradient of 1 in 12 on its 4½-mile spiral round the mountain, it was designed on the Fell system which utilizes a raised centre rail which can be engaged by grippers on the cars for braking purposes on the descent, the ascent being effected by adhesion only. The wider car bogies needed to accommodate the grippers meant a wider gauge (3ft 6in) than the MER, so ruling out

THE MANX
ELECTRIC RAILWAY
COMPANY, LTD.

GLORIOUS WEATHER
FOR
SNAEFELL SUMMIT !

— TAKE THE —
Electric Cars
FROM
DERBY CASTLE.

A Delightful and Exhilirating Run.
HAROLD BROWN,
PRINTED AT "HERALD" OFFICE, DOUGLAS.   **General Manager.**

Early advertisement for the Manx Electric Railway and Snaefell Mountain Railway.

through running. The Fell rail is not installed on the level ground at Laxey where the tracks parallel those of the MER, giving the line the appearance of a tramway, but once the long climb begins on its own reserved sleeper track the resemblance quickly vanishes.

Bibliography: *Manx Electric* Mike Goodwyn (Platform 5 Publishing, 1993) 1 872524 52 4

Tramways of the Channel Islands

Despite their comparatively small size the Channel Islands have been, over the years, rich in rail transport systems. At one time or another the four largest islands of Jersey, Guernsey, Alderney and Herm could boast narrow and standard gauge public railways, narrow and standard gauge freight-only lines, a network of military railways laid during the German occupation of the islands in World War II – but only one tramway.

Elsewhere in the British Isles, proposals for tramways far outnumbered those actually constructed and in this respect the Channel Islands were no different. The main focus for these schemes was Jersey, a fact reflected in the title of the Jersey Railways & Tramways Co. Ltd which, despite its name, never succeeded in bringing tramways to that island.

Whether railway or tramway, public rail transport did not survive on the islands beyond the 1930s. The reasons for this demise are not hard to find: the short length of the lines, no centres of population large enough to support an urban system, the increase in car ownership and, above all, the development after World War I of competing bus services. In this last respect too the Channel Islands were no different from any other of the British Isles and, for their solitary tramway, the outcome was sadly much the same.

GUERNSEY RAILWAY
Authority: Order in Council 1877
Gauge: 4ft 8½in
Traction: Steam, overhead electric
Opened: 6 June 1879
Closed: 9 June 1934
System: Single line
Length: 2.81 miles
Stock: 8 locos, 7 sd, 2 dd steam; 6 sd, 14 dd electric
Livery: Chocolate & stone
Last Car: No 6

Running from the harbour in the capital

St Peter Port, to the harbour at St Sampson's, this short line was operated originally by the Guernsey Steam Tramway Co. Ltd (registered in London on 29 May 1878) to replace the existing horse bus service between these two major centres of population on the island's east coast. The scheme, the concession for which was granted by the States of Guernsey on 2 May 1877 and confirmed by an Order in Council later that year, was fine on paper – and initially successful – but the locomotives proved prone to breakdowns and the bus competition refused to accept defeat; in 1888 the Company went into liquidation and on 5 January of the following year services were suspended, not to be resumed until 2 December, this time operated by the re-formed and renamed Guernsey Railway Co. Ltd.

The single-track tramway hugged the shore for almost all of its length, running northeastwards from St Peter Port via the various esplanades, Bas Courtils Road and Bulwer Avenue to St Sampson's. The track was a mixture of flat-bottomed and grooved rails, ballasted or paved, depending on their roadway or roadside location.

Ten or so years later the Company decided to electrify the line, the work being completed enough for trials by October 1891; public running of the new cars began on 20 February 1892 but teething troubles necessitated the retention of the steam trams for another four years. Steam workings finally ceased in November 1896 when a fire in the sheds on Bulwer Avenue destroyed one of the last three locos. The other two were sold later for scrap and a new depot built at Hougue-à-la-Perre, roughly halfway along the route and close to the line's power station.

Following trials in 1877-8 with a Merryweather tram loco, two had been ordered for the start of services in 1879; these were numbered 1 and 2 and in 1890

Postcard view of the Guernsey Railway's St Sampson's terminus with No 1 of 1905 to the fore. (Lens of Sutton)

named *Shooting Star* and *Sampson* respectively. Later in 1879 these were joined by No 3 from Stephen Lewin of Poole and by four Hughes engines (Nos 4-7) in 1882-3; the last arrival, in 1890, was No 8 *Haro* from Hawthorns. Only the three named locos survived until the end of steam on the line, the one destroyed by fire being *Sampson*.

Information regarding the passenger trailers is patchy, especially as regards makers; what seems likely is that services began with two single-deck saloons (Nos 1 and 2) and three roofed toastracks (Nos 3-5) though in December 1879 the last two of these were rebuilt as saloon cars. These were joined at an unknown date by a curious open passenger car (No 6) that looked as much like a coke wagon as No 7, the official coke wagon, did! In 1881 a roofed, double-deck bogie car (No 8) was purchased, followed in 1884 by a single-deck bogie saloon (No 9) from Starbuck. The last arrival, in 1890, was replacement No 4, another roofed double-deck bogie car. Trains of up to three trailers were run behind a single loco.

Electric services were worked by a combination of new vehicles and rebuilt steam trailers and, as in the steam days, trailer workings were the norm. Original new motor cars were Nos 7, 10 and 11 built by Falcon in 1891 as open-top double-deckers; these were followed by Nos 5 and 6 in 1893 (bogie cars this time) while former steam trailers 9 of 1884 and 4 of 1890 were electrified in 1891 as motor cars. Another bogie car, No 8, arrived from Milnes in 1896 and in 1903 and 1905 another two open-toppers, Nos 2 and 1, were bought from Brush. Original trailers were Nos 12-14, roofed Falcon toastracks, joined in 1897 by two more (Nos 14 and 15) from Milnes following the depot fire, together with an open-top double-decker (No 3) which was converted in 1901 to a motor car. The last trailers to be bought were Nos 16-19 in 1903, four ex-Cardiff double-deck horse cars.

In 1895 the Company bought out its bus rival, the Guernsey Omnibus Co., and operated its horse buses until 1909 when they were joined by three motor buses; the horse buses were withdrawn two years later. By the 1930s though, bus competition from other operators was being felt by the tramway and in 1934 it closed for good. The Company however remained very much in existence – as it does today – under the same title, though solely a bus operator.

Bibliography: *The Guernsey Railway* (The Railways of the Channel Islands Vol 3, The Oakwood Library of Railway History No 58A) N. R. P. Bonsor (The Oakwood Press, 1967) 0 85361 329 X

JERSEY RAILWAYS & TRAMWAYS

The Jersey Railways & Tramways Co. Ltd was incorporated in 1896 to take over the assets of the Jersey Railway Co. which operated a 3ft 6in gauge steam railway, some 6 miles in length, from the capital St Helier to Corbiere on the west coast of the island. Despite its title the Company never built or operated any tramways (or indeed any other railways) although electrification of the line was considered at one time.

The first section of the railway (from St Helier to St Aubin) had opened as a standard gauge line in 1870; the whole railway closed in 1936 after a fire destroyed much of its passenger stock.

Bibliography: *The Jersey Railway* (J.R.&T.) (The Railways of the Channel Islands Vol 1, The Oakwood Library of Railway History No 58) N. R. P. Bonsor (The Oakwood Press, 1962)

Section 7

Preserved, Museum and other Pleasure Lines

There is one last category of working tramways to be considered which, for want of a better name, may be called 'pleasure lines': tramways whose sole reason for existence has been to give pleasure rides in much the same way as seaside miniature railways do. Like the miniature railway, the pleasure tramway is a surprisingly ancient animal, the oldest traced being that opened in SHIPLEY GLEN more than a hundred years ago. Although this venerable example was possibly unique, the number of pleasure lines has received a boost in recent years, first, with the construction of several permanent working museum lines, secondly with the opening of a number of semi-permanent miniature tramways and, thirdly, with their temporary use at recent Garden Festivals.

Tramcar preservation is as old as tramway modernization for when horse traction was displaced by (usually) electricity several operators were heritage-minded enough to set aside the odd vehicle for museum display. The precedent for doing this had been set by the railway companies but not until 1951 however was there a precedent for the preservation of a whole line – the narrow gauge Talyllyn Railway in Wales – but even with this example to encourage enthusiasts, the prospect of running even part of an existing or restored tramway proved unobtainable at the very time when the last great wave of system closures was taking place.

The main obstacle in the preservationists' path was the fact that by and large local authorities wanted shot of tramways completely, citing such reasons as that they impeded traffic flow (often true) or that they were holding up road improvement schemes (where there could have been compromises made). Whatever the pros and cons of the tramways v the private car, or even tramways v buses arguments, the fact remains that no local authority was willing to countenance a bunch of amateurs operating trams through its streets – and it was even more unlikely

that national authorities such as the BoT would have done so. Thus, by their very nature, most tramways were ruled out immediately as candidates for preservation; all that were left as possible projects were those lines – or portions of lines – which occupied their own reserved rights of way. Two such schemes, both consistently canvassed over many years now, have centred on the former Swansea & Mumbles and Llandudno & Colwyn Bay lines but with no success as yet.

Inevitably, the number of potential locations (never great to begin with) has decreased as reserved roadside stretches have been swallowed up by road widenings and open-field sections have been built upon. Only one genuine length of tramway route has been preserved for operational use – in MANCHESTER's Heaton Park – and only then because of possibly unique circumstances.

Until 1963 tramway preservation, then, meant tramcar or relic preservation (anything from shelters and standards down to tickets and uniform buttons); in that year though a new, purpose-built museum line was opened at CRICH in Derbyshire in order to operate preserved cars in passenger service once more. Since then similar lines have opened whilst the overall total of preserved cars, working or static (and including imported foreign examples) is now well over the three hundred mark.

As with their railway counterparts, the difference between a miniature and a narrow gauge tramway is not primarily one of size – or even gauge – but rather proportions. Thus a very narrow gauge (2ft) line such as Fairbourne in Wales used cut-down stock still in proportion to its riders whereas a miniature line such as EASTBOURNE (also 2ft gauge), used scaled-down stock in the model engineering tradition not in harmony with its full-sized passengers.

Whilst miniature railways are thick on the ground in Britain, miniature tramways are

not. There is a simple reason for this: on a miniature railway usually only the locomotive is a scale model with the passengers riding in or on non-scale carriages; with a tramway, a model tramcar has somehow to accommodate passengers as well. A secondary but still important reason is an economic one: a miniature train driven by one man might easily carry 30 or more fare-paying passengers whereas a one-man tram is limited to half a dozen or so. For these two reasons miniature tramways have generally been short, portable exhibition lines operated by private individuals or model engineering societies and the like; because of their ephemeral nature these have not been included here though the handful of more permanent ones are described below.

The Garden Festivals held on various sites during the 1980s and early 1990s were the latest in a long line of Shows, Exhibitions and Expositions dating back to the great grandaddy of them all, the 1851 Great Exhibition. What set them apart from their predecessors however was that in addition to providing an entertaining day out and a showcase for manufacturers and other exhibitors, their sites were areas of industrial dereliction chosen deliberately so that the preparatory landscaping and other improvements would result in long-term benefits to their locality.

In all, five Garden Festivals were held: Liverpool (1984), Stoke-on-Trent (1986), Glasgow (1988), Gateshead (1990) and Ebbw Vale (1992). All provided forms of rail transport to move visitors around the site – miniature railways proving especially popular – but of relevance here is that both GLASGOW and GATESHEAD laid full-size working tramways (albeit only temporarily) for both pleasure and utility.

Although the Garden Festival movement has now ended (in the sense that no future ones are planned), the principle of using similar semi-permanent tramways as crowd-movers (and pullers) has been demonstrated successfully and there can be little doubt that the idea will be repeated someday, somewhere, in a different guise. Indeed, with the number of rescued, renovated, imported and operational tramcars growing yearly, and with a concommitant steady increase in the number of working museum and pleasure lines operational or planned (alongside the modern hi-tech systems of Manchester and Sheffield), the outlook for the tramway enthusiast/lover/historian/supporter looks brighter today than it has done for half a century or more.

BEAMISH: NORTH OF ENGLAND OPEN AIR MUSEUM

Occupying a huge, 300-acre rural site in County Durham, this museum recreates the flavour of early 20th century town and country life in the North of England. A 4ft 8½in gauge overhead electric tramway, opened in 1973 to carry visitors to various parts of the site, has been extended in stages and now provides a circular 1¼-mile ride around the perimeter of the site, operating on a year-round basis with a variety of preserved northern tramcars on long-term loan from elsewhere (plus an Oporto single-decker rebuilt as Beamish 196).

BETWS-Y-COED: CONWY VALLEY RAILWAY MUSEUM

In October 1991 Conwy Valley Railway Museum opened a 15in gauge overhead electric miniature tramway beside the BR branch line at its premises in Betws-y-Coed. Running over ½ mile of single track is a single-deck cross-bench saloon built in 1989 by TMA Engineering of Birmingham. The partially open-sided red and white car seats 14 passengers and operates during the summer months only.

BLACK COUNTRY MUSEUM *see* DUDLEY: BLACK COUNTRY MUSEUM

BRADFORD: TRANSPERIENCE DISCOVERY PARK

Britain's newest pleasure tramway seems destined to be a short standard gauge line at the West Yorkshire Transport Trust's Transperience Discovery Park at Low Moor on the outskirts of Bradford. This £11.5m leisure complex (also featuring motor and trolleybuses) opened on 1 July 1995 though

Gateshead & District No 10 restored and running at Beamish. (North of England Open Air Museum)

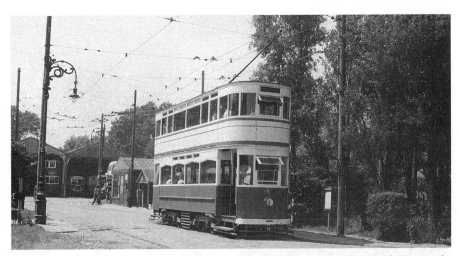

One of many preserved Blackpool trams: balcony car 159 of 1927 (enclosed in 1930) at the East Anglia Transport Museum, Carlton Colville. (Author)

at the time of writing (late 1995) the tramway, which will be operated with an ex-Budapest 1904 car, was not completed.

CARDIFF: HEATH PARK TRAMWAY

This 18in gauge miniature overhead electric line was constructed in 1973 for the 25th

A warning sign to motorists that the tram line was about to approach the kerb, now at the East Anglia Transport Museum. (Author)

anniversary of the Whitchurch & District Model Engineering Society and was designed and built by F. J. Cunuder, formerly Chief Engineer with Cardiff Corporation Tramways. It was laid on a short stretch of ex-BR trackbed incorporated into the Society's premises in Highfield Road, Cardiff, and eventually reached 125yd in length.

The first car (No 1) was a roofed toastrack seating eight passengers and was followed in

1976 by No 3, a semi-closed bogie vehicle seating 20, both in Cardiff crimson lake and cream livery. In 1985 the line was forced to close by housing development but a new, public site was found nearby in Heath Park and the first 80yd of relaid line opened on 5 September 1987 during the Summer Bank Holiday.

The line, now 350yd in length, is operated by Society members on Bank Holiday weekends and certain Sundays and is laid in a horseshoe shape with a passing loop and two-road depot.

CARLTON COLVILLE: EAST ANGLIA TRANSPORT MUSEUM

Run by members of the East Anglia Transport Museum Society, this museum occupies a small rural site just outside Lowestoft, its genesis being the 1961 acquisition of Lowestoft 14 for preservation. A short working 4ft 8½in gauge electric tramway was opened in 1972 and later extended as a single-track, out-and-back run some 500yd in length.

Current stock (operational and non-operational) includes tramcars from Amersterdam, Blackpool, Glasgow, London, Lowestoft and Norwich; buses, trolleybuses and other period road vehicles are also displayed, plus a short narrow-gauge railway. Opening is summer season only.

Restored Lanarkshire car No 53 at the Summerlee Heritage Museum, Coatbridge. (David Peace, Summerlee Heritage Trust)

COATBRIDGE: SUMMERLEE HERITAGE MUSEUM

Opened in March 1988 east of Glasgow near Airdrie on the site of the former Summerlee Ironworks (opened 1832 and later levelled for a crane factory), this museum is designed to show the industrial, engineering, transport and social history of central Scotland.

To help visitors around the 25-acre site a 300-yard long 4ft 8½in gauge electric tramway was installed for the opening and this has since been extended to some two-thirds of a mile. At the time of writing duties are shared between three Continental single-deckers (Brussels 9062, Graz 225 and Oporto 150) and the recently rescued and restored Lanarkshire 53 (though a number of other Scottish cars are undergoing long-term restoration here).

CONWY VALLEY RAILWAY MUSEUM *see* BETWS-Y-COED: CONWY VALLEY RAILWAY MUSEUM

CRICH: NATIONAL TRAMWAY MUSEUM

The idea of a National Tramway Museum had its seed in the formation in 1955 of the Tramway Museum Society, a body dedicated to preserving and displaying what could be salvaged of Britain's rapidly-vanishing tramway heritage. In 1959 a site was acquired at Crich in Derbyshire where a mineral railway had once served a limestone quarry, and the Society set about laying its first section of 4ft 8½in gauge track and converting existing buildings into car sheds and

The street terminus at the National Tramway Museum, Crich, with Paisley District No 68 of 1919 departing. (M. Donnison)

workshops for its growing number of rescued vehicles.

Horse traction began in 1963 and electric traction a year later. Since then the line has been extended gradually to its present length of a mile, new sheds added and a Victorian/Edwardian street scene created at one end of the line with buildings and street furniture from all over Britain re-erected there (much to the joy of film and TV directors needing

authentic-looking tramway shots).

The museum is a working museum in all senses of the word. New exhibits (including a number of foreign cars) have to be restored to exhibition standard after years of neglect and service as chicken houses or whatever, and existing exhibits have to be maintained to keep them in display or working order. Not all of the fifty-plus cars, locomotives and works vehicles are in running condition, often for reasons of gauge (though a number have been regauged to suit the line). In addition, one or two of the museum's cars are usually out on loan at any time, in service at Blackpool, at Garden Festivals or at one of the other working museums such as BEAMISH.

DUDLEY: BLACK COUNTRY MUSEUM

The object of this museum, opened in 1979 on a 26-acre site adjacent to Dudley Castle in the heart of the Black Country, is to recreate as faithfully as possible a slice of the late 19th century urban and industrial landscape of the area with genuine buildings saved from demolition elsewhere and moved to the site, in situ coal and limestone workings, an existing canal basin and tunnel, and a new overhead electric tramway which opened in 1980 on the local 'standard' gauge of 3ft 6in.

The year-round tramway service is operated by restored Dudley & Stourbridge single-decker No 5 (the only electric car of this gauge currently running in Great Britain) although a number of other Black

Works vehicles are a vital part of any tramway's car fleet. These three examples at Crich are (from left) a 1927 Blackpool loco used for coal and rail haulage, a tower wagon for servicing the overhead and Sheffield rail-grinder No 330. (Author)

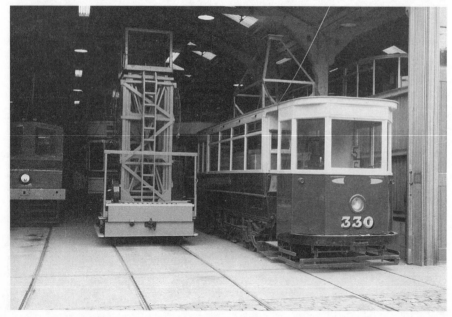

Country cars are awaiting or undergoing restoration here.

The single-track line runs from the museum's main entrance to the rebuilt village some 600yd away, though it is hoped to extend it in the near future via the castle and zoo to the edge of the town centre itself.

DUDLEY: HIMLEY PARK TRAMWAY

In September 1992 a 600mm gauge tramway was opened at Himley Hall, just outside Dudley. Laid by railway engineers Alan Keef Ltd of Cote, partly on the trackbed of a resited miniature railway, the line was built as a showcase for its unusual tramcar. This is a four-wheeled red and white single-deck saloon built by Parry People Movers Ltd of nearby Cradley Heath on an Alan Keef chassis. What is distinctive about this vehicle is that it is a ¾-sized prototype of what PPM hope will be an environmentally-friendly minitram system.

The car is powered by a large flywheel mounted horizontally beneath the floor driving the wheels via a stepless variable transmission – an old idea made practicable by modern technology. At the 'stations' a conducting connection under the low platform powers briefly a small electric motor on the car which recharges the flywheel. Full sized-cars (on a 2ft 6in gauge) have operated on short demonstration lines around the country and it is highly likely that this clean, quiet and efficient transportation system will soon be seen installed in a wide variety of locations. The tramway wheel has indeed come full circle.

EAST ANGLIA TRANSPORT MUSEUM *see* CARLTON COLVILLE: EAST ANGLIA TRANSPORT MUSEUM

EASTBOURNE ELECTRIC TRAMWAY

This was the previous incarnation of the Seaton tramway (see Section 1), operating before that line and after the one at RHYL. With the move from Wales in 1953-54 to a larger site, a wider gauge of 2ft was chosen to allow the construction of more spacious cars. The new line was laid at Princes Park, Eastbourne, with the tramway running from a terminus at Royal Parade to the Crumbles (part of the route having been used for a short demonstration line in September 1953 for the benefit of local Councillors and Chief Officers whose permission was needed to construct the tramway).

The line was constructed by Lane's company, Modern Electric Tramways Ltd, during 1954-55 with the first section opening on 4 July 1954 and the official opening the

The Parry People Mover at Himley Park, Dudley – the shape of short lines to come? (Courtesy JPM Parry & Associates Ltd)

following Whitsun. Two new cars were built to help Rhyl Nos 3 and 225 work the line, both being based on Blackpool prototypes: No 226 (another 'Boat') and No 238 (a model of a 'Balloon' but without the upper floor). Further cars were to follow: freelance design bogie open-toppers No 6 (1956) and 7 (1958), followed in 1961 by No 4, another Blackpool 'Boat'. These last three cars all incorporated parts such as seats and controllers from withdrawn British full-size tramcars.

By 1958 the track had reached its final limit at the borough boundary (1 mile in all) and although MET's five-year concession was extended it became clear during the 1960s that the Corporation's road-building plans might affect the tramway – and so it proved when, in 1967, formal notice was given that the line would be severed by a new roadway. The Company accordingly began looking for yet another site, the search resulting in the removal of the whole operation to Seaton after its closure on 14 September 1969, at the end of its last summer season.

Postcard of Eastbourne miniature tramcar No 6 of 1956. (Author's Collection)

Bibliography: *Eastbourne Tramways* Lionel J.
   Boylett (Ian Allan)

GATESHEAD GARDEN FESTIVAL

The Gateshead Garden Festival site occupied 180 acres of derelict land at Dunston on
the south bank of the River Tyne and a
4ft 8½in gauge electric tramway 660yd long
was laid in the southwest corner using track
and overhead poles from the GLASGOW
GARDEN FESTIVAL line. It was a single
line of single track with a passing loop at
each end and operated during the summer of
1990 from 18 May to 21 October.

Cars used were Blackpool 167, Gateshead
5, Newcastle 102 and Sunderland 100, all
from the National Tramway Museum at
CRICH.

GLASGOW GARDEN FESTIVAL

The Glasgow Garden Festival was held
in Govan on the south bank of the River
Clyde on a 120-acre site that had previously
been disused dockland. A single 4ft 8½in
gauge track ran for about ½ mile along
the former quayside whilst a return track
parallel to this a short distance away
completed an out-and-back circuit of the
electric tramway. Five cars were used
throughout the duration of the festival (from
28 April to 26 September 1988): Glasgow 22
and 1297, Edinburgh 35 and Paisley 68, all
from the National Tramway Museum at
CRICH. Two years later the track and overhead were used for a similar purpose at
GATESHEAD.

HEATH PARK TRAMWAY see CARDIFF: HEATH PARK TRAMWAY

HEATON PARK VINTAGE TRAMWAY see MANCHESTER: HEATON PARK VINTAGE TRAMWAY

HIMLEY PARK TRAMWAY see DUDLEY: HIMLEY PARK TRAMWAY

MANCHESTER: HEATON PARK VINTAGE TRAMWAY

The Heaton Park tramway is unique amongst
the pleasure lines in that it operates on a
stretch of original tramway restored for the
running of preserved tramcars, the special
circumstances of it not being on a public
highway making this possible.

The surviving portion of the former
Manchester Corporation Tramways (see
Section 1) was a 380-yard long double-track
branch off Middleton Road into Heaton
Park itself. The Middleton Road route
opened on 1 April 1904 and on 21 April of

the following year the branch opened as
sidings to cope with the large numbers of
visitors to the park (at 600 acres one of
Britain's largest). During the Manchester
closures of the 1930s the branch was dis-
connected (on 19 January 1934) and two
tracks were tarred over for use as a carpark.
(A third track was removed.)

There the matter – and the rails – rested
until the 1970s when the Manchester
Transport Museum Society proposed
reopening the branch for the operating
of preserved vehicles, adapting a large
and conveniently-sited park shelter as
a depot. Refurbishment work took place during 1978 with a trial opening that summer
and a formal opening on 28 March of the
following year (though public services did
not commence until 1 September).

Such was the immediate popularity of the
line, even though it is operated (by volun-
teers) primarily on summer Sundays and
Bank Holidays only, that in 1984 work began
on extending it nearly ¼ mile to the boating
lake (making a total length of 810yd). The
trial opening of the extension took place at
the end of the 1985 season with the formal
opening at the beginning of the next.

The current service is provided by Hull 96
and Manchester 765 (on loan from the
National Tramway Museum at CRICH) and
Blackpool 600 (on loan from there).

Bibliography: *The Manchester Tramways* Ian
   Yearsley and Philip Groves (Transport
   Publishing Company, 1988)
   0 86317 144 3

NATIONAL TRAMWAY MUSEUM see CRICH: NATIONAL TRAMWAY MUSEUM

NORTH OF ENGLAND OPEN AIR MUSEUM see BEAMISH: NORTH OF ENGLAND OPEN AIR MUSEUM

RHYL MINIATURE TRAMWAY

Although this 15in gauge miniature tramway
ran for just a few summer seasons
(Whitsun–September) it played an important
role in the evolution of the present-day
Seaton line (see Section 1). It was the brainchild of Mr C. W. Lane, a New Barnet engineer and manufacturer of battery-electric
delivery vehicles, and began life as a portable
15in gauge line for use at fetes and the like.
Lane decided – after trials in the summer of
1951 on a short temporary track on St
Leonard's seafront in Sussex – that it
deserved a permanent site and chose Voryd
Amusement Park, Rhyl as a suitable location.

The single-track overhead electric line,
which opened at Whitsun 1952, ran for ¼
mile from the Promenade (West Parade) to
Wellington Road where it curved sharply

westwards to the car park. There were two
roads at each terminus and a two-road car
shed at the Wellington Road curve.

The three cars used were a one-third
scale version of Llandudno & Colwyn Bay
No 23 constructed in 1948, a 1949 model
of Blackpool 'Boat' No 225 and No 3 of
1952, a freelance design Edwardian-style
open-top double-decker. Accommodation
on top of the double-deckers – especially the
enclosed No 23 – was more than somewhat
cramped!

The line's popularity meant that very soon
a larger site was sought and, in the winter of
1953-54, Lane moved the operation to
EASTBOURNE where the tramway re-
opened in 1954 in a new guise with
cars 3 and 225 regauged to 2ft. A bogie open
toastrack (No 6) was built to work the
Rhyl line with No 23 for its last season,
after which it was sold to the Twigdon family
who extended the tramway a short distance
at the Promenade end. They operated it until
the close of the 1957 season, after which the
equipment reverted to Lane. Car No 6 (which
only worked at Rhyl in 1954) was drastically
rebuilt as a double-decker and regauged for
use at Eastbourne (and later Seaton) and No
23 sold into private ownership.

Bibliography: *North Wales Tramways*
   Keith Turner (David & Charles, 1979)
   0 7153 7769 8

SHIPLEY GLEN POND TRAMWAY

This early pleasure line was laid round Glen
Pond in Shipley Glen, a beauty spot to the
north of Bradford in Yorkshire. During the
1880s and 1890s a number of attractions
were constructed in the Glen by the owner,
Col. Maude, including a boating pool, a
switchback railway and an aerial runway.
The horse tramway was built by a local
engineer and entrepreneur, Sam Wilson,
who had purchased six open toastrack cars
used on a temporary line at the 1887 Saltaire
Exhibition; two of these were used on the
Shipley Glen line and the other four put in
store and later used on the Shipley Glen
Tramway (see Section 1). As the gauge of
this latter line was 1ft 8in it is likely that the
gauge of the horse line was the same. It is not
known when the line closed – probably
sometime before World War I – nor indeed
many other details.

Bibliography: *1d. Up – ½d. Down: the story
   of Shipley Glen and its Tramway* Alan
   Whitrick & Michael J. Leak (Bradford
   Trolleybus Association, 1982)
   0 86275 014 8

SKEGNESS ELECTRIC TRAMWAY

The latest miniature line to be opened in the

British Isles (at the time of writing) is a 12¼in gauge tramway which began operations on 29 May 1994 on a 460yd seafront route, running from Princes Parade to the Tower Esplanade, a site previously occupied by a miniature railway. The tramway's first, battery-powered vehicle is a green and cream roofed articulated toastrack which, at the end of the 1994 season was rebuilt into a three-car unit by the line's owner, the Cleethorpes Coast Light Railway.

SUMMERLEE HERITAGE
MUSEUM *see* COATBRIDGE:
SUMMERLEE HERITAGE
MUSEUM

TELFORD TOWN PARK TRAMWAY

This short-lived 2ft gauge pleasure line was constructed by the staff and pupils of Phoenix School on the trackbed of a portion of the former LNWR's branch line from Hadley Junction to Coalport which opened in 1861 and closed in 1960. A decade later the northern part of the trackbed in what had become Telford New Town was landscaped as a pathway in the new Town Park.

The informal opening of the 300yd single-track line took place on 8 September 1979 during Telford Development Corporation's annual carnival and show in the park. Motive power was a small 0-4-0 vertical-boilered tram locomotive (built by local engineers Kierstead Ltd with a s team unit by Pontis Steam Plant of Peterborough) hauling a matching 16-seater coach by Alan Keef Ltd of Cote, Oxfordshire.

The line's formal opening, followed by regular services, took place on 9 April 1980 and was performed by the Rev. W. Awdry of 'Thomas the Tank Engine' fame. The loco was named *Thomas* in honour of this, Thomas Telford after whom the New Town was named, and Emyr Thomas, General Manager of the TDC. Somewhat surprisingly, in view of its population clusters and industrial history – after all, the Industrial Revolution began in the Ironbridge Gorge here – this was Shropshire's only passenger tramway. It was however soon realised that the line did not have legal authority to operate and the stock was put into store. *Thomas* is now in residence at the nearby Horsehay Steam Trust premises.

TRANSPERIENCE DISCOVERY
PARK *see* BRADFORD:
TRANSPERIENCE DISCOVERY
PARK

Major Landmarks in British Tramway History

1807   World's first railed passenger service inaugurated on the Oystermouth Tramroad in Wales

1859   William Curtis runs his patent omnibuses on a line in Liverpool Docks

1860   George Train opens the first genuine street railway in the British Isles (Birkenhead)

       Tramways Act (Ireland)

1863   First Act of Parliament for a street tramway (Portsmouth)

1864   First trials of steam traction (Ryde Pier)

1870   Tramways Act

1876   First regular use of steam traction (Wantage)

1877   First regular use of steam traction on a street tramway (Vale of Clyde)

1879   Use of Mechanical Power on Tramways Act

1883   Giant's Causeway, Portrush & Bush Valley pioneers the use of electricity (third rail)

       Huddersfield becomes the first municipal operator

       Tramways and Public Companies (Ireland) Act

1884   Highgate Hill Cable Tramway pioneers the use of cable traction (London)

1885   First (conduit) electric tramway opens (Blackpool)

1889   Light Railways (Ireland) Act

1891   First overhead electric tramway opens (Leeds)

1896   Light Railways Act

1909   Last regular use of steam traction on a street tramway (Rossendale Valley)

1917   First abandonment of an electric system (Sheerness)

1924   Last new system for 46 years opens (Dearne District)

1927   Last steam passenger service outside Ireland ceases (Wisbech & Upwell)

1928   Last use of horse traction outside the Isle of Man (Pwllheli & Llanbedrog)

1934   Channel Islands' only tramway closes (Guernsey)

1952   Largest system closes (London)

1959   Ireland's last tramway closes (Hill of Howth)

       Last steam passenger service (Arigna)

1960   Swansea & Mumbles closes leaving the Great Orme as Wales' sole surviving tramway

1961   Grimsby & Immingham closes leaving Blackpool as England's sole surviving tramway

1962   Scotland's last tramway closes (Glasgow)

1963   National Tramway Museum opens at Crich in England

1970   First tramway to be built since 1924 opens (Seaton)

1992   Manchester Metrolink ushers in a new era of urban tramways

English Passenger Tramway Locations by Former County

BEDFORDSHIRE
Luton

BERKSHIRE
Reading; Wantage

BUCKINGHAMSHIRE
Wolverton & Stony Stratford

CAMBRIDGESHIRE
Cambridge; Wisbech & Upwell (part)

CHESHIRE
Birkenhead; Chester; Manchester and district (part); Stalybridge and district (part); Stockport (part); Wallasey; Warrington (part)

CORNWALL
Camborne & Redruth

CUMBERLAND
Carlisle

DERBYSHIRE
Burton & Ashby (part); Chesterfield; Derby; Glossop; Ilkeston; Matlock; Nottinghamshire & Derbyshire (part)

DEVON
Exeter; Plymouth; Seaton; Torquay and district

DORSET
Poole

DURHAM
Darlington; Gateshead; The Hartlepools; Jarrow; South Shields; Stockton & Thornaby (part); Sunderland and district

ESSEX
Barking; Canvey Island; Colchester; East Ham; Ilford; Leyton; London (part); Southend-on-Sea; Walthamstow; West Ham

GLOUCESTERSHIRE
Bristol (part); Cheltenham; Gloucester

HAMPSHIRE & ISLE OF WIGHT
Aldershot & Farnborough; Bournemouth; Gosport & Farnham; Portsmouth and district; Ryde; Southampton

HERTFORDSHIRE
London (part)

HUNTINGDONSHIRE
Peterborough

KENT
Bexley (part); Chatham; Dartford; Dover; Erith; Folkestone, Hythe & Sandgate; Gravesend & Northfleet; Herne Bay; Isle of Thanet; Maidstone; Sheerness; South Metropolitan (part)

LANCASHIRE
Accrington and district; Ashton-under-Lyne; Barrow-in-Furness; Blackburn; Blackpool and district; Bolton; Burnley; Bury; Colne & Trawden; Darwen; Farnworth; Heywood; Lancaster and district; Liverpool and district; Lytham St Annes and district; Manchester; Middleton; Morecambe; Nelson; Oldham; Preston; Rawtenstall and district; Rochdale; St Helens: Salford; South Lancashire; Southport; Stalybridge and district (part); Stockport (part); Warrington (part); Waterloo & Great Crosby; Wigan

LEICESTERSHIRE
Burton & Ashby (part); Leicester

LINCOLNSHIRE
Alford & Sutton; Grimsby and district; Lincoln; Skegness

LONDON
Bexley (part); London (part)

MIDDLESEX
London (part)

NORFOLK
Norwich; Wisbech & Upwell (part); Great Yarmouth

NORTHAMPTONSHIRE
Northampton

NORTHUMBERLAND
Newcastle; Tynemouth; Tyneside

NOTTINGHAMSHIRE
Mansfield; Nottingham; Nottinghamshire & Derbyshire (part)

OXFORDSHIRE
Oxford

SOMERSET
Bath; Bristol (part); Taunton; Weston-super-Mare

STAFFORDSHIRE
Birmingham (part); Black Country (part); Burton and district (part); Kinver (part); Potteries; Walsall; Wolverhampton

SUFFOLK
Ipswich; Lowestoft

SURREY
Croydon; South Metropolitan (part)

SUSSEX
Brighton and district; Shoreham and district; Hastings

WARWICKSHIRE
Birmingham (part); Coventry; Leamington & Warwick; Stratford & Moreton

WILTSHIRE
Swindon

WORCESTERSHIRE
Black Country (part); Kidderminster & Stourport; Worcester

YORKSHIRE
Barnsley; Batley; Bradford; Dearne District; Doncaster; Huddersfield; Hull and district; Keighley; Mexborough & Swinton; Middlesbrough; Rotherham; Scarborough; Sheffield; Shipley; Stockton & Thornaby (part); Wakefield and district; York; Yorkshire (West Riding); Yorkshire (Woollen District)

Herefordshire, Rutland, Shropshire and Westmoreland have had no regular passenger tramways.

Appendix 2

Welsh Passenger Tramway Locations by Former County
(Including Monmouthshire)

CAERNARVONSHIRE
Llandudno and district (part); Pwllheli and district

CARMARTHENSHIRE
Llanelly

DENBIGHSHIRE
Colwyn Bay and district (part); Glyn Valley; Wrexham

GLAMORGAN
Aberdare; Cardiff; Merthyr Tydfil; Neath; Pontypridd; Rhondda; Swansea and district

MERIONETHSHIRE
Barmouth Junction & Arthog; Fairbourne; Harlech

MONMOUTHSHIRE
Newport

Anglesey, Brecknockshire, Cardiganshire, Flintshire, Montgomeryshire, Pembrokeshire and Radnorshire have had no regular passenger tramways.

Scottish Passenger Tramway Locations by Former County

ABERDEENSHIRE
Aberdeen; Cruden Bay; Strabathie & Blackdog

ANGUS
Dundee and district

AYRSHIRE
Ayr; Kilmarnock

BUTESHIRE
Rothesay

DUNBARTONSHIRE
Dumbarton

FIFE
Dunfermline; Kirkcaldy; Wemyss

LANARKSHIRE
Airdrie & Coatbridge; Glasgow; Lanarkshire

MIDLOTHIAN
Edinburgh; Leith; Musselburgh

PERTHSHIRE
Perth

RENFREWSHIRE
Greenock & Port Glasgow; Paisley

STIRLINGSHIRE
Falkirk; Stirling & Bridge of Allan

Argyllshire, Banffshire, Berwickshire, Caithness, Clackmannanshire, Dumfries-shire, East Lothian, Inverness-shire, Kincardineshire, Kinross-shire, Kircudbrightshire, Morayshire, Nairn, Orkney, Pebbles-shire, Ross & Cromarty, Roxburghshire, Selkirkshire, Sutherland, West Lothian, Wigtownshire and Zetland have had no regular passenger tramways.

Irish Passenger Tramway Locations by County

ANTRIM
Belfast (part)

ARMAGH
Glenanne & Loughgilly

CORK
Cork

DOWN
Belfast (part); Warrenpoint & Rostrevor

DUBLIN
Dublin and district (part); Hill of Howth

FERMANAGH
Clogher Valley (part)

GALWAY
Galway & Salthill

LEITRIM
Arigna (part)

LONDONDERRY
Derry; Portstewart

ROSCOMMON
Arigna (part)

TYRONE
Clogher Valley (part); Castlederg & Victoria Bridge

WICKLOW
Dublin and district (part)

Carlow, Cavan, Clare, Donegal, Kerry, Kildare, Kilkenny, Laois, Limerick, Longford, Louth, Mayo, Meath, Monaghan, Offaly, Sligo, Tipperary, Waterford, Westmeath and Wexford have had no regular passenger tramways.

Appendix 5

Horse-Only Tramways

Although the normal course of events for early British tramways was to start with horse traction and then modernize with electrification around the end of the 19th century (sometimes experimenting with steam traction along the way), a significant number of lines remained faithful to horse traction until the end without it being replaced (or the tramway rebuilt in some other form). The reason was normally financial with low traffic receipts not justifying the cost of conversion. These latter systems are listed below with their dates of operation and the Sections where their main entries can be found.

BARMOUTH JUNCTION & ARTHOG	1899 - 1903?	WALES
CAMBRIDGE	1880 - 1914	ENGLAND
DERRY	1897 - 1919	IRELAND
DOUGLAS BAY	1876 -	ISLE OF MAN
FAIRBOURNE	1890? - 1915?	WALES
FOLKESTONE, HYTHE & SANDGATE	1891 - 1921	ENGLAND
GALWAY & SALTHILL	1879 - 1918	IRELAND
GLENANNE & LOUGHGILLY	1897 - 1918?	IRELAND
HARLECH	1878 - 1880s	WALES
LANCASTER & DISTRICT	1890 - 1921	ENGLAND
MORECAMBE CORPORATION	1898 - 1926	ENGLAND
OXFORD	1881 - 1914	ENGLAND
PWLLHELI	1899 - 1919	WALES
PWLLHELI & LLANBEDROG	1894 - 1928	WALES
SKEGNESS	c1880 - c1882	ENGLAND
WARRENPOINT & ROSTREVOR	1877 - 1915	IRELAND

Appendix 6

Steam-Only
Tramways

Lines which employed steam traction were of two broad types: urban street tramways and isolated rural roadside lines. The type of locomotives used corresponded generally with the type of line: box-like, purpose-built tramway engines for the street systems and adapted railway engines for the others. In the towns, steam traction lasted little more than twenty years, from c1880 to c1900; in rural areas its use survived well into the 20th century, and sometimes right up to a line's closure (often with internal-combustion traction as well.) The following list is of those tramways which used steam traction exclusively with their dates of operation and the Sections where their main entries can be found.

ALFORD & SUTTON	1884 - 1889	ENGLAND
ARIGNA	1887 - 1959	IRELAND
BRIGHTON & SHOREHAM	1884 - 1913	ENGLAND
HULL: Drypool & Marfleet	1889 - 1901	ENGLAND
PORTSTEWART	1882 - 1926	IRELAND
WISBECH & UPWELL	1883 - 1927*	ENGLAND
WOLVERTON & STONY STRATFORD	1887 - 1926	ENGLAND

* retained steam (later diesel) traction for goods trains

Appendix 7

Cable Tramways

Cable traction on tramways, because of the complicated mechanical arrangements needed if more than one route was involved, was almost exclusively limited to short, single-line systems where steep gradients had to be conquered. (The one exception was Edinburgh.) The list below includes all British cable lines with their dates of cable operation and the Sections where their main entries can be found.

BIRMINGHAM: Hockley Hill	1888 - 1911*	ENGLAND
DOUGLAS: Upper Douglas	1896 - 1929	ISLE OF MAN
EDINBURGH	1888 - 1922*	SCOTLAND
LONDON: Brixton Hill	1892 - 1904*	ENGLAND
LONDON: Highgate Hill	1884 - 1909*	ENGLAND
LLANDUDNO: Great Orme	1902 -	WALES
MATLOCK	1893 - 1927	ENGLAND
SWANSEA: Constitution Hill	1898 - 1902?	WALES

* converted to electric traction

Appendix 8

Pier Tramways

Many of Britain's piers and jetties have had, at one time or another, lines laid on them. In many cases these were simple extensions of the national railway system and used for the loading and unloading of passengers and goods from ferry boats and pleasure steamers; occasionally railway vehicles themselves would be transhipped. A few piers though possessed their own self-contained lines to carry passengers and their luggage between pier head and shore and, when there were no steamers to service, to give rides to holidaymakers. Most of these lines were railways, fenced-off from the rest of the pier decking (a necessary precaution as many were electrified on the third-rail system) but a handful were true tramways laid flush with the decking. These are listed below with their dates of operation and the Sections where their main entries can be found.

BLACKPOOL	1991 -	ENGLAND
HERNE BAY (1)	1833?- 1864	ENGLAND
HERNE BAY (2)	1899 - 1939	ENGLAND
RAMSEY	1899 - 1981	ISLE OF MAN
RYDE	1864 - 1886?	ENGLAND
SOUTHEND	1874?- 1880	ENGLAND
SOUTHPORT	1863	ENGLAND

Appendix 9

Railway-Owned Tramways

A small number of tramways were owned and/or operated by railway companies, for reasons almost as numerous as the lines themselves. The following list includes all such lines with the original operating railways and the Sections where the tramways' main entries can be found.

ARIGNA	Cavan & Leitrim Rly	IRELAND
BURTON & ASHBY	MR	ENGLAND
CRUDEN BAY	GNSR	SCOTLAND
FOLKESTONE, HYTHE & SANDGATE	SER	ENGLAND
GRIMSBY & IMMINGHAM	GCR	ENGLAND
HILL OF HOWTH	GNR(I)	IRELAND
HOYLAKE & BIRKENHEAD	Hoylake Rly	ENGLAND
PORTSTEWART	BNCR	IRELAND
WATERLOO & GREAT CROSBY	Liverpool Overhead	ENGLAND
WISBECH & UPWELL	GER	ENGLAND
WOLVERTON & STONY STRATFORD	LNWR	ENGLAND

Although it was not uncommon for a seaside local authority to own both a tramway and a pier or cliff railway, or a multi-interest conglomerate to own a small line (eg the Imperial group's ownership of the Corris Railway in Wales), it was unusual for a single-system tramway company to own a railway of any sort. Only the TORQUAY and BRISTOL operators did so, possessing respectively the Babbacombe and Clifton Rocks cliff railways.

Postscript

Future Tramways

In January 1996 construction work began on the first stage (Birmingham–Wolverhampton) of the Midland Metro, the most advanced in a growing list of modern tramway projects for other towns and cities in the British Isles. (Croydon, Leeds, Glasgow and Dublin to name but four.)